PENGUIN BOOKS

THE PORTABLE CONSERVATIVE READER

Each volume in The Viking Portable Library either presents a representative selection from the works of a single outstanding writer or offers a comprehensive anthology on a special subject. Averaging 700 pages in length and designed for compactness and readability, these books fill a need not met by other compilations. All are edited by distinguished authorities, who have written introductory essays and included much other helpful material.

"The Viking Portables have done more for good reading and good writers than anything that has come along since I can remember."

—Arthur Mizener

Russell Kirk, critic, historian of ideas, biographer, novelist, and editor of *The University Bookman*, is director of the social-science program of the Educational Research Council of America. He is the author of twenty-two books, including *The Conservative Mind, Eliot and His Age, John Randolph of Roanoke*, and *The Roots of American Order*. Mr. Kirk lives in his ancestral village of Mecosta, Michigan, with his wife, Annette, who is a member of the new federal Commission on Excellence in Education.

The Portable

CONSERVATIVE READER

*Edited, with an
Introduction and Notes,
by Russell Kirk*

PENGUIN BOOKS

To Cecilia Abigail Kirk,
conservative at the age of thirteen

PENGUIN BOOKS
Published by the Penguin Group
Viking Penguin Inc., 40 West 23rd Street, New York, New York 10010, U.S.A.
Penguin Books Ltd, 27 Wrights Lane, London W8 5TZ, England
Penguin Books Australia Ltd, Ringwood, Victoria, Australia
Penguin Books Canada Ltd, 2801 John Street,
Markham, Ontario, Canada L3R 1B4
Penguin Books (N.Z.) Ltd, 182–190 Wairau Road,
Auckland 10, New Zealand

Penguin Books Ltd, Registered Offices:
Harmondsworth, Middlesex, England

First published in the United States of America
in simultaneous hardcover and paperback editions by
Viking Penguin Inc. 1982

7 9 10 8 6

LIBRARY OF CONGRESS CATALOGING IN PUBLICATION DATA
Main entry under title:
The Portable conservative reader.
(The Viking portable library)
Bibliography: p.
Includes index.
1. Political science. 2. Conservatism. I. Kirk, Russell.
JC131.P67 320.5'2 81-15381
ISBN 0 14 015.095 1 AACR2

Printed in the United States of America
Set in CRT Janson

Page 725 constitutes an extension of the copyright page.

CONTENTS

Contents

INTRODUCTION

1. Succinct Description

"What is conservatism?" Abraham Lincoln inquired rhetorically, as he campaigned for the presidency of the United States. "Is it not adherence to the old and tried, against the new and untried?" By that test, the candidate told his audience, Abraham Lincoln was a conservative.

Other definitions have been offered. In Ambrose Bierce's *Devil's Dictionary* one encounters this: "Conservative, *n.* A statesman who is enamored of existing evils, as distinguished from the Liberal, who wishes to replace them with others."

Definition of these words "conservative" and "conservatism" is not easily accomplished. In this anthology we examine a body of opinions, or a set of general political principles, which were enunciated during the French Revolution. These views of society have been more fully developed during the past two centuries; they have exerted a strong influence upon the practical politics and the political speculation of Europe and the Americas.

As a coherent body of political thought, what we call conservatism is a modern development. It is approximately as old as the different body of opinions called liberalism, and some decades older than the ideologies called socialism, communism, and anarchism. The roots of conservative thought, for all that, extend deep into the history of ideas and of social institutions.

In various medieval cities, particularly in Italy, the title of "conservator" was given to guardians of the laws.

English justices of the peace originally were styled *custodes pacis*—conservators of the peace. Chaucer, in "The House of Fame," uses the word "conservatif" in its sense of protection and preservation. Jeremy Taylor, in the seventeenth century, wrote that "the Holy Spirit is the great conservative of the new life." The word, in short, implied security—a commendatory word. But not until the third decade of the nineteenth century was the word incorporated into the English lexicon of political controversy.

True, one might trace a continuity of conservative political thought (though not of the word itself) back into the seventeenth century. Lord Falkland, during the English Civil Wars, touched upon the essence of conservative convictions in declaring, "When it is not necessary to change, it is necessary not to change." A rudimentary conservatism may be discerned in colonial America, too, assuming definite form just after the American Revolution in the most successful conservative device, the Constitution of the United States.

For that matter, conservative impulses and interests have existed ever since a civil social order came into being. By analogy, it is possible to speak of Aristophanes as a conservative, or Plato, or Cicero. But in this present volume we have space for conservative beliefs and attitudes only in their modern context. Indeed, the looming bulk of able writing by eminent conservatives requires us to confine ourselves, in this collection, almost wholly to British and American literature.

So we commence with the age of Edmund Burke—the last quarter of the eighteenth century. Modern use of the word "conservatism" implies those principles of social thought and action that are set against radical innovation after the pattern of the French Revolution. Edmund Burke opposed his "moral imagination" to what has been called the "idyllic imagination" of Jean-Jacques Rousseau. From that contest arose what Walter Bagehot called "the conservatism of reflection." Almost by definition, ever since Burke published his *Reflections on the Revolution in France*, the principal conservatives in the Western world have been conscious or unconscious disciples of Burke.

Burke himself did not employ the word "conservative," speaking rather of "preservation"—as in his aphorism "Change is the means of our preservation," or his remark that the able statesman is one who combines with a disposition to preserve an ability to reform. During Burke's own lifetime there existed no sharp demarcation between the words "conservative" and "liberal."

As a term of politics, the word "conservative" arose in France during and just after the Napoleonic era. Philosophical statesmen as varied in opinion and faction as Guizot, Bonald, Maistre, Chateaubriand, and Tocqueville all were influenced by Burke's writings. Seeking for a word to describe a policy of moderation, intended to reconcile the best in the old order with the necessities of the nineteenth century, French political writers hit upon the concept of the *conservateur*, the guardian of the heritage of civilization and of the principles of justice.

From France, this concept passed into England. The editors of *The Quarterly Review*, in 1830, approved "conservative" over "Tory" to describe the British party of order. By the 1840s, the word "conservative" had attained popularity in the United States, being employed with approbation by John C. Calhoun, Daniel Webster, and Orestes Brownson.

Burke's political concepts spread rapidly across Europe, especially in the Germanys and the Austrian system. The European revolutionary movements of 1829–30 and of 1848 caused greater emphasis to be placed upon distinctions among conservatives, liberals, and radicals. Throughout Europe, conservatism came to mean hostility toward the principles of the French Revolution, with its violent leveling innovations; while liberalism increasingly signified sympathy with the revolutionary ideals of liberty, equality, fraternity, and material progress.

Conservatives, especially in Britain, soon found themselves opposing another radicalism than the theories of Rousseau: that is, the radical utilitarianism of Jeremy Bentham, called by John Stuart Mill "the great subversive." Thus the intellectual heirs of Burke, and the conservative interest generally, did battle on two fronts: against the successors of the Jacobins, with their "armed doctrine"; and against the economists of Manchester, with their reliance upon the nexus of cash payment.

Our first necessity here, then, is to endeavor to describe (rather than to define) the conservatives' understanding of society. In recent years the term "conservatism" often has been employed to mean "reactionary" or "obscurantist" or "oldfangled"; it has even been confounded with the economic dogmas of the Manchester School. What does the word really signify?

Strictly speaking, conservatism is not a political system, and certainly not an ideology. In the phrase of H. Stuart Hughes, "Conservatism is the negation of ideology." Instead, conservatism is a way of looking at the civil social order. Although certain general principles held by most conservatives may be described, there exists wide variety in application of these ideas from age to age and country to country. Thus conservative views and parties have existed under monarchical, aristocratic, despotic, and democratic regimes, and in a considerable range of economic systems. The conservatives of Peru, for instance, differ much from those of Australia, say; they may share a preference for the established order of society, these conservatives of the Spanish and of the English heritages; yet the institutions and customs which these conservative factions respectively wish to preserve are by no means identical.

Unlike socialism, anarchism, and even liberalism, then, conservatism offers no universal pattern of politics for adoption everywhere. On the contrary, conservatives reason that social institutions always must differ considerably from nation to nation, since any land's politics must be the product of that country's dominant religion, ancient customs, and historic experience.

Although it is no ideology, conservatism may be apprehended reasonably well by attention to what leading writers and politicians, generally called conservative, have said and done. So this anthology itself is a convenient means for ascertaining what a conservative is. "Conservatism," to put the matter another way, amounts to the consensus of the leading conservative thinkers and actors over the past two centuries. For our present purpose, however, we may set down below several general principles upon which most eminent conservatives in some degree may be said to have agreed implicitly. The following first principles are best discerned in the theoretical and practical politics of British and American conservatives.

First, conservatives generally believe that there exists a transcendent moral order, to which we ought to try to conform the ways of society. A divine tactic, however dimly descried, is at work in human society. Such convictions may take the form of belief in "natural law" or may assume some other expression; but with few exceptions conservatives recognize the need for enduring moral authority. This conviction contrasts strongly with the liberals' utilitarian view of the state (most consistently expressed by Bentham's disciples), and with the radicals' detestation of theological postulates.

Second, conservatives uphold the principle of social continuity. They prefer the devil they know to the devil they don't know. Order and justice and freedom, they believe, are the artificial products of a long and painful social experience, the results of centuries of trial and reflection and sacrifice. Thus the body social is a kind of spiritual corporation, comparable to the church; it may even be called a community of souls. Human society is no machine, to be treated mechanically. The continuity, the life-blood, of a society must not be interrupted. Burke's reminder of the social necessity for prudent change is in the minds of conservatives. But necessary change, they argue, ought to be gradual and discriminatory, never "unfixing old interests at once." Revolution slices through the arteries of a culture, a cure that kills.

Third, conservatives believe in what may be called the principle of prescription. "The wisdom of our ancestors" is one of the more important phrases in the writings of Burke; presumably Burke derived it from Richard Hooker. Conservatives sense that modern men and women are dwarfs on the shoulders of giants, able to see farther than their ancestors only because of the great stature of those who have preceded us in time. Therefore conservatives very frequently emphasize the importance of "prescription"—that is, of things established by immemorial usage, so "that the mind of man runneth not to the contrary." There exist rights of which the chief sanction is their antiquity—including rights in property, often. Similarly, our morals are prescriptive in great part. Conservatives argue that we are unlikely, we moderns, to make any brave new discoveries in morals or politics or taste. It is perilous to weigh every passing issue on the basis of private judgment and private rationality. "The individual is foolish, but the species is wise," Burke declared. In politics we do well to abide by precedent and precept and even prejudice, for "the great mysterious incorporation of the human race" has acquired habits, customs, and conventions of remote origin which are woven into the fabric of our social being; the innovator, in Santayana's phrase, never knows how near to the taproot of the tree he is hacking.

Fourth, conservatives are guided by their principle of prudence. Burke agrees with Plato that in the statesman, prudence is chief among virtues. Any public measure ought to be judged by its probable long-run consequences, not merely by temporary advantage or popularity. Liberals and radicals, the conservative holds, are imprudent: for they dash at their objectives without giving much heed to the risk of new abuses worse than the evils they hope to sweep away. Human society being complex, remedies cannot be simple if they are to be effective. The conservative declares that he acts only after sufficient reflection, having weighed the consequences. Sudden and slashing reforms are perilous as sudden and slashing surgery. The march of providence is slow; it is the devil who always hurries.

Fifth, conservatives pay attention to the principle of variety. They feel affection for the proliferating intricacy of long-established social institutions and modes of life, as distinguished from the narrowing uniformity and deadening egalitarianism of radical systems. For the preservation of a healthy diversity in any civilization, there must survive orders and classes, differences in material condition, and many sorts of inequality. The only true forms of equality are equality in the Last Judgment and equality before a just court of law; all other attempts at leveling lead, at best, to social stagnation. Society longs for honest and able leadership; and if natural and institutional differences among people are destroyed, presently some tyrant or host of squalid oligarchs will create new forms of inequality. Similarly, conservatives uphold the institution of private property as productive of human variety: without private property, liberty is reduced and culture is impoverished.

Sixth, conservatives are chastened by their principle of imperfectibility. Human nature suffers irremediably from certain faults, the conservatives know. Man being imperfect, no perfect social order ever can be created. Because of human restlessness, mankind would grow rebellious under any utopian domination, and would break out once more in violent discontent—or else expire of boredom. To aim for utopia is to end in disaster, the conservative says:

we are not made for perfect things. All that we reasonably can expect is a tolerably ordered, just, and free society, in which some evils, maladjustments, and suffering continue to lurk. By proper attention to prudent reform, we may preserve and improve this tolerable order. But if the old institutional and moral safeguards of a nation are forgotten, then the anarchic impulses in man break loose: "the ceremony of innocence is drowned."

Such are six of the major premises of what Walter Bagehot, a century ago, called "reflective conservatism." To have set down some principal convictions of conservative thinkers, in the fashion above, may be misleading: for conservative thought is not a body of immutable secular dogmas. Our purpose here has been broad description, not fixed definition. If one requires a single sentence—why, let it be said that for the conservative, politics is the art of the possible, not the art of the ideal.

Edmund Burke turned to first principles in politics only with reluctance, believing that "metaphysical" politicians let loose dreadful mischief by attempting to govern nations according to abstract notions. Conservatives have believed, following Burke, that general principles always must be tempered, in any particular circumstances, by what Burke called expedience, or prudence; for particular circumstances vary infinitely, and every nation must observe its own traditions and historical experience—which should take precedence over universal notions drawn up in some quiet study. Yet Burke did not abjure general ideas; he distinguished between "abstraction" (or *a priori* notions divorced from a nation's history and necessities) and "principle" (or sound general ideas derived from a knowledge of human nature and of the past). Principles are necessary to a statesman, but they must be applied discreetly and with infinite caution to the workaday world. The preceding six conservative principles, therefore, are to be taken as a rough catalog of the general assumptions of conservatives, and not as a tidy system of doctrines for governing a state.

So much, just now, for our attempt at honest description of the character of conservative writing. Let us turn for a moment to some account of what this conservatism is *not*.

2. *Misapprehensions of Conservatism*

Misunderstandings of the conservative mentality and of conservative arguments may be divided into two categories: first, the errors of scholars; second, popular confusions. Turn we to the blunders of the learned.

A failure to grasp Burke's distinction between abstraction and principle has led to considerable error as to the theoretical basis of conservatism, from the day of rationalistic historians such as Henry Buckle down to the present day. This controversy takes four principal forms, all at loggerheads with one another. They may be summarized thus: (1) conservatism is metaphysically mystical; (2) conservatism has no philosophical foundation; (3) conservatism is empirical; (4) conservatism is pragmatic. These views require reasoned examination.

(1) Conservatism by its nature is not "mystical," "abstract," or "doctrinaire." Burke and his school, as practical statesmen, did not think that political and metaphysical schemes should be created out of whole cloth. Rather than enveloping politics in mysterious theories of a General Will or of Thesis and Antithesis, Burke and his followers accepted as given the political institutions of their country and their age; as for moral postulates, they took those from the King James Version and the Book of Common Prayer. It is true that some Continental men of the Right, and some English scholars toward the end of the nineteenth century, came under the influence of Hegel's idealism. But (as Alexis de Tocqueville foresaw) Hegel's

influence came to be far stronger upon socialist theorists than upon conservative writers and politicians.

(2) Conservatism, despite Burke's contempt for desiccated rationality and abstract speculation, does not lack some theoretical basis. Burke proclaimed that he knew nothing more wicked than the heart of an abstract metaphysician—that is, of some coffeehouse philosopher who would presume to write a new constitution for the human race on the basis of arid intellectual abstractions. The intellectual foundation which Burke and his associates took for granted was what since has been called the Great Tradition—that is, the classical and Christian intellectual patrimony which then still formed the curriculum of schools. Burke referred to "the Schoolmen of the fourteenth century" and other Christian philosophers. In the view of the eighteenth-century conservatives, a man is afflicted by *hubris*, overweening presumption, if he tries to cast aside the wisdom of his ancestors and to create out of his tiny private stock of reason some brand-new structure of metaphysical doctrines. Burke's metaphysics, in short, were the philosophical postulates of Richard Hooker, John Bramhall, and other English divines.

(3) Conservatism is empirical only in the sense that conservatives respect the wisdom of the species and think that history, the recorded experience of mankind, should be constantly consulted by the statesman. Yet mere practical experience, "empiricism" in the sense of being guided simply by yesterday's pains or pleasures, is not enough for the conservative, who believes that we can apply our knowledge of the remote or the immediate past with prudence only if we are guided by some general principles, which have been laid down for us over the centuries by prophets and philosophers. Burke broke with Locke's empiricism.

(4) Conservatism is pragmatic only in the sense that it disavows utopian speculation and experiment, putting its faith instead in prudence and moderation. Modern prag-

matism is intent upon experiment—that is, groping forward with scant respect for the past; conservatism, on the contrary, relies upon tradition and the bank and capital of the ages. Conservatives think that mere change may as easily be retrogression as progress, and that to tamper experimentally with great states and human nature, out of a vague faith in Progress and Process, is infinitely perilous.

Some doctors of the schools notwithstanding, then, the conservative school of politics cannot be thrust into any mystical, empirical, pragmatic, or nondescript pigeonhole. Recent studies by Peter Stanlis, Francis Canavan, Charles Parkin, and other scholars have sufficiently undone earlier notions about Burke's first principles. Yet even today a good many professors of politics or of history remain afflicted by rather a muddy notion of the intellectual sources of conservative belief.

Such a confusion is more readily pardoned among the mass of men and women, as the twentieth century nears its end, two hundred years after the events that brought forth conservative politics. The word "conservative," at this writing, enjoys a renewed popularity in both the United States and Britain. Whether those who exalt "conservative" to the condition of a god-term, or those who condemn it to the condition of a devil-term, actually know what the word has meant—why, that's another matter.

Some of the extracts and essays in this anthology may suggest adequately that conservatives are not the rich faction, per se; or the stupid, per se; or the belligerent, per se; or the neurotic, per se. (All those charges have been made against conservatives in recent years.) Doubtless there are conservatives who are at once rich, stupid, belligerent, and neurotic, quite as there are liberals and radicals similarly afflicted; yet the generality of the breed are even as you and I.

It is not surprising that in some quarters (especially in America) there lingers an impression that the conservative is "some sort of radical"—a paradox no more startling than many other paradoxes of popular opinion. For decades popular jounalists often have used the word "conservative" in a sense considerably different from the intellectual conservatism described earlier in this Introduction. Among many people unfamiliar with the writings of Burke or of the Adamses there does flourish, after all, a set of opinions which Walter Bagehot once unflatteringly described as "the ignorant Democratic Conservatism of the masses." There endures also "shop-and-till conservatism," or mere attachment to one's little property, out of fear that radical political measures would injure or destroy the material interests of anyone possessing property. This "party of order," as it was called in France and elsewhere in Europe during the nineteenth century, is animated by fear, Bagehot wrote: "dread that their shop, their house, their life—not so much their physical life as their whole mode and sources of existence—will be destroyed and cast away." Just so; precisely that has happened in half the world since Bagehot wrote; so the high-spirited conservatism of Burke has been reinforced by the shop-and-till victims of twentieth-century ideological fanaticism.

So it is that some conservatives are learned, and some ignorant; some rich, and some poor. It is not easy to show a close correspondence between political conservatism and personal prosperity. At several general elections, the Conservative party in Britain has won the votes of millions of trade-union members; while in the United States hardpressed small farmers generally are a bulwark of the conservative interest on many issues, and so increasingly is a large proportion of the "blue-collar" vote.

Between religious convictions and conservative political views, there is a nearer alliance, despite the radicalism of many modern clergy (very like the English clergy of Burke's day). Because ideology is by essence antireligious, Christians tend to be attracted to ideology's negation, conservatism.

Do most of the men and women who vote for conservative candidates and conservative policies thoroughly apprehend the six conservative principles sketched earlier in this introductory essay? No, of course not—no more than the typical liberal or the typical radical voter can set up as a political philosopher.

Most conservatives, like their liberal and radical adversaries, are not metaphysicians; they hold their convictions somewhat vaguely, as prejudices rather than reasoned conclusions. Even more than liberals and radicals, typical conservatives (sensing that politics is not the whole of life) remain indifferent to political action so long as possible; there are more interesting things to do. It was for this reason that John Stuart Mill called conservatives "the stupid party." The conservative scholar F. J. C. Hearnshaw wrote in this century that "It is commonly sufficient for practical purposes if conservatives, without saying anything, just sit and think, or even if they merely sit." The conservative has on his side the mighty power of inertia; the radical has on his side the grim power of love of change. In the modern world, the love of change has been gaining at the expense of the love of things established, with a consequent weakening of the conservative interest—at least until very late in the day.

Conservatives, it should be understood, are neither angels nor devils. Conservatism has its vice, and that vice is selfishness. Self-centered conservatives mutter, with Fafnir, "Let me rest: I lie in possession." Radicalism, too, has its vice, and that vice is envy. Such radicals growl, as in *Dr. Faustus*, "Why shouldst thou sit, and I stand?" (As for the liberals, nowadays they seem in the sere and yellow leaf, so that it would be cruel to tax them with vices.) Most conservatives hold by their particular social convictions because of early prejudices and experiences; their minds are not susceptible to temperate argument, nor can they express with much lucidity the postulates from which they draw their professed opinions. That, however, is true of the majority of political partisans of whatever persuasion; indeed, probably it is less true of conservatives than of their adversaries, conservatism being no ideology—and therefore not so overwhelmed by the passions of political religion. And it must be kept in mind that in any country, in any age, there exists more than one sort of conservative.

Walter Bagehot, in his brief essay "Intellectual Conservatism" (included in this volume), distinguishes three types of conservatives: the conservatives of enjoyment, loyal to old ways, like the Cavaliers; the conservatives of fear, like the French middle classes in the nineteenth century; and the conservatives of reflection. These last always are relatively few in number, and yet they leaven the whole of the conservative interest. This conservatism of reflection is the strong rope connecting the essays and speeches and stories and poems that make up this anthology.

3. The Course of Conservative Politics in America

In this Introduction it is not possible to make room for a history of conservative parties and factions. We can only suggest, in these few pages, the endeavors and the vicissitudes of the conservative interest during the past two centuries.

Although American conservatism did not become self-aware, so to speak, until the close of the Revolution, nevertheless strongly conservative influences and factions may be discerned in the colonial era. The planter societies of Virginia, Maryland, and South Carolina, especially, were governed for the most part by constitutions (written or unwritten) which we should call conservative. New York, with its great landed estates and its established mercantile interests, was socially conservative; so was New Jersey. Even the colonies founded upon dissent, the New

England settlements and Pennsylvania, became relatively conservative shortly after they acquired wealth and population: only a few years after the landing at Plymouth, for instance, Governor Bradford was writing of the mischievous illusion that property should be held in common, and laying emphasis on the necessity for order, authority, and true community.

Yet a Tory party in the old English sense scarcely existed in America. Political debates in the colonies usually occurred between two factions of Whigs, both attached to the Whig idea of liberty, but differing as to means and the relationship with the Crown. Neither of these Whig factions was radical essentially, although some leveling elements were to be found among the Patriots. The triumph of the Patriots in the Revolution expelled from the Thirteen Colonies what little Toryism had existed there, and along with it many of the moderate Whigs. For all that, recent scholarship inclines toward the view that the American Revolution was no revolution truly, but simply a War of Independence—a revolution (in Burke's phrase concerning the Glorious Revolution of 1688) "not made, but prevented."

The intellectual leaders of the Americans during the troubled period of Confederation were men, most of them, of conservative tendency—John Adams, Gouverneur Morris, John Jay, Hamilton, Madison. Even Jefferson, despite certain French influences upon his mind, was no frantic innovator. Most other Southern leaders, such as Pinckney or Mason, differed more about means than about the ends of society: their view of the state was conservative—viewed, that is, from a twentieth-century vantage point. Even some eminent radicals of the time, notably Patrick Henry, grew steadily more conservative as responsibility settled upon them.

Out of the discussions and compromises of these masterful politicians grew the Federal Constitution, which Sir Henry Maine called the most successful conservative device in the history of government. And the Federalist Papers, written to obtain acceptance of the Constitution, reflect the conservative concepts of moderation, balance, order, and prudence—together with those conservative guarantees of prescriptive usage, arrangement of political checks, restrictions upon power, protection for private property, and restraints upon popular impulses.

During the early years of the United States, the chief political contests may be regarded as a long acrimonious debate between two powerful conservative interests—the mercantile interest of the North, the agricultural interest of the South—confused by lesser issues and personalities. At first, the two types of conservatism were represented respectively by John Adams and James Madison. As the slavery question began to divide the country, John Randolph and John C. Calhoun came to speak for the conservative impulse of the South, and Daniel Webster for that of the North. On the eve of the Civil War, the two most interesting conservative thinkers were men of letters, rather than politicians: Nathaniel Hawthorne and Orestes Brownson; but they could not prevail against Abolitionists and Fire-Eaters.

The catastrophe of the Civil War dealt a grim blow to reflective conservatism, North or South. In the Gilded Age, little political principle of any kind could be distinguished. In the writings of Henry Adams lingered something of the old New England conservatism; in the books of John W. Burgess was expressed a new sort of conservative liberalism, heavily influenced by German thought. Yet amidst the material aggrandizement of America during the concluding third of the nineteenth century, the better public men in both parties retained conservative attitudes: Grover Cleveland and Theodore Roosevelt, for examples.

As the United States grew into the greatest power in the world, with corresponding duties and hard choices, conservative concepts were discussed again, notably by such writers as Paul Elmer More, Irving Babbitt, and George Santayana. The Great Depression and the ascendancy of Franklin Roosevelt seemed to quash this renewal of conservative thought. Until the first administration of Franklin Roosevelt, the term "liberal" had not been popular among American politicians; but Rooseveltian liberalism swept everything before it during the 1930s and 1940s. Not until the early 1950s did there appear, or reappear, a strong body of conservative thought, expressed in books and periodical literature, to challenge the dominant liberalism. This latter-day intellectual renewal of the conservative mind, sometimes awkwardly styled a "New Conservatism," is represented by several selections in the concluding section of this anthology.

America has known many conservative politicians and men of ideas, but no national Conservative party—or, for that matter, a national Liberal party, let alone a powerful Radical party. The United States ordinarily has been spared ideological passions in its great parties. In the past, the absence of a distinct aristocracy and the numerous opportunities for personal advancement tended to discourage the formation of class parties or ideological parties.

The triumph of merciless ideologies in half of the world, nevertheless, and the national interest of the United States in restraining the ambitions of Hitlerian Germany, the Soviet Union, and Communist China, have been important causes of the revival of political thought in America. Ideology of any sort being radical, a consequence of America's opposition to the totalist powers has been the stimulating of conservative ideas. At this writing, it seems probable that conservative concepts will be reflected in American foreign and domestic policies for some years or decades to come.

In America, as in other countries, the particular forms assumed by the conservative impulse tend to be shaped by the nation's established social and political modes. Thus an American political conservative, at least as the term is employed popularly, is a person who believes strongly that the old pattern of American society ought not to be much altered. Typically, such a person holds by the Constitution, maintaining that it should be strictly interpreted; he endeavors to oppose the drift toward political centralization; he dislikes organizations on the grand scale, in government, in business and industry, in organized labor; he is a defender of private property; he resents the heavy increase of taxation and many of the "transfer payments" of the welfare state; he is unalterably opposed to the Communist ideology and the aspirations of the Soviet Union; he sighs, or perhaps shouts, *O tempora! O mores!* at the decay of private and public morality. In former years this typical conservative was a Protestant; but from the early 1940s, for a number of reasons, more and more American Catholics have moved toward conservative political attitudes, and often have taken the lead in conservative causes.

We never step in the same river twice. This representative conservative American of the 1980s is not identical with a Federalist of the 1780s. Yet some continuity of belief and institution connects those two figures; and it seems probable that the literature of American conservative thought and character may endure as long as the Republic.

4. English Conservatism

Under various names, political parties founded on conservative concepts appeared throughout Europe early in the nineteenth century. Of these, only Britain's Conservative party—now the oldest political party of any sort, anywhere in the world—has remained powerful right down to the present day.

The history of conservative parties and movements in Germany and France is an important and lively subject which cannot be examined here. Until the Bolshevik Revolution and Soviet imperialism extirpated the old social order in Eastern Europe, every European country had some political party or faction which deserved to be classified as conservative—the aims and complexion of the party varying from one state to another. In Northern Europe, these parties were sustained particularly by the landed gentry; they also enjoyed a good deal of support from peasants and from a part of the middle classes. In the Austrian system and in Southern Europe, links between the conservative parties and the Catholic Church existed. But throughout the Continent, in the face of vigorous liberal parties and of armed risings against the established order, the conservatives gradually lost ground; and after the revolutions of 1848, with the flight of Metternich from Austria and of Louis Philippe from France, conservative regimes surrendered power to liberals and nationalists or else clung to influence only in coalition with other political groups.

The coming of modern industrialism, too, hastened the decline of old-style conservatism, transferring wealth and power to new hands and breaking what Bagehot called "the cake of custom." Industrialism undermined the habitual acceptance of things long established that is bound up with the conservative understanding of community. Between 1830 and 1880, roughly speaking, liberalism beat down the conservative ascendancy in much of Europe. Even in Russia and Prussia, liberal assumptions and measures were adopted by the reigning monarchs.

Only in Britain did a party—and a climate of opinion—unabashedly conservative maintain ascendancy much of the time throughout the whole of the nineteenth century, obtaining the support of at least half the electorate. Originally taking form as a coalition of Tories and Portland Whigs in William Pitt's ministry during the war with revolutionary France, the English conservatives began to use the word "conservative" as early as 1824, implying by that word their discipleship to Burke; and gradually "Conservative" became the name of their party.

The English people's marked aversion to change made the Conservative party palatable to a great part of the public. (Had most of Britain's electors belonged to the "Celtic fringe" of Scotland, Wales, and Ireland, the Conservative party would have found itself in a permanent minority.) When the French socialist speculator Saint-Simon visited Britain during the formative years of the Conservative party, he predicted that British society, already industrialized, soon would be overwhelmed by a rising of the proletariat. Nothing of the sort occurred, in that time or later in the century. After the passing of a century and a half, indeed, the British Conservative party still can win general elections.

Although shaken by the Whig Reform Bill of 1832 and by the passage of other Whig and Liberal measures that undermined the agricultural interest, the Conservatives were rescued by the fertile imagination and astute management of Benjamin Disraeli. From the time of the French Revolution to the Reform Bill of 1867, the backbone of the Conservative party was formed by the landed proprietors—the squirearchy. Disraeli's reform of 1867 attached to the Conservatives a considerable part of the artisan classes. As the Liberals turned their attention toward egalitarian measures and humanitarian projects, successive segments of the middle classes and of the surviving Whig interest went over to the Conservatives—most notably, the Liberal Unionists, in 1886. At the end of the nineteenth century, under the leadership of Lord Salisbury, the conservatives stood seemingly at the summit of their popularity.

An overwhelming Liberal victory in the general election of 1906 terminated this ascendancy—but only temporarily, for the rise of socialism was pressing the Liberals hard, and the Labour victory of 1924 meant the end of the

Liberal party as an effective force. During the following four decades, conservatives formed the government most of the time. Since the Second World War, Labour and Conservative governments have alternated in power.

In absorbing much of the former Liberal interest, the British Conservative party has adopted also some elements of Liberal policy, so that the Conservative party has become a union of old Tory and Liberal factions, combined against Labour. Although the Conservatives yielded much ground to their opponents as the decades passed, what they have succeeded in retaining is more remarkable. The monarchy remains so popular as to be quite unchallenged; an aristocratic element survives both *de jure* and *de facto;* parliamentary government is not menaced; most property remains in private possession; the welfare state is being modified by the Conservatives; there is still a church by law established; intellectually, the conservative interest has recovered from the shaken state in which it lay after the Second World War.

The more interesting conservative public men have been Burke, Pitt, Canning, Wellington, Peel, Disraeli, Salisbury, Balfour, and Winston Churchill; the chief conservative thinkers (in the larger sense of "conservative"), Burke, Coleridge, Newman, Stephen, Maine, Mallock, and Eliot. Most of these are represented in this anthology. In recent years a scholarly political conservatism has produced several important writers—whose center is more London University and the London School of Economics (once allegedly forcing-beds for liberalism and radicalism) than Oxford or Cambridge.

5. *Prospects for Conservative Thought and Policy*

Despite the persistence, or perhaps recrudescence, of the conservative impulse in America and Britain, can conservative views and interests long endure in an age of ideol-

ogy, when two of the three great powers in the world are
ruled by Marxist doctrinaires, and while technological and
economic and cultural change continue to tear apart the
cake of custom everywhere? The English-speaking peoples aside, in what it has become fashionable to call "the
Post-Modern Age" or "the Post-Christian Era" indeed it
seems as if (fulfilling Burke's vaticinations) "generation
will not link with generation, and men will be as the flies
of a summer." Brooks Adams wrote that "With conservative populations, slaughter is nature's remedy." The conservative populations of Vietnam, Cambodia, and Laos
have been butchered very recently. Will people after people be devoted to the Savage God of ideology?

Consider the European continent. After suffering sup-
pression under the dictatorial regimes of the 1930s and
during the Second World War, European conservative
groups began to regain vigor about 1946. Soviet power
had extirpated effectual conservatism in Poland, Hungary,
Czechoslovakia, Rumania, Bulgaria, and lesser states; but
to the chagrin of the Communists, and indeed of the socialist parties of Western Europe, conservative parties—
or, more commonly, Christian Democratic parties in
which various conservative and liberal elements were
leagued—won national elections in several countries; elsewhere, except under Marxist governments, they exercised
a moderating influence.

Yet this revived conservatism was shorn of many of its
old associations and had come to terms, in most countries,
with old-fashioned economic liberalism. Paradoxically,
the conservatives' partial success was brought about by
the menace of Marxism: after the failure of the Nazi and
Fascist regimes, and the ineffectuality of postwar "democratic" socialism, many Europeans turned once more to
quasi-conservative policies as the only alternatives to a totalist order. "Conservative" governments in France, Germany, Italy, Austria, and some other European states
today may be conservative in the broader and comparative

sense of the term, but they differ markedly from the conservative parties and their views before 1914. It may be argued that in truth these recent "conservative" governments have been substantially liberal governments in the nineteenth-century sense, with some admixture of conservative elements and conservative rhetoric. How long such regimes might stand, were they shorn of American protection, nobody knows.

Turn to Latin America. Ever since their wars of independence, the Latin American states have striven to establish stable political orders. They have not succeeded. Their formal constitutions, usually imitating European or North American models, rarely have reflected the real social circumstances of their peoples; and so have not exerted a conservative influence like that of the Constitution of the United States. Except for relatively long periods in the history of Chile and Colombia, and shorter periods in the history of Venezuela, Argentina, Costa Rica, and El Salvador, dictatorship or oligarchy ordinarily has triumphed over the representative institutions that characterize Anglo-American and most European states. Social and racial conflicts have swept away many of the bulwarks of conservatism. Struggles with the Catholic Church in several countries have weakened the religious foundations of the conservative interest. The triumph of a Marxist regime in Cuba illustrated the feebleness of conservative elements in much of Latin America. Joseph Conrad's novel *Nostromo* remains as accurate a picture of Latin American social instability as it was at its publication in 1904. One cannot look to Latin America for signs of conservative imagination and hope.

In Asia, Western ideology and Western technology, both blending with a new ferocious nationalism in some countries, have so thoroughly broken up the old order of things that it scarcely is possible to speak of conservative politics anywhere except in Japan and some of the Muslim states. Japanese conservatism, now recovering from the injuries inflicted by war and military occupation, is an interesting development, arising out of old Japanese concepts of piety, duty, and honor. This subtle conservatism gradually may reassert itself: as Lafcadio Hearn wrote, Japan wears successively, and perhaps sincerely, a series of Western masks; but these are discarded in turn, for beneath the masks the old Japanese character lives. The present mask of Western materialism and technocracy will not endure forever; but it does not follow that it must be succeeded by the mask of proletarian dictatorship.

In India, Western socialist and liberal ideas are dominant, though yielding perhaps to Marxist influences. Western conservatism on the English pattern, never deep-rooted in India, has become negligible. A powerfully conservative body of Hindu culture does provide some check upon Western ideology. A somewhat similar struggle between Western progressivism and conservative Muslim tradition continues in Pakistan, Indonesia, and elsewhere.

In short, it is not to be expected that there can be brought to pass any concert of conservative political regimes, throughout the world, with the intention of withstanding Marxist ideology. Conservatism on the American or the British model would be an impossible exotic in central Africa or in other regions where nothing comparable to the British or the American historical experience ever has occurred. As Daniel Boorstin puts it, "The American Constitution is not for export." If sovereign states cooperate to resist Soviet imperialism, that will be on the ground of the national interest of each state, not because of a general political consensus. Conservatism not being an ideology with pretensions to universality and infallibility, there can be no Capitalist Manifesto to set against the Communist Manifesto. For that matter, not many conservatives would be happy to enlist under the banner of one abstraction, Capitalism, against another abstraction, Communism—or to die, absurdly, for "a higher standard of living."

And yet, transcending the differences of culture and history and race and national frontiers, something that we may call the conservative impulse or the conservative yearning does exist among all peoples. Without this instinct, any society would fall to pieces. Coleridge wrote that in any state there must be its Permanence, or elements of stability and continuity; and its Progression, or elements of growth and experiment. If the restraining conservative influence were destroyed, any society would fly apart from the vertiginous speed of change.

In that sense, a kind of universal conservatism may be glimpsed. It has not been stamped out even in Soviet Russia. Under tribulation, it is nurtured by an instinct for veneration almost inextinguishable in some people; by an insight best expressed by Richard Hooker: "The reason first why we do admire those things which are greatest, and second those things which are ancientest, is because the one are the least distant from the infinite substance, the other from the infinite continuance, of God."

At bottom, then, conservatism is not a matter of economic interests and economic theories; not a matter of political advantages and political systems; not a matter of power or preferment. If we penetrate to the root, we discover that "conservatism" is a way of looking at the human condition. As a conservative Polish proverb puts it, "Old truths, old laws, old boots, old books, and old friends are the best." The conservative impulse is a man's desire to walk in the paths that his father followed; it is a woman's desire for the sureties of hearth and home.

In every culture, what does the imaginative conservative aspire to conserve? Why, to conserve order: both order in the soul and order in the state. With Luke, the man of conservative impulses says to himself, "No man having drunk old wine straightway desireth new; for he saith, The old is better." Out of the deep well of the past comes order; and as Simone Weil reminds us, "Order is the first need of all."

From revelation, from right reason, from poetic vision, from much study, from the experience of the species—so the conservative argues—we human beings have learned certain ways and principles of order. Were we lacking these, we would lie at the mercy of will and appetite—in private life, in public concerns. It is this order, this old safeguard against private and public anarchy, which the conservative refuses to surrender to the evangels of Progress.

That love of order is the common element of the writings of the men and women—otherwise differing in much—whose thoughts are included in this anthology. Were there no ordering of the soul and of the state, no human society could survive; indeed, no civilized individual could endure. That being so, conservative beliefs will not cease to be unless the civil social order ceases to be. Many voices nowadays tell us that the Liberal Era is far gone in senescence; the Marxist Era, already repudiated by men of letters and false to its own promises, may not endure long; so there may come round again a time for the restoration of old standards.

Or it may come to pass that Kipling's Gods of the Copybook Headings with fire and slaughter return. Even so, something worth saving may be raked from the ashes.

6. *The Literature of Conservatism*

In practical affairs, during the past two centuries, the rearguard actions of conservatives very often have fallen into routs. In the realm of letters, nevertheless, often conservative writers have won the day, from the triumph of Burke's rhetoric to the ascendancy of Eliot's poetry and criticism. Liberals have become painfully aware of this seeming paradox.

An embarrassment of riches is the principal difficulty with this anthology. Complaints that some first-rate conservative writers have been omitted altogether are anticipated; and we confess to the impeachment. In a collection extending over two centuries, we simply lack space sufficient to include every author we ought to include; and sometimes our exclusions are arbitrary merely.

Certain general principles, nevertheless, have been employed in our exclusions.

For lack of space, we include only writing in the English language; German and French and Spanish and other conservative writers must await some other anthology. Our only exception is Tocqueville, admitted to this book because he wrote about America and because his works have exerted so powerful an influence in Britain and America.

For lack of space, we have emphasized in our selections depth of thought and power of style, rather than the practical political success of the men and women whose writings are included here. True, we do find space for Burke, John Adams, Disraeli, John Randolph, Calhoun, and several other active politicians—because certain of their writings happen to fit into the pattern of this anthology, and because those writings meet our other criteria. But we have found it necessary, for a variety of reasons, to omit many important conservative men of affairs—among them Theodore Roosevelt and Winston Churchill, able writers though those two were. We cannot be comprehensive here.

For lack of space, we have not attempted to treat economic questions systematically. This neglect does not result from contempt for the Dismal Science, but rather from the impossibility of discussing in our compass any technical aspects of economics; and from the fact that relatively few economists have called themselves conservatives. We do include some selections by Lecky, Godkin, and others which take up economic concerns in their political and moral aspects.

For lack of space, we have refrained from including writers who have objected to being labeled "conservative"—among them the self-styled "Old Whig" F. A. Hayek, the "Edwardian Radical" Hilaire Belloc, and the philosophical historians Eric Voegelin and John Lukacs (who prefer to be exempted from any tags). Also it would be difficult to extract from some of the above scholars meaningful portions of their books succinct enough for this anthology.

For lack of space, then, we have committed many sins of omission. Yet we hope that we may be found to have dealt fairly with several varieties of the conservative impulse. We have divided our anthology into seventeen parts, with a brief prefatory page for each part; these sections of the book run roughly in chronological order.

And we have given primacy to the *literature* of conservatives' thought and emotion. Some other collections of conservative writing consist mainly of politicians' speeches—though nothing is deader than dead practical politics of the ephemeral sort. Yet other anthologies are made of articles by professors of political science or of sociology—as a breed, dull dogs! This Viking Portable reader is sufficiently liberal (in the root sense of that abused word) to extend to poems, short stories, and chapters from novels; for conservative literature has been imaginative and evocative, as well as polemical and expository. Yet we have made no attempt to include the whole range of important poets whose political sentiments were conservative, or at least antiliberal: the reader must turn, if he wishes, to the collected poems of Yeats, Eliot, and Frost. (We do make room for a specimen of Eliot's prose.)

All in all, what we have tried to accomplish in this collection is a display of the range and power of the conservative *imagination*. In his essay on Disraeli, Paul Elmer More mentions a "positive factor of conservatism—its trust in the controlling power of the imagination," which More contrasts with the liberal's lack of imagination and the radical's misplaced confidence in human nature. The conservative statesman's task is difficult, More remarks.

The liberal exercises "an honourable opportunism," and lets the future take care of itself. The radical, employing flattery, finds it easy to convince the public "at a time when man's innate restlessness has been lifted by false deductions from evolutionary science into a philosophy which regards all change as life and progress and condemns stability as stagnation and death."

Amen to that. Yet "imagination governs the human race." Who said that? No poet: instead, Napoleon, master of the big battalions. He knew that in the long run, the power of the moral imagination exceeds the power of a whiff of grapeshot. If the world is entering upon the Post-Modern Age (John Lukacs setting A.D. 1945 as the Year Zero of this Post-Modern Age), new-seeming ideas and new-seeming sentiments and new-seeming modes of statecraft may grow popular during the next few decades. The Post-Modern imagination stands ready to be captured. And the seemingly novel ideas and sentiments and modes may turn out, after all, to be revived truths and institutions, well known to surviving conservatives. Lionel Trilling, more than thirty years ago, found the liberal imagination nearly bankrupt; that kind of imagination has not prospered since then. It may be the conservative imagination which is to guide the Post-Modern Age, particularly in America. The aim of Burke, says Paul Elmer More, was "to use the imagination as a force for order and self-restraint and political health." It is just conceivable that such conservative imagination may attain its fullness in the twenty-first century.

However that may be—whether the reader of this collection takes the literature of conservatism for a vestige of forgotten days or for the prolegomenon of a great work yet to be produced—the selections in this anthology stand in their own right, worthy of being read for their wit and passion and vision. At the least, this reader may be found enlightening by the many people uncertain as to the signification of "conservative."

If not altogether voices of a forlorn and dispossessed orthodoxy, the conservative voices in this anthology have been misunderstood or ignored by those dominant liberals whom Trilling vainly tried to rouse from complacency. Others than liberals can profit from his admonition. This book may help to diminish that ignorance of the nominally educated.

Part One

~~~~~~

THE TENSION OF ORDER AND FREEDOM

Edmund Burke (1729–1797) is the most important of
modern political philosophers, says Hans Barth in his
book *The Idea of Order*, because Burke understood
better than did anyone else that a tension must be
maintained between the claims of freedom and the
claims of order. That knowledge lies at the heart of
conservative politics. And that principle runs
through the selections from Burke's writings which
form the first section of this anthology.

THE TRUTH ABOUT
CIVIL LIBERTY
Edmund Burke

At the height of the American Revolution, Burke—
then member of Parliament from Bristol—addressed
to his constituents this public *Letter to the Sheriffs of
Bristol*, in which he discusses the true character of
civil freedom. The conservative dislike of extremes
may be noted here. This extract is taken from the Rivington edition (London, 1826) of *The Works of the
Right Honourable Edmund Burke*, Vol. III, pp.
156-57, 183-86.

Believe me, gentlemen, the way still before you is intricate, dark, and full of perplexed and treacherous mazes.
Those who think they have the clue may lead us out of
this labyrinth. We may trust them as amply as we think
proper; but as they have most certainly a call for all the
reason which their stock can furnish, why should we think
it proper to disturb its operation by inflaming their passions? I may be unable to lend an helping hand to those
who direct the state; but I should be ashamed to make
myself one of a noisy multitude to halloo and hearten
them into doubtful and dangerous courses. A conscien-
tious man would be cautious how he dealt in blood. He
would feel some apprehension at being called to a tremendous account for engaging in so deep a play, without any
sort of knowledge of the game. It is no excuse for presumptuous ignorance, that it is directed by insolent passion. The poorest being that crawls on earth, contending

to save itself from injustice and oppression, is an object respectable in the eyes of God and man. But I cannot conceive any existence under Heaven, (which, in the depths of its wisdom, tolerates all sorts of things) that is more truly odious and disgusting, than an impotent helpless creature, without civil wisdom or military skill, without a consciousness of any other qualification for power but his servility to it, bloated with pride and arrogance, calling for battles which he is not to fight, contending for a violent dominion which he can never exercise, and satisfied to be himself mean and miserable, in order to render others contemptible and wretched.

If you and I find our talents not of the great and ruling kind, our conduct, at least, is conformable to our faculties. No man's life pays the forfeit of our rashness. No desolate widow weeps tears of blood over our ignorance. Scrupulous and sober in a well-grounded distrust of ourselves, we would keep in the port of peace and security; and pehaps in recommending to others something of the same diffidence, we should shew ourselves more charitable to their welfare, than injurious to their abilities. . . .

If there be one fact in the world perfectly clear, it is this: "That the disposition of the people of America is wholly averse to any other than a free government"; and this is indication enough to any honest statesman, how he ought to adapt whatever power he finds in his hands to their case. If any ask me what a free government is, I answer that, for any practical purpose, it is what the people think so; and that they, and not I, are the natural, lawful, and competent judges of this matter. If they practically allow me a greater degree of authority over them than is consistent with any correct ideas of perfect freedom, I ought to thank them for so great a trust, and not to endeavour to prove from thence, that they have reasoned amiss, and that having gone so far, by analogy, they must hereafter have no enjoyment but by my pleasure.

If we had seen this done by any others, we should have

concluded them far gone in madness. It is melancholy as
well as ridiculous, to observe the kind of reasoning with
which the publick has been amused, in order to divert our
minds from the common sense of our American policy.
There are people, who have split and anatomised the doctrine of free government, as if it were an abstract question
concerning metaphysical liberty and necessity; and not a
matter of moral prudence and natural feeling. They have
disputed, whether liberty be a positive or a negative idea;
whether it does not consist in being governed by laws;
without considering what are the laws, or who are the
makers; whether man has any rights by nature; and
whether all the property he enjoys be not the alms of his
government, and his life itself their favour and indulgence.
Others corrupting religion, as these have perverted philosophy, contend, that Christians are redeemed into captiv-
ity; and the blood of the Saviour of mankind has been
shed to make them the slaves of a few proud and insolent
sinners. These shocking extremes provoking to extremes
of another kind, speculations are let loose as destructive to
all authority, as the former are to all freedom; and every
government is called tyranny and usurpation which is not
formed on their fancies. In this manner the stirrers-up of
this contention, not satisfied with distracting our depen-
dencies and filling them with blood and slaughter, are
corrupting our understandings: they are endeavouring to
tear up, along with practical liberty, all the foundations of
human society, all equity and justice, religion and order.

Civil freedom, gentlemen, is not, as many have endeavoured to persuade you, a thing that lies hid in the depth of
abstruse science. It is a blessing and a benefit, not an abstract speculation; and all the just reasoning that can be
upon it is of so coarse a texture, as perfectly to suit the ordinary capacities of those who are to enjoy, and of those
who are to defend it. Far from any resemblance to those
propositions in geometry and metaphysicks, whch admit
no medium, but must be true or false in all their latitude;

social and civil freedom, like all other things in common life, are variously mixed and modified, enjoyed in very different degrees, and shaped into an infinite diversity of forms, according to the temper and circumstances of every community. The *extreme* of liberty (which is its abstract perfection, but its real fault) obtains nowhere, nor ought to obtain anywhere. Because extremes, as we all know, in every point which relates either to our duties or satisfactions in life, are destructive both to virtue and enjoyment. Liberty too must be limited in order to be possessed. The degree of restraint it is impossible in any case to settle precisely. But it ought to be the constant aim of evey wise, publick council, to find out by cautious experiments, and rational, cool endeavours, with how little, not how much of this restraint, the community can subsist. For liberty is a good to be improved, and not an evil to be lessened. It is not only a private blessing of the first order, but the vital spring and energy of the state itself, which has just so much life and vigour as there is liberty in it. But whether liberty be advantageous or not (for I know it is a fashion to decry the very principle), none will dispute that peace is a blessing; and peace must in the course of human affairs be frequently bought by some indulgence and toleration at least to liberty. For as the sabbath (though of divine institution) was made for man, not man for the sabbath, government, which can claim no higher origin or authority, in its exercise at least, ought to conform to the exigences of the time, and the temper and character of the people, with whom it is concerned; and not always to attempt violently to bend the people to their theories of subjection. The bulk of mankind on their part are not excessively curious concerning any theories, whilst they are really happy; and one sure symptom of an ill-conducted state is the propensity of the people to resort to them.

LIBERTY AND POWER
Edmund Burke

Even before the triumph of the Jacobins in France, Burke published his prophetic *Reflections on the Revolution in France* (1789), one of the few works of political philosophy to exercise an immediate influence upon events. This was the beginning of Burke's intellectual defense of the ordered civilized world against the revolutionary "antagonist world." This extract—from the Rivington edition of Burke's *Works*, Vol. V, pp. 35–38—is an analysis of abstract doctrines of liberty as a menace to real freedom.

I flatter myself that I love a manly, moral, regulated liberty as well as any gentleman of that society, be he who he will: and perhaps I have given as good proofs of my attachment to that cause, in the whole course of my publick conduct. I think I envy liberty as little as they do, to any other nation. But I cannot stand forward, and give praise or blame to any thing which relates to human actions, and human concerns, on a simple view of the object, as it stands stripped of every relation, in all the nakedness and solitude of metaphysical abstraction. Circumstances (which with some gentlemen pass for nothing) give in reality to every political principle its distinguishing colour and discriminating effect. The circumstances are what render every civil and political scheme beneficial or noxious to mankind. Abstractedly speaking, government, as well as liberty, is good; yet could I, in common sense, ten years ago, have felicitated France on her enjoyment of a government (for she then had a government) without inquiry what the nature of that government was, or how it was administered? Can I now congratulate the same nation upon its freedom? Is it because liberty in the abstract may be classed amongst the blessings of mankind, that I am seriously to felicitate a mad-man, who has escaped from the protecting restraint and wholesome darkness of his cell, on his restoration to the enjoyment of light and liberty? Am I to congratulate a highwayman and murderer, who has broke prison, upon the recovery of his natural rights? This would be to act over again the scene of the criminals condemned to the gallies, and their heroick deliverer, the metaphysick knight of the sorrowful countenance.

When I see the spirit of liberty in action, I see a strong principle at work; and this, for a while, is all I can possibly know of it. The wild *gas*, the fixed air, is plainly broke loose: but we ought to suspend our judgment until the first effervescence is a little subsided, till the liquor is cleared, and until we see something deeper than the agitation of a troubled and frothy surface. I must be tolerably sure, before I venture publickly to congratulate men upon a blessing, that they have really received one. Flattery corrupts both the receiver and the giver; and adulation is not of more service to the people than to kings. I should therefore suspend my congratulations on the new liberty of France, until I was informed how it had been combined with government; with publick force; with the discipline and obedience of armies; with the collection of an effective and well-distributed revenue; with morality and religion; with solidity and property; with peace and order; with civil and social manners. All these (in their way) are good things too; and, without them, liberty is not a benefit whilst it lasts, and is not likely to continiue long. The effect of liberty to individuals, is, that they may do what they please: we ought to see what it will please them to do, before we risk congratulations, which may be soon turned into complaints. Prudence would dictate this in the case of separate, insulated, private men; but liberty, when men act in bodies, is *power*. Considerate people, before they declare themselves, will observe the use which is made of *power*; and particularly of so trying a thing as *new* power in *new* persons, of whose principles, tempers, and dispositions, they have little or no experience, and in situations, where those who appear the most stirring in the scene may possibly not be the real movers.

CHANGE AND CONSERVATION
Edmund Burke

In another passage from the *Reflections* (*Works*, Rivington edition, Vol. V, pp. 59–60, 77–81) Burke discusses the relationship between change and conservation, and the social necessity for continuity in "the great mysterious incorporation of the human race."

A state without the means of some change is without the means of its conservation. Without such means it might even risk the loss of that part of the constitution which it wished the most religiously to preserve. The two principles of conservation and correction operated strongly at the two critical periods of the Restoration and Revolution, when England found itself without a king. At both those periods the nation had lost the bond of union in their ancient edifice; they did not, however, dissolve the whole fabrick. On the contrary, in both cases they regenerated the deficient part of the old constitution through the parts which were not impaired. They kept these old parts exactly as they were, that the part recovered might be suited to them. They acted by the ancient organized states in the

shape of their old organization, and not by the organick
moleculae of a disbanded people. At no time, perhaps, did
the sovereign legislature manifest a more tender regard to
that fundamental principle of British constitutional policy, than at the time of the Revolution, when it deviated
from the direct line of hereditary succession. The crown
was carried somewhat out of the line in which it had before moved; but the new line was derived from the same
stock. It was still a line of hereditary descent; still an hereditary descent qualified with protestantism. When the
legislature altered the direction, but kept the principle,
they shewed that they held it inviolable.

On this principle, the law of inheritance had admitted
some amendment in the old time, and long before the æra
of the revolution. Some time after the conquest great
questions arose upon the legal principles of hereditary descent. It became a matter of doubt, whether the heir *per
capita* or the heir *per stirpes*[1] was to succeed; but whether
the heir *per capita* gave way when the heirdom *per stirpes*
took place, or the catholic heir when the protestant was
preferred, the inheritable principle survived with a sort of
immortality through all transmigrations—*multosque per
annos stat fortuna domus et avi numerantur avorum.*[2]
This is the spirit of our constitution, not only in its settled
course, but in all its revolutions. Whoever came in, or
however he came in, whether he obtained the crown by
law, or by force, the hereditary succession was either continued or adopted. . . .

The same policy pervades all the laws which have since
been made for the preservation of our liberties. In the 1st
of William and Mary, in the famous statute, called the

1. *Per capita:* by the head, the right of succession divided equally
among individuals. *Per stirpes:* by familial stocks, the right of succession applied in equal degrees to the branches of a family. [R. K.]
2. Throughout many years the fortune of the house remains, and the
ancestors of ancestors are numbered. [R. K.]

Declaration of Right, the two houses utter not a syllable of "a right to frame a government for themselves." You will see, that their whole care was to secure the religion, laws, and liberties, that had been long possessed, and had been lately endangered. "Taking into their most serious consideration the *best* means for making such an establishment, that their religion, laws, and liberties, might not be in danger of being again subverted," they auspicate all their proceedings, by stating as some of those *best* means, "in the *first place*" to do "as their *ancestors in like cases have usually* done for vindicating their *ancient* rights and liberties, to *declare*";—and then they pray the king and queen, "that it may be *declared* and enacted, that *all and singular* the rights and liberties *asserted and declared* are the true *ancient* and indubitable rights and liberties of the people of this kingdom."

You will observe, that from Magna Carta to the Declaration of Right, it has been the uniform policy of our constitution to claim and assert our liberties, as an *entailed inheritance* derived to us from our forefathers, and to be transmitted to our posterity; as an estate specially belonging to the people of this kingdom, without any reference whatever to any other more general or prior right. By this means our constitution preserves an unity in so great a diversity of its parts. We have an inheritable crown; an inheritable peerage; and a house of commons and a people inheriting privileges, franchises, and liberties, from a long line of ancestors.

The policy appears to me to be the result of profound reflection; or rather the happy effect of following nature, which is wisdom without reflection, and above it. A spirit of innovation is generally the result of a selfish temper, and confined views. People will not look forward to posterity, who never look backward to their ancestors. Besides, the people of England well know that the idea of inheritance furnishes a sure principle of conservation, and a sure principle of transmission; without at all excluding a principle of improvement. It leaves acquisition free; but it secures what it acquires. Whatever advantages are obtained by a state proceeding on these maxims, are locked fast as in a sort of family settlement; grasped as in a kind of mortmain for ever. By a constitutional policy working after the pattern of nature, we receive, we hold, we transmit our government and our privileges, in the same manner in which we enjoy and transmit our property and our lives. The institutions of policy, the goods of fortune, the gifts of Providence, are handed down to us, and from us, in the same course and order. Our political system is placed in a just correspondence and symmetry with the order of the world, and with the mode of existence decreed to a permanent body composed of transitory parts; wherein, by the disposition of a stupendous wisdom, moulding together the great mysterious incorporation of the human race, the whole, at one time, is never old, or middle-aged, or young, but, in a condition of unchangeable constancy, moves on through the varied tenour of perpetual decay, fall, renovation, and progression. Thus, by preserving the method of nature in the conduct of the state, in what we improve, we are never wholly new; in what we retain, we are never wholly obsolete. By adhering in this manner and on those principles to our forefathers, we are guided not by the superstition of antiquarians, but by the spirit of philosophick analogy. In this choice of inheritance we have given to our frame of polity the image of a relation in blood; binding up the constitution of our country with our dearest domestick ties; adopting our fundamental laws into the bosom of our family affections; keeping inseparable, and cherishing with the warmth of all their combined and mutually reflected charities, our state, our hearths, our sepulchres, and our altars.

Through the same plan of a conformity to nature in our artificial institutions, and by calling in the aid of her unerring and powerful instincts, to fortify the fallible and feeble contrivances of our reason, we have derived several other, and those no small benefits, from considering our liberties in the light of an inheritance. Always acting as if in the presence of canonized forefathers, the spirit of freedom, leading in itself to misrule and excess, is tempered with an awful gravity. This idea of a liberal descent inspires us with a sense of habitual native dignity, which prevents that upstart insolence almost inevitably adhering to and disgracing those who are the first acquirers of any distinction. By this means our liberty becomes a noble freedom. It carries an imposing and majestick aspect. It has a pedigree and illustrating ancestors. It has its bearings and its ensigns armorial. It has its gallery of portraits; its monumental inscriptions; its records, evidences, and titles. We procure reverence to our civil institutions on the principle upon which nature teaches us to revere individual men; on account of their age, and on account of those from whom they are descended. All your sophisters cannot produce any thing better adapted to preserve a rational and manly freedom than the course that we have pursued, who have chosen our nature rather than our speculations, our breasts rather than our inventions, for the great conservatories and magazines of our rights and privileges.

NATURAL RIGHTS AND REAL RIGHTS
Edmund Burke

Continuing his argument in the *Reflections* (*Works*, Rivington edition, vol. V, pp. 119–127) Burke distinguishes between the "real" and the "pretended" rights of people in a civil social order, and touches upon the necessity for a governing power.

It is no wonder therefore, that with these ideas of every thing in their [the French Revolutionaries] constitution and government at home, either in church or state, as illegitimate and usurped, or, at best as a vain mockery, they look abroad with an eager and passionate enthusiasm. Whilst they are possessed by these notions, it is vain to talk to them of the practice of their ancestors, the fundamental laws of their country, the fixed form of a constitution, whose merits are confirmed by the solid test of long experience, and an encreasing publick strength and national prosperity. They despise experience as the wisdom of unlettered men; and as for the rest, they have wrought under-ground a mine that will blow up, at one grand explosion, all examples of antiquity, all precedents, charters, and acts of parliament. They have "rights of men." Against these there can be no prescription; against these no argument is binding: these admit no temperament, and no compromise: any thing withheld from their full demand is so much of fraud and injustice. Against these their rights of men let no government look for security in the length of its continuance, or in the justice and lenity of its administration. The objections of these speculatists, if its forms do not quadrate with their theories, are as valid against such an old and beneficient government, as against the most violent tyranny, or the greenest usurpation. They are always at issue with governments, not on a question of abuse, but a question of competency, and a question of title. I have nothing to say to the clumsy subtilty of their political metaphysicks. Let them be their amusement in the schools—"*Illa se jactat in aula—Eolus, et clauso ventorum carcere regnet.*"[1]—But let them not break prison to burst like a *Levanter*, to sweep the earth

---

1. "Let Aeolus boast in that hall and reign in the locked prison of the winds." (Virgil, *Aeneid* I.140-1.) [R. K.]

with their hurricane, and to break up the fountains of the great deep to overwhelm us.

Far am I from denying in theory, full as far is my heart from withholding in practice (if I were of power to give or to withhold) the *real* rights of men. In denying their false claims of right, I do not mean to injure those which are real, and are such as their pretended rights would totally destroy. If civil society be made for the advantage of man, all the advantages for which it is made become his right. It is an institution of beneficence; and law itself is only beneficence acting by a rule. Men have a right to live by that rule; they have a right to do justice; as between their fellows, whether their fellows are in politick function or in ordinary occupation. They have a right to the fruits of their industry; and to the means of making their industry fruitful. They have a right to the acquisitions of their parents; to the nourishment and improvement of their offspring; to instruction in life, and to consolation in death. Whatever each man can separately do, without trespassing upon others, he has a right to do for himself; and he has a right to a fair portion of all which society, with all its combinations of skill and force, can do in his favour. In this partnership all men have equal rights; but not to equal things. He that has but five shillings in the partnership, has as good a right to it, as he that has five hundred pounds has to his larger proportion. But he has not a right to an equal dividend in the product of the joint stock; and as to the share of power, authority, and direction which each individual ought to have in the management of the state, that I must deny to be amongst the direct original rights of man in civil society; for I have in my contemplation the civil social man, and no other. It is a thing to be settled by convention.

If civil society be the offspring of convention, that convention must be its law. That convention must limit and modify all the descriptions of constitution which are

formed under it. Every sort of legislature, judicial, or exe-
cutory power, are its creatures. They can have no being in
any other state of things; and how can any man claim,
under the conventions of civil society, rights which do not
so much as suppose its existence? Rights which are absolutely repugnant to it? One of the first motives to civil society, and which becomes one of its fundamental rules, is,
that no man should be judge in his own cause. By this
each person has at once divested himself of the first fundamental right of uncovenanted man, that is, to judge for
himself, and to assert his own cause. He abdicates all right
to be his own governour. He inclusively, in a great measure abandons the right of self-defence, the first law of nature. Men cannot enjoy the rights of an uncivil and of a
civil state together. That he may obtain justice, he gives
up his right of determining, what it is in points the most
essential to him. That he may secure some liberty, he
makes a surrender in trust of the whole of it.

   Government is not made in virtue of natural rights,
which may and do exist in total independence of it; and
exist in much greater clearness, and in a much greater degree of abstract perfection: but their abstract perfection is
their practical defect. By having a right to every thing
they want every thing. Government is a contrivance of
human wisdom to provide for human *wants.* Men have a
right that these wants should be provided for by this wisdom. Among these wants is to be reckoned the want, out
of civil society, of a sufficient restraint upon their passions.
Society requires not only that the passions of individuals
should be subjected, but that even in the mass and body as
well as in the individuals, the inclinations of men should
frequently be thwarted, their will controlled, and their
passions brought into subjection. This can only be done
by a power out of themselves; and not, in the exercise of its
function, subject to that will and to those passions which
it is its office to bridle and subdue. In this sense the restraints on men, as well as their liberties, are to be reck-

oned among their rights. But as the liberties and the restrictions vary with times and circumstances, and admit of infinite modifications, they cannot be settled upon any abstract rule; and nothing is so foolish as to discuss them upon that principle.

The moment you abate any thing from the full rights of men, each to govern himself, and suffer any artificial, positive limitation upon those rights, from that moment the whole organization of government becomes a consideration of convenience. This it is which makes the constitution of a state, and the due distribution of its powers, a matter of the most delicate and complicated skill. It requires a deep knowledge of human nature and human necessities, and of the things which facilitate or obstruct the various ends, which are to be pursued by the mechanism of civil institutions. The state is to have recruits to its strength, and remedies to its distempers. What is the use of discussing a man's abstract right to food or medicine? The question is upon the method of procuring and administering them. In that deliberation I shall always advise to call in the aid of the farmer and the physician, rather than the professor of metaphysicks.

The science of constructing a commonwealth, or renovating it, or reforming it, is, like every other experimental science, not to be taught *a priori.* Nor is it a short experience that can instruct us in that practical science; because the real effects of moral causes are not always immediate; but that which in the first instance is prejudicial may be excellent in its remoter operation; and its excellence may arise even from the ill effects it produces in the beginning. The reverse also happens; and very plausible schemes, with very pleasing commencements, have often shameful and lamentable conclusions. In states there are often some obscure and almost latent causes, things which appear at first view of little moment, on which a very great part of its prosperity or adversity may most essentially depend. The science of government being therefore so practical in itself, and intended for such practical purposes, a matter which requires experience, and even more experience than any person can gain in his whole life, however sagacious and observing he may be, it is with infinite caution that any man ought to venture upon pulling down an edifice, which has answered in any tolerable degree for ages the common purposes of society, or on building it up again, without having models and patterns of approved utility before his eyes.

These metaphysick rights entering into common life, like rays of light which pierce into a dense medium, are, by the laws of nature, refracted from their straight line. Indeed in the gross and complicated mass of human passions and concerns, the primitive rights of men undergo such a variety of refractions and reflections, that it becomes absurd to talk of them as if they continued in the simplicity of their original direction. The nature of man is intricate; the objects of society are of the greatest possible complexity: and therefore no simple disposition or direction of power can be suitable either to man's nature, or to the quality of his affairs. When I hear the simplicity of contrivance aimed at and boasted of in any new political constitutions, I am at no loss to decide that the artificers are grossly ignorant of their trade, or totally negligent of their duty. The simple goverments are fundamentally defective, to say no worse of them. If you were to contemplate society in but one point of view, all these simple modes of polity are infinitely captivating. In effect each would answer its single end much more perfectly than the more complex is able to attain all its complex purposes. But it is better that the whole should be imperfectly and anomalously answered, than that, while some parts are provided for with great exactness, others might be totally neglected, or perhaps materially injured, by the over-care of a favorite member.

The pretended rights of these theorists are all extremes: and in proportion as they are metaphysically true, they are morally and politically false. The rights of men are in a sort of *middle*, incapable of definition, but not impossible to be discerned. The rights of men in governments are their advantages; and these are often in balances between differences of good; in compromises sometimes between good and evil, and sometimes between evil and evil. Political reason is a computing principle; adding, subtracting, multiplying, and dividing, morally and not metaphysically or mathematically, true moral denominations.

By these theorists the right of the people is almost always sophistically confounded with their power. The body of the community, whenever it can come to act, can meet with no effectual resistance; but till power and right are the same, the whole body of them has no right inconsistent with virtue, and the first of all virtues, prudence. Men have no right to what is not reasonable, and to what is not for their benefit; for though a pleasant writer said, *Liceat perire poetis,* when one of them, in cold blood, is said to have leaped into the flames of a volcanick revolution, *Ardentem frigidus Etnam insiluit,*[2] I consider such a frolick rather as an unjustifiable poetick licence, than as one of the franchises of Parnassus; and whether he were poet or divine, or politician, that chose to exercise this kind of right, I think that more wise, because more charitable thoughts would urge me rather to save the man, than to preserve his brazen slippers as the monuments of his folly.

The kind of anniversary sermons to which a great part of what I write refers, if men are not shamed out of their present course, in commmemorating the fact, will cheat many out of the principles, and deprive them of the benefits of the revolution they commemorate. I confess to you, Sir, I never liked this continual talk of resistance, and rev-

---

2. *Liceat perire poetis: "Let poets be permitted to perish." Ardentem frigidus Etnam insiluit:* "In cold blood he [Empedocles] jumped into fiery Aetna." (Horace, *Ars Poetica* 465.) [R. K.]

olution, or the practice of making the extreme medicine of the constitution its daily bread. It renders the habit of society dangerously valetudinary: it is taking periodical doses of mercury sublimate, and swallowing down repeated provocatives of cantharides to our love of liberty.

THE MORAL IMAGINATION
Edmund Burke

Immediately after his famous apostrophe to Marie Antoinette in the *Reflections* (*Works*, Vol. V, pp. 148–55) Burke takes up his concept of the moral imagination, the mark of true civilization; and he discusses the two principles which sustained the European world—the spirit of a gentleman and the spirit of religion.

It is now sixteen or seventeen years since I saw the queen of France, then the dauphiness, at Versailles; and surely never lighted on this orb, which she hardly seemed to touch, a more delightful vision. I saw her just above the horizon, decorating and cheering the elevated sphere she just began to move in—glittering like the morning-star, full of life, and splendour, and joy. Oh! what a revolution! and what an heart must I have, to contemplate without emotion that elevation and that fall! Little did I dream when she added titles of veneration to those of enthusiastick, distant, respectful love, that she should ever be obliged to carry the sharp antidote against disgrace concealed in that bosom; little did I dream that I should have lived to see such disasters fallen upon her in a nation of gallant men, in a nation of men of honour, and of cavaliers. I thought ten thousand swords must have leaped from their scabbards to avenge even a look that threatened her with insult. But the age of chivalry is gone. That of so-phisters, economists, and calculators, has succeeded; and the glory of Europe is extinguished for ever. Never, never more, shall we behold that generous loyalty to rank and sex, that proud submission, that dignified obedience, that subordination of the heart, which kept alive, even in ser-vitude itself, the spirit of an exalted freedom. The un-bought grace of life, the cheap defence of nations, the nurse of manly sentiment and heroick enterprise is gone! It is gone, that sensibility of principle, that chastity of honour, which felt a stain like a wound, which inspired courage whilst it mitigated ferocity, which ennobled whatever it touched, and under which vice itself lost half its evil, by losing all its grossness.

This mixed system of opinion and sentiment had its origin in the ancient chivalry; and the principle, though varied in its appearance by the varying state of human af-fairs, subsisted and influenced through a long succession of generations, even to the time we live in. If it should ever be totally extinguished, the loss I fear will be great. It is this which has given its character to modern Europe. It is this which has distinguished it under all its forms of gov-ernment, and distinguished it to its advantage, from the states of Asia, and possibly from those states which flourished in the most brilliant periods of the antique world. It was this, which, without confounding ranks, had produced a noble equality, and handed it down through all the gradations of social life. It was this opinion which mitigated kings into companions, and raised private men to be fellows with kings. Without force, or opposition, it subdued the fierceness of pride and power; it obliged sov-ereigns to submit to the soft collar of social esteem, com-pelled stern authority to submit to elegance, and gave a domination vanquisher of laws, to be subdued by man-ners.

But now all is to be changed. All the pleasing illusions, which made power gentle, and obedience liberal, which harmonized the different shades of life, and which, by a bland assimilation, incorporated into politicks the sentiments which beautify and soften private society, are to be dissolved by this new conquering empire of light and reason. All the decent drapery of life is to be rudely torn off. All the superadded ideas, furnished from the wardrobe of a moral imagination, which the heart owns, and the understanding ratifies, as necessary to cover the defects of our naked, shivering nature, and to raise it to dignity in our own estimation, are to be exploded as a ridiculous, absurd, and antiquated fashion.

On this scheme of things, a king is but a man, a queen is but a woman; a woman is but an animal; and an animal not of the highest order. All homage paid to the sex in general as such, and without distinct views, is to be regarded as romance and folly. Regicide, and parricide, and sacrilege, are but fictions of superstition, corrupting jurisprudence by destroying its simplicity. The murder of a king, or a queen, or a bishop, or a father, are only common homicide; and if the people are by any chance, or in any way gainers by it, a sort of homicide much the most pardonable, and into which we ought not to make too severe a scrutiny.

On the scheme of this barbarous philosophy, which is the offspring of cold hearts and muddy understandings, and which is as void of solid wisdom, as it is destitute of all taste and elegance, laws are to be supported only by their own terrours, and by the concern, which each individual may find in them, from his own private speculations, or can spare to them from his own private interest. In the groves of *their* academy, at the end of every vista, you see nothing but the gallows. Nothing is left which engages the affections on the part of the commonwealth. On the principles of this mechanick philosophy, our institutions can never be embodied, if I may use the expression, in persons; so as to create in us love, veneration, admiration, or attachment. But that sort of reason which banishes the affections is incapable of filling their place. These publick affections, combined with manners, are required sometimes as supplements, sometimes as correctives, always as aids to law. The precept given by a wise man, as well as a great critick, for the construction of poems, is equally true as to states:—*Non satis est pulchra esse poemata, dulcia sunto.*[1] There ought to be a system of manners in every nation, which a well-formed mind would be disposed to relish. To make us love our country, our country ought to be lovely.

But power, of some kind or other, will survive the shock in which manners and opinions perish; and it will find other and worse means for its support. The usurpation which, in order to subvert ancient institutions, has destroyed ancient principles, will hold power by arts similar to those by which it has acquired it. When the old feudal and chivalrous spirit of *fealty*, which, by freeing kings from fear, freed both kings and subjects from the precaution of tyranny, shall be extinct in the minds of men, plots and assassinations will be anticipated by preventive murder and preventive confiscation, and that long roll of grim and bloody maxims, which form the political code of all power, not standing on its own honour, and the honour of those who are to obey it. Kings will be tyrants from policy, when subjects are rebels from principle.

When ancient opinions and rules of life are taken away, the loss cannot possibly be estimated. From that moment we have no compass to govern us; nor can we know distinctly to what port we steer. Europe, undoubtedly, taken in a mass, was in a flourishing condition the day on which your revolution was completed. How much of that prosperous state was owing to the spirit of our old manners

---

1. "It is not enough for poems to be beautiful, let them be pleasing." (Horace, *Ars Poetica* 99.) [R. K.]

and opinions is not easy to say; but as such causes cannot be indifferent in their operation, we must presume, that, on the whole, their operation was beneficial.

We are but too apt to consider things in the state in which we find them, without sufficiently adverting to the causes by which they have been produced, and possibly may be upheld. Nothing is more certain, than that our manners, our civilization, and all the good things which are connected with manners, and with civilization, have, in this European world of ours, depended for ages upon two principles; and were indeed the result of both combined; I mean the spirit of a gentleman, and the spirit of religion. The nobility and the clergy, the one by profession, the other by patronage, kept learning in existence, even in the midst of arms and confusions, and whilst governments were rather in their causes, than formed. Learning paid back what it received to nobility and to priesthood; and paid it with usury, by enlarging their ideas, and by furnishing their minds. Happy if they had all continued to know their indissoluble union, and their proper place! Happy if learning, not debauched by ambition, had been satisfied to continue the instructor, and not aspired to be the master! Along with its natural protectors and guardians, learning will be cast into the mire; and trodden down under the hoofs of a swinish multitude.

If, as I suspect, modern letters owe more than they are always willing to own to ancient manners, so do other interests which we value full as much as they are worth. Even commerce, and trade, and manufacture, the gods of our economical politicians, are themselves perhaps but creatures; are themselves but effects, which, as first causes, we choose to worship. They certainly grew under the same shade in which learning flourished. They too may decay with their natural protecting principles. With you, for the present at least, they all threaten to disappear together. Where trade and manufactures are wanting to a people, and the spirit of nobility and religion remains, sentiment supplies, and not always ill supplies, their place; but if commerce and the arts should be lost in an experiment to try how well a state may stand without these old fundamental principles, what sort of a thing must be a nation of gross, stupid, ferocious, and, at the same time, poor and sordid barbarians, destitute of religion, honour, or manly pride, possessing nothing at present, and hoping for nothing hereafter?

PREJUDICE, RELIGION, AND THE ANTAGONIST WORLD
Edmund Burke

The meaning of "prejudice," and the link between prejudice and religious faith, are examined in this passage from the *Reflections* (*Works*, Vol. V, pp. 168-70, 173-85). Then Burke develops his concept "the contract of eternal society," set against the "antagonist world of madness, discord, vice, confusion, and unavailing sorrow."

You see, Sir, that in this enlightened age I am bold enough to confess, that we are generally men of untaught feelings; that instead of casting away all our old prejudices, we cherish them to a very considerable degree, and, to take more shame to ourselves, we cherish them because they are prejudices; and the longer they have lasted, and the more generally they have prevailed, the more we cherish them. We are afraid to put men to live and trade each on his own private stock of reason; because we suspect that the stock in each man is small, and that the individuals would do better to avail themselves of the general bank and capital of nations and of ages. Many of our men of speculation, instead of exploding general prejudices, employ their sagacity to discover the latent wisdom which prevails in them. If they find what they seek, and they seldom fail, they think it more wise to continue the prejudice, with the reason involved, than to cast away the coat of prejudice, and to leave nothing but the naked reason; because prejudice, with its reason, has a motive to give action to that reason, and an affection which will give it permanence. Prejudice is of ready application in the emergency; it previously engages the mind in a steady course of wisdom and virture, and does not leave the man hesitating in the moment of decision, sceptical, puzzled, and unresolved. Prejudice renders a man's virtue his habit: and not a series of unconnected acts. Through just prejudice, his duty becomes a part of his nature.

Your literary men, and your politicians, and so do the whole clan of the enlightened among us, essentially differ in these points. They have no respect for the wisdom of others; but they pay it off by a very full measure of confidence in their own. With them it is a sufficient motive to destroy an old scheme of things, because it is an old one. As to the new, they are in no sort of fear with regard to the duration of a building run up in haste; because duration is no object to those who think little or nothing has been done before their time, and who place all their hopes in discovery. They conceive, very systematically, that all things which give perpetuity are mischievous, and therefore they are at inexpiable war with all establishments. They think that government may vary like modes of dress, and with as little ill effect: that there needs no principle of attachment, except a sense of present conveniency, to any constitution of the state. They always speak as if they were of opinion that there is a singular species of compact between them and their magistrates, which binds the magistrate, but which has nothing reciprocal in it, but that the majesty of the people has a right to dissolve it without any reason, but its will. Their attachment to their country itself is only so far as it agrees with some of their fleeting projects; it begins and ends with that scheme of polity which falls in with their momentary opinion.

These doctrines, or rather sentiments, seem prevalent with your new statesmen. But they are wholly different from those on which we have always acted in this country....

We know, and what is better, we feel inwardly, that religion is the basis of civil society, and the source of all good and of all comfort. In England we are so convinced of this, that there is no rust of superstition, with which the accumulated absurdity of the human mind might have crusted it over in the course of ages, that ninety-nine in a hundred of the people of England would not prefer to impiety. We shall never be such fools as to call in an enemy to the substance of any system to remove its corruptions, to supply its defects, or to perfect its construction. If our religious tenets should ever want a further elucidation, we shall not call on atheism to explain them. We shall not light up our temple from that unhallowed fire. It will be illuminated with other lights. It will be perfumed with other incense, than the infectious stuff which is imported by the smugglers of adulterated metaphysicks. If our ecclesiastical establishment should want a revision, it is not avarice or rapacity, publick or private, that we shall employ for the audit, or receipt, or application of its consecrated revenue. Violently condemning neither the Greek nor the Armenian, nor, since heats are subsided, the Roman system of religion, we prefer the Protestant; not because we think it has less of the Christian religion in it, but because, in our judgment, it has more. We are protestants, not from indifference, but from zeal.

We know, and it is our pride to know, that man is by his constitution a religious animal; that atheism is against, not only our reason, but our instincts; and that it cannot prevail long. But if, in the moment of riot, and in a drunken delirium from the hot spirit drawn out of the alembick of hell, which in France is now so furiously boiling, we should uncover our nakedness, by throwing off that Christian religion which has hitherto been our boast and comfort, and one great source of civilization amongst us, and among many other nations, we are apprehensive (being well aware that the mind will not endure a void) that some uncouth, pernicious and degrading superstition might take place of it.

For that reason, before we take from our establishment the natural, human means of estimation, and give it up to contempt, as you have done, and in doing it have incurred the penalties you well deserve to suffer, we desire that some other may be presented to us in the place of it. We shall then form our judgment.

On these ideas, instead of quarrelling with establishments, as some do, who have made a philosophy and a religion of their hostility to such institutions, we cleave closely to them. We are resolved to keep an established church, an established monarchy, an established aristocracy, and an established democracy, each in the degree it exists, and in no greater. I shall shew you presently how much of each of these we possess.

It has been the misfortune (not as these gentlemen think it, the glory) of this age, that every thing is to be discussed, as if the constitution of our country were to be always a subject rather of altercation, than of enjoyment. For this reason, as well as for the satisfaction of those among you (if any such you have among you) who may wish to profit of examples, I venture to trouble you with a few thoughts upon each of these establishments. I do not think they were unwise in ancient Rome, who, when they wished to new model their laws, set commissioners to examine the best constituted republicks within their reach.

First, I beg leave to speak of our church establishment, which is the first of our prejudices, not a prejudice destitute of reason, but involving in it profound and extensive wisdom. I speak of it first. It is first, and last, and midst in our minds. For, taking ground on that religious system, of which we are now in possession, we continue to act on the early received, and uniformly continued sense of mankind. That sense not only, like a wise architect, hath built up the august fabrick of states, but like a provident proprietor, to preserve the structure from profanation and ruin, as a sacred temple, purged from all the impurities of fraud, and violence, and injustice, and tyranny, hath solemnly and for ever consecrated the commonwealth, and all that officiate in it. This consecration is made, that all who administer in the government of men, in which they stand in the person of God himself, should have high and worthy notions of their function and destination; that their hope should be full of immortality; that they should not look to the paltry pelf of the moment, nor to the temporary and transient praise of the vulgar, but to a solid, permanent existence, in the permanent part of their nature, and to a permanent fame and glory, in the example they leave as a rich inheritance to the world.

Such sublime principles ought to be infused into persons of exalted situations; and religious establishments provided, that they may continually revive and enforce them. Every sort of moral, every sort of civil, every sort of politick institution, aiding the rational and natural ties that connect the human understanding and affections to the divine, are not more than necessary, in order to build up that wonderful structure, Man; whose prerogative it is, to be in a great degree a creature of his own making; and who, when made as he ought to be made, is destined to hold no trivial place in the creation. But whenever man is put over men, as the better nature ought ever to preside, in that case more particularly, he should as nearly as possible be approximated to his perfection.

The consecration of the state, by a state religious establishment, is necessary also to operate with a wholesome awe upon free citizens; because, in order to secure their freedom, they must enjoy some determinate portion of power. To them therefore a religion connected with the state, and with their duty towards it, becomes even more necessary than in such societies, where the people, by the terms of their subjection, are confined to private sentiments, and the management of their own family concerns. All persons possessing any portion of power ought to be strongly and awfully impressed with an idea that they act in trust; and that they are to account for their conduct in that trust to the one great Master, Author and Founder of society.

This principle ought even to be more strongly impressed upon the minds of those who compose the collective sovereignty, than upon those of single princes. Without instruments, these princes can do nothing. Whoever uses instruments, in finding helps, finds also impediments. Their power is therefore by no means complete; nor are they safe in extreme abuse. Such persons, however elevated by flattery, arrogance, and self-opinion, must be sensible, that, whether covered or not by positive law, in some way or other they are accountable even here for the abuse of their trust. If they are not cut off by a rebellion of their people, they may be strangled by the very janissaries kept for their security against all other rebellion. Thus we have seen the king of France sold by his soldiers for an increase of pay. But where popular authority is absolute and unrestrained, the people have an infinitely greater, because a far better founded confidence in their own power. They are themselves, in a great measure, their own instruments. They are nearer to their objects. Besides, they are less under responsibility to one of the greatest controlling powers on earth, the sense of fame and estimation. The share of infamy, that is likely to fall to the lot of each individual in publick acts, is small indeed; the operation of opinion being in the inverse ratio to the number of those who abuse power. Their own approbation of their own acts has to them the appearance of a publick judgment in their favour. A perfect democracy is therefore the most shameless thing in the world. As it is the most shameless, it is also the most fearless. No man apprehends in his person that he can be made subject to punishment. Certainly the people at large never ought: for as all punishments are for example towards the conservation of the people at large, the people at large can never become the subject of punishment by any human hand. It is therefore of infinite importance that they should not be suffered to imagine that their will, any more than that of kings, is the standard of right and wrong. They ought to be persuaded that they are full as little entitled, and far less qualified, with safety to themselves, to use any arbitrary power whatsoever; that therefore they are not, under a false show of liberty, but, in truth, to exercise an unnatural, inverted domination, tyrannically to exact, from those who officiate in the state, not an entire devotion to their interest, which is their right, but an abject submission to their occasional will; extinguishing thereby, in all those who serve them, all moral principle, all sense of dignity, all use of judgment, and all consistency of character; whilst by the very same process they give themselves up as a proper, a suitable, but a most contemptible prey to the servile ambition of popular sycophants, or courtly flatterers.

When the people have emptied themselves of all the lust of selfish will, which without religion it is utterly impossible they ever should, when they are conscious that they exercise, and exercise perhaps in a higher link of the order of delegation, the power, which to be legitimate must be according to that eternal, immutable law, in which will and reason are the same, they will be more careful how they place power in base and incapable hands. In their nomination to office, they will not appoint to the exercise of authority, as to a pitiful job, but as to a holy function; not according to their sordid, selfish interest, nor to their wanton caprice, nor to their arbitrary will; but they will confer that power (which any man may well tremble to give or to receive) on those only, in whom they may discern that predominant proportion of active virtue and wisdom, taken together and fitted to the charge, such, as in the great and inevitable mixed mass of human imperfections and infirmities, is to be found.

When they are habitually convinced that no evil can be acceptable, either in the act or the permission, to him whose essence is good, they will be better able to extirpate out of the minds of all magistrates, civil, ecclesiastical, or military, any thing that bears the least resemblance to a proud and lawless domination.

But one of the first and most leading principles on which the commonwealth and the laws are consecrated, is lest the temporary possessors and life-renters in it, unmindful of what they have received from their ancestors, or of what is due to their posterity, should act as if they were the entire masters; that they should not think it amongst their rights to cut off the entail, or commit waste on the inheritance, by destroying at their pleasure the whole original fabric of their society; hazarding to leave to those who come after them a ruin instead of an habitation—and teaching these successors as little to respect their contrivances, as they had themselves respected the institutions of their forefathers. By this unprincipled facility of changing the state as often, and as much, and in as many ways, as there are floating fancies or fashions, the whole chain and continuity of the commonwealth would be broken. No one generation could link with the other. Men would become little better than the flies of a summer.

And first of all, the science of jurisprudence, the pride of the human intellect, which, with all its defects, redundancies, and errours, is the collected reason of ages, combining the principles of original justice with the infinite variety of human concerns, as a heap of old exploded errours, would be no longer studied. Personal self-sufficiency and arrogance (the certain attendants upon all those who have never experienced a wisdom greater than their own) would usurp the tribunal. Of course no certain laws, establishing invariable grounds of hope and fear, would keep the actions of men in a certain course, or direct them to a certain end. Nothing stable in the modes of holding property, or exercising function, could form a solid ground on which any parent could speculate in the education of his offspring, or in a choice for their future establishment in the world. No principles would be early worked into the habits. As soon as the most able instructor had completed his laborious course of institution, instead of sending forth his pupil, accomplished in a virtuous discipline, fitted to procure him attention and respect, in his place in society, he would find every thing altered; and that he had turned out a poor creature to the contempt and derision of the world, ignorant of the true grounds of estimation. Who would insure a tender and delicate sense of honour to beat almost with the first pulses of the heart, when no man could know what would be the test of honour in a nation, continually varying the standard of its coin? No part of life would retain its acquisitions. Barbarism with regard to science and literature, unskilfulness with regard to arts and manufactures, would infallibly succeed to the want of a steady education and settled principle; and thus the commonwealth itself would, in a few generations, crumble away, be disconnected into the dust and powder of individuality, and at length dispersed to all the winds of heaven.

To avoid therefore the evils of inconstancy and versatility, ten thousand times worse than those of obstinacy and the blindest prejudice, we have consecrated the state, that no man should approach to look into its defects or corruptions but with due caution; that he should never dream of beginning its reformation by its subversion; that he should approach to the faults of the state as to the wounds of a father, with pious awe, and trembling solicitude. By this wise prejudice we are taught to look with horrour on those children of their country, who are prompt rashly to hack that aged parent in pieces, and put him into the kettle of magicians, in hopes that by their poisonous weeds, and wild incantations, they may regenerate the paternal constitution, and renovate their father's life.

Society is indeed a contract. Subordinate contracts for objects of mere occasional interest may be dissolved at pleasure—but the state ought not to be considered nothing better than a partnership agreement in a trade of pepper and coffee, calico or tobacco, or some other such low concern, to be taken up for a little temporary interest, and to be dissolved by the fancy of the parties. It is to be looked on with other reverence; because it is not a partnership in things subservient only to the gross animal existence of a temporary and perishable nature. It is a partnership in all science; a partnership in all art; a partnership in every virtue, and in all perfection. As the ends of such a partnership cannot be obtained in many generations, it becomes a partnership not only between those who are living, but between those who are living, those who are dead, and those who are to be born. Each contract of each particular state is but a clause in the great primaeval contract of eternal society, linking the lower with the higher natures, connecting the visible and invisible world, according to a fixed compact sanctioned by the inviolable oath which holds all physical and all moral natures, each in their appointed place. This law is not subject to the will of those, who by an obligation above them, and infinitely superiour, are bound to submit their will to that law. The municipal corporations of that universal kingdom are not morally at liberty at their pleasure, and on their speculations of a contingent improvement, wholly to separate and tear asunder the bands of their subordinate community, and to dissolve it into an unsocial, uncivil, unconnected chaos of elementary principles. It is the first and supreme necessity only, a necessity that is not chosen, but chooses, a necessity paramount to deliberation, that admits no discussion, and demands no evidence, which alone can justify a resort to anarchy. This necessity is no exception to the rule; because this necessity itself is a part too of that moral and physical disposition of things, to which man must be obedient by consent of force: but if that which is only submission to necessity should be made the object of choice, the law is broken, nature is disobeyed, and the rebellious are outlawed, cast forth, and exiled, from this world of reason, and order, and peace, and virtue, and fruitful penitence, into the antagonist world of madness, discord, vice, confusion, and unavailing sorrow.

PRESERVING AND REFORMING
Edmund Burke

Unable to construct, the French radicals hasten to pull down—so Burke argues in the *Reflections* (*Works*, Vol. V, pp. 302–309). He proceeds to describe the true statesman's duty of at once preserving and reforming social institutions.

It is this inability to wrestle with difficulty which has obliged the arbitrary Assembly of France to commence their schemes of reform with abolition and total destruction.[1] But is it in destroying and pulling down that skill is

---

1. A leading member of the Assembly, M. Rabaud de St. Etienne, has expressed the principle of all their proceedings as clearly as possible—nothing can be more simple:—"*Tous les établissemens en France couronnent le malheur du peuple: pour le rendre heureux il faut rénouveler; changer ses idées; changer ses loix; changér les moeurs;... changer les hommes; changer les choses; changer les mots.... tout détruire; oui, tout détruire; puisque tout est à*

displayed? Your mob can do this as well at least as your assemblies. The shallowest understanding, the rudest hand, is more than equal to that task. Rage and frenzy will pull down more in half an hour, than prudence, deliberation, and foresight can build up in an hundred years. The errours and defects of old establishments are visible and palpable. It calls for little ability to point them out; and, where absolute power is given, it requires but a word wholly to abolish the vice and the establishment together. The same lazy but restless disposition, which loves sloth and hates quiet, directs these politicians, when they come to work for supplying the place of what they have destroyed. To make every thing the reverse of what they have seen is quite as easy as to destroy. No difficulties occur in what has never been tried. Criticism is almost baffled in discovering the defects of what has not existed; and eager enthusiasm and cheating hope have all the wide field of imagination, in which they may expatiate with little or no opposition.

At once to preserve and to reform is quite another thing. When the useful parts of an old establishment are kept, and what is superadded is to be fitted to what is retained, a vigorous mind, steady, persevering attention, various powers of comparison and combination, and the resources of an understanding fruitful in expedients, are to be exercised; they are to be exercised in a continued con-

---

recréer." [All the establishments of France crown the misery of the people: to make them happy it is necessary to renew them, change their ideas, change their laws, change their manners . . . change men, change things, change words . . . destroy everything; yes, destroy everything, since everything is to be recreated.] This gentleman was chosen president in an assembly not sitting at Quinze-vingt [a hospital for the blind], or the Petits Maisons [an insane asylum]; and composed of persons giving themselves out to be rational beings; but neither his ideas, language, or conduct, differ in the smallest degree from the discourses, opinions, and actions of those within and without the Assembly, who direct the operations of the machine now at work in France.

flict with the combined force of opposite vices, with the obstinacy that rejects all improvement, and the levity that is fatigued and disgusted with every thing of which it is in possession. But you may object—"A process of this kind is slow. It is not fit for an assembly, which glories in performing in a few months the work of ages. Such a mode of reforming, possibly, might take up many years." Without question it might; and it ought. It is one of the excellencies of a method in which time is amongst the assistants, that its operation is slow, and in some cases almost imperceptible. If circumspection and caution are a part of wisdom, when we work only upon inanimate matter, surely they become a part of duty too, when the subject of our demolition and construction is not brick and timber, but sentient beings, by the sudden alteration of whose state, condition, and habits, multitudes may be rendered miserable. But it seems as if it were the prevalent opinion in Paris, that an unfeeling heart, and an undoubting confidence, are the sole qualifications for a perfect legislator. Far different are my ideas of that high office. The true lawgiver ought to have a heart full of sensibility. He ought to love and respect his kind, and to fear himself. It may be allowed to his temperament to catch his ultimate object with an intuitive glance; but his movements towards it ought to be deliberate. Political arrangement, as it is a work for social ends, is to be only wrought by social means. There mind must conspire with mind. Time is required to produce that union of minds which alone can produce all the good we aim at. Our patience will achieve more than our force. If I might venture to appeal to what is so much out of fashion in Paris, I mean to experience, I should tell you, that in my course I have known, and, according to my measure, have co-operated with great men; and I have never yet seen any plan which has not been mended by the observations of those who were much inferiour in understanding to the person who took the lead in the business. By a slow but well-sustained progress, the effect of each step is watched; the good or ill success of the first gives light to us in the second; and so, from light to light, we are conducted with safety through the whole series. We see that the parts of the system do not clash. The evils latent in the most promising contrivances are provided for as they arise. One advantage is as little as possible sacrificed to another. We compensate, we reconcile, we balance. We are enabled to unite into a consistent whole the various anomalies and contending principles that are found in the minds and affairs of men. From hence arises, not an excellence in simplicity, but, one far superior, an excellence in composition. Where the great interests of mankind are concerned through a long succession of generations, that succession ought to be admitted into some share in the councils which are so deeply to affect them. If justice requires this, the work itself requires the aid of more minds than one age can furnish. It is from this view of things that the best legislators have been often satisfied with the establishment of some sure, solid, and ruling principle in government; a power like that which some of the philosophers have called a plastic nature; and having fixed the principle, they have left it afterwards to its own operation.

To proceed in this manner, that is, to proceed with a presiding principle, and a prolifick energy, is with me the criterion of profound wisdom. What your politicians think the marks of a bold, hardy genius, are only proofs of a deplorable want of ability. By their violent haste, and their defiance of the process of nature, they are delivered over blindly to every projector and adventurer, to every alchymist and emperick. They despair of turning to account any thing that is common. Diet is nothing in their system of remedy. The worst of it is, that this their despair of curing common distempers by regular methods, arises not only from defect of comprehension, but, I fear, from some malignity of disposition. Your legislators seem to have taken their opinions of all professions, ranks, and offices, from the declamations and buffooneries of satirists; who would themselves be astonished if they were held to the letter of their own descriptions. By listening only to these, your leaders regard all things only on the side of their vices and faults, and view those vices and faults under every colour of exaggeration. It is undoubtedly true, though it may seem paradoxical; but in general, those who are habitually employed in finding and displaying faults, are unqualified for the work of reformation: because their minds are not only unfurnished with patterns of the fair and good, but by habit they come to take no delight in the contemplation of those things. By hating vices too much, they come to love men too little. It is therefore not wonderful, that they should be indisposed and unable to serve them. From hence arises the complexional disposition of some of your guides to pull every thing in pieces. At this malicious game they display the whole of their *quadrimanous* activity. As to the rest, the paradoxes of eloquent writers, brought forth purely as a sport of fancy, to try their talents, to rouze attention, and excite surprise, are taken up by these gentlemen, not in the spirit of the original authors, as means of cultivating their taste and improving their style. These paradoxes become with them serious grounds of action, upon which they proceed in regulating the most important concerns of the state. Cicero ludicrously describes Cato as endeavouring to act, in the commonwealth, upon the school paradoxes, which exercised the wits of the junior students in the Stoick philosophy. If this was true of Cato, these gentlemen copy after him in the manner of some persons who lived about his time—*pede nudo Catonem.*[2] Mr. Hume told me, that he had from Rousseau himself the secret of his principles of composition. That acute, though eccentrick observer, had perceived, that to strike and interest the publick, the marvellous must be produced; that the marvellous of the hea-

---

2. "Bare-footed Cato." [R. K.]

then mythology had long since lost is effects; that giants, magicians, fairies, and heroes of romance which succeeded, had exhausted the portion of credulity which belonged to their age; that now nothing was left to a writer but that species of the marvellous, which might still be produced, and with as great an effect as ever, though in another way; that is, the marvellous in life, in manners, in characters, and in extraordinary situations, giving rise to new and unlooked-for strokes in politicks and morals. I believe, that were Rousseau alive, and in one of his lucid intervals, he would be shocked at the practical frenzy of his scholars, who in their paradoxes are servile imitators; and even in their incredulity discover an implicit faith.

WHO SPEAKS FOR THE PEOPLE?

Edmund Burke

As the Whig party was torn apart by opinions concerning the French Revolution, Burke published his *Appeal to the Old Whigs from the New* (1791), from which this extract is taken (*Works*, Vol. VI, pp. 210–219, 249–60). A nation's people, he declares, are not a mere temporary majority; and he explains the composition of a natural aristocracy.

When the supreme authority of the people is in question, before we attempt to extend or to confine it, we ought to fix in our minds, with some degree of distinctness, an idea of what it is we mean, when we say the PEOPLE.

In a state of *rude* nature there is no such thing as a people. A number of men in themselves have no collective capacity. The idea of a people is the idea of a corporation. It is wholly artificial; and made like all other legal fictions by common agreement. What the particular nature of that agreement was, is collected from the form into which the particular society has been cast. Any other is not *their* covenant. When men, therefore, break up the original compact or agreement which gives its corporate form and capacity to a state, they are no longer a people; they have no longer a corporate existence; they have no longer a legal, coactive force to bind within, nor a claim to be recognised abroad. They are a number of vague, loose individuals, and nothing more. With them all is to begin again. Alas! they little know how many a weary step is to be taken before they can form themselves into a mass, which has a true, politick personality.

We hear much from men, who have not acquired their hardiness of assertion from the profundity of their thinking, about the omnipotence of a *majority*, in such a dissolution of an ancient society as hath been taken place in France. But amongst men so disbanded, there can be no such thing as majority or minority; or power in any one person to bind another. The power of acting by a majority, which the gentlemen theorists seem to assume so readily, after they have violated the contract out of which it has arisen, (if at all it existed) must be grounded on two assumptions; first, that of an incorporation produced by unanimity; and secondly, an unanimous agreement, that the act of a mere majority (say of one) shall pass with them and with others as the act of the whole.

We are so little affected by things which are habitual, that we consider this idea of the decision of a *majority* as if it were a law of our original nature: but such constructive whole, residing in a part only, is one of the most violent fictions of positive law, that ever has been or can be made on the principles of artificial incorporation. Out of civil society nature knows nothing of it; nor are men, even when arranged according to civil order, otherwise than by very long training, brought at all to submit to it. The mind is brought far more easily to acquiesce in the proceedings of one man, or a few, who act under a general procuration for the state, than in the vote of a victorious majority in councils, in which every man has his share in the deliberation. For there the beaten party are exasperated and soured by the previous contention, and mortified by the conclusive defeat. This mode of decision, where wills may be so nearly equal, where, according to circumstances, the smaller number may be the stronger force, and where apparent reason may be all upon one side, and on the other little else than impetuous appetite; all this must be the result of a very particular and special convention, confirmed afterwards by long habits of obedience, by a sort of discipline in society, and by a strong hand, vested with stationary, permanent power, to enforce this sort of constructive general will. What organ it is that shall declare the corporate mind is so much a matter of positive arrangement, that several states, for the validity of several of their acts, have required a proportion of voices much greater than that of a mere majority. These proportions are so entirely governed by convention, that in some cases the minority decides. The laws in many countries to *condemn* require more than a mere majority; less than an equal number to *acquit*. In our judicial trials we require unanimity either to condemn or to absolve. In some incorporations one man speaks for the whole; in others, a few. Until the other day, in the constitution of Poland, unanimity was required to give validity to any act of their great national council or diet. This approaches much more nearly to rude nature than the institutions of any other country. Such, indeed, every commonwealth must be, without a positive law to recognise in a certain number the will of the entire body.

If men dissolve their ancient incorporation, in order to regenerate their community, in that state of things each man has a right, if he pleases, to remain an individual. Any number of individuals, who can agree upon it, have an undoubted right to form themselves into a state apart, and wholly independent. If any of these is forced into the fellowship of another, this is conquest and not compact. On every principle, which supposes society to be in virtue of a free covenant, this compulsive incorporation must be null and void.

As a people can have no right to a corporate capacity without universal consent, so neither have they a right to hold exclusively any lands in the name and title of a corporation. On the scheme of the present rulers in our neighbouring country, regenerated as they are, they have no more right to the territory called France than I have. I have a right to pitch my tent in any unoccupied place I can find for it; and I may apply to my own maintenance any part of their unoccupied soil. I may purchase the house or vineyard of any individual proprietor who refuses his consent (and most proprietors have, as far as they dared, refused it) to the new incorporation. I stand in his independent place. Who are these insolent men calling themselves the French nation, that would monopolize this fair domain of nature? Is it because they speak a certain jargon? Is it their mode of chattering, to me unintelligible, that forms their title to my land? Who are they who claim by prescription and descent from certain gangs of banditti called Franks, and Burgundians, and Visigoths, of whom I may have never heard, and ninety-nine out of an hundred of themselves certainly never have heard; whilst at the very time they tell me, that prescription and long possession form no title to property? Who are they that presume to assert that the land which I purchased of the individual, a natural person, and not a fiction of state, belongs to them who in the very capacity in which they make their claim can exist only as an imaginary being, and in virtue of the very prescription which they reject and disown? This mode of arguing might be pushed into all the detail, so as to leave no sort of doubt, that on their principles, and on the sort of footing on which they have thought proper to place themselves, the crowd of men, on the one side of the channel, who have the impudence to call themselves a people, can never be the lawful, exclusive possessors of the soil. By what they call reasoning without prejudice, they leave not one stone upon another in the fabrick of human society. They subvert all the authority which they hold, as well as all that which they have destroyed.

As in the abstract, it is perfectly clear, that, out of a state of civil society, majority and minority are relations which can have no existence; and that, in civil society, its own specifick conventions in each corporation determine what it is that constitutes the people, so as to make their act the signification of the general will: to come to particulars, it is equally clear, that neither in France nor in England has the original, or any subsequent compact of the state, expressed or implied, constituted *a majority of men, told by the head,* to be the acting people of their several communities. And I see as little of policy or utility, as there is of right, in laying down a principle that a majority of men told by the head are to be considered as the people, and that as such their will is to be law. What policy can there be found in arrangements made in defiance of every political principle? To enable men to act with the weight and character of a people, and to answer the ends for which they are incorporated into that capacity, we must suppose them (by means immediate or consequential) to be in that state of habitual social discipline, in which the wiser, the more expert, and the more opulent conduct, and by conducting enlighten and protect the weaker, the less knowing, and the less provided with the goods of fortune. When the multitude are not under this discipline, they can scarcely be said to be in civil society. Give once a certain constitution of things, which produces a variety of conditions and circumstances in a state, and there is in nature and reason a principle which, for their own benefit, post-

pones, not the interest but the judgment, of those who are
numero plures, to those who are *virtute et honore majores.*[1] Numbers in a state (supposing, which is not the
case in France, that a state does exist) are always of con-
sideration—but they are not the whole consideration. It is
in things more serious than a play, that it may be truly
said *satis est equitatem mihi plaudere.*[2]

A true natural aristocracy is not a separate interest in
the state, or separable from it. It is an essential integrant
part of any large body rightly constituted. It is formed out
of a class of legitimate presumptions, which, taken as generalities, must be admitted for actual truths. To be bred in
a place of estimation; to see nothing low and sordid from
one's infancy; to be taught to respect one's self; to be habituated to the censorial inspection of the publick eye; to
look early to publick opinion; to stand upon such elevated
ground as to be enabled to take a large view of the widespread and infinitely diversified combinations of men and
affairs in a large society; to have leisure to read, to reflect,
to converse; to be enabled to draw the court and attention
of the wise and learned wherever they are to be found;—
to be habituated in armies to command and to obey; to be
taught to despise danger in the pursuit of honour and
duty; to be formed to the greatest degree of vigilance,
foresight, and circumspection, in a state of things in which
no fault is committed with impunity, and the slightest
mistakes draw on the most ruinous consequences—to be
led to a guarded and regulated conduct, from a sense that
you are considered as an instructor of your fellow-citizens
in their highest concerns, and that you act as a reconciler
between God and man—to be employed as an administrator of law and justice, and to be thereby amongst the first
benefactors to mankind—to be a professor of high science,

---

1. *Numero plures:* greater in number. *Virtute et honore majores:*
greater in virtue and honor. [R. K.]
2. "It is enough for me to applaud justice." [R. K.]

or of liberal and ingenuous art—to be amongst rich traders, who from their success are presumed to have sharp and vigorous understandings, and to possess the virtues of diligence, order, constancy, and regularity, and to have cultivated an habitual regard to commutative justice— these are the circumstances of men, that form what I should call a *natural* aristocracy, without which there is no nation.

The state of civil society, which necessarily generates this aristocracy, is a state of nature; and much more truly so than a savage and incoherent mode of life. For man is by nature reasonable; and he is never perfectly in his natural state, but when he is placed where reason may be best cultivated, and most predominates. Art is man's nature. We are as much, at least, in a state of nature in formed manhood, as in the immature and helpless infancy. Men, qualified in the manner I have just described, form in nature, as she operates in the common modification of society, the leading, guiding, and governing part. It is the soul to the body, without which the man does not exist. To give therefore no more importance, in the social order, to such descriptions of men, than that of so many units, is a horrible usurpation.

When great multitudes act together, under that discipline of nature, I recognise the PEOPLE. I acknowledge something that perhaps equals, and ought always to guide the sovereignty of convention. In all things the voice of this grand chorus of national harmony ought to have a mighty and decisive influence. But when you disturb this harmony; when you break up this beautiful order, this array of truth and nature, as well as of habit and prejudice; when you separate the common sort of men from their proper chieftains so as to form them into an adverse army, I no longer know that venerable object called the people in such a disbanded race of deserters and vagabonds. For a while they may be terrible indeed; but in such a manner as wild beasts are terrible. The mind owes to them no sort of submission. They are, as they have always been reputed, rebels. They may lawfully be fought with, and brought under, whenever an advantage offers. Those who attempt by outrage and violence to deprive men of any advantage which they hold under the laws, and to destroy the natural order of life, proclaim war against them.

PASSION AND CONTROL
Edmund Burke

Replying to a Frenchman during 1791 in his *Letter to a Member of the National Assembly* (*Works*, Vol. VI, pp. 63–64), Burke touches upon the need for personal morality to prevent liberty from being perverted into license.

I am constantly of opinion, that your states, in three orders, on the footing on which they stood in 1614, were capable of being brought into a proper and harmonious combination with royal authority. This constitution by estates, was the natural and only just representation of France. It grew out of the habitual conditions, relations, and reciprocal claims of men. It grew out of the circumstances of the country, and out of the state of property. The wretched scheme of your present masters is not to fit the constitution to the people, but wholly to destroy conditions, to dissolve relations, to change the state of the nation, and to subvert property, in order to fit their country to their theory of a constitution.

Until you make out practically that great work, a combination of opposing forces, "a work of labour long, and endless praise," the utmost caution ought to have been used in the reduction of the royal power, which alone was capable of holding together the comparatively heterogeneous mass of your states. But, at this day, all these considerations are unseasonable. To what end should we discuss the limitations of royal power? Your king is in prison. Why speculate on the measure and standard of liberty? I doubt much, very much indeed, whether France is at all ripe for liberty on any standard. Men are qualified for civil liberty in exact proportion to their disposition to put moral chains upon their own appetites; in proportion as their love of justice is above their rapacity; in proportion as their soundness and sobriety of understanding is above their vanity and presumption; in proportion as they are more disposed to listen to the counsels of the wise and good, in preference to the flattery of knaves. Society cannot exist unless a controlling power upon will and appetite be placed somewhere, and the less of it there is within, the more there must be without. It is ordained in the eternal constitution of things, that men of intemperate minds cannot be free. Their passions forge their fetters.

Part Two

AMERICAN LIBERTY UNDER LAW

In America, the Federalists became as resolutely opposed to the ideas and consequences of the French Revolution as was Edmund Burke. Federalist thought, indeed—especially that of the Federalist with the greatest practical influence, John Marshall—owed a great deal to Burke. But the chief Federalists were also men possessed of remarkable minds of their own. In this section of the *Reader* we find room for some passages by John Adams, Alexander Hamilton, and Fisher Ames.

THE PRUDENT
CONSTITUTIONS OF AMERICA
John Adams

The learned and mordant John Adams (1735–1826) was America's first minister to the British court when the Constitutional Convention assembled at Philadelphia. To refute the abstract and doctrinaire criticisms made by Turgot and other enlightenment reformers of the political institutions of the infant United States, Adams wrote his huge *Defence of the Constitutions of Government of the United States of America*, in three volumes. This extract from the Preface to his first volume (1787) is a good sample of Adams as both practical statesman and historical scholar. See *The Works of John Adams*, edited by Charles Francis Adams (Boston, 1851), Vol. IV, pp. 283–94.

The arts and sciences, in general, during the three or four last centuries, have had a regular course of progressive improvement. The inventions in mechanic arts, the discoveries in natural philosophy, navigation, and commerce, and the advancement of civilization and humanity, have occasioned changes in the condition of the world, and the human character, which would have astonished the most refined nations of antiquity. A continuation of similar exertions is every day rendering Europe more and more like one community, or single family. Even in the theory and practice of government, in all the simple monarchies, considerable improvements have been made. The checks and balances of republican governments have been in some degree adopted at the courts of princes. By the erection of various tribunals, to register the laws, and exercise the judicial power—by indulging the petitions and remonstrances of subjects, until by habit they are regarded as rights—a control has been established over ministers of state, and the royal councils, which, in some degree, approaches the spirit of republics. Property is generally secure, and personal liberty seldom invaded. The press has great influence, even where it is not expressly tolerated; and the public opinion must be respected by a minister, or his place becomes insecure. Commerce begins to thrive; and if religious toleration were established, personal liberty, a little more protected, by giving an absolute right to demand a public trial in a certain reasonable time, and the states were invested with a few more privileges, or rather restored to some that have been taken away, these governments would be brought to as great a degree of perfection, they would approach as near to the character of governments of laws and not of men, as their nature will probably admit of. In so general a refinement, or more properly a reformation of manners and improvement in science, is it not unaccountable that the knowledge of the principles and construction of free governments, in which the happiness of life, and even the further progress of improvement in education and society, in knowledge and virtue, are so deeply interested, should have remained at a full stand for two or three thousand years?

According to a story in Herodotus, the nature of monarchy, aristocracy, and democracy, and the advantages and inconveniences of each, were as well understood at the time of the neighing of the horse of Darius, as they are at this hour. A variety of mixtures of these simple species were conceived and attempted, with various success, by the Greeks and Romans. Representations, instead of collections, of the people; a total separation of the executive from the legislative power, and of the judicial from both;

and a balance in the legislature, by three independent, equal branches, are perhaps the only three discoveries in the constitution of a free government, since the institution of Lycurgus. Even these have been so unfortunate, that they have *never* spread: the first has been given up by all the nations, excepting one, which had once adopted it; and the other two, reduced to practice, if not invented, by the English nation, have never been initiated by any other, except their own descendants in America.

While it would be rash to say, that nothing further can be done to bring a free government, in all its parts, still nearer to perfection, the representations of the people are most obviously susceptible of improvement. The end to be aimed at, in the formation of a representative assembly, seems to be the sense of the people, the public voice. The perfection of the portrait consists in its likeness. Numbers, or property, or both, should be the rule; and the proportions of electors and members an affair of calculation. The duration should not be so long that the deputy should have time to forget the opinions of his constituents. Corruption in elections is the great enemy of freedom. Among the provisions to prevent it, more frequent elections, and a more general privilege of voting, are not all that might be devised. Dividing the districts, diminishing the distance of travel, and confining the choice to residents, would be great advances towards the annihilation of corruption. The modern aristocracies of Holland, Venice, Bern, etc., have tempered themselves with innumerable checks, by which they have given a great degree of stability to that form of government; and though liberty and life can never be there enjoyed so well as in a free republic, none is perhaps more capable of profound sagacity. We shall learn to prize the checks and balances of a free government, and even those of the modern aristocracies, if we recollect the miseries of Greece, which arose from its ignorance of them. The only balance attempted against the ancient kings was a body of nobles; and the consequences were perpetual alternations of rebellion and tyranny, and the butchery of thousands upon every revolution from one to the other. When kings were abolished, aristocracies tyrannized; and then no balance was attempted but between aristocracy and democracy. This, in the nature of things, could be no balance at all, and therefore the pendulum was forever on the swing.

It is impossible to read in Thucydides,[1] his account of the factions and confusions throughout all Greece, which were introduced by this want of an equilibrium, without horror. . . .

"Such things ever will be," says Thucydides, "so long as human nature continues the same." But if this nervous historian had known a balance of three powers, he would not have pronounced the distemper so incurable, but would have added—*so long as parties in cities remain unbalanced.* . . .

Such were the fashionable outrages of unbalanced parties. In the name of human and divine benevolence, is such a system as this to be recommended to Americans, in this age of the world? Human nature is as incapable now of going through revolutions with temper and sobriety, with patience and prudence, or without fury and madness, as it was among the Greeks so long ago. The latest revolution that we read of was conducted, at least on one side, in the Grecian style, with laconic energy; and with a little Attic salt, at least, without too much patience, foresight, and prudence, on the other. Without three orders, and an effectual balance between them, in every American constitution, it must be destined to frequent unavoidable revolutions; though they are delayed a few years, they must come in time. The United States are large and populous nations, in comparison with the Grecian commonwealths, or even the Swiss cantons; and they are growing every day more disproportionate, and therefore less capable of being

1. Lib. iii. 81, 82.

held together by simple governments. Countries that increase in population so rapidly as the States of America did, even during such an impoverishing and destructive war as the last was, are not to be long bound with silken threads; lions, young or old, will not be bound by cobwebs. It would be better for America, it is nevertheless agreed, to ring all the changes with the whole set of bells, and go through all the revolutions of the Grecian States, rather than establish an absolute monarchy among them, notwithstanding all the great and real improvements which have been made in that kind of government.

The objection to it is not because it is supported by nobles, and a subordination of ranks; for all governments, even the most democratical, are supported by a subordination of offices, and of ranks too. None ever existed without it but in a state of anarchy and outrage, in a contempt of law and justice, no better than no government. But the nobles, in the European monarchies, support them more by opposing than promoting their ordinary views. The kings are supported by their armies; the nobles support the crown, as it is in full possession of the gift of all employments; but they support it still more by checking its ministers, and preventing them from running into abuses of power and wanton despotism; otherwise the people would be pushed to extremities and insurrections. It is thus that the nobles reconcile the monarchical authority to the obedience of the subjects; but take away the standing armies, and leave the nobles to themselves, and in a few years, they would overturn every monarchy in Europe, and erect aristocracies.

It is become a kind of fashion among writers, to admit, as a maxim, that if you could be always sure of a wise, active, and virtuous prince, monarchy would be the best of governments. But this is so far from being admissible, that it will forever remain true, that a free government has a great advantage over a simple monarchy. The best and wisest prince, by means of a freer communication with his people, and the greater opportunities to collect the best advice from the best of his subjects, would have an immense advantage in a free state over a monarchy. A senate consisting of all that is most noble, wealthy, and able in the nation, with a right to counsel the crown at all times, is a check to ministers, and a security against abuses, such as a body of nobles who never meet, and have no such right, can never supply. Another assembly, composed of representatives chosen by the people in all parts, gives free access to the whole nation, and communicates all its wants, knowledge, projects, and wishes to government; it excites emulation among all classes, removes complaints, redresses grievances, affords opportunities of exertion to genius, though in obscurity, and gives full scope to all the faculties of man; it opens a passage for every speculation to the legislature, to administration, and to the public; it gives a universal energy to the human character, in every part of the state, such as never can be obtained in a monarchy.

There is a third particular which deserves attention both from governments and people. In a simple monarchy, the ministers of state can never know their friends from their enemies; secret cabals undermine their influence, and blast their reputation. This occasions a jealousy ever anxious and irritated, which never thinks the government safe without an encouragement of informers and spies, throughout every part of the state, who interrupt the tranquillity of private life, destroy the confidence of families in their own domestics and in one another, and poison freedom in its sweetest retirements. In a free government, on the contrary, the ministers can have no enemies of consequence but among the members of the great or little council, where every man is obliged to take his side, and declare his opinion, upon every question. This circumstance alone, to every manly mind, would be sufficient to decide the preference in favor of a free government. Even secrecy, where the executive is entire in one hand, is as easily and surely preserved in a free government, as in a simple monarchy; and as to despatch, all the simple monarchies of the whole universe may be defied to produce greater or more numerous examples of it than are to be found in English history. An Alexander, or a Frederic, possessed of the prerogatives only of a king of England, and leading his own armies, would never find himself embarrassed or delayed in any honest enterprise. He might be restrained, indeed, from running mad, and from making conquests to the ruin of his nation, merely for his own glory; but this is no argument against a free government.

There can be no free government without a democratical branch in the constitution. Monarchies and aristocracies are in possession of the voice and influence of every university and academy in Europe. Democracy, simple democracy, never had a patron among men of letters. Democratical mixtures in government have lost almost all the advocates they ever had out of England and America. Men of letters must have a great deal of praise, and some of the necessaries, conveniences, and ornaments of life. Monarchies and aristocracies pay well and applaud liberally. The people have almost always expected to be served gratis, and to be paid for the honor of serving them; and their applauses and adorations are bestowed too often on artifices and tricks, on hypocrisy and superstition, on flattery, bribes, and largesses. It is no wonder then that democracies and democratical mixtures are annihilated all over Europe, except on a barren rock, a paltry fen, an inaccessible mountain, or an impenetrable forest. The people of England, to their immortal honor, are hitherto an exception; but, to the humiliation of human nature, they show very often that they are like other men. The people in America have now the best opportunity and the greatest trust in their hands, that Providence ever committed to so small a number, since the transgression of the first pair; if they betray their trust, their guilt will merit even greater punishment than other nations have suffered, and the indignation of Heaven. If there is one certain truth to be collected from the history of all ages, it is this; that the people's rights and liberties, and the democratical mixture in a constitution, can never be preserved without a strong executive, or, in other words, without separating the executive from the legislative power. If the executive power, or any considerable part of it, is left in the hands either of an aristocratical or a democratical assembly, it will corrupt the legislature as necessarily as rust corrupts iron, or as arsenic poisons the human body; and when the legislature is corrupted, the people are undone.

The rich, the well-born, and the able, acquire an influence among the people that will soon be too much for simple honesty and plain sense, in a house of representatives. The most illustrious of them must, therefore, be separated from the mass, and placed by themselves in a senate; this is, to all honest and useful intents, an ostracism. A member of a senate, of immense wealth, the most respected birth, and transcendent abilities, has no influence in the nation, in comparison of what he would have in a single representative assembly. When a senate exists, the most powerful man in the state may be safely admitted into the house of representatives, because the people have it in their power to remove him into the senate as soon as his influence becomes dangerous. The senate becomes the great object of ambition; and the richest and the most sagacious wish to merit an advancement to it by services to the public in the house. When he has obtained the object of his wishes, you may still hope for the benefits of his exertions, without dreading his passions; for the executive power being in other hands, he has lost much of his influence with the people, and can govern very few votes more than his own among the senators.

It was the general opinion of ancient nations, that the Divinity alone was adequate to the important office of giving laws to men. The Greeks entertained this prejudice throughout all their dispersions; the Romans cultivated the same popular delusion; and modern nations, in the consecration of kings, and in several superstitious chimeras of divine right in princes and nobles, are nearly unanimous in preserving remnants of it. Even the venerable magistrates of Amersfort devoutly believe themselves God's vicegerents. Is it that obedience to the laws can be obtained from mankind in no other manner? Are the jealousy of power, and the envy of superiority, so strong in all men, that no considerations of public or private utility are sufficient to engage their submission to rules for their own happiness? Or is the disposition to imposture so prevalent in men of experience, that their private reviews of ambition and avarice can be accomplished only by artifice? It was a tradition in antiquity that the laws of Crete were dictated to Minos by the inspiration of Jupiter. This legislator and his brother Rhadamanthus were both his sons; once in nine years they went to converse with their father, to propose questions concerning the wants of the people; and his answers were recorded as laws for their government. The laws of Lacedaemon were communicated by Apollo to Lycurgus; and, lest the meaning of the deity should not have been perfectly comprehended, or correctly expressed, they were afterwards confirmed by his oracle at Delphos. Among the Romans, Numa was indebted for those laws which procured the prosperity of his country to his conversations with Egeria. The Greeks imported these mysteries from Egypt and the East, whose despotisms, from the remotest antiquity to this day, have been founded in the same solemn empiricism; their emperors and nobles being all descended from their gods. Woden and Thor were divinities too; and their posterity ruled a thousand years in the north by the strength of a like credulity. Manco Capac was the child of the sun, the visible deity of the Peruvians; and transmitted his divinity, as well as his earthly dignity and authority, through a line of incas. And the rudest tribes of savages in North

America have certain families from which their leaders are always chosen, under the immediate protection of the god War. There is nothing in which mankind have been more unanimous; yet nothing can be inferred from it more than this, that the multitude have always been credulous, and the few are always artful.

The United States of America have exhibited, perhaps, the first example of governments erected on the simple principles of nature; and if men are now sufficiently enlightened to disabuse themselves of artifice, imposture, hypocrisy, and superstition, they will consider this event as an era in their history. Although the detail of the formation of the American governments is at present little known or regarded either in Europe or in America, it may hereafter become an object of curiosity. It will never be pretended that any persons employed in that service had interviews with the gods, or were in any degree under the inspiration of Heaven, more than those at work upon ships or houses, or laboring in merchandise or agriculture; it will forever be acknowledged that these governments were contrived merely by the use of reason and the senses, as Copley painted Chatham; West, Wolf; and Trumbull, Warren and Montgomery; as Dwight, Barlow, Trumbull, and Humphries composed their verse, and Belknap and Ramsay history; as Godfrey invented his quadrant and Rittenhouse his planetarium; as Boylston practised inoculation, and Franklin electricity; as Paine exposed the mistakes of Raynal, and Jefferson those of Buffon, so unphilosophically borrowed from the despicable dreams of De Pan. Neither the people, nor their conventions, committees, or sub-committees, considered legislation in any other light than as ordinary arts and sciences, only more important. Called without expectation, and compelled without previous inclination, though undoubtedly at the best period of time, both for England and America, suddenly to erect new systems of laws for their future government, they adopted the method of a wise architect, in erecting a new palace for the residence of his sovereign. They determined to consult Vitruvius, Palladio, and all other writers of reputation in the art; to examine the most celebrated buildings, whether they remain entire or in ruins; to compare these with the principles of writers; and to inquire how far both the theories and models were founded in nature, or created by fancy; and when this was done, so far as their circumstances would allow, to adopt the advantages and reject the inconveniences of all. Unembarrassed by attachments to noble families, hereditary lines and successions, or any considerations of royal blood, even the pious mystery of holy oil had no more influence than that other one of holy water. The people were universally too enlightened to be imposed on by artifice; and their leaders, or more properly followers, were men of too much honor to attempt it. Thirteen governments thus founded on the natural authority of the people alone, without a pretence of miracle or mystery, and which are destined to spread over the northern part of that whole quarter of the globe, are a great point gained in favor of the rights of mankind. The experiment is made, and has completely succeeded; it can no longer be called in question, whether authority in magistrates and obedience of citizens can be grounded on reason, morality, and the Christian religion, without the monkery of priests, or the knavery of politicians. As the writer was personally acquainted with most of the gentlemen in each of the states, who had the principal share in the first draughts, the following work was really written to lay before the public a specimen of that kind of reading and reasoning which produced the American constitutions. . . .

If Cicero and Tacitus could revisit the earth, and learn that the English nation had reduced the great idea to practice, and brought it nearly to perfection, by giving each division a power to defend itself by a negative; had found it the most solid and durable government, as well as the most free; had obtained by means of a prosperity among civilized nations, in an enlightened age, like that of the Romans among barbarians; and that the Americans, after having enjoyed the benefits of such a constitution a century and a half, were advised by some of the greatest philosophers and politicians of the age to renounce it, and set up the governments of ancient Goths and modern Indians,—what would they say? That the Americans would be more reprehensible than the Cappadocians, if they should listen to such advice.

It would have been much to the purpose, to have inserted a more accurate investigation of the form of government of the ancient Germans and modern Indians; in both, the existence of the three divisions of power is marked with a precision that excludes all controversy. The democratical branch, especially, is so determined, that the real sovereignty resided in the body of the people, and was exercised in the assembly of king, nobles, and commons together. These institutions really collected all authority into one centre of kings, nobles, and people. But, small as their numbers and narrow as their territories were, the consequence was confusion; each part believed it governed the whole; the chiefs thought they were sovereigns; the nobles believed the power to be in their hands; and the people flattered themselves that all depended upon them. Their purposes were well enough answered, without coming to an explanation, so long as they were few in number, and had no property; but when spread over large provinces of the Roman empire, now the great kingdoms of Europe, and grown populous and rich, they found the inconvenience of each not knowing its place. Kings, nobles, and people claimed the government in turn; and after all the turbulence, wars, and revolutions, which compose the history of Europe for so many ages, we find simple monarchies established everywhere. Whether the system will now become stationary, and last forever, by means of a few further improvements in monarchical government, we know not; or whether still further revolutions are to come. The most probable, or rather the only probable change, is the introduction of democratical branches into those governments. If the people should ever aim at more, they will defeat themselves; as they will, indeed, if they aim at this by any other than gentle means and by gradual advances, by improvements in general education, and by informing the public mind.

The systems of legislators are experiments made on human life and manners, society and government. Zoroaster, Confucius, Mithras, Odin, Thor, Mahomet, Lycurgus, Solon, Romulus, and a thousand others, may be compared to philosophers making experiments on the elements. Unhappily, political experiments cannot be made in a laboratory, nor determined in a few hours. The operation once begun, runs over whole quarters of the globe, and is not finished in many thousands of years. The experiment of Lycurgus lasted seven hundred years, but never spread beyond the limits of Laconia. The process of Solon expired in one century; that of Romulus lasted but two centuries and a half; but the Teutonic institutions, described by Caesar and Tacitus, are the most memorable experiment, merely political, ever yet made in human affairs. They have spread all over Europe, and have lasted eighteen hundred years. They afford the strongest argument that can be imagined in support of the position assumed in these volumes. Nothing ought to have more weight with America, to determine her judgment against mixing the authority of the one, the few, and the many, confusedly in one assembly, than the wide-spread miseries and final slavery of almost all mankind, in consequence of such an ignorant policy in the ancient Germans. What is the ingredient which in England has preserved the democratical authority? The balance, and that only. The English have, in reality, blended together the feudal institutions with those of the Greeks and Romans, and out of all have made that noble composition, which avoids the inconveniences, and retains the advantages of both.

The institutions now made in America will not wholly wear out for thousands of years. It is of the last importance, then, that they should begin right. If they set out wrong, they will never be able to return, unless it be by accident, to the right path. After having known the history of Europe, and of England in particular, it would be the height of folly to go back to the institutions of Woden and of Thor, as the Americans are advised to do. If they had been counselled to adopt a single monarchy at once, it would have been less mysterious.

Robertson, Hume, and Gibbon have given such admirable accounts of the feudal institutions and their consequences, that it would have been, perhaps, more discrete to have referred to them, without saying any thing more upon the subject. To collect together the legislation of the Indians would take up much room, but would be well worth the pains. The sovereignty is in the nation, it is true, but the three powers are strong in every tribe; and their royal and aristocratical dignities are much more generally hereditary, from the popular partiality to particular families, and the superstitious opinion that such are favorites of the God of War, than late writers upon this subject have allowed.

IDEOLOGY AND IDEOCRACY
John Adams

In this holograph note written in the margin of his own copy of his volume *Discourses on Davila,* John Adams expresses his detestation of ideology and his contempt for governments founded merely upon abstract ideas. (*Discourses on Davila* was published in 1805, but the book's substance appeared in 1790 in *The Gazette of the United States;* Adams' marginal note is dated 3 March, 1813.) Napoleon, here quoted by Adams, was referring to Destutt de Tracy's volumes entitled *Principles of Ideology;* and Adams, in this gloss, somewhat sardonically endorses Napoleon's denunciation. See *The Works of John Adams,* Vol. VI, pp. 402–03.

The contents of the foregoing volume are summarily comprehended in a few sentences in the following

Comment
by Napoleon, Emperor of France:—

"On the twentieth of December, 1812, the council of state were conducted into the imperial presence, and presented by His Serene Highness, the Prince Arch-Chancellor of the empire (Cambacérès).

"His Excellency, Count de Fermon, Minister of State, President of the Section of Finance, made an address. To which the Emperor made the following answer:—

"It is to ideology, to that obscure metaphysics, which, searching with subtlety after first causes, wishes to found upon them the legislation of nations, instead of adapting the laws to the knowledge of the human heart and to the lessons of history, that we are to attribute all the calamities that our beloved France has experienced. Those errors necessarily produced the government of the men of blood. Indeed, who proclaimed the principle of insurrection as a duty? Who flattered the people, by proclaiming for them a sovereignty which they were incapable of exercising? Who destroyed the sanctity and the respect to the laws, by making them to depend, not upon the sacred principles of justice, upon the nature of things, and upon civil justice, but only upon the will of an assembly of men, composed of men strangers to the knowledge of the civil, criminal, administrative, political, and military laws?

"When we are called to regenerate a state, we must act

upon opposite principles. History paints the human heart. It is in history that we are to seek for the advantages and disadvantages of different systems of law. These are the principles of which the council of state of a great empire ought never to lose sight. It ought to add to them a courage equal to every emergency, and like the Presidents Harlay and Molé, be ready to perish in defence of the sovereign, the throne, and the laws."

Comments on the Comment

Napoleon! Mutato nomine, de te fabula narratur.[1] This book is a prophecy of your empire, before your name was heard!

The political and literary world are much indebted for the invention of the new word IDEOLOGY.

Our English words, Idiocy or Idiotism, express not the force or meaning of it. It is presumed its proper definition is the science of Idiocy. And a very profound, abstruse, and mysterious science it is. You must descend deeper than the divers in the Dunciad to make any discoveries, and after all you will find no bottom. It is the bathos, the theory, the art, the skill of diving and sinking in government. It was taught in the school of folly; but alas! Franklin, Turgot, Rochefoucauld, and Condorcet, under Tom Paine, were the great masters of the academy!

It may be modestly suggested to the Emperor, to coin another word in his new mint, in conformity or analogy with Ideology, and call every constitution of government in France, from 1789 to 1799, an IDEOCRACY.

---

1. "With the name changed, the story is about you." [R.K.]

ON NATURAL ARISTOCRACY
John Adams

Writing to John Taylor of Carolina on April 15, 1814, Adams declares the natural inequality of men. (The complete text of the letter is in Adams' *Works*, Vol. VI, pp. 451–54.)

By *natural aristocracy*, in general, may be understood those superiorities of influence in society which grow out of the constitution of human nature. By *artificial aristocracy*, those inequalities of weight and superiorities of influence which are created and established by civil laws. Terms must be defined before we can reason. By aristocracy, I understand all those men who can command, influence, or procure more than an average of votes; by an aristocrat, every man who can and will influence one man to vote besides himself. Few men will deny that there is a natural aristocracy of virtues and talents in every nation and in every party, in every city and village. Inequalities are a part of the natural history of man.

I believe that none but Helvetius will affirm, that all children are born with equal genius.

None will pretend, that all are born of dispositions exactly alike,—of equal weight; equal strength; equal length; equal delicacy of nerves; equal elasticity of muscles; equal complexions; equal figure, grace, or beauty.

I have seen, in the Hospital of Foundlings, the *"Enfans Trouvés,"* at Paris, fifty babes in one room;—all under four days old; all in cradles alike; all nursed and attended alike; all dressed alike; all equally neat. I went from one end to the other of the whole row, and attentively observed all their countenances. And I never saw a greater variety, or more striking inequalities, in the streets of Paris or London. Some had every sign of grief, sorrow, and despair; others had joy and gayety in their faces. Some were sinking in the arms of death; others looked as if they might live to fourscore. Some were as ugly and others as beautiful, as children or adults ever are; these were stupid; those sensible. These were all born to equal rights, but to very different fortunes; to very different success and influence in life.

The world would not contain the books, if one should produce all the examples that reading and experience would furnish. One or two permit me to hint.

Will any man say, would Helvetius say, that all men are born equal in strength? Was Hercules no stronger than his neighbors? How many nations, for how many ages, have been governed by his strength, and by the reputation and renown of it by his posterity? If you have lately read Hume, Robertson, or the Scottish Chiefs, let me ask you, if Sir William Wallace was no more than equal in strength to the average of Scotchmen? and whether Wallace could have done what he did without that extraordinary strength?

Will Helvetius or Rousseau say that all men and women are born equal in beauty? Will any philosopher say, that beauty has no influence in human society? If he does, let him read the histories of Eve, Judith, Helen, the fair Gabrielle, Diana of Poitiers, Pompadour, Du Barry, Susanna, Abigail, Lady Hamilton, Mrs. Clark, and a million others. Are not despots, monarchs, aristocrats, and democrats, equally liable to be seduced by beauty to confer favors and influence suffrages?

Socrates calls beauty a short-lived tyranny; Plato, *the privilege of nature*; Theophrastus, a mute eloquence; Diogenes, the best letter of recommendation; Carneades, a queen without soldiers; Theocritus, a serpent covered with flowers; Bion, a good that does not belong to the possessor, because it is impossible to give ourselves beauty, or to preserve it. Madame du Barry expressed the philosophy of Carneades in more laconic language, when she said, "*La véritable royauté, c'est beauté,*"—the genuine royalty is beauty. And she might have said with equal truth, that it is genuine aristocracy; for it has as much influence in one form of government as in any other; and produces aristocracy in the deepest democracy that ever was known or imagined, as infallibly as in any other form of government. What shall we say to all these philosophers, male and female? Is not beauty a privilege granted by nature, according to Plato and to truth, often more influential in society, and even upon laws and government, than stars, garters, crosses, eagles, golden fleeces, or any hereditary titles or other distinctions? The grave elders were not proof against the charms of Susanna. The Grecian sages wondered not at the Trojan war when they saw Helen. Holofernes's guards, when they saw Judith, said, "one such woman let go would deceive the whole earth."

Can you believe, Mr. Taylor, that the brother of such a sister, the father of such a daughter, the husband of such a wife, or even the gallant of such a mistress, would have but one vote in your moral republic? Ingenious,—but not historical, philosophical, or political,—learned, classical, poetical Barlow! I mourn over thy life and thy death. Had truth, instead of popularity and party, been thy object, your pamphlet on privileged orders would have been a very different thing!

That all men are born to equal rights is true. Every being has a right to his own, as clear, as moral, as sacred, as any other being has. This is as indubitable as a moral government in the universe. But to teach that all men are born with equal powers and faculties, to equal influence in society, to equal property and advantages through life, is as gross a fraud, as glaring an imposition on the credulity of the people, as ever was practised by monks, by Druids, by Brahmins, by priests of the immortal Lama, or by the self-styled philosophers of the French revolution. For honor's sake, Mr. Taylor, for truth and virtue's sake, let American philosophers and politicians despise it.

Mr. Adams leaves to Homer and Virgil, to Tacitus and Quintilian, to Mahomet and Calvin, to Edwards and Priestley, or, if you will, to Milton's angels reasoning high in pandemonium, all their acute speculations about fate, destiny, foreknowledge absolute, necessity, and predestination. He thinks it problematical, whether there is, or ever will be, more than one Being capable of understanding this vast subject. In his principles of legislation, he has nothing to do with these interminable controversies. He considers men as free, moral, and accountable agents; and he takes men as God has made them. And will Mr. Taylor deny, that God has made some men deaf and some blind, or will he affirm that these will infallibly have as much influence in society, and be able to procure as many votes as any who can see and hear?

SAFETY IN UNION
Alexander Hamilton

The need for a strong general government of the United States is the subject of these two essays by Alexander Hamilton (1757–1804); they were published in the papers entitled *The Continentalist*, July 1781 (included in Henry Cabot Lodge's edition of *The Works of Alexander Hamilton*, New York, 1901, Vol. I, pp. 243–54). These essays commenced the movement which led to the adoption of the Constitution of the United States.

It would be the extreme of vanity in us not to be sensible that we began this revolution with very vague and confined notions of the practical business of government. To the greater part of us it was a novelty; of those who under the former constitution had had opportunities of acquiring experience, a large proportion adhered to the opposite side, and the remainder can only be supposed to have possessed ideas adapted to the narrow colonial sphere in which they had been accustomed to move, not of that enlarged kind suited to the government of an independent nation.

There were, no doubt, exceptions to these observations,—men in all respects qualified for conducting the public affair with skill and advantage. But their number was small; they were not always brought forward in our councils; and when they were, their influence was too commonly borne down by the prevailing torrent of ignorance and prejudice.

On a retrospect, however, of our transactions, under the disadvantages with which we commenced, it is perhaps more to be wondered at that we have done so well than that we have not done better. There are, indeed, some traits in our conduct as conspicuous for sound policy as others for magnanimity. But, on the other hand, it must also be confessed, there have been many false steps, many chimerical projects and utopian speculations, in the management of our civil as well as of our military affairs. A part of these were the natural effects of the spirit of the times, dictated by our situation. An extreme jealousy of power is the attendant on all popular revolutions, and has seldom been without its evils. It is to this source we are to trace many of the fatal mistakes which have so deeply endangered the common cause; particularly that defect which will be the object of these remarks—a want of power in Congress.

The present Congress, respectable for abilities and integrity, by experience convinced of the necessity of change, are preparing several important articles, to be submitted to the respective States, for augmenting the powers of the Confederation. But though there is hardly at this time a man of information in America who will not acknowledge, as a general proposition, that in its present form it is unequal either to a vigorous prosecution of the war or to the preservation of the Union in peace; yet when the principle comes to be applied to practice, there seems not to be the same agreement in the modes of remedying the defect; and it is to be feared, from a disposition which appeared in some of the States on a late occasion, that the salutary intentions of Congress may meet with more delay and opposition than the critical posture of the States will justify.

It will be attempted to show, in a course of papers, what ought to be done, and the mischiefs of a contrary policy.

In the first stages of the controversy, it was excusable to err. Good intentions, rather than great skill, were to have been expected from us. But we have now had sufficient time for reflection, and experience as ample as unfortunate, to rectify our errors. To persist in them becomes disgraceful, and even criminal, and belies that character of good sense, and a quick discernment of our interests, which, in spite of our mistakes, we have been hitherto allowed. It will prove that our sagacity is limited to interests of inferior moment, and that we are incapable of those enlightened and liberal views necessary to make us a great and a flourishing people.

History is full of examples where, in contests for liberty, a jealousy of power has either defeated the attempts to recover or preserve it, in the first instance, or has afterward subverted it by clogging government with too great precautions for its felicity, or by leaving too wide a door for sedition and popular licentiousness. In a government framed for durable liberty, not less regard must be paid to giving the magistrate a proper degree of authority to make and execute the laws with rigor, than to guard against encroachments upon the rights of the community. As too much power leads to despotism, too little leads to anarchy, and both, eventually, to the ruin of the people. These are maxims well known, but never sufficiently attended to, in adjusting the frames of governments. Some momentary interest or passion is sure to give a wrong bias, and pervert the most favorable opportunities.

No friend to order or to rational liberty can read without pain and disgust the history of the Commonwealths of Greece. Generally speaking, they were a constant scene of the alternate tyranny of one part of the people over the other, or of a few usurping demagogues over the whole. Most of them had been originally governed by kings, whose despotism (the natural disease of monarchy) had obliged their subjects to murder, expel, depose, or reduce them to a nominal existence, and institute popular governments. In these governments, that of Sparta excepted, the jealousy of power hindered the people from trusting out of their own hands a competent authority to maintain the repose and stability of the Commonwealth; whence originated the frequent revolutions and civil broils with which they were distracted. This, and the want of a solid federal union to restrain the ambition and rivalship of the different cities, after a rapid succession of bloody wars, ended in their total loss of liberty, and subjugation to foreign powers.

In comparison of our governments with those of the ancient republics, we must, without hesitation, give the preference to our own; because every power with us is exercised by representation, not in tumultuary assemblies of the collective body of the people, where the art or impudence of the *Orator* or *Tribune*, rather than the utility or justice of the measure, could seldom fail to govern. Yet, whatever may be the advantage on our side in such a comparison, men who estimate the value of institutions, not from prejudices of the moment, but from experience and reason, must be persuaded that the same *jealousy* of *power* has prevented our reaping all the advantages from the examples of other nations which we ought to have done, and has rendered our constitutions in many respects feeble and imperfect.

Perhaps the evil is not very great in respect to our State constitutions; for, notwithstanding their imperfections, they may for some time be made to operate in such a manner as to answer the purposes of the common defence and the maintenance of order; and they seem to have, in themselves, and in the progress of society among us, the seeds of improvement.

But this is not the case with respect to the Federal Government; if it is too weak at first, it will continually grow weaker. The ambition and local interests of the respective members will be constantly undermining and usurping upon its prerogatives till it comes to a dissolution, if a partial combination of some of the more powerful ones does not bring it to a more *speedy* and *violent end.*

In a single state where the sovereign power is exercised by delegation, whether it be a limited monarchy or a republic, the danger most commonly is, that the sovereign will become too powerful for his constituents. In federal governments, where different states are represented in a general council, the danger is on the other side—that the members will be an overmatch for the common head; or, in other words, that it will not have sufficient influence and authority to secure the obedience of the several parts of the confederacy.

In a single state the sovereign has the whole legislative power as well as the command of the national forces—of course an immediate control over the persons and property of the subjects; every other power is subordinate and dependent. If he undertakes to subvert the constitution, it can only be preserved by a general insurrection of the people. The magistrates of the provinces, counties, or towns into which the State is divided, having only an executive and police jurisdiction, can take no decisive measures for counteracting the first indications of tyranny;

but must content themselves with the ineffectual weapon of petition and remonstrance. They cannot raise money, levy troops, nor form alliances. The leaders of the people must wait till their discontents have ripened into a general revolt, to put them in a situation to confer the powers necessary for their defence. It will always be difficult for this to take place; because the sovereign, possessing the appearance and forms of legal authority, having the forces and revenues of the state at his command, and a large party among the people besides,—which with those advantages he can hardly fail to acquire—he will too often be able to baffle the first motions of the discontented, and prevent that union and concert essential to the success of their opposition.

The security, therefore, of the public liberty must consist in such a distribution of the sovereign power, as will make it morally impossible for one part to gain an ascendency over the others, or for the whole to unite in a scheme of usurpation.

In federal governments, each member has a distinct sovereignty, makes and executes laws, imposes taxes, distributes justice, and exercises every other function of government. It has always within itself the means of revenue; and on an emergency, can levy forces. If the common sovereign should meditate or attempt any thing unfavorable to the general liberty, each member, having all the proper organs of power, can prepare for defence with celerity and vigor. Each can immediately sound the alarm to the others, and enter into leagues for mutual protection. If the combination is general, as is to be expected, the usurpers will soon find themselves without the means of recruiting their treasury or their armies; and for want of continued supplies of men and money, must, in the end, fall a sacrifice to the attempt. If the combination is not general, it will imply that some of the members are interested in that which is the cause of dissatisfaction to others, and this cannot be an attack upon the common liberty, but upon the interests of one part in favor of another part; and it will be a war between the members of the federal union with each other, not between them and the federal government. From the plainest principles of human nature, two inferences are to be drawn: one, that each member of a political confederacy will be more disposed to advance its own authority upon the ruins of that of the confederacy, than to make any improper concession in its favor, or support it in unreasonable pretensions; the other, that the subjects of each member will be more devoted in their attachments and obedience to their own particular governments, than to that of the union.

It is the temper of societies as well as of individuals to be impatient of constraint, and to prefer partial to general interest. Many cases may occur where members of a confederacy have, or seem to have, an advantage in things contrary to the good of the whole, or a disadvantage in others conducive to that end. The selfishness of every part will dispose each to believe that the public burdens are unequally apportioned, and that itself is the victim. These and other circumstances will promote a disposition for abridging the authority of the federal government; and the ambition of men in office in each state will make them glad to encourage it. They think their own consequence connected with the power of the government of which they are a part; and will endeavor to increase the one as the means of increasing the other.

The particular governments will have more empire over the minds of their subjects than the general one, because their agency will be more direct, more uniform, and more apparent. The people will be habituated to look up to them as the arbiters and guardians of their personal concerns, by which the passions of the vulgar, if not of all men, are most strongly affected; and in every difference with the confederated body, will side with them against the common sovereign.

Experience confirms the truth of these principles. The

chief cities of Greece had once their council of Amphyctions, or States-general, with authority to decide and compose the differences of the several cities, and to transact many other important matters relative to the common interest and safety. At their first institution, they had great weight and credit; but never enough to preserve effectually the balance and harmony of the confederacy; and in time their decrees only served as an additional pretext to that side whose pretensions they favored. When the cities were not engaged in foreign wars, they were at perpetual variance among themselves. Sparta and Athens contended twenty-seven years for the precedence, or rather dominion, of Greece, till the former made herself mistress of the whole; and till, in subsequent struggles, having had recourse to the pernicious expedient of calling in the aid of foreign enemies, the Macedonians first and afterward the Romans became their masters.

The German Diet had formerly more authority than it now has, though like that of Greece never enough to hinder the great potentates from disturbing the repose of the empire, and mutually wasting their own territories and people.

The Helvetic League is another example. It is true it has subsisted nearly five hundred years; but in that period the cantons have had repeated and furious wars with each other, which would have made them an easy prey to their more powerful neighbors, had not the reciprocal jealousy of these prevented either from taking advantage of their dissensions. This and their poverty have hitherto saved them from total destruction, and kept them from feeling the miseries of foreign conquest, added to those of civil war. The federal government is too weak to hinder their renewal, whenever the ambition or fanaticism of the principal cantons shall be disposed to rekindle the flame. For some time past, indeed, it has been in a great measure nominal; the Protestants and Catholics have had separate diets, to manage almost all matters of importance; so that in fact, the general diet is only kept up to regulate the affairs of the common bailliages and preserve a semblance of union; and even this, it is probable would cease, did not the extreme weakness of the cantons oblige them to a kind of coalition.

If the divisions of the United Provinces have not proceeded to equal extremities, there are peculiar causes to be assigned. The authority of the Stadt-holder pervades the whole frame of the republic, and is a kind of common link by which the provinces are bound together. The jealousy of his progressive influence, in which more or less they all agree, operates as a check upon their ill-humors against one another. The inconsiderableness of each province separately, and the imminent danger to which the whole would be exposed of being overrun by their neighbors in case of disunion, is a further preservative against the phrensy of hostility; and their importance and even existence depending entirely upon frugality, industry, and commerce, peace both at home and abroad is of necessity the predominant object of their policy.

THE SPECTACLE OF REVOLUTIONARY FRANCE
Alexander Hamilton

The Federalists' abhorrence of the French Revolution is expressed here by the masterly Hamilton, writing under the pseudonym of Titus Manlius on April 7, 1798, shortly before the enactment of the Alien and Sedition Acts, in the series of papers called *The Stand.* See Lodge's edition of Hamilton's *Works*, Vol. VI, pp. 257–81.

In reviewing the disgusting spectacle of the French Revolution, it is difficult to avert the eye entirely from those features of it which betray a plan to disorganize the human mind itself, as well as to undermine the venerable pillars that support the edifice of civilized society. The attempt by the rulers of a nation to destroy all religious opinion, and to pervert a whole nation to atheism, is a phenomenon of profligacy reserved to consummate the infamy of the unprincipled reformers of France. The proofs of this terrible design are numerous and convincing.

The animosity to the Christian system is demonstrated by the single fact of the ridiculous and impolite establishment of the decades, with the evident object of supplanting the Christian Sabbath. The inscriptions by public authority on the tombs of the deceased, affirming death to be an eternal sleep, witness the desire to discredit the belief of the immortality of the soul. The open profession of atheism in the convention,[1] received with acclamations; the honorable mention on its journals of a book professing to prove the nothingness of all religion[2]; the institution of a festival to offer public worship to a courtesan decorated with the pompous title of "Goddess of Reason"; the congratulatory reception of impious children appearing in the hall of the convention to lisp blasphemy against the King of kings, are among the dreadful proofs of a conspiracy to establish atheism on the ruins of Christianity,—to deprive mankind of its best consolations and most animating hopes, and to make a gloomy desert of the universe.

Latterly, the indications of this plan are not so frequent as they were, but from time to time something still escapes which discovers that it is not renounced. The late

---

[1] By Dupont, Danton, etc.
[2] Written and presented by Anacharsis Clootz, calling himself orator of the human race.

address of Buonaparte to the Directory is an example. That unequalled conqueror, from whom it is painful to detract, in whom one would wish to find virtues worthy of his shining talents, profanely unites religion (not superstition) with royalty and the feudal system as the scourges of Europe for centuries past. The decades likewise remain the *catapulta* which are to batter down Christianity.

Equal pains have been taken to deprave the morals as to extinguish the religion of the country, if indeed morality in a community can be separated from religion. It is among the singular and fantastic vagaries of the French Revolution, that while the Duke of Brunswick was marching to Paris a new law of divorce was passed, which makes it as easy for a husband to get rid of his wife, and a wife of her husband, as to discard a worn-out habit.[3] To complete the dissolution of those ties, which are the chief links of domestic and ultimately of social attachment, the journals of the convention record with guilty applause the accusations preferred by children against their parents.

It is not necessary to heighten the picture by sketching the horrid group of proscriptions and murders which have made France a den of pillage and slaughter; blackening with eternal opprobrium the very name of man.

The pious and moral weep over these scenes as a sepulchre destined to entomb all they revere and esteem. The politician who loves liberty, sees them with regret as a gulf that may swallow up the liberty to which he is devoted. He knows that morality overthrown (and morality *must* fall with religion), the terrors of despotism can alone curb the impetuous passions of man, and confine him within the bounds of social duty.

But let us return to the conduct of revolutionary France

---

[3] This law, it was understood, had been lately modified in consequence of its manifestly pernicious tendency: but upon a plan which, according to the opinions of the best men in the two councils lately banished, would leave the evil in full force.

towards other nations, as more immediately within our purpose.

It has been seen that she commenced her career as the champion of universal liberty; and proclaiming destruction to the governments which she was pleased to denominate despotic, made a tender of fraternity and assistance to the nations whom they oppressed. She at the same time disclaimed conquest and aggrandizement.

But it has since clearly appeared that at the very moment she was making these professions, and while her diplomatic agents were hypocritically amusing foreign courts[4] with conciliatory explanations and promises of moderation, she was exerting every faculty, by force and fraud, to accomplish the very conquest and aggrandizement which she insidiously disavowed. The people of Belgium, ensnared by fair pretences, believed that in abandoning the defence of their country and the cause of their ancient sovereign, they acquired a title to enjoy liberty under a government of their own choice, protected by France. Contrary to the hopes which were inspired—contrary to the known will of a large majority of that people—contrary to all their religious and national prejudices, they have been compelled to become departments of France. And their violated temples have afforded a rich plunder to aliment further conquest and oppression. The Dutch, seduced by the same arts to facilitate rather than obstruct the entrance of a French army into their country, thought they were only getting rid of their Stadt-holder and nobles, and were to retain their territory and their wealth, secured by such a civil establishment as they should freely choose. Their reward is the dismemberment of their country and the loss of their wealth by exhausting contributions; and they are obliged to take a government, dictated by a faction openly countenanced and supported by France. Completely a province of France, in imitation

---

[4] England among the rest.

of their frantic masters they are advancing with rapid strides to a lawless tyranny at home.[5] France, professing eternal hatred to kings, was to be the tutelary genius of republics. Holland, Genoa, Venice, the Swiss Canton, and the United States, are agonizing witness of her sincerity.

Of undone Holland no more need be said; nothing remains for us but to exercise tender sympathy in the unfortunate fate of a country which generously lent its aid to establish our independence, and to deduce from her melancholy example an instructive lesson to repel with determined vigor the mortal embrace of her seducer and destroyer.

Genoa, a speck on the globe, for having at every hazard resisted the efforts of the enemies of France to force her from a neutral station, is recompensed with a subversion of her government and the pillage of her wealth, by compulsory and burthensome contributions.

Venice is no more! In vain had she preserved a faithful neutrality, when, perhaps, her interposition might have inclined the scale of victory in Italy against France. A few of her citizens[6] kill some French soldiers. Instant retaliation takes place. Every atonement is offered. Nothing will suffice but the overthrow of her government. 'T is effected. Her own citizens, attracted by the lure of democracy, become accessory to it, and receive a popular government at the hand of France. What is the sequel? what the faith kept with them? It suits France to bribe the emperor to a surrender of the Netherlands and to peace, that she may pursue her projects elsewhere with less obstacle. It suits France to extend her power and commerce by the acquisitions of portions of the Venetian territories. The bribe is offered and accepted. Venice is divided. She disappears from the map of nations. The tragedy of Po-

---

[5] By the last accounts, some of the most independent citizens have been seized and imprisoned merely for the constitutional exercise of their opinion.

[6] Were they not French agents employed to create the pretext?

land is re-enacted with circumstances of aggravated atrocity. France is perfidious enough to sacrifice a people who at her desire, had consented to abrogate their privileged castes to the chief of those despots against whom she had vowed eternal hatred.

The Swiss Cantons—the boast of republicans—the model to which they have been glad to appeal in proof that a republican government may consist with the order and happiness of society—the old and faithful allies of France, who are not even pretended to have deviated from sincere neutrality,—what are they at this moment? Perhaps like Venice, a *story told!* The despots of France had found pretences to quarrel with them; commotions were excited; the legions of France were in march to second the insurgents. Little other hope remains than that the *death* of this respectable people will be as glorious as their life; that they will sell their independence as dearly as they bought it. But why despair of a brave and virtuous people who appear determined to meet the impending danger with a countenance emulous of their ancient renown?

The United States—what is their situation? Their sovereignty trampled in the dust, and their commerce bleeding at every pore, speak in loud accents the spirit of oppression and rapine which characterizes the usurpers of France. But of this a distinct view is requisite, and will be taken.

In these transactions we discover ambition and fanaticism marching hand in hand—bearing the ensigns of hypocrisy, treachery, and rapine. The dogmas of a false and fatal creed second the weapons of ambition. Like the prophet of Mecca, the tyrants of France press forward with the alcoran of their faith in one hand and the sword in the other. They proselyte, subjugate, and debase; no distinction is made between republic and monarchy; all must alike yield to the aggrandizement of the *"great nation"*—the distinctive, the arrogant appellation lately assumed by France to assert in the face of nations her superiority and ascendency. Nor is it a mere title with which vanity decorates itself—it is the substantial claim of dominion. France, swelled to a gigantic size, and aping ancient Rome, except in her virtues, plainly meditates the control of mankind, and is actually giving the law to nations. Unless they quickly rouse and compel her to abdicate her insolent claim, they will verify the truth of that philosophy, which makes man in his natural state a quadruped, and it will only remain for the miserable animal, converting his hands into paws in the attitude of prone submission, to offer his patient and servile back to whatever burthens the *lordly* tyrants of France may think fit to impose.

CONSERVATIVE FOREBODINGS
Fisher Ames

Fisher Ames (1758–1808) of Massachusetts, the gloomiest and most eloquent of the Federalists, wrote in 1803 this essay, "The Dangers of American Liberty," which was not published until after his death. He predicts that Jeffersonian democracy will ruin the United States. See *Works of Fisher Ames* (Boston, 1809), pp. 379–85, 418–37.

I am not positive, that it is of any immediate use to our country, that its true friends should better understand one another; nor am I apprehensive, that the crudities, which my ever hasty pen confides to my friends, will essentially mislead their opinion in respect either to myself or to publick affairs. At a time when men eminently wise cherish almost any hopes, however vain, because they choose to be blind to their fears, it would be neither extraordinary nor disreputable for me to mistake the degree of maturity, to which our political vices have arrived, nor to err in computing how near or how far off we stand from the term of their fatal consummation.

I fear, that the future fortunes of our country no longer depend on *counsel*. We have persevered in our errours too long to change our propensities by now enlightening our convictions. The political sphere, like the globe we tread upon, never stands still, but with a silent swiftness accomplishes the revolutions, which, we are too ready to believe, are effected by our wisdom, or might have been controlled by our efforts. There is a kind of fatality in the affairs of republicks, that eludes the foresight of the wise, as much as it frustrates the tolls and sacrifices of the patriot and the hero. Events proceed, not as they were expected or intended, but as they are impelled by the irresistible laws of our political existence. Things inevitable happen, and we are astonished, as if they were miracles, and the course of nature had been overpowered or suspended to produce them. Hence it is, that, till lately, more than half our countrymen believed our publick tranquillity was firmly established, and that our liberty did not merely rest upon dry land, but was wedged, or rather rooted high above the flood in the rocks of granite, as immovably as the pillars that prop the universe. They, or at least the discerning of them, are at length no less disappointed than terrified to perceive that we have all the time floated, with a fearless and unregarded course, down the stream of events, till we are now visibly drawn within the revolutionary suction of Niagara, and every thing that is liberty will be dashed to pieces in the descent.

We have been accustomed to consider the pretension of Englishmen to be free, as a proof how completely they were broken to subjection, or hardened in imposture. We have insisted, that they had no constitution, because they never made one; and that their boasted government, which is just what time and accident have made it, was palsied with age, and blue with the plague-sores of corruption. We have believed, that it derived its stability, not from reason, but from prejudice; that it is supported; not because it is favourable to liberty, but as it is dear to national pride; that it is reverenced, not for its excellence, but because ignorance is naturally the idolater of antiquity; that it is not sound and healthful, but derives a morbid energy from disease, and an unaccountable aliment from the canker that corrodes its vitals.

But we maintained, that the federal constitution, with all the bloom of youth and splendour of innocence, was gifted with immortality. For, if time should impair its force, or faction tarnish its charms, the people, ever vigilant to discern its wants, ever powerful to provide for them, would miraculously restore it to the field, like some wounded hero of the epick, to take a signal vengeance on its enemies, or like Antaeus, invigorated by touching his mother earth, to rise the stronger for a fall.

There is, of course, a large portion of our citizens, who will not believe, even on the evidence of facts, that any publick evils exist, or are impending. They deride the apprehensions of those who foresee, that licentiousness will prove, as it ever has proved, fatal to liberty. They consider her as a nymph, who need not be coy to keep herself pure, but that, on the contrary, her chastity will grow robust by frequent scuffles with her seducers. They say, while a faction is a minority, it will remain harmless by being outvoted; and if it should become a majority, all its acts, however profligate or violent, are then legitimate. For, with the democrats, the people is a sovereign who can do no wrong, even when he respects and spares no existing right, and whose voice, however obtained or however counterfeited, bears all the sanctity and all the force of a living divinity.

Where, then, it will be asked, in a tone both of menace and of triumph, can the people's dangers lie, unless it be with the persecuted federalists? *They* are the partisans of monarchy, who propagate their principles in order, as soon as they have increased their sect, to introduce a king; for by this only avenue they foretell his approach. Is it possible the people should ever be their own enemies? If all government were dissolved to-day, would they not re-establish it to-morrow, with no other prejudice to the publick liberty, than some superfluous fears of its friends, some abortive projects of its enemies? Nay, would not liberty rise resplendent with the light of fresh experience, and coated in the seven-fold mail of constitutional amendments?

These opinions are fiercely maintained, not only as if there were evidence to prove them, but as if it were a merit to believe them, by men who tell you, that, in the most desperate extremity of faction or usurpation, we have an unfailing resource in the *good sense of the nation*. They assure us there is at least as much wisdom *in the people*, as in these ingenious tenets of their creed.

For any purpose, therefore, of popular use or general impression, it seems almost fruitless to discuss the question, whether our publick liberty can subsist, and what is to be the conditon of that awful futurity to which we are hastening. The clamours of party are so loud, and the resistance of national vanity is so stubborn, it will be impossible to convince any but the very wise (and in every state they are the very few), that our democratick liberty is utterly untenable; that we are devoted to the successive struggles of factions, who will rule by turns, the worst of whom will rule last, and triumph by the sword. But for the wise this unwelcome task is, perhaps, superfluous: they, possibly, are already convinced.

All such men are, or ought to be, agreed, that simple governments are despotisms; and of all despotisms a democracy, though the least durable, is the most violent. It is also true, that all the existing governments we are acquainted with are more or less *mixed*, or balanced and checked, however imperfectly, by the ingredients and principles that belong to the other simple sorts. It is, nevertheless, a fact, that there is scarcely any civil constitution in the world, that, according to American ideas, is *so mixed* and combined as to be favourable to the liberty of the subject—none, absolutely none, that an American patriot would be willing to adopt for, much less to impose on, his country. Without pretending to define that liberty, which writers at length agree is incapable of any precise and comprehensive definition, all the European governments, except the British, admit a most formidable portion of arbitrary power; whereas, in America, no plan of government, without a large and preponderating commixture of democracy, can, for a moment, possess our confidence and attachment.

It is unquestionable, that the concern of the people in the affairs of such a government, tends to elevate the character and enlarge the comprehension, as well as the enjoyments, of the citizens; and, supposing the government wisely constituted, and the laws steadily and firmly carried into execution, these effects, in which every lover of mankind must exult, will not be attended with a corresponding depravation of the publick manners and morals. I have never yet met with an American of any party, who seemed willing to exclude the people from their temperate and well-regulated share of concern in the government. Indeed, it is notorious, that there was scarcely an advocate for the federal constitution, who was not anxious, from the first, to hazard the experiment of an unprecedented, and almost unqualified proportion of democracy, both in constructing and administering the government, and who did not rely with confidence, if not blind presumption, on its success. This is certain, the body of the federalists were always, and yet are essentially democratick in their political notions. The truth is, the American nation, with ideas and prejudices wholly democratick, undertook to frame, and expected tranquilly, and with energy and success, to administer a *republican* government.

It is, and ever has been my belief, that the federal constitution was as good, or very nearly as good, as our country could bear; that the attempt to introduce a mixed monarchy was never thought of, and would have failed, if it had been made; and could have proved only an inveterate curse to the nation, if it had been adopted cheerfully, and even unanimously, by the people. Our materials for a government were all democratick, and whatever the hazard of their combination may be, our Solons and Lycurguses in the convention had no alternative, nothing to consider, but how to combine them, so as to ensure the longest duration to the constitution, and the most favourable chance for the publick liberty in the event of those changes, which the frailty of the structure of our government, the operation of time and accident, and the maturity and development of the national character were well understood to portend. We should have succeeded worse, if we had trusted to our metaphysicks more. Experience must be our physician, though his medicines may kill.

The danger obviously was, that a species of government, in which the people choose all the rulers, and then, by themselves, or ambitious demagogues pretending to be the people, claim and exercise an effective control over what is called the government, would be found on trial no better than a turbulent, licentious democracy. The danger was, that their best interests would be neglected, their dearest rights violated, their sober reason silenced, and the worst passions of the worst men not only freed from legal restraint, but invested with publick power. The known propensity of a democracy is to licentiousness, which the ambitious call, and the ignorant believe to be liberty.

The great object, then, of political wisdom in framing our constitution, was to guard against licentiousness, that inbred malady of democracies, that deforms their infancy with grey hairs and decrepitude.

The federalists relied much on the efficiency of an independent judiciary, as a check on the hasty turbulence of the popular passions. They supposed the senate proceeding from the states, and chosen for six years, would form a sort of balance to the democracy, and realise the hope, that a *federal republick of states might subsist*. They counted much on the information of the citizens; that they would give their unremitted attention to publick affairs; that either dissensions would not arise in our happy country, or, if they should, that the citizens would remain calm, and would walk, like the three Jews in Nebuchadnezzar's furnace, unharmed amidst the fires of party.

It is needless to ask, how rational such hopes were, or how far experience has verified them.

The progress of party has given to Virginia a preponderance, that, perhaps, was not foreseen. Certainly, since the late amendment in the article for the choice of president and vice-president, there is no existing provision of any efficacy to counteract it.

The project of arranging states in a federal union, has long been deemed by able writers and statesmen more promising than the scheme of a single republick. The experiment, it has been supposed, has not yet been fairly tried; and much has been expected from the example of America.

If states were neither able nor inclined to obstruct the federal union, much, indeed, might be hoped from such a confederation. But Virginia, Pennsylvania, and New-York are of an extent sufficient to form potent monarchies, and, of course, are too powerful, as well as too proud, to be *subjects* of the federal laws. Accordingly, one of the first schemes of *amendment*, and the most early executed, was, to exempt them in form from the obligations of justice. States are not liable to be sued. Either the federal head or the powerful members must govern. Now, as it is a thing ascertained by experience, that the great states are not willing, and cannot be compelled to obey the union, it is manifest, that their ambition is most singularly invited to aspire to the usurpation or control of the powers of the confederacy. A confederacy of many states, all of them small in extent and population, not only might not obstruct, but happily facilitate the federal authority. But the late presidential amendment demonstrates the overwhelming preponderance of several great states, combining together to engross the control of federal affairs. . . .

Now, though such leaders may have many occasions of jealousy and discord with one another, especially in the division of power and booty, is it not absurd to suppose, that any set of them will endeavour to restore both to the right owners? Do we expect a self-denying ordinance from the sons of violence and rapine? Are not those remarkably inconsistent with themselves, who say, our republican system is a government of justice and order, that was freely adopted in peace, subsists by morals, and whose office it is to ask counsel of the wise and to give protection to the good, yet who console themselves in the storms of the state with the fond hope, that order will spring out of confusion, because innovators will grow weary of change, and the ambitious will contend about their spoil. Then we are to have a new system exactly like the old one, from the fortuitous concourse of atoms, from the crash and jumble of all that is precious or sacred in the state. It is said, the popular hopes and fears are the gales that impel the political vessel. Can any disappointment of such hopes be greater than their folly?

It is true, the men now in power may not be united together by patriotism, or by any principle of faith or integrity. It is also true, that they have not, and cannot easily have, a military force to awe the people into submission. But on the other hand, they have no need of an army; there is no army to oppose them. They are held together by the ties, and made irresistible by the influence of party. With the advantage of acting as the government, who can oppose them? Not the federalists, who neither have any force, nor any object to employ it for, if they had. Not any subdivision of their own faction, because the opposers, if they prevail, will become the government, so much the less liable to be opposed for their recent victory; and if the new sect should fail, they will be nothing. The conquerors will take care, that an unsuccessful resistance shall strengthen their domination.

Thus it seems, in every event of the division of the ruling party, the friends of true liberty have nothing to hope. Tyrants may thus be often changed, but the tyranny will remain.

A democracy cannot last. Its nature ordains, that its next change shall be into a military despotism, of all known governments, perhaps, the most prone to shift its head, and the slowest to mend its vices. The reason is, that the tyranny of what is called the people, and that by the sword, both operate alike to debase and corrupt, till there are neither men left with the spirit to desire liberty, nor morals with the power to sustain justice. Like the burning pestilence that destroys the human body, nothing can subsist by its dissolution but vermin.

A military government may make a nation great, but it cannot make them free. There will be frequent and bloody struggles to decide who shall hold the sword; but the conqueror will destroy his competitors and prevent any permanent division of the empire. Experience proves, that in all such governments there is a continual tendency to *unity*.

Some kind of balance between the two branches of the Roman government had been maintained for several ages, till at length every popular demagogue, from the two Gracchi to Cesar, tried to gain favour, and by favour to gain power by flattering the multitude with new pretensions to power in the state. The assemblies of the people disposed of every thing; and intrigue and corruption, and often force disposed of the votes of those assemblies. It appears, that Catulus, Cato, Cicero, and the wisest of the Roman patriots, and perhaps wiser never lived, kept on, like the infatuated federalists, hoping to the last, that the people would see their errour and return to the safe old path. They laboured incessantly to reestablish the commonwealth; but the deep corruption of those times, not more corrupt than our own, rendered that impossible. Many of the friends of liberty were slain in the civil wars; some, like Lucullus, had retired to their farms; and most of the others, if not banished by the people, were without commands in the army, and, of course, without power in the state. Catiline came near being chosen consul, and Piso and Gabinius, scarcely less corrupt, *were* chosen. A people so degenerate could not maintain liberty; and do we find bad morals or dangerous designs any obstruction to the election of any favourite of the reigning party? It is remarkable, that when by a most singular concurrence of circumstances, after the death of Cesar, an opportunity was given to the Romans to re-establish the republick, there was no effective disposition among the people to concur in that design. It seemed as if the republican party, consisting of the same class of men as the Washington federalists, had expired with the dictator. The truth is, when parties rise and resort to violence, the moment of calm, if one should happen to succeed, leaves little to wisdom and nothing to choice. The orations of Cicero proved feeble against the arms of Mark Antony. Is not all this apparent in the United States? Are not the federalists as destitute of hopes as of power? What is there left for them to do? When a faction has seized the republick, and established itself in power, can the true federal republicans any longer subsist? After having seen the republick expire, will it be asked, why they are not immortal?

But the reason why such governments are not severed by the ambition of contending chiefs, deserves further consideration.

As soon as the Romans had subdued the kingdoms of Perseus, Antiochus, and Mithridates, it was necessary to keep on foot great armies. As the command of these was

bestowed by the people, the arts of popularity were studied by all those, who pretended to be the friends of the
people, and who really aspired to be their masters. The
greatest favourites became the most powerful generals;
and, as at first there was nothing which the Roman assemblies were unwilling to give, it appeared very soon that
they had nothing left to withhold. The armies disposed of
all power in the state, and of the state itself; and the generals of course assumed the control of the armies.

It is a very natural subject of surprise, that, when the
Roman empire was rent by civil war, as it was, perhaps,
twenty times from the age of Marius and Sylla to that of
Constantine, some competitor for the imperial purple did
not maintain himself with his veteran troops in his province; and found a new dynasty on the banks of the
Euphrates or the Danube, the Ebro or the Rhine. This
surprise is augmented by considering the distractions and
weakness of an elective government, as the Roman was;
the wealth, extent, and power of the rebellious provinces,
equal to several modern first rate kingdoms; their distance
from Italy; and the resource that the despair, and shame,
and rage of so many conquered nations would supply on
an inviting occasion to throw off their chains and rise once
more to independence; yet the Roman power constantly
prevailed, and the empire remained one and indivisible.
Sertorius was as good a general as Pompey; and it seems
strange that he did not become emperour of Spain. Why
were not new empires founded in Armenia, Syria, Asia
Minor, in Gaul or Britain? Why, we ask, unless because
the very nature of a military democracy, such as the
Roman was, did not permit it? Every civil war terminated
in the re-union of the provinces, that a rebellion had for a
time severed from the empire. Britain, Spain, and Gaul,
now so potent, patiently continued to wear their chains,
till they dropped off by the total decay of the Western
Empire.

The first conquests of the Romans were made by the

superiority of their discipline. The provinces were permitted to enjoy their municipal laws, but all political and military power was exercised by persons sent from Rome. So that the spirit of the subject nations was broken or rendered impotent, and every contest in the provinces was conducted, not by the provincials, but by Roman generals and veteran troops. These were all animated with the feelings of the Roman democracy. Now a democracy, a party, and an army bear a close resemblance to each other: they are all creatures of emotion and impulse. However discordant all the parts of a democracy may be, they all seek a centre, and that centre is the single arbitrary power of a chief. In this we see how exactly a democracy is like an army: they are equally governments by downright force.

A multitude can be moved only by their passions; and these, when their gratification is obstructed, instantly impel them to arms. *Furor arma ministrat.*[1] The club is first used, and then, as more effectual, the sword. The *disciplined* is found by the leaders to be more manageable than the *mobbish* force. The rabble at Paris that conquered the bastile were soon formed into national guards. But, from the first to the last, the nature, and character, and instruments of power remain the same. A *ripe* democracy will not long want sharp tools and able leaders: in fact, though not in name, it is an army. It is true, an army is not constituted as a deliberative body, and very seldom pretends to deliberate; but, whenever it does, it is a democracy in regiments and brigades, somewhat the more orderly as well as more merciful for its discipline. It always will deliberate, when it is suffered to feel its own power, and is indiscreetly provoked to exert it. At those times, is there much reason to believe it will act with less good sense, or with a more determined contempt for the national interest and opinion, than a giddy multitude

---

1. "Fury supplies weapons." [R.K.]

managed by worthless leaders? Now though an army is
not indulged with a vote, it cannot be stripped of its feelings, feelings that may be managed, but cannot be resisted. When the legions of Syria or Gaul pretended to
make an emperour, it was as little in the power as it was in
the disposition of Severus to content himself with Italy,
and to leave those fine provinces to Niger and Albinus.
The military town meeting must be satisfied; and nothing
could satisfy it but the overthrow of a rival army. If Pompey before the battle of Pharsalia had joined his lieuten-
ants in Spain, with the design of abandoning Italy, and
erecting Spain into a separate republick, or monarchy,
every Roman citizen would have despised, and every
Roman soldier would have abandoned him. After that
fatal battle, Cato and Scipio never once thought of keeping
Africa as an independent government; nor did Brutus and
Cassius suppose, that Greece and Macedonia, which they
held with an army, afforded them more than the means of
contesting with Octavius and Antony the dominion of
Rome. No hatred is fiercer than such as springs up among
those who are closely allied and nearly resemble each
other. Every common soldier would be easily made to feel
the personal insult and the intolerable wrong of another
army's rejecting his emperour and setting up one of their
own—not only so, but he knew it was both a threat and a
defiance. The shock of the two armies was therefore inevitable. It was a sort of duel, and could no more stop short of
destruction, than the combat of Hector and Achilles. We
greatly mistake the workings of human nature, when we
suppose the soldiers in such civil wars are mere machines.
Hope and fear, love and hatred, on the contrary, exalt
their feelings to enthusiasm. When Otho's troops had received a check from those of Vitellius, he resolved to kill
himself. His soldiers, with tears, besought him to live, and
swore they would perish, if necessary, in his cause. But he
persisted in his purpose, and killed himself; and many of
his soldiers, overpowered by their grief, followed his ex-

ample. Those, whom false philosophy makes blind, will suppose, that national wars will justify, and, therefore, will excite all a soldier's ardour; but that the strife between two ambitious generals will be regarded by all men with proper indifference. National disputes are not understood, and their consequences not foreseen, by the multitude; but a quarrel that concerns the life, and fame, and authority of a military favourite takes hold of the heart, and stirs up all the passions.

A democracy is so like an army, that no one will be at a loss in applying these observations. The great spring of action with the people in a democracy, is their fondness for one set of men, the men who flatter and deceive, and their outrageous aversion to another, most probably those who prefer their true interest to their favour.

A mob is no sooner gathered together, than it instinctively feels the want of a leader, a want that is soon supplied. They may not obey him as long, but they obey him as implicitly, and will as readily fight and burn, or rob and murder, in his cause, as the soldiers will for their general.

As the Roman provinces were held in subjection by Roman troops, so every American state is watched with jealousy, and ruled with despotick rigour by the partisans of the faction that may happen to be in power. The successive struggles, to which our licentiousness may devote the country, will never be of state against state, but of rival factions diffused over our whole territory. Of course, the strongest army, or that which is best commanded will prevail, and we shall remain subject to one indivisible bad government.

This conclusion may seem surprising to many; but the event of the Roman republick will vindicate it on the evidence of history. After faction, in the time of Marius, utterly obliterated every republican principle that was worth anything, Rome remained a military despotism for almost six hundred years; and, as the re-establishment of republican liberty in our country after it is once lost, is a thing not to be expected, what can succeed its loss but a government by the sword? It would be certainly easier to prevent than to retrieve its fall.

The jacobins are indeed ignorant or wicked enough to say, a *mixed monarchy* on the model of the British will succeed the failure of our republican system. Mr. Jefferson in his famous letter to Mazzei has shewn the strange condition both of his head and heart, by charging this design upon Washington and his adherents. It is but candid to admit, that there are many weakminded democrats, who really think a *mixed monarchy* the next stage of our politicks. As well might they promise, that, when their factious fire has burned the plain dwelling-house of our liberty, her temple will rise in royal magnificence and with all the proportions of Grecian architecture from the ashes. It is impossible sufficiently to elucidate, yet one could never be tired of elucidating the matchless absurdity of this opinion. An *unmixed* monarchy, indeed, there is almost no doubt awaits us; but it will not be called a monarchy. Cesar lost his life by attempting to take the name of *king*. A president, whose election cannot be hindered, may be well content to wear that title, which inspires no jealousy, yet disclaims no prerogative that party can usurp to confer. Old forms may be continued, till some inconvenience is felt from them; and then the same faction that has made them *forms*, can make them less, and substitute some new *organick decree* in their stead.

But a mixed monarchy would not only offend fixed opinions and habits, but provoke a most desperate resistance. The people, long after losing the substance of republican liberty, maintain a reverence for the name; and would fight with enthusiasm for the tyrant, who has left them the name, and taken from them every thing else. Who, then, are to set it up? and how are they to do it? Is it by an army? Where are their soldiers? Where are their resources and means to arm and maintain them? Can it be established by free popular consent? Absurd. A people once trained to republican principles, will feel the degradation of submitting to a king. It is far from certain, that their opposition would be soothed, by restricting the powers of such a king to the one half of what are now enjoyed by Mr. Jefferson. That would make a difference, but the many would not discern it. The aversion of a republican nation to kingship is sincere and warm, even to fanaticism; yet it has never been found to exact of a favourite demagogue, who aspired to reign, any other condescension than an ostentatious scrupulousness of regard to names, to appearances, and forms. Augustus, whose despotism was not greater than his cunning, professed to be the obsequious minister of his slaves in the senate; and Roman pride not only exacted, but enjoyed to the last, the pompous hypocrisy of the phrase, the majesty of the Roman *commonwealth*.

To suppose, therefore, a monarchy established by vote of the people, by the free consent of a majority, is contrary to the nature of man and the uniform testimony of his experience. To suppose it introduced by the disciples of Washington, who are with real or affected scorn described by their adversaries as a fallen party, a despicable handful of malcontents, is no less absurd than inconsistent. The federalists cannot command the consent of a majority, and they have no consular or imperial army to extort it. Every thing of that sort is on the side of their foes, and, of course, an unsurmountable obstacle to their pretended enterprise.

It will weigh nothing in the argument with some persons, but with men of sense it will be conclusive, that the mass of the federalists are the owners of the commercial and monied wealth of the nation. Is it conceivable, that such men will plot a revolution in favour of monarchy, a revolution that would make them beggars as well as traitors, if it should miscarry; and, if it should succeed ever so well, would require a century to take root and acquire stability enough to ensure justice and protect property? In these convulsions of the state property is shaken, and in

almost every radical change of government actually shifts
hands. Such a project would seem audacious to the conception of needy adventurers who risk nothing but their
lives; but to reproach the federalists of New England, the
most independent farmers, opulent merchants, and thriving mechanicks, as well as pious clergy, with such a conspiracy, requires a degree of impudence that nothing can
transcend. As well might they suspect the merchants of a
plot to choak up the entrance of our harbours by sinking
hulks, or that the directors of the several banks had
confederated to blow up the money vaults with gunpowder. The Catos and the Ciceros are accused of conspiring
to subvert the commonwealth—and who are the accusers?
The Clodii, the Antonies, and the Catilines.

Let us imagine, however, that by some miracle a *mixed*
monarchy is established, or rather put into operation; and
surely no man will suppose an *unmixed* monarchy can
possibly be desired or contemplated by the federalists.
The charge against them is, that they like the British
monarchy too well. For the sake of argument, then, be it
the British monarchy. To-morrow's sun shall rise and gild
it with hope and joy, and the dew of to-morrow's evening
shall moisten its ashes. Like the golden calf, it would be
ground to powder before noon. Certainly, the men, who
prate about an American monarchy copied from the British, are destitute of all sincerity or judgment. What could
make such a monarchy? Not parchment—We are beginning to be cured of the insane belief, that an engrossing
clerk can make a constitution. Mere words, though on
parchment, though sworn to, are wind, and worse than
wind, because they are perjury. What could give effect to
such a monarchy? It might have a right to command, but
what could give it power? Not an army, for that would
make it a military tyranny, of all governments the most
odious, because the most durable. The British monarchy
does not govern by an army, nor would their army suffer
itself to be employed to destroy the national liberties. It is

officered by the younger sons of noble and wealthy parents, and by many distinguished commanders who are in avowed opposition to the ministry. In fact, democratick opinions take root and flourish scarcely less in armies than in great cities, and infinitely more than they are found to do, or than it is possible they should in the cabals of any ruling party in the world.

Great Britain, by being an island, is secured from foreign conquest; and by having a powerful enemy within sight of her shore is kept in sufficient dread of it to be inspired with patriotism. That virtue, with all the fervour and elevation that a society which mixes so much of the commercial with the martial spirit can display, has other kindred virtues in its train; and these have had an influence in forming the habits and principles of action, not only of the English military and nobles, but of the mass of the nation. There is much, therefore, there is every thing in that island to blend self-love with love of country. It is impossible, that an Englishman should have fears for the government without trembling for his own safety. How different are these sentiments from the immovable apathy of those citizens, who think a constitution no better than any other piece of paper, nor so good as a blank on which a more perfect one could be written!

Is *our* monarchy to be supported by the national habits of subordination and implicit obedience? Surely, when they hold out this expectation, the jacobins do not mean to answer for themselves. Or do we really think it would still be a monarchy, though we should set up, and put down at pleasure, a town meeting king?

By removing or changing the relation of any one of the pillars that support the British government, its identity and excellence would be lost, a revolution would ensue. When the house of commons voted the house of peers useless, a tyranny of the committees of that body sprang up. The English nation have had the good sense, or, more correctly, the good fortune, to alter nothing, till time and circumstances enforced the alteration, and then to abstain from speculative innovations. The evil spirit of metaphysicks has not been conjured up to demolish, in order to lay out a new foundation by the line, and to build upon plan. The present happiness of that nation rests upon old foundations, so much the more solid, because the meddlesome ignorance of professed builders has not been allowed to new lay them. We may be permitted to call it a *matter of fact* government. No correct politician will presume to engage, that the same form of government would succeed equally well, or even succeed at all, any where else, or even in England under any other circumstances. Who will dare to say, that their monarchy would stand, if this generation had raised it? Who, indeed, will believe, if it did stand, that the weakness produced by the novelty of its institution would not justify and, even from a regard to self preservation, compel an almost total departure from its essential principles?

Now is there one of those essential principles, that it is even possible for the American people to adopt for their monarchy? Are old habits to be changed by a vote, and new ones to be established without experience? Can we have a monarchy without a peerage? or shall our governours supply that defect by giving commissions to a sufficient number of nobles of the quorum? Where is the American hierarchy? Where, above all, is the system of English law and justice, which would support liberty in Turkey, if Turkey could achieve the impossibility of supporting such justice?

It is not recollected, that any monarchy in the world was ever introduced by consent; nor will any one believe, on reflection, that it could be maintained by any nation, if nothing but consent upheld it. It is a rare thing, for a people to choose their government; it is beyond all credibility, that they will enjoy the still rarer opportunity of changing it by choice.

The notion, therefore, of an American *mixed monarchy*

is supremely ridiculous. It is highly probable, our country will be eventually subject to a monarchy, but it is demonstrable that it cannot be such as the British; and, whatever it may be, that the votes of the citizens will not be taken to introduce it.

It cannot be expected, that the tendency towards a change of government, however obvious, will be discerned by the multitude of our citizens. While demagogues enjoy their favour, their passions will have no rest, and their judgment and understanding no exercise. Otherwise, it might be of use to remind them, that more essential breaches have been made in our constitution within four years than in the British in the last hundred and forty. In that *enslaved* country, every executive attempt at usurpation has been spiritedly and perseveringly resisted, and substantial improvements have been made in the constitutional provisions for liberty. Witness the habeas corpus, the independence of the judges, and the perfection, if any thing human is perfect, of their administration of justice, the result of the famous Middlesex election, and that on the right of issuing general search-warrants. Let every citizen who is able to think, and who can bear the pain of thinking, make the contrast at his leisure.

They are certainly blind who do not see, that we are descending from a supposed orderly and stable republican government into a licentious democracy, with a progress that baffles all means to resist, and scarcely leaves leisure to deplore its celerity. The institutions and the hopes that Washington raised are nearly prostrate; and his name and memory would perish, if the rage of his enemies had any power over history. But they have not—history will give scope to her vengeance, and posterity will not be defrauded.

But, if our experience had not clearly given warning of our approaching catastrophe, the very nature of democracy would inevitably produce it.

A government by the passions of the multitude, or, no

less correctly, according to the vices and ambition of their leaders, is a democracy. We have heard so long of the indefeasible sovereignty of the people, and have admitted so many specious theories of the rights of man, which are contradicted by his nature and experience, that few will dread at all, and fewer still will dread as they ought, the evils of an American democracy. They will not believe them near, or they will think them tolerable or temporary. Fatal delusion!

When it is said, there may be a tyranny of the *many* as well as of the *few*, every democrat will yield at least a cold and speculative assent; but he will at all times act, as if it were a thing incomprehensible, that there should be any evil to be apprehended in the uncontrolled power of the people. He will say, arbitrary power may make a tyrant, but how can it make its possessor a slave?

In the first place, let it be remarked, the power of individuals is a very different thing from their liberty. When I vote for the man I prefer, he may happen not to be chosen; or he may disappoint my expectations, if he is; or he may be out-voted by others in the publick body to which he is elected. I may, then, hold and exercise all the power that a citizen can have or enjoy, and yet such laws may be made and such abuses allowed as shall deprive me of all liberty. I may be tried by a jury, and that jury may be culled and picked out from my political enemies by a federal marshal. Of course, my life and liberty may depend on the good pleasure of the man who appoints that marshal. I may be assessed arbitrarily for my faculty, or upon conjectural estimation of my property, so that all I have shall be at the control of the government, whenever its displeasure shall exact the sacrifice. I may be told, that I am a federalist, and, as such, bound to submit, in all cases whatsoever, to the will of the majority, as the ruling faction ever pretend to be. My submission may be tested by my resisting or obeying commands that will involve me in disgrace, or drive me to despair. I may become a fugitive, because the ruling party have made me afraid to stay at home; or, perhaps, while I remain at home, they may, nevertheless, think fit to inscribe my name on the list of emigrants and proscribed persons.

All this was done in France, and many of the admirers of French examples are impatient to imitate them. All this time the people may be told, they are the freest in the world; but what ought my opinion to be? What would the threatened clergy, the *aristocracy* of wealthy merchants, as they have been called already, and thirty thousand more in Massachusetts, who vote for Governour Strong, and whose case might be no better than mine, what would they think of their condition? Would they call it liberty? Surely, here is oppression sufficient in extent and degree to make the government that inflicts it both odious and terrible; yet this and a thousand times more than this was practised in France, and will be repeated, as often as it shall please God in his wrath to deliver a people to the dominion of their licentious passions.

The people, as a body, cannot deliberate. Nevertheless, they will feel an irresistible impulse to act, and their resolutions will be dictated to them by their demagogues. The consciousness, or the opinion, that they possess the supreme power, will inspire inordinate passions; and the violent men, who are the most forward to gratify those passions, will be their favourites. What is called the government of the people is in fact too often the arbitrary power of such men. Here, then, we have the faithful portrait of democracy. What avails the boasted *power* of individual citizens? or of what value is the will of the majority, if that will is dictated by a committee of demagogues, and law and right are in fact at the mercy of a victorious faction? To make a nation free, the crafty must be kept in awe, and the violent in restraint. The weak and the simple find their liberty arise not from their own individual sovereignty, but from the power of law and justice over all. It is only by the due restraint of others, that I am free.

Popular sovereignty is scarcely less beneficent than awful, when it resides in their courts of justice; there its office, like a sort of human providence, is to warn, enlighten, and protect; when the people are inflamed to seize and exercise it in their assemblies, it is competent only to kill and destroy. Temperate liberty is like the dew, as it falls unseen from its own heaven; constant without excess, it finds vegetation thirsting for its refreshment, and imparts to it the vigour to take more. All nature, moistened with blessings, sparkles in the morning ray. But democracy is a water spout, that bursts from the clouds, and lays the ravaged earth bare to its rocky foundations. The labours of man lie whelmed with his hopes beneath masses of ruin, that bury not only the dead, but their monuments.

It is the almost universal mistake of our countrymen, that democracy would be mild and safe in America. They charge the horrid excesses of France not so much to human nature, which will never act better, when the restraints of government, morals, and religion are thrown off, but to the characteristick cruelty and wickedness of Frenchmen.

The truth is, and let it humble our pride, the most ferocious of all animals, when his passions are roused to fury and are uncontrolled, is man; and of all governments, the worst is that which never fails to excite, but was never found to restrain those passions, that is, democracy. It is an illuminated hell, that in the midst of remorse, horrour, and torture, rings with festivity; for experience shews, that one joy remains to this most malignant description of the damned, the power to make others wretched. When a man looks round and sees his neighbours mild and merciful, he cannot feel afraid of the abuse of their power over him: and surely if they oppress me, he will say, they will spare their own liberty, for that is dear to all mankind. It is so. The human heart is so constituted, that a man loves liberty as naturally as himself. Yet liberty is a rare thing in the world, though the love of it is so universal.

Before the French Revolution, it was the prevailing opinion of our countrymen, that other nations were not free, because their despotick governments were too strong for the people. Of course, we were admonished to detest all existing governments, as so many lions in liberty's path; and to expect by their downfall the happy opportunity that every emancipated people would embrace to secure their own equal rights for ever. France is supposed to have had this opportunity, and to have lost it. Ought we not, then, to be convinced, that something more is necessary to preserve liberty than to love it? Ought we not to see, that, when the people have destroyed all power but their own, they are the nearest possible to a despotism, the more uncontrolled for being new, and ten-fold the more cruel for its hypocrisy?

The steps by which a people must proceed to change a government, are not those to enlighten their judgment or to sooth their passions. They cannot stir without following the men before them, who breathe fury into their hearts and banish nature from them. On whatever grounds and under whatever leaders the contest may be commenced, the revolutionary work is the same, and the characters of the agents will be assimilated to it. A revolution is a mine that must explode with destructive violence. The men who were once peaceable like to carry firebrands and daggers too long. Thus armed, will they submit to salutary restraint? How will you bring them to it? Will you undertake to reason down fury? Will you satisfy revenge without blood? Will you preach banditti into habits of self-denial? If you can, and in times of violence and anarchy, why do you ask any other guard than sober reason for your life and property in times of peace and order, when men are most disposed to listen to it? Yet even at such times, you impose restraints; you call out for your defence the whole array of law with its instruments of punishment and terrour; you maintain ministers to strengthen force with opinion, and to make religion the auxiliary of morals. With all this, however, crimes are still perpetrated; society is not any too safe or quiet. Break down all these fences; make what is called law an assassin; take what it ought to protect, and divide it; extinguish by acts of rapine and vengeance the spark of mercy in the heart; or, if it should be found to glow there, quench it in that heart's blood; make your people scoff at their morals, and unlearn an education to virtue; displace the Christian sabbath by a profane one, for a respite once in ten days from the toils of murder, because men, who first shed blood for revenge, and proceed to spill it for plunder, and in the progress of their ferocity, for sport, want a festival—what sort of society would you have? Would not rage grow with its indulgence? The coward fury of a mob rises in proportion as there is less resistance; and their inextinguishable thirst for slaughter grows more ardent as more blood is shed to slake it. In such a state is liberty to be gained or guarded from violation? It could not be kept an hour from the daggers of those who, having seized despotick power, would claim it as their lawful prize.—I have written the history of France. Can we look back upon it without terrour, or forward without despair?

The nature of arbitrary power is always odious; but it cannot be long the arbitrary power of the multitude. There is, probably, no form of rule among mankind, in which the progress of the government depends so little on the particular character of those who administer it. Democracy is the creature of impulse and violence; and the intermediate stages towards the tyranny of one are so quickly passed, that the vileness and cruelty of men are displayed with surprising uniformity. There is not time for great talents to act. There is no sufficient reason to be-

lieve, that we should conduct a revolution with much
more mildness than the French. If a revolution find the
citizens lambs, it will soon make them carnivorous, if not
cannibals. We have many thousands of the Paris and St.
Domingo assassins in the United States, not as fugitives,
but as patriots, who merit reward, and disdain to take any
but power. In the progress of our confusion, these men
will effectually assert their claims and display their skill.
There is no governing power in the state but party. The
moderate and thinking part of the citizens are without
power or influence; and it must be so, because all power
and influence are engrossed by a factious combination of
men, who can overwhelm uncombined individuals with
numbers, and the wise and virtuous with clamour and
fury.

It is indeed a law of politicks as well as of physicks, that
a body in action must overcome an equal body at rest. The
attacks that have been made on the constitutional barriers
proclaim in a tone that would not be louder from a trumpet, that party will not tolerate any resistance to its will.
All the supposed independent orders of the commonwealth must be its servile instruments, or its victims. We
should experience the same despotism in Massachusetts,
New Hampshire, and Connecticut, but the battle is not
yet won. It will be won; and they who already display the
temper of their Southern and French allies, will not linger
or reluct in imitating the worst extremes of their example.

What, then, is to be our condition?

Faction will inevitably triumph. Where the government
is both stable and free, there may be parties. There will be
differences of opinion, and the pride of opinion will be
sufficient to generate contests, and to inflame them with
bitterness and rancour. There will be rivalships among
those whom genius, fame, or station have made great, and
these will deeply agitate the state without often hazarding
its safety. Such parties will excite alarm, but they may be

safely left, like the elements, to exhaust their fury upon each other.

The object of their strife is to get power *under* the government; for, where that is constituted as it should be, the power *over* the government will not seem attainable, and, of course, will not be attempted.

But in democratick states there will be *factions*. The sovereign power being nominally in the hands of all, will be effectively within the grasp of a FEW; and, therefore, by the very laws of our nature, a few will combine, intrigue, lie, and fight to engross it to themselves. All history bears testimony, that this attempt has never yet been disappointed.

Who will be the associates? Certainly not the virtuous, who do not wish to control the society, but quietly to enjoy its protection. The enterprising merchant, the thriving tradesman, the careful farmer will be engrossed by the toils of their business, and will have little time or inclination for the unprofitable and disquieting pursuits of politicks. It is not the industrious, sober husbandman, who will plough that barren field; it is the lazy and dissolute bankrupt, who has no other to plough. The idle, the ambitious, and the needy will band together to break the hold that law has upon them, and then to get hold of law. Faction is a Hercules, whose first labour is to strangle this lion, and then to make armour of his skin. In every democratick state the ruling faction will have law to keep down its enemies; but it will arrogate to itself an undisputed power over law. If our ruling faction has found any impediments, we ask, which of them is now remaining? And is it not absurd to suppose, that the conquerors will be contented with half the fruits of victory?

We are to be subject, then, to a *despotick* faction, irritated by the resistance that has delayed, and the scorn that pursues their triumph, elate with the insolence of an arbitrary and uncontrollable domination, and who will exercise their sway, not according to the rules of integrity or national policy, but in conformity with their own exclusive interests and passions.

This is a state of things, which admits of progress, but not of reformation: it is the beginning of a revolution, which must *advance*. Our affairs, as first observed, no longer depend on counsel. The opinion of a majority is no longer invited or permitted to control our destinies, or even to retard their consummation. The men in power may, and, no doubt, will give place to some other faction, who will succeed, because they are abler men, or, possibly, in candour we say it, because they are worse. Intrigue will for some time answer instead of force, or the mob will supply it. But by degrees force only will be relied on by those who are *in*, and employed by those who are *out*. The vis major will prevail, and some bold chieftain will *conquer* liberty, and triumph and reign in her name.

Yet, it is confessed we have hopes, that this event is not very near. We have no cities as large as London or Paris; and, of course, the ambitious demagogues may find the ranks of their STANDING ARMY too thin to rule by them alone. It is also worth remark, that our mobs are not, like those of Europe, excitable by the cry of *no bread*. The dread of famine is every where else a power of political electricity, that glides through all the haunts of filth, and vice, and want in a city with incredible speed, and in times of insurrection rives and scorches with a sudden force, like heaven's own thunder. Accordingly, we find the sober men of Europe more afraid of the despotism of the rabble than of the government.

But, as in the United States we see less of this description of low vulgar, and as, in the essential circumstance alluded to, they are so much less manageable by their demagogues, we are to expect, that our affairs will be long guided by courting the mob, before they are violently changed by employing them. While the passions of the multitude can be conciliated to confer power and to overcome all impediments to its action, our rulers have a plain and easy task to perform. It costs them nothing but hypocrisy. As soon, however, as rival favourites of the people may happen to contend by the practice of the same arts, we are to look for the sanguinary strife of ambition. Brissot will fall by the hand of Danton, and *he* will be supplanted by Robespiere. The revolution will proceed in exactly the same way, but not with so rapid a pace, as that of France.

Part Three

~~~~~~

THE REPLY OF THE POETS

Reacting from an early enthusiasm for the French Revolution, Samuel Taylor Coleridge, William Wordsworth, and Robert Southey set their faces, and their pens, against radicalism. Walter Scott, in his romances, popularized the convictions of Burke. Wits like George Canning and John Hookham Frere drubbed radicals and liberals in *The Anti-Jacobin Review*. Despite the radicalism of Shelley, Godwin, and some other writers of the Romantic period, the general tendency of English men of letters during the first three decades of the nineteenth century was Tory. Here we have space only for specimens from Coleridge and Southey.

FRANCE: AN ODE
Samuel Taylor Coleridge

Samuel Taylor Coleridge (1772–1834), philosopher
and poet, expresses in this ode, written in 1798, the
abhorrence of Jacobinism and the discipleship to
Burke which many among the rising generation
shared in the concluding years of the eighteenth century.

Ye Clouds! that far above me float and pause,
    Whose pathless march no mortal may control!
    Ye Ocean-Waves! that, wheresoe'er ye roll,
Yield homage only to eternal laws!
Ye Woods! that listen to the night-birds singing,
    Midway the smooth and perilous slope reclined,
Save when your own imperious branches swinging
    Have made a solemn music of the wind!
Where, like a man beloved of God,
Through glooms, which never woodman trod,
    How oft, pursuing fancies holy,
My moonlight way o'er flowering weeds I wound,
    Inspired, beyond the guess of folly,
By each rude shape and wild unconquerable sound!
O ye loud Waves! and O ye Forests high!
    And O ye Clouds that far above me soared!
Thou rising Sun! thou blue rejoicing Sky!
    Yea, every thing that is and will be free!
    Bear witness for me, wheresoe'er ye be,
With what deep worship I have still adored
    The spirit of divinest Liberty.

II

When France in wrath her giant-limbs upreared,
  And with that oath, which smote air, earth and sea,
  Stamped her strong foot and said she would be free,
Bear witness for me, how I hoped and feared!
With what a joy my lofty gratulation
  Unawed I sang, amid a slavish band:
And when to whelm the discenchanted nation,
  Like fiends embattled by a wizard's wand,
    The Monarchs marched in evil day,
    And Britain joined the dire array;
  Though dear her shores and circling ocean,
Though many friendships, many youthful loves
  Had swoln the patriot emotion
And flung a magic light o'er all her hills and groves;
Yet still my voice, unaltered, sang defeat
  To all that braved the tyrant-quelling lance,
And shame too long delayed and vain retreat!
For ne'er, O Liberty! with partial aim
I dimmed thy light or damped thy holy flame;
  But blessed the paeans of delivered France,
And hung my head and wept at Britain's name.

III

"And what," I said, "though Blasphemy's loud scream
  With that sweet music of deliverance strove?
  Though all the fierce and drunken passions wove
A dance more wild than e'er was maniac's dream?
Ye storms, that round the dawning east assembled,
The Sun was rising, though ye hid his light!"
  And when, to soothe my soul, that hoped and trembled,
The dissonance ceased, and all seemed calm and bright;
  When France her front deep-scarred and gory;
  Concealed with clustering wreaths of glory;
    When, insupportably advancing,

Her arm made mockery of the warrior's tramp;
    While timid looks of fury glancing,
Domestic treason, crushed beneath her fatal stamp,
Writhed like a wounded dragon in his gore;
    Then I reproached my fears that would not flee;
"And soon," I said, "shall Wisdom teach her lore
In the low huts of them that toil and groan!
And, conquering by her happiness alone,
    Shall France compel the nations to be free,
Till Love and Joy look round, and call the Earth their
        own."

IV

Forgive me, Freedom! O forgive those dreams!
    I hear thy voice, I hear thy loud lament,
    From bleak Helvetia's icy caverns sent—
I hear thy groans upon her blood-stained streams!
    Heroes, that for your peaceful country perished,
And ye that, fleeing, spot your mountain-snows
    With bleeding wounds; forgive me, that I cherished
One thought that ever blessed your cruel foes!
    To scatter rage and traitorous guilt,
    Where Peace her jealous home had built;
        A patriot-race to disinherit
Of all that made their stormy wilds so dear;
        And with inexpiable spirit
To taint the bloodless freedom of the mountaineer—
O France, that mockest Heaven, adulterous, blind,
    And patriot only in pernicious toils,
Are these thy boasts, Champion of human kind?
    To mix with Kings in the low lust of sway,
    Yell in the hunt, and share the murderous prey;
To insult the shrine of Liberty with spoils
    From freemen torn; to tempt and to betray?

v

The Sensual and the Dark rebel in vain,
  Slaves by their own compulsion! In mad game
They burst their manacles and wear the name
    Of Freedom, graven on a heavier chain!
O Liberty! with profitless endeavour
Have I pursued thee, many a weary hour;
  But thou nor swell'st the victor's strain, nor ever
Didst breathe thy soul in forms of human power.
    Alike from all, howe'er they praise thee,
    (Nor prayer, nor boastful name delays thee)
    Alike from Priestcraft's harpy minions,
  And factious Blasphemy's obscener slaves,
    Thou speedest on thy subtle pinions,
The guide of homeless winds, and playmate of the waves!
And there I felt thee!—on that sea-cliff's verge,
  Whose pines, scarce travelled by the breeze above,
Had made one murmur with the distant surge!
Yes, while I stood and gazed, my temples bare,
And shot my being through earth, sea and air,
  Possessing all things with intensest love,
    O Liberty! my spirit felt thee there.

THE IDEA OF THE CONSTITUTION
Samuel Taylor Coleridge

Coleridge's principal work of political theory is *The Constitution of the Church and State, According to the Idea of Each* (1830). In this brief extract (fourth edition, London, 1852, pp. 18–21) Coleridge points out that a constitution is an idea, a concept, rather than merely a document.

Ask any of our politicians what is meant by the Constitution, and it is ten to one that he will give a false explanation; as for example, that it is the body of our laws, or that it is the Bill of Rights; or perhaps, if he have read Thomas Payne, he may say that we do not yet possess one, and yet not an hour may have elapsed, since we heard the same individual denouncing, and possibly with good reason, this or that code of laws, the excise and revenue laws, or those for including pheasants, or those for excluding Roman Catholics, as altogether unconstitutional; and such and such acts of Parliament as gross outrages on the Constitution. Mr. Peel, who is rather remarkable for groundless and unlucky concessions, owned that the late Act broke in on the Constitution of 1688: whilst in 1689 a very imposing minority of the then House of Lords, with a decisive majority in the Lower House of Convocation, denounced this very Constitution of 1688, as breaking in on the English Constitution.

But a Constitution is an idea arising out of the idea of a State; and because our whole history from Alfred onwards demonstrates the continued influence of such an idea, or ultimate aim, on the minds of our forefathers, in their characters and functions as public men, alike in what they resisted and in what they claimed; in the institutions and forms of polity, which they established, and with regard to those against which they more or less successfully contended; and because the result has been a progressive, though not always a direct or equable, advance in the gradual realisation of the idea; and because it is actually, though even because it is an idea not adequately, represented in a correspondent scheme of means really existing; we speak, and have a right to speak, of the idea itself, as actually existing, that is, as a principle existing in the only way in which a principle can exist,—in the minds and consciences of the persons whose duties it prescribes, and whose rights it determines. In the same sense that the sciences of arithmetic and of geometry, that mind, that life itself, have reality; the Constitution has real existence, and does not the less exist in reality, because it both is, and exists as, an idea.

THE SINS OF MANCHESTER
Robert Southey

The English conservatives of the Romantic era generally—and the poets in particular—sternly criticized the new industrial order for its inhumanity; they denounced the economic and social theories of Thomas Malthus, Jeremy Bentham, and the Manchesterian economists. Here Robert Southey (1774–1843), who received the gold medal of the Royal Society of Literature, reproaches British industrialism of the Bleak Age for the harm it inflicted upon community, the family, and older forms of economic production. This is Letter XXXVIII from Southey's *Letters from England*, first published in 1807 (pp. 207–217 in the Cresset Press edition, London, 1951). These purport to be the observations of a Spanish traveler in England—a literary device of Southey which at first a large part of the public mistook as genuine.

J. had provided us with letters to a gentleman in Manchester; we delivered them after breakfast, and were received with that courtesy which a foreigner when he takes with him the expected recommendations is sure to experience in England. He took us to one of the great cotton manufactories, showed us the number of children who were at work there, and dwelt with delight on the infinite good which resulted from employing them at so early an age. I listened without contradicting him, for who would lift up his voice against Diana in Ephesus!—proposed my questions in such a way as not to imply, or at least not to advance, any difference of opinion, and returned with a feeling at heart which makes me thank God I am not an Englishman.

There is a shrub in some of the East Indian islands which the French called *veloutier*; it exhales an odour that is agreeable at a distance, becomes less so as you draw nearer, and, when you are quite close to it, is insupportably loathsome. Alciatus himself could not have imagined an emblem more appropriate to the commercial prosperity of England.

Mr. —— remarked that nothing could be so beneficial to a country as manufactures. "You see these children, sir," said he. "In most parts of England poor children are a burthen to their parents and to the parish; here the parish, which would else have to support them, is rid of all expense; they get their bread almost as soon as they can run about, and by the time they are seven or eight years old bring in money. There is no idleness among us:—they come at five in the morning; we allow them half an hour for breakfast, and an hour for dinner; they leave work at six, and another set relieves them for the night; the wheels never stand still." I was looking, while he spoke, at the unnatural dexterity with which the fingers of these little creatures were playing in the machinery, half giddy myself with the noise and the endless motion: and when he told me there was no rest in these walls, day nor night, I thought that if Dante had peopled one of his hells with children, here was a scene worthy to have supplied him with new images of torment.

"These children, then," said I, "have no time to receive instruction." "That, sir," he replied, "is the evil which we have found. Girls are employed here from the age you see them till they marry, and then they know nothing about domestic work, not even how to mend a stocking or boil a potatoe. But we are remedying this now, and send the children to school for an hour after they have done work." I asked if so much confinement did not injure their health. "No," he replied, "they are as healthy as any children in the world could be. To be sure, many of them as they grew up went off in consumptions, but consumption was the disease of the English." I ventured to inquire afterwards concerning the morals of the people who were trained up in this monstrous manner, and found, what was to be expected, that in consequence of herding together such numbers of both sexes, who are utterly uninstructed in the commonest principles of religion and morality, they were as debauched and profligate as human beings under the influence of such circumstances must inevitably be; the men drunken, the women dissolute; that however high the wages they earned, they were too improvident ever to lay-by for a time of need; and that, though the parish was not at the expense of maintaining them when children, it had to provide for them in diseases induced by their mode of life, and in premature debility and old age; the poor-rates were oppressively high, and the hospitals and work-houses always full and overflowing. I inquired how many persons were employed in the manufactory, and was told, children and all about two hundred. What was the firm of the house?—There were two partners. So! thought I,—a hundred to one!

"We are well off for hands in Manchester," said Mr. ——; "manufactures are favourable to population, the poor are not afraid of having a family here, the parishes therefore have always plenty to apprentice, and we take them as fast as they can supply us. In new manu-facturing towns they find it difficult to get a supply. Their only method is to send people round the country to get children from their parents. Women usually undertake this business; they promise the parents to provide for the children; one party is glad to be eased of a burthen, and it answers well to the other to find the young ones in food, lodging and clothes, and receives their wages." "But if these children should be ill-used?" said I. "Sir," he replied, "it never can be the interest of the women to use them ill, nor of the manufacturers to permit it."

It would have been in vain to argue had I been disposed to it. Mr. —— was a man of humane and kindly nature, who would not himself use any thing cruelly, and judged of others by his own feelings. I thought of the cities in Arabian romance, where all the inhabitants were enchanted: here Commerce is the queen witch, and I had no talisman strong enough to disenchant those who were daily drinking of the golden cup of her charms.

We purchase English cloth, English muslins, English buttons, etc., and admire the excellent skill with which they are fabricated, and wonder that from such a distance they can be afforded to us at so low a price, and think what a happy country is England! A happy country indeed it is for the higher orders; no where have the rich so many enjoyments, no where have the ambitious so fair a field, no where have the ingenious such encouragement, no where have the intellectual such advantages; but to talk of English happiness is like talking of Spartan freedom, the Helots are overlooked. In no other country can such riches be acquired by commerce, but it is the one who grows rich by the labour of the hundred. The hundred, human beings like himself, as wonderfully fashioned by Nature, gifted with the like capacities, and equally made for immortality, are sacrificed body and soul. Horrible as it must needs appear, the assertion is true to the very letter. They are deprived in childhood of all instruction and all enjoyment; of the sports in which childhood instinctively indulges, of fresh air by day and of natural sleep by night. Their health physical and moral is alike destroyed; they die of diseases induced by unremitting task work, by confinement in the impure atmosphere of crowded rooms, by the particles of metallic or vegetable dust which they are continually inhaling; or they live to grow up without decency, without comfort, and without hope, without morals, without religion, and without shame, and bring forth slaves like themselves to tread in the same path of misery.

The dwellings of the labouring manufacturers are in narrow streets and lanes, blocked up from light and air, not as in our country to exclude an insupportable sun, but crowded together because every inch of land is of such value, that room for light and air cannot be afforded them. Here in Manchester a great proportion of the poor lodge in cellars, damp and dark, where every kind of filth is suffered to accumulate, because no exertions of domestic care can ever make such homes decent. These places are so many hotbeds of infection; and the poor in large towns are rarely or never without an infectious fever among them, a plague of their own, which leaves the habitations of the rich, like a Goshen of cleanliness and comfort, unvisited.

Wealth flows into the country, but how does it circulate there? Not equally and healthfully through the whole system; it sprouts into wens and tumours, and collects in aneurisms which starve and palsy the extremities. The government indeed raises millions now as easily as it raised thousands in the days of Elizabeth: the metropolis is six times the size which it was a century ago; it has nearly doubled during the present reign; a thousand carriages drive about the streets of London, where, three generations ago, there were not an hundred; a thousand hackney coaches are licensed in the same city, where at the same distance of time there was not one; they whose grandfathers dined at noon from wooden trenchers, and upon the produce of their own farms, sit down by the light of waxen tapers to be served upon silver, and to partake of delicacies from the four quarters of the globe. But the number of the poor, and the sufferings of the poor, have continued to increase; the price of every thing which they consume has always been advancing, and the price of labour, the only commodity which they have to dispose of, remains the same. Work-houses are erected in one place, and infirmaries in another; the poor-rates increase in proportion to the taxes; and in times of dearth the rich even purchase food, and retail it to them at a reduced price, or supply them with it gratuitously: still every year adds to their number. Necessity is the mother of crimes; new prisons are built, new punishments enacted; but the poor become year after year more numerous, more miserable, and more depraved; and this is the inevitable tendency of the manufacturing system.

This system is the boast of England,—long may she continue to boast it before Spain shall rival her! Yet this is the system which we envy, and which we are so desirous to imitate. Happily our religion presents one obstacle; that incessant labour which is required in these task-houses can never be exacted in a Catholic country, where the Church has wisely provided so many days of leisure for the purposes of religion and enjoyment. Against the frequency of these holydays much has been said; but Heaven forbid that the clamour of philosophizing commercialists should prevail, and that the Spaniard should ever be brutalized by unremitting task-work, like the negroes in America and the labouring manufacturers in England! Let us leave to England the boast of supplying all Europe with her wares; let us leave to these lords of the sea the distinction of which they are so tenacious, that of being the white slaves of the rest of the world, and doing for it all its dirty work. The poor must be kept miserably poor, or such a state of things could not continue; there must be laws to regulate their wages, not by the value of their work, but by the pleasure of their masters; laws to prevent their removal from one place to another within the kingdom, and to prohibit their emigration out of it. They would not be crowded in hot task-houses by day, and herded together in damp cellars at night; they would not toil in unwholesome employments from sun-rise till sun-set, whole days, and

whole days and quarters, for with twelve hours labour the
avidity of trade is not satisfied; they would not sweat night
and day, keeping up this *laus perennis* of the Devil, before
furnaces which are never suffered to cool, and breathing-
in vapours which inevitably produce disease and death;—
the poor would never do these thing unless they were
miserably poor, unless they were in that state of abject
poverty which precludes instruction, and by destroying
all hope for the future, reduces man, like the brutes, to
seek for nothing beyond the gratification of present wants.

How England can remedy this evil, for there are not
wanting in England those who perceive and confess it to
be an evil, it is not easy to discover, nor is it my business
to inquire. To us it is of more consequence to know how
other countries may avoid it, and, as it is the prevailing
system to encourage manufactures every where, to inquire
how we may reap as much good and as little evil as possible. The best methods appear to be by extending to the
utmost the use of machinery, and leaving the price of labour to find its own level: the higher it is the better. The
introduction of machinery in an old manufacturing country always produces distress by throwing workmen out of
employ, and is seldom effected without riots and execu-
tions. Where new fabrics are to be erected it is obvious
that this difficulty does not exist, and equally obvious that,
when hard labour can be performed by iron and wood, it
is desirable to spare flesh and blood. High wages are a general benefit, because money thus distributed is employed
to the greatest general advantage. The labourer, lifted up
one step in society, acquires the pride and the wants, the
habits and the feelings, of the class now next above him.
Forethought, which the miserably poor necessarily and
instinctively shun, is, to him who earns a comfortable
competence, new pleasure; he educates his children, in the
hope that they may rise higher than himself, and that he is
fitting them for better fortunes. Prosperity is said to be
more dangerous than adversity to human virtue; both are

wholesome when sparingly distributed, both in the excess perilous always, and often deadly: but if prosperity be thus dangerous, it is a danger which falls to the lot of few; and it is sufficiently proved by the vices of those unhappy wretches who exist in slavery, under whatever form or in whatever disguise, that hope is essential to prudence, and to virtue, as to happiness.

Part Four

~~~~~~

SOUTHERN CONSERVATISM

Northern Federalists and Whigs held no monopoly of conservative opinion in the United States. What Henry Adams called "the Sable Genius of the South" produced, south of Mason's and Dixon's Line, a passionate attachment to old ways, to rural society, and to the South's peculiar institutions. In the Civil War, this southern conservatism would be beaten down by the stronger North. John Randolph of Roanoke (1773–1833) was the most eloquent champion of this school, and John C. Calhoun (1782–1850) its most systematic advocate.

KING NUMBERS
John Randolph

Randolph of Roanoke, the brilliant and eccentric adversary of Jefferson and the Virginia Dynasty, led the "Old Republicans" for decades in the House of Representatives. At Virginia's constitutional convention of 1829–30, the dying Randolph denounced centralization, the lust for political innovation, and "King Numbers"—the tyranny of a majority. Here Randolph defends the old constitution of Virginia against the proposed new constitution. This speech is from *Proceedings of the Virginia Convention of 1829–30,* reprinted in Kirk, *John Randolph of Roanoke* (third edition, Indianapolis, 1978), pp. 542–67.

Mr. Randolph rose, and addressed the Committee as follows:

Mr. Chairman: It has been with great disappointment, and yet deeper regret, that I have perceived an invincible repugnance on the part of gentlemen representing here a large portion of the Commonwealth extending from Cape Henry to the Mountains, along the whole length of the North Carolina line, that portion of it in which my own district is situated, to take a share in this debate—a repugnance not resulting—I say so from my personal knowledge of many of them—not resulting from any want of ability, nor from the want of a just, modest, and manly confidence in the abilities they possess. I have looked to Norfolk; I have looked to Southampton; I have looked to

Dinwiddie; I have looked to Brunswick, for the display of talent which I knew to exist; but Sir, I have looked in vain.

And it is this circumstance only—I speak it with a sincerity I have too much self-respect to vouch for, which has induced me to overcome the insuperable aversion—(insuperable until now)—that I have felt, to attract towards myself the attention of the Committee.

As long as I have had my fixed opinions, I have been in the habit of considering the Constitution of Virginia, under which I have lived for more than half a century, with all its faults and failings, and with all the objections which practical men—not theorists and visionary speculators—have urged, or can urge against it, as the very best Constitution; not for Japan; not for China; not for New England; or for Old England; but for this, our ancient Commonwealth of Virginia.

But, I am not such a bigot as to be unwilling, under any circumstances, however imperious, to change the Constitution under which I was born; I may say, certainly, under which I was brought up, and under which I had hoped to be carried to my grave. My principles on that subject are these: the grievance must first be clearly specified, and fully proved; it must be vital, or rather, deadly in its effect; its magnitude must be such as will justify prudent and reasonable men in taking the always delicate, often dangerous step, of making innovations in their fundamental law; and the remedy proposed must be reasonable and adequate to the end in view. When the grievance shall have been thus made out, I hold him to be not a loyal subject, but a political bigot, who would refuse to apply the suitable remedy.

But, I will not submit my case to a political physician, come his diploma from whence it may, who would at once prescribe all the medicines in the Pharmacopoeia, not only for the disease I now have, but for all the diseases of every possible kind I ever might have in future. These are my principles, and I am willing to carry them out; for, I will not hold any principles which I may not fairly carry out in practice.

Judge then, with what surprise and pain, I found that not one department of this government—no, not one— Legislative, Executive, or Judicial—nor one branch of either, was left untouched by the spirit of *innovation*— (for I cannot call it reform). When even the Senate—yes, Sir, the Senate, which had so lately been swept by the besom of innovation—even the Senate had not gone untouched or unscathed. Many innovations are proposed to be made without any one practical grievance having been even suggested, much less shown.

Take that branch of the Government which was so thoroughly reformed in 1816, and even that is not untouched. Sir, who ever heard a whisper, *ab urbe condita* to this day, that the Senators of Virginia were too *youthful?* I never heard such a sentiment in my life. And in the House of Delegates, what men ever heard that the members—I speak of them, of course, in the aggregate—that the members were too young? Yet, even there, it is to be declared, that all men who might be elected to that body between the ages of twenty-one and twenty-four, are to be disfranchised; and as regards the Senate, all between the ages of twenty-one and thirty. Yes, Sir, not only the spring and seed-time, but the summer and harvest of life—that delightful season which neither you, Sir, nor I can ever recall—the dearest and the best portion of our lives; during this period of nine years, the very prime of human life, men are to be disfranchised. And for what? For a political megrim, a freak—no evil is suggested.

The case is certainly very rare that a man under thirty is elected a member of the Senate. It will then be said, there is no privation, and, therefore, no injury. But, Sir, there is a wide difference between a man's being not elected, and a fundamental law stamping a stigma upon him by which he is excluded from the noblest privilege to which no merit or exertion on his part can restore him.

But, all this, I suppose, is in obedience to the all-prevailing principle that *vox populi, vox dei;* aye, Sir, the all-prevailing principle that Numbers, and Numbers alone, are to regulate all things in political society, in the very teeth of those abstract natural rights of man which constitute the only shadow of claim to exercise this monstrous tyranny.

With these general remarks, permit me to attempt—I am afraid it will prove an abortive attempt—to say something on the observations of other gentlemen, to which I have given the most profound attention I am capable of. Sir, I have no other preparation for this task than a most patient attention to what has been said here, and in the Committee of which I was a member, and deep, intense, and almost annihilating thought on the subjects before us. This is all the preparation that I have made. I cannot follow the example which has been set me. I cannot go into the history of my past life, or defend my political consistency here or elsewhere. I will not do this for this reason: I have always held it unwise to plead 'til I am arraigned, and arraigned before a tribunal having competent and ample jurisdiction. My political consistency requires no such defence. My claim to Republicanism rests on no patent taken out yesterday, or to be taken our tomorrow. My life itself is my only voucher, a life spent for thirty years in the service of the most grateful of constituents.

The gentleman from Augusta, who occupies so large a space, both in the time and in the eye of the House, has told us that he fought gallantly by the side of his noble friend from Chesterfield, so long as victory was possible, and that it was not until he was conquered, that he grounded his arms. The gentleman further told us that, finding his native country and his early friends on this side the mountain, on whose behalf he had waged that gallant war—he found he hesitated what part to take *now*, until his constituents, aye, Sir—and more than that, his property, lay on the other side—and he has taken his course accordingly. Well, Sir, and will he not allow, on our part, that some consideration is due to our constituents, although they happen to be our neighbours, or to *our property*, although we reside upon it? Are either or both less dear on that account?

But, Sir, I put it to the Committee, whether the gentleman is not mistaken in point of fear? Whether the victory *is* indeed won? Every one, to be sure, is the best judge whether he is beaten or not. But, I put it to the gentleman himself, whether, if he were now fighting along side of his noble friend from Chesterfield, the scale might not possibly turn the other way? No man, however, is compelled to fight after he feels himself vanquished.

Sir, I mean no ill-timed pleasantry, either as it regards the place where it is uttered, the person to whom it refers, and least of all, as it respects him by whom the remark is made, when I say that in this prudent resolution of the gentleman from Augusta he could not have been exceeded in caution and forcast by a certain renowned Captain Dugald Dalgetty himself. Sir, the war being ended, he takes service on the other side: the sceptre having passed from Judah, the gentleman stretches out his arm from Richmond to Rockfish Gap to intercept and clutch it in its passage.

Among various other observations with which he favoured the committee, he protested with great earnestness against opinions relating to the Federal Government or its administration being introduced here. Sir, the gentleman is too great a lawyer not to know that the Federal Government is *our* Government: it is the Government of Virginia—and if a man were disposed to shut his eyes to the constitution, and the administration of the Federal Government, he could not do it: they would be forced open, Sir, by the interests, and feelings, aye, and by the passions too, which have existed, do exist, and will continue to exist, as long as Virginia herself shall have existence.

It is not the least of my regrets that one of the most inevitable consequences of these changes, if they shall take effect, will be totally to change all the politics of Virginia in reference to the Federal Government—(without considering the hands in which it may happen to be placed)—and I do confidently believe that the very greatest cause of them is to be found in the hope of producing that all-desired change. In many cases I know it to exist, of my own personal knowledge.

Sir, we can't shut our eyes to the Federal Government.

When in 1788, the Convention of Virginia adopted the Federal Government as a part of her Constitution, they effected a greater change in our Constitution than the wildest reformer now suggests to us. To estimate the amount of that change we must have reference to her interests and power at that day; if not, we may call *ourselves* Statesmen, but the world will apply to us a very different epithet. Among innumerable causes why I now oppose a change is my full recollection of the change which was then brought about. I have by experience learned that changes, even in the ordinary law of the land, do not always operate as the drawer of the bill, or the Legislative body, may have anticipated: and of all the things in the world, a Government, whether ready made to suit casual customers or made per order, is the very last that operates as its framers intended. Governments are like revolutions: you may put them in motion, but I defy you to control them after they are *in* motion.

Sir, if there is any one thing clearer than another, it is that the Federal Constitution intended that the State Governments should issue no paper money; and by giving the Federal Government power *"to coin money"* it was intended to insure the result that this should be a hard money Government. And what is it? It is a paper-money Government. If this be the result, in spite of all precautions to the contrary—(Sir, this is no time, as the late illustrious President of the Court of Appeals was wont to say, to mince words)—and these Governments have turned out to be two most corrupt paper-money Governments, and you could not prevent it. How can we except now to define and limit the operation of new and untried principles? For new and untried they are, and if God lends me strength, I will prove it.

I have very high authority—the authority of the gentleman from Augusta—to say that the Federal Government was intended to be charged only with the external relations of the country; but, by a strange transformation, it has become the regulator (abandoning the Colonial trade by negligence, or incapacity, or both, and crippling all our other trade), it has become the regulator of the interior of the country: its roads, its canals, and, more than that, of its productive, or rather, its *unproductive* labour—for they have made it so.

Yet, with these facts staring us in the face, we are gravely told not to look at the Federal Government at all: And this in the Government of Virginia, where, to use a very homely phrase, but one that exactly suits the case: we can't take a step without breaking our shins over some Federal obstacle.

Sir, I can readily see a very strong motive for wishing to do away with all past distinctions in politics, to obliterate the memory of old as well as of recent events, and once more to come with something like equal chances into the political lottery.

Let me return to my illustration. What provision is there, Mr. Chairman, either in the Constitution of Virginia or the Constitution of the United States, which establishes it as a principle that the Commonwealth of Virginia should be the sole restraining and regulating power on the mad and unconstitutional usurpations of the Federal Government? There is no such provision in either:—yet in practice and in fact, the Commonwealth of Virginia has been, to my certain knowledge, for more than thirty years, the sole counterpoise and check on the usurpations of the Federal Government—so far as they have checked at all: I wish they had been checked more effectually.

For a long time, our brethren of the South, because we were the frontier state of the great Southern division of the Union, were dead to considerations to which they have, I fear, awaked too late. Virginia was left alone and unsupported, unless by the feeble aid of her distant offspring, Kentucky. It is because I am unwilling to give up this check or to diminish its force, that I am unwilling to pull down the edifice of our State Government from the garret to the cellar, aye, down to the foundation stone. I will not put in hazard this single good for all the benefits the warmest advocate of reform can hope to derive from the results of this body.

The gentleman from Augusta told us, yesterday, I believe, or the day before, or the day before that—I really do not remember which—that slaves have always been a subject of taxation in Virginia, and that a long while ago, neat cattle had also been taxed. In regard to these horned cattle, I think they have occupied full as much attention as they are entitled to in this debate. But, let it be remembered, that we were then not taxing the cattle *of the West*, for there was no West, but a few scattered settlements beyond the mountain; and what we have been discussing was the proportion of taxes paid by the East and the West. No sooner was an interest in this subject established beyond the mountains, than the tax was laid aside. At that time, Sir, the Commonwealth of Virginia was throughout, a slave-holding Commonwealth: (would to God she were so now). And is it then so wonderful that slaves should have been a subject of taxation? Yes, Sir: Virginia was then not only throughout, a slave-holding, but a tobacco-planting Commonwealth. You can't open the Statute Book—I mean one of the old Statute Books, not those that have been defaced by the finger of reform—and not see that tobacco was, in fact, the currency as well as staple of the State. We paid our clerks' fees in tobacco; verdicts were given in tobacco; and bonds were executed payable in tobacco. That accounts for it all. While a large portion of the State has ceased to be a slave-holding, and a still larger portion has ceased to be a tobacco-planting community, the burden has rested on the necks of a comparatively small, unhappy, and I will say it, a proscribed caste in the community. Not that any such effect was intended, when all were tobacco-planters, taxes on slaves and tobacco were fair and equal. But time, the greatest of innovators, has silently operated to produce this great and grinding oppression. My nativity cast my lot there. I am one of them. I participate in all their interests and feelings. And if I had been told, until I had the evidence of fact to prove it, that one of the great slave-holding and tobacco-planting districts would lend itself to the support of the report of the Legislative Committee, unmitigated, or—to use a term for which I am indebted to the gentleman from Spottsylvania—*unmollified,* or *undulcified* by anything to give it a wholesome operation, I would not have believed it. Nothing but ocular and auricular demonstration would have made me believe it possible. For my part, I had not only, as the gentleman from Chesterfield has said, never have been born, but, being born, and grown up as I am, it were better for me that a mill-stone were hanged about my neck and I cast into the uttermost depths of the sea, than to return to my constituents after having given a naked vote for the report of the Committee.

Sir, when I speak of danger, from what quarter does it come? From whom? From the corn and oat growers on the Eastern Shore, the Rappahannock and the Pamunkey? From the fishermen on the Chesapeake? The pilots of Elizabeth City? No, Sir—from ourselves—from the great slave-holding and tobacco-planting districts of the State. I could not have brought myself to believe it—nothing could have persuaded me to believe, that the real danger which threatens this great interest should spring from those districts themselves. And, arrogant and presumptuous as it may appear in me (these epithets have been applied to us by the gentleman from Augusta), I will risk any thing short of my eternal salvation on the fact that when the people of that region come to understand the real question, you will as soon force ratsbane down their throats as a Constitution with such a principle in it.

The gentleman from Augusta told us, yesterday, or the day before—I cannot be certain as to the precise day—with some appearance as if it were a grievance, that the people had interfered; and he asked if we are to be instructed out of our seats? I answer: yes. Such as cannot be instructed *in* their seats must be instructed *out* of their seats. He says the voices of the people from county meetings and crossroads and taverns will come here and interrupt the harmony of our deliberations.

I trust they will. Though the people have hitherto been supine, on this side of the mountains, I trust they will take the matter into their own hands. I hope they are beginning to rouse from their torpor: and I know it. I will state one fact, to show that the current of public sentiment is fast setting in on our side. I do not say whether it was for or against us before. I have heard, not one, not ten, not fifty (and when I say not fifty, I mean not less but more than that number), of intelligent men declare that, if by any possibility, they could have foreseen (poor innocents) that such were to be the results, they never would have voted for this Convention. In the mean while, not a single convert has been made from our cause; if there has, name the man. I could name ten, twenty, aye, fifty; and if I were to resort to documentary evidence, I could name more. So far am I from being one of those who wish to precipitate the question, I am glad, I rejoice in the prospect, that our Session will run into that of the Virginia Assembly. In politics, I am always for getting the last advices. You can never get at the true temper of the public mind 'til the occasion presents itself for decisive action.

I have made, and shall make, no disclaimer of having intended offence to any person or party in this body—and this for the same reason I before stated. I never will plead 'til I am arraigned by a competent tribunal, and the disclaimer would be misplaced. Gentlemen on all sides have spoken of the *intention* with which they are demanding power (for the gentleman from Augusta lifted the veil and owned to us that power, and power alone, is the object he is in pursuit of). Sir, I mean no disrespect when I say, that however important it may be to themselves, to me it is a matter of perfect indifference—I speak in reference to the operation of their measures—whether their intents be wicked or charitable. I say, the demand which they make is such as ought to alarm every considerate and fore-thoughted man; and that there is nothing to mitigate that alarm in the stern, unrelenting, inexorable, remorseless cry which they raise for power, and their determination to listen to no compromise. One gentleman, indeed, has abated somewhat of his tone of triumph. Perhaps, the prospect of speedy enjoyment has claimed his exultation and sobered him down.

Mr. Chairman, since I have been here, the scene has recalled many old recollections. At one time I thought myself in the House of Representatives, listening to the debate on the Tariff; at another time, I imagined myself listening to the debate on the Missouri Question; and sometimes I fancied myself listening to both questions debated at once. Are we men? met to consult about the affairs of men? Or are we, in truth, a Robinhood Society discussing rights in the abstract? Have we no house over our heads? Do we forget that we are living under a Constitution which has shielded us for more than half a century?—that we are not a parcel of naked and forlorn savages on the shores of New Holland; and that the worst that can come is that we shall live under the same Constitution that we have lived under, freely and happily, for half a century? To their monstrous claims of power, we plead this prescription; but then we are told: *nullum tempus occurrit Regi.*[1] King who? King Numbers. And they will not listen to a prescription of fifty-four years—a period greater by four years than would secure a title to the best estate in the Commonwealth, unsupported by any other shadow of right. Nay, Sir, in this case, prescription operates *against* possession. They tell us it is only a case of long-continued, and therefore of aggravated, injustice. They say to us, in words the most courteous and soft—but I am not so soft as to swallow them—"we shall be—we will be—we must be your masters, and you shall submit." To whom do they hold this language? To dependents? weak, unprotected, and incapable of defence? Or is it to the great tobacco-growing and slave-holding interest, and to every other interest on this side the Ridge? "We are numbers, you have property." I am not so obtuse as to require any further explanation on this head. "We are numbers, you have property." Sir, I understand it perfectly.

Mr. Chairman, since the days of the French Revolution, when the Duke of Orleans, who was the richest subject not only in France but in all Europe, lent himself to the *mountain* party in the Convention, in the vain and weak hope of grasping political power, perhaps of mounting the throne—still slippery with the blood of the last incumbent—from that day to this, so great a degree of infatuation has not been shown by any individual as by the tobacco-grower and slave-holder of Virginia who shall lend his aid to rivet this yoke on the necks of his brethren, and on his own. Woe betide that man! Even the Duke of Orleans himself, profligate and reprobate as he was, would have halted in his course had he foreseen in the end, his property confiscated to the winds, and his head in the sack of the executioner.

I enter into no calculations of my own, for I have made

---

1. "At no time does one oppose the King." [R.K.]

none, nor shall I follow the example which has been set me. I leave that branch of the argument, if argument it can be called, of the gentleman from Augusta, to be answered by himself.

The gentleman told us, the day before yesterday, that in fifteen minutes of the succeeding day, he would conclude all he had to say; and he then kept us two hours, not by the Shrewsbury clock, but by as good a watch as can be made in the city of London. (*Drawing out and opening his watch.*) As fifteen minutes are to two hours in the proportion of one to eight, such is the approximation to truth in the gentleman's calculations. If all the calculations and promises of the gentleman from Augusta, which he held out to gull us—I speak not of his intentions, but only of the effect that would have ensued—shall be no nearer the truth than these, where then should we be who trust them?

In the course of what I fear will be thought my very wearisome observations, I spoke of the Tariff Law. When the people of the United States threw off their allegiance to Great Britain, and established Republican Governments here, whether State or Federal, one discovery since made in politics had not yet entered into the head of any man in the Union, which, if not arrested by the good sense and patriotism of the country, will destroy all Republican Government as certainly and inevitably as time will one day destroy us. That discovery is this: that a bare majority—(the majority on the Tariff was, I believe, but two—my friend behind me [Mr. P. P. Barbour] tells me that I am right—and on one important branch of that law, that, I mean, which relates to cotton bagging, the majority was but one, and *that* consisted of the casting vote of the Speaker)—that a bare majority may oppress, harass, and plunder the minority at pleasure, but that it is their interest to keep up the minority to the highest possible point consistent with their subjugation, because, the larger that minority shall be, in proportion to the majority, by that same proportion are the profits of the majority enhanced, which they have extracted and extorted from the minority. And after all our exclamations against this crying oppression; after all our memorials and remonstrances; after all our irrefragable arguments against it—(I refer not to the share I had in them; I speak of the arguments of other gentlemen, and not of my own)—shall we in Virginia introduce this deadly principle into our own Government? and give power to a bare majority to tax us *ad libitum*, and that when the strongest temptation is at the same time held out to them to do it? It is now a great while since I learned from the philosopher of Malmesbury that a state of nature is a state of war; but if we sanction this principle, we shall prove that a state, not of nature, but of society, and of Constitutional Government, is a state of interminable war. And it will not stop here. Instructed by this most baneful, yes, and most baleful example, we shall next have one part of a county conspiring to throw their share of the burden of the levy upon the other part. Sir, if there is a destructive principle in politics, it is that which is maintained by the gentleman from Augusta.

But we are told we are to have a stay of execution. "We will give you time," say the gentlemen: "only give us a bond binding all your estate, secured by a deed of trust on all your slaves." Why, Sir, there is not a hard-hearted Shylock in the Commonwealth who will not, on such conditions, give you time. Are we so weak that, like the spend-thrift who runs to the usurer, we are willing to encounter this calamity because it is not to come upon us 'til the year 1856? a period not as long as some of us have been in public life? Sir, I would not consent to it if it were not to come 'til the year 2056! I am at war with the principle! Let me not be told that I am at war with the Bill of Rights. I subscribe to every word in the Bill of Rights. I need not show how this can be. It has been better done already by the gentleman from Spottsylvania (Mr. Stanard), to whom I feel personally indebted as a tobacco-planter and a slave-holder, for the speech he has made. The Bill of Rights contains unmodified principles. The declarations it contains are our lights and guides, but when we come to apply these great principles, we must modify them for use; we must set limitations to their operation, and the enquiry then is *quousque?* How far? It is a question not of principle but of degree. The very moment this immaculate principle of theirs is touched, it becomes what all principles are: materials in the hands of men of sense, to be applied to the welfare of the Commonwealth. It is not an incantation. It is no Talisman. It is not witchcraft. It is not a torpedo to benumb us. If the naked principle of numbers only is to be followed, the requisites for the Statesman fall far below what the gentleman from Spottsylvania rated them at. He needs not the four rules of arithmetic. No, Sir, a negro boy with a knife and a tally-stick is a Statesman complete in this school. Sir, I do not scoff, jeer or flout—(I use, I think, the very words of the gentleman from Augusta; two of them certainly were employed by him)—at the principles of the Bill of Rights, and so help me Heaven, I have not heard of any who did. But I hold with one of the greatest masters of political philosophy, that "no rational man ever did govern himself by abstractions and universals. I do not put abstract ideas wholly out of any question, because I know well that under that name I should dismiss principles; and that without the guide and light of sound, well understood principles, all reasonings in politics, as in every thing else, would be only a confused jumble of particular facts and details, without the means of drawing out any sort of theoretical or practical conclusion.

"A Statesman differs from a Professor in a University. The latter has only the general view of society; the former, the Statesman, has a number of circumstances to combine with those general ideas, and to take into his consideration. Circumstances are infinite, are infinitely combined, are variable and transient: he who does not take them into consideration is not erroneous, but stark mad—*dat operam ut cum ratione insaniat*[2]—he is metaphysically mad. A Statesman, never losing sight of principles, is to be guided by circumstances, and judging contrary to the exigencies of the moment, he may ruin his country forever."

Yes, Sir—and after that ruin has been effected, what a poor consolation is derived from being told, "I had not thought it." *Stulti est dixisse non putaram.*[3] "Who would have thought it?" "Lord bless me! I never thought of such a thing, or I never would have voted for a Convention."

If there is any country on earth where circumstances have a more important bearing than in another, it is here, in Virginia. Nearly half the population are in bondage— yes, Sir, more than half in the country below the Ridge. And is this no circumstance? Yet, let me say with the gentleman from Accomac (Mr. Joynes), whose irresistible array of figures set all figures of speech at defiance, that if there were not a negro in Virginia, I would still contend for the principle in the amendment. And why? Because I will put it in the power of no man or set of men who ever lived, or who ever shall live, to tax me without my consent. It is wholly immaterial whether this is done without my having any representation at all, or, as it was done in the case of the Tariff Law, by a phalanx stern and inexorable who, being the majority, and having the power, prescribe to me the law that I shall obey. Sir, what was it to all the Southern interest that we came within two votes of defeating that iniquitous measure? Do not our adversaries (for adversaries they are), know that they have the power? and that we must submit? Yes, Sir. This whole slave-holding country, the whole of it, from the Potomac to Mexico, was placed under the ban and anathema of a majority of two! And will you introduce such a principle into your own State Government? Sir, at some times dur-

---

2. "He labors so that he goes mad with reason." [R.K.]
3. "It is foolish to say, 'I didn't think of that.' " [R.K.]

ing this debate I doubted if I were in my right mind. From the beginning of time 'til now, there is no case to be found of a rational and moral people subverting a Constitution under which they had lived for half a century—aye, for two centuries, by a majority of *one*. When revolutions have happened in other countries, it was the effect of a political storm, a Levanter, a tornado, to which all opposition was fruitless. But did any body ever hear of a revolution affecting the entire condition of one half of a great State being effected by a majority of one? Did it ever enter the head of the wildest visionary, from the days of Peter the Hermit to—a day I will not name—to accomplish a revolution by a majority of *one?* Sir, to change your constitution by such a majority is nothing more than to sound the tocsin for a civil war. It may be at first a war of words, a weaponless war, but it is one of those cases in which, as the lawyers tell us, fury supplies arms. Sir, this thing cannot be: it must not be. I was about to say, it *shall* not be. I tell gentlemen now, with the most perfect deliberation and calmness, that we cannot submit to this outrage on our rights. It surpasses that measure of submission and forebearance which is due from every member of an organized Government to that Government. And why do I so tell them? Sir, we are not a company of naked savages on the coast of New Holland, or Van Diemans Land. We have a Government; we have rights; and do you think that we shall tamely submit, and let you deprive us of our vested rights, and reduce us to bondage? Yes, vested rights! that we shall let you impose on us a yoke hardly lighter than that of the *villeins regardant*[4] of the manor? We are now little better than the trustees of slave-labour for the nabobs of the East, and of the North (if there be any such persons in our country), and to the speculators of the West. They regulate our labour. Are we to have *two*

---

4. Vigilant peasants, those charged to perform all the menial tasks within the manor. [R.K.]

masters? When every vein has been sluiced—when our whole system presents nothing but one pitiful enchymosis—are we to be patted and tapped to find yet another vein to breathe, not for the Federal Government, but for our own? Why, Sir, the richest man in Virginia, be that man who he may, would make a good bargain to make you a present of his estate, provided you give him a bond upon that estate allowing him to tax it as he pleases, and to spend the money as he pleases. It is of the very essence of property that none shall tax it but the owner himself, or one who has a common feeling and interest with him. It does not require a plain planter to tell an Assembly like this, more than half of whose members are gentlemen of the law, that no man may set his foot on your land without your permission but as a trespasser, and that he renders himself liable to an action for damages. This is of the very essence of property. But, he says, "thank you, for nothing, with all my heart, I don't mean to set my foot on your land, but, not owning one foot of land myself, I will stand here in the highway, which is as free to me as it is to you, and I will tax your land, not to your heart's content but to *mine*, and spend the proceeds as I please. I cannot enter upon it myself, but I will send the Sheriff of the county, and he shall enter upon it, and do what I cannot do in my own person."

Sir, is this to be endured? It is not to be endured. And unless I am ignorant of the character and feelings and— what is dearer to me than all—the prejudices of the people of the lower country, it will not be endured. You may as well adjourn *sine die*. We are too old birds to be taken with chaff, or else we are not old enough: I don't know which. We will not give up this question for the certainty, and far less for the hope, that the evil will be rectified in the other branch of the Legislature. We know, every body knows, that it is impossible. Why, Sir, the British House of Peers, which contains four hundred members, holding a vast property, much more now, it is true, than when

Chatham said they were but as a drop in the ocean compared with the wealth of the Commons: if they, holding their seats for life, and receiving and transmitting them by hereditary descent, have never been able to resist the House of Commons in any measure on which that House chose to insist, do you believe that twenty-four gentlemen upstairs can resist one hundred and twenty below? especially when the one hundred and twenty represent their own districts, and are to go home with them to their common constituents? Sir, the case has never yet happened, I believe, when a Senator has been able to resist the united delegation from his district in the lower House.

Mr. Chairman, I am a practical man. I go for solid security, and I never will, knowingly, take any other. But, if the security on which I have relied is insufficient, and my property is in danger, it is better that I should know it in time, and I may prepare to meet the consequences while it is yet called today, than to rest on a security that is fallacious and deceptive. Sir, I would not give you a button for your mixed basis in the Senate. Give up this question, and I have nothing more to lose. This is the entering wedge, and every thing else must follow. We are told, indeed, that we must rely on a restriction of the Right of Suffrage; but, gentlemen, know that after you shall have adopted the report of the Select Committee, you can place no restriction upon it. When this principle is in operation, the waters are out. It is as if you would ask an industrious and sagacious Hollander that you may cut his dykes, provided you make your cut only of a certain width. A rat hole will let in the ocean. Sir, there is an end to the security of all property in the Commonwealth, and he will be unwise who shall not abandon the ship to the underwriters. It is the first time in my life that I ever heard of a Government which was to divorce property from power. Yet this is seriously and soberly proposed to us. Sir, I know it is practicable, but it can be done only by a violent divulsion, as in France, but the moment you have separated the two, that very moment property will go in search of power, and power in search of property. "Male and female created He them"; and the two sexes do not more certainly, nor by a more unerring law, gravitate to each other, than power and property. You can only cause them to change hands. I could almost wish, indeed, for the accommodation of the gentleman from Augusta, that God had ordained it otherwise; but so it is, and so it is obliged to be. It is of the nature of man. Man always has been in society—we always find him in possession of property, and with a certain appetite for it which leads him to seek it, if not *per fas*, sometimes *per nefas*[5]; and hence the need of laws to protect it, and to punish its invaders.

But I am subjecting myself, I know, to a most serious reproach. It will be said that I am not a friend to the poor. Sir, the gentleman from Chesterfield and the gentleman from Spottsylvania have dealt with the "friends of the people" to my entire satisfaction. I wish to say a word now as to the "friends of the poor." Whenever I see a man, especially a rich man, endeavouring to rise and to acquire consequence in society by standing out as the especial champion of the poor, I am always reminded of an old acquaintance of mine, one Señor Manuel Ordonez, who made a comfortable living, and amassed an opulent fortune by administering the funds of the poor. Among the strange notions which have been broached since I have been on the political theatre, there is one which has lately seized the minds of men: that all things must be done for them by the Government, and that they are to do nothing for themselves. The Government is not only to attend to the great concerns which are its province, but it must step in and ease individuals of their natural and moral obligations. A more pernicious notion cannot prevail. Look at that ragged fellow staggering from the whiskey shop, and

---

5. *Per fas:* rightly, by fair means. *Per nefas:* wrongly, by foul means. [R.K.]

see that slattern who has gone there to reclaim him; where are their children? Running about, ragged, idle, ignorant, fit candidates for the penitentiary. Why is all this so? Ask the man and he will tell you, "Oh, the Government has undertaken to educate our children for us. It has given us a premium for idleness, and I now spend in liquor what I should otherwise be obliged to save to pay for their schooling. My neighbor there, that is so hard at work in his field yonder with his son, can't spare that boy to attend, except in the winter months, the school which he is taxed to support for mine. He has to scuffle hard to make both ends meet at the end of the year, and keep the wolf from the door. His children can't go to this school, yet he has to pay a part of the tax to maintain it." Sir, is it like friends of the poor to absolve them from what Nature, what God himself has made their first and most sacred duty? For the education of their children is the first and most obvious duty of every parent, and one which the worthless alone are ever known wholly to neglect.

Mr. Chairman, these will be deemed, I fear, unconnected thoughts; but they have been the aliment of my mind for years. Rumination and digestion can do no more; they are thoroughly concocted.

In the course of not a short or uneventful life, I have had correspondence with various persons in all parts of the Union, and I have seen gentlemen on their return from the North and East, as well as from the new States of the West; and I have never heard from any of them but one expression of opinion as it related to us in Virginia. It was in the sentiment, if not in the language of Virgil: Oh, fortunate, if we knew our own blessedness. They advise us with one voice, "Stick to what you have got; stick to your Constitution; stick to your Right of Suffrage. Don't give up your freehold representation. We have seen enough of the opposite system, and too much." I have received and seen letters breathing this spirit from men who dare not promulgate such a sentiment at home because it would only destroy their hopes of usefulness—from North Carolina, from South Carolina, from Georgia, from Alabama, from Pennsylvania, and from New York.

Sir, the day, come when it may, which sees this old and venerable fabric of ours scattered in ruins, and the mattock and the spade digging the foundation for a new political edifice, will be a day of jubilee to all those who have been, and who must be, in conflict with those principles which have given to Virginia her weight and consequence, both at home and abroad. If I understand aright the plans which are in agitation, I had sooner the day should arrive that must close my eyes forever, than witness their accomplishment. Yes, Sir, to this Constitution we owe all that we have preserved—(much I know is lost, and of great value)—but all that we have preserved from the wreck of our political fortunes. This is the mother which has reared all our great men. Well may she be called *magna mater virum.*[6] She has, indeed, produced men, and mighty men.

But, I am told, that so far is this from being true, we have been living for fifty-four years under a Government which has no manner of authority, and is a mere usurpation at best. Yet, Sir, during that time, we have changed our Government; and I call the attention of this body to the manner in which that change was made. The Constitution of '88 was submitted to the people, and a Convention was called to ratify it, and what was that Convention? It was the old House of Burgesses with a nickname—the old House of Delegates, Sir, with a nickname—in which the same municipal divisions of the State were regarded—the same qualifications required—the same qualified freeholders were returned from the same districts and by the same sheriffs—and yet, by waving of a magic wand, they were converted into a Convention in which Warwick was made equal with Culpeper, then by far the

---

6. The Great Mother of men. [R.K.]

largest county in the state. Do not gentlemen see where the point of their own argument leads to? If it is a *sine qua non* of a legitimate Government that it must have the assent of a majority of the people told by the head, then is the Federal Government an usurpation to which the people *per capita*—King Numbers—has never given his assent.

It is now thought necessary to have another Convention, and what is it? It is nothing but the Senate of Virginia, elected from the same districts, by the same voters, and returned by the same sheriffs—many of them the self-same men; yet when multiplied by four, by talismanic touch they become a Convention. Yes, Sir. You can't trust the House of Delegates and Senate with your affairs, but you can trust a smaller body. You can't trust the whole, but you can trust a part. You can't trust the Senate, but you can trust the same men from the same districts if multiplied by four. Sir, are we men? Or are we children?

For my share, this is the first Convention in which I ever had a seat; and I trust in God it will be the last. I never had any taste for Conventions; or for new Constitutions made per order, or kept ready made to suit casual customers. I need not tell *you*, Sir, that I was not a member of the Staunton Convention. No Sir, nor was I a member of the Harrisburg Convention—nor the Charlottesville Convention. No, Sir, nor the anti-Jackson Convention—though I had the honour (in very good company) of being put to the ban and anathema of that august Assembly—and when, to their very great surprise and alarm, we returned their fire, they scattered like a flock of wild geese.

Mr. Chairman, the wisest thing this body could do, would be to return to the people from whom they came, *re infecta.*[7] I am willing to lend my aid to any very small and moderate reforms which I can be made to believe that

---

7. Without accomplishing the matter. [R.K.]

this our ancient Government requires. But, far better would it be that they were never made, and that our Constitution remained unchangeable like that of Lycurgus, than that we should break in upon the main pillars of the edifice.

Sir, I have exhausted myself, and tried you. I am physically unable to recall or to express the few thoughts I brought with me to this Assembly. Sir, that great master of the human heart, who seemed to know it as well as if he had made it, I mean Shakespeare—when he brings before our eyes an old and feeble monarch, not only deserted, but oppressed by his own pampered and ungrateful offspring, describes him as finding solace and succour, only in his discarded and disinherited child. If this, our venerable parent, must perish, deal the blow who will, it shall never be given by my hand. I will avert it if I can, and if I cannot, in the sincerity of my heart I declare, I am ready to perish with it. Yet, as the gentleman from Spottsylvania says, I am no candidate for martyrdom. I am too old a man to remove; my associations, my habits, and my property, nail me to the Commonwealth. But, were I a young man, I would, in case this monstrous tyranny shall be imposed upon us, do what a few years ago I should have thought parricidal. I would withdraw from your jurisdiction. I would not live under King Numbers. I would not be his steward, nor make him my taskmaster. I would obey the principle of self-preservation, a principle we find even in the brute creation, in flying from this mischief.

ON THE VETO POWER
John C. Calhoun

On the floor of the United States Senate, in Febru-
ary, 1842, John C. Calhoun spoke against Henry
Clay's proposed constitutional amendment to limit
the presidential veto power. Calhoun's arguments in
this speech concerning checks upon the will of a majority later were expanded in his *Disquisition on
Government.* His doctrine of "concurrent majorities" is an important element in this address, which is
reprinted in John M. Anderson (ed.) *Calhoun: Basic
Documents* (State College, Pennsylvania, 1952),
pp. 229–51.

The Senator from Kentucky, in support of his amendment, maintained that the people of these States constitute
a nation; that the nation has a will of its own; that the numerical majority of the whole was the appropriate organ
of its voice; and that whatever derogated from it, to that
extent departed from the genius of the Government, and
set up the will of the minority against the majority. We
have thus presented at the very threshold of the discussion, a question of the deepest import, not only as it regards the subject under consideration, but the nature and
character of our Government; and that question is, are
these propositions of the Senator true? If they be, then he
admitted the argument against the veto would be conclusive; not, however, for the reason assigned by him, that it
would make the voice of a single functionary of the Government, (the President,) equivalent to that of some six
Senators and forty members of the other House; but, for
the far more decisive reason, according to his theory, that

the President is not chosen by the voice of the numerical majority, and does not, therefore, according to his principle, represent truly the will of the nation.

It is a great mistake to suppose that he is elected simply on the principle of numbers. They constitute, it is true, the principal element in his election; but not the exclusive. Each State is, indeed, entitled to as many votes in his election, as it is to representatives in the other House; that is, to its Federal population; but to these, two others are added, having no regard to numbers for their representation in the Senate, which greatly increases the relative influence of the small States, compared to the large, in the Presidential election. What effect this latter element may have on the numbers necessary to elect a President, may be made apparent by a very short and simple calculation.

The population of the United States, in Federal numbers, by the late census, is 15,908,376. Assuming that sixty-eight thousand, the number reported by the committee of the other House, will be fixed on for the ratio of representation there, it will give, according to the calculation of the committee, two hundred and twenty-four members to the other House. Add fifty-two, the number of the Senators, and the electoral college will be found to consist of two hundred and seventy-six, of which one hundred and thirty-nine is a majority. If nineteen of the smaller States, excluding Maryland, be taken, beginning with Delaware and ending with Kentucky inclusive, they will be found to be entitled to one-hundred and forty votes, one more than a majority, with a federal population of only 7,227,869; while the seven other States, with a population of 8,680,507, would be entitled to but one hundred and thirty-six votes, three less than a majority, with a population of almost a million and a half greater than the others. Of the one hundred and forty electoral votes of the smaller States, thirty-eight would be on account of the addition of two to each State for their representation in this body, while of the larger there would be but fourteen on that account; making a difference of twenty-four votes on that account, being two more than the entire electoral votes of Ohio, the third State in point of numbers in the Union.

The Senator from Kentucky, with these facts, but acts in strict conformity to his theory of the Government, in proposing the limitation he has on the veto power; but as much cannot be said in favor of the substitute he has offered. The argument is as conclusive against the one, as the other, or any other modification of the veto that could possibly be devised. It goes farther, and is conclusive against the Executive department itself, as elected; for there can be no good reason offered why the will of the nation, if there be one, should not be as fully and perfectly represented in that department as in the Legislative.

But it does not stop there. It would be still more conclusive, if possible, against this branch of the Government. In constituting the Senate, numbers are totally disregarded. The smallest State stands on a perfect equality with the largest; Delaware, with her seventy-seven thousand, with New York with her two million and a half. Here a majority of States control, without regard to population; and fourteen of the smallest States, with a federal population of but 4,064,457, little less than a fourth of the whole, can, if they unite, overrule the twelve others, with a population of 11,844,919. Nay, more; they could virtually destroy the Government, and put a veto on the whole system, by refusing to elect Senators; and yet this equality among States, without regard to numbers, including the branch where it prevails, would seem to be the favorite with the Constitution. It cannot be altered without the consent of every State, and this branch of the Government where it prevails, is the only one that participates in the powers of all the others. As a part of the Legislative Department, it has full participation with the other, in all matters of legislation, except originating money bills, while it participates with the Executive in two of its highest functions, that of appointing to office and making treaties, and in that of the Judiciary, in being the high court before which all impeachments are tried.

But we have not yet got to the end of the consequences. The argument would be as conclusive against the Judiciary as against the Senate, or the Executive and his veto. The judges receive their appointments from the Executive and the Senate; the one nominating, and the other consenting to and advising the appointment; neither of which departments, as has been shown, is chosen by the numerical majority. In addition, they hold their office during good behavior, and can only be turned out by impeachment, and yet they have the power, in all cases in law and equity brought before them, in which an act of Congress is involved, to decide on its constitutionality—that is, in effect, to pronounce an absolute veto.

If, then, the Senator's theory be correct, its clear and certain result, if carried out in practice, would be to sweep away, not only the veto, but the Executive, the Senate, and the Judiciary, as now constituted, and to leave nothing standing in the midst of the ruins but the House of Representatives where only, in the whole range of the Government, numbers exclusively prevail. But as desolating as would be its sweep, in passing over the Government, it would be far more destructive in its whirl over the Constitution. There it would not leave a fragment standing amidst the ruin in its rear.

In approaching this topic, let me premise, what all will readily admit, that if the voice of the people may be sought for any where with confidence it may be in the Constitution, which is conceded by all to be the fundamental and paramount law of the land. If, then, the people of these States do really constitute a nation, as the Senator supposes; if the nation has a will of its own, and if the numerical majority of the whole is the only appropriate and true organ of that will, we may fairly expect to find that will, pronounced through the absolute majority, pervading every part of that instrument, and stamping its authority on the whole. Is such the fact? The very reverse. Throughout the whole—from first to last—from beginning to the end—in its formation, adoption, and amendment, there is not the slightest evidence, trace, or vestige of the existence of the facts on which the Senator's theory rests; neither of the nation, nor its will, nor of the numerical majority of the whole, as its organ, as I shall next proceed to show.

The convention which formed it was called by a portion of the States; its members were all appointed by the States; received their authority from their separate States; voted by States in forming the Constitution; agreed to it, when formed, by States; transmitted it to Congress to be submitted to the States for their ratification; it was ratified by the people of each State in convention, each ratifying by itself, for itself, and bound exclusively by its own ratification, and by express provision it was not to go into operation, unless nine out of twelve States should ratify, and then to be binding only between the States ratifying. It was thus put in the power of any four States, large or small, without regard to numbers, to defeat its adoption, which might have been done by a very small proportion of the whole, as will appear by reference to the first census. That census was taken very shortly after the adoption of the Constitution at which time the Federal population of the then twelve States was 3,462,279, of which the four smallest, Delaware, Rhode Island, Georgia, and New Hampshire, with a population of only 241,490, something more than the fourteenth part of the whole, could have defeated the ratification. Such was the total disregard of population in the adoption and formation of the Constitution.

It may, however, be said, it is true that the Constitution is the work of the States, and that there was no nation prior to its adoption; but that its adoption fused the people of the States into one so as to make a nation of what before

constituted separate and independent sovereignties. Such
an assertion would be directly in the teeth of the Constitution, which says that, when ratified, "it should be binding" (not over the States ratifying, for that would imply
that it was imposed by some higher authority, nor between the individuals composing the States, for that
would imply that they were all merged in one, but), "between the States ratifying the same"; and thus by the
strongest implication, recognising them as the parties to
the instrument, and as maintaining their separate and independent existence as States, after its adoption. But let
that pass. I need it not to rebut the Senator's theory—to
test the truth of the assertion, that the Constitution has
formed a nation of the people of these States. I go back to
the grounds already taken, that if such be the fact—if they
really form a nation, since the adoption of the Constitution, and the nation has a will, and the numerical majority
is its only proper organ, in that case, the mode prescribed
for the amendment of the Constitution would furnish
abundance and conclusive evidence of the fact. But here
again, as in its formation and adoption, there is not the
slightest trace or evidence, that such is the fact; on the
contrary, most conclusive to sustain the very opposite
opinion.

There are two modes in which amendments to the
Constitution may be proposed. The one, such as that now
proposed, by a resolution to be passed by two-thirds of
both Houses; and the other by a call of a convention, by
Congress, to propose amendments, on the application of
two-thirds of the States; neither of which give the least
countenance to the theory of the Senator. In both cases
the mode of ratification, which is in the material point, is
the same, and requires the concurring assent of three-
fourths of the States, regardless of population, to ratify an
amendment. Let us now pause for a moment to trace the
effects of this provision.

There are now twenty-six States, and the concurring

assent, of course, of twenty States, is sufficient to ratify an amendment. It then results that twenty of the smaller States, of which Kentucky would be the largest, are sufficient for that purpose, with a population in federal numbers of only 7,652,097, less by several hundred thousand than the numerical majority of the whole, against the united voice of the other six, with a population of 8,216,-279, exceeding the former by more than half a million. And yet this minority, under the amending power, may change, alter, modify or destroy every part of the Constitution, except that which provides for an equality of representation of the States in the Senate, while as if in mockery and derision of the Senator's theory, nineteen of the larger States, with a population, in federal numbers, of 14,526,073, cannot, even if united to a man, alter a letter in the Constitution, against the seven others, with a population of only 1,382,303; and this, too, under the existing Constitution, which is supposed to form the people of these States into a nation. Finally, Delaware, with a population of little more than 77,000, can put her veto on all the other States, on a proposition to destroy the equality of the States in the Senate. Can facts more clearly illustrate the total disregard of the numerical majority, as well in the process of amending, as in that of forming and adopting the Constitution?

All this must appear anomalous, strange and unaccountable, on the theory of the Senator, but harmonious and easily explained on the opposite; that ours is an union, not of individuals, united by what is called a social compact, for that would make it a nation; nor of Governments, for that would have formed a mere Confederacy, like the one superceded by the present Constitution; but an union of States, founded on a written, positive compact, forming a Federal Republic, with the same equality of rights among the States composing the Union, as among the citizens composing the States themselves. Instead of a nation, we are in reality an assemblage of nations, or peoples (if the plural noun may be used where the language affords none), united in their sovereign character immediately and directly by their own act, but without losing their separate and independent existence.

It results from all that has been stated, that either the theory of the Senator is wrong, or that our political system is throughout a profound and radical error. If the latter be the case, then that complex system of ours, consisting of so many parts, but blended, as was supposed, into one harmonious and sublime whole, raising its front on high and challenging the admiration of the world, is but a misshapen and disproportionate structure that ought to be demolished to the ground, with the single exception of the apartment allotted to the House of Representatives. Is the Senator prepared to commence the work of demolition? Does he believe that all other parts of this complex structure are irregular and deformed appendages; and that if they were taken down, and the Government erected exclusively on the will of the numerical majority, would effect as well, or better, the great objects for which it was instituted: "to establish justice; ensure domestic tranquillity; provide for the common defence; promote the general welfare; and secure the blessings of liberty to ourselves and our posterity."? Will the Senator—will any one—can any one—venture to assert that? And if not, why not? There is the question, on the proper solution of which hangs not only the explanation of the veto, but that of the real nature and character of our complex, but beautiful and harmonious system of Government. To give a full and systematic solution, it would be necessary to descend to the elements of political science, and discuss principles little suited to a discussion in a deliberate assembly. I waive the attempt, and shall content myself with giving a much more matter of fact solution.

It is sufficient, for that purpose, to point to the actual operation of the Government, through all the stages of its existence, and the many and important measures which have agitated it from the beginning; the success of which one portion of the people regarded as essential to their prosperity and happiness, while other portions have viewed them as destructive of both. What does this imply, but a deep conflict of interests, real or supposed, between the different portions of the community, on subjects of the first magnitude—the currency, the finances, including taxation and disbursements; the Bank, the protective tariff, distribution, and many others; on all of which the most opposite and conflicting views have prevailed? And what would be the effect of placing the powers of the Government under the exclusive control of the numerical majority—of 8,000,000 over 7,900,000, of six States over all the rest—but to give the dominant interest, or combination of interests, an unlimited and despotic control over all others? What, but to vest it with the power to administer the Government for its exclusive benefit, regardless of all others, and indifferent to their oppression and wretchedness? And what, in a country of such vast extent and diversity of condition, institutions, industry, and productions, would that be, but to subject the rest to the most grinding despotism and oppression? But what is the remedy? It would be but to increase the evil, to transfer the power to a minority, to abolish the House of Representatives, and place the control exclusively in the hands of the Senate—in that of the four millions, instead of the eight. If one must be sacrificed to the other, it is better that the few should be to the many, than the many to the few.

What then is to be done, if neither the majority nor the minority, the greater nor the less part, can be safely trusted with the exclusive control? What but to vest the powers of the Government in the whole—the entire people—to make it in truth and reality the Government of the people, instead of the Government of a dominant over a subject part, be it the greater or less—of the whole people—self-government; and if this should prove impossible in practice, then to make the nearest approach to it, by requiring the concurrence in the action of the government, of the greatest possible number consistent with the great ends for which Government was instituted—justice and security, within and without. But how is that to be effected? Not certainly by considering the whole community as one, and taking its sense as a whole by a single process, which, instead of giving the voice of all, can but give that of a part. There is but one way by which it can possibly be accomplished; and that is by a judicious and wise division and organization of the Government and community, with reference to its different and conflicting interests, and by taking the sense of each part separately, and the concurrence of all as the voice of the whole. Each may be imperfect of itself, but if the construction be good and all the keys skilfully touched, there will be given out in one blended and harmonious whole, the true and perfect voice of the people.

But on what principle is such a division and organization to be made to effect this great object, without which it is impossible to preserve free and popular institutions? To this no general answer can be given. It is the work of the wise and experienced, having full and perfect knowledge of the country and the people in every particular for whom the Government is intended. It must be made to fit, and when it does, it will fit no other, and will be incapable of being imitated or borrowed. Without, then, attempting to do what cannot be done, I propose to point out, how that which I have stated has been accomplished in our system of Government, and the agency the veto is intended to have in effecting it.

I begin with the House of Representatives. There each State has a representation according to its federal numbers, and when met, a majority of the whole number of members controls its proceedings; thus giving to the numerical majority the exclusive control throughout. The effect is to place its proceedings in the power of eight millions of people over all the rest, and six of the largest States, if united, over the other twenty; and the consequence, if the House was the exclusive organ of the voice of the people, would be the domination of the stronger over the weaker interests of the community, and the establishment of an intolerable and oppressive despotism. To find the remedy against what would be so great an evil, we must turn to this body. Here an entirely different process is adopted to take the sense of the community. Population is entirely disregarded, and States, without reference to the number of people, are made the basis of representation; the effect of which is to place the control here in a majority of the States, which, had they the exclusive power, would exercise it as despotically and oppressively as would the House of Representatives.

Regarded, then, separately, neither truly represents the sense of the community, and each is imperfect of itself; but when united, and the concurring voice of each is made necessary to enact laws, the one corrects the defects of the other; and, instead of the less popular derogating from the more popular, as is supposed by the Senator, the two together give a more full and perfect utterance to the voice of the people than either would separately. Taken separately, six States might control the House, and a little upwards of four millions might control the Senate, by a combination of the fourteen smaller States; but by requiring the concurrent votes of the two, the six largest States must add eight others to have the control in both bodies. Suppose, for illustration, they should unite with the eight smallest, which would give the least number by which an act could pass both Houses, it will be found, by adding the population in federal numbers of the six largest to the eight smallest States, that the least number by which an act can pass both Houses, if the members should be true to those they represent, would be 9,788,570 against a minority of 6,119,797, instead of 8,000,000, against 7,900,000, if the assent of the most popular branch alone was required.

This more full and perfect expression of the voice of the people by the concurrence of the two, compared to either separately, is a great advance towards a full and perfect expression of their voice; but great as it is, it falls far short, and the framers of the Constitution were accordingly not satisfied with it. To render it still more perfect, their next step was to require the assent of the President, before an act of Congress could become a law, and, if he disapproved, to require two-thirds of both Houses to overrule his veto. We are thus brought to the point immediately under discussion, and which, on that account, claims a full and careful examination.

One of the leading motives for vesting the President with this high power, was, undoubtedly, to give him the means of protecting the portion of the powers allotted to him by the Constitution, against the encroachment of Congress. To make a division of power effectual, a veto in one form or another is indispensable. The right of each to judge for itself of the extent of the power alloted to its share, and to protect itself in its exercise, is what in reality is meant by a division of power. Without it, the allotment to each department would be a mere partition, and no division at all. Acting under this impression, the framers of the Constitution have carefully provided that his approval should be necessary, not only to the acts of Congress, but to every resolution, vote or order, requiring the consent of the two Houses, so as to render it impossible to elude it by any conceivable device. This of itself was an adequate motive for the provision, and were there no other, ought to be a sufficient reason for the rejection of this resolution. Without it, the division of power between the legislative and Executive departments, would have been merely nominal.

But it is not the only motive. There is another and deeper, to which the division itself of the Government into departments is subordinate; to enlarge the popular basis, by increasing the number of voices necessary to its action.

As numerous as are the voices required to obtain the assent of the people through the Senate and the House to an act, it was not thought by the framers of the Constitution sufficient for the action of the Government in all cases. Nine thousand eight hundred, as large as is the number, were regarded as still too few, and six thousand one hundred too many to remove all motives for oppression; the latter being not too few to be plundered, and the former not too large to divide the spoils of plunder among. Till the increase of numbers on one side, and the decrease on the other reaches that point, there is no security for the weaker against the stronger, especially in so extensive a country as ours. Acting in the spirit of these remarks, the authors of the Constitution, although they deemed the concurrence of the Senate and the House as sufficient, with the approval of the President, to the enactment of laws in ordinary cases, yet, when he dissented, they deem it a sufficient presumption against the measure to require a still greater enlargement of the popular basis for its enactment. With this view, the assent of two-thirds of both Houses were required to overrule his veto, that is eighteen States in the Senate, and a constituency of ten millions six hundred thousand in the other House.

But it may be said that nothing is gained towards enlarging the popular basis of the Government by the veto powers; because the number necessary to elect a majority to the two Houses, without which the act could not pass, would be sufficient to elect him. That is true. But he may have been elected by a different portion of the people, or if not, great changes may take place during his four years, both in the Senate and the House, which may change the majority that brought him into power, and with it the measures and policy to be pursued. In either case he might find it necessary to interpose his veto to maintain his views of the Constitution, or the policy of the party of which he is the head, and which elevated him to power.

But a still stronger consideration for vesting him with

the power may be found in the difference of the manner of his election, compared with that of the members of either House. The Senators are elected by the vote of the Legislatures of the respective States, and the members of the House by the people, who, in almost all the States, elect by districts. In neither is there the least responsibility of the members of any one State, to the Legislature or people of any other State. They are, as far as their responsibility may be concerned, solely and exclusively under the influence of the States and people, who respectively elect them. Not so the President. The votes of the whole are counted in his election, which makes him more or less responsible to every part—to those who voted against him, as well as those to whom he owes his election, which he must feel sensibly. If he should be an aspirant for re-election, he will desire to gain the favorable opinion of States that opposed him, as well as to retain that of those which voted for him. Even if he should not be a candidate for re-election, the desire of having a favorite elected, or maintaining the ascendency of his party, may have, to a considerable extent, the same influence over him. The effect, in either case, would be to make him look more to *the interest of the whole*—to soften sectional feelings and asperity—to be more of a patriot, than the partisan of any particular interest; and through the influence of these causes to give a more general character to the politics of the country, and thereby render the collision between sectional interests less fierce than it would be if legislation depended solely on the members of the two Houses, who owe no responsibility but to those who elected them. The same influence acts even on the aspirants for the Presidency, and is followed to a very considerable extent by the same softening and generalizing effects. In the case of the President, it may lead to the interposing of his veto against oppressive and dangerous sectional measures, even when supported by those to whom he owes his election. But, be the cause of interposing his veto what it may, its effect in all cases is to require a greater body of constituency, through the legislative organs, to put the Government in action against it—to require another key to be struck, and to bring out a more full and perfect response from the voice of the people.

There is still another impediment, if not to the enactment of laws, to their execution, to be found in the Judiciary Department. I refer to the right of the courts, in all cases coming before them in law or equity, where an act of Congress comes in question, to decide on its unconstitutionality, which, if decided against the law in the Supreme Court, is in effect a permanent veto. But here a difference must be made between a decision against the constitutionality of a law of Congress and that of States. The former acts as a restriction on the powers of this Government, but the latter as an enlargement.

Such are the various processes of taking the sense of the people through the divisions and organization of the different departments of the Government, all of which, acting through their appropriate organs, are intended to widen its basis and render it more popular, instead of less, by increasing the number necessary to put it in action, and having for their object to prevent one portion of the community from aggrandizing or enriching itself at the expense of the other, and to restrict the whole to the sphere intended by the framers of the Constitution. Has it effected these objects? Has it prevented oppression and usurpation on the part of the Government? Has it accomplished the objects for which the Government was ordained, as enumerated in the preamble of the Constitution? Much, very much, certainly has been done, but not all. Many instances might be enumerated, in the history of the Government, of the violation of the Constitution—of the assumption of powers not delegated to it—of the perversion of those delegated to uses never intended—and of their being wielded by the dominant interest, for the time, for its aggrandizement, at the expense of the rest of the community—instances that may be found in every period of its existence, from the earliest to the latest, beginning with the Bank and bank connection at its outset, and ending with the Distribution act, at its late extraordinary session. How is this to be accounted for? What is the cause?

The explanation and cause will be found in the fact, that, as fully as the sense of the people is taken in the action of the Government, it is not taken fully enough. For, after all that has been accomplished in that respect, there are but two organs through which the voice of the community acts directly on the Government, and which, taken separately, or in combination, constitute the elements of which it is composed; the one is the majority of the States regarded in their corporate character as bodies politic, which in its simple form constitutes the Senate; and the other is the majority of the people of the States, of which, in its simple form, the House of Representatives is composed. These combined, in the proportions already stated, constitute the Executive Department, and that department and the Senate appoint the judges, who constitute the Judiciary. But it is only in their simple form in the Senate and the other House, that they have a steady and habitual control over the legislative acts of the Government. The veto of the Executive is rarely interposed; not more than about twenty times during the period of more than fifty years that the Government has existed. Their effects have been beneficially felt, but only casually, at long intervals, and without steady and habitual influence over the action of the Government. The same remarks are substantially applicable to what, for the sake of brevity, may be called the veto of the Judiciary; the right of negativing a law for the want of constitutionality, when it comes in question, in a case before the courts.

The Government, then, of the Union, being under no other habitual and steady control but these two majorities, acting through this and the other House, is, in fact, placed substantially under the control of the portion of the community, which the united majorities of the two Houses represent for the time, and which may consist of but fourteen States with a federal population of less than ten millions, against a little more than six, as has been already explained. But as large as is the former, and as small as is the latter, the one is not large enough, in proportion, to prevent it from plundering, under the forms of law, and the other small enough from being plundered; and hence the many instances of violation of the Constitution, of usurpation, of powers perverted, and wielded for selfish purposes, which the history of the Government affords. They furnish proof conclusive that the principle of plunder, so deeply implanted in all Governments, has not been eradicated in ours by all the precaution taken by its framers against it.

But in estimating the number of the constituency necessary to control the majority in the two Houses of Congress at something less than ten millions, I have estimated it altogether too high, regarding the practical operation of the Government. To form a correct conception of its practical operation in this respect, another element, which has in practice an important influence, must be taken into the estimate, and which I shall next proceed to explain.

Of the two majorities, which, acting either separately or in combination, control the Government, the numerical majority is by far the most influential. It has the exclusive control in the House of Representatives, and preponderates more than five to one in the choice of the President, assuming that the ratio of representation will be fixed at sixty-eight thousand, under the late census. It also greatly preponderates in appointment of the judges the right of nominating having much greater influence in making appointments than that of advising and consenting. From these facts, it must be apparent that the leaning of the President will be to that element of power to which he mainly owes his elevation, and on which he must principally rely, to secure his re-election, or maintain the ascendancy of the party and its policy, the head of which he usually is. This leaning of his must have a powerful effect on the inclination and tendency of the whole Government. In his hands are placed, substantially, all the honors and emoluments of the Government, and these, when greatly increased, as they are and ever must be when the powers of the Government are greatly stretched and increased, must give the President a corresponding influence over, not only the members of both Houses, but also public opinion, and through that, a still more powerful indirect influence over them; and thus they may be brought to sustain or oppose, through his influence measures which otherwise they would have opposed or sustained, and the whole Government be made to lean in the same direction with the Executive.

From these causes the Government, in all of its departments, gravitates steadily towards the numerical majority, and has been moving slowly towards it from the beginning; sometimes, indeed, retarded, or even stopped or thrown back, but, taking any considerable period of time, always advancing towards it. That it begins to make near approach to that fatal point, ample proof may be found in the oft-repeated declaration of the mover of this resolution and of many of his supporters at the extraordinary session, that the late Presidential election decided all the great measures which he so ardently pressed through the Senate. Yes, even here, in this chamber, in the Senate, which is composed of the opposing element, and on which the only effectual resistance to this fatal tendency exists that is to be found in the Government, we are told that the popular will as expressed in the presidential election is to decide not only the election, but every measure which may be agitated in the canvass in order to influence the result. When what was thus boldly insisted on comes to be an established principle of action, the end will be near.

As the Government approaches nearer and nearer to the one absolute and single power, the will of the greater number, its action will become more and more disturbed and irregular; faction, corruption, and anarchy, will more and more abound; patriotism will daily decay, and affection and reverence for the Government grow weaker and weaker, until the final shock occurs, when the system will rush to ruin; and the sword take the place of law and Constitution.

Let me not be misunderstood. I object not to that structure of the Government which makes the numerical majority the predominant element: it is, perhaps, necessary it should be so in all popular constitutional Governments like ours, which excludes classes. It is necessarily the exponent of the strongest interest, or combination of interests, in the community; and it would seem to be necessary to give it the preponderance, in order to infuse into the Government the necessary energy to accomplish the ends for which it was instituted. The great question is, How is due preponderance to be given to it, without subjecting the whole, in time, to its unlimited sway? which brings up the question, Is there anywhere, in our complex system of Government, a guard, check, or contrivance, sufficiently strong to arrest so fearful a tendency of the Government? Or, to express it in more direct and intelligible language, Is there anywhere in the system a more full and perfect expression of the voice of the people of the States calculated to counteract this tendency to the concentration of all the powers of the Government in the will of the numerical majority, resulting from the partial and imperfect expression of their voice through its organs?

Yes, fortunately, doubly fortunately, there is; not only a more full and perfect, but a full and perfect expression to be found in the Constitution, acknowledged by all to be the fundamental and supreme law of the land. It is full and perfect, because it is the expression of the voice of each State, adopted by the separate assent of each, by itself, and for itself, and is the voice of all by being that of each component part, united and blended into one harmonious whole. But it is not only full and perfect, but as just as it is full and perfect; for combining the sense of each, and therefore all, there is nothing left on which injustice, or oppression, or usurpation can operate. And, finally, it is as supreme as it is just, because, comprehending the will of all, by uniting that of each of the parts, there is nothing within or above to control it. It is indeed, the *vox populi vox Dei;* the creating voice that called the system into existence, and of which the Government itself is but a creature, clothed with delegated powers to execute its high behests.

We are thus brought to a question of the deepest import, and on which the fate of the system depends: How can this full, perfect, just, and supreme voice of the people, embodied in the Constitution, be brought to bear habitually and steadily in counteracting the fatal tendency of Government to the absolute and despotic control of the numerical majority? Or, if I may be permitted to use so bold an expression, how is this, the Deity of our political system, to be successfully invoked, to interpose its all powerful creating voice to save from perdition the creature of its will and the work of its hand? If it cannot be done, ours, like all free Governments preceding it, must go the way of all flesh; but if it can be, its duration may be from generation to generation, to the latest posterity. To this all-important question, I will not attempt a reply at this time. It would lead me far beyond the limits properly belonging to this discussion. I descend from the digression nearer to the subject immediately at issue, in order to reply to an objection to the veto power, taken by the Senator from Virginia, on this side the chamber [Mr. Archer.] He rests his support of this resolution on the ground that the object intended to be effected by the veto has failed; that the framers of the Constitution regard the legislative department of the Government, as the one most to be dreaded, and that their motive for vesting the Executive with the veto, was to check its encroachments on the other departments; but that the Executive, and not the Legislature, had proved to be the most dangerous, and that the veto had become either useless or mischievous by being converted into a sword to attack, instead of a shield to defend as was originally intended.

I make no issue with the Senator, as to the correctness of his statement. I assume the facts to be as he supposes; not because I agree with him, but simply with the view of making my reply more brief.

Assuming, then, that the Executive Department has proved to be the more formidable, and that it requires to be checked, rather than to have the power of checking others, the first inquiry on that assumption, should be into the cause of its increase of power, in order to ascertain the seat and the nature of the danger; and the next, whether the measure proposed—that of divesting it of the veto, or modifying it as proposed—would guard against the danger apprehended.

I began with the first, and in entering on it, assert with confidence, that if the Executive has become formidable to the liberty or safety of the country or other departments of the Government, the cause is not in the Constitution, but in the acts and omissions of Congress itself.

According to my conception, the powers vested in the President by the Constitution, are few and effectually guarded, and are not of themselves at all formidable. In order to have a just conception of the extent of his powers, it must be borne in mind that there are but two classes of power known to the Constitution; and they are powers that are expressly granted, and those that are necessary to carry the granted powers into execution. Now, by a positive provision of the Constitution, all powers necessary to the execution of the granted powers, are expressly delegated to Congress, be they powers granted to the Legislative, Executive or Judicial department, and can only be exercised by the authority of Congress, and in the manner prescribed by law. This provision wil be found in what is called the residuary clause, which declares that Congress shall have power "to make all laws which shall be necessary and proper to carry into execution the foregoing powers," (those granted to Congress,) "and all other powers vested by this Constitution in the Government of the United States, or in any department or officer thereof." A more comprehensive provision cannot be imagined. It carries with it all powers necessary and proper to the execution of the granted powers, be they lodged where they may, and vests the whole, in terms not less explicit, in Congress; and here let me add, in passing, that the provision is as wise as it is comprehensive. It deposits the right of deciding what powers are necessary for the execution of the granted powers, where, and where only it can be lodged with safety, in the hands of the law-making power, and forbids any department or officer of the Government from exercising any power not expressly authorized by the Constitution or the laws, thus making ours emphatically a Government of *law and Constitution.*

Having now shown that the President is restricted by the Constitution to powers expressly granted to him, and that if any of his granted powers be such that they require other powers to execute them, he cannot exercise them without the authority of Congress, I shall now show that there is not one power vested in him that is any way dangerous, unless made so by the acts or permission of Congress. I shall take them in the order they stand in the Constitution.

He is, in the first place, made Commander-in-chief of the army and navy of the United States, and the militia, when called into actual service. Large and expensive military and naval establishments and numerous corps of militia, called into service, would no doubt increase very dangerously the power and patronage of the President; but neither can take place but by the action of Congress. Not a soldier can be enlisted, a ship of war built, nor a militiaman called into service, without its authority; and very fortunately our situation is such, that there is no necessity, and, probably, will be none, why his power and patronage should be dangerously increased by either of those means.

He is next vested with the power to make treaties and to appoint officers, with the advice and consent of the Senate; and here again his power can only be made dangerous by the action of one or both Houses of Congress. In the formation of treaties two-thirds of the Senate must concur; and it is difficult to conceive of a treaty that could materially enlarge his powers, that would not require an act of Congress to carry into effect. The appointing power may, indeed, dangerously increase this patronage, if officers be uselessly multiplied and too highly paid; but if such should be the case, the fault would be in Congress, by whose authority exclusively they can be created or their compensation regulated.

But much is said in this connection, of the power of removal, justly accompanied by severe condemnation of the many and abusive instances of the use of the power, and the dangerous influence it gives the President, in all of which I fully concur. It is, indeed, a corrupting and dangerous power, when officers are greatly multiplied, and highly paid, and when it is perverted from its legitimate object, to the advancement of personal or party purposes. But I find no such power in the list of powers granted to the Executive, which is proof conclusive that it belongs to the class necessary and proper to execute some other power, if it exists at all, which none can doubt; and, for reasons already assigned, cannot be exercised without authority of law. If then, it has been abused, it must be because Congress has not done its duty in permitting it to be exercised by the President without the sanction of law authorizing its exercise, and guarding against the abuses to which it is so liable.

The residue of the list are rather duties than rights; that of recommending to Congress such measures as he may deem expedient; of convening both Houses on extraordinary occasions; of adjourning them when they cannot agree on the time; of receiving ambassadors and other ministers; of taking care that the laws be faithfully executed, and commissioning the officers of the United States. Of all these, there is but one which claims particular notice, in connection with the point immediately under consideration; and that is his power as the administrator of the laws. But whatever power he may have in that capacity depends on the action of Congress. If Congress should limit its legislation to the few great subjects confided to it; so frame its laws as to leave as little as possible to discretion, and take care to see that they are duly and faithfully executed, the administrative powers of the President would be proportionally limited, and divested of all danger. But if, on the contrary, it should extend its legislation in every direction; draw within its action subjects never contemplated by the Constitution; multiply its acts, create numerous offices, and increase the revenue and expenditures proportionally, and, at the same time, frame its laws vaguely and loosely, and withdraw, in a great measure, its supervising care over their execution, his power would indeed become truly formidable and alarming. Now I appeal to the Senator and his friend, the author of this resolution, whether the growth of Executive power has not been the result of such a course on the part of Congress. I ask them whether his power has not in fact increased or decreased, just in proportion to the increase and decrease of the system of legislation, such as has been described? What was the period of its maximum increase, but the very period which they have so frequently and loudly denounced as the one most distinguished for the prevalence of Executive power and usurpation? Much of that power certainly depended on the remarkable man, then at the head of that Department, but much—far more, on the system of legislation, which the author of this resolution had built up with so much zeal and labor, and which carried the powers of the Government to a point beyond that to which it had ever before attained, drawing many and important powers into its vortex, of which the framers of the Constitution never dreamed. And here let me say to both of the Senators, and the party of which they are prominent members, that they labor in vain to bring down Executive power, while they support the system they so zealously advocate. The power they complain of is but its necessary fruit. Be assured that as certain as Congress transcends its assigned limits, and usurps powers never conferred, or stretches those conferred beyond the proper limits, so surely will the fruits of its usurpation pass into the hands of the Executive. In seeking to become master, it but makes a master in the person of the President. It is only by confining itself to its alloted sphere, and a discreet use of its acknowledged powers, that it can retain that ascendency in the Government which the Constitution intended to confer on it.

Having now pointed out the cause of the great increase of the Executive power on which the Senator rested his objection to the veto power, and having satisfactorily shown, as I trust I have, that, if it has proved dangerous in fact, the fault is not in the Constitution, but in Congress, I would next ask him, in what possible way could the divesting the President of his veto, or modifying it as he proposes, limit his power? Is it not clear, that so far from the veto being the cause of the increase of his power, it would have acted as a limitation on it if it had been more freely and frequently used? If the President had vetoed the original Bank—the connection with the banking system—the tariffs of '24 and '28, and the numerous acts appropriating money for roads, canals, harbors, and a long list of other measures not less unconstitutional, would his power have been half as great as it now is? He has grown great and powerful, not because *he used* his veto, but because *he abstained* from using it. In fact, it is difficult to imagine a case in which its application can tend to enlarge his power, except it be the case of an act intended to repeal a law calculated to increase his power, or to restore the authority of one which, by an arbitrary construction of his power, he has set aside.

Now let me add, in conclusion, that this is a question, in its bearings, of vital importance to that wonderful and sublime system of Government which our patriotic ancestors established, not so much by their wisdom, as wise and experienced as they were, as by the guidance of a kind Providence, who, in his divine dispensation, so disposed events as to lead to the establishment of a system of government wiser than those who framed it. The veto, of itself, as important as it is, sinks into nothing compared to the principle involved. It is but one, and that by no means the most considerable, of those many wise devices which I have attempted to explain, and which were intended to strengthen the popular basis of our Government, and resist its tendency to fall under the control of the dominant interest, acting through the mere numerical majority. The introduction of this resolution may be regarded as one of the many symptoms of that fatal tendency, and of which we had such fearful indications in the bold attempt at the late extraordinary session, of forcing through a whole system of measures of the most threatening and alarming character, in the space of a few weeks, on the ground that they were all decided in the election of the late President; thus attempting to substitute the will of a majority of the people, in the choice of a Chief Magistrate, as the legislative authority of the Union, in lieu of the beautiful and profound system established by the Constitution.

Part Five

AMERICAN
DEMOCRATIC
LEVELING

The modern passion for equality of condition alarmed conservatives on either side of the Atlantic, as both Britain and America moved toward universal suffrage during the 1830s and 1840s. Alexis de Tocqueville (1805–1859) repeatedly discusses the impulse toward egalitarianism, and restraints upon democratic equality, in his *Democracy in America*, the great work which was to be much heeded in both America and Europe. About the time Tocqueville traveled in the United States, James Fenimore Cooper (1789–1851) was mulling over the reflections which form his book *The American Democrat*.

ON EQUALITY
James Fenimore Cooper

Cooper's chapter "On Equality" from *The American Democrat* (1838) was published two years before the appearance of the American edition of Tocqueville's second volume, concerned with the social influence of democracy. Like Walter Scott, Cooper believed in order, class, and the idea of a gentleman—convictions that run through the historical novels of both writers. An extract is combined here with others from the 1931 (New York) reprint of *The American Democrat*, pp. 37–51, 112–13, 138–43.

Equality, in a social sense, may be divided into that of condition, and that of rights. Equality of condition is incompatible with civilization, and is found only to exist in those communities that are but slightly removed from the savage state. In practice, it can only mean a common misery.

Equality of rights is a peculiar feature of democracies. These rights are properly divided into civil and political, though even these definitions are not to be taken as absolute, or as literally exact.

Under the monarchies of the old world, there exist privileged classes, possessed of exclusive rights. For a long period the nobles were exempted from taxes, and many other charges, advantages that are still enjoyed by them, in certain countries. In England, even, the nobles are entitled to hereditary advantages that are denied to those who are of inferior birth. All these distinctions are done away with in principle, in countries where there exists a professed equality of rights, though there is probably no community that does not make some distinctions between the political privileges of men. If this is true, there is strictly no equality of political rights, any where, although there may be, and is, a nearer approach to an equality of civil rights.

By political rights we understand, the suffrage, eligibility to office, and a condition of things that admits of no distinction between men, unless on principles that are common to all. Thus, though a man is not qualified to vote until he has reached the age of twenty-one, the regulation does not effect political equality, since all are equally subjected to the rule, and all become electors on attaining the same age.

With an equality of civil rights, all men are equal before the law; all classes of the community being liable equally to taxation, military service, jury duties, and to the other impositions attendant on civilization, and no one being exempted from its control, except on general rules, which are dependent on the good of all, instead of the exemption's belonging to the immunities of individuals, estates, or families. An equality of civil rights may be briefly defined to be an absence of privileges.

The distinction between the equality of civil and of political rights is material, one implying mere equality before the administration of the law, the other, equality in the power to frame it.

An equality of civil rights is never absolute, but we are to understand by the term, such an equality only, as is compatible with general justice and the relations between the different members of families. Thus, women nowhere possess precisely the same rights as men, or men the same rights as women. The wife, usually, can neither sue nor be sued, while the husband, except in particular cases, is made liable to all legal claims on account of the wife.

Minors are deprived of many of their civil rights, or, it would be better to say, do not attain them, until they reach a period of life that has been arbitrarily fixed, and which varies in different countries, according to their several policies.

Neither is equality of political rights ever absolute. In those countries where the suffrage is said to be universal, exceptions exist, that arise from the necessity of things, or from that controlling policy which can never be safely lost sight of in the management of human affairs. The interests of women being thought to be so identified with those of their male relatives as to become, in a great degree, inseparable, females are, almost generally, excluded from the possession of political rights. There can be no doubt that society is greatly the gainer, by thus excluding one half its members, and the half that is best adapted to give a tone to its domestic happiness, from the strife of parties, and the fierce struggles of political controversies. Men are also excluded from political rights previously to having attained the age prescribed by law. Paupers, those who have no fixed abodes, and aliens in law, though their lives may have been principally passed in the country, are also excluded from the enjoyment of political rights, every where. Thus birth-right is almost universally made a source of advantage. These exceptions, however, do not very materially affect the principle of political equality, since the rules are general, and have been made solely with a reference to the good of society, or to render the laws less liable to abuses in practice.

It follows, that equality, whether considered in connection with our civil or political rights, must not be taken as a general and absolute condition of society, but as such an equality as depends on principles that are equitable, and which are suited to the actual wants of men.

The equality of the United States is no more absolute than that of any other country. There may be less inequality in this nation than in most others, but inequality exists, and, in some respects, with stronger features than it is usual to meet with in the rest of christendom.

The rights of property being an indispensable condition of civilization, and its quiet possession every where guaranteed, equality of condition is rendered impossible. One man must labor, while another may live luxuriously on his means; one has leisure and opportunity to cultivate his tastes, to increase his information, and to refine his habits, while another is compelled to toil, that he may live. One is reduced to serve, while another commands, and, of course, there can be no equality in their social conditions.

The justice and relative advantage of these differencies, as well as their several duties, will be elsewhere considered.

By the inequality of civil and political rights that exists in certain parts of the Union, and the great equality that exists in others, we see the necessity of referring the true character of the institutions to those of the states, without a just understanding of which, it is impossible to obtain any general and accurate ideas of the real polity of the country.

The same general exceptions to civil and political equality, that are found in other free countries, exist in this, though under laws peculiar to ourselves. Women and minors are excluded from the suffrage, and from maintaining suits at law, under the usual provisions, here as well as elsewhere. None but natives of the country can fill many of the higher offices, and paupers, felons and all those who have not fixed residences, are also excluded from the suffrage. In a few of the states property is made the test of political rights, and, in nearly half of them, a large portion of the inhabitants, who are of a different race from the original European occupants of the soil, are entirely excluded from all political, and from many of the civil rights, that are enjoyed by those who are deemed citizens. A slave can neither choose, nor be chosen to office, nor, in most of the states, can even a free man, unless a white man. A slave can neither sue nor be sued; he can not hold property, real or personal, nor can he, in many of the states be a witness in any suit, civil or criminal.

It follows from these facts, that absolute equality of condition, of political rights, or of civil rights, does not exist in the United States, though they all exist in a much greater degree in some states than in others, and in some of the states, perhaps, to as great a degree as is practicable. In what are usually called the free states of America, or those in which domestic slavery is abolished, there is to be found as much equality in every respect as comports with safety, civilization and the rights of property. This is also true, as respects the white population, in those states in which domestic slavery does exist; though the number of the bond is in a large proportion to that of the free.

As the tendency of the institutions of America is to the right, we learn in these truths, the power of facts, every question of politics being strictly a question of practice. They who fancy it possible to frame the institutions of a country, on the pure principles of abstract justice, as these principles exist in theories, know little of human nature, or of the restraints that are necessary to society. Abuses assail us in a thousand forms, and it is hopeless to aspire to any condition of humanity, approaching perfection. The very necessity of a government at all, arises from the impossibility of controlling the passions by any other means than that of force.

The celebrated proposition contained in the declaration of independence is not to be understood literally. All men are not "created equal," in a physical, or even in a moral sense, unless we limit the signification to one of political rights. This much is true, since human institutions are a human invention, with which nature has had no connection. Men are not born equals, physically, since one has a good constitution, another a bad; one is handsome, another ugly; one white, another black. Neither are men born equals morally, one possessing genius, or a natural aptitude, while his brother is an idiot. As regards all human institutions men are born equal, no sophistry being able to prove that nature intended one should inherit power and wealth, another slavery and want. Still artificial inequalities are the inevitable consequences of artificial ordinances, and in founding a new governing principle for the social compact, the American legislators instituted new modes of difference.

The very existence of government at all, infers inequality. The citizen who is preferred to office becomes the superior of those who are not, so long as he is the repository of power, and the child inherits the wealth of the parent as a controlling law of society. All that the great American proposition, therefore, can mean, is to set up new and juster notions of natural rights than those which existed previously, by asserting, in substance, that God has not instituted political inequalities, as was pretended by the advocates of the Jus Divinum, and that men possessed a full and natural authority to form such social institutions as best suited their necessities.

There are numerous instances in which the social inequality of America may do violence to our notions of abstract justice, but the compromise of interests under which all civilized society must exist, renders this unavoidable. Great principles seldom escape working injustice in particular things, and this so much the more, in establishing the relations of a community, for in them many great, and frequently conflicting principles enter, to maintain the more essential features of which sacrifices of parts become necessary. If we would have civilization and the exertion indispensable to its success, we must have property; if we have property, we must have its rights; if we have the rights of property, we must take those consequences of the rights of property which are inseparable from the rights themselves.

The equality of rights in America, therefore, after allowing for the striking exception of domestic slavery, is only a greater extension of the principle than common, while there is no such thing as an equality of condition. All that can be said of the first, is that it has been carried as far as a prudent discretion will at all allow, and of the last, that the inequality is the simple result of civilization, unaided by any of those factitious plans that have been elsewhere devised in order to augment the power of the strong, and to enfeeble the weak.

Equality is no where laid down as a governing principle of the institutions of the United States, neither the word, nor any inference that can be fairly deduced from its meaning, occurring in the constitution. As respect the states, themselves, the professions of an equality of rights are more clear, and slavery excepted, the intention in all their governments is to maintain it, as far as practicable, though equality of condition is no where mentioned, all political economists knowing that it is unattainable, if, indeed, it be desirable. Desirable in practice, it can hardly be, since the result would be to force all down to the level of the lowest.

All that a good government aims at, therefore, is to add no unnecessary and artificial aid to the force of its own unavoidable consequences, and to abstain from fortifying and accumulating social inequality as a means of increasing political inequalities.

Liberty, like equality, is a word more used than understood. Perfect and absolute liberty is as incompatible with the existence of society, as equality of condition. It is impracticable in a state of nature even, since, without the protection of the law, the strong would oppress and enslave the weak. We are then to understand by liberty, merely such a state of the social compact as permits the members of a community to lay no more restraints on themselves, than are required by their real necessities, and obvious interests. To this definition may be added, that it is a requisite of liberty, that the body of a nation should retain the power to modify its institutions, as circumstances shall require.

The natural disposition of all men being to enjoy a perfect freedom of action, it is a common error to suppose that the nation which possesses the mildest laws, or laws that impose the least personal restraints, is the freest. This opinion is untenable, since the power that concedes this freedom of action, can recall it. Unless it is lodged in the body of the community itself, there is, therefore, no pledge for the continuance of such a liberty. A familiar, supposititious case will render this truth more obvious.

A slave holder in Virginia is the master of two slaves: to one he grants his liberty, with the means to go to a town in a free state. The other accompanies his old associate clandestinely. In this town, they engage their services voluntarily, to a common master, who assigns to them equal shares in the same labor, paying them the same wages. In time, the master learns their situation, but, being an indulgent man, he allows the slave to retain his present situation. In all material things, these brothers are equal; they labor together, receive the same wages, and eat of the same food. Yet one is bond, and the other free, since it is in the power of the master, or of his heir, or of his assignee, at any time, to reclaim the services of the one who was not legally manumitted, and reduce him again to the condition of slavery. One of these brothers is the master of his own acts, while the other, though temporarily enjoying the same privileges, holds them subject to the will of a superior.

This is an all important distinction in the consideration of political liberty, since the circumstances of no two countries are precisely the same, and all municipal regulations ought to have direct reference to the actual condition of a community. It follows, that no country can properly be deemed free, unless the body of the nation possesses, in the last resort, the legal power to frame its laws according to its wants. This power must also abide in the nation, or it becomes merely an historical fact, for he that was once free is not necessarily free always, any more than he that was once happy, is to consider himself happy in perpetuity.

This definition of liberty is new to the world, for a government founded on such principles is a novelty. Hitherto, a nation has been deemed free, whose people were possessed of a certain amount of franchises, without any reference to the general repository of power. Such a nation may not be absolutely enslaved, but it can scarcely be considered in possession of an affirmative political liberty, since it is not the master of its own fortunes.

Having settled what is the foundation of liberty, it remains to be seen by what process a people can exercise this authority over themselves. The usual course is to refer all matters of choice to the decision of majorities. The common axiom of democracies, however, which says that "the majority must rule," is to be received with many limitations. Were the majority of a country to rule without restraint, it is probable as much injustice and oppression would follow, as are found under the dominion of one. It belongs to the nature of men to arrange themselves in parties, to lose sight of truth and justice in partizanship and prejudice, to mistake their own impulses for that which is proper, and to do wrong because they are indisposed to seek the right. Were it wise to trust power, unreservedly, to majorities, all fundamental and controlling laws would be unnecessary, since they might, as occasion required, emanate from the will of numbers. Constitutions would be useless.

The majority rules in prescribed cases, and in no other. It elects to office, it enacts ordinary laws, subject however to the restrictions of the constitution, and it decides most of the questions that arise in the primitive meetings of the people; questions that do not usually affect any of the principal interests of life.

The majority does not rule in settling fundamental laws, under the constitution; or when it does rule in such cases, it is with particular checks produced by time and new combinations; it does not pass judgment in trials at law, or under impeachment, and it is impotent in many matters touching vested rights. In the state of New York, the majority is impotent, in granting corporations, and in appropriating money for local purposes.

Though majorities often decide wrong, it is believed that they are less liable to do so than minorities. There can be no question that the educated and affluent classes of a country, are more capable of coming to wise and intelligent decisions in affairs of state, than the mass of a population. Their wealth and leisure afford them opportunities for observation and comparison, while their general information and greater knowledge of character, enable them to judge more accurately of men and measures. That these opportunities are not properly used, is owing to the unceasing desire of men to turn their advantages to their own particular benefit, and to their passions. All history proves, when power is the sole possession of a few, that it is perverted to their sole advantage, the public suffering in order that their rulers may prosper. The same nature which imposes the necessity of governments at all, seems to point out the expediency of confiding its control, in the last resort, to the body of the nation, as the only lasting protection against gross abuses.

We do not adopt the popular polity because it is perfect, but because it is less imperfect than any other. As man, by his nature, is liable to err, it is vain to expect an infallible whole that is composed of fallible parts. The government that emanates from a single will, supposing that will to be pure, enlightened, impartial, just and consistent, would be the best in the world, were it attainable for men. Such is the government of the universe, the result of which is perfect harmony. As no man is without spot in his justice, as no man has infinite wisdom, or infinite mercy, we are driven to take refuge in the opposite extreme, or in a government of many.

It is common for the advocates of monarchy and aristocracy to deride the opinions of the mass, as no more than the impulses of ignorance and prejudices. While experience unhappily shows that this charge has too much truth, it also shows that the educated and few form no exemption to the common rule of humanity. The most intelligent men of every country in which there is liberty of thought and action, yielding to their interests or their passions, are always found taking the opposite extremes of contested questions, thus triumphantly refuting an arrogant proposition, that of the exclusive fitness of the few to govern, by an unanswerable fact. The minority of a country is never known to agree, except in its efforts to reduce and oppress the majority. Were this not so, parties would be unknown in all countries but democracies, whereas the factions of aristocracies have been among the fiercest and least governable of any recorded in history.

Although real political liberty can have but one character, that of a popular base, the world contains many modifications of governments that are, more or less, worthy to be termed free. In most of these states, however, the liberties of the mass, are of the negative character of franchises, which franchises are not power of themselves, but merely an exemption from the abuses of power. Perhaps no state exists, in which the people, either by usage, or by direct concessions from the source of authority, do not possess some of these franchises; for, if there is no such thing, in practice, as perfect and absolute liberty, neither is there any such thing, in practice, as total and unmitigated slavery. In the one case, nature has rendered man incapable of enjoying freedom without restraint, and in the other, incapable of submitting, entirely without resistance, to oppression. The harshest despots are compelled to acknowledge the immutable principles of eternal justice, affecting necessity and the love of right, for their most ruthless deeds.

England is a country in which the franchises of the subject are more than usually numerous. Among the most conspicuous of these are the right of trial by jury, and that of the *habeas corpus*. Of the former it is unnecessary to speak, but as the latter is a phrase that may be unintelligible to many, it may be well to explain it.

The literal signification of *Habeas Corpus* is, "thou may'st have the body." In arbitrary governments, it is much the usage to oppress men, under the pretence of justice, by causing them to be arrested on false, or trivial charges, and of subjecting them to long and vexatious imprisonments, by protracting, or altogether evading the day of trial. The issue of a writ of *Habeas Corpus*, is an order to bring the accused before an impartial and independent judge, who examines into the charge, and who orders the prisoner to be set at liberty, unless there be sufficient legal ground for his detention.

This provision of the English law has been wisely retained in our system, for without some such regulation, it would be almost as easy to detain a citizen unjustly, under a popular government, as to detain the subject of a monarchy; the difference in favor of the first, consisting only in the greater responsibility of its functionaries.

By comparing the privileges of the *Habeas Corpus*, where it exists alone, and as a franchise, with those of the citizen who enjoys it merely as a provision of his own, against the abuses of ordinances that he had a voice in framing, we learn the essential difference between real liberty and franchises. The Englishman can appeal to a tribunal, against the abuse of an existing law, but if the law be not with him, he has no power to evade it, however unjust, or oppressive. The American has the same appeal against the abuse of a law, with the additional power to vote for its repeal, should the law itself be vicious. The one profits by a franchise to liberate his person only, submitting to his imprisonment however, if legality has been respected; while the other, in addition to this privilege, has a voice in getting rid of the obnoxious law, itself, and in preventing a recurrence of the wrong.

Some countries have the profession of possessing a government of the people, because an ancient dynasty has been set aside in a revolution, and a new one seated on the throne, either directly by the people, or by a combination that has been made to assume the character of a popular decision. Admitting that a people actually had an agency in framing such a system, and in naming their ruler, they cannot claim to be free, since they have parted with the power they did actually possess. No proposition can be clearer than that he who has given away a thing is no longer its master.

Of this nature is the present government of France. In that country the ancient dynasty has been set aside by a combination of leaders, through the agency of a few active spirits among the mass, and a prince put upon the throne, who is virtually invested with all the authority of his predecessor. Still, as the right of the last sovereign is clearly derived from a revolution, which has been made to assume the appearance of popular will, his government is termed a government of the people. This is a fallacy that can deceive no one of the smallest reflection. Such a system may be the best that France can now receive, but it is a mystification to call it by any other than its proper name. It is not a government of consultation, but one of pure force as respects a vast majority of Frenchmen.

A good deal of the same objection lies against the government of Great Britain, which, though freer in practice than that of France, is not based on a really free system. It may be said that both these governments are as free as comports with discretion, as indeed may be said of Turkey, since men get to be disqualified for the possession of any advantage in time; but such an admission is only an avowal of unfitness, and not a proof of enjoyment.

It is usual to maintain, that in democracies the tyranny of majorities is a greater evil than the oppression of minorities in narrow systems. Although this evil is exaggerated, since the laws being equal in their action it is not easy to oppress the few without oppressing all, it undeniably is the weak side of a popular government. To guard against this, we have framed constitutions, which point out the cases in which the majority shall decide, limiting their power, and bringing that they do possess within the circle of certain general and just principles. It will be elsewhere shown that it is a great mistake for the American citizen to take sides with the public, in doubtful cases affecting the rights of individuals, as this is the precise form in which oppression is the most likely to exhibit itself in a popular government.

Although it is true, that no genuine liberty can exist without being based on popular authority in the last resort, it is equally true that it can not exist when thus based, without many restraints on the power of the mass. These restraints are necessarily various and numerous. A familiar example will show their action. The majority of the people of a state might be in debt to its minority. Were the power of the former unrestrained, circumstances might arise in which they would declare depreciated bank notes a legal tender, and thus clear themselves of their liabilities, at the expense of their creditors. To prevent this, the constitution orders that nothing shall be made a legal tender but the precious metals, thus limiting the power of majorities in a way that the government is not limited in absolute monarchies, in which paper is often made to possess the value of gold and silver.

Liberty therefore may be defined to be a controlling authority that resides in the body of a nation, but so restrained as only to be exercised on certain general principles that shall do as little violence to natural justice, as is compatible with the peace and security of society. . . .

Some changes of the language are to be regretted, as they lead to false inferences, and society is always a loser by mistaking names for things. Life is a fact, and it is seldom any good arises from a misapprehension of the real circumstances under which we exist. The word "gentleman" has a positive and limited signification. It means one elevated above the mass of society by his birth, manners, attainments, character and social condition. As no civilized society can exist without these social differences, nothing is gained by denying the use of the term. If blackguards were to be *called* "gentlemen," and "gentlemen," "blackguards," the difference between them would be as obvious as it is today.

The word "gentleman," is derived from the French gentilhomme, which originally signified one of noble birth. This was at a time when the characteristics of the condition were never found beyond a caste. As society advanced, ordinary men attained the qualifications of nobility, without that of birth, and the meaning of the word was extended. It is now possible to be a gentleman without birth, though, even in America, where such distinctions are purely conditional, they who have birth, except in extraordinary instances, are classed with gentlemen. To call a laborer, one who has neither education, manners, accomplishments, tastes, associations, nor any one of the ordinary requisites, a gentleman, is just as absurd as to call one who is thus qualified, a fellow. The word must have some especial signification, or it would be synonymous with man. One may have gentlemanlike feelings, principles and appearance, without possessing the liberal attainments that distinguish the gentleman. Least of all does money alone make a gentleman, though, as it becomes a means of obtaining the other requisites, it is usual to give it a place in the claims of the class. Men may be, and often

are, very rich, without having the smallest title to be
deemed gentlemen. A man may be a distinguished gentleman, and not possess as much money as his own foot-
man. . . .

There is a disposition, under popular governments, to
mistake the nature and authority of the publick. Publick
opinion, as a matter of course, can only refer to that portion of the community that has cognizance of the particular circumstances it affects, but in all matters of law, of
rights, and of principles, as they are connected with the
general relations of society, the publick means the entire
constituency, and that, too, only as it is authorized to act,
by the fundamental laws, or the constitution. Thus the
citizen who asserts his legal rights in opposition to the
wishes of a neighborhood, is not opposing the publick, but
maintaining its intentions, while the particular neighborhood is arrogating to itself a power that is confided to the
whole body of the state.

Tyranny can only come from the publick, in a democracy, since individuals are powerless, possessing no more
rights than it pleases the community to leave in their
hands. The pretence that an individual oppresses the publick, is, to the last degree, absurd, since he can do no more
than exercise his rights, as they are established by law;
which law is enacted, administered and interpreted by the
agents of the publick.

As every man forms a portion of the publick, if honest
and influenced by right principles, the citizen will be cautious how he takes sides against particular members of the
community, for he is both deciding in his own case, a circumstance under which few make impartial judges, and
combining with the strong to oppress the weak.

In this country, in which political authority is the possession of the body that wields opinion, influences that
elsewhere counteract each other, there is a strong and dangerous disposition to defer to the publick, in opposition to

truth and justice. This is a penalty that is paid for liberty, and it depends on the very natural principle of flattering power. In a monarchy, adulation is paid to the prince; in a democracy to the people, or the publick. Neither hears the truth, as often as is wholesome, and both suffer for the want of the corrective. The man who resists the tyranny of a monarch, is often sustained by the voices of those around him; but he who opposes the innovations of the publick in a democracy, not only finds himself struggling with power, but with his own neighbors. It follows that the oppression of the publick is of the worst description, and all real lovers of liberty should take special heed not to be accessaries to wrongs so hard to be borne. As between the publick and individuals, therefore, the true bias of a democrat, so far as there is any doubt of the real merits of the controversy, is to take sides with the latter. This is opposed to the popular notion, which is to fancy the man who maintains his rights against the popular will, an aristocrat, but it is none the less true; the popular will, in cases that affect popular pleasure, being quite as likely to be wrong, as an individual will, in cases that affect an individual interest.

It ought to be impressed on every man's mind, in letters of brass, *"That, in a democracy, the publick has no power that is not expressly conceded by the institutions, and that this power, moreover, is only to be used under the forms prescribed by the constitution. All beyond this, is oppression, when it takes the character of acts, and not unfrequently when it is confined to opinion."* Society has less need of the corrective of publick opinion, under such a system, than under a narrow government, for possessing all the power, the body of the community, by framing the positive ordinances, is not compelled to check abuses by resisting, or over-awing the laws. Great care should be had, therefore, to ascertain facts, before the citizen of a free country suffers himself to inflict the punishment of publick opinion, since it is aiding oppression in its worst form, when in error, and this too, without a sufficient object.

Another form of oppression practised by the publick, is arrogating to itself a right to inquire into, and to decide on the private acts of individuals, beyond the cognizance of the laws.

Men who have designs on the favor of the publick invite invasions on their privacy, a course that has rendered the community less scrupulous and delicate than it ought to be. All assumptions of a power to decide on conduct, that is unaccompanied by an authority to investigate facts, is adding the danger of committing rank injustice, to usurpation. The practice may make hypocrites, but it can never mend morals.

The publick, every where, is proverbially soulless. All feel when its rights, assumed or real, are invaded, but none feel its responsibilities. In republicks, the publick is, also, accused of ingratitude to its servants. This is true, few citizens of a democracy retaining the popular favor, without making a sacrifice of those principles, which conflict with popular caprices. The people, being sovereign, require the same flattery, the same humoring of their wishes, and the same sacrifices of truths, as a prince.

It is not more true, however, that the people in a democracy, are ungrateful, than that monarchs are ungrateful. The failing is common to all power, which, as a rule, is invariably as forgetful of services as it is exacting. The difference in the rewards of the servants of a prince, and the rewards of the servants of a democracy, is to be found in the greater vigilance of the first, who commonly sees the necessity of paying well. No dignities or honors conferred on a subject, moreover, can raise him to a level with his master, while a people reluctantly yield distinctions that elevate one of their own number above themselves.

In America, it is indispensable that every well wisher of true liberty should understand that acts of tyranny can only proceed from the publick. The publick, then, is to be watched, in this country, as, in other countries kings and aristocrats are to be watched.

The end of liberty is the happiness of man, and its means, that of leaving the greatest possible personal freedom of action, that comports with the general good. To supplant the exactions of the laws, therefore, by those of an unauthorized public, is to establish restraints without the formalities and precision of legal requirements. It is putting the prejudices, provincialisms, ignorance and passions of a neighborhood in the place of statutes; or, it is establishing a power equally without general principles, and without responsibility.

Although the political liberty of this country is greater than that of nearly every other civilized nation, its personal liberty is said to be less. In other words, men are thought to be more under the control of extra-legal authority, and to defer more to those around them, in pursuing even their lawful and innocent occupations, than in almost every other country. That there is much truth in this opinion, all observant travellers agree, and it is a reproach to the moral civilization of the country that it should be so. It is not difficult to trace the causes of such a state of things, but the evil is none the less because it is satisfactorily explained. One principal reason, beyond a question, is the mistake that men are apt to make concerning the rights and powers of the publick in a popular government.

The pretence that the publick has a right to extend its jurisdiction beyond the reach of the laws, and without regard to the principles and restraints of the fundamental compact that binds society together, is, indeed, to verify the common accusation of the enemies of democracy, who affirm that, by substituting this form of government for that of a despotism, people are only replacing one tyrant by many. This saying is singularly false as respects the political action of our institutions, but society must advance farther, the country must collect more towns, a denser population, and possess a higher degree of general civilization, before it can be as confidently pronounced that it is untrue as respects the purely social.

The disgraceful desire to govern by means of mobs, which has lately become so prevalent, has arisen from misconceiving the rights of the publick. Men know that the publick, or the community, rules, and becoming impatient of any evil that presses on them, or which they fancy presses on them, they overstep all the forms of law, overlook deliberation and consultation, and set up their own local interests, and not unfrequently their passions, in the place of positive enactments and the institutions. It is scarcely predicting more than the truth will warrant, to say, that if this substitution of the caprices, motives and animosities of a portion of the publick, for the solemn ordinances of the entire legal publick, should continue, even those well affected to a popular government, will be obliged to combine with those who wish its downfall, in order to protect their persons and property, against the designs of the malevolent; for no civilized society can long exist, with an active power in its bosom that is stronger than the law.

THE NEW SOCIAL MORALITY
Alexis de Tocqueville

For sixteen years Tocqueville carried on a correspondence with Arthur de Gobineau, the theorist of race. In this letter of 1843, Tocqueville asserts that the new social morality of egalitarianism is supplanting Christian morals. The letter is printed in English translation in Lukacs (ed.), *"The European Revolution" and Correspondence with Gobineau* (New York, 1960), pp. 190–95.

Your letter, monsieur, arrived the day I left for the *conseil général*. I found it upon my return. I want to anwer you at once.

I shall ask you now to put all your books aside for a moment and to make a rapid mental survey of your recent readings and of your earlier studies, so as to answer this question in conversational form: What is there really *new* in the works or in the discoveries of the modern moral philosophers? By *modern* I mean not merely those of the last fifty years but those who immediately preceded them, those who belong to that generation which had decisively broken with the Middle Ages. Did they really see the obligations of mankind in such a new light? Did they really discover new motives for human actions? Did they really establish new foundations, or even new explanations, for human duties? Have they placed the sanctions of moral laws elsewhere? Through the darkness all I think I can recognize is this: to me it is Christianity that seems to have accomplished the revolution—you may prefer the word change—in all the ideas that concern duties and rights; ideas which, after all, are the basic matter of all moral knowledge.

Christianity did not exactly create new duties or, to put it in other terms, it did not establish entirely new virtues; but it changed their relative position. Certain rude and half-savage virtues had been on the top of the list; Christianity put them on the bottom. The milder virtues, such as neighborly love, pity, leniency, the forgetfulness even of injuries had been on the bottom of the antique list; Christianity placed them above all others. Here was the first change.

The realm of duties had been limited. Christianity broadened it. It had been limited to certain citizenries; Christianity extended it to all men. It had been restricted and confirmed the position of masters; Christianity gave it to the slaves. Thus Christianity put in grand evidence the equality, the unity, the fraternity of all men. Here was the second change.

The sanction of moral laws had existed for this world rather than for the other. Christianity put the ultimate aim of human life beyond this world; it gave thus a finer, purer, less material, less interested, and higher character to morality. Here was the last change.

All of these things had been seen, shown, and preached before it came. But Christianity alone bound them together, making this new morality into a religion, and the minds of men were absorbed therewith.

We have lived with the rule of this morality for a long chain of centuries. Have we added much to it that is essential? This is what I do not see clearly. We may have put a few shades into the colors of the picture, but I do not see that we have added really new colors. The morality of our own time—the way I see it revealed through words and through action and through the ceaseless patter of our loquacious society—our modern morality (and I am leaving aside what is being printed in fat volumes about this subject) may have reverted in some of its facets to the notions of the ancients, yet for the most part it has merely developed and expanded the consequences of Christian morality without affecting the essential principles of the latter. Our society is much more alienated from the theology than it is from the philosophy of Christianity. As our religious beliefs have become less strong and our view of the life hereafter less clear, morality has become more concerned with the legitimacy of material needs and pleasures. This is the idea that I think the followers of Saint-Simon expressed by saying that *the flesh must be rehabilitated.* It is probably the same tendency that, for some time now, appears in the writings and in the doctrines of our moral philosophers.

For this reason some people have now felt the urge to find the sanctions of moral laws in this life. They could no longer place them with absolute certainty in the life thereafter. From this came the doctrine of benevolent interest, about honesty paying dividends and vice leading to misery. The English Utilitarians are upholders of this new trend of ideas, ideas rather unfamiliar to the Christian moralists of the past.

Christianity and consequently its morality went beyond all political powers and nationalities. Its grand achievement is to have formed a human community beyond national societies. The duties of men among themselves as well as in their capacity of *citizens*, the duties of citizens to their fatherland, in brief, the public virtues seem to me to have been inadequately defined and considerably neglected within the moral system of Christianity. This seems to me the only weak facet of that admirable moral system, just as this seems the only strong facet of the moral system of the antique nations. Though the Christian idea of human brotherhood may seem to dominate contemporary minds, those public virtues have also advanced in the meantime; and I am convinced that the moralists of the past hundred years are preoccupied with it far more than were their predecessors. This is due to the resurgence of political passions. They are, at the same time, causes and effects of the great changes we are now witnessing. Thus the modern world re-established a part of antique morality and inserted it within the moral principles of Christianity.

But the most noteworthy innovation of our modern moral teaching, to me, consists in the tremendous development and in the new form that is now given to two principles which Christianity had first put in grand evidence: the equal rights of every man in the goods of this world, and the duty of those who have more to help those who have less. The revolutions that displaced the old European ruling class, the general extension of wealth and education which has made individuals more and more alike have given an immense and unexpected impetus to the principle of equality, which Christianity had established in the spiritual rather than in the tangible material sphere. The idea that *all* men have a right to certain goods, to certain pleasures, and that our primary moral duty is to procure these for them—this idea, as I said above, has now gained immense breadth, and it now appears in an endless variety of aspects. This first innovation led to another. Christianity made charity a personal virtue. Every day now we are making a social duty, a political obligation, a public virtue out of it. And the growing number of those who must be supported, the variety of needs which we are growing accustomed to provide for, the disappearance of great personalities to whom previously one could turn with these problems of succor, now makes every eye turn to the State. Governments now are compelled to redress certain inequalities, to mollify certain hardships, to offer support to all the luckless and helpless. Thus a new kind of social and political morality is being established, a kind which the antique peoples hardly knew but which is, in reality, a combination of some of their political ideas with the moral principles of Christianity.

Here, my dear Gobineau, is all that I can now distinguish through the fog that surrounds me. You see that I speak only of what I see in the habits of people; I am unable to say whether the same signs are registered in books or whether they reappear elsewhere. These reflections of mine are not supposed to give you a foundation or a basic framework, but rather an example of what I think we should search for. We have to find whatever new concepts of morality may exist. I have tried hard, while attempting to keep close to realities. Do my propositions strike you as true? Do you have others to propose? Do these modern moral theories justify them? My own mental habit has made me look exclusively for these newer things which might directly influence the actions of our contemporaries. But I cannot afford to neglect those different moralistic innovations, the new theses, new concepts, new explications which I might be permitted to call sterile fantasies, were it not for my academic affiliation that obliges me to term them "interesting products of the human intellect."

Only after we shall have *outlined* whatever there is new in the moral doctrines and tendencies of our age will we begin to follow the consequences of these primary data in some detail. We should ascertain them before all. So, my dear collaborator, put your head in your hands and think about the above. What I ask from you is no longer the work of a student but of a master, yet I am certain that this does not surpass your powers. Once we have this foundation the rest of the work will be easier and at the same time much more interesting. . . .

Farewell, monsieur. Please trust the expression of my very genuine affection.

P.S. Don't destroy this letter, as I might wish to reread it someday when I finally get down to writing.

Part Six

~~~~~~~~~~~~~~~~~~~~~~~~~~~~~~~~~~~~

AGAINST UTILITARIAN RADICALISM

Until the middle of the nineteenth century, conservatives in Britain and America had for their adversaries chiefly the utilitarians, egalitarians, and progressivists whose views of society were highly individualistic. Later, conservatives changed their front—but not their ground—to resist socialists and other collectivists.

Whigs of the old school like Thomas Babington Macaulay (1800–1859), Tories like Benjamin Disraeli (1804–1881), and Catholic leaders like John Henry Newman (1801–1890) disagreed about much; but they had in common a strong dislike of the intellectual heirs of Jeremy Bentham, and of radical political movements. So here we turn to several varieties of conservative thought before the ideology of Marxism loomed large.

A RADICAL
WAR-SONG

Thomas Babington Macaulay

The young Macaulay, not yet a famous historian, wrote in 1820 these satirical stanzas on the English radical Reform movement that had been dealt a rough blow some months earlier by the "Peterloo Massacre." The poem is included in the various editions of Macaulay's *Critical, Historical, and Miscellaneous Essays and Poems.*

Awake, arise, the hour is come,
    For rows and revolutions;
There's no receipt like pike and drum
    For crazy constitutions.
Close, close the shop! Break, break the loom!
    Desert your hearths and furrows,
And throng in arms to seal the doom
    Of England's rotten boroughs.

We'll stretch that tort'ring Castlereagh
    On his own Dublin rack, sir;
We'll drown the King in Eau de vie,
    The Laureate in his sack, sir;
Old Eldon and his sordid hag
    In molten gold we'll smother,
And stifle in his own green bag
    The Doctor and his brother.

In chains we'll hang in fair Guildhall
   The City's famed Recorder,
And next on proud St. Stephen's fall,
   Though Wynne should squeak to order.
In vain our tyrants then shall try
   To 'scape our martial law, sir;
In vain the trembling Speaker cry
   That "Strangers must withdraw," sir.

Copley to hang offends no text;
   A rat is not a man, sir:
With schedules and with tax bills next
   We'll bury pious Van, sir.
The slaves who loved the Income Tax,
   We'll crush by scores, like mites, sir,
And him, the wretch who freed the blacks,
   And more enslaved the whites, sir.

The peer shall dangle from his gate,
   The bishop from his steeple,
Till all recanting, own, the State
   Means nothing but the People.
We'll fix the church's revenues
   On Apostolic basis,
One coat, one scrip, one pair of shoes
   Shall pay their strange grimaces.

We'll strap the bar's deluding train
   In their own darling halter,
And with his big church bible brain
   The parson at the altar.
Hail glorious hour, when fair Reform
   Shall bless our longing nation,
And Hunt receives command to form
   A new administration.

Carlisle shall sit enthroned, where sat
  Our Cranmer, and our Secker;
And Watson show his snow-white hat
  In England's rich Exchequer.
The breast of Thistlewood shall wear
  Our Wellesley's star and sash, man;
And many a mausoleum fair
  Shall rise to honest Cashman.

Then, then beneath the nine-tailed cat
  Shall they who used it writhe, sir;
And curates lean, and rectors fat,
  Shall dig the ground they tithe, sir.
Down with your Bayleys, and your Bests,
  Your Giffords and your Gurneys:
We'll clear the island of the pests,
  Which mortals name attorneys.

Down with your sheriffs, and your mayors,
  Your registrars, and proctors,
We'll live without the lawyer's cares,
  And die without the doctor's.
No discontented fair shall pout
  To see her spouse so stupid;
We'll tread the torch of Hymen out,
  And live content with Cupid.

Then, when the high-born and the great
  Are humbled to our level,
On all the wealth of Church and State,
  Like aldermen, we'll revel.
We'll live when hushed the battle's din,
In smoking and in cards, sir,
In drinking unexcised gin,
  And wooing fair Poissardes, sir.

ALL SAIL AND NO ANCHOR
Thomas Babington Macaulay

In 1857, old Lord Macaulay exchanged several letters
with Henry S. Randall, an American biographer of
Jefferson. Randall discovered that Macaulay held no
high opinion of either Jefferson or the American democracy. These two letters express Macaulay's misgivings for the future of the United States. The
complete text of the correspondence may be found in
a slim volume published by the New York Public Library in 1925: H. M. Lyndenberg (ed.), *What Did
Macaulay Say about America?*

Sir,

I beg you to accept my thanks for your letter enclosing
the autograph of Washington, which reached me three
weeks ago, and for the History of the State of New York,
which I received the day before yesterday.

I shall look forward with curiosity to the appearance of
your Life of Jefferson. I cannot say that he is one of my
Heroes: but it is very probable that you may convince me
that I have formed an erroneous estimate of his character.

I am a little surprised to learn from you that Americans
generally consider him as a foil to Washington, as the Ari-
manes of the republic contending against the Oromasdes.
There can, I apprehend, be no doubt that your institutions have, during the whole of the nineteenth century,
been constantly becoming more Jeffersonian and less
Washingtonian. It is surely strange that, while this process
has been going on, Washington should have been exalted
into a God, and Jefferson degraded into a Demon.

If there were any chance of my living to write the history of your Revolution, I should eagerly and gratefully accept your kind offer of assistance. But I now look to the accession of the House of Hanover as my extreme goal. . . .

Dear Sir,

The four volumes of the Colonial History of New York reached me safely. I assure you that I shall value them highly. They contain much to interest an English as well as an American reader. Pray accept my thanks, and convey them to the Regents of the University.

You are surprised to learn that I have not a high opinion of Mr. Jefferson, and I am a little surprised at your surprise. I am certain that I never wrote a line, and that I never, in Parliament, in conversation, or even on the hustings,—a place where it is the fashion to court the populace,—uttered a word indicating an opinion that the supreme authority in a state ought to be intrusted to the majority of citizens told by the head, in other words, to the poorest and most ignorant part of society. I have long been convinced that institutions purely democratic must, sooner or later, destroy liberty, or civilisation, or both. In Europe, where the population is dense, the effect of such institutions would be almost instantaneous. What happened lately in France is an example. In 1848 a pure democracy was established there. During a short time there was reason to expect a general spoliation, a national bankruptcy, a new partition of the soil, a maximum of prices, a ruinous load of taxation laid on the rich for the purpose of supporting the poor in idleness. Such a system would, in twenty years, have made France as poor and barbarous as the France of the Carlovingians. Happily the danger was averted; and now there is a despotism, a silent tribune, an enslaved press. Liberty is gone, but civilisation has been saved. I have not the smallest doubt that, if we had a purely democratic government here, the effect would be the same. Either the poor would plunder the rich, and civilisation would perish, or order and property would be saved by a strong military government, and liberty would perish. You may think that your country enjoys an exemption from these evils. I will frankly own to you that I am of a very different opinion. Your fate I believe to be certain, though it is deferred by a physical cause. As long as you have a boundless extent of fertile and unoccupied land, your labouring population will be far more at ease than the labouring population of the old world; and, while that is the case, the Jeffersonian polity may continue to exist without causing any fatal calamity. But the time will come when New England will be as thickly peopled as old England. Wages will be as low, and will fluctuate as much with you as with us. You will have your Manchesters and Birminghams, and in those Manchesters and Birminghams, hundreds of thousands of artisans will assuredly be sometimes out of work. Then your institutions will be fairly brought to the test. Distress everywhere makes the labourer mutinous and discontented, and inclines him to listen with eagerness to agitators who tell him that it is a monstrous iniquity that one man should have a million while another cannot get a full meal. In bad years there is plenty of grumbling here, and sometimes a little rioting. But it matters little. For here the sufferers are not the rulers. The supreme power is in the hands of a class, numerous indeed, but select; of an educated class, of a class which is, and knows itself to be, deeply interested in the security of property and the maintenance of order. Accordingly, the malcontents are firmly, yet gently, restrained. The bad time is got over without robbing the wealthy to relieve the indigent. The springs of national prosperity soon begin to flow again: work is plentiful: wages rise; and all is tranquillity and cheerfulness. I have seen England pass three or four times through such critical seasons as I have described. Through such seasons the United States will have to pass, in the course of the next century, if not of this. How will you pass through them. I heartily wish you a good deliverance. But my reason and my wishes are at war; and I cannot help foreboding the worst. It is quite plain that your government will never be able to restrain a distressed and discontented majority. For with you the majority is the government, and has the rich, who are always a minority, absolutely at its mercy. The day will come when, in the State of New York, a multitude of people, none of whom has had more than half a breakfast, or expects to have more than half a dinner, will choose a Legislature. Is it possible to doubt what sort of a Legislature will be chosen? On one side is a statesman preaching patience, respect for vested rights, strict observance of public faith. On the other is a demagogue ranting about the tyranny of capitalists and usurers, and asking why anybody should be permitted to drink Champagne and to ride in a carriage, while thousands of honest folks are in want of necessaries. Which of the two candidates is likely to be preferred by a working man who hears his children cry for more bread? I seriously apprehend that you will, in some such season of adversity as I have described, do things which will prevent prosperity from returning; that you will act like people who should in a year of scarcity, devour all the seed corn, and thus make the next year a year, not of scarcity, but of absolute famine. There will be, I fear, spoliation. The spoliation will increase the distress. The distress will produce fresh spoliation. There is nothing to stop you. Your Constitution is all sail and no anchor. As I said before, when a society has entered on this downward progress, either civilisation or liberty must perish. Either some Caesar or Napoleon will seize the reins of government with a strong hand; or your republic will be as fearfully plundered and laid waste by barbarians in the twentieth Century as the Roman Empire was in the fifth;—with this difference, that the Huns and Vandals who ravaged the Roman Empire came from

without, and that your Huns and Vandals will have been
engendered within your own country by your own institutions.

Thinking thus, of course, I cannot reckon Jefferson
among the benefactors of mankind. I readily admit that
his intentions were good and his abilities considerable.
Odious stories have been circulated about his private life;
but I do not know on what evidence those stories rest; and
I think it probable that they are false, or monstrously exaggerated. I have no doubt that I shall derive both pleasure and information from your account of him.

UTILITARIAN FOLLIES
Benjamin Disraeli

The rising Benjamin Disraeli published in 1835 his
book *A Vindication of the English Constitution*. Although it was through his novels and his lively
speeches that Disraeli rose to be prime minister, this
early book of his established him as a serious political
thinker. In these extracts from Chapters I, II, and III,
Disraeli endeavors to demolish the radical Utilitarianism which would have swept aside the old English
Constitution. The *Vindication* is most readily available in William Hutcheon (ed.), *Whigs and Whiggism: Political Writings by Benjamin Disraeli*
(London, 1913), pp. 113–21.

A political sect has sprung up avowedly adverse to the
Estates of the Realm, and seeking by means which, of
course, it holds legal, the abrogation of a majority of them.
These anti-constitutional writers, like all new votaries, are
remarkable for their zeal and activity. They omit no

means of disseminating their creed: they are very active missionaries: there is no medium of the public press of which they do not avail themselves: they have their newspapers, daily and weekly, their magazines, and their reviews. The unstamped press takes the cue from them, and the members of the party who are in Parliament lose no opportunity of dilating on the congenial theme at the public meetings of their constituents. . . .

The avowed object of this new sect of statesmen is to submit the institutions of the country to the test of UTILITY and to form a new Constitution on the abstract principles of theoretic science. I think it is Voltaire who tells us that there is nothing more common than to read and to converse to no purpose, and that in history, in morals, and in divinity, we should beware of EQUIVOCAL TERMS. I do not think that politics should form an exception to this salutary rule; and, for my own part, it appears to me that this term, UTILITY, is about as equivocal as any one which, from the time of the Nominalists and Realists to our present equally controversial and equally indefinite days, hath been let loose to breed sects and set men a-brawling. The fitness of a material object for a material purpose is a test of its utility which our senses and necessities can decide; but what other test there is of moral and political utility than the various and varying opinions of mankind I am at a loss to discover; and that this is utterly unsatisfactory and insufficient, all, I apprehend, must agree.

Indeed, I have hitherto searched in vain in the writings of the Utilitarian sect for any definition of their fundamental phrase with which it is possible to grapple. That they pretend to afford us a definition it would be disingenuous to conceal, and we are informed that Utility is "the principle which produces the greatest happiness of the greatest number." Does this advance us in comprehension? Who is to decide upon the greatest happiness of the greatest number? According to Prince Metternich, the government of Austria secures the greatest happiness of the greatest number: it is highly probable that the effect of the Austrian education and institutions may occasion the majority of the Austrian population to be of the same opinion. Yet the government of Austria is no favourite with the anti-constitutional writers of our own country. Gross superstition may secure the greatest happiness of the greatest number, as it has done in Spain and Portugal: a military empire may secure the greatest happiness of the greatest number, as it has done in Rome and France: a coarse and unmitigated despotism may secure the greatest happiness of the greatest number, as it does to this day in many regions of Asia and Africa. Every government that ever existed, that has enjoyed any quality of duration, must have been founded on this "greatest happiness principle," for, had not the majority thought or felt that such were its result, the government could never have endured. There have been times, and those too not far gone, when the greatest happiness of Christian nations has been secured by burning men alive for their religious faith; and unless we are prepared to proclaim that all religious creeds which differ from our own are in fact not credited by their pretended votaries, we must admit that the greatest happiness of the greatest number of mankind is even now secured by believing that which we know to be false. If the greatest happiness of the greatest number, therefore, be the only test of the excellence of political institutions, that may be the plea for institutions which, according to the Utilitarians especially, are monstrous or absurd: and if to avoid this conclusion we maintain that the greatest number are not the proper judges of the greatest happiness, we are only referred to the isolated opinions of solitary philosophers, or at the best to the conceited conviction of some sectarian minority. UTILITY, in short, is a mere phrase, to which any man may ascribe any meaning that his interests prompt or his passions dictate. With this plea, a nation may consider it in the highest degree useful that all the statues scattered throughout the museums of Christendom should be collected in the same capital, and conquer Christendom in consequence to obtain their object; and by virtue of the same plea, some Iconoclastic enemy may declare war upon this nation of Dilettanti tomorrow, and dash into fragments their cosmopolite collection.

Viewed merely in relation to the science of government, the effect of the test of utility, as we have considered it, would in all probability be harmless, and its practical tendency, if any, would rather lead to a spirit of conservation and optimism than to one of discontent and change. But optimism is assuredly not the system of the Utilitarians: far from thinking everything is for the best, they decidedly are of opinion that everything is for the worst. In order, therefore, that their test of utility should lead to the political results which they desire, they have dovetailed their peculiar system of government into a peculiar system of morals, in connection with which we must alone subject it to our consideration. The same inventive sages, who have founded all political science on UTILITY, have founded all moral science on SELF-INTEREST, and have then declared that a system of government should be deduced alone from the principles of human nature. If mankind could agree on a definition of Self-interest, I willingly admit that they would not be long in deciding upon a definition of Utility. But what do the Utilitarians mean by the term Self-interest? I at once agree that man acts from no other principle than self-interest, but I include in self-interest, and I should think every accurate reasoner must do the same, every motive that can possibly influence man. If every motive that can possibly influence man be included in self-interest, then it is impossible to form a science on a principle which includes the most contrary motives. If the Utilitarians will not admit all the motives, but only some of the motives, then their science of government is not founded on human nature, but only on a part of human nature, and must be consequently and proportionately imperfect. But the Utilitarian only admits one or two of the motives that influence man; a desire of power and desire of property; and therefore infers that it is the interest of man to tyrannise and to rob.

The blended Utilitarian system of morals and politics, then, runs thus: Man is only influenced by self-interest: it is the interest of man to be a tyrant and a robber: a man does not change his nature because he is a king; therefore a king is a tyrant and a robber. If it be the interest of one man to be a tyrant and a robber, it is the interest of fifty or five thousand to be tyrants and robbers; therefore we cannot trust an aristocracy more than a monarch. But the eternal principle of human nature must always hold good. A privileged class is always an aristocracy, whether it consists of five thousand or fifty thousand, a band of nobles or a favoured sect; therefore the power of government should be entrusted to all; therefore the only true and useful government is a representative polity, founded on universal suffrage. This is the Utilitarian system of morals and government, drawn from their "great works" by one who has no wish to misrepresent them. Granting for a moment their premises, I do not see that their deduction, even then, is logically correct. It is possible to conceive a state of society where the government may be in the hands of a favoured majority; a community of five millions, of which three might form a privileged class. Would not the greatest happiness of the greatest number be secured by such an arrangement? and, if so secured, would or would not the utilitarian, according to his theory, feel justified in disturbing it? If he oppose such a combination, he overthrows his theory; if he consents to such a combination, his theory may uphold tyranny and spoliation.

But I will not press this point: it is enough for me to show that, to render their politics practical, they are obliged to make their metaphysics impossible. Let the

Utilitarian prove that the self-interest of man always leads him to be a tyrant and a robber, and I will grant that universal suffrage is a necessary and useful institution. A nation that conquers the world acts from self-interest; a nation that submits to a conqueror acts from self-interest. A spendthrift and a miser alike act from self-interest: the same principle animated Messalina and Lucretia, Bayard and Byng. To say that when a man acts he acts from self-interest is only to announce that when a man does act he acts. An important truth, a great discovery, calling assuredly for the appearance of prophets, or, if necessary, even ghosts. But to announce that when a man acts he acts from self-interest, and that the self-interest of every man prompts him to be a tyrant and a robber, is to declare that which the experience of all human nature contradicts; because we all daily and hourly feel and see that there are a thousand other motives which influence human conduct besides the idea of exercising power and obtaining property; every one of which motives must rank under the term Self-interest, because every man who acts under their influence must necessarily believe that in so acting he acts for his happiness, and therefore for his self-interest. Utility, Pain, Power, Pleasure, Happiness, Self-interest, are all phrases to which any man may annex any meaning he pleases, and from which any acute and practised reasoner may most syllogistically deduce any theory he chooses. "Such words," says Locke, "no more improve our understanding than the move of a jack will fill our bellies." This waste of ingenuity on nonsense is like the condescending union that occasionally occurs between some high-bred steed and some long-eared beauty of the Pampas: the base and fantastical embrace only produces a barren and mulish progeny.

We have before this had an *a priori* system of celestial mechanics, and its votaries most syllogistically sent Galileo to a dungeon, after having triumphantly refuted him.

We have before this had an *a priori* system of metaphysics, but where now are the golden volumes of Erigena, and Occam, and Scotus, and Raymond Lully? And now we have an *a priori* system of politics. The schoolmen are revived in the nineteenth century, and are going to settle the State with their withering definitions, their fruitless logomachies, and barren dialectics.

I should suppose that there is no one of the Utilitarian sages who would not feel offended if I were to style him the Angelical Doctor, like Thomas Aquinas; and I regret from bitter experience, that they have not yet condescended sufficiently to cultivate the art of composition to entitle them to the style of the Perspicuous Doctor, like Walter Burley.

These reflections naturally lead me to a consideration of the great object of our new school of statesmen in general, which is to form political institutions on abstract principles of theoretic science, instead of permitting them to spring from the course of events, and to be naturally created by the necessities of nations. It would appear that this scheme originated in the fallacy of supposing that theories produce circumstances, whereas the very converse of the proposition is correct, and circumstances indeed produce theories. If we survey the career of an individual, we shall on the whole observe a remarkable consistency in his conduct; yet it is more than possible that the individual has never acted from that organised philosophy which we style *system*. What, then, has produced this consistency? what, then, has occasioned this harmony of purpose? His individual character. Nations have characters as well as individuals, and national character is precisely the quality which the new sect of statesmen in their schemes and speculations either deny or overlook. The ruling passion, which is the result of organisation, regulates the career of an individual, subject to those superior accidents of fortune whose secondary influence is scarcely inferior to the impulse of his nature. The blended influences of nature and fortune form his character; 'tis the same with nations. There were important events in the career of an individual which force the man to ponder over the past, and, in these studies of experience and struggles for self-knowledge, to ascertain certain principles of conduct which he recognises as the cause of past success, and anticipates as the guarantee of future prosperity: and there are great crises in the fortunes of an ancient people which impel them to examine the nature of the institutions which have gradually sprung up among them. In this great national review, duly and wisely separating the essential character of their history from that which is purely adventitious, they discover certain principles of ancestral conduct, which they acknowledge as the causes that these institutions have flourished and descended to them; and in their future career, and all changes, reforms, and alterations, that they may deem expedient, they resolve that these principles shall be their guides and their instructors. By these examinations they become more deeply intimate with their national character; and on this increased knowledge, and on this alone, they hold it wise to act. This, my Lord, I apprehend to be the greatest amount of theory that ever enters into those political institutions, which, from their permanency, are alone entitled to the consideration of a philosophical statesman; and this moderate, prudent, sagacious, and eminently practical application of principles to conduct has ever been, in the old time, the illustrious characteristics of our English politicians.

WHO'S TO BLAME?
John Henry Newman

John Henry Newman, not yet Cardinal when in 1855 he published "Who's to Blame?" (his only directly political essay), wrote this defense of stable constitutions during the disasters of the Crimean War. Protection and Liberty, he says, are the great and contrary advantages of the social union; and it is not the British Constitution that should be blamed for the follies of the time. Sections 3 and 6 (extracted here) of this long essay are to be found in Newman's *Discussions and Arguments on Various Subjects;* in the Longmans edition of 1891 (London), on pp. 317–24, 339–44.

It is a common saying that political power is founded on opinion; this is true, if the word "opinion" be understood in the widest sense of which it is capable. A State depends and rests, not simply on force of arms, not on logic, not on anything short of the sentiment and will of those who are governed. This doctrine does not imply instability and change as inherent characteristics of a body politic. Since no one can put off his opinions in a moment, or by willing it, since those opinions may be instincts, principles, beliefs, convictions, since they may be self-evident, since they may be religious truths, it may be easily understood how a national polity, as being the creation and development of a multitude of men having all the same opinions, may stand of itself, and be most firmly established, and may be practically secure against reverse. And thus it is that countries become settled, with a definite form of social union, and an ascendancy of law and order; not as if that particular settlement, union, form, order, and law were self-sanctioned and self-supported, but because it is founded in the national mind, and maintained by the force of a living tradition. This, then, is what I mean by a State; and, being the production and outcome of a people, it is necessarily for the good of the people, and it has two main elements, power and liberty,—for without power there is no protection, and without liberty there is nothing to protect. The seat of power is the Government; the seat of liberty is the Constitution.

You will say that this implies that every State must have a Constitution; so I think it has, in the sense in which I have explained the word. As the governing power may be feeble and unready, so the check upon its arbitrary exercise may be partial and uncertain; it may be rude, circuitous, abrupt, or violent; it need not be scientifically recognized and defined; but there never has been, there never can be, in any political body, an instance of unmitigated absolutism. Human nature does not allow of it. In pure despotisms, the practical limitation of the ruler's power lies in his personal fears, in the use of the dagger or the bowstring. These expedients have been brought into exercise before now, both by our foes, the Russians, and, still more so, by our friends, the Turks. Nay, when the present war began, some of our self-made politicians put forward the pleasant suggestion that the Czar's assassination at the hands of his subjects, maddened by taxes and blockades, was a possible path to the triumph of the allies.

Such is the lawless remedy which nature finds for a lawless tyranny; and no one will deny that such a savage justice is national in certain states of Society, and has a traditional authority, and may in a certain sense be called Constitutional. As society becomes civilized, the checks on arbitrary power assume a form in accordance with a more cultivated morality. We have one curious specimen of a Constitutional principle, preserved to us in the Medo-Persian Empire. It was a wholesome and subtle provision, adopting the semblance of an abject servility suitable to the idea of a despotism, which proclaimed the judgment of the despot infallible, and his word irrevocable. Alexander felt what it was to do irrevocable acts in the physical order, when, in the plenitude of his sovereignty, he actually killed his friend in the banquet; and, as to the vulgar multitude, this same natural result, the remedy or penalty of reckless power, is expressed in the unpolite proverb, "Give a rogue rope enough, and he will hang himself." With a parallel significance, then, it was made a sacred principle among the Medo-Persians, which awed and sobered the monarch himself, from its surpassing inconvenience, that what he once had uttered had the force of fate. It was the punishment of his greatness, that, when Darius would have saved the prophet Daniel from the operation of a law, which the king had been flattered into promulgating, he could not do so.

A similar check upon the tyranny of power, assuming the character of veneration and homage, is the form and etiquette which is commonly thrown round a monarch. By irresistible custom, a ceremonial more or less stringent has been made almost to enter into his essential idea, for we know majesty without its externals is a jest; and, while to lay it aside is to relinquish the discriminating badge which is his claim upon the homage of his subjects, to observe it is to surrender himself manicled and fettered into their hands. It is said a king of Spain was roasted to death because the proper official was not found in time to wheel away his royal person from the fire. If etiquette hindered him from saving his own life, etiquette might also interpose an obstacle to his taking the life of another. If it was so necessary for Sancho Panza, governor of Barataria, to eat his dinner with the sanction of the court physician on every dish, other great functionaries of State might possibly be conditions of other indulgences on his part which were less reasonable and less imperative. As for our own most gracious Sovereign, she is honoured with the Constitutional prerogative that "the king can do no wrong"; that is, he can do no political act of his own mere will at all.

It is, then, no paradox to say that every State has in some sense a Constitution; that is, a set of traditions, depending, not on formal enactment, but on national acceptance, in one way or other restrictive of the ruler's power; though in one country more scientifically developed than another, or more distinctly recognized, or more skilfully and fully adapted to their end. There is a sort of analogy between the political and the physical sense of the word. A man of good constitution is one who has something more than life,—viz., a bodily soundness, organic and functional, which will bring him safely through hardships, or illnesses, or dissipations. On the other hand, no one is altogether without a constitution: to say he has nothing to fall back upon, when his health is tried, is almost to pronounce that his life is an accident, and that he may at any moment be carried off. And, in like manner, that must be pronounced no State, but a mere fortuitous collection of individuals, which has no unity stronger than despotism, or deeper than law.

I am not sure how far it bears upon the main proposition to which these remarks are meant to conduct us, but at least it will illustrate the general subject, if I ask your leave to specify, as regards the depository of political power, four Constitutional principles, distinct in kind from each other, which, among other parallel ones, have had an historical existence. If they must have names given them, they may be called respectively the principles of co-ordination, subordination, delegation, and participation.

1. As all political power implies unity, the word *co-ordination* may seem inconsistent with its essential idea: and yet there is a state of society, in which the limitation of despotism is by the voice of the people so unequivocally committed to an external authority, that we must speak of

it as the Constitution of such a State, in spite of the seeming anomaly. Such is the recognition of the authority of Religion, as existing in its own substantive institutions, external to the strictly political framework, which even in pagan countries has been at times successfully used to curb the extravagances of absolute power. Putting paganism aside, we find in the history both of Israel and of Judah the tyranny of kings brought within due limits by the priests and prophets, as by legitimate and self-independent authorities. The same has been the case in Christian times. The Church is essentially a popular institution, defending the cause and encouraging the talents of the lower classes, and interposing an external barrier in favour of high or low against the ambition and the rapacity of the temporal power. "If the Christian Church had not existed," says M. Guizot, "the whole world would have been abandoned to unmitigated material force." However, as the corrective principle is in this instance external to the State, though having its root internally in national opinion, it cannot, except improperly, be termed Constitutional.

2. Next I come to the principle of *subordination*, which has been commonly found in young, semi-barbarous states both in Europe and Asia, and has attained its most perfect form in what is called the Feudal System. It has had a military origin; and, after the pattern of an army, is carried out in an hierarchy of chiefs, one under the other, each of whom in consequence had direct jurisdiction only over a few. First came the *suzerain*, or lord paramount, who had the allegiance of a certain number of princes, dukes, counts, or even kings. These were his feudatories,—that is, they owed him certain military services, and held their respective territories of him. Their vassals, in turn, were the barons, each under his own prince or duke, and owing him a similar service. Under the barons were the soldiers, each settled down on his own portion of

land, with the peasants of the soil as his serfs, and with similar feudal duties to his own baron. A system like this furnished a most perfect expedient against absolutism. Power was distributed among many persons, without confusion or the chance of collision; and, while the paucity of vassals under one and the same rule gave less scope to tyrannical excesses, it created an effective public opinion, which is strongest when the relation between governor and governed is most intimate. Moreover, if any one were disposed to play the tyrant, there were several distinct parties in a condition to unite against him; the barons and lower class against the king, the king and the lower class against the barons. The barbarities of the middle ages have been associated in men's minds with this system; but, whatever they were, they surely took place in spite of it, not through it,—just as the anti-Catholic virulence of the present race of Englishmen is mitigated, not caused, by the British Constitution.

3. By the principle of *delegation*, I mean that according to which power is committed for a certain time to individuals, with a commensurate responsibility, to be met whenever that time has expired. Thus the Roman Dictator, elected on great emergencies, was autocrat during the term of his rule. Thus a commander of an army has unfettered powers to do what he will, while his command continues; or the captain of a ship; but afterwards his acts are open to inquiry, and, if so be, to animadversion. There are great advantages to a system like this; it is the mode of bringing out great men, and of working great measures. You choose the fittest man for each department; you frankly trust him, you heap powers upon him, you generously support him with your authority, you let him have his own way, you let him do his best. Afterwards you review his proceedings; you reward or censure him. Such, again, in fact, is with us the liberty of the press, censorship being simply unconstitutional, and the court of

law, the remedy against seditious, libellous, or demoralizing publications. Here, too, your advantage is great; you form public opinion, and you ascertain the national mind.

4. The very opposite to this is the principle of *participation*. It is that by which a People would leave nothing to its rulers, but has itself, or by its immediate instruments, a concurrent part in everything that is done. Acting on the notion that no one is to be trusted, even for a time, and that every act of its officials is to be jealously watched, it never commits power without embarrassing its exercise. Instead of making a venture for the transcendent, it keeps fast by a safe mediocrity. It rather trusts a dozen persons than one to do its work. This is the great principle of boards and officers, engaged in checking each other, with a second apparatus to check the first apparatus, and other functionaries to keep an eye on both of them,—Tom helping Jack, and Jack waiting for Bill, till the end is lost in the means. Such seems to have been the principle of the military duties performed by the Aulic Council in Germany, which virtually co-operated with Napoleon in his victories in that country. Such is the great principle of committees of taste, which have covered this fair land with architectural monstrosities. And as being closely allied to the principle of comprehension and compromise (a principle, necessary indeed, in some shape, but admitting of ruinous excess), it has had an influence on our national action in matters more serious than architecture or sculpture. And it has told directly upon our political efficiency.

The social union promises two great and contrary advantages, Protection and Liberty,—such protection as shall not interfere with liberty, and such liberty as shall not interfere with protection. How much a given nation can secure of the one, and how much of the other, depends on its peculiar circumstances. As there are small frontier territories, which find it their interest to throw themselves into the hands of some great neighbour, sacrificing their liberties as the price of purchasing safety from barbarians or rivals, so too there are countries which, in the absence of external danger, have abandoned themselves to the secure indulgence of freedom, to the jealous exercise of self-government, and to the scientific formation of a Constitution. And as, when liberty has to be surrendered for protection, the Horse must not be surprised if the Man whips or spurs him, so, when protection is neglected for the sake of liberty, he must not be surprised if he suffers from the horns of the Stag.

Protected by the sea, and gifted with a rare energy, self-possession, and imperturbability, the English people have been able to carry out self-government to its limits, and to absorb into its constitutional action many of those functions which are necessary for the protection of any country, and commonly belong to the Executive; and triumphing in their marvellous success they have thought no task too hard for them, and have from time to time attempted more than even England could accomplish. Such a crisis has come upon us now, and the Constitution has not been equal to the occasion. For a year past we have been conducting a great war on our Constitutional *routine*, and have not succeeded in it. If we continue that *routine*, we shall have more failures, with France or Russia (whichever you please) to profit by it:—if we change it, we change what after all is Constitutional. It is this dilemma which makes me wish for peace,—or else some *Deus è machinâ*, some one greater even than Wellington, to carry us through. We cannot depend upon Constitutional *routine*.

People abuse *routine*, and say that all the mischief which happens is the fault of *routine;*—but can they get out of *routine*, without getting out of the Constitution? That is the question. The fault of a *routine* Executive, I suppose, is not that the Executive always goes on in one way,—else, system is in fault,—but that it goes on in a bad way, or on a bad system. We must either change the sys-

tem, then,—our Constitutional system; or not find fault
with its *routine*, which is according to it. The present Parliamentary Committee of Inquiry, for instance, is either a
function and instrument of the *routine* system,—and
therefore is making bad worse,—or is not,—and then perhaps it is only the beginning of an infringement of the
Constitution. There may be Constitutional failures which
have no Constitutional remedies, unwilling as we may be
to allow it. They may be necessarily incidental to a free
self-governing people.

The Executive of a nation is the same all over the world,
being, in other words, the administration of the nation's
affairs; it differs in different countries, not in its nature and
office, nor in its ends, acts, or functions, but in its characteristics, as being prompt, direct, effective, or the contrary;
that is, as being strong or feeble. If it pursues its ends earnestly, performs its acts vigorously and discharges its
functions successfully, then it is a strong Executive; if
otherwise, it is feeble. Now, it is obvious, the more it is
concentrated, that is, the fewer are its springs, and the
simpler its mechanism, the stronger it is, because it has
least friction and loss of power; on the other hand, the
more numerous and widely dispersed its centres of action
are, and the more complex and circuitous their interaction, the more feeble it is. It is strongest, then, when it is
lodged in one man out of the whole nation; it is feeblest,
when it is lodged, by participation or conjointly, in every
man in it. How can we help what is self-evident? If the
English people lodge power in the many, not in the few,
what wonder that its operation is roundabout, clumsy,
slow, intermittent, and disappointing? And what is the
good of finding fault with the *routine*, if it is after all the
principle of the *routine*, or the system, or the Constitution, which causes the hitch? You cannot eat your cake
and have it; you cannot be at once a self-governing nation
and have a strong government. Recollect Wellington's
question in opposition to the Reform Bill, "How is the

King's Government to be carried on?" We are beginning to experience its full meaning.

A people so alive, so curious, so busy as the English, will be a power in themselves, independently of political arrangements; and will be on that very ground jealous of a rival, impatient of a master, and strong enough to cope with the one and to withstand the other. A government is their natural foe; they cannot do without it altogether, but they will have of it as little as they can. They will forbid the concentration of power; they will multiply its seats, complicate its acts, and make it safe by making it inefficient. They will take care that it is the worst-worked of all the many organizations which are found in their country. As despotisms keep their subjects in ignorance, lest they should rebel, so will a free people maim and cripple their government, lest it should tyrannize.

This is human nature; the more powerful a man is, the more jealous is he of other powers. Little men endure little men; but great men aim at a solitary grandeur. The English nation is intensely conscious of itself; it has seen, inspected, recognized, appreciated, and warranted itself. It has erected itself into a personality, under the style and title of John Bull. Most neighbourly is he when let alone; but irritable, when commanded or coerced. He wishes to form his own judgment in all matters, and to have everything proved to him; he dislikes the thought of generously placing his interests in the hands of others, he grudges to give up what he cannot really keep himself, and stickles for being at least a sleeping partner in transactions which are beyond him. He pays his people for their work, and is as proud of them, if they do it well, as a rich man of his tall footmen.

Policy might teach him a different course. If you want your work done well, which you cannot do yourself, find the best man, put it into his hand, and trust him implicitly. An Englishman is too sensible not to understand this in private matters; but in matters of State he is afraid of such a policy. He prefers the system of checks and counter-checks, the division of power, the imperative con-currence of disconnected officials, and his own supervision and revision,—the method of hitches, cross-purposes, col-lisions, deadlocks, to the experiment of treating his public servants as gentlemen. I am not quarrelling with what is inevitable in his system of self-government; I only say that he cannot expect his work done in the best style, if this is his mode of providing for it. Duplicate functionaries do but merge responsibility; and a jealous master is paid with formal, heartless service. Do your footmen love you across the gulf which you have fixed between them and you? and can you expect your store-keepers and harbour-masters at Balaklava not to serve you by rule and prece-dent, not to be rigid in their interpretation of your orders, and to commit themselves as little as they can, when you show no belief in their zeal, and have no mercy on their failures?

England, surely, is the paradise of little men, and the purgatory of great ones. May I never be a Minister of State or a Field-Marshal! I'd be an individual, self-respecting Briton, in my own private castle, with the *Times* to see the world by, and pen and paper to scribble off withal to some public print, and set the world right. Public men are only my *employés;* I use them as I think fit, and turn them off without warning. Aberdeen, Gladstone, Sidney Herbert, Newcastle, what are they muttering about services and ingratitude? were they not paid? hadn't they their regular quarter-day? Raglan, Burgoyne, Dundas,—I cannot recollect all the fellows' names,—can they merit aught? can they be profitable to me their lord and master? And so, having no tenderness or respect for their persons, their antecedents, or their age,—not caring that in fact they are serving me with all their strength, not asking whether, if they manage ill, it be not, perchance, because they are in the fetters of Constitutional red tape, which have weighed on their hearts and deadened their energies, till the hazard of failure and the fear of censure have quenched the spirit of daring, I think it becoming and generous,—during, not after their work, not when it is ended, but in the very agony of conflict,—to institute a formal process of inquiry into their demerits, not secret, not indulgent to their sense of honour, but in the hearing of all Europe, and amid the scorn of the world,—hitting down, knocking over, my workhouse apprentices, in order that they may get up again, and do my matters for me better.

How far these ways of managing a crisis can be amended in a self-governing Nation, it is most difficult to say. They are doubly deplorable, as being both unjust and impolitic. They are kind, neither to ourselves, nor to our public servants; and they so unpleasantly remind one of certain passages of Athenian history, as to suggest that perhaps they must ever more or less exist, except where a despotism, by simply extinguishing liberty, effectually prevents its abuse.

INTELLECTUAL CONSERVATISM
Walter Bagehot

Walter Bagehot (1826–1877), political essayist and economist, was a Liberal—yet a conservative one. In this short essay first published in *The Saturday Review* of April 26, 1856, Bagehot calls for a conservatism of reflection. See Barrington (ed.), *The Works and Life of Walter Bagehot* (London, 1915), Vol. IX, pp. 254–58.

At first sight it does not seem difficult to be a Conservative. The *status quo* is a plain creed—you have to discover nothing, and to invent nothing. Very heavy men have been able to say, *Nolumus leges Angliae mutari*.[1] Yet when the matter is more carefully looked at, we may see reason to change our opinion. Father Newman used to teach at Oxford that true opinions might become false because of the *manner* of holding them. He viewed—or seemed to view—truth as a succession of perpetual oscillations, like the negative and positive signs of an alternate series, in which you were constantly more or less denying or affirming the same proposition; and he deemed it certain that a person who unthinkingly rested at the beginning of the series, although he affirmed the truth, might really be farther from it than the thoughtful inquirer, some steps on, who actually denied it. The realisation—such was the creed in those days—which you gained in the process of inquiry, and which was on the point of bringing you to more effectual belief, was more than a compensation for the error of the momentary denial. And, whatever may be the inference from these severe metaphysics as to the mind of the inquirer himself, there is no doubt that, as to those around him, and among whom he desires to diffuse his belief, his power of so doing is directly proportioned to his realisation of what he holds, to his insight into its features and principles—to his mastery of it. The very plainness of the Conservative creed is here a difficulty. People in the country fancy they understand it. A rural dinner-party is rarely remarkable for adventurous conversation, but a good opinion-extractor will not have the least difficulty in eliciting from the average inhabitant—squire or rector—an admission that he knows what is, ought to be; and if you try to show an oddness in anything, the sentiment of society will be against you.

If we look at the political party, the traces of the fact are

---

1. "Let us not change England's laws." [R.K.]

evident. We do not speak of the leaders. The final cause of Mr. Disraeli is the "great Asian mystery" that is not yet revealed—his partiality for the Caucasian and ancient races has drawn him back to "the times before morality." When a man is infinitely above having an opinion, it would be illogical to inquire how he holds that opinion. But take the average follower of this great man—any member of the plain and simple party which resisted Catholic Emancipation, which clove to Protection, which hates Maynooth, which could not understand Sir Robert Peel—of how few can even the most partial friend maintain that they really know what they are holding—that they have sounded the complicated depths of English society—that they understand the traditional maxims which they repeat—that they appreciate and comprehend the nice adjustment of the institutions which they would risk their lives to uphold. Their plain intellect seems unequal, their simple temperament seems opposed, to so elaborate an investigation. Does not the very fact of their being led by Mr. Disraeli at once evince that they do not themselves possess that full mastery of principles which is necessary for their argumentative exposition—that they scarcely appreciate the moral thoughtfulness which accompanies careful and rational conviction?

Looking back to the past fortunes and history of this great party, we observe too great sentiments or feelings which have in great part—sometimes worthily, and sometimes unworthily—supplied the place of intellectual conviction. The first is the old cavalier feeling of loyalty—the belief that all existence is a *regium donum*[2]—that the very fact of doubt or inquiry is a misdeed—that the first duty of life is to accept that which is given, because of the king from whom it comes. Traces, few and faint, of this feeling may still be discerned among us, especially among those to whom a happy organisation gives a daily enjoyment. In

---

2. A royal gift. [R.K.]

old customs and ancient associations it would not be difficult to show the vestiges of this curious and often noble
feeling. It can, however, at least in that form, be only
looked on as a great thing of the past. When once the
change in politics is made from the one heaven-appointed
monarch to a divided, shifting, constitutional system, the
romance of royalty passes away—we are governed by a
cabinet, and who ever found sentiment for a managing
Committee?

Another feeling of a different kind is that which ani-
mates what they call on the Continent the Party of Order.
This is nothing more or less than fear. It finds expression
in excellent sentences as to the safety of society, the protection of the "results of ages"; but when you analyse it, it
simply comes to this,—that those who feel it dread that
their shop, their house, their life—not so much their physical life as their whole mode and sources of existence—
will be destroyed and cast away. The English Tory party,
at the end of the last century, shared largely in this sentiment. The French Revolution terrified mankind all
through the period which Arnold called "the misused
trial-time of modern Europe." The old cavalier feeling had
been gradually melting down into a simple acquiescence
in a comfortable existence. The whole life of the higher
classes—as it remains to us in books, so agreeable that we
can hardly blame what they describe—was a succession of
careless enjoyments. They accepted that which was given
them—and well they might accept it; for on few generations have the comforts of intellectual cultivation been bestowed in so large measure, and so unchecked by the cares
and evils which, in most days, as in ours, that cultivation
at once reveals. It is not necessary to say how the danger
was speedily revealed. The "French volcano," as Sir Ar-
chibald Alison always terms it, soon burst, and brought
on, among other effects, Lord Eldon—the man who objected to volcanoes. He was the chief of the party of order
at that time. The mass of the people lived in fear that any

alteration—anything touching the crust of outward existence—might bring on an eruption. Lord Eldon told them
it would bring on an eruption, but if they would keep him
Chancellor there should be no eruption. He held up the
Court of Chancery to mankind, and said, "While that
moves slowly you are safe—accelerate it and you are lost."
No generation more closely observed the signs which
were given them. The history of England for thirty years
is the history of a craven maintenance of misunderstood
institution. The consequence—the nearly fatal consequence—of this has been admitted by those most likely to
form a contrary judgment. "A few more drops," said the
Quarterly Review, "of *Eldonine,* and we should have had
the People's Charter." Nothing, indeed, could have been
more likely to foster an all-destroying Radicalism than the
consecutive omnipotence of the two most contemptible
conservatisms—first, of the careless enjoyment which
does not regard the evil of others—next, of a shrinking
terror when the possible personal consequences of that
evil are suddenly comprehended.

It would be very unjust to cast on any portion of the
Conservatives of the present day any greater share in
either of these reproaches. A spirit of earnestness has gone
out into society, which forbids the diffusion of reckless
and selfish enjoyment. The high-minded pluck of the
English gentleman detests the Conservatism of fear. But it
yet can hardly be said that we possess a Conservatism of
reflection—at least we do not possess it in the degree
which we should. How few, even of those who are most
anxious to claim the title, have a real mastery of the reasons, a real familiarity with the moral grounds—to say
nothing of the political consequences—of the existing
state of things! How few of the vaunted arguments which
are paraded before minds already convinced would be in
the face of an enemy—in the face of those who doubt!
How little toleration is there for the refinements of necessary reasoning—for the complexities of political investiga-

tion! How strong a tendency to exact a narrow consistency of result, in place of a statesmanlike consideration of problems—a wise and patent weighing of facts. Nor is this a mere party misfortune. It is not because we deem our institutions perfect that we regret the defects of the Conservative party—our grounds are national. To a great extent, every Liberal is now a Conservative. That moral and intellectual state—that predominance of the politically intelligent—that gradual training of the politically unintelligent—that unity of order and freedom which it is the aim of Liberalism to produce, already exists. Yet our institutions are daily assailed by the "uneasy classes"—by the lovers of correct bureaucracy, all-involving democracy, and quickly striking despotism. In the face of questioning classes, every unthinking Conservative endangers what he defends—he is a vexation to the Liberal, and a misfortune to his country.

Part Seven

〜〜〜〜〜〜〜〜〜〜〜〜〜〜

PROGRESS AND HUMAN FRAILTY

Two Yankees, Nathaniel Hawthorne (1804–1864) and Orestes Brownson (1803–1876), reminded the evangels of Progress in the nineteenth century that human nature and society are not perfectible. Hawthorne's allegorical tales and meditative novels are probably the most thoroughly studied body of American literature; but Brownson's abundant polemical writings were neglected from his death until recently.

EARTH'S HOLOCAUST
Nathaniel Hawthorne

As Baudelaire was to write, the only true progress consists in diminishing the marks of original sin. That, in substance, is the moral of Hawthorne's fantasy "Earth's Holocaust," included in his collection *Mosses from an Old Manse* (1846) and often reprinted.

Once upon a time—but whether in the time past or time to come is a matter of little or no moment—this wide world had become so overburdened with an accumulation of wornout trumpery that the inhabitants determined to rid themselves of it by a general bonfire. The site fixed upon at the representation of the insurance companies, and as being as central a spot as any other on the globe, was one of the broadest prairies of the west, where no human habitation would be endangered by the flames, and where a vast assemblage of spectators might commodiously admire the show. Having a taste for sights of this kind, and imagining, likewise, that the illumination of the bonfire might reveal some profundity of moral truth heretofore hidden in mist or darkness, I made it convenient to journey thither and be present. At my arrival, although the heap of condemned rubbish was as yet comparatively small, the torch had already been applied. Amid that boundless plain, in the dusk of the evening, like a far-off star alone in the firmament, there was merely visible one tremulous gleam, whence none could have anticipated so fierce a blaze as was destined to ensue. With every moment, however, there came foot travellers, women holding up their aprons, men on horseback, wheelbarrows, lumbering baggage wagons, and other vehicles, great and small, and from far and near, laden with articles that were judged fit for nothing but to be burned.

"What materials have been used to kindle the flame?" inquired I of a bystander; for I was desirous of knowing the whole process of the affair from beginning to end.

The person whom I addressed was a grave man, fifty years old or thereabout, who had evidently come thither as a looker on. He struck me immediately as having weighed for himself the true value of life and its circumstances, and therefore as feeling little personal interest in whatever judgment the world might form of them. Before answering my question, he looked me in the face by the kindling light of the fire.

"O, some very dry combustibles," replied he, "and extremely suitable to the purpose—no other, in fact, than yesterday's newspapers, last month's magazines, and last year's withered leaves. Here now comes some antiquated trash that will take fire like a handful of shavings."

As he spoke, some rough-looking men advanced to the verge of the bonfire, and threw in, as it appeared, all the rubbish of the herald's office—the blazonry of coat armor, the crests and devices of illustrious families, pedigrees that extended back, like lines of light, into the mist of the dark ages, together with stars, garters, and embroidered collars, each of which, as paltry a bawble as it might appear to the uninstructed eye, had once possessed vast significance, and was still, in truth, reckoned among the most precious of moral or material facts by the worshippers of the gorgeous past. Mingled with this confused heap, which was tossed into the flames by armfuls at once, were innumerable badges of knighthood, comprising those of all the European sovereignties, and Napoleon's decoration of the Legion of Honor, the ribbons of which were entangled with those of the ancient order of St. Louis. There, too, were the medals of our own Society of Cincinnati, by means of which, as history tells us, an order of hereditary knights came near being constituted out of the king quellers of the revolution. And besides, there were the patents of nobility of German counts and barons, Spanish grandees, and English peers, from the wormeaten instruments signed by William the Conqueror down to the brand new parchment of the latest lord who has received his honors from the fair hand of Victoria.

At sight of the dense volumes of smoke, mingled with vivid jets of flame, that gushed and eddied forth from this immense pile of earthly distinctions, the multitude of plebeian spectators set up a joyous shout, and clapped their hands with an emphasis that made the welkin echo. That was their moment of triumph, achieved, after long ages, over creatures of the same clay and the same spiritual infirmities, who had dared to assume the privileges due only to Heaven's better workmanship. But now there rushed towards the blazing heap a grayhaired man, of stately presence, wearing a coat, from the breast of which a star, or other badge of rank, seemed to have been forcibly wrenched away. He had not the tokens of intellectual power in his face; but still there was the demeanor, the habitual and almost native dignity, of one who had been born to the idea of his own social superiority, and had never felt it questioned till that moment.

"People," cried he, gazing at the ruin of what was dearest to his eyes with grief and wonder, but nevertheless with a degree of stateliness,—"people, what have you done? This fire is consuming all that marked your advance from barbarism, or that could have prevented your relapse thither. We, the men of the privileged orders, were those who kept alive from age to age the old chivalrous spirit; the gentle and generous thought; the higher, the purer, the more refined and delicate life. With the nobles, too, you cast off the poet, the painter, the sculptor—all the beautiful arts; for we were their patrons, and created the atmosphere in which they flourish. In abolishing the majestic distinctions of rank, society loses not only its grace, but its steadfastness—"

More he would doubtless have spoken; but here there arose an outcry, sportive, contemptuous, and indignant, that altogether drowned the appeal of the fallen nobleman, insomuch that, casting one look of despair at his own half-burned pedigree, he shrunk back into the crowd, glad to shelter himself under his new-found insignificance.

"Let him thank his stars that we have not flung him into the same fire!" shouted a rude figure, spurning the embers with his foot. "And henceforth let no man dare to show a piece of musty parchment as his warrant for lording it over his fellows. If he have strength of arm, well and good; it is one species of superiority. If he have wit, wisdom, courage, force of character, let these attributes do for him what they may; but from this day forward no mortal must hope for place and consideration by reckoning up the mouldy bones of his ancestors. That nonsense is done away."

"And in good time," remarked the grave observer by my side, in a low voice, however, "if no worse nonsense comes in its place; but, at all events, this species of nonsense has fairly lived out its life."

There was little space to muse or moralize over the embers of this time-honored rubbish; for, before it was half burned out, there came another multitude from beyond the sea, bearing the purple robes of royalty, and the crowns, globes, and sceptres of emperors and kings. All these had been condemned as useless bawbles, playthings at best, fit only for the infancy of the world or rods to govern and chastise it in its nonage, but with which universal manhood at its full-grown stature could no longer brook to be insulted. Into such contempt had these regal insignia now fallen that the gilded crown and tinselled robes of the player king from Drury Lane Theatre had been thrown in among the rest, doubtless as a mockery of his brother monarchs on the great stage of the world. It was a strange sight to discern the crown jewels of England glowing and flashing in the midst of the fire. Some of them had been delivered down from the time of the Saxon princes; others were purchased with vast revenues, or perchance ravished from the dead brows of the native potentates of Hindostan; and the whole now blazed with a dazzling lustre, as if a star had fallen in that spot and been shattered into fragments. The splendor of the ruined monarchy had no reflection save in those inestimable precious stones. But enough on this subject. It were but tedious to describe how the Emperor of Austria's mantle was converted to tinder, and how the posts and pillars of the French throne became a heap of coals, which it was impossible to distinguish from those of any other wood. Let me add, however, that I noticed one of the exiled Poles stirring up the bonfire with the Czar of Russia's sceptre, which he afterwards flung into the flames.

"The smell of singed garments is quite intolerable here," observed my new acquaintance, as the breeze enveloped us in the smoke of a royal wardrobe. "Let us get to windward and see what they are doing on the other side of the bonfire."

We accordingly passed around, and were just in time to witness the arrival of a vast procession of Washingtonians,—as the votaries of temperance call themselves nowadays,—accompanied by thousands of the Irish disciples of Father Mathew, with that great apostle at their head. They brought a rich contribution to the bonfire— being nothing less than all the hogsheads and barrels of liquor in the world, which they rolled before them across the prairie.

"Now, my children," cried Father Mathew, when they reached the verge of the fire, "one shove more, and the work is done. And now let us stand off and see Satan deal with his own liquor."

Accordingly, having placed their wooden vessels within reach of the flames, the procession stood off at a safe distance, and soon beheld them burst into a blaze that reached the clouds and threatened to set the sky itself on fire. And well it might; for here was the whole world's stock of spirituous liquors, which, instead of kindling a frenzied light in the eyes of individual topers as of yore, soared upwards with a bewildering gleam that startled all mankind. It was the aggregate of that fierce fire which would otherwise have scorched the hearts of millions. Meantime numberless bottles of precious wine were flung into the blaze, which lapped up the contents as if it loved them, and grew, like other drunkards, the merrier and fiercer for what it quaffed. Never again will the insatiable thirst of the fire fiend be so pampered. Here were the treasures of famous bon vivants—liquors that had been tossed on ocean, and mellowed in the sun, and hoarded long in the recesses of the earth—the pale, the gold, the ruddy juice of whatever vineyards were most delicate— the entire vintage of Tokay—all mingling in one stream with the vile fluids of the common pothouse, and contributing to heighten the selfsame blaze. And while it rose in a gigantic spire that seemed to wave against the arch of the firmament and combine itself with the light of stars, the multitude gave a shout as if the broad earth were exulting in its deliverance from the curse of ages.

But the joy was not universal. Many deemed that human life would be gloomier than ever when that brief illumination should sink down. While the reformers were at work I overheard muttered expostulations from several respectable gentlemen with red noses and wearing gouty shoes; and a ragged worthy, whose face looked like a hearth where the fire is burned out, now expressed his discontent more openly and boldly.

"What is this world good for," said the last toper, "now that we can never be jolly any more? What is to comfort the poor man in sorrow and perplexity? How is he to keep his heart warm against the cold winds of this cheerless earth? And what do you propose to give him in exchange for the solace that you take away? How are old friends to sit together by the fireside without a cheerful glass between them? A plague upon your reformation! It is a sad world, a cold world, a selfish world, a low world, not worth an honest fellow's living in, now that good fellowship is gone forever!"

This harangue excited great mirth among the bystanders; but, preposterous as was the sentiment, I could not help commiserating the forlorn condition of the last toper, whose boon companions had dwindled away from his side, leaving the poor fellow without a soul to countenance him in sipping his liquor, nor indeed any liquor to sip. Not that this was quite the true state of the case; for I had observed him at a critical moment filch a bottle of fourth-proof brandy that fell beside the bonfire and hide it in his pocket.

The spirituous and fermented liquors being thus disposed of, the zeal of the reformers next induced them to replenish the fire with all the boxes of tea and bags of coffee in the world. And now came the planters of Virginia, bringing their crops of tobacco. These, being cast upon the heap of inutility, aggregated it to the size of a mountain, and incensed the atmosphere with such potent fragrance that methought we should never draw pure breath again. The present sacrifice seemed to startle the lovers of the weed more than any that they had hitherto witnessed.

"Well, they've put my pipe out," said an old gentleman, flinging it into the flames in a pet. "What is this world coming to? Every thing rich and racy—all the spice of life—is to be condemned as useless. Now that they have kindled the bonfire, if these nonsensical reformers would fling themselves into it, all would be well enough!"

"Be patient," responded a stanch conservative; "it will come to that in the end. They will first fling us in, and finally themselves."

From the general and systematic measures of reform I now turned to consider the individual contributions to this memorable bonfire. In many instances these were of a very amusing character. One poor fellow threw in his empty purse, and another a bundle of counterfeit or insolvable bank notes. Fashionable ladies threw in their last season's bonnets, together with heaps of ribbons, yellow lace, and much other half-worn milliner's ware, all of which proved even more evanescent in the fire than it had been in the fashion. A multitude of lovers of both sexes— discarded maids or bachelors and couples mutually weary of one another—tossed in bundles of perfumed letters and enamored sonnets. A hack politician, being deprived of bread by the loss of office, threw in his teeth, which happened to be false ones. The Rev. Sidney Smith—having voyaged across the Atlantic for that sole purpose—came up to the bonfire with a bitter grin and threw in certain repudiated bonds, fortified though they were with the broad seal of a sovereign state. A little boy of five years old, in the premature manliness of the present epoch, threw in his playthings; a college graduate his diploma; an apothecary, ruined by the spread of homœopathy, his whole stock of drugs and medicines; a physician his library; a parson his old sermons; and a fine gentleman of the old school his code of manners, which he had formerly written down for the benefit of the next generation. A widow, resolving on a second marriage, slyly threw in her dead husband's miniature. A young man, jilted by his mistress, would willingly have flung his own desperate heart into the flames, but could find no means to wrench it out of his bosom. An American author, whose works were neglected by the public, threw his pen and paper into the bonfire and betook himself to some less discouraging occupation. It somewhat startled me to overhear a number of ladies, highly respectable in appearance, proposing to fling their gowns and petticoats into the flames, and assume the garb, together with the manners, duties, offices, and responsibilities, of the opposite sex.

What favor was accorded to this scheme I am unable to say, my attention being suddenly drawn to a poor, deceived, and half-delirious girl, who, exclaiming that she was the most worthless thing alive or dead, attempted to cast herself into the fire amid all that wrecked and broken trumpery of the world. A good man, however, ran to her rescue.

"Patience, my poor girl!" said he, as he drew her back from the fierce embrace of the destroying angel. "Be patient, and abide Heaven's will. So long as you possess a living soul, all may be restored to its first freshness. These things of matter and creations of human fantasy are fit for nothing but to be burned when once they have had their day; but your day is eternity!"

"Yes," said the wretched girl, whose frenzy seemed now to have sunk down into deep despondency,—"yes, and the sunshine is blotted out of it!"

It was now rumored among the spectators that all the weapons and munitions of war were to be thrown into the bonfire with the exception of the world's stock of gunpowder, which as the safest mode of disposing of it, had already been drowned in the sea. This intelligence seemed to awaken great diversity of opinion. The hopeful philanthropist esteemed it a token that the millennium was already come; while persons of another stamp, in whose view mankind was a breed of bulldogs, prophesied that all the old stoutness, fervor, nobleness, generosity, and magnanimity of the race would disappear—these qualities, as they affirmed, requiring blood for their nourishment. They comforted themselves, however, in the belief that the proposed abolition of war was impracticable for any length of time together.

Be that as it might, numberless great guns, whose thunder had long been the voice of battle,—the artillery of the

Armada, the battering trains of Marlborough, and the adverse cannon of Napoleon and Wellington,—were trundled into the midst of the fire. By the continual addition of dry combustibles, it had now waxed so intense that neither brass nor iron could withstand it. It was wonderful to behold how these terrible instruments of slaughter melted away like playthings of wax. Then the armies of the earth wheeled around the mighty furnace, with their military music playing triumphant marches, and flung in their muskets and swords. The standard bearers, likewise, cast one look upward at their banners, all tattered with shot holes and inscribed with the names of victorious fields; and, giving them a last flourish on the breeze, they lowered them into the flame, which snatched them upward in its rush towards the clouds. This ceremony being over, the world was left without a single weapon in its hands, except possibly a few old king's arms and rusty swords and other trophies of the revolution in some of our state armories. And now the drums were beaten and the trumpets brayed all together, as a prelude to the proclamation of universal and eternal peace and the announcement that glory was no longer to be won by blood, but that it would henceforth be the contention of the human race to work out the greatest mutual good, and that beneficence, in the future annals of the earth, would claim the praise of valor. The blessed tidings were accordingly promulgated, and caused infinite rejoicings among those who had stood aghast at the horror and absurdity of war.

But I saw a grim smile pass over the seared visage of a stately old commander,—by his warworn figure and rich military dress he might have been one of Napoleon's famous marshals,—who, with the rest of the world's soldiery, had just flung away the sword that had been familiar to his right hand for half a century.

"Ay! ay!" grumbled he. "Let them proclaim what they please; but, in the end, we shall find that all this foolery has only made more work for the armorers and cannon founders."

"Why, sir," exclaimed I, in astonishment, "do you imagine that the human race will ever so far return on the steps of its past madness as to weld another sword or cast another cannon?"

"There will be no need," observed, with a sneer, one who neither felt benevolence nor had faith in it. "When Cain wished to slay his brother, he was at no loss for a weapon."

"We shall see," replied the veteran commander. "If I am mistaken, so much the better; but in my opinion, without pretending to philosophize about the matter, the necessity of war lies far deeper than these honest gentlemen suppose. What! is there a field for all the petty disputes of individuals? and shall there be no great law court for the settlement of national difficulties? The battle field is the only court where such suits can be tried."

"You forget, general," rejoined I, "that, in this advanced stage of civilization, Reason and Philanthropy combined will constitute just such a tribunal as is requisite."

"Ah, I had forgotten that, indeed!" said the old warrior, as he limped away.

The fire was now to be replenished with materials that had hitherto been considered of even greater importance to the well being of society than the warlike munitions which we had already seen consumed. A body of reformers had travelled all over the earth in quest of the machinery by which the different nations were accustomed to inflict the punishment of death. A shudder passed through the multitude as these ghastly emblems were dragged forward. Even the flames seemed at first to shrink away, displaying the shape and murderous contrivance of each in a full blaze of light, which of itself was sufficient to convince mankind of the long and deadly error of human law. Those old implements of cruelty; those horrible monsters of mechanism; those inventions which it seemed to demand something worse than man's natural heart to contrive, and which had lurked in the dusky nooks of ancient prisons, the subject of terror-stricken legend,—were now brought forth to view. Headsmen's axes, with the rust of noble and royal blood upon them, and a vast collection of halters that had choked the breath of plebeian victims, were thrown in together. A shout greeted the arrival of the guillotine, which was thrust forward on the same wheels that had borne it from one to another of the bloodstained streets of Paris. But the loudest roar of applause went up, telling the distant sky of the triumph of the earth's redemption, when the gallows made its appearance. An ill-looking fellow, however, rushed forward, and, putting himself in the path of the reformers, bellowed hoarsely, and fought with brute fury to stay their progress.

It was little matter of surprise, perhaps, that the executioner should thus do his best to vindicate and uphold the machinery by which he himself had his livelihood and worthier individuals their death; but it deserved special note that men of a far different sphere—even of that consecrated class in whose guardianship the world is apt to trust its benevolence—were found to take the hangman's view of the question.

"Stay, my brethren!" cried one of them. "You are misled by a false philanthropy; you know not what you do. The gallows is a Heaven-ordained instrument. Bear it back, then, reverently, and set it up in its old place, else the world will fall to speedy ruin and desolation!"

"Onward! onward!" shouted a leader in the reform. "Into the flames with the accursed instrument of man's bloody policy! How can human law inculcate benevolence and love while it persists in setting up the gallows as its chief symbol? One heave more, good friends, and the world will be redeemed from its greatest error."

A thousand hands, that nevertheless loathed the touch,

now lent their assistance, and thrust the ominous burden far, far into the centre of the raging furnace. There its fatal and abhorred image was beheld, first black, then a red coal, then ashes.

"That was well done!" exclaimed I.

"Yes, it was well done," replied, but with less enthusiasm than I expected, the thoughtful observer who was still at my side; "well done, if the world be good enough for the measure. Death, however, is an idea that cannot easily be dispensed with in any condition between the primal innocence and that other purity and perfection which perchance we are destined to attain after travelling round the full circle; but, at all events, it is well that the experiment should now be tried."

"Too cold! too cold!" impatiently exclaimed the young and ardent leader in this triumph. "Let the heart have its voice here as well as the intellect. And as for ripeness, and as for progress, let mankind always do the highest, kindest, noblest thing that, at any given period it has attained the perception of; and surely that thing cannot be wrong nor wrongly timed."

I know not whether it were the excitement of the scene, or whether the good people around the bonfire were really growing more enlightened every instant; but they now proceeded to measures in the full length of which I was hardly prepared to keep them company. For instance, some threw their marriage certificates into the flames, and declared themselves candidates for a higher, holier, and more comprehensive union than that which had subsisted from the birth of time under the form of the connubial tie. Others hastened to the vaults of banks and to the coffers of the rich—all of which were open to the first comer on this fated occasion—and brought entire bales of paper money to enliven the blaze and tons of coin to be melted down by its intensity. Henceforth, they said, universal benevolence, uncoined and exhaustless, was to be the golden currency of the world. At this intelligence the bankers and speculators in the stocks grew pale, and a pickpocket, who had reaped a rich harvest among the crowd, fell down in a deadly fainting fit. A few men of business burned their day books and legers, the notes and obligations of their creditors, and all other evidences of debts due to themselves; while perhaps a somewhat larger number satisfied their zeal for reform with the sacrifice of any uncomfortable recollection of their own indebtment. There was then a cry that the period was arrived when the title deeds of landed property should be given to the flames, and the whole soil of the earth revert to the public, from whom it had been wrongfully abstracted and most unequally distributed among individuals. Another party demanded that all written constitutions, set forms of government, legislative acts, statute books, and every thing else on which human invention had endeavored to stamp its arbitrary laws, should at once be destroyed, leaving the consummated world as free as the man first created.

Whether any ultimate action was taken with regard to these propositions is beyond my knowledge; for, just then, some matters were in progress that concerned my sympathies more nearly.

"See! see! What heaps of books and pamphlets!" cried a fellow, who did not seem to be a lover of literature. "Now we shall have a glorious blaze!"

"That's just the thing!" said a modern philosopher. "Now we shall get rid of the weight of dead men's thought, which has hitherto pressd so heavily on the living intellect that it has been incompetent to any effectual self-exertion. Well done, my lads! Into the fire with them! Now you are enlightening the world indeed!"

"But what is to become of the trade?" cried a frantic bookseller.

"O, by all means, let them accompany their merchandise," coolly observed an author. "It will be a noble funeral pile!"

The truth was, that the human race had now reached a

stage of progress so far beyond what the wisest and wit-
tiest men of former ages had ever dreamed of that it would
have been a manifest absurdity to allow the earth to be
any longer encumbered with their poor achievements in
the literary line. Accordingly a thorough and searching
investigation had swept the booksellers' shops, hawkers'
stands, public and private libraries, and even the little
book shelf by the country fireside, and had brought the
world's entire mass of printed paper, bound or in sheets,
to swell the already mountain bulk of our illustrious bonfire. Thick, heavy folios, containing the labors of lexicog-
raphers, commentators, and encyclopedists, were flung in,
and, falling among the embers with a leaden thump,
smouldered away to ashes like rotten wood. The small,
richly gilt French tomes of the last age, and the hundred
volumes of Voltaire among them, went off in a brilliant
shower of sparkles and little jets of flame; while the current literature of the same nation burned red and blue, and
threw an infernal light over the visages of the spectators,
converting them all to the aspect of partycolored fiends. A
collection of German stories emitted a scent of brimstone.
The English standard authors made excellent fuel, generally exhibiting the properties of sound oak logs. Milton's
works, in particular, sent up a powerful blaze, gradually
reddening into a coal, which promised to endure longer
than almost any other material of the pile. From Shakespeare there gushed a flame of such marvellous splendor
that men shaded their eyes as against the sun's meridian
glory; nor even when the works of his own elucidators
were flung upon him did he cease to flash forth a dazzling
radiance from beneath the ponderous heap. It is my belief
that he is still blazing as fervidly as ever.

"Could a poet but light a lamp at that glorious flame,"
remarked I, "he might then consume the midnight oil to
some good purpose."

"That is the very thing which modern poets have been
too apt to do, or at least to attempt," answered a critic.

"The chief benefit to be expected from this conflagration of past literature undoubtedly is, that writers will henceforth be compelled to light their lamps at the sun or stars."

"If they can reach so high," said I; "but that task requires a giant, who may afterwards distribute the light among inferior men. It is not every one that can steal the fire from heaven like Prometheus; but, when once he had done the deed, a thousand hearths were kindled by it."

It amazed me much to observe how indefinite was the proportion between the physical mass of any given author and the property of brilliant and long-continued combustion. For instance, there was not a quarto volume of the last century—nor, indeed, of the present—that could compete in that particular with a child's little gilt-covered book, containing Mother Goose's Melodies. The Life and Death of Tom Thumb outlasted the biography of Marlborough. An epic, indeed a dozen of them, was converted to white ashes before the single sheet of an old ballad was half consumed. In more than one case, too, when volumes of applauded verse proved incapable of any thing better than a stifling smoke, an unregarded ditty of some nameles bard—perchance in the corner of a newspaper—soared up among the stars with a flame as brilliant as their own. Speaking of the properties of flame, methought Shelley's poetry emitted a purer light than almost any other productions of his day, contrasting beautifully with the fitful and lurid gleams and gushes of black vapor that flashed and eddied from the volumes of Lord Byron. As for Tom Moore, some of his songs diffused an odor like a burning pastil.

I felt particular interest in watching the combustion of American authors, and scrupulously noted by my watch the precise number of moments that changed most of them from shabbily-printed books to indistinguishable ashes. It would be invidious, however, if not perilous, to betray these awful secrets; so that I shall content myself with observing that it was not invariably the writer most frequent in the public mouth that made the most splendid appearance in the bonfire. I especially remember that a great deal of excellent inflammability was exhibited in a thin volume of poems by Ellery Channing; although, to speak the truth, there were certain portions that hissed and spluttered in a very disagreeable fashion. A curious phenomenon occurred in reference to several writers, native as well as foreign. Their books, though of highly respectable figure, instead of bursting into a blaze or even smouldering out their substance in smoke, suddenly melted away in a manner that proved them to be ice.

If it be no lack of modesty to mention my own works, it must here be confessed that I looked for them with fatherly interest, but in vain. Too probably they were changed to vapor by the first action of the heat; at best, I can only hope that, in their quiet way, they contributed a glimmering spark or two to the splendor of the evening.

"Alas! and woe is me!" thus bemoaned himself a heavy-looking gentleman in green spectacles. "The world is utterly ruined, and there is nothing to live for any longer. The business of my life is snatched from me. Not a volume to be had for love or money!"

"This," remarked the sedate observer beside me, "is a bookworm—one of those men who are born to gnaw dead thoughts. His clothes, you see, are covered with the dust of libraries. He has no inward fountain of ideas; and, in good earnest, now that the old stock is abolished, I do not see what is to become of the poor fellow. Have you no word of comfort for him?"

"My dear sir," said I to the desperate bookworm, "is not Nature better than a book? Is not the human heart deeper than any system of philosophy? Is not life replete with more instruction than past observers have found it possible to write down in maxims? Be of good cheer. The great book of Time is still spread wide open before us; and, if we read it aright, it will be to us a volume of eternal truth."

"O, my books, my books, my precious printed books!" reiterated the forlorn bookworm. "My only reality was a bound volume; and now they will not leave me even a shadowy pamphlet!"

In fact, the last remnant of the literature of all the ages was now descending upon the blazing heap in the shape of a cloud of pamphlets from the press of the New World. These likewise were consumed in the twinkling of an eye, leaving the earth, for the first time since the days of Cadmus, free from the plague of letters—an enviable field for the authors of the next generation.

"Well, and does any thing remain to be done?" inquired I somewhat anxiously. "Unless we set fire to the earth itself, and then leap boldly off into infinite space, I know not that we can carry reform to any farther point."

"You are vastly mistaken, my good friend," said the observer. "Believe me, the fire will not be allowed to settle down without the addition of fuel that will startle many persons who have lent a willing hand thus far."

Nevertheless there appeared to be a relaxation of effort for a little time, during which, probably, the leaders of the movement were considering what should be done next. In the interval, a philosopher threw his theory into the flames—a sacrifice which, by those who knew how to estimate it, was pronounced the most remarkable that had yet been made. The combustion, however, was by no means brilliant. Some indefatigable people, scorning to take a moment's ease, now employed themselves in collecting all the withered leaves and fallen boughs of the forest, and thereby recruited the bonfire to a greater height than ever. But this was mere by-play.

"Here comes the fresh fuel that I spoke of," said my companion.

To my astonishment, the persons who now advanced into the vacant space around the mountain fire bore surplices and other priestly garments, mitres, crosiers, and a confusion of Popish and Protestant emblems, with which it seemed their purpose to consummate the great act of faith. Crosses from the spires of old cathedrals were cast upon the heap with as little remorse as if the reverence of centuries, passing in long array beneath the lofty towers, had not looked up to them as the holiest of symbols. The font in which infants were consecrated to God, the sacramental vessels whence piety received the hallowed draught, were given to the same destruction. Perhaps it most nearly touched my heart to see among these devoted relics fragments of the humble communion tables and undecorated pulpits which I recognized as having been torn from the meeting houses of New England. Those simple edifices might have been permitted to retain all of sacred embellishment that their Puritan founders had bestowed, even though the mighty structure of St. Peter's had sent its spoils to the fire of this terrible sacrifice. Yet I felt that these were but the externals of religion, and might most safely be relinquished by spirits that best knew their deep significance.

"All is well," said I cheerfully. "The woodpaths shall be the aisles of our cathedral—the firmament itself shall be its ceiling. What needs an earthly roof between the Deity and his worshippers? Our faith can well afford to lose all the drapery that even the holiest men have thrown around it, and be only the more sublime in its simplicity."

"True," said my companion; "but will they pause here?"

The doubt implied in his question was well founded. In the general destruction of books already described, a holy volume, that stood apart from the catalogue of human literature, and yet, in one sense, was at its head, had been spared. But the Titan of innovation—angel or fiend, double in his nature, and capable of deeds befitting both characters,—at first shaking down only the old and rotten shapes of things, had now, as it appeared, laid his terrible hand upon the main pillars which supported the whole edifice of our moral and spiritual state. The inhabitants of the earth had grown too enlightened to define their faith within a form of words or to limit the spiritual by any analogy to our material existence. Truths which the heavens trembled at were now but a fable of the world's infancy. Therefore, as the final sacrifice of human error, what else remained to be thrown upon the embers of that awful pile except the book which, though a celestial revelation to past ages, was but a voice from a lower sphere as regarded the present race of man? It was done! Upon the blazing heap of falsehood and wornout truth—things that the earth had never needed, or had ceased to need, or had grown childishly weary of—fell the ponderous church Bible, the great old volume that had lain so long on the cushion of the pulpit, and whence the pastor's solemn voice had given holy utterance on so many a Sabbath day. There, likewise, fell the family Bible, which the long-buried patriarch had read to his children—in prosperity or sorrow, by the fireside and in the summer shade of trees—and had bequeathed downward as the heirloom of generations. There fell the bosom Bible, the little volume that had been the soul's friend of some sorely-tried child of dust, who thence took courage, whether his trial were for life or death, steadfastly confronting both in the strong assurance of immortality.

All these were flung into the fierce and riotous blaze; and then a mighty wind came roaring across the plain with a desolate howl, as if it were the angry lamentation of the earth for the loss of heaven's sunshine; and it shook the gigantic pyramid of flame and scattered the cinders of half-consumed abominations around upon the spectators.

"This is terrible!" said I, feeling that my cheek grew pale, and seeing a like change in the visages about me.

"Be of good courage yet," answered the man with whom I had so often spoken. He continued to gaze steadily at the spectacle with a singular calmness, as if it concerned him merely as an observer. "Be of good courage, nor yet exult too much; for there is far less both of good and evil in the effect of this bonfire than the world might be willing to believe."

"How can that be? exclaimed I, impatiently. "Has it not consumed every thing? Has it not swallowed up or melted down every human or divine appendage of our mortal state that had substance enough to be acted on by fire? Will there be any thing left us to-morrow morning better or worse than a heap of embers and ashes?"

"Assuredly there will," said my grave friend. "Come hither to-morrow morning, or whenever the combustible portion of the pile shall be quite burned out, and you will find among the ashes every thing really valuable that you have cast into the flames. Trust me, the world of to-morrow will again enrich itself with the gold and diamonds which have been cast off by the world of to-day. Not a truth is destroyed nor buried so deep among the ashes but it will be raked up at last."

This was a strange assurance. Yet I felt inclined to credit it, the more especially as I beheld among the wallowing flames a copy of the Holy Scriptures, the pages of which, instead of being blackened into tinder, only assumed a more dazzling whiteness as the finger marks of human imperfection were purified away. Certain marginal notes and commentaries, it is true, yielded to the intensity of the fiery test, but without detriment to the smallest syllable that had flamed from the pen of inspiration.

"Yes; there is the proof of what you say," answered I, turning to the observer; "but if only what is evil can feel the action of the fire, then, surely, the conflagration has been of inestimable utility. Yet, if I understand aright, you intimate a doubt whether the world's expectation of benefit would be realized by it."

"Listen to the talk of these worthies," said he, pointing to a group in front of the blazing pile; "possibly they may teach you something useful without intending it."

The persons whom he indicated consisted of that brutal

and most earthy figure who had stood forth so furiously in defence of the gallows,—the hangman, in short,—together with the last thief and the last murderer, all three of whom were clustered about the last toper. The latter was liberally passing the brandy bottle, which he had rescued from the general destruction of wines and spirits. This little convivial party seemed at the lowest pitch of despondency, as considering that the purified world must needs be utterly unlike the sphere that they had hitherto known, and therefore but a strange and desolate abode for gentlemen of their kidney.

"The best counsel for all of us is," remarked the hangman, "that, as soon as we have finished the last drop of liquor, I help you, my three friends, to a comfortable end upon the nearest tree, and then hang myself on the same bough. This is no world for us any longer."

"Poh, poh, my good fellows!" said a dark-complexioned personage who now joined the group—his complexion was indeed fearfully dark, and his eyes glowed with a redder light than that of the bonfire; "be not so cast down, my dear friends; you shall see good days yet. There is one thing that these wiseacres have forgotten to throw into the fire, and without which all the rest of the conflagration is just nothing at all; yes, though they had burned the earth itself to a cinder."

"And what may that be?" eagerly demanded the last murderer.

"What but the human heart itself?" said the dark-visaged stranger, with a portentous grin. "And, unless they hit upon some method of purifying that foul cavern, forth from it will reissue all the shapes of wrong and misery—the same old shapes or worse ones—which they have taken such a vast deal of trouble to consume to ashes. I have stood by this livelong night and laughed in my sleeve at the whole business. O, take my word for it, it will be the old world yet!"

This brief conversation supplied me with a theme for

lengthened thought. How sad a truth, if true it were, that man's agelong endeavor for perfection had served only to render him the mockery of the evil principle, from the fatal circumstance of an error at the very root of the matter! The heart, the heart,—there was the little yet boundless sphere wherein existed the original wrong of which the crime and misery of this outward world were merely types. Purify that inward sphere, and the many shapes of evil that haunt the outward, and which now seem almost our only realities, will turn to shadowy phantoms and vanish of their own accord; but if we go no deeper than the intellect, and strive, with merely that feeble instrument, to discern and rectify what is wrong, our whole accomplishment will be a dream, so unsubstantial that it matters little whether the bonfire, which I have so faithfully described, were what we choose to call a real event and a flame that would scorch the finger, or only a phosphoric radiance and a parable of my own brain.

LIBERALISM AND PROGRESS
Orestes Brownson

Written while the result of the Civil War still was in question, this essay (first published in *Brownson's Quarterly Review* for October, 1864) is a good example of Brownson's resolute candor. Here Brownson makes a penetrating analysis of American conservatism, and flays the liberal tendency to create wants beyond the possibility of satisfaction. He protests that constitutions founded merely upon the consent of the governed lack that transcendent sanction which is the source of justice and of peace. A supporter of the Union, he does not hesitate, for all that, to declare his preference for Southern society and his detestation of the gospel of material success and of radical notions of human progress. Brownson looked upon the terrible struggle between North and South as a contest between just authority and anarchic impulse—not a doctrinaire crusade of democratic ideologues against a conservative society. This essay is included in Brownson's *Works* (1882–1887), Vol. XX; and in Kirk (ed.), *Orestes Brownson: Select Essays* (Chicago, 1955), pp. 161–90.

This work, which has not yet found a publisher, and which exists only in the author's autograph, has come honestly into our possession, with permissions to make such use of it as we see proper.[1] The author seems to have been only a civilian general, as his name does not appear in the army Register, and we suspect that he has never served in any army, hardly in a band of filibusters. From his English, and his inability to see any thing in our habits or manners, in our civil or military service, to commend, we should judge him some disappointed foreigner, who at the breaking out of our civil war, had offered his services to the government and had them refused. He regards himself as qualified for any post from pathmaster to president, or from corporal to commander-in-chief of the armies of the United States, which makes against the theory that he is a foreigner, and would indicate that he is a native, and "to the manner born." He finds every thing amiss with us, and that things can come right only by his being placed at the head of our civil and military affairs.

The general (?) is very profuse in his military criticisms, and shows a very hostile spirit towards our military academy. He blames the government for intrusting im-

---

1. *Tendencies of Modern Society, with Remarks on the American People, Government, and Military Administration.* By General Croaker. MS.

portant commands to men who have been educated at West Point, and insists that if it will appoint Americans to the commands of its armies, it should appoint civilians, who have not been narrowed, belittled, and cramped by the pedantry of a military education. He prefers instinct to study, and the happy inspirations of ignorance to the calculations of science. He thinks our true course is to invite hither the military adventurers so numerous on the continent of Europe, and who can find, in consequence of their devotion to democracy, no employment at home, and give them the command of our armies. He does not seem to be aware that we have tried his theory pretty thoroughly in both respects, and have found it not to work well. We passed in the beginning over the army, and made nearly all our high military appointments from civil life. In our first batch of major-generals, not one was taken from the army, and only one was taken who had been educated at West Point. The government commenced with as great a distrust of West Point and a military education and military experience, and with as great a confidence in the military instincts and inspirations of civilians or political aspirants, as our author himself could desire, and with what wisdom the country knows, to its sorrow. Most of our civilian generals have proved sad failures; West Point is now at a premium, and would remain so, but for the wretched policy of making most new appointments in the army from the ranks, thereby spoiling good sergeants and making poor officers. Something besides bravery even is demanded of an officer. Gentlemanly tastes, habits, education, and manners, a knowledge of his profession, and an aptitude to command men, are necessary. Appointments from the ranks, as a reward of extraordinary merit, is well; but they should be sparingly and judiciously made. When we make appointments from the ranks the rule, they cease to be the reward of merit, and degrade the army and impair its efficiency.

In the beginning of the war, we had almost any number

of foreign adventurers in our service, but we have been obliged to get rid of the larger portion of them. Some among the foreign officers who have received commissions from our government are men of real merit, and have served with intelligence and success; but the majority of them have proved to be men "who left their country for their country's good." No national army can be worth any thing that is to any considerable extent officered by foreigners. If the nation cannot from itself officer its own army, it had better not go to war; for it is pretty sure to fail if it does. Then war as made here assumes a peculiar character. Carried on over our vast extent of country, much of it either a wilderness, or sparingly settled, in a manner so different from what the training and experience acquired in European armies and wars fit one for, that foreign officers can be of little use to us. Neither the strategy nor the tactics of a Napoleon would secure success here. The men who enter a foreign service are, besides, rarely the best officers in the army of their native country, and are usually such as their own government does not care to employ. We maintain, too, that though West Point is susceptible of improvement, nowhere are young men better trained for the profession of arms, and it is very little that the men from abroad, who seek commissions in our army, can teach our West Pointers. The great objection to our army officers at the opening of the war was their lack of experience in commanding, moving, and manoeuvring large bodies of men; but the foreigners who seek to enter our armies equally lack that experience. They have had only a lieutenant's, a captain's, a major's, or at most a colonel's command in their own country, or in the foreign service to which they had been attached. At the opening of the war, there were some who were mad enough to wish the government to invite Garibaldi to come and take command of our army; but Garibaldi, however successful he might have been as the tool of Piedmont or Mazzini in stirring up insurrection, and as a partisan commander, never commanded nor proved himself capable of commanding an army of thirty thousand men. Besides, his proper place in this country would not have been in the federal army, but in that of the rebels. To fight against rebellion and revolution in defence of legal authority and established government would have been a novelty to him, and contrary to his native instincts.

Our author is a decided democrat, in the European sense of the word, and complains that the American people are not truly and thoroughly democratic. He has no sympathy with our people, and thinks them false to their own democratic principles. What brought him here, if a foreigner, and induced him to offer us his valuable services, which appear to have been rejected, was his sympathy with democracy, and hostility to all other actual or possible forms of government. He wanted to sustain democracy here, not for our sake, but as a *point d'appui* for his operations against monarchy and aristocracy in Europe. All this may be very well in him, only he is on the wrong side, as would have been his friend Garibaldi. The struggle in which we are engaged, notwithstanding what some silly journalists write and publish, is not a struggle for the triumph of democracy. So to understand it is to misunderstand it; and we always regret to find friends of the Union urging the war as a war between the Northern democracy and the Southern aristocracy. Such many have tried and are still trying to make it; but such is not its real legitimate character. On our side it is a war in defence of government, of authority, and the supremacy of law. It is a war in vindication of national integrity, and in defence of American constitutionalism. The very thing our author would have us make the principle and end of the war, is that which the war is waged against. We wish to abolish slavery as far as it can be done without appealing to humanitarian or revolutionary principles: but we have neither the right nor the wish to seek to revolutionize Southern society. Politically, Southern society is no more aristocratic in its constitution than northen society: if socially it is more so, that is an advantage, not a disadvantage. In the present struggle, southern society has proved relatively stronger and more energetic than northern society, because in southern society the people are marshalled under their natural leaders, under men who are intrinsically superior to the mass, and felt to be so; while in the northern states they have been marshalled under no leaders or under artificial leaders, not superior, and often inferior, to those they are commissioned to lead. No society that has not a natural aristocracy, if we may borrow a phrase from Thomas Jefferson, has any really cohesive power, or any more strength than a rope of sand.

We have some madmen amongst us who talk of exterminating the southern leaders, and of new-englandizing the South. We wish to see the free-labor system substituted for the slave-labor system, but beyond that we have no wish to exchange or modify southern society, and would rather approach northern society to it, than it to northern society. The New Englander has excellent points, but is restless in body and mind, always scheming, always in motion, never satisfied with what he has, and always seeking to make all the world like himself, or as uneasy as himself. He is smart, seldom great; educated, but seldom learned; active in mind, but rarely a profound thinker; religious, but thoroughly materialistic: his worship is rendered in a temple founded on Mammon, and he expects to be carried to heaven in a softly-cushioned railway car, with his sins carefully checked and deposited in the baggage crate with his other luggage, to be duly delivered when he has reached his destination. He is philanthropic, but makes his philanthropy his excuse for meddling with everybody's business as if it were his own, and under pretence of promoting religion and morality, he wars against every generous and natural instinct, and aggravates the very evils he seeks to cure. He has his use in the community; but a whole nation composed of such as he would be short-lived, and resemble the community of the lost rather than that of the blest. The Puritan is a reformer by nature, but he never understands the true law of progress, and never has the patience to wait till the reform he wishes for can be practically effected. He is too impatient for the end ever to wait the slow operations of the means, and defeats his own purpose by his inconsiderate haste. He needs the slower, the more deliberate, and the more patient and enduring man of the South to serve as his counterpoise.

The South has for its natural leaders, not simply men of property, but men of large landed estates, and who are engaged in agricultural pursuits: the North has for its natural leaders business men and their factors, who may or may not be men of wealth, or who, if rich to-day, may be poor to-morrow, and who necessarily seek to subordinate every thing to business interests. They of course are less fitted, in a country like ours, to lead than the landholders, because agriculture with us is a broader and more permanent interest of the nation than trade or manufactures.

We insist that it were a gross perversion of the war to make it a war against Southern society or the Southern people. The war is just and defensible only when it is conducted as a war of the nation for its own existence and rights against an armed rebellion. In the war the nation seeks to reduce the rebels to their allegiance, not to destroy them, not to exile them, not to deprive them of their property or their franchise; it seeks to make them once more loyal citizens, and an integral portion of the American people, standing on a footing of perfect equality with the rest, not slaves or tributaries. Southern society must be respected, and any attempt to build up a new South out of the few Union men left there, northern speculators, sharpers, adventurers, and freed negroes, is not only impolitic, but unconstitutional and wrong. Such a South would be a curse to itself and to the whole nation; we want it not. With here and there an individual exception, the real people of the South are united in the rebellion, and under their natural leaders, and any scheme of settlement that does not contemplate their remaining with their natural leaders, the real, substantial, ruling people of the southern states, will not only fail, but ought not to be entertained. They must have the control of affairs in their respective states, and represent them in the councils of the nation. The nation cannot afford to lose them; if it could, it need not have gone to war against them. The bringing of the negro element, except in states where it is too feeble to amount to any thing, into American political society will never be submitted to by either the North or the South. We must suppress the rebellion; but with the distinct understanding that the Southern states are to be restored, when they submit, to all the rights of self-government in the Union, and that no attempt in the mean time shall be made to revolutionize their society in favor of Northern or European ideas. If in our haste, our wrath, or our zeal we have said any thing that can bear a different sense, it must be retracted.

Friends of constitutional government, and of liberty with law, may justly sympathize with our government in the present struggle; but no European radicals, democrats, and revolutionists, for the principle of the struggle is as hostile to them as it is to the southern rebels. In this war the nation is fighting Northern democracy or Jacobinism as much as it is Southern aristocracy, and the evidence of it is in the fact, that the people cease to support willingly the war just in proportion as it assumes a Jacobinical character, and loses its character of a war in defence of government and law. The administration may not see it; and the philosophers of the *New York Tribune* and *Evening Post*, well convinced as they may be that something is wrong, may deny it, and propose to cure the evil by doubling the dose of radicalism; even the people, while they instinctively feel, may not be fully aware that it is that which holds them back; but so it is, and nothing for years has given us so much hope for our country as this very fact. It proves that, after all, the popular instincts are right, and that while the people are ready to carry on a war to preserve the constitution and government, they are not prepared to carry on a war for revolutionizing either. These foreign radicals and revolutionists who complain of our democracy, that it is not thorough-going and consistent, and does not press straight to its end, ought to understand that there is no legitimate sympathy between them and us, and that they cannot fight their battles in ours. We are not fighting their battles, and those of our countrymen who think we are, begin already to find themselves deserted by the nation. The American people, however ready they have been to sympathize with revolution, and encourage insurrection and rebellion in foreign nations, therein imitating the English Whigs, are yet very far from being revolutionists in the interior of their souls, and for their own country.

Our author, who professes to side with the Federalists, keeps an eye on the revolutionary movements in Europe, and a considerable part of his work is written with the express intention of forwarding them. He rejoices at the spread of democratic ideas in England, in Germany, and in Italy, and he expresses his hope that the democratic party will rise again in France, and hurl the emperor from his throne. We trust we love liberty and free government as much as does this disappointed foreigner, or American with foreign sympathies and notions: but, in our judgment, what Europe most wants at present is repose in the interior of her several nations, and freedom for their respective governments to devote themselves to the welfare and progress of the people, for which they can do nothing, so long as they have to use all their power and energy to maintain their own existence. Every enlightened well-wisher to European society would rejoice to see the whole race of European revolutionists exterminated, or converted into loyal and peaceful subjects. True liberty was never yet advanced by subverting the established government of a country. Europe has lost far more than it has gained by its century of insurrections, revolutions, and civil wars, and the new *régimes* introduced have left fewer effective guaranties of civil freedom and personal liberty than existed before them. Providence may overrule evil for good, but good is never the natural product of evil.

We know, in censuring the revolutionary spirit of modern society, we are placing ourselves in opposition to the whole so-called liberal party of the civilized world; but that is not our fault. The liberal party so called has its good side and its bad side. Some things in it are to be commended, and other things in it, whoever would not stultify himself must condemn. Man is by nature a social being, and cannot live and thrive out of society; society is impracticable without strong and efficient government; and strong and efficient government is impracticable, where the people have no loyal sentiments, and hold themselves free to make war on their government and subvert it whenever they please. Men and governments, no doubt, are selfish, and prone to abuse power when they have it; but no government can stand that rests only on the selfishness of the human heart, or on what in the last century they called "enlightened self-interest," *L'intérêt bien entendu,* and not on the sense of duty, strengthened by loyal affection. People must feel not only that it is their interest to sustain government, but that it is their moral and religious duty to sustain it; and when they have no moral sense, no religion, and no loyal affection, they should know that they cannot sustain it, and society must cease to exist. A nation of atheists were a solecism in history. A few atheists may, perhaps, live in society, and even serve it for a time, where the mass of the people are believers and worshippers, but an entire nation of real atheists was never yet founded, and never could subsist any longer than it would take to dissipate the moral wealth acquired while it was as yet a religious nation. It was well said by the Abbé de La Mennais, before his unhappy fall: "Religion is always found by the cradle of nations, philosophy only at their tombs"—meaning, as he did, philosophy in the sense of unbelief and irreligion; not philosophy in the sense of the rational exercise of the faculties of the human mind on divine and human things, aided by the light of revelation. The ancient lawgivers always sought for their laws not only a moral, but a religious sanction, and where the voice of God does not, in some form, speak to men's consciences, and bid them obey the higher power, government can subsist only as a craft or as sheer force, which nobody is bound to respect or obey.

The great misfortune of modern liberalism is, that it was begotten of impatience and born of a reaction against the tyranny and oppression, the licentiousness and despotism of governments and the governing classes; and it is more disposed to hate than to love, and is abler to destroy than to build up. Wherever you find it, it bears traces of its origin, and confides more in human passion than in divine Providence. The great majority of its adherents, even if they retain a vague and impotent religious sentiment, and pay some slight outward respect to the religion of their country, yet place the state above the church, the officers of government above the ministers of religion, and maintain that priests have nothing to do with the affairs of this world. They forget that it is precisely to introduce the elements of truth, justice, right, duty, conscience into the government of individuals and nations in this world, as the means of securing the next, that institutions of religion exist, and priests are consecrated. Politicians may do as they please, so long as they violate no rule of right, no principle of justice, no law of God; but in no world, in no order, in no rank, or condition, have men the right to do wrong. Religion, if any thing is the *lex suprema*,[1] and

---

1. Supreme law. [R.K.]

what it forbids, no man has the right to do. This is a lesson liberalism has forgotten, or never learned.

In our last *Review* we defended civil and religious freedom and pointed out to the *obscurantists* in church and state, wherein and wherefore they mistake this age, are laboring for an impossibility, and fail to recall men to faith, and to reëstablish in its integrity the unity of Christendom; but whoever inferred from what we then said that we have any sympathy with political atheism, reasoned from premises of his own, not from any we ever laid down or entertained. Almost entire volumes of this *Review* are filled with refutations, such as they are, of political atheism, and the defence of the authority of religion for the human conscience in all the affairs of human life. There are elements in modern liberalism that it will not do to oppose, because, though liberalism misapplies them, they are borrowed from the Gospel, are taken from Christian civilization, and are, in themselves, true, noble, just, and holy. Nor can we recall modern society to that old order of things, that liberalism began by opposing, even if it were desirable, which it is not. Many things we may seek to save from being overthrown, which, when overthrown, it would be madness to attempt to reëstablish. But we have never denied that modern liberalism has an odor of infidelity and irreligion, and assumes an independence of religion, that is, of conscience, of God, which is alike incompatible with the salvation of souls and the progress of society. Liberals, if they would study the question, would soon find that religion offers no obstacle to any thing true and good they wish to effect, and even offers them that very assistance without which they cannot effect or preserve it.

It is the mad attempt to separate the progress of society from religion that has rendered modern liberalism everywhere destructive, and everywhere a failure. It has sapped the foundation of society, and rendered government, save as a pure despotism, impracticable, by taking from law its

sacredness, and authority its inviolability, in the understanding and consciences of men. The world, since the
opening of modern history, in the fifteenth century, has
displayed great activity, and in all directions; but its
progress in the moral and intellectual orders has been in
losing rather than in gaining. Its success in getting rid of
old ideas, old beliefs, old doctrines, old sentiments, old
practices, and in cutting itself loose from all its old moor-
ings, has been marvellous, and well-nigh complete. Taste
has, indeed, been refined, and manners, habits, and sentiments have been softened, and become more humane, but
we have not learned that they have gained much in purity
or morality. There has been a vast development of material resources, great progress in the application of science
to the productive arts, and a marvellous augmentation of
material goods; but it may well be doubted if there has
been any increase even of material happiness. Happiness
is not in proportion to what one is able to consume, as our
political economists would lead one to suppose, but in
proportion of the supply to one's actual wants. We, with
our present wants and habits, would be perfectly miserable for a time, if thrown back into the condition of the
people of the middle ages; and yet it is probable they were
better able to satisfy even such material or animal wants as
were developed in them than we are to satisfy those developed in us. Human happiness is not augmented by multiplying human wants, without diminishing the proportion
between them and the means of satisfaction, and that proportion has not been diminished, and cannot be, because
such is human nature, that men's wants multiply always
in even a greater ratio than the means of meeting them, as
affirmed by our political economists, in their maxims of
trade and production, that demand creates a supply, and
supply creates a demand. Under the purely material relation, as a human animal, there is no doubt that the negro
slave, well fed and well clothed, and not unkindly treated,
is happier than the free laborer at wages. We suspect that

it would be difficult to find in the world's history any age, in which the means of supply were less in proportion to the wants actually developed than in our own. There was more wisdom than our liberals are disposed to admit in the old maxim: If you would make a man happy, study not to augment his goods; but to diminish his wants. One of the greatest services Christianity has rendered the world has been its consecration of poverty, and its elevation of labor to the dignity of a moral duty. The tendency of modern society is in the opposite direction. England and the United States, the most modern of all modern nations, and the best exponents the world has of tendencies of modern civilization, treat poverty as a crime, and hold honest labor should be endured by none who can escape it.

There is no question that education has been more generally diffused than it was in the middle ages, but it is doubtful if the number of thinkers has been increased, or real mental culture extended. Education loses in thoroughness and depth what it gains in surface. Modern investigators have explored nature to a greater extent than it appears to have ever been done by the ancients, and accumulated a mass of facts, or materials of science, at which many heads are turned; but little progress has been made in their really scientific classification and explanation. Theories and hypotheses in any number we have, each one of which is held by the simpletons of the age to be a real contribution to science when it is first put forth, but most of them are no better than soap-bubbles, and break and disappear as soon as touched. Christianity has taught the world to place a high estimate on the dignity of human nature, and has developed noble and humane sentiments, but under the progress of modern society in losing it, characters have been enfeebled and debased, and we find no longer the marked individuality, the personal energy, the manliness, the force, the nobility of thought and purpose, and the high sense of honor, so common in the mediaeval world, and the better periods of antiquity. There is in our characters a littleness, a narrowness, a meanness, coupled with an astuteness and unscrupulousness to be matched only in the later stages of the Roman empire. In military matters we have introduced changes, but may still study with advantage the Grecian phalanx and the Roman legion. Ulpian and Papinian can still, save in what we have learned from Christianity, teach us law, and we improve modern legislation and jurisprudence only by borrowing from the civil law as digested by the lawyers of Justinian, in the *Institutes* and *Novellae*. In political science, properly so called, Aristotle, and any of the great mediaeval doctors, are still competent to be our masters. He who has read Aristotle's *Politics* has read the history of American democracy, and the unanswerable refutation of all the democratic theories and tendencies of modern liberals. For the most part we are prone to regard what is new to us as new to the world, and, what is worse, what is new to us as a real scientific acquisition, and a real progress of the race.

We have never read or heard of any age that had so high an opinion of its own acquisitions, that believed so firmly in its own intelligence, and that so little questioned its own immense superiority over all preceding ages, as the eighteenth century. It believed itself enlightened, highly cultivated, profound, philosophic, humane, and yet the doctrines and theories that it placed in vogue, and over which the upper classes grew enthusiastic in their admiration, are so narrow, so shallow, so directly in the face and eyes of common sense, so manifestly false and absurd that one finds it difficult to believe that anybody out of a madhouse ever entertained them. What think you of a philosopher who defines man—"A digesting tube, open at both ends"? and of another who ascribes all the difference between a man and a horse, for instance, to "the fact that man's fore limbs terminate in hands and flexible fingers, while those of a horse terminate in hoofs"? Yet these philosophers were highly esteemed in their day, and gave a tone to public opinion. We laugh at them as they did with the disciples of Epicurus, at the superstitions of past ages, the belief of sorcery, magic, necromancy, demons, witches, wizards, magicians, and yet all these things flourished in the eighteenth century, are believed in this nineteenth century in our own country, in England, France, and Germany, by men of all professions, and in all ranks of society. Wherein then, consists the progress of our enlightenment?

But "we are more liberal, more tolerant in matters of opinion, and have ceased to persecute men for religious differences," says our author. Hardly; yet if so, it may as well be because we are more indifferent, and less in earnest than our predecessors, believe less in mind, and more in matter. We have read no public document more truly liberal and more tolerant in its spirit and provisions than the edict of Constantine the Great, giving liberty to Christians, and not taking it from pagans. Even Julian the Apostate professed as much liberality and tolerance as Voltaire, or Mazzini, and practised them as well as the liberals in Europe usually do, when in power. "But the age tends," replies our author, "to democracy, and, therefore, to the amelioration, and social and political elevation of the people." Fine words; but, in fact, while demagogues spout democracy, and modern literature sneers at law, mocks at loyalty, and preaches insubordination, insurrection, revolution, governments have a fine pretext for tightening their bonds, and rendering their power despotic; nay, in some respects, are compelled to do so, as the only means left of preventing the total dissolution of society and the lapse of the race into complete barbarism. If the system of repression is carried too far and threatens its own defeat, the exaggerations of liberalism provoke, and in part justify it, for the liberalistic tendencies, if unchecked, could lead only to anarchy. Democracy, understood not as a form of government, but as the end government is to seek, to wit, the common good, the advance in civilization of the people, the poorer and more numerous, as well as the richer and less numerous classes, not of a privileged caste or class, is a good thing, and a tendency towards it is really an evidence of social progress. But this is only what the great doctors of the church have always taught, when they have defined the end of government to be the good of the community, the public good, or the common good of all,—not the special good of a few, nor yet the greatest good of the greatest number, as taught by that grave and elaborate humbug, Jeremy Bentham, but the common good of all, that good which is common to all the members of the community, whether great or small, rich or poor.

But that democracy as the form of the government is the best practicable means of securing this end, unless restrained by constitutions, the most earnest and enlightened faith, and by the most pure and rigid religious discipline, is, to say the least, a perfectly gratuitous assumption. We defend here and everywhere, now and always, the political order established in our country, and our failure—for failed, substantially, we have—is owing solely to our lack of real Christian faith, of the Christian conscience, and to our revolutionary attempts to interpret that order by the democratic theory. Our political order is republican, not democratic. But, in point of fact, the liberals have never advocated democracy for the end we have stated, from love of liberty, or for sake of ameliorating the condition of the people, though they may have so pretended, and at times even so believed, but really as a means of elevating themselves to power. Their democracy is, practically,—I am as good as you, and you have no more right than I to be in power or place. We believe in the disinterestedness or the patriotism of no man who can conspire to overthrow the government of his country, and whenever we hear a man professing great love for the dear people, praising their wisdom and virtue, their intelligence and sagacity, and telling that they are sovereign, and their will ought to prevail, we always regard him as a self-seeker, and as desirous of using the people simply to elevate himself to be one of their rulers. Democracy elevates to places of honor, profit, and trust, men who could not be so elevated under any other form of government; but that this operates to the advantage of the public we have yet to learn.

What our author praises as the tendency of democracy, is the tendency to reduce all things to a low average, and to substitute popular opinion for truth, justice, reason, as the rule of action, and the criterion even of moral judgment. Democracy, when social as well as political, elevates not the best men to office, but the most available men, usually the most cunning, crafty, or empty-headed demagogues. When, two years ago, the editor of this *Review* received the nomination in his district for member of congress, he was interiorly alarmed, and began a self-examination to ascertain what political folly or iniquity he had committed; and he became reconciled to himself, and his conscience was at ease, only when he found his election defeated by an overwhelming majority. His own defeat consoled him for his nomination, and restored his confidence in his own integrity, loyalty, and patriotism. The men democracy usually elevates are petty attorneys or small lawyers, men of large selfishness and small capacity, and less political knowledge. The Southern states, whose democracy is less socially diffused than that of the northern states, has always as a rule elevated abler men than has the North, which has given them an ascendency in the Union that has provoked northern jealousy. They have selected to represent them in congress, in diplomacy, in the cabinet, in the presidential chair, their ablest men while we have selected our feeblest men; or, if abler men, we have, with rare exception, "rotated" them from their places before they could acquire experience enough to be useful. Democracy, in the sense we are considering it, has shown what men it selects, when left to itself, in the present administration, and in the last and present congresses. Were there no better men in the country? Then is democracy condemned, as tending to degrade intellect and abase character, for greater and better men we certainly had, who were formed while we were yet British colonies. If there were greater or better men, and democracy passed them over as unavailable, then it is incapable of employing the best talent and the highest character produced by the country in its service, and therefore should also be condemned. President Lincoln we need not speak of; we have elsewhere given his character. But we have not had a single statesman, worthy of the name, in his cabinet or in congress since the incoming of the present administration, and hardly one from the free states since the Whigs, in 1840, descended into the forum, took the people by the hand, and, led on by the *Boston Atlas* and the *New York Tribune*, undertook to be more democratic than the Democratic party itself, and succeeded in out-heroding Herod. When they dropped the name *Whig*, and assumed that of *Republican*, which we had recommended in place of *Democratic*, we, in our simplicity, supposed that they really intended to abandon Jacobinism and to contend for constitutionalism, else had we never for a moment supported them. But they did, and intended to do nothing of the sort.

There is nothing in the American experiment thus far to justify the liberals in identifying the progress of liberty and social well-being with the progress of democracy. On this point our author is wholly at fault. Since Mr. Van Buren, more incompetent men in the presidential chair we could not have had, if we had depended on the hereditary principle, than popular election has given us. Prince John [Van Buren] would have been better than Harrison or Taylor, and Prince Bob [Lincoln] can hardly fall below his father. We want no hereditary executive, but probably the chances of getting a wise man for president, if the executive were hereditary, would be greater than they have been under the elective principle, as our elections have been, for a long time, conducted. Seldom has our senate been equal to the English house of peers. Democracy opens a door to office to men who, under no other system, could ever attain to office; but their attainment to office is of no conceivable advantage to the public, and very little to themselves. It opens a door to every man's ambition, at least permits every man to indulge ambitious aspirations. When such a man as Abraham Lincoln can become president, who may not hope one day also to be president? It stimulates every one's ambition, every one's hope of office, perhaps of the highest in the gift of the people, but it does not stimulate any one to study or to labor to qualify himself for honorably discharging the duties of office. It is rare to find any man who does not think himself qualified for any office to which the people can be induced to elect him. The plurality of votes is a sovereign indorsement of his qualification. The people, in electing me, have judged me qualified, and would you, proud aristocrat, arraign the judgment of the people? Enough said.

The same tendency to democracy, lauded by our author, leads in nearly every thing, every one to struggle to be other than he is, to get what he has not, and to fill another place than the one he is in, and hence produces universal competition, and general uneasiness and discontent in society. No man is contented to live and die in the social position in which he was born, and pride and vanity, not love and humility, become the principle of all individual and social action. I am as good as Abraham Lincoln, and why should he be president and not I? He was a rail-splitter and I am a hod-carrier. Let me throw down the hod, as he did the beetle and wedge, become an attorney, and I may one day be president as well as he. John Jacob Astor was once a poor German boy, who landed alone and friendless in the streets of New York, and he died worth, some say, twenty-five millions, all made by himself in trade; and why not I do as much, and make as much money as he? So every boy is discontented to remain at home and follow the occupation of his father, that of a mechanic or small farmer, and becomes anxious to get a place in a counting-house, and to engage in trade and speculation. Where all are free to aim to be first no one is contented to be second, especially to be last. This is the effect of liberalism, and an effect which our author cites as an evidence of its merit. He dwells on it with enthusiasm, and contrasts the movement, the activity, the aspirations of the common people at present with that of the lower classes under feudalism, and even the monarchical *régime* of the sixteenth and seventeenth centuries.

We, although a true-born Yankee, think very differently. Liberalism, taken in its practical workings in a society, with weak faith, a movable religion, and no loyalty, tends to develop wants which it is impossible to satisfy, because the wants it develops all demand their satisfaction from the material order. In the moral, intellectual, and spiritual world, the multiplication of wants is in itself not an evil, because the means of satisfaction are liberally supplied, and even the very craving for moral or spiritual good,—what the Gospel calls "a hungering and thirsting after righteousness," is itself a good, and blessed are they that do so, for they shall be filled. But the multiplication of wants which can be satisfied only with material or sensible goods, is not a good, but an evil. Political equality and equality before the law is practicable, but social equality, equality of wealth and social condition, is impracticable, and even undesirable. Only one man, once in four years, out of many millions, can be president of the United States; and if all set their hearts on it, all but the one must be disappointed. The sufferings of disappointed office-seekers more than overbalance the pleasures of office-holders. All cannot be rich, for if all were rich, paradoxical as it may sound, all would be poor. Real wealth is not in the magnitude of one's possessions, but in the amount of labor of others one is able to command; and if all are rich, no one can command any labor of another at all, for there is no one to sell his labor, and the rich man is reduced precisely to the level of the poor man. Though his possessions are counted by millions, he must produce for himself, and actually have only what he can produce with the labor of his own hands. All your schemes of an equal division of property, and for keeping all the members of a community equal in their condition, are fallacious, and, if they could be carried out, would end only in establishing universal poverty, universal ignorance, and universal barbarism. The human race would soon sink everywhere below the condition of our North American savages and, indeed, liberalism is practically a tendency to the savage state, as any one may learn even from Jean Jacques Rousseau.

We want no privileged caste or class; we want no political aristocracy, recognized and sustained as such by law. Let all be equal before the law. But we do want a social aristocracy, families elevated by their estates, their public services, their education, culture, manners, tastes, refinement, above the commonalty; and we do not believe a community can long even subsist where such an aristocracy is wanting, to furnish models and leaders for the people. It is the presence of such an aristocracy, that in the present fearful struggle gives to the Southern states their unity and strength. It is the want of such a class, enjoying the confidence and respect of the people in the loyal states, that constitutes our national weakness, as we have elsewhere shown. The people, we have said, and we all know, must have leaders and leaders must be born, not made. The number in a nation who have the qualities to be leaders, whether in peace or war, are comparatively few. All cannot lead; the mass must follow, and those who are born to follow should be content to follow, and not aspire to lead. If you stir up in them the ambition to lead, make them discontented with their lot, and determined to pass from followers to leaders, you reverse the natural order of things, introduce confusion into society, disorder into all ranks, and do good to nobody. We ourselves, we know it well, were never born to lead, and should only be misplaced, and ruin ourselves and others, were we put in the position of a leader. Our author professes to be a philosopher, and to have mastered what just now is called the science of sociology,—a barbarous term, which we detest,—and therefore he ought to understand that he is calling things by wrong names; that practically he says, Evil be thou my good! and, if successful, would erect a pandaemonium, not a well ordered human society, or a temple of liberty and peace.

Yet our author swims with the current, and is sustained by all the force of what is regarded as the advanced opinion of the age, and for the moment is stronger than we, who are sustained only by certain moral instincts and traditions which are generally unheeded. He has, too, the ear of the public, if not for himself personally, yet for innumerable others who agree with him, and can speak with even far more force and eloquence than he; while we are repudiated by all parties, by all sects, and only a few will listen to or heed our voice, harsh and discordant as it is in most ears. We are neither an *obscurantist* nor a liberal, but agreeing in some things, and disagreeing in others, with both; precisely the sort of a man, no party likes, for we can support no party through thick and thin,—a legitimate child of the nineteenth century, yet believing that all wisdom was neither born nor will die with it. We believe there were "brave men before Agamemnon," and that there will be brave men even after we are dead and forgotten. We belong not to the party that would restore the past, but to that which would retain what was true and good, and for all ages, in the past; we are not of those who would destroy the past, and compel the human race to begin *de novo*, but of those, few in number they may be, who see something good even in liberalism, and would accept it without breaking the chain of tradition, or severing the continuity of the life of the race, separate it from the errors and falsehoods, and bitter and hateful passions with which it is mixed up, and carry it onward. We are too much of the present to please the men of the past, and too much of the past to please the men of the present; so we are not only doomed, Cassandra-like, to utter prophecies which nobody believes, but prophecies which nobody heeds either to believe or disbelieve. We know it well, and therefore we said, We were not born to be a leader, although we have been long since spoiled as a follower, like most of our contemporaries. Hence, though we know that we speak the words of truth and soberness, we expect not our words to be heeded. Popular opinion decides with us all questions of wisdom and folly, of truth and falsehood, and popular opinion we do not and cannot echo.

Our author is a liberal, and ultra-democrat, a revolutionist,—has been, and probably still is, a conspirator,—a man who sees no sacredness in law, no inviolability in authority, and no charm in loyalty. His political creed is short, and very precise. It is: "The people are sovereign; the people are divine; the people are infallible and impeccable; I and my fellow-conspirators and revolutionists are the people; and because you Americans will not permit us to assume the direction of your civil and military affairs, you are no true liberals, no consistent democrats, and are really hostile to the progressive tendencies of the modern world." This is his creed, and the creed of all such as he, whether at home or abroad. We do not believe his creed, and have no wish to see it prevail. Many Americans profess it: few of them, however, really believe it, or, in fact, much else. They have been in the habit of hearing it, of reading it in newspapers and novels, and listening to it from the lips of impassioned orators on the Fourth of July, and in political meetings, and they have repeated it, as a matter of course, without giving it one moment's serious thought; but their instincts are truer than the creed they now and then fancy they believe, and there still linger in their minds faint reminiscences of something better, which was once believed by most men, and approved by Christian faith and conscience.

If the American people could only once understand that the present war is not a war between democracy and aristocracy, but a war in defence of government and law, that is, in defence of authority in principle as well as in practice, against popular license and revolutionism, the war, however it might terminate, would prove the richest boon they have ever as a people received from the hand of Heaven. It would arrest that lawless and revolutionary tendency they have hitherto thoughtlessly followed, which they have fancied it belonged to them to encourage both at home and abroad, and which at times has threatened to make us the pest of the civilized world. We trust it will yet have this effect. We are radical, if you will, in our determination, at the earliest moment it can be legally done, to get rid of the system of slave-labor, but, thank God, a radical in nothing else, and sympathize in little else with those who are called radicals: and, after all, we suspect the mass of the American people agree more nearly with us than with our General Croaker, and that we are a truer exponent of their real interior convictions and social instincts than he, although they will never believe it because they will never read us; and the jounals, if they notice us at all, will only misrepresent and pervert our words. Yet we rely greatly on military discipline and the effect of the war, to bring back the people to sounder political and social views.

Part Eight

~~~~~~~~~~~~~~~~~~~~~~~~~~~~~~~~~~~~~

LEGAL AND HISTORICAL CONSERVATISM

Several great Victorians took up their cudgels against the tendency of the times. Among the more redoubtable of these conservatives were Henry Maine (1822–1888), a famous scholar in the law, and W. E. H. Lecky (1838–1903), the learned historian of rationalism, morals, England, and Ireland. Although they wrote at the height of British power and prosperity, they perceived the grim shape of things to come.

THE MISCHIEF OF
ROUSSEAU AND BENTHAM
Sir Henry Maine

Sir Henry Maine, the author of *Ancient Law* and other enduring studies in jurisprudence, saw the rule of law dissolving beneath the acid of egalitarian and utilitarian notions. His *Popular Government* (1886) describes the process. This selection (pp. 159–74 in Liberty Classics edition, Indianapolis, 1976) is a succinct, telling criticism of the ideas of Rousseau and Bentham.

I do not think it likely to be denied, that the activity of popular government is more and more tending to exhibit itself in legislation, or that the materials for legislation are being constantly supplied in ever-increasing abundance through the competition of parties, or, lastly, that the keen interest which the community takes in looking on, as a body of spectators, at the various activities of popular government, is the chief reason of the general impression that ours is an Age of Progress, to be indefinitely continued. There are, however, other causes of this impression or belief, which are much less obvious and much less easily demonstrated to the ordinary English politician. At the head of them, are a group of words, phrases, maxims, and general propositions, which have their root in political theories, not indeed far removed from us by distance of time, but as much forgotten by the mass of mankind as if they had belonged to the remotest antiquity. How is one to convince the advanced English politician who announces with an air of pride that he is Radical, and indeed a Radical and something more, that he is calling himself by a name which he would never have had the courage to adopt, so deep was its disrepute, if Jeremy Bentham had not given it respectability by associating it with a particular theory of legislation and politics? How is one to persuade him, when he speaks of the Sovereign People, that he employs a combination of words which would never have occurred to his mind if in 1762 a French philosopher had not written a speculative essay on the origin of society, the formation of States, and the nature of government? Neither of these theories, the theory of Rousseau which starts from the assumed Natural Rights of Man, or the theory of Bentham which is based on the hypothetical Greatest Happiness principle, is now-a-days explicitly held by many people. The natural rights of man have indeed made their appearance in recent political discourse, producing much the same effect as if a professed lecturer on astronomy were to declare his belief in the Ptolemaic spheres and to call upon his audience to admire their music; but, of the two theories mentioned above, that of Rousseau which recognises these rights is much the most thoroughly forgotten. For the attempt to apply it led to terrible calamities, while the theory of Bentham has at present led to nothing worse than a certain amount of disappointment. How is it then that these wholly or partially exploded speculations still exercise a most real and practical influence on political thought? The fact is that political theories are endowed with the faculty possessed by the hero of the Border-ballad. When their legs are smitten off they fight upon their stumps. They produce a host of words, and of ideas associated with those words, which remain active and combatant after the parent speculation is mutilated or dead. Their posthumous influence often extend a good way beyond the domain of politics. It does not seem to me a fantastic assertion that the ideas of one of the great novelists of the last generation may be traced to Bentham, and those of another to Rousseau. Dickens, who spent his early manhood among the politicians of 1832 trained in Bentham's school, hardly ever wrote a novel without attacking an abuse. The procedure of the Court of Chancery and of the Ecclesiastical Courts, the delays of the Public Offices, the costliness of divorce, the state of the dwellings of the poor, and the condition of the cheap schools in the North of England, furnished him with what he seemed to consider, in all sincerity, the true moral of a series of fictions. The opinions of Thackeray have a strong resemblance to those to which Rousseau gave popularity. It is a very just remark of Mill, that the attraction which Nature and the State of Nature had for Rousseau may be partly accounted for as a reaction against the excessive admiration of civilisation and progress which took possession of educated men during the earlier part of the eighteenth century. Theoretically, at any rate, Thackeray hated the artificialities of civilisation, and it must be owned that some of his favourite personages have about them something of Rousseau's natural man as he would have shown himself if he had mixed in real life—something, that is, of the violent blackguard.

The influence which the political theory originating in France and the political theory originating in England still exercise over politics seems to me as certain as anything in the history of thought can be. It is necessary to examine these theories, because there is no other way of showing the true value of the instruments, the derivative words and derivative ideas, through which they act. I will take first the famous constitutional theory of Rousseau, which, long unfamiliar or discredited in this country, is the fountain of many notions which have suddenly become popular and powerful among us. There is much difficulty in the attempt to place it in a clear light, for reasons well known to all who have given attention to the philosophy of the remarkable man who produced it. This philosophy is the most striking example extant of a confusion which may be detected in all corners of non-scientific modern thought, the confusion between what is and what ought to be, between what did as a fact occur and what under certain conditions would have occurred. The *Contrat Social*, which sets forth the political theory on which I am engaged, appears at first sight to give an historical account of the emergence of mankind from a State of Nature. But whether it is meant that mankind did emerge in this way, whether the writer believes that only a happily circumstanced part of the human race had this experience, or whether he thinks that Nature, a beneficent legislatress, intended all men to have it, but that her objects were defeated, it is quite impossible to say with any confidence. The language of Rousseau sometimes suggests that he meant his picture of early social transformations to be regarded as imaginary;[1] but nevertheless the account given of them is so precise, detailed, and logically built up, that it is quite inconceivable its author should not have intended it to express realities. This celebrated theory is briefly as follows. Rousseau, who in his earlier writings had stongly insisted on the disadvantages which man had sustained through the loss of his natural rights, begins the *Contrat Social* with the position that Man was originally in the State of Nature. So long as he remained in it, he was before all things free. But, in course of time, a point is

---

1. *"Comment ce changement s'est-il fait? Je l'ignore."* [How did this change come about? I don't know.]—*Contrat social*, chap. i. I have myself no doubt that very much of the influence of Rousseau over the men of his own generation, and of the next, arose from the belief widely spread among them that his account of natural and of early political society was literally true. There is a remarkable passage in the *Pensées* of Pascal (III. 8) which describes the powerful revolutionary effects which may be produced by contrasting an existing institution with some supposed "fundamental and primitive law" of the State. The reflection was obviously suggested by the sedition of the Fronde. The Parliament of Paris firmly believed in the "fundamental and primitive laws" of France; and, a century later, the disciples of Rousseau had exactly the same faith in the State of Nature and the Social Compact.

reached at which the obstacles to his continuance in the natural condition become insuperable. Mankind then enter into the Social Compact under which the State, society, or community is formed. Their consent to make this compact must be unanimous; but the effect of its completion is the absolute alienation or surrender, by every individual human being, of his person and all his rights to the aggregate community.[2] The community then becomes the sovereign, the true and original Sovereign People, and it is an autocratic sovereign. It ought to maintain liberty and equality among its subjects, but only because the subjection of one individual to another is a loss of force to the State, and because there cannot be liberty without equality.[3] The collective despot cannot divide, or alienate, or delegate his power. The Government is his servant, and is merely the organ of correspondence between the sovereign and the people. No representation of the people is allowed. Rousseau abhorred the representative system; but periodical assemblies of the entire community are to be held, and two questions are to be submitted to them— whether it is the pleasure of the sovereign to maintain the present form of government—and whether the sovereign pleases to leave the administration of its affairs to the persons who now conduct it.[4] The autocracy of the aggregate community and the indivisibility, perpetuity, and incommunicable character of its power, are insisted upon in

---

2. "*Le pacte social se réduit aux termes suivants: chacun de nous mit en commun sa personne et toute sa puissance sous la suprême direction de la volonté générale; et nous recevons encore chaque membre comme partie individuelle du tout.*" [The social compact reduces itself to the following conditions: each one of us places his person and all his power in common under the supreme direction of the general will; and furthermore, we receive each member as an individual part of the whole.]—*Contrat Social,* c. i. 6.

3. *Contrat Social,* ii. 11.

4. *Contrat social,* iii. 18. The decision is in this case to be by majority; Rousseau requires unanimity for the consent to enter into the Social Compact, but not otherwise.

every part of the *Contrat Social* and in every form of words.

As is almost always the case with sweeping theories, portions of Rousseau's ideas may be discovered in the speculations of older writers. A part may be found, a century earlier, in the writings of Hobbes; another part in those of the nearly contemporary school of French Economists. But the theory, as he put it together, owes to him its extraordinary influence; and it is the undoubted parent of a host of phrases and associated notions which, after having long had currency in France and on the Continent, are beginning to have serious effect in this country, as the democratic element in its Constitution increases. From this origin sprang the People (with a capital P), the Sovereign People, the People the sole source of all legitimate power. From this came the subordination of Governments, not merely to electorates but to a vaguely defined multitude outside them, or to the still vaguer mastership of floating opinion. Hence began the limitation of legitimacy in governments to governments which approximate to democracy. A vastly more formidable conception bequeathed to us by Rousseau is that of the omnipotent democratic State rooted in natural right; the State which has at its absolute disposal everything which individual men value, their property, their persons, and their independence; the State which is bound to respect neither precedent nor prescription; the State which may make laws for its subjects ordaining what they shall drink or eat, and in what way they shall spend their earnings; the State which can confiscate all the land of the community, and which, if the effect on human motives is what it may be expected to be, may force us to labour on it when the older incentives to toil have disappeared. Nevertheless this political speculation, of which the remote and indirect consequences press us on all sides, is of all speculations the most baseless. The natural condition from which it starts is a simple figment of the imagination. So far as any research into the nature of primitive human society has any bearing on so mere a dream, all inquiry has dissipated it. The process by which Rousseau supposes communities of men to have been formed, or by which at all events he wishes us to assume that they were formed, is again a chimera. No general assertion as to the way in which human societies grew up is safe, but perhaps the safest of all is that none of them were formed in the way imagined by Rousseau.

The true relation of some parts of the theory to fact is very instructive. Some particles of Rousseau's thought may be discovered in the mental atmosphere of his time. "Natural Law" and "natural rights" are phrases properly belonging to a theory not of politics, but of jurisprudence, which, originating with the Roman jurisconsults, had a great attraction for the lawyers of France. The despotic sovereign of the *Contrat Social,* the all-powerful community, is an inverted copy of the King of France invested with an authority claimed for him by his courtiers and by the more courtly of his lawyers, but denied to him by all the highest minds in the country, and specially by the great luminaries of the French Parliaments. The omnipotent democracy is the King-Proprietor, the lord of all men's fortunes and persons; but it is the French King turned upside down. The mass of natural rights absorbed by the sovereign community through the Social Compact is, again, nothing more than the old divine right of kings in a new dress. As for Rousseau's dislike of representative systems and his requirement that the entire community should meet periodically to exercise its sovereignty, his language in the *Contrat Social* suggests that he was led to these opinions by the example of the ancient tribal democracies. But at a later date he declared that he had the Constitution of Geneva before his mind;[5] and he cannot but have known that the exact method of government

---

5. *Lettres écrites de la Montagne,* part i., letter 6, p. 328.

which he proposed still lived in the oldest cantons of Switzerland.

This denial to the collective community of all power of acting in its sovereign capacity through representatives is so formidable, as apparently to forbid any practical application of Rousseau's theory. Rousseau, indeed, expressly says[6] that his principles apply to small communities only, hinting at the same time that they may be adapted to States having a large territory by a system of confederation; and in this hint we may suspect that we have the germ of the opinion, which has become an article of faith in modern Continental Radicalism, that freedom is best secured by breaking up great commonwealths into small self-governing communes. But the time was not ripe for such a doctrine at the end of the last century; and real vitality was for the first time given to the speculation of Rousseau by that pamphlet of Siéyès, *Qu'est-ce que le Tiers État?* which did so much to determine the early stages of the French Revolution. As even the famous first page[7] of this pamphlet is often misquoted, what follows it is not perhaps always carefully read, and it may have escaped notice that much of it[8] simply reproduces the theory of Rousseau. But then Siéyès reproduces this theory with a difference. The most important claim which he advanced, and which he succeeded in making good, was that the Three Orders should sit together and form a National Assembly. The argument by which he reaches this conclusion is substantially that of the *Contrat Social.* With

---

6. *Contrat Social*, iii. 15.

7. The first page runs: "*1. Qu'est-ce que le Tiers État?—Tout. 2. Qu'a-t-il été jusquâ présent dans l'ordre politique?—Rien. 3. Que demande-t-il?—A être quelque chose.*" [1. What is the common man?—Everything. 2. Until now what has he been in the political order?—Nothing. 3. What does he ask?—To be something.] It is misquoted by Alison, *History of Europe during the French Revolution*, vol. i. c. iii. p. 453.

8. The argument fills the long chapter v. The edition before me is the third, published in 1789.

Siéyès, as with Rousseau, man begins in the natural condition; he enters society by a social compact; and by virtue of this compact an all-powerful community is formed. But then Siéyès had not the objection of Rousseau to representation, which indeed was one of his favourite subjects of speculation during life. He allows the community to make a large preliminary delegation of its powers by representation. Thus is formed the class of representative bodies to which the future National Assembly of France was to belong. Siéyès calls them *extraordinary*, and describes them as exercising their will like men in a state of nature, as standing in place of the nation, as incapable of being tied down to any particular decision or line of legislation . *Ordinary* representative bodies are, on the other hand, legislatures deriving their powers from a Constitution which the extraordinary Assembly has formed and strictly confined to the exercise of these powers. The extraordinary assembly is thus the sovereign community of Rousseau; the ordinary assembly is his government. To the first class belong those despotic bodies which, under the name of National Assembly or Convention, have four times governed France, never successfully and sometimes disastrously. To the second belong the Legislative Assemblies and Chambers of Deputies so often overthrown by revolution.

The other theory, from which a number of political phrases and political ideas now circulating among us have descended, is of English origin, and had Jeremy Bentham for its author. Its contribution to this currency is at this moment smaller than that which may be traced to a French source in the *Contrat Social*, but it was at one time much larger. It must be carefully borne in mind that during the earlier and greater part of his long life Bentham was not a reformer of Constitutions, but a reformer of Law. He was the first Englishman to see clearly how the legislative powers of the State, very sparingly employed for this object before, could be used to rearrange and recon-

struct civil jurisprudence and adapt it to is professed ends.
He became a Radical reformer—an expression to which,
as I said before, he gave a new respectability—through
sheer despair.[9] The British Constitution in his day might
no doubt have been improved in many of its parts, but, in
his impatience of delay in legislative reforms, he attributed to inherent defects in the Constitution obstructions
which were mainly owing to the effects produced on the
entire national mind by detestation of principles, strongly
condemned by himself, which had brought on France the
Reign of Terror and on the entire Continent the military
despotism of Napoleon Bonaparte. Superficially, the ideal
political system for which he argued in a series of pamphlets has not a little resemblance to that of Rousseau and
Siéyès. There was to be a single-chambered democracy,
one all-powerful representative assembly, with powers
unrestricted theoretically, but with its action facilitated
and guided by a strange and complex apparatus of subordinate institutions.[10] The real difference between his plans
and those of the French theorist lay in their philosophical
justification. The system of Rousseau was based on the
pretended Natural Rights of men, and it owes to this basis
a hold on weaker and less instructed minds, which is
rather increasing than diminishing. But Bentham utterly
repudiated those Natural Rights, and denounced the conception of them as absurd and anarchical. During the first
or law-reforming period of his life, which lasted till he was
more than sixty years old, he had firmly grasped the
"greatest happiness of the greatest number" (a form of
words found in Beccaria) as the proper standard of legislative reform; but, observing the close association of law
with morals, he had made the bolder attempt to reform
moral ideas on the same principle, and by a sort of legisla-

9. See the Introduction to his plan of Parliamentary Reform. *Works*,
iii. 436.
10. *Constitutional Code. Works*, ix. 1.

tion to force men to think and feel, as well as to act, in conformity with his standard. As the great war proceeded, the
time became more and more unfavourable for Bentham's
experiment, and finally he himself declared that the cause
of reform was lost on the plains of Waterloo. It was then
that he began his attack on the British Constitution, and
published his proposals for reconstructing it from base to
apex. As the classes which it placed in power refused to
recognise or promote the greatest happiness of the greatest
number, he proposed to displace them and to hand over all
political authority to the greatest number itself. It must
necessarily follow his standard, he argued; every man and
every number of men seeks its own happiness, and the
greatest number armed with legislative power must legislate for its own happiness. This reasoning had great effect
on some of the most powerful minds of Bentham's day.
His disciples—Grote, the two Mills, Molesworth, the two
Austins, and Roebuck—did really do much to transform
the British Constitution. Some of them, however, lived
long enough to be disenchanted by the results;[11] and, I
have attempted to show in a former Essay, many of these
results would have met with the deepest disapproval from
Bentham himself. The truth is, there was a serious gap in
his reasoning. Little can be said against "the greatest happiness of the greatest number" as a standard of legislation,
and indeed it is the only standard which the legislative

---

11. I quote the following passage from the Preface to John Austin's
Plea for the Constitution. "In the course of the following Essay I
have advanced opinions which are now unpopular, and which may
possibly expose me to some obloquy, though I well remember the
time (for I was then a Radical) when the so-called Liberal opinions
which are now predominant exposed the few who professed them to
political and social proscription. I have said that the bulk of the
working-classes are not yet qualified for political power. . . . I have
said this because I think so. I am no worshipper of the great and rich,
and have no fancy for their style of living. I am by origin, and by my
strongest sympathies, a man of the people; and I have never desired,
for a single moment, to ascend from the modest station which I have
always occupied."

power, when once called into action, can possibly follow. It is inconceivable that any legislator should deliberately propose or pass a measure intended to diminish the happiness of the majority of the citizens. But when this multitudinous majority is called to the Government for the purpose of promoting its own happiness, it now becomes evident that, independently of the enormous difficulty of obtaining any conclusion from a multitude of men, there is no security that this multitude will know what its own happiness is, or how it can be promoted. On this point it must be owned that Rousseau shows himself wiser than Bentham. He claimed for the entire community that it should be sovereign and that it should exercise its sovereignty in the plenitude of power, because these were its Natural Rights; but, though he claimed for it that it should be all-powerful, he did not claim that it was all-wise, for he knew that it was not. The People, he said, always meant well; but it does not always judge well.

Comment une multitude aveugle, qui souvent ne sait ce qu'elle veut, parce qu'elle sait rarement ce qui lui est bon, exécuterait-elle d'elle-même une entreprise aussi grande, aussi difficile, qu'un système de législation? De lui-même le peuple veut toujours le bien, mais de lui-même il ne le voit pas toujours. La volonté générale est toujours droite, mais le jugement qui la guide n'est pas toujours éclairé.[12]

[How can a blind multitude, which often does not know what it wants, because it rarely knows what is good for it, carry out for itself such an enormous and difficult enterprise as a system of legislation? Of themselves the people always desire the good, but by themselves they do not always see it. The general will is always right, but the judgment which guides it is not always enlightened.]

---

12. *Contrat Social*, ii. 6. The latter part of this chapter is replete with good sense.

Rousseau was led by these misgivings almost to doubt the practical possibility of wise legislation by his ideal democracy. He seems to have thought that the legislator who could properly guide the people in the exercise of their sovereign powers would only appear at long intervals, and must virtually be semi-divine. In connection with these ideas, he made a prediction which has contributed nearly as much to his fame as any of his social and political speculations. Sharing the general interest and sympathy which the gallant struggle of the Corsicans for independence had excited in his day, he persuaded himself that the ideal legislator would most probably arise in Corsica. "J'ai quelque pressentiment," he writes, "qu'un jour, cette petite île étonnera L'Europe."[13] The prophecy has been repeatedly taken to mean that Rousseau foresaw the birth in Corsica, seven years later, of a military genius after whom the Code Civil of France would be named.

One further remark, not perhaps at first sight obvious, ought to be made of these political theories of Rousseau and Bentham which contribute so largely to the mental stock of the classes now rising to power in Europe. These theories were, in their origin, theories not of constitutional reform, but of law-reform. It is unnecessary to give new proof of this assertion as respects Bentham. But it is also true of Rousseau. The conceptions of Nature, of Natural Law, and of Natural Right, which prompted and shaped his political speculations, are first found in the language of the Roman lawyers. It is more than doubtful whether these illustrious men ever believed in the State of Nature as a reality, but they seem to have thought that, under all the perverse technicalities of ancient law, there lay a simple and symmetrical system of rules which were in some sense those of Nature. Their natural law was, for all prac-

---

13. "I have a premonition that one day this little island will shake Europe." [R.K.]

tical purposes, simple or simplified law. This view, with all its philosophical defects, led to a great simplification of law both in the Roman State and in modern Europe, and indeed was the chief source of law-reform until the system of Bentham, which also aimed at the simplification of law, made its appearance. But the undoubted descent both of the French and the English political theory from theories of law-reform points to a serious weakness in them. That because you can successfully reform jurisprudence on certain principles, you can successfully reform Constitutions on the same principles, is not a safe inference. In the first place, the simplification of civil law, its disentanglement from idle forms, technicalities, obscurities, and illogicalities, can scarcely be other than a beneficial process. It may indeed lead to disappointment. Bentham thought that, if law were reformed on his principles, litigation would be easy, cheap, and expeditious; yet, now that nearly all his proposals have been adopted, the removal of legal difficulties seems to have brought into still greater nakedness the difficulties of questions of fact. But, though the simplification of law may lead to disappointment, it can scarcely lead to danger. It is, however, idle to conceal from oneself that the simplification of political institutions leads straight to absolutism, the absolutism not of an expert judge, but of a single man or of a multitude striving to act as if it were a single man. The illogicalities swept away in the process may really be buttresses which helped to support the vast burden of government, or checks which mitigated the consequences of the autocrat's undeniable fallibility. Again, a mistake in law-reform is of small importance. It mainly affects a class of whose grievances, I may observe, Bentham had far too exalted a notion, the small part of the community which actually "goes to law." If committed, it can be corrected with comparative ease. But a mistake in constitutional innovation directly affects the entire community and every part of it. It may be fraught with calamity or ruin, public or private. And correction is virtually impossible. It is practically taken for granted among us, that all constitutional changes are final and must be submitted to, whatever their consequences. Doubtless this assumption arises from a general belief that, in these matters, we are propelled by an irresistible force on a definite path towards an unavoidable end—towards Democracy, as towards Death.

RUINOUS TAXATION
W. E. H. Lecky

The "progressive" or "graduated" income tax was in its infancy when Lecky published the two volumes of *Democracy and Liberty* (London, 1896);.that was in the green tree; now we are in the dry. This famous historian's general thesis is that of Tocqueville, reinforced by policies of the latter half of the nineteenth century: the more democracy, the greater the perils to personal liberty. Here we set down Lecky's prediction (Vol. I, pp. 346–60) of the consequences of graduated taxation.

Recent discussions have made the arguments which have been adduced by economists against graduated taxation very familiar. It is obvious that a graduated tax is a direct penalty imposed on saving and industry, a direct premium offered to idleness and extravagance. It discourages the very habits and qualities which it is most in the interest of the State to foster, and it is certain to operate forcibly where fortunes approach the limits at which a higher scale of taxation begins. It is a strong inducement at that period, either to cease to work or to cease to save. It is at the same time perfectly arbitrary. When the principle of taxing all fortunes on the same rate of computation is abandoned, no definite rule or principle remains. At what point the higher scale is to begin, or to what degree it is to be raised, depends wholly on the policy of Governments and the balance of parties. The ascending scale may at first be very moderate, but it may at any time, when fresh taxes are required, be made more severe, till it reaches or approaches the point of confiscation. No fixed line or amount of graduation can be maintained upon principle, or with any chance of finality. The whole matter will depend upon the interests and wishes of the electors; upon party politicians seeking for a cry and competing for the votes of very poor and very ignorant men. Under such a system all large properties may easily be made unsafe, and an insecurity may arise which will be fatal to all great financial undertakings. The most serious restraint on parliamentary extravagance will, at the same time, be taken away, and majorities will be invested with the easiest and most powerful instrument of oppression. Highly graduated taxation realises most completely the supreme danger of democracy, creating a state of things in which one class imposes on another burdens which it is not asked to share, and impels the State into vast schemes of extravagance, under the belief that the whole cost will be thrown upon others.

The belief is, no doubt, very fallacious, but it is very natural, and it lends itself most easily to the clap-trap of dishonest politicians. Such men will have no difficulty in drawing impressive contrasts between the luxury of the rich and the necessities of the poor, and in persuading ignorant men that there can be no harm in throwing great burdens of exceptional taxation on a few men, who will still remain immeasurably richer than themselves. Yet, no truth of political economy is more certain than that a heavy taxation of capital, which starves industry and employment, will fall most severely on the poor. Graduated taxation, if it is excessive or frequently raised, is inevitably largely drawn from capital. It discourages its accumulation. It produces an insecurity which is fatal to its stability, and it is certain to drive great masses of it to other lands.

The amount to be derived from this species of taxation is also much exaggerated. The fortunes of a few millionaires make a great show in the world, but they form in reality a very insignificant sum, compared with the aggregate of moderate fortunes and small savings. Unless the system of graduation be extended, as in Switzerland, to very moderate fortunes, it will produce little, and even then the exemptions that accompany it will go far to balance it. It is certain, too, that it will be largely evaded. There is, it is true, a great distinction to be drawn in this respect between real and personal property. Land is of such a nature that it cannot escape the burden which is imposed on it, but there are many ways in which personal property can escape. Confidential arrangements between members of a family or partners in a business, foreign investments payable to foreign bankers, an increasing portion of wealth sunk in life annuities, insurances made in companies that are not subject to British taxation, securities payable to bearer, which it will be impossible to trace, will all multiply, and the frauds that are so much complained of in income-tax returns will certainly increase. No graver error can be made by a financier than to institute a system which is so burdensome and so unjust that men will be disposed to employ all their ingenuity to evade it. With the vast and various field of international investment that is now open to them they are sure, in innumerable instances, to succeed, and no declaration, no oath, no penalty will effectually prevent it. Taxation is, ultimately, the payment which is made by the subject for the security and other advantages which he derives from the State. If the taxation of one class is out of all proportion to the cost of the protection they enjoy; if its members are convinced that it is not an equitable payment, but an exceptional and confiscatory burden imposed upon them by an act of power because they are politically weak, very many of them will have no more scruple in defrauding the Government than they would have in deceiving a highwayman or a burglar.

It would be pressing these arguments too far to maintain that a graduated scale of taxation is always and necessarily an evil. In this, as in most political questions, much will depend upon circumstances and degrees. It is, however, sufficiently clear that any financier who enters on this field is entering on a path surrounded with grave and various dangers. Graduated taxation is certain to be contagious, and it is certain not to rest within the limits that its originators desired. No one who clearly reads the signs of the times as they are shown in so many lands can doubt that this system of taxation is likely to increase. It would be hardly possible that it should be otherwise when political power is placed mainly in the lands of the working-classes; when vast masses of landed property are accumulated in a few hands; when professional politicians are continually making changes in the incidence of taxation a prominent part of their electioneering programmes; when almost every year enlarges the functions, and therefore the expenditure, of the State; when nearly all the prevalent Utopias take a socialistic form, and point to an equalisation of conditions by means of taxation. Under such conditions the temptation to enter upon this path becomes almost invincible.

It is a question of great importance to consider to what result it is likely to lead. To suppose that any system of taxation can possibly produce a real equality of fortunes, or prevent the accumulation of great wealth, seems to me wholly chimerical; though it is quite possible that legislators in aiming at these objects may ruin national credit, and bring about a period of rapid commercial decadence. Highly graduated taxation, however, is likely to have great political and social effects in transforming the character of wealth. It will probably exercise a special influence on landed property, breaking up or greatly diminishing those vast estates which are so distinctive a feature of English life. The tendencies which are in operation acting in this direction are very powerful. Land, as it is at present held by the great proprietors, is usually one of the least profitable forms of property. The political influence attached to it has greatly diminished. The magisterial and other administrative functions, that once gave the great landlord an almost commanding influence in his county, are being steadily taken away, and county government in all its forms is passing into other hands. If government is effectually divorced from property, and if a system of graduated taxation intended to equalise fortunes becomes popular, great masses of immovable land must become one of the most undesirable forms of property. No other excites so much cupidity, or is so much exposed to predatory legislation. Under all these circumstances, we may expect to see among the great landowners a growing desire to diminish gradually their stake in the land, thus reversing the tendency to agglomeration which for many generations has been dominant.

The change, in my opinion, will not be wholly evil. It is not a natural thing that four or five country places should be held by one man; that whole counties should be almost included in one gigantic property; that square miles of territory should be enclosed in a single park. The scale of luxury and expenditure in English country life is too high. The machinery of life is too cumbersome. Its pleasures are costly out of all proportion to the enjoyment they give. Nor, on the other hand, is it desirable that great landed properties should be held together when the fixed and necessary charges are so great that they become overwhelming whenever agricultural depression, or any other form of adversity, arrives, while the girls and younger children of the family are left to a poverty which seems all the more acute from the luxurious surroundings in which they have been brought up. If the result of graduated taxation should be to produce a more equal division of property between the members of a family; if rich men, instead of making an allowance to their sons, should seek to avoid death duties by capitalising and at once handing over the amount; if the preservation of game should be on a less extravagant scale; if estates should become smaller and less encumbered, and the habits of great country houses somewhat less luxurious than at present, these things would not injure the country.

Other consequences, however, of a far less desirable character are certain to ensue, and they are consequences that will fall more heavily upon the poor than upon the rich. Only a very small fraction of the expenditure of a great landowner can be said to contribute in any real degree to his own enjoyment. The vast cost of keeping up a great place, and the scale of luxurious hospitality which the conventionalities of society impose, count for much. Parks maintained at great expense, and habitually thrown open to public enjoyment; the village school, or church, or institute established and endowed; all local charities, all county enterprises largely assisted; costly improvements, which no poor landlord could afford; much work given for the express purpose of securing steady employment to the poor,—these things form the largest items in the budget of many of the great landowners. Nor should we omit to mention remissions of rent in times of depression which no poor man could afford to make, and very low rents kept unchanged during long periods of increasing prosperity.

In every considerable class there will be the good and the bad, the generous and the grasping; but, on the whole, no candid man will deny the extremely liberal spirit in which the large landed properties in England have been administered. Whatever ultimate benefits may be obtained by their dissolution, it is certain that the first effect will be to extinguish great centres of beneficence and civilisation, to diminish employment, to increase the severity of contracts, and in many other ways to curtail the pleasures and augment the hardships of the deserving poor. It is often said that wealthy Americans, not having the ambition of founding families, give more than wealthy Englishmen for public purposes; but I believe that an examination of the unselfish expenditure of the larger English landlords on objects connected with their estates would show that they in this respect fall little, if at all, below the Transatlantic example. It is, probably, only in England that we frequently see the curious spectacle of men with incomes of several thousands a year overwhelmed by lifelong pecuniary troubles, not because of any improvidence, or luxurious habits or tastes, but simply because their incomes are insufficient to bear the necessary expenses of their great position.

It seems likely, under the influences I have described, that a great change, both for good and evil, will take place. Land will probably, in future, be more divided, will change hands more frequently, will be treated in a more purely commercial spirit than in the past. Country places taken for mere pleasure, and unconnected with any surrounding property or any landlord duties, will be more frequent. It is not probable that yeomen farmers will multiply as long as it is economically more advantageous for a farmer to rent than to purchase his farm; but land will be bought and sold more frequently, in moderate quantities, as a speculation, let at its extreme value, and divested of all the feudal ideas that are still connected with it. The old historic houses will, no doubt, remain, but they will remain, like the French castles along the Loire, memories of a state of society that has passed away. Many will be in the hands of rich merchants or brewers, and perhaps American millionaires. They will often be shut up, as a measure of economy, for long periods. They will no longer be the centres of great landed properties, or represent a great county influence or a long train of useful duties. Parks will be divided. Picture-galleries will be broken up. Many noble works of art will cross the Atlantic. The old type of English country life will be changed, and much of its ancient beauty will have passed away.

Assuming, as is most probable, that these changes are effected gradually and without violent convulsion, they by no means imply the impoverishment of those who are now the great landed proprietors. No one can doubt that, at the present day, the members of this class would be better off if they had less land and more money; if their properties were in such forms that they had more power of modifying their expenditure according to their means. They will have to pass through a trying period of transition, but, as they are remarkably free from the prejudices and narrow conventionalities that incapacitate some Continental aristocracies in the battle of life, they will, probably, soon adapt themselves to their new circumstances. With ordinary good fortune, with skilful management, with the rich marriages they can always command, with the excellent legal advice that is always at their disposal, they will probably succed in many instances in keeping together enormous fortunes, and the time is far distant when a really able man, bearing an historic name, does not find that name an assistance to him in his career. But the class will have lost their territorial influence. Public life, dominated, or at least largely influenced, by professional politicians of the American type, will become more distasteful to them. They will find themselves with few landlord or county duties, and with much less necessary hospitality to perform, and they will probably content themselves with smaller country establishments, and spend much more of their time in brighter lands beyond the sea.

The effects of highly graduated taxation on personal property will also be considerable, but probably not so great as on real property. It will strengthen the disposition of a rich man to divide as much as possible his investments, as all great masses of homogeneous, immovable property will become specially insecure. It will, in this respect, increase a movement very dangerous to English commercial supremacy, which labour troubles and organisations have already produced. Most good observers have come to the conclusion that an appreciable influence in the commercial depression of the last few years has been the reluctance of rich men to embark on extensive enterprises at a time when labour troubles are so acute, so menacing, and so likely to exercise an influence on legislation. Far-seeing men hesitate to commit themselves to undertakings which can only slowly arrive at maturity when they see the strong bias of popular legislation against property, and the readiness with which a considerable number of modern statesmen will purchase a majority in the House of Commons by allying themselves with the most dishonest groups, and countenancing the most subversive theories. Every influence which, in any department of industrial life, increases risks and diminishes profits must necessarily divert capital, and, whatever other consequences may flow from the frequent strikes and the formidable labour organisations of our time, it cannot be denied that they have both of these effects. If, in addition to these things, it becomes the policy of Governments to seek to defray national expenditure more and more by exceptional taxation, levied for the sake of popularity exclusively on the rich, the tendency to abstain from large manufacturing and commercial enterprises will be greatly accentuated. Such enterprises will not cease, but they will become less numerous. Many manufacturers will probably follow the example which some have already set, and throw out branch establishments in foreign countries. A manufacturer who has some thousand pounds on hand, instead of employing them, as he would once have done, in extending his business, will be inclined to divide them in distant investments. It need scarcely be pointed out how dangerous all this is to a country which has a population much beyond its natural resources, and mainly dependent upon the enormous, unflagging, ever-extending manufacturing and commercial enterprise which vast accumulations and concentrations of capital can alone produce.

Another consequence, which has, perhaps, not been sufficiently considered, is the tendency of large fortunes to take forms which bring with them no clear and definite duties. The English landed system, which seems now gradually passing away, had, to a very eminent degree, associated great fortunes and high social position with an active life spent in the performance of a large number of administrative county and landlord duties. It in this way provided, perhaps as far as any social institution can provide, that the men who most powerfully influence others by their example should on the whole lead useful, active, and patriotic lives. A great manufacturer and the head of a great commercial undertaking is still more eminently a man whose wealth is indissolubly connected with a life of constant and useful industry.

Wealth, however, takes many other forms than these, and, if I mistake not, a conspicuous characteristic of our century has been the rapid multiplication of the idle rich. In the conditions of modern life it is quite possible for a man to have a colossal fortune in forms that require absolutely no labour, and bring with them no necessary or obvious duties. If he is content with the low rate of interest of the very best securities, he need scarcely give a thought to the sources of his income. If, as is probable, the whole or a portion of his fortune is invested in more speculative securities, it will require from him some time and thought, but it will not necessarily bring with it any imperative duties towards his fellow-creatures. It is true that a rich man of this kind is in reality a large employer of labour. As a shareholder he is part proprietor of railroads, steam-packets, dockyards, mines, and many other widely different, and probably widely scattered, industrial enterprises and organisations. But he has no real voice in the management of these concerns. He knows nothing of the conditions of the countless labourers who, in many countries and many climes, are toiling for his profit. He looks on his investments simply as sources of income. His sole information concerning them is probably confined to a few statistics about dividends, traffic returns, encumbrances, and trade prospects.

We are all familiar with great numbers of more or less wealthy men whose fortunes are of this description. Under the influences that I have described such fortunes seem to me likely to multiply. The tendency of most great forms of industry is evidently towards vast joint-stock companies with many shareholders. With improved means of communication, the securities and enterprises of many countries are easily thrown into a common market, and national and municipal debts, which create one of the easiest and most important forms of investment, are rapidly increasing. One of the first signs that a barbarous nation is adopting the manners of Occidental civilisation is, usually, the creation of a national debt, and democracies are certainly showing themselves in no degree behind the most extravagant monarchies in the rapidity with which they accumulate national and local indebtedness. Nor should we forget the effect which frequent revolutions and violent social and industrial perturbations always exercise on the disposition of fortunes. These things seldom fail to depress credit, to increase debt, to destroy industry, to impoverish nations; but they also furnish many opportunities by which the skilful, the fortunate, and the unscrupulous rise rapidly to easily acquired wealth. If we take them in conjunction with the influences that are in so many directions dissociating great wealth from landed property and administrative functions, and adding to the risks of extensive industrial undertakings, it will appear probable that the fortunes of the future will be much less connected with active duties than those of the past.

The prospect is not an encouraging one. A man of very superior powers will, no doubt, always find his work, and to such a man a fortune of this description will be an incalculable blessing. It will save him from years of drudgery and anxiety, and it will give him at the outset of his career the priceless advantage of independence. To men of lofty moral qualities it will at least be no injury. Such men will feel strongly the inalienable responsibilities of wealth, and will find in the fields of social and philanthropic activity ample scope for their exertions. Many, too, who are not men of conspicuous mental or moral force will have some strong taste for art, or literature, or country pursuits, or science, or research, which will secure for them useful and honourable lives. Yet it can scarcely be doubted that even these will always be exceptions. The majority of men fail to find their work unless it is brought before them prominently by circumstances, or forced upon them by the strong pressure of necessity. Wealth which brings with it no ties and is obtained and enjoyed with no effort is to most men a temptation and a snare. All the more dissipated capitals and watering-places of Europe and America are full of examples of men in this position, living lives of absolute frivolity, dissociated from all serious interests, ever seeking with feverish eagerness for new forms of pleasure, raising the standard of luxury and ostentation, and often, in still graver ways, depressing the moral tone of the society in which they live.

Considerations of this kind will probably be treated with much disdain by Radical critics. They will truly say, that the section of society referred to forms only a very small portion of the population, and they will ask whether nations are to frame their institutions with the object of providing occupation for the spoilt children of fortune, and saving them from their own frivolity or vice. No one, I suppose, would maintain that they should do so; but, in estimating the advantages and disadvantages of different institutions, many weights enter into either scale which would not of themselves be sufficient to turn the balance.

It is, however, a grave error to suppose that the evils I have described can be confined to the classes who are immediately concerned. It is impossible that the upper class of a nation can become corrupt, frivolous, or emasculated without affecting deeply and widely the whole body of the community. Constituted as human nature is, rich men will always contribute largely to set the tone of society, to form the tastes, habits, ideals and aspirations of other classes. In this respect, as in many others, the gradual dissociation of the upper classes from many forms of public duty is likely to prove a danger to the community.

It is an evil which appears wherever democracy becomes ascendant, though its progress varies much in different countries. The strong traditions, the firmly knit organisation of English life, has hitherto resisted it much more effectively than most nations. No one can say that the upper classes in England have as yet abandoned politics. Those who fear this change may derive some consolation from observing how largely the most Radical Cabinets of our time have consisted of peers and connections of peers, and from counting up the many thousands of pounds at which the average private incomes of their members may be estimated. Nor, indeed, can it be said that English democracy, on either side of the Atlantic, shows any special love for a Spartan, or Stoical, or Puritan simplicity. Mr. Cecil Rhodes once described a prominent politician as 'a cynical sybarite who was playing the demagogue'; and it must be owned that professions of a very austere democracy have not unfrequently been found united with the keenest appetite for wealth, for pleasure, and even for titles. The political and economical influences, however, which I have endeavoured to trace have established in England, as elsewhere, a tendency which is not the less real because it has not yet triumphed, and the experience of American political and municipal life throws much light upon the path along which we are moving. The change in the House of Commons is becoming visible to every eye, and one of the most important questions for the future is the possibility of maintaining an Upper Chamber as a permanent and powerful element in the Constitution.

Part Nine

~~~~~~

CONSERVATIVE IMPULSES AMID AMERICAN MATERIALISM

During the "Gilded Age" that followed the Civil War, and down to the First World War, some brave voices were raised against the political and economic corruption of the time, and against America's materialism generally. E. L. Godkin (1831–1902), an Englishman of Liberal background who became editor of the New York *Nation;* Henry Adams (1838–1918), the historian, descendant of John Adams and John Quincy Adams; and Brooks Adams (1848–1927), Henry's brother, gloomily original— these three all foresaw how easily an abstraction called Capitalism might succumb to another abstraction called Communism.

WHO WILL PAY THE BILLS
OF SOCIALISM?

Edwin Lawrence Godkin

Edwin Lawrence Godkin, a journalist of high endowments, fought hard against the abuses of American society in the closing decades of the nineteenth century. But he knew that he would relish still less than his own era some collectivistic domination. This essay (pp. 225–48) from his *Problems of Modern Democracy* (New York, 1896) assails the "ethical economists" of socialism.

If I were to visit a friend of very moderate means, who was living very simply in a flat, in a remote part of the city, and he were to tell me that he was going to move into a house on Fifth or Madison Avenue; that he was tired, as was his family, of the very restricted life he had been leading; that he meant to give his children better quarters, better clothing, a better education, and more frequent access to the world of fashion and amusements, than they had previously had, I should conclude that he had received, in some way, a considerable addition to his income. But if I found, on inquiry, that not one cent or only a few hundred dollars had been added to it, I should conclude that the poor fellow was insane; that he was laboring under the well-known hallucination called plutomania.

Now I am very much in the same state of mind about the Socialists and ethical economists that I would be about him. I have, during the last two years, been reading a great deal of socialistic literature, ending the other day with

Kidd's "Social Evolution." The principal thing which I have learned from it all is that we are on the eve of a great social transformation. The régime of slavery has passed away; and the régime of feudalism has passed away; and the régime of competition is to pass away, and that before very long. The process began a few years ago, I am told, with the overthrow of the Manchester School. That school taught the doctrine of *laissez faire* as the best rule of living for the community. It taught individualism. It taught that the least possible government was the best. It reasoned about all social topics from the "economic man," a person whose main desire was to get money with the least posssible amount of exertion. It was willing to let the ablest man get the best things in life, and so on.

I learn that this is all now to be changed, not because it is not scientific, but because it is disagreeable or inhuman. Government is to interfere a good deal. It is first of all to take possession of the gas- and water-works, the railroads and telegraphs of the country. By and by it is to take possession of all the instruments of production, and see that nobody ever wants work. All the very rich men and the idle men are to disappear, and everybody is to be moderately well off. The differences, whatever they are, between workingmen and other people are to come to an end. According to Kidd, the workingmen are to have the same "social position" as every one else, because "moderate income is to give as good a social position as a large one." "The position of the lower classes is to be raised at the expense of the wealthier classes." "Education in its highest forms"—which I suppose means college education—is to be within the reach of everybody, and not, as now, the privilege of the well-to-do only. "The sphere of action of the State is to extend to every department of our social life." I might quote indefinitely to this effect from Marshall, from the Fabian "school" of economists, the "historical school" in Germany, and the Ely "school" in this country. In the world which they not only promise us, but which they say is now really near at hand, there will be no distinction of classes. Workingmen and their children will have exactly the same opportunities which professional men and people of moderate means now have. They will have their dinners, their balls, their theatres, their summer trips, their short hours of labor, their libraries, museums, and so forth. I am told this great change is coming very fast, though, as far as I can see, the signs of it are only to be found, as yet, in authors' studies and in college lecture-rooms. Mr. Kidd's authorities about it are chiefly the monthly magazines, Marshall, and an interview with W. T. Stead. The Fabian School cites no authorities at all, producing the whole change deductively out of its own head. Professor Ely bases his beliefs also on his own intuitions. A very large part of the work is to be wrought through "ethics," or "the science of ethics," which, I believe, is the name given by the various schools to the opinions of some of their members about the injustices of the competitive or present system.

I do not, as I have said, see any signs of the new régime in the world outside, except in extension of government interference to some enterprises, "affected," as our courts say, "with a public use." But no hard-and-fast line between government business and private business was ever drawn, even by the unfortunate Manchester School. What John Stuart Mill—whom I suppose I may describe as speaking for them, at all events to some extent—said, was that the question what things government should take charge of itself, and not leave to private enterprise, is to be settled by judgment, just as the question what things the head of a family should buy and what make at home, has to be settled by judgment. Government is, from the outset, a joint-stock enterprise. To say that it may run a post-office, but must on no account carry on a gas-factory or water-works, would be absurd. But whether, besides running a post-office, it should also run gas-works and water-works, depends on time and place and circumstances. To allow the city government of New York to do things which it is perfectly safe to let the corporation of Birmingham or Berlin do, would be extremely foolish. The truth is that the business of man in this world is to make himself as happy and comfortable as liability to death and disease will let him, and not to carry out the theories of "schools" or doctrinaires.

I make this little digression to get rid of the supposition that anything the civilized governments of the world are doing—and have done—for the convenience of their citizens, is to be considered the beginning of any great "movement" or "evolution." They have done nothing as yet which interferes seriously with any man's rational liberty. It makes no difference to me where I get my gas, or water, or transportation, provided I get it good and pure, provided I am not forced to take it if I do not want it, and provided I am not compelled to pay for anybody else's supply. I may say much the same thing of the education of children. Numerous experiments have shown me in various countries that if the State does not undertake the education of children, they will not be educated, and I am so sensible of the value of education to our civilization that I am well satisfied if the State should do it; nay, I insist that the State shall do it. I maintain, therefore, that no beginning of an evolution, or of an organic change in human society, has yet been made by any State. Whatever we are to have in that line is still to come, and it is of what is to come—that is, of what we are promised or threatened with—that I here concern myself.

As I said at the beginning of this article, when a man is about to move into a larger house and change his whole manner of life, he is, if sane, sure to ask himself what the change will cost, that is, what increase in his expenditures it will make necessary. If sane, also, he will follow this question by another, namely, Have I got the money? Now, in reading these stories to which I have referred, of the social evolution through which modern communities are to pass shortly, I find absolutely no allusion to cost. It is quite evident that, when the change comes about, it will make a great increase in the mere living expenses of every civilized population, without any increase of income that I can see or hear of. In this it will differ from all previous evolutions or revolutions. When the world gave up slavery, it substituted for a very wasteful form of labor a much more productive one. When, in the eighteenth century, it emancipated the peasantry from the kings and nobles, it gave a great impetus to their industry. It relieved them of enormous burdens incurred for the benefit of idle and frivolous men, and it greatly increased the motives for saving. The French Revolution gave a powerful stimulus to agriculture, and much enlarged the income of the working farmer. In like manner, in England, the introduction of the factory régime made large additions to the national income, and, through this, raised the wages and the standard of living of the working population. What Sidney Godolphin Osborne did by sending the Wiltshire farm-laborers to the North tells the whole story. In fact, the history of all the social and industrial changes of the civilized world during the past hundred years is, in the main, the history of great improvements in money-making, the history of additions both to the national and the individual income. The Manchester School has been much blamed for attaching too much importance to this, for thinking too much of additions to wealth without concerning itself as to the manner in which it was distributed. I am not concerned to defend it against this charge. My point is, that, ever since the fall of the Roman Empire, changes in the social condition of the civilized world have meant great improvements in the social income. No matter who got the money, more of it came in. Everybody who changed his style of living—barring, of course, spendthrifts and swindlers—did so because he knew his means permitted it.

The peculiarity of the social evolution which the phi-

losophers say is now impending is, that it is to be not a
money-making, but a spending evolution. Everybody is to
live a great deal better than he has been in the habit of living, and to have far more fun. Poverty is to disappear, and
real destitution—what the French call *"la misère"*—to
become unknown except as the result of gross misconduct.
I was one day last winter in the University Settlement in
Delancey Street, New York, and paid a visit to the rooms
in the top story of the building occupied by Dr. Stanton
Coit and his fellow-laborers. They were very neatly and
comfortably furnished, but perfectly simple and plain. Dr.
Coit explained to me that the aim of those who furnished
them was to show the kind of rooms every workingman
would have "if justice were done." I have since inquired
what the rent of those rooms would be to-day in that
neighborhood, and am told it would be about $750 a year,
or about $14.50 per week. But I am also told that $14.50 is
about the rent which the better class of laborers now pay
for their rooms *per month*. The general run of unskilled
laborers do not pay over $10 per month; so that, to do
"justice" to a workingman in this one particular, would
cost somebody about $43 a month. Who is this to be? A
rent of $58 per month ought, according to the ordinary
calculations, to argue an income of $290 per month. What
workingman gets this? If he does not get it, and ought to
have it, who is keeping him out of it?

What is the real working-class trouble? What is it that
makes their condition a "problem?" Why has it become a
question of growing importance in the politics of all European countries, as well as in our own? Why are so many
books and pamphlets written about it? Why do so many
people feel or affect a deep interest in it? Why does it call
out so much "ethical" discussion? Why are we threatened
with "social evolution" as a means of settling it?

The answer to all these questions is very simple. It is
the workingman's want of money which makes him the
object of so much pity, and dread, and speculation. If he

were better paid—as well paid as a clerk, a clergyman, a lawyer, a doctor, a business man—all the fuss we make about him would be an impertinence. We should bestow no consideration on his food, or clothing, or education, or on his "elevation," or on the elevation of his family. We should have no "ethical concepts" about him. So that the labor question is the question why the workingman does not have more money. The answer is that he gets now all there is for him, and that, if he is to have more, it must come from some great and sudden increase of production unattended with a great increase of population. The income of this and every other country in the world, since the plunder of foreign nations has ceased, is the product of its land an labor. Some of this income goes to pay wages, some goes to repair machinery and buildings, and some goes to pay profits to capital, or, in other words, to reward men for saving or for supplying long-felt wants. Consequently, to do justice to the laborer and greatly increase his comforts, so that he shall be as well off as anybody else, we must cut down the profits or interest on capital, or seize the capital, unless some hitherto unknown source of supply has been discovered.

Now let us see what would be the result of distributing among labor *all* the profit and interest on capital of the entire country. It must be observed, however, that, if we took it all, capital would promptly disappear, and next year, or the year after, labor would have to depend on its own resources. Besides this, the socialistic programme makes no provision for saving; the money is all to go in furniture, or amusements, and transportation. The capitalistic or saving class—or, in other words, the class which every year keeps back part of the national income for use next year—will vanish from the scene. We believe "the State" is, in the new régime, to play the part of the capitalist, but it could not withhold from labor the means of living with the comfort required by the new creed.

The total wealth of the United States, according to the

census of 1890—that is, the total existing product of land, labor, and saving—was $65,037,091,197; the population of the country was at the same date 62,622,250. Evenly divided, this would give $1,039 per caput, or a little more than $5,000 per family on the commonly accepted basis of five persons to a family. If the laborer spent his $5,000 at once in making himself comfortable, of course, he would, as well as the country at large, be worse off than ever. He would, in fact, be plunged at once into a very hopeless kind of poverty. But suppose he invested it; it would not yield him over, say, six per cent. at present rates of interest. This would make his income $300 a year, or about $6 a week. It is evident that he could on this make no material change in his style of living. Six dollars a week does not go far in rent and furniture and dinners and amusements. We have no statistics showing the annual income of the United States, but if we put it down as six per cent on the total accumulated wealth, we shall certainly not underestimate it. This interest would be $3,902,225,472, which, divided among the population, would give $62.31 a head, or $311.55 per family of five persons—that is, less than a dollar a day.

This does not differ materially from the results obtained in Great Britain. Robert Giffen, the English statistician, in one of his most elaborate articles a few years ago, estimated the total capital of the people of the United Kingdom, or the accumulated wealth of the nation, at £8,500,000,000 sterling, the population at that time being almost exactly 34,000,000, thus giving each individual $1,250 per caput, or about $6,000 per family, counting, as before, five to a family. If this were invested in England, it would hardly give more than four per cent., or $240 a year, which would be a pleasant addition to wages, but would leave no margin for amusements, travel, books, or "swell" clothing. We have no means of getting at the wealth of well-to-do people in the United States, there being as yet no reliable statistics bearing on that subject;

but an analysis of the income-tax returns in Great Britain shows that in a year when 456,680 persons were assessed, 118,830 had incomes over £300 a year, the total being £110,565,955. On the assumption that these people ought to be despoiled and made to share with their less fortunate brethren, let us see what would happen. The population of the kingdom in the year these returns were made was 37,176,464. If the income, then, of people having more than £300 a year were divided among the masses per capita, it would give each individual an income of about £3, or $15, annually. I always wonder, when reading the romances of the ethical economists, whether they have ever taken the trouble to look at these figures. Apparently they have not. If they had, we should assuredly, unless they have gone clean daft, hear less talk about what "the State" or the municipality can and ought to do for the elevation of the poor. The State has no money which it does not wring from the hard earnings of sorely pressed people. If it took as we see here, every cent they had, it would not be able to make a very noticeable change in the laborer's condition, even for a single year. What the rich spend on themselves is only a drop in the bucket, and they can secure none of their luxuries without sharing with the laborer, through investment.

The notion that there is a reservoir of wealth somewhere, either in the possession of the Government or the rich, which might be made to diffuse "plenty through a smiling land," is a delusion which nearly all the writings of the ethical economists tend to spread, and it is probably the most mischievous delusion which has ever taken hold on the popular mind. It affects indirectly large numbers of persons, who, if it were presented to them boldly and without drapery, would probably repudiate it. But it steals into their brains through sermons, speeches, pamphlets, Fabian essays, and Bellamy utopias, and disposes them, on humanitarian grounds, to great public extravagances, in buildings, in relief work, in pensions, in schools, in high State wages, and philanthropic undertakings which promise at no distant day to land the modern world in bankruptcy. It will be very well if the century closes without witnessing this catastrophe in France or Italy, or both—the two countries in which the democratic theory of the inexhaustibility of State funds has been carried furthest. It is diffusing through the working class of all countries, also, more and more every day, not only envy and hatred of the rich, but an increasing disinclination to steady industry, and an increasing disposition to rely on politics for the bettering of their condition. The Unions in England have already announced openly that it is no longer to strikes, but to Parliament, they must look for elevation, and, of course, all that Parliament can do for them is either to give them more money for less labor, or to spend other people's money on them in increasing their comforts.

This indifference to cost, or unwillingness to say where the money is to come from to make all the world happy and comfortable, is not confined, by any means, to our American and English Socialists. It is an equally marked characteristic of those of the Continent. Says the Paris *Temps*, speaking of that latest scheme of pensioning all old people:

> What are the usual tactics of Radicals and Socialists? They call with loud cries for reforms of all sorts, and vote the principle of them, but always refuse to discuss their financial consequences. More than this, they are among the first to vote remissions of taxes. On one side they swell the expenses; on the other they diminish the resources.

At Roubaix, the other day, the mayor proposed the following resolution: "All invalid laborers and all children should be supported by the Commune and the State." Somebody then asked him where the Commune and the State were to get the money. His answer was: "The money will be taken wherever it can be found." As Director Ely says, it was to be done from a "broad social standpoint," and "the general social effect" only—not cost—was to be considered.

Next in importance to the delusion that there is somewhere a great reservoir of wealth, which can still be drawn on for the general good, is the delusion that there is somewhere a reservoir of wisdom still untapped which can be drawn on for the execution of a new law of distribution. Not only is this current, but some of the philosophers have got into their heads that if our politicians had more money to spend, and more places to bestow, they would become purer and nobler and more public-spirited. This theory is so much opposed to the experience of the human race, that we are hardly more called on to argue against it than against the assertion that there will be no winter next year. We must take it for granted that what is meant is that there is somewhere a class of men whose services are now lost to the world, who would come into the field for the work of production and distribution under the new régime, and display a talent and discretion and judgment, which now cannot be had either for love or money, for the ordinary work of the world. Any salary is, to-day, small for a competent railroad, mining, or mill-manager; but we are asked to believe that when the State took charge of the great work of clothing and feeding and employing the community, men would be found in abundance to see that "ideal justice" was done, at about $3,000 a year. Well, there is no sign of such men at present. Nobody knows of their existence. The probabilities of biology, physiology, psychology, and sociology are all against their existence. The opportunities for display of their talents even now are immense, and yet they do not appear. Nobody says he has ever seen them. Nobody pretends that they could be found, except the ethical economists, and they never mention their names or habitat. In fact, as in Bellamy's case, the writers of the social romances are compelled to make

them unnecessary by predicting a change in human nature
which will make us all wise, just, industrious, and self-
denying.

I think, on the whole, it would not be an exaggeration to
say that such a social evolution as the ethical economists
have planned could not be accomplished, even for a single
year, without doubling the wealth of every country which
tried it, while making no increase in the population. And
this arrest of the growth of the population is just as necessary as the increase of wealth. For it is the exertions of
mankind in keeping up and increasing their numbers
which have prevented the poor from profiting more by the
recent improvements in production. Statistics show readily that, thus far, subsistence increases more rapidly than
population, and this does much to cheer up the optimists
and the revilers of Malthus. But to make a man of any use
to civilization, he must in some manner be able to pay for
his board. If wheat costs only ten cents a bushel, the man
who has not and cannot get the ten cents is clearly a bit of
surplus population. He has to depend on some one else for
his support, and is thus a burden to the community. Employing him at the public expense does not change the situation, for his neighbors are the public. If they really
wanted the work done, he would have something to exchange. If they do it in order to keep him from starving,
the demand for his labor is not legitimate, and is only a
thin disguise for charity. Population and subsistence are
equally balanced, in an economical sense, only when there
is a full demand for all the labor that offers itself, a state of
things which is never seen now in any of the great towns
of the world. Let a strike but take place in any branch of
unskilled or only slightly skilled labor, and the swarm of
applicants for the vacant places, who instantly appear,
shows that there is in that spot an excess of people. That is
to say, statistics may prove that food has far outrun the
population of the United States at large, and yet there will
be in New York and Boston and Philadelphia thousands

who find it very difficult to purchase it at any price. The Socialists have no plan of dealing with this, except making the successful support the unsuccessful, the industrious the idle, on the same scale of comfort as their own.

I have also learned from my reading that a new "law of distribution" is under consideration in the colleges and ethical schools of the world, and that there is a fair prospect that one which will satisfy all existing needs will be evolved. Now, there are only three laws of distribution of which I can form any conception. One would be a natural law, like the law of gravitation, which automatically divided among all concerned, as soon as completed, the results of any given piece of production, without any care on the part of anybody, and of which nobody could complain any more than of the earth's attraction. Another would be a law formed by some authority, which everybody would acknowledge as final, and to which all would submit, either owing to the overwhelming force at its command, or to the universal confidence in its justice. The third would be the present law, which I may call the law of general agreement, under which everybody gets the least for which he will labor, and the least for which he will save and invest. If there be any other than these, I am unable to think it.

The first of these, I presume, does not need discussion. There never will be any natural distributive force to which we shall all have to submit as we submit to the law of chemical affinity or proportion. The division of the products of labor and capital will always be the subject of some sort of human arrangement, in which the human will will play a more or less prominent part. So that the second of these laws would have to be the result of some kind of understanding as to who or what the deciding authority should be, to which all would have to submit without murmuring. Thus far in the history of mankind it has never been possible to come to such an agreement even on matters touching the feelings much less nearly than one's share of the products of one's labor. No government, spiritual or temporal, has ever existed, which had not to keep in subjection a hostile minority by the use of force in some shape. The Pope in the Middle Ages came nearer seeming the voice of pure justice than any other power that has ever appeared in the Western world. But Christendom was never unanimously willing to let him arrange even its political concerns, and I do not think it ever entered into the head of the most enthusiastic papist to let him arrange his domestic affairs—so far as to say what his wages or his profits should be. The guilds came near doing this in various trades, but their authority was maintained by the power of expulsion. When the whole of civil society becomes a guild, this power cannot be exercised, because there will be no place for the expelled man to go. To make him submit, there would have to be some sort of compulsion put upon him. In other words, he would have to be enslaved by being compelled to labor against his will for a reward which he deemed inadequate. Except on the assumption, which the smallest knowledge of human nature makes ridiculous, that everybody is sure to be satisfied with what he gets for his work, any law of distribution emanating from a human authority would necessarily result in slavery. In truth it is impossible to conceive any plan of State socialism which would not involve the slavery of some portion of the population, unless we can picture to ourselves unanimity concerning the things on which men under all previous régimes have been most apt to differ.

It is hardly necessary to discuss the chances of a "State" composed of men of such acknowledged wisdom and goodness that nobody would dispute their ordering of his domestic concerns. But, improbable as this is, it is by no means so improbable as a State composed of men competent to meet the Socialists' demands in their business capacity. The ethical economists never go into details on this subject. They assume, as does Schmoller, that the State—

that is, the small body of men charged with the enormous responsibilities of a socialist or semi-socialist community, both with its production and distribution, and the care of its health and morals—would in some manner be a sort of concentration of the virtue and morals of the whole community; that it would, in addition, have an amount of administrative power, for which railroads, mines, and mills now vainly offer almost any salary, and for which nations would give every conceivable earthly honor and reward—fame, power, money, and enthusiastic homage—could they get them for the management of their finances or the command of their armies. As this assumption is so gross and bold that there is curiously little discussion about it, and as its basis is never explained, it may be dismissed as chimaera.

Mr. Kidd makes mention, among Socialists' expectations, the expectation that some day the laborer will have the same "social position" as the more well-to-do classes, that is, what the French call the *bourgeoisie*—the men who wear black coats and do no manual labor. "Social position" is an extremely vague phrase, and yet I think there is probably more hope for the working classes in this direction than in any other. The Socialists mean, I presume, by sameness of social position, association for purposes of social enjoyment on a footing of equality and with reciprocity of pleasure. But the difficulties in the way of this consummation, though on the surface trifling, and, like the thing itself, hard to define, are nevertheless likely to prove very troublesome. The old feudal feeling which made the man who employed labor look down on the laborer as an inferior or semi-menial person, has hardly reached this country, or, if it ever did reach it, has died out. Society is consequently divided by what we may call natural lines—that is, by differences of taste, of personal habits, of mental culture, and social experience. People of the same "social position" are, as a rule, people who live in much the same way—that is, with about the same expenditure in clothes, furniture, and cookery, and are drawn together by some sort of community either of ideas or of intersts.

But any change which goes on in the way of development or "evolution," in this arrangement, is in the direction of bringing people together socially who do *not* live in exactly the same way, do not belong to the same caste or circle or class. In those countries in which the democratic movement has made most advances and made most impression on the manners—France, Italy, and the United States, for instance—differences of fortune are less and less potent in preventing social intercourse. But in no country has the workingman made his way as yet into anything that can be called "society," that is, into any circle which gives "social position." Nor could he be introduced into it by any sort of legislation or any species of compulsion. "Social position" is something beyond the reach of armies or fleets or parliaments. It must be won in some manner. It cannot be accorded or decreed. The difference between a lady's drawing-room full of guests, and a wigwam packed with squaws and warriors, tells better than even science, or art, or laws, or government, the distance the community has travelled in its upward course.

CORRUPT WASHINGTON
Henry Adams

Henry Adams' *Education*, his *Mont-Saint-Michel and Chartres*, and his nine-volume *History of the United States during the Administrations of Jefferson and Madison* have kept his memory much alive. His two novels have been less admired. Yet this chapter from his novel *Democracy* (1908), with its burning contempt for democratic corruption, is not easy to forget. The scene is a Washington drawing room during the Gilded Age. There one encounters Baron Jacobi, the Bulgarian minister; Mrs. Lightfoot Lee, Madeleine, a charming high-minded widow; Count Popoff of the Russian legation; John Carrington, a Washington lawyer from Virginia; Hartbeest Schneidekoupon, a genteel lobbyist from Philadelphia; Nathan Gore of Massachusetts, historian and man of letters, dancing attendance upon power; and Senator Ratcliffe, sufficiently ruthless, from the Middle West. All are drawn from the life. This is Chapter IV of *Democracy* (pp. 66–82 in the reprint of New York, 1933).

Sunday evening was stormy, and some enthusiasm was required to make one face its perils for the sake of society. Nevertheless, a few intimates made their appearance as usual at Mrs. Lee's. The faithful Popoff was there, and Miss Dare also ran in to pass an hour with her dear Sybil; but as she passed the whole evening in a corner with Popoff, she must have been disappointed in her object. Carrington came, and Baron Jacobi. Schneidekoupon and his sister dined with Mrs. Lee, and remained after dinner, while Sybil and Julia Schneidekoupon compared conclusions about Washington society. The happy idea also occurred to Mr. Gore that, inasmuch as Mrs. Lee's house was but a step from his hotel, he might as well take the chance of amusement there as the certainty of solitude in his rooms. Finally, Senator Ratcliffe duly made his appearance, and, having established himself with a cup of tea by Madeleine's side, was soon left to enjoy a quiet talk with her, the rest of the party by common consent occupying themselves with each other. Under cover of the murmur of conversation in the room, Mr. Ratcliffe quickly became confidential.

"I came to suggest that, if you want to hear an interesting debate, you should come up to the Senate to-morrow.

I am told that Garrard, of Louisiana, means to attack my last speech, and I shall probably in that case have to answer him. With you for a critic I shall speak better."

"Am I such an amiable critic?" asked Madeleine.

"I never heard that amiable critics were the best," said he; "justice is the soul of good criticism, and it is only justice that I ask and expect from you."

"What good does this speaking do?" inquired she. "Are you any nearer the end of your difficulties by means of your speeches?"

"I hardly know yet. Just now we are in dead water; but this can't last long. In fact, I am not afraid to tell you, though of course you will not repeat it to any human being, that we have taken measures to force an issue. Certain gentlemen, myself among the rest, have written letters meant for the President's eye, though not addressed directly to him, and intended to draw out an expression of some sort that will show us what to expect."

"Oh!" laughed Madeleine, "I knew about that a week ago."

"About what?"

"About your letter to Sam Grimes, of North Bend."

"What have you heard about my letter to Sam Grimes, of North Bend?" ejaculated Ratcliffe, a little abruptly.

"Oh, you do not know how admirably I have organised my secret service bureau," said she. "Representative Cutter cross-questioned one of the Senate pages, and obliged him to confess that he had received from you a letter to be posted, which letter was addressed to Mr. Grimes, of North Bend."

"And, of course, he told this to French, and French told you," said Ratcliffe; "I see. If I had known this I would not have let French off so gently last night, for I prefer to tell you my own story without his embellishments. But it was my fault. I should not have trusted a page. Nothing is a secret here long. But one thing that Mr. Cutter did not find out was that several other gentlemen wrote letters at the same time, for the same purpose. Your friend, Mr. Clinton, wrote; Krebs wrote; and one or two members."

"I suppose I must not ask what you said?"

"You may. We agreed that it was best to be very mild and conciliatory, and to urge the President only to give us some indication of his intentions, in order that we might not run counter to them. I drew a strong picture of the effect of the present situation on the party, and hinted that I had no personal wishes to gratify."

"And what do you think will be the result?"

"I think we shall somehow manage to straighten things out," said Ratcliffe. "The difficulty is only that the new President has little experience, and is suspicious. He thinks we shall intrigue to tie his hands, and he means to tie ours in advance. I don't know him personally, but those who do, and who are fair judges, say that, though rather narrow and obstinate, he is honest enough, and will come round. I have no doubt I could settle it all with him in an hour's talk, but it is out of the question for me to go to him unless I am asked, and to ask me to come would be itself a settlement."

"What, then, is the danger you fear?"

"That he will offend all the important party leaders in order to conciliate unimportant ones, perhaps sentimental ones, like your friend French; that he will make foolish appointments without taking advice. By the way, have you seen French to-day?"

"No," replied Madeleine; "I think he must be sore at your treatment of him last evening. You were very rude to him."

"Not a bit," said Ratcliffe; "these reformers need it. His attack on me was meant for a challenge. I saw it in his manner."

"But is reform really so impossible as you describe it? Is it quite hopeless?"

"Reform such as he wants is utterly hopeless, and not even desirable."

Mrs. Lee, with much earnestness of manner, still pressed her question: "Surely something can be done to check corruption. Are we for ever to be at the mercy of thieves and ruffians? Is a respectable government impossible in a democracy?"

Her warmth attracted Jacobi's attention, and he spoke across the room. "What is that you say, Mrs. Lee? What is it about corruption?"

All the gentlemen began to listen and gather about them.

"I am asking Senator Ratcliffe," said she, "what is to become of us if corruption is allowed to go unchecked."

"And may I venture to ask permission to hear Mr. Ratcliffe's reply?" asked the baron.

"My reply," said Ratcliffe, "is that no representative government can long be much better or much worse than the society it represents. Purify society and you purify the government. But try to purify the government artificially and you only aggravate failure."

"A very statesmanlike reply," said Baron Jacobi, with a formal bow, but his tone had a shade of mockery. Carrington, who had listened with a darkening face, suddenly turned to the baron and asked him what conclusion he drew from the reply.

"Ah!" exclaimed the baron, with his wickedest leer, "what for is my conclusion good? You Americans believe yourselves to be excepted from the operation of general laws. You care not for experience. I have lived seventy-five years, and all that time in the midst of corruption. I am corrupt myself, only I do have courage to proclaim it, and you others have it not. Rome, Paris, Vienna, Petersburg, London, all are corrupt; only Washington is pure! Well, I declare to you that in all my experience I have found no society which has had elements of corruption like the United States. The children in the street are corrupt, and know how to cheat me. The cities are all corrupt, and also the towns and the counties and the States' legislatures and the judges. Everywhere men betray trusts both public and private, steal money, run away with public funds. Only in the Senate men take no money. And you gentlemen in the Senate very well declare that your great United States, which is the head of the civilized world, can never learn anything from the example of corrupt Europe. You are right—quite right! The great United States needs not an example. I do much regret that I have not yet one hundred years to live. If I could then come back to this city, I should find myself very content—much more than now. I am always content where there is much corruption, and *ma parole d'honneur!*[1] broke out the old man with fire and gesture, "the United States will then be more corrupt than Rome under Caligula; more corrupt than the Church under Leo X.; more corrupt than France under the Regent!"

As the baron closed his little harangue, which he delivered directly at the senator sitting underneath him, he had the satisfaction to see that every one was silent and listening with deep attention. He seemed to enjoy annoying the senator, and he had the satisfaction of seeing that the senator was visibly annoyed. Ratcliffe looked sternly at the baron and said, with some curtness, that he saw no reason to accept such conclusions. Conversation flagged, and all except the baron were relieved when Sybil, at Schneidekoupon's request, sat down at the piano to sing what she called a hymn. So soon as the song was over, Ratcliffe, who seemed to have been curiously thrown off his balance by Jacobi's harangue, pleaded urgent duties at his rooms, and retired. The others soon afterwards went off in a body, leaving only Carrington and Gore, who had seated himself by Madeleine, and was at once dragged by her into a discussion of the subject which perplexed her, and for the moment threw over her mind a net of irresistible fascination.

---

1. "Upon my word." [R.K.]

"The baron discomfited the senator," said Gore, with a certain hesitation. "Why did Ratcliffe let himself be trampled upon in that manner?"

"I wish you would explain why," replied Mrs. Lee; "tell me, Mr. Gore—you who represent cultivation and literary taste hereabouts—please tell me what to think about Baron Jacobi's speech. Who and what is to be believed? Mr. Ratcliffe seems honest and wise. Is he a corruptionist? He believes in the people, or says he does. Is he telling the truth or not?"

Gore was too experienced in politics to be caught in such a trap as this. He evaded the question. "Mr. Ratcliffe has a practical piece of work to do; his business is to make laws and advise the President; he does it extremely well. We have no other equally good practical politician; it is unfair to require him to be a crusader besides."

"No!" interposed Carrington, curtly; "but he need not obstruct crusades. He need not talk virtue and oppose the punishment of vice."

"He is a shrewd practical politician," replied Gore, "and he feels first the weak side of any proposed political tactics."

With a sigh of despair Madeleine went on:

"Who, then, is right? How *can* we all be right? Half of our wise men declare that the world is going straight to perdition; the other half that it is fast becoming perfect. Both cannot be right. There is only one thing in life," she went on, laughing, "that I must and will have before I die. I must know whether America is right or wrong. Just now this question is a very practical one, for I really want to know whether to believe in Mr. Ratcliffe. If I throw him overboard, everything must go, for he is only a specimen."

"Why not believe in Mr. Ratcliffe?" said Gore; "I believe in him myself, and am not afraid to say so."

Carrington, to whom Ratcliffe now began to represent the spirit of evil, interposed here, and observed that he imagined Mr. Gore had other guides besides, and steadier

ones than Ratcliffe, to believe in; while Madeleine, with a
certain feminine perspicacity, struck at a much weaker
point in Mr. Gore's armour, and asked point-blank
whether he believed also in what Ratcliffe represented:
"Do you yourself think democracy the best government,
and universal suffrage a success?"

Mr. Gore saw himself pinned to the wall, and he turned
at bay with almost the energy of despair:

"These are matters about which I rarely talk in society;
they are like the doctrine of a personal God; of a future
life; of revealed religion; subjects which one naturally reserves for private reflection. But since you ask for my political creed, you shall have it. I only condition that it shall
be for you alone, never to be repeated or quoted as mine. I
believe in democracy. I accept it. I will faithfully serve
and defend it. I believe in it because it appears to me the
inevitable consequence of what has gone before it. Democracy asserts the fact that the masses are now raised to
a higher intelligence than formerly. All our civilisation
aims at this mark. We want to do what we can to help it. I
myself want to see the result. I grant it is an experiment,
but it is the only direction society can take that is worth
its taking; the only conception of its duty large enough to
satisfy its instincts; the only result that is worth an effort
or a risk. Every other possible step is backward, and I do
not care to repeat the past. I am glad to see society grapple
with issues in which no one can afford to be neutral."

"And supposing your experiment fails," said Mrs. Lee;
"suppose society destroys itself with universal suffrage,
corruption, and communism."

"I wish, Mrs. Lee, you would visit the Observatory
with me some evening, and look at Sirius. Did you ever
make the acquaintance of a fixed star? I believe astron-
omers reckon about twenty millions of them in sight, and
an infinite possibility of invisible millions, each one of
which is a sun, like ours, and may have satellites like our
planet. Suppose you see one of these fixed stars suddenly

increase in brightness, and are told that a satellite has fallen into it and is burning up, its career finished, its capacities exhausted? Curious, is it not; but what does it matter? Just as much as the burning up of a moth at your candle."

Madeleine shuddered a little. "I cannot get to the height of your philosophy," said she. "You are wandering among the infinites, and I am finite."

"Not at all! But I have faith; not perhaps in the old dogmas, but in the new ones; faith in human nature; faith in science; faith in the survival of the fittest. Let us be true to our time, Mrs. Lee! If our age is to be beaten, let us die in the ranks. If it is to be victorious, let us be first to lead the column. Anyway, let us not be skulkers or grumblers. There! have I repeated my catechism correctly? You would have it! Now oblige me by forgetting it. I should lose my character at home if it got out. Good night!"

Mrs. Lee duly appeared at the Capitol the next day, as she could not but do after Senator Ratcliffe's pointed request. She went alone, for Sybil had positively refused to go near the Capitol again, and Madeleine thought that on the whole this was not an occasion for enrolling Carrington in her service. But Ratcliffe did not speak. The debate was unexpectedly postponed. He joined Mrs. Lee in the gallery, however, sat with her as long as she would allow, and became still more confidential, telling her that he had received the expected reply from Grimes, of North Bend, and that it had enclosed a letter written by the President-elect to Mr. Grimes in regard to the advances made by Mr. Ratcliffe and his friends.

"It is not a handsome letter," said he; "indeed, a part of it is positively insulting. I would like to read you one extract from it and hear your opinion as to how it should be treated." Taking the letter from his pocket, he sought out the passage, and read as follows: " 'I cannot lose sight, too, of the consideration that these three Senators' (he means Clinton, Krebs, and me) 'are popularly considered to be the most influential members of that so-called senatorial ring, which has acquired such general notoriety. While I shall always receive their communications with all due respect, I must continue to exercise complete freedom of action in consulting other political advisers as well as these, and I must in all cases make it my first object to follow the wishes of the people, not always most truly represented by their nominal representatives.' What say you to that precious piece of presidential manners?"

"At least I like his courage," said Mrs. Lee.

"Courage is one thing; common sense is another. This letter is a studied insult. He has knocked me off the track once. He means to do it again. It is a declaration of war. What ought I to do?"

"Whatever is most for the public good," said Madeleine, gravely.

Ratcliffe looked into her face with such undisguised delight—there was so little possibility of mistaking or ignoring the expression of his eyes, that she shrank back with a certain shock. She was not prepared for so open a demonstration. He hardened his features at once, and went on:

"But what *is* most for the public good?"

"That you know better than I," said Madeleine; "only one thing is clear to me. If you let yourself be ruled by your private feelings, you will make a greater mistake than he. Now I must go, for I have visits to make. The next time I come, Mr. Ratcliffe, you must keep your word better."

When they next met, Ratcliffe read to her a part of his reply to Mr. Grimes, which ran thus: "It is the lot of every party leader to suffer from attacks and to commit errors. It is true, as the President says, that I have been no exception to this law. Believing as I do that great results can only be accomplished by great parties, I have uniformly yielded my own personal opinions where they have failed to obtain general assent. I shall continue to follow this course, and the President may with perfect confidence count upon my disinterested support of all party measures, even though I may not be consulted in originating them."

Mrs. Lee listened attentively, and then said:

"Have you never refused to go with your party?"

"Never!" was Ratcliffe's firm reply.

Madeleine still more thoughtfully inquired again: "Is nothing more powerful than party allegiance?"

"Nothing, except national allegiance," replied Ratcliffe, still more firmly.

THE REVOLT OF MODERN DEMOCRACY AGAINST STANDARDS OF DUTY
Brooks Adams

The degradation of woman and art by an insensate materialistic individualism: this is the evil scourged here by Brooks Adams, a conservative of Jeremiah's school. This speech was published in *Proceedings of the American Academy of Arts and Letters*, Vol. 9 (New York, November, 1916), pp. 8–12.

I know not how it may be with others, but I am aware of a growing reluctance to express my views in public, which of late has approached absolute repugnance. Perhaps this feeling may be due to the sombreness of age, but I rather incline to ascribe it to an apprehension of the future which dawned on me long ago, but which of late has deepened with a constantly augmenting acceleration. If I thought that anything that I could do would affect the final issue, I might be more inclined to effort; but I perceive myself to be so far sundered from most of my countrymen that I shrink exceedingly from thrusting on them opinions which will give offense or, more likely still, excite derision. For when I look about me I see the American people as a whole quite satisfied that they have solved the riddle of the universe, and firmly convinced that by means of plenty of money, popular education, cheap transportation, universal suffrage, unlimited amusements, the moral uplift, and the "democratic ideal," they have only one more step to take to land them in perfection.

I cannot altogether share this optimism, and particularly I have doubts touching the American "democratic ideal." It is of these doubts that I intend to speak to-day, as I consider this apotheosis of the "democratic ideal" the profoundest and most far-reaching phenomenon of our age. Yet I so much dislike assuming the critical attitude that I should have declined the flattering invitation you have given me to address you had I deemed it quite becoming for a member of an association like this to refuse to participate in your proceedings when requested to do so by your officers. I have only this one claim to urge to your indulgence: at least I have not sought to vex you by obtruding my speculations on you.

I start with this proposition, which to me is self-evident, and which I therefore assume as axiomatic: that no organized social system, such as we commonly call a national civilization, can cohere against those enemies which must certainly beset it, if it fail to recognize as its primary standard of duty the obligation of the individual man and woman to sacrifice themselves for the whole community in time of need. And, furthermore, that this standard may be effective and not theoretical, it must be granted that the power to determine when the moment of need has arisen lies not with the individual, but with society in its corporate capacity. This last crucial attribute can never be admitted to inhere in private judgment.

I shall ask you to consider with me first the nature of the American "democratic ideal," and subsequently to test it by this standard. For my part, for the last twelve months this subject has been constantly in my thoughts, fixed there by the war now raging.

Last August I chanced to be in Paris when hostilities began, and I came home filled with the solemn impression of the French sense of duty made on me by seeing the whole manhood of France march to the frontier without a murmur and without a quaver. I knew that the same thing was going on in Germany. I thought that men could do no more. Now, the rights and wrongs of this war are, for my present purpose, immaterial; all that concerns me is the national standard it illustrates of self-sacrifice and of duty. And on both sides of the Rhine I found that standard good. It seemed to me also to be the true standard of pure democracy. For what can be more democratic than that prince and peasant, plutocrat and pauper, shall serve their country together side by side, marching in the same regiment, wearing the same uniform, submitting to the same discipline, enduring the same hardships, and dying the same death? In mass universal service is absolute equality. Some men, it is true, serve as officers, but these men are officers only because, by lives devoted to obedience, to self-denial, and to study, they have made themselves fit for command, and when the hour of danger is at hand this fitness for command is recognized by their countrymen who have chosen more lucrative or easier walks in life.

I had supposed that in our democracy these great facts would be appreciated and honored by all, even though it might possibly be argued that in America the necessity for such self-abnegation had not yet arisen. I never fell into greater error. Familiar as I am with American idiosyncrasies, I was astonished, on landing in New York, to find the German military system bitterly assailed as conflicting with the American "democratic ideal," and I asked myself why this should be. It is true that the German system of universal military service had been the first to be thoroughly organized, but that could not impeach its principle or make it conflict with a sound "democratic ideal."

I beg you to grant me an instant in which to explain myself. I wish to make it clear that I have never admired Germany as a whole, although I have known her rather intimately. A generation ago, when it was the fashion here almost to worship the Germans, even to their art, their literature, their language, and their manners, when eminent gentlemen who have no good word for Germany now used to insist to me at college that nothing but a Germanized education could suffice for the student, I rebelled. I protested that Germany had made no such contribution to our civilization, in comparison, for instance, with France, as to justify in us any such servile attitude, and that I could not admit her claims. In later years I have distrusted her ambitions, I have detested her manners, I have abhorred her language and her art, I have feared her competition, and I have been jealous of her navy, but I have never questioned in my heart that her military system of universal service is truly democratic, and I have wished that it might be adopted here. It never occurred to me that it could be denounced as undemocratic, or reviled as a tool of the Junker class, used by them for their own aggrandizement and for the oppression of the German people. Such an accusation would have seemed to me too shallow to be noticed. I could not comprehend how any sober-minded man who knew the history of the Seven Years War and of Jena could fail to perceive that the German military system was an effect of a struggle of a people for existence, and that the German people and the German army are one. Their vices and their virtues are the same. To imagine that a handful of Prussian squires, most of whom are far from rich, could coerce millions of their countrymen from all ranks in life, who equally with the Junkers are trained and armed soldiers, into doing something which they thought harmful, and waging wars which they hated as ruinous or wrong, was and is to me a proposition too absurd to deserve serious refutation. What, then, I asked myself, could be the secret of the hostility of Americans to German universal military service, a hostility which Americans disguised under the phrase of faith in "democratic ideals"? And as I watched this phenomenon and meditated upon what I saw and heard, the suspicion which had long lain half-consciously in my mind ripened into the conviction that the real tyranny against which my countrymen revolted was the tyranny of universal self-sacrifice, and that they hated German universal military service because it rigorously demanded a sacrifice from every man from which they personally shrank; for, enforced in America, as it might be were Germany to prevail in this war, they would perhaps be constrained to give one year of their lives to their country.

If this inference were sound, it occurred to me that not improbably our "democratic ideal" consisted in the principle that men or women should not be obliged to conform to any standard of duty against their will, or, in short, in the principle of universal selfishness. Then I turned to our women for enlightenment, as the female sex is supposed to set ours an example in unselfishness. To instruct myself I read the modern feminist literature and followed a little the feminist debate, and very shortly I found my question answered.

Since civilization first dawned on earth the family has been the social unit on which all authority, all order, and all obedience has reposed. Therefore the family has been the cement of society, and the chief element in cohesion. To preserve the family, and thus to make society stable, the woman has always sacrificed herself for it, as the man has sacrificed himself for her upon the field of battle. The obligations and the sacrifices have been correlative. But I beheld our modern women shrilly repudiating such a standard of duty and such a theory of self-sacrifice. On the contrary, they denied that as individual units they owed society any duty as mothers or as wives, and maintained that their first duty was to themselves. If they found the bonds of the family irksome, they might renounce them and wander whither they would through the world in order to obtain a fuller life for themselves. This phase of individualism would appear to be an ultimate form of self-ishness, and the final resolution of society into atoms, but none the less it would also appear to be the feminine in-terpretation of the American "democratic ideal."

Proceeding a little further, I come to the capitalistic class—a class which I take to be a far more powerful class with us than are the Prussian Junkers in Germany. Noth-ing, therefore, can be more important to our present pur-pose than to appreciate the standard recognized by them. I shall take but one test of many I applied, because time is pressing.

The railways are to a modern country what the arteries are to the human body. The national life-blood flows through them. They are a prime factor in our prosperity and contentment in time of peace, and our first means of defense in time of war. Though they are vital to our cor-porate life, our Government confides their administration to capitalists as trustees, who are supposed to collect for their work as trustees a reasonable compensation, which they levy on the public by a tax on transportation which we call rates. Very clearly no injustice could be more fla-grant and no injury deeper than that such taxes should be unequal or excessive. I ask in what spirit this most sacred of trusts has been performed? The legislation that cumbers our statute-books, the cases that cram our law reports, and the wrecks upon the stock-market tell the tale better than could any words of mine. It is hardly a tale of self-abnegation to meet a standard of public duty, though it may well be an exemplification of the American "demo-cratic ideal."

Next in order would naturally come labor. The specta-cle in democratic England of hundreds of thousands of coal miners utilizing the extremity of their country's agony as a means of extorting from society a selfish pecuniary advantage for themselves brings before us vividly enough the workman's understanding of the "democratic ideal."

Supposing, for our own edification, we contemplate *ourselves*, we who are artists and literary men, and ask ourselves what our interpretation is of our "democratic ideal." At this suggestion there rises before my mind a vision of long ago. I was one evening conversing in a club with a well-known painter about some decorations which were attracting attention and were very costly, but which offended my taste as being frankly plutocratic. I observed that though they brought high prices, I questioned whether they conformed to any true canon of art. Like a flash he turned on me and said:

"And who are you to talk of artistic standards? In our world there is but one standard, and that the standard of price. That which sells is good art, that which does not sell is bad art. There can be no appeal from price."

I made no answer, for I saw that he was right. Art is a form of expression, and art can, therefore, express only the society which environs it, and our standard is money, or, in other words, the means of self-indulgence. I had been unconsciously thinking of the civilization which produced the old tower of Chartres and the Virgin's Portal at Paris, when monks, safe in their convents, could concentrate their souls on expressing the aspirations and the self-devotion of their age. I wondered whether we as literary men have in mind, when we do our work, an ideal which is our standard, as religion was their standard or as the verdict at Olympia was the standard of the Greeks; or do we worry little over the form or the substance of our labor, and think mostly of the artifices which may attract the public, and charm the publisher by stimulating sales. If we do the latter, we exemplify the American "democratic ideal," which denies any standard save the standard of self-interest which is incarnated in price.

I had reached this point in my reflections when it occurred to me to test my inferences by applying them to our collective public thought. After some hesitation I have concluded that, as a unified organism, we Americans are nearly incapable of continuous collective thought except at long intervals under the severest tension. For instance, during the Civil war one-half of our country sustained what might be called a train of partly digested collective thought through some four years, but on the return to the Union of the Southern States our thought became more disorderly than ever. Ordinarily we cannot think except individually or locally. Hence the particular interest must, as a rule, dominate the collective interest, so that scientific legislation is impossible, and no fixed policy can be long maintained. Thus we can formulate no scientific tariff, since our tariffs are made by combinations of private and local interests, with little or no relation to collective advantage. We can organize no effective army, because the money and the effort needed to construct an effective army must be frittered away to gratify localities; nor can we have a well-adjusted navy, because we can persist in no plan developed by a central intelligence. We call our appropriation bill for public works our pork-barrel, probably with only too good reason. But the point to be marked is that in our national legislature the instinct of unity, continuity, and order seldom prevails over individualism or disorder, with the result that our collective administration of public affairs may not unreasonably be termed chaotic.

Descending from the Union to the State, the same rule holds. This year a constitution was submitted to the voters of New York, the object of which was to check in some small measure the chaos of individualism in state affairs. It was defeated by an enormous majority because the "democratic ideal" does not tolerate the notion of unity or order at the cost of private self-interest.

But after all the most perfect exemplification of the American "democratic ideal," or the principle of selfishness in public affairs, occurs in our cities. In America there is one city administered on the principle of unity and self-restraint. It is Washington, but I suppose that no other municipality in the land would endure such a yoke, and the reason is plain. In Washington private interests are subordinated to public interests, but our "democratic ideal" contemplates a municipal system which yields an opposite result. Self-interest requires that our municipalities should be so organized that every rich man may buy such franchises as he needs to enrich himself, while every poor man may obtain his job at the public cost. This is the complete subordination of the principle of unity to that of diversity, of order to chaos, of the community to the individual, of self-sacrifice to selfishness. It is in fine the pure American "democratic ideal."

I submit most humbly that untold ages of human experience have proved to us that nature is inexorable and demands of us self-sacrifice if we would have our civilization, our country, our families, our art, or our literature survive. Unselfishness is what the words patriotism and maternal love mean. Those words mean that we cannot survive and live for ourselves alone. We cannot be individualistic, or selfish to an extreme, we cannot hope for salvation through our "democratic ideal." For, if we accept that, we accept the conclusion that our country can never exert her strength in the hour of peril, because we leave to private judgment the sacrifice which every citizen shall make her. We renounce a standard of duty. But surely sooner or later that mortal peril must arise which none can hope to escape, either from within or from without, and when we least expect it. "But of that day and hour knoweth no man, for ye know not what hour our Lord may come."

If it be true, as I do apprehend, that our "democratic ideal" is only a phrase to express our renunciation as a nation of all standards of duty, and the substitution therefor of a reference to private judgment; if we men are to leave to ourselves as individual units the decision as to how and when our country may exact from us our lives; if each woman may dissolve the family bond at pleasure; if, in fine, we are to have no standard of duty, of obedience, or, in substance, of right and wrong save selfish caprice; if we are to resolve our society from a firmly cohesive mass, unified by a common standard of duty and self-sacrifice, into a swarm of atoms selfishly fighting one another for money, as beggars scramble for coin, then I much fear that the hour cannot be far distant when some superior, because more cohesive and intelligent organism, such as nature has decreed shall always lie in wait for its victim, shall spring upon us and rend us as the strong have always rent those wretched, because feeble, creatures who are cursed with an aborted development.

Part Ten

~~~~~~~~~~~~~~~~~~~~~~~~~~~~~~

THE CRUMBLING COUNTRY HOUSE

Although the Marquess of Salisbury loomed largest among Britain's public men during the last three decades of the nineteenth century, and the Conservative party held office most of the time, still the old society of England and Scotland and Ireland was insecure. That society's politics and taste and tone long had been set by the landed gentry, even after the smoky triumph of British industrialism. As Queen Victoria's Jubilee approached, men began to ask themselves whether the country house could stand forever.

THE FOUR REFORMERS
Robert Louis Stevenson

Robert Louis Stevenson (1850–1894), was not disposed to surrender to some new regime of dreariness. His essay on the gentleman is worth reading several times over; but we must be content here with his "The Four Reformers," from his *Fables* (1888).

Four reformers met under a bramble bush. They were all agreed the world must be changed. "We must abolish property," said one.

"We must abolish marriage," said the second.

"We must abolish God," said the third.

"I wish we could abolish work," said the fourth.

"Do not let us get beyond practical politics," said the first. "The first thing is to reduce men to a common level."

"The first thing," said the second, "is to give freedom to the sexes."

"The first thing," said the third, "is to find out how to do it."

"The first step," said the first, "is to abolish the Bible."

"The first thing," said the second, "is to abolish the laws."

"The first thing," said the third, "is to abolish mankind."

THE DISSOLUTION
OF FAITH
W. H. Mallock

A charming country house is the setting for this
chapter from that winning satire *The New Republic,
or Culture, Faith, and Philosophy in an English
Country House* (London, 1877), by W. H. Mallock
(1849–1923). The most versatile and tireless of conservative writers, during his long career Mallock was
wit, novelist, social critic, economist, literary essayist,
autobiographer. In this chapter of *The New Republic*
(pp. 269–82 in J. C. Squire's edition, 1945), the
guests at the country-house weekend are treated to a
sermon by Mr. Herbert, whose thought and style
strongly resemble John Ruskin's. His exhortation is
not approved by Dr. Jenkinson, a very liberal clergyman. For Herbert foretells the coming wrath, "an
undreamed-of anarchy for all," if the faith which has
created and sustained civilization gives place to a
"liberal" nihilism.

Once more the theatre was brightly lighted; and once
more the congregation was assembled in the tier of boxes.
There was not so much excitement as there had been in
the morning; indeed, the reserved decorum that reigned
might have been said to partake almost of the nature of apathy. When, however, Dr. Seydon entered, none could
deny that he did indeed look a reverend man; and the very
aspect of the place seemed to grow devotional at his presence. Lady Ambrose perceived with a full heart that he
was duly habited in a surplice; and her bosom warmed
with a sense of safety and of comfort as he took his place

and solemnly produced his prayer-book. Nor was Lady Ambrose alone in this sudden stir of feeling. There was another of the worshippers who was moved even more strongly, though in a slightly different way. Many starts had been given on the stage in that theatre; but none of these, it may be safely said, ever equalled one now given in the boxes, as Dr. Jenkinson, who had been kneeling with his face hid in his hands, raised his eyes, and saw for the first time who it was confronting him—no obscure rural clergyman, as he had anticipated, but that illiberal apologist of superstition, whose officious bigotry had robbed the Upper House of its most enlightened spiritual peer. Dr. Jenkinson, however, with the heroism of a true martyr, suffered bravely for his faith in the comprehensiveness of Christianity. His face assumed, in another moment, an expression of cherubic suavity; in his gentlest and devoutest tones he was soon taking his part in the whole service, and that too with such an exquisite clearness of articulation, that, amongst the confused murmurs of the rest, the entire evening office sounded like a duet between him and Dr. Seydon. It is true that there was something in the ring of this one audible voice that gave the latter a sense of something being wrong somewhere; but luckily, being a little short-sighted, he could not recognise the owner of it; and Dr. Jenkinson, feeling no manner of call to endure the sermon, retired furtively as soon as the prayers were over.

'Weren't they read beautifully!' said Lady Ambrose to Lady Grace in a whisper. 'Oh, how glad I shall be to hear him preach once again!' she added, as Dr. Seydon, having risen from his knees, retired, his hands clasped before him, through the side door. Lady Ambrose, however, was entirely alone in this gladness. Most of the others dreaded the sermon that was imminent, and some even meditated following Dr. Jenkinson. But events were too quick for them. Hardly, it seemed, had Dr. Seydon left the stairs, than the curtain drew rapidly up, and displayed again the gorge in the Indian Caucasus, only with a preacher in it very different from the one who had stood there in the morning. The whole congregation gave a sudden gasp of surprise. It was not Dr. Seydon that they saw. It was Mr. Herbert.

With a gracious gravity he advanced towards the footlights; and made a slight bow to the house—a bow of deprecation and apology.

'A little while ago, in the garden,' he said, 'I confessed to our kind host, Mr. Laurence, that there were a few things that I should like quietly to say to you; and Mr. Laurence has become sponsor for you all, and has promised, in your names, that you would suffer me to say them here. It is true,' Mr. Herbert went on, with a smile and a wave of his hand, 'that when I look round me at this glittering semicircle, I begin to feel not a little shy of you, and to repent of my own temerity. You, however, have given me to-day so much good food for reflection, that I feel bound, in the commonest honesty, to make what poor return I can. So remember, that if I weary you, you have really brought it upon yourselves.

'Well—to begin, then. You think me—you need not deny it, for I know you think me—a somewhat crotchety and melancholy individual, averse to modern knowledge and to modern progress, and seeing, as a rule, everything very yellow indeed, with his jaundiced eyes. But I think myself that I am not by any means so obstinate and so wrong-headed as I am quite aware that I appear to you; nay, my own opinion is that I err, rather, in not being quite obstinate enough. It is true that I have persistently pointed out that England is at present given over wholly to ignoble pursuits, and is ruining herself with deadly industries. But I have never said hitherto, so far as I know, that we might not rally, and that a brighter future might not be in store for us. Nay, I hailed a piece of news to-day with the most unfeigned delight, which seemed an omen to me that such a brighter future actually was in store for

us. In a paper that reached me this afternoon there was a
letter on the prospects of the English iron trade; and I read
in that letter that nineteen foundries in Middlesborough
have been closed within the last three months, and the
Moloch fires in their blast-furnaces extinguished; that ten
more foundries in the same place are scarcely able to continue work, and must very shortly be closed likewise; and
that the dense smoke-cloud that so long has darkened that
whole country is beginning to clear away, and will open
ere long upon astonished human eyes, that have never yet
beheld it, the liquid melted blue of the deep wells of the
sky. It is quite true that this indication of a reviving prosperity for our country suggests more than it proves. But at
any rate it put me this afternoon, when I joined your
party, into quite a right and hopeful mood for appreciat-
ing your conceptions of a better order of things. It is in
fact simply to explain my appreciation that I am, in this
most unconscionable way, now detaining you.

'Let me say in the first place, then, how profoundly
right I consider the manner in which you set to work. For
it is one of the most vital of all truths, that in a perfect
state all the parts will be perfect; and that if the highest
classes be as good as they can be, so also will be all the
other classes. And I want to tell you, in the next place,
how entirely fair and lovely did all the elements seem to
be, out of which you composed for your higher classes
their ideal existence. For you gave them every outward
grace that could adorn life, and every inward taste and
emotion that could enrich it, and every species of intellectual activity that could stimulate it. Your society was indeed to be truly the *crème de la crème;* it was to be made
beautiful, and profound, and brilliant, by lovers, and theologians, and wits, and men of science, and poets, and philosophers, and humourists—all men and women of the
world, and fit to live in society, as well as to educate it.
This would indeed be, as was said at dinner, Rome and
Athens and Florence, at their best, and let me add Paris

also, united and reanimated, and enriched by the possession of yet wider knowledge, and the possibilities of freer speculation. That truly is a dazzling picture. But even that is not all. There was your city itself too, of which a lovely glimpse was given us, with its groves, its gardens, it palaces, and its exquisite reproductions of the world's noblest architectures; and all this under our softest English skies, and by our bluest English seas. Ah,' exclaimed Mr. Herbert, smiling, and clasping his hands gently, 'how I should like to live in a city like that! I can literally see it now with my mind's eye, whilst I am talking. I see its private houses with their wonders of wrought marble; I see its theatres, its museums, its chapels and churches of all denominations, its scientific lecture rooms, and its convents. For what strikes me more forcibly than anything is that all forms of faith and philosophy seem to find here an impartial home, and to unite in animating one harmonious social life. In fact, so vividly do I see this scene which your words have called up before me, that I want very much, if you will let me, to add one small feature to it, myself. It is a very humble detail, this of mine. In the eyes of the men of science, who lead modern thought, it is simply a sanitary matter. It relates to the way in which you shall dispose of your dead. Now in this, at least, you will be surprised to hear I quite keep pace with the times, being a sincere advocate for cremation; and what I should want to do in your city, would be to supply it with an establishment, hidden underground, where the bodies of the dead should be turned into gas, in properly devised retorts; the gas from each body being received in a small separate gasometer. Above these gasworks, and amongst your fair towers and spires, and your superb institutions, and art-galleries, I would build a circular domed temple of umbered marble, blind and blank upon the face of it, without carved work, and without window; only there should be written above the portal, not as in Dante's vision,

Per me si va nell' eterno dolore,
Per me si va tra la perduta gente—[1]

but one verse out of our English translation of the Bible,
for women and little children to read; and another verse
out of a Latin poet, which is, I believe, an equivalent for
the original of that translation, for men and scholars to
read. The first should be, "Though after my skin worms
destroy this body, yet in my flesh shall I see God." And
the other:

Quaeris quo jaceas post obitum loco?
Quo non nata jacent.[2]

And within, around the dark walls, should be a number of
separate shrines, like—to use the simile that Dante would
have chosen—the stalls in a great stable; and to each
shrine there should be a separate gas-jet. And when the
life of any was over, after the fire had done its work upon
the dead body, that man or woman who felt most bitterly
the loss of the one that had been, should repair to this
temple, to an appointed shrine, and there, in silence
kneeling before it, should light the gas-jet; and thus evok-
ing for the last time that which was once so loved and lov-
ing, pass, with what thoughts might be, a brief vigil before
it, till its flicker grew slowly faint upon the watcher's face,
and at length it went out and ended utterly and for ever.
And above, over these sanctuaries of bereavement and
final leave-taking, there should hang from the domed roof
one rude iron lamp, always burning—casting a pale flare
upwards upon the darkness. This would be the common
lamp of the poor, for whose sake, dying, no one felt be-

---

1. "Through me the way to eternal woe,
Through me the way among the lost people."
   (Dante, *Inferno*, Canto III, 2-3.) [R.K.]
2. "Do you seek the place where you will lie after death?
Where those lie who have not been born." [R.K.]

reavement, or whom no one at any rate could find time to say good-bye to; but who thus united together, apart by themselves, would do all that would be at all seemly in them—would remind you mutely and unobtrusively by their joint light, that one thing at least they shared with you, namely death. It is not of the poor, however, that I am mainly thinking now. It is of your higher classes, who have leisure to feel sorrow and all its holy influences. And these, I say, would find in this simple funeral service one that would meet all their diverse needs, and be in tune with all their diverse feelings. It would suit all. For to some it would symbolise an absolute disbelief in any life beyond; and to all the rest it would symbolise a bewildered doubt about my life beyond. For in one or other of these states of mind everyone would be.

'Do you deny it?' exclaimed Mr. Herbert, raising his voice suddenly and looking round the theatre with a passionate anger, at which the whole audience were literally electrified. 'Do you deny it?' he exclaimed. 'I tell you that it is so. I tell you too that that is your own case, and that in your Utopia you have aggravated the evil, and have not remedied it. You are all deniers or doubters, I tell you, every one of you. The deniers, I know, will not contradict me; so at present I need not speak to them. It is to you—the majority, you who *will* contradict me; you who are so busy with your various affirmations, with your prayers, your churches, your philosophies, your revivals of old Christianities, or your new improvement on them; with your love of justice, and humanity, and toleration; it is to you that I speak. It is to you that I say that, however enlightened and however sure you may be about all other matters, you are darkened and uncertain as to this—whether there really is any God at all who can hear all the prayers you utter to Him, or whether there really is any other life at all, where the aspirations you are so proud of will be realised, and where the wrongs you are so pitiful over will be righted. There is not one amongst you who, watching a dead friend flickering for the last time before you in the form of a gas-flame, and seeing how a little while and this flame was with you, and again a little while and it was not with you, would be at all sure whether this was really because, as your hearts would suggest to you, it went to the Father, or because, as your men of science would assert to you, it went simply—out.

'Listen to me for a moment and I can prove that this is so to you. You are rich, and you have leisure to think of things in what light you will, and your life is to a great extent made easy for you by the labour of others. I do not complain of that. There can be no civilisation without order, and there can be no order without subordination. Outward good must be apportioned unequally, or there would be no outward goods to apportion. But you who have the larger share of these are bound to do something for those who have the less. I say you are *bound* to do so; or else sooner or later that large share will be taken away from you. Well, and what is it you propose to do? I know your answer—I have heard it a thousand times. You will educate them—you will teach them. And truly if you know how to do that properly, you will have done all you need do. But,' exclaimed Mr. Herbert, his voice again rising, and quivering with excitement, 'that is just what you do not know. I am not casting my words at random. Out of your own mouths will I judge you. There never was a time when you talked so much as now about teaching the people, and yet do not you yourselves confess that you cannot agree together as to what to teach them? You can agree about teaching them—I know this too well—countless things that you think will throw light upon life; but life itself you leave a blank darkness upon which no light can be thrown. You say nothing of what is good in it, and of what is evil. Does success in it lie in the enjoyment of bodily pleasures, or in the doing of spiritual duty? Is there anything in it that is right for its own sake, or are all things right only because of their consequences? And seeing that, if we struggle for virtue, our struggles can never be quite successful here, is there any other place where they may have, I do not say their reward, but their consummation? To these questions only two answers can be given, and one must be entirely true, and the other entirely false. But you—you dare not give either; you are too enlightened. It is true that *you* can afford to be liberal about these matters; you can afford to consider truth and falsehood equally *tolerable*. But for the poor man surely it is not so. It must make some difference to him what you teach him, whether your teaching is to open his eyes to his God and to his duty, and so place his noblest happiness in his own hands, or whether it is to open his eyes to those *verified* Utilitarian principles from which he will learn that his own life and labour are only not utterly contemptible, because they conduce to a material well-being in which he himself can have no share. If, with entire belief yourselves, you are prepared to give him the former teaching, why then it is well and good both for him and you. But if not, beware of teaching him at all. You will but be removing a cataract from his mind's eye that he may stare aghast and piteous at his own poverty and nakedness, or that he may gaze with a wild beast's hunger at your own truly noble prosperity which he can never taste, save in the wild beast's way.

'But enough of the poor: enough of this division of happiness. Let me ask you to consider now what sort of happiness there is to divide—I say divide, meaning that you will get the whole of it. And as I have said before, this happiness is very fair in seeming. Knowledge, and culture, and freedom, and toleration—you have told us what fine things all these can do for you. And I admit it myself too; I feel it myself too. Lovely, indeed, to look upon are the faiths, the philosophies, the enthusiasms of the world— the ancient products of the ages—as the sunshine of the modern intellect falls on them. See, they look clearer, and brighter, and more transparent—see, they form them-

selves into more exquisite and lucid shapes, more aërial
structures. But why? Do not deceive yourselves; it is for a
terrible reason. It is because, like a fabric of snow, they are
one and all dissolving.

'Listen, and I will show you that this is so. Aristotle
says that what is truly a man's Self is the thinking part of
him. This sooner or later all the other parts obey—sooner
or later, willingly or unwillingly; and if this Self be base,
the whole man will be base; if the Self be noble, the whole
man will be noble. And as it is with the individual man, so
it is with the ages and the generations. They obey their
several Selves, whatever these Selves may be. The world
once had a Self whose chief spokesman was a Jewish peasant called Jesus; and sooner or later the world followed
him. Later on, it had a Self whose chief spokesmen were
Dominics or Luthers or Loyolas; and in like manner the
world followed them. Later still, it had got another Self,
and the chief spokesmen of this were Voltaires and Rous-
seaus. And in each case the world was convinced at heart,
consciously or unconsciously, that the vital truths of life
were to be sought for only where these Selves sought for
them. With Jesus and with Luther it sought them in duty
and in a turning to the true God; with Voltaire and Rousseau, in justice, and in a turning from the false God. And
now, where do you seek them? Where does the Self of
your age seek them—your Self, that thinking part of you
before which you all either quail or worship? Does it seek
them either in justice, or loving-kindness, or in the vision
of the most high God! No—but in the rotting bodies of
dead men, or in the writhing bodies of live cats. And in
your perplexity, and your amazed despair, ever and again
you cry to it, What shall we do to be saved? Show us the
Father! Show us the high and holy One that inhabiteth
Eternity! And what does your Self answer you? It answers you with a laugh. "There is no high and holy One at
all. How say ye then to me, Show us the Father? For the
Earth saith, He is not with me; and the depth saith, He is

not with me; and our filthy phials of decaying animal matter say, He is not with us. Argal, ye poor foolish seekers, He is nowhere." You may try to escape from your own Self, but you cannot; you may try to forget its answer, but you cannot. Loudly you may affirm with your lips; but the importunate denial is ever at your heart. *Patriae quis exsul se quoque fugit?*[3]

'What do you do then in this perplexity—this halting between two opinions? Why, you do this. You try to persuade yourselves that neither opinion is of much moment—that the question cannot be decided absolutely—that it should not be decided absolutely—in fact, that it is one of your chief glories that you leave it undecided. But I tell you, in that case, that though you say you are rich, and increased with goods, and have need of nothing; you are, in reality, wretched, and miserable, and poor, and blind, and naked. I am not casting my words at random. Again out of your own mouths will I judge you. All your culture, you say, is based ultimately upon this— a discrimination between right and wrong. True, profoundly true. But will you be able to say what is right and what is wrong any longer, if you don't know *for whom* anything is right and *for whom* anything is wrong— whether it is for men with immortal souls, or only with mortal bodies—who are only a little lower than the angels, or only a little better than the pigs? Whilst you can still contrive to doubt upon this matter, whilst the fabric of the old faith is still dissolving only, life still for you, the enlightened few, may preserve what happiness it has now. But when the old fabric is all dissolved, what then? When all divinity shall have gone from love and heroism, and only utility and pleasure shall be left, what then? Then you will have to content yourselves with complete denial; or build up again the faith that you have just pulled

---

3. "What exile from his homeland escapes himself as well?" (Horace, *Odes* II.16.19.) [R.K.]

down—you will have to be born again, and to seek for a new Self.

'But suppose we accept denial, you will say, what then? Many deniers have lived noble lives, though they have looked neither for a God nor for a heaven. Think of Greece, you will say to me, and that will answer you. No—but that is not so, and that will not answer me. The Greeks never, in your sense, denied God; they never, in your sense, denied eternal life—never, because they never knew them. They *felt* God only; they felt Him unconsciously; and in denying the God they knew, they were really affirming the God they felt. But you—do not you deceive yourselves. Do not think you can ever again be as the Greeks. The world's progress has a twofold motion. History moves onwards round some undiscovered centre, as well as round what you consider its discovered axis; and though it seems to repeat itself, it never can repeat itself. The Atheism of the modern world is not the Atheism of the ancient: the long black night of the winter is not the swift clear night of the vanished summer. The Greek philosopher could not darken his life, for he knew not from what mysterious source the light fell upon it. The modern philosopher does know, and he knows that it is called God, and thus knowing the source of light he can at once quench it.

'What will be left you then if this light be quenched? Will art, will painting, will poetry be any comfort to you? You have said that these were magic mirrors which reflected back your life for you. Well—will they be any better than the glass mirrors in your drawing-rooms, if they have nothing but the same listless orgy to reflect? For that is all that will be at last in store for you; nay, that is the best thing that possibly can be in store for you; the only alternative being not a listless orgy for the few, but an undreamed-of anarchy for all. I do not fear that, however. Some will be always strong, and some will be always weak; and though, if there is no God, no divine and fa-

therly source of order, there will be, trust me, no aristocracies, there will still be tyrannies. There will still be rich
and poor; and that will then mean happy and miserable;
and the poor will be—as I sometimes think they are already—but a mass of groaning machinery, without even
the semblance of rationality; and the rich, with only the
semblance of it, but a set of gaudy, dancing mario-
nettes, which it is the machinery's one work to keep in
motion.

'What, then, shall you do to be saved? Rend your
hearts, I say, and do not mend your garments. Seek God
earnestly, and peradventure you still may find Him—and
I—even I may find Him also. For I—who am I that speak
to you? Am I a believer? No, I am a doubter too. Once I
could pray every morning, and go forth to my day's labour stayed and comforted. But now I can pray no longer.
You have taken my God away from me, and I know not
where you have laid Him. My only consolation in my
misery is that at least I am inconsolable for His loss. Yes,'
cried Mr. Herbert, his voice rising into a kind of threatening wail, 'though you have made me miserable, I am not
yet content with my misery. And though I too have said
in my heart that there is no God, and that there is no more
profit in wisdom than in folly, yet there is one folly that I
will not give tongue to. I will not say Peace, peace, when
there is no peace. I will not say we are still Christians,
when we can sip our wine smilingly after dinner, and talk
about some day defining the Father; and I will only pray
that if such a Father be, He may have mercy alike upon
those that hate Him, because they *will* not see Him; and
on those who love and long for Him although they no
longer *can* see Him.'

Mr. Herbert's voice ceased. The curtain fell. The
whirlwind was over; the fire was over; and after the fire,
from one of the side boxes came a still small voice.

'Very poor taste—very poor taste.'

It was perceived that Dr. Jenkinson, having discovered

almost immediately who was really to be the preacher, had stolen back silently into the theatre.

THE CONSERVATIVE ENGLISHMAN
George Gissing

For most of his life, George Gissing (1857–1903) labored in Grub Street and was a connoisseur of poverty. His novels of London's lower-class life still ring true. Emancipating himself from socialism, Gissing came to accept politics as the art of the possible. In this little essay from *The Private Papers of Henry Ryecroft* (1903), he remarks at the time of Victoria's Second Jubilee the English reliance, in their politics, upon Common Sense. In the numerous editions of *Ryecroft*, this is "Summer," Part XX.

It is the second Jubilee. Bonfires blaze upon the hills, making one think of the watchman on Agamemnon's citadel. (It were more germane to the matter to think of Queen Elizabeth and the Armada.) Though wishing the uproar happily over, I can see the good in it as well as another man. English monarchy, as we know it, is a triumph of English common sense. Grant that men cannot do without an over-lord: how to make that over-lordship consist with the largest practical measure of national and individual liberty? We, at all events, have for a time solved the question. For a time only, of course; but consider the history of Europe, and our jubilation is perhaps justified.

For sixty years has the British Republic held on its way under one President. It is wide of the mark to object that other Republics, which change their President more frequently, support the semblance of over-lordship at considerably less cost to the people. Britons are minded for the present that the Head of their State shall be called King or Queen; the name is pleasant to them; it corresponds to a popular sentiment, vaguely understood, but still operative, which is called loyalty. The majority thinking thus, and the system being found to work more than tolerably well, what purpose could be served by an attempt at *novas res?* The nation is content to pay the price; it is the nation's affair. Moreover, who can feel the least assurance that a change to one of the common forms of Republicanism would be for the general advantage? Do we find that countries which have made the experiment are so very much better off than our own in point of stable, quiet government and of national welfare? The theorist scoffs at forms which have survived their meaning, at privilege which will bear no examination, at compromises which sound ludicrous, at submissions which seem contemptible; but let him put forward his practical scheme for making all men rational, consistent, just. Englishmen, I imagine, are not endowed with these qualities in any extraordinary degree. Their strength, politically speaking, lies in a recognition of expediency, complemented by respect for the established fact. One of the facts particularly clear to them is the suitability to their minds, their tempers, their habits, of a system of polity which has been established by the slow effort of generations within this sea-girt realm. They have nothing to do with ideals; they never trouble themselves to think about the Rights of Man. If you talk to them (long enough) about the rights of the shopman, or the ploughman, or the cat's-meat-man, they will lend ear, and, when the facts of any such case have been examined, they will find a way of dealing with them. This characteristic of theirs they call Common Sense. To them, all things considered, it has been of vast service; one may even say that the rest of the world has profited by it not a little. That Uncommon Sense might now and then have stood them even in better stead is nothing to the point. The Englishman deals with things as they are, and first and foremost accepts his own being.

This Jubilee declares a legitimate triumph of the average man. Look back for threescore years, and who shall affect to doubt that the time has been marked by many improvements in the material life of the English people? Often have they been at loggerheads among themselves, but they have never flown at each other's throats, and from every grave dispute has resulted some substantial gain. They are a cleaner people and a more sober; in every class there is a diminution of brutality; education—stand for what it may—has notably extended; certain forms of tyranny have been abolished; certain forms of suffering, due to heedlessness or ignorance, have been abated. True, these are mere details; whether they indicate a solid advance in civilization cannot yet be determined. But assuredly the average Briton has cause to jubilate; for the progressive features of the epoch are such as he can understand and approve, whereas the doubt which may be cast upon its ethical complexion is for him either non-existent or unintelligible. So let cressets flare into the night from all the hills! It is no purchased exultation, no servile flattery. The People acclaims itself, yet not without genuine gratitude and affection towards the Representative of its glory and its power. The Constitutional Compact has been well preserved. Review the record of kingdoms, and say how often it has come to pass that sovereign and people rejoiced together over bloodless victories.

TORYISM

George Saintsbury

George Saintsbury (1845–1933), critic, historian of
literature, connoisseur of wines, and genial essayist,
took it as a compliment when an unknown man muttered, as Saintsbury passed, "There goes the biggest
Tory in England." This brief musing upon Toryism
(from *A Scrap Book*, London, 1922, pp. 42–49) suggests that Toryism is integral to the English civil social order.

There lies open before me, with inside end-paper and fly-
leaf exposed, a small volume inscribed as follows in a very
comely hand, names only blanked:

To
——

One of two Tories in England,
from the other,
——

January 1892.

"The other" is, alas! dead, and "the one" (whose hand is
not comely) probably has not long to live, so that unless
some recruits have sprung up in the last thirty years,
Toryism would seem, on the authority of this document,
to be in a rather bad way. If I remember right, Victor
Hugo, in *his* Victorian manner, announced once, *je serai
celui-là!*[1] in the case of its coming to a definitely last man
of another (quite other) sort of political creed, and
seemed rather to enjoy the prospect. I am afraid I should

---

1. I shall be that one!" [R.K.]

not possess μεγαλοψυχία[2] of that kind to that extent if I were in the case above suggested.

For it would not only be a great pity, from various minor points of view, but would show, rather uncomfortably, that the human brain is returning rapidly to that ape-stage in which some of us still don't believe. (Everything that I have ever seen of or read about monkeys inclines me to believe that there is pretty complete democracy among them.) Toryism—however contrary this may go to Radical chatter about it—is at least a political creed which can stand the tests of rational examination of the physical and historical *facts* of life. It rests, in the first place, on the recognition of the facts that all men and women are born *un*equal; that no men or women are born free (if one could play the hackneyed "time-reversal" game it would be cruelly amusing to catch a future democrat at his birth, leave him entirely free from all interference, and see what happened to him); and that if you leave two healthy brothers or sisters alone together they will frequently, if not continually, fight. In the second, being well acquainted with history, it knows that all attempts to establish Liberty, Equality, and Fraternity have failed more or less disastrously and disgustingly, whatever *camouflage* of success they may have kept up; while acceptance and judicious regulation of the contraries have always (barring the faults of individuals, or more rarely of systems) done well. For the sentimental pleas of Socialist Democracy, it has the answer of Religious Charity. For the arithmetical plausibility of "share and share alike," it has the irresistible replies in kind that the "alikeness" will not last a year, a month, a week, a day, nay, not an hour, and that in a very short time there will be nothing to share afresh. "Why should there be kings?" Because there always *are* kings—whether by Divine Right, as in some cases, or by Diabolic Selection, as in others. "Why should

---

2. Magnanimity. [R.K.]

there be peers?" Because you want in all, or nearly all, cases some court of political appeal; and when your first line of government is elective, there should clearly be a second with which direct popular election has as little to do as possible. Now the hereditary principle supplies this, as it also does in the case of kingship, better, by all experience, than anything else.

Behind all this, and any amount more which anybody can have who wants it, there is the vague-seeming but rationally inpregnable background-argument, provided once more by age-long experience, that change is rarely for the better, and that continual change, for the sake of changing, will certainly sometimes, and probably often, be for the worse. The goods you have are real, and the ills, in all probability and experience, to a large extent imaginary—certainly bearable in that they have been borne. The goods that are to come may, and by experience to a large extent will, be imaginary, and the ills very real indeed. Nothing has been said here—purposely nothing—of the non-practical side of Toryism; which is, of course, giving away masses of weight. Some of the more generous iconoclasts themselves admit the beauty of the icons they would destroy. For my part, their own ideals seem to me more hideously ugly and uninteresting the more they elaborate them. Put away all thought of the crime and agony which would have to be gone through in order to bring about the Socialist Utopia; get it somehow brought about by fairy agency; could there, even then, be anything more loathsome than one wide waste of proletariat-Cocqcigrue[3] comfort; everybody as good as the President; everybody as "well educated" as everybody else; everybody stationed, rationed, regulated by some kind of abstract "State"—as equal, and really about as free, as pigs in a sty, and not much better deserving the name of man,

---

3. A fabulous animal in French folkore, here signifying an idle utopian fantasy. [R.K.]

or the manly chances of position, possession, genius, ancestry, and all that differentiates us from brutes?

If any one says, "But you have no business to assume that there is no *via media* between this and Toryism," history and not I shall answer him. Whiggery, Liberalism, Moderate Radicalism—all have failed more or less: the only reason why, in this or that case, they have not failed utterly, or have held out for a long time, being that they have not been "extreme," that the remnant of the principles of Toryism itself—Inequality, Individualism, Heredity, Property, etc.—which they have retained, has kept them alive.

Part Eleven

~~~~~~

THE FABULISTS

The conservative imagination has been at work
within many novelists; and often the conservative
understanding of society is more clearly expressed
through perceptive image and fable than through
governmental blue-books. "Unless we please, we are
not heard at all," Rudyard Kipling says in his poem
"The Fabulists." The first two decades of the twentieth century are especially endowed with such imaginative writing. One would like, for instances, to
include here G. K. Chesteron's short story "The Yellow Bird," concerning the Russian anarchist professor who aspired to eliminate all limits; or a chapter
from Conrad's *Nostromo*, the keenest picture of
Latin-American politics. But it is necessary to confine ourselves to one story by Joseph Conrad
(1857–1924) and a fable by Rudyard Kipling
(1865–1936).

THE INFORMER
Joseph Conrad

Joseph Conrad—a conservative in both his Polish and his English aspects—portrays anarchist conspirators in his novels *Under Western Eyes* and *The Secret Agent*. In this story from *A Set of Six* (London, 1908) we encounter the genteel cynical anarchist moved by the *libido dominandi*.

Mr. X came to me, preceded by a letter of introduction from a good friend of mine in Paris, specifically to see my collection of Chinese bronzes and procelain.

My friend in Paris is a collector, too. He collects neither porcelain, nor bronzes, nor pictures, nor medals, nor stamps, nor anything that could be profitably dispersed under an auctioneer's hammer. He would reject, with genuine surprise, the name of a collector. Nevertheless, that's what he is by temperament. He collects acquaintances. It is delicate work. He brings to it the patience, the passion, the determination of a true collector of curiosities. His collection does not contain any royal personages. I don't think he considers them sufficiently rare and interesting; but, with that exception, he has met with and talked to everyone worth knowing on any conceivable ground. He observes them, listens to them, penetrates them, measures them, and puts the memory away in the galleries of his mind. He has schemed, plotted, and travelled all over Europe in order to add to his collection of distinguished personal acquaintances.

As he is wealthy, well connected, and unprejudiced, his
collection is pretty complete, including objects (or should
I say subjects?) whose value is unappreciated by the vulgar, and often unknown to popular fame. Of those specimens my friend is naturally the most proud.

He wrote to me of X: "He is the greatest rebel (*révolté*)
of modern times. The world knows him as a revolutionary
writer whose savage irony has laid bare the rottenness of
the most respectable institutions. He has scalped every
venerated head, and has mangled at the stake of his wit
every received opinion and every recognized principle of
conduct and policy. Who does not remember his flaming
red revolutionary pamphlets? Their sudden swarmings
used to overwhelm the powers of every Continental police
like a plague of crimson gadflies. But this extreme writer
has been also the active inspirer of secret societies, the
mysterious unknown Number One of desperate conspiracies suspected and unsuspected, matured or baffled. And
the world at large has never had an inkling of that fact!
This accounts for him going about amongst us to this day,
a veteran of many subterranean campaigns, standing aside
now, safe within his reputation of merely the greatest destructive publicist that ever lived."

Thus wrote my friend, adding that Mr. X was an enlightened connoisseur of bronzes and china, and asking me
to show him my collection.

X turned up in due course. My treasures are disposed in
three large rooms without carpets and curtains. There is
no other furniture than the étagères and the glass cases
whose contents shall be worth a fortune to my heirs. I
allow no fires to be lighted, for fear of accidents, and a
fire-proof door separates them from the rest of the house.

It was a bitter cold day. We kept on our overcoats and
hats. Middle-sized and spare, his eyes alert in a long,
Roman-nosed countenance, X walked on his neat little
feet, with short steps, and looked at my collection intelligently. I hope I looked at him intelligently, too. A snow-

white moustache and imperial made his nut-brown complexion appear darker than it really was. In his fur coat and shiny tall hat that terrible man looked fashionable. I believe he belonged to a noble family, and could have called himself Vicomte X de la Z if he chose. We talked nothing but bronzes and porcelain. He was remarkably appreciative. We parted on cordial terms.

Where he was staying I don't know. I imagine he must have been a lonely man. Anarchists, I suppose, have no families—not, at any rate, as we understand that social relation. Organization into families may answer to a need of human nature, but in the last instance it is based on law, and therefore must be something odious and impossible to an anarchist. But, indeed, I don't understand anarchists. Does a man of that—of that—persuasion still remain an anarchist when alone, quite alone and going to bed, for instance? Does he lay his head on the pillow, pull his bedclothes over him, and go to sleep with the necessity of the *chambardement général*, as the French slang has it, of the general blow-up, always present to his mind? And if so how can he? I am sure that if such a faith (or such a fanaticism) once mastered my thoughts I would never be able to compose myself sufficiently to sleep or eat or perform any of the routine acts of daily life. I would want no wife, no children; I could have no friends, it seems to me; and as to collecting bronzes or china, that, I should say, would be quite out of the question. But I don't know. All I know is that Mr. X took his meals in a very good restaurant which I frequented also.

With his head uncovered, the silver top-knot of his brushed-up hair completed the character of his physiognomy, all bony ridges and sunken hollows, clothed in a perfect impassiveness of expression. His meagre brown hands emerging from large white cuffs came and went breaking bread, pouring wine, and so on, with quiet mechanical precision. His head and body above the tablecloth had a rigid immobility. This firebrand, this great agitator, exhibited the least possible amount of warmth and animation. His voice was rasping, cold, and monotonous in a low key. He could not be called a talkative personality; but with his detached calm manner he appeared as ready to keep the conversation going as to drop it at any moment.

And his conversation was by no means commonplace. To me, I own, there was some excitement in talking quietly across a dinner-table with a man whose venomous pen-stabs had sapped the vitality of at least one monarchy. That much was a matter of public knowlege. But I knew more. I knew of him—from my friend—as a certainty what the guardians of social order in Europe had at most only suspected, or dimly guessed at.

He had had what I may call his underground life. And as I sat, evening after evening, facing him at dinner, a curiosity in that direction would naturally arise in my mind. I am a quiet and peaceable product of civilization, and know no passion other than the passion for collecting things which are rare, and must remain exquisite even if approaching to the monstrous. Some Chinese bronzes are monstrously precious. And here (out of my friend's collection), here I had before me a kind of rare monster. It is true that this monster was polished and in a sense even exquisite. His beautiful unruffled manner was that. But then he was not of bronze. He was not even Chinese, which would have enabled one to contemplate him calmly across the gulf of racial difference. He was alive and European; he had the manner of good society, wore a coat and hat like mine, and had pretty near the same taste in cooking. It was too frightful to think of.

One evening he remarked, casually, in the course of conversation. "There's no amendment to be got out of mankind except by terror and violence."

You can imagine the effect of such a phrase out of such a man's mouth upon a person like myself, whose whole scheme of life had been based upon a suave and delicate

discrimination of social and artistic values. Just imagine!
Upon me, to whom all sorts and forms of violence appeared as unreal as the giants, ogres, and seven-headed
hydras whose activities affect, fantastically, the course of
legends and fairy-tales!

I seemed suddenly to hear above the festive bustle and
clatter of the brilliant restaurant the mutter of a hungry
and seditious multitude.

I suppose I am impressionable and imaginative. I had a
disturbing vision of darkness, full of lean jaws and wild
eyes, amongst the hundred electric lights of the place. But
somehow this vision made me angry, too. The sight of that
man, so calm, breaking bits of white bread, exasperated
me. And I had the audacity to ask him how it was that the
starving proletariat of Europe to whom he had been
preaching revolt and violence had not been made indignant by his openly luxurious life. "At all this," I said,
pointedly, with a glance round the room and at the bottle
of champagne we generally shared between us at dinner.

He remained unmoved.

"Do I feed on their toil and their heart's blood? Am I a
speculator or a capitalist? Did I steal my fortune from a
starving people? No! They know this very well. And they
envy me nothing. The miserable mass of the people is generous to its leaders. What I have acquired has come to me
through my writings; not from the millions of pamphlets
distributed gratis to the hungry and the oppressed, but
from the hundreds of thousands of copies sold to the well-
fed bourgeoisie. You know that my writings were at one
time the rage, the fashion—the thing to read with wonder
and horror, to turn your eyes up at my pathos . . . or else,
to laugh in ecstasies at my wit."

"Yes," I admitted. "I remember, of course; and I confess frankly that I could never understand that infatuation."

"Don't you know yet," he said, "that an idle and selfish
class loves to see mischief being made, even if it is made at

its own expense? Its own life being all a matter of pose and gesture, it is unable to realize the power and the danger of a real movement and of words that have no sham meaning. It is all fun and sentiment. It is sufficient, for instance, to point out the attitude of the old French aristocracy towards the philosophers whose words were preparing the Great Revolution. Even in England, where you have some common-sense, a demagogue has only to shout loud enough and long enough to find some backing in the very class he is shouting at. You, too, like to see mischief being made. The demagogue carries the amateurs of emotion with him. Amateurism in this, that, and the other thing is a delightfully easy way of killing time, and feeding one's own vanity—the silly vanity of being abreast with the ideas of the day after to-morrow. Just as good and otherwise harmless people will join you in ecstasies over your collection without having the slightest notion in what its marvellousness really consists."

I hung my head. It was a crushing illustration of the sad truth he advanced. The world is full of such people. And that instance of the French aristocracy before the Revolution was extremely telling, too. I could not traverse his statement, though its cynicism—always a distasteful trait—took off much of its value to my mind. However, I admit I was impressed. I felt the need to say something which would not be in the nature of assent and yet would not invite discussion.

"You don't mean to say," I observed, airily, "that extreme revolutionists have ever been actively assisted by the infatuation of such people?"

"I did not mean exactly that by what I said just now. I generalized. But since you ask me, I may tell you that such help has been given to revolutionary activities, more or less consciously, in various countries. And even in this country."

"Impossible!" I protested with firmness. "We don't play with fire to that extent."

"And yet you can better afford it than others, perhaps. But let me observe that most women, if not always ready to play with fire, are generally eager to play with a loose spark or so."

"Is this a joke?" I asked, smiling.

"If it is, I am not aware of it," he said, woodenly. "I was thinking of an instance. Oh! mild enough in a way ..."

I became all expectation at this. I had tried many times to approach him on his underground side, so to speak. The very word had been pronounced between us. But he had always met me with his impenetrable calm.

"And at the same time," Mr. X continued, "it will give you a notion of the difficulties that may arise in what you are pleased to call underground work. It is sometimes difficult to deal with them. Of course there is no hierarchy amongst the affiliated. No rigid system."

My surprise was great, but short-lived. Clearly, amongst extreme anarchists there could be no hierarchy; nothing in the nature of a law of precedence. The idea of anarchy ruling among anarchists was comforting, too. It could not possibly make for efficiency.

Mr. X startled me by asking, abruptly. "You know Hermione Street?"

I nodded doubtful assent. Hermione Street has been, within the last three years, improved out of any man's knowledge. The name exists till, but not one brick or stone of the old Hermione Street is left now. It was the old street he meant, for he said:

"There was a row of two-storied brick houses on the left, with their backs against the wing of a great public building—you remember. Would it surprise you very much to hear that one of these houses was for a time the centre of anarchist propaganda and of what you would call underground action?"

"Not at all," I declared. Hermione Street had never been particularly respectable, as I remembered it.

"The house was the property of a distinguished government official," he added, sipping his champagne.

"Oh, indeed!" I said, this time not believing a word of it.

"Of course he was not living there," Mr. X continued. "But from ten till four he sat next door to it, the dear man, in his well-appointed private room in the wing of the public building I've mentioned. To be strictly accurate, I must explain that the house in Hermione Street did not really belong to him. It belonged to his grown-up children—a daughter and a son. The girl, a fine figure, was by no means vulgarly pretty. To more personal charm than mere youth could account for, she added the seductive appearance of enthusiasm, of independence, of courageous thought. I suppose she put on these appearances as she put on her picturesque dresses and for the same reason: to assert her individuality at any cost. You know, women would go to any length almost for such a purpose. She went to a great length. She had acquired all the appropriate gestures of revolutionary convictions—the gestures of pity, of anger, of indignation against the anti-humanitarian vices of the social class to which she belonged herself. All this sat on her striking personality as well as her slightly original costumes. Very slightly original; just enough to mark a protest against the philistinism of the overfed taskmasters of the poor. Just enough, and no more. It would not have done to go too far in that direction—you understand. But she was of age, and nothing stood in the way of her offering her house to the revolutionary workers."

"You don't mean it!" I cried.

"I assure you," he affirmed, "that she made that very practical gesture. How else could they have got hold of it? The cause is not rich. And, moreover, there would have been difficulties with any ordinary house-agent, who would have wanted references and so on. The group she came in contact with while exploring the poor quarters of the town (you know the gesture of charity and personal service which was so fashionable some years ago) accepted with gratitude. The first advantage was that Hermione Street is, as you know, well away from the suspect part of the town, specially watched by the police.

"The ground floor consisted of a little Italian restaurant, of the flyblown sort. There was no difficulty in buying the proprietor out. A woman and a man belonging to the group took it on. The man had been a cook. The comrades could get their meals there, unnoticed amongst the other customers. This was another advantage. The first floor was occupied by a shabby Variety Artists' Agency—an agency for performers in inferior music-halls, you know. A fellow called Bomm, I remember. He was not disturbed. It was rather favourable than otherwise to have a lot of foreign-looking people, jugglers, acrobats, singers of both sexes, and so on, going in and out all day long. The police paid no attention to new faces, you see. The top floor happened, most conveniently, to stand empty then."

X interrupted himself to attack impassively, with measured movements, a *bombe glacée* which the waiter had just set down on the table. He swallowed carefully a few spoonfuls of the iced sweet, and asked me, "Did you ever hear of Stone's Dried Soup?"

"Hear of *what?*"

"It was," X pursued, evenly, "a comestible article once rather prominently advertised in the dailies, but which never, somehow, gained the favour of the public. The enterprise fizzled out, as you say here. Parcels of their stock could be picked up at auctions at considerably less than a penny a pound. The group bought some of it, and an agency for Stone's Dried Soup was started on the top floor. A perfectly respectable business. The stuff, a yellow powder of extremely unappetizing aspect, was put up in large square tins, of which six went to a case. If anybody ever came to give an order, it was, of course, executed. But the advantage of the powder was this, that things could be

concealed in it very conveniently. Now and then a special
case got put on a van and sent off to be exported abroad
under the very nose of the policeman on duty at the corner. You understand?"

"I think I do," I said, with an expressive nod at the
remnants of the *bombe* melting slowly in the dish.

"Exactly. But the cases were useful in another way too.
In the basement, or in the cellar at the back, rather, two
printing-presses were established. A lot of revolutionary
literature of the most inflammatory kind was got away
from the house in Stone's Dried Soup cases. The brother
of our anarchist young lady found some occupation there.
He wrote articles, helped to set up type and pull off the
sheets, and generally assisted the man in charge, a very
able young fellow called Sevrin.

"The guiding spirit of that group was a fanatic of social
revolution. He is dead now. He was an engraver and
etcher of genius. You must have seen his work. It is much
sought after by certain amateurs now. He began by being
revolutionary in his art, and ended by becoming a revolutionist, after his wife and child had died in want and misery. He used to say that the bourgeoisie, the smug,
overfed lot, had killed them. That was his real belief. He
still worked at his art and led a double life. He was tall,
gaunt, and swarthy, with a long, brown beard and deep-
set eyes. You must have seen him. His name was Horne."

At this I was really startled. Of course years ago I used
to meet Horne about. He looked like a powerful, rough
gipsy, in an old top hat, with a red muffler round his
throat and buttoned up in a long, shabby overcoat. He
talked of his art with exaltation, and gave one the impression of being strung up to the verge of insanity. A
small group of connoisseurs appreciated his work. Who
would have thought that this man . . . Amazing! And yet it
was not, after all, so difficult to believe.

"As you see," X went on, "this group was in a position
to pursue its work of propaganda, and the other kind of

work, too, under very advantageous conditions. They were all resolute, experienced men of a superior stamp. And yet we became struck at length by the fact that plans prepared in Hermione Street almost invariably failed."

"Who were 'we'?" I asked, pointedly.

"Some of us in Brussels—at the centre," he said, hastily. "Whatever vigorous action originated in Hermione Street seemed doomed to failure. Something always happened to baffle the best planned manifestations in every part of Europe. It was a time of general activity. You must not imagine that all our failures are of a loud sort, with arrests and trials. That is not so. Often the police work quietly, almost secretly, defeating our combinations by clever counter-plotting. No arrests, no noise, no alarming of the public mind and inflaming the passions. It is a wise procedure. But at that time the police were too uniformly successful from the Mediterranean to the Baltic. It was annoying and began to look dangerous. At last we came to the conclusion that there must be some untrustworthy elements amongst the London groups. And I came over to see what could be done quietly.

"My first step was to call upon our young Lady Amateur of anarchism at her private house. She received me in a flattering way. I judged that she knew nothing of the chemical and other operations going on at the top of the house in Hermione Street. The printing of anarchist literature was the only 'activity' she seemed to be aware of there. She was displaying very strikingly the usual signs of severe enthusiasm, and had already written many sentimental articles with ferocious conclusions. I could see she was enjoying herself hugely, with all the gestures and grimaces of deadly earnestness. They suited her big-eyed, broad-browed face and the good carriage of her shapely head, crowned by a magnificent lot of brown hair done in an unusual and becoming style. Her brother was in the room, too, a serious youth, with arched eyebrows and wearing a red necktie, who struck me as being abolutely in the dark about everything in the world, including himself. By and by a tall young man came in. He was clean-shaved with a strong bluish jaw and something of the air of a taciturn actor or of a fanatical priest: the type with thick black eyebrows—you know. But he was very presentable indeed. He shook hands at once vigorously with each of us. The young lady came up to me and murmured sweetly, 'Comrade Sevrin.'

"I had never seen him before. He had little to say to us, but sat down by the side of the girl, and they fell at once into earnest conversation. She leaned forward in her deep armchair, and took her nicely rounded chin in her beautiful white hand. He looked attentively into her eyes. It was the attitude of love-making, serious, intense, as if on the brink of the grave. I suppose she felt it necessary to round and complete her assumption of advanced ideas, of revolutionary lawlessness, by making believe to be in love with an anarchist. And this one, I repeat, was extremely presentable, notwithstanding his fanatical black-browed aspect. After a few stolen glances in their direction, I had no doubt that he was in earnest. As to the lady, her gestures were unapproachable, better than the very thing itself in the blended suggestion of dignity, sweetness, condescension, fascination, surrender, and reserve. She interpreted her conception of what that precise sort of love-making should be with consummate art. And so far, she, too, no doubt, was in earnest. Gestures—but so perfect!

"After I had been left alone with our Lady Amateur I informed her guardedly of the object of my visit. I hinted at our suspicions. I wanted to hear what she would have to say, and half expected some perhaps unconscious revelation. All she said was, 'That's serious,' looking delightfully concerned and grave. But there was a sparkle in her eyes which meant plainly, 'How exciting!' After all, she knew little of anything except of words. Still, she undertook to put me in communication with Horne, who was not easy to find unless in Hermione Street, where I did not wish to show myself just then.

"I met Horne. This was another kind of a fanatic altogether. I exposed to him the conclusion we in Brussels had arrived at, and pointed out the significant series of failures. To this he answered with irrelevant exaltation:

" 'I have something in hand that shall strike terror into the heart of these gorged brutes.'

"And then I learned that, by excavating in one of the cellars of the house, he and some companions had made their way into the vaults under the great public building I have mentioned before. The blowing up of a whole wing was a certainty as soon as the materials were ready.

"I was not so appalled at the stupidity of that move as I might have been had not the usefulness of our centre in Hermione Street become already very problematical. In fact, in my opinion it was much more of a police trap by this time than anything else.

"What was necessary now was to discover what, or rather who, was wrong, and I managed at last to get that idea into Horne's head. He glared, perplexed, his nostrils working as if he were sniffing treachery in the air.

"And here comes a piece of work which will no doubt strike you as a sort of theatrical expedient. And yet what else could have been done? The problem was to find out the untrustworthy member of the group. But no suspicion could be fastened on one more than another. To set a watch upon them all was not very practicable. Besides, that proceeding often fails. In any case, it takes time, and the danger was pressing. I felt certain that the premises in Hermione Street would be ultimately raided, though the police had evidently such confidence in the informer that the house, for the time being, was not even watched. Horne was positive on that point. Under the circumstances it was an unfavourable symptom. Something had to be done quickly.

"I decided to organize a raid myself upon the group. Do you understand? A raid of other trusty comrades personating the police. A conspiracy within a conspiracy. You see the object of it, of course. When apparently about to be arrested I hoped the informer would betray himself in some way or other; either by some unguarded act or simply by his unconcerned demeanour, for instance. Of course there was the risk of complete failure and the no lesser risk of some fatal accident in the course of resistance, perhaps, or in the efforts at escape. For, as you will easily see, the Hermione Street group had to be actually and completely taken unawares, as I was sure they would be by the real police before very long. The informer was amongst them, and Horne alone could be let into the secret of my plan.

"I will not enter into the detail of my preparations. It was not very easy to arrange, but it was done very well, with a really convincing effect. The sham police invaded the restaurant, whose shutters were immediately put up. The surprise was perfect. Most of the Hermione Street party were found in the second cellar, enlarging the hole communicating with the vaults of the great public building. At the first alarm, several comrades bolted through impulsively into the aforesaid vault, where, of course, had this been a genuine raid, they would have been hopelessly trapped. We did not bother about them for the moment. They were harmless enough. The top floor caused considerable anxiety to Horne and myself. There, surrounded by tins of Stone's Dried Soup, a comrade, nick-named the Professor (he was an ex-science student) was engaged in perfecting some new detonators. He was an abstracted, self-confident, sallow little man, armed with large round spectacles, and we were afraid that under a mistaken impression he would blow himself up and wreck the house about our ears. I rushed upstairs and found him already at the door, on the alert, listening, as he said, to 'suspicious noises down below.' Before I had quite finished explaining to him what was going on he shrugged his shoulders disdainfully and turned away to his balances and test tubes. His was the true spirit of an extreme revolutionist. Explosives were his faith, his hope, his weapon, and his shield. He perished a couple of years afterwards in a secret laboratory through the premature explosion of one of his improved detonators.

"Hurrying down again, I found an impressive scene in the gloom of the big cellar. The man who personated the inspector (he was no stranger to the part) was speaking harshly, and giving bogus orders to his bogus subordinates for the removal of his prisoners. Evidently nothing enlightening had happened so far. Horne, saturnine and swarthy, waited with folded arms, and his patient, moody expectation had an air of stoicism well in keeping with the situation. I detected in the shadows one of the Hermione street group surreptitiously chewing up and swallowing a small piece of paper. Some compromising scrap, I suppose; perhaps just a note of a few names and addresses. He was a true and faithful 'companion.' But the fund of secret malice which lurks at the bottom of our sympathies caused me to feel amused at that perfectly uncalled-for performance.

In every other respect the risky experiment, the theatrical *coup*, if you like to call it so, seemed to have failed. The deception could not be kept up much longer; the explanation would bring about a very embarrassing and even grave situation. The man who had eaten the paper would be furious. The fellows who had bolted away would be angry, too.

"To add to my vexation, the door communicating with the other cellar, where the printing-presses were, flew open, and our young lady revolutionist appeared, a black silhouette in a close-fitting dress and a large hat, with the blaze of gas flaring in there at her back. Over her shoulder I perceived the arched eyebrows and the red necktie of her brother.

"The last people in the world I wanted to see then! They had gone that evening to some amateur concert for the delectation of the poor people, you know; but she had insisted on leaving early, on purpose to call in Hermione Street on the way home, under the pretext of having some work to do. Her usual task was to correct the proofs of the Italian and French editions of the *Alarm Bell* and the *Firebrand*. . . ."

"Heavens!" I murmured. I had been shown once a few copies of these publications. Nothing, in my opinion, could have been less fit for the eyes of a young lady. They were the most advanced things of the sort; advanced, I mean, beyond all bounds of reason and decency. One of them preached the dissolution of all social and domestic ties; the other advocated systematic murder. To think of a young girl calmly tracking printers' errors all along the sort of abominable sentences I remembered was intolerable to my sentiment of womanhood. Mr. X, after giving me a glance, pursued steadily.

"I think, however, that she came mostly to exercise her fascinations upon Sevrin, and to receive his homage in her queenly and condescending way. She was aware of both—her power and his homage—and enjoyed them with, I dare say, complete innocence. We have no ground in expediency or morals to quarrel with her on that account. Charm in woman and exceptional intelligence in man are a law unto themselves. Is it not so?"

I refrained from expressing my abhorrence of that licentious doctrine because of my curiosity.

"But what happened then?" I hastened to ask.

X went on crumbling slowly a small piece of bread with a careless left hand.

"What happened, in effect," he confessed, "is that she saved the situation."

"She gave you an opportunity to end your rather sinister farce," I suggested.

"Yes," he said, preserving his impassive bearing. "The

farce was bound to end soon. And it ended in a very few minutes. And it ended well. Had she not come in, it might have ended badly. Her brother, of course, did not count. They had slipped into the house quietly some time before. The printing-cellar had an entrance of its own. Not finding any one there, she sat down to her proofs, expecting Sevrin to return to his work at any moment. He did not do so. She grew impatient, heard through the door the sounds of a disturbance in the other cellar and naturally came in to see what was the matter.

Sevrin had been with us. At first he had seemed to me the most amazed of the whole raided lot. He appeared for an instant as if paralyzed with astonishment. He stood rooted to the spot. He never move a limb. A solitary gas-jet flared near his head; all the other lights had been put out at the first alarm. And presently, from my dark corner, I observed on his shaven actor's face an expression of puzzled, vexed watchfulness. He knitted his heavy eyebrows. The corners of his mouth dropped scornfully. He was angry. Most likely he had seen through the game, and I regretted I had not taken him from the first into my complete confidence.

"But with the appearance of the girl he became obviously alarmed. It was plain. I could see it grow. The change of his expression was swift and startling. And I did not know why. The reason never occurred to me. I was merely astonished at the extreme alteration of the man's face. Of course he had not been aware of her presence in the other cellar; but that did not explain the shock her advent had given him. For a moment he seemed to have been reduced to imbecility. He opened his mouth as if to shout, or perhaps only to gasp. At any rate, it was somebody else who shouted. This somebody else was the heroic comrade whom I had detected swallowing a piece of paper. With laudable presence of mind he let out a warning yell.

" 'It's the police! Back! Back! Run back, and bolt the door behind you.'

"It was an excellent hint; but instead of retreating the girl continued to advance, followed by her long-faced brother in his knickerbocker suit, in which he had been singing comic songs for the entertainment of a joyless proletariat. She advanced not as if she had failed to understand—the word 'police' has an unmistakable sound—but rather as if she could not help herself. She did not advance with the free gait and expanding presence of a distinguished amateur anarchist amongst poor, struggling professionals, but with slightly raised shoulders, and her elbows pressed close to her body, as if trying to shrink within herself. Her eyes were fixed immovably upon Sevrin. Sevrin the man, I fancy; not Sevrin the anarchist. But she advanced. And that was natural. For all their assumption of independence, girls of that class are used to the feeling of being specially protected, as, in fact, they are. This feeling accounts for nine tenths of their audacious gestures. Her face had gone completely colourless. Ghastly. Fancy having it brought home to her so brutally that she was the sort of person who must run away from the police! I believe she was pale with indignation, mostly, though there was, of course, also the concern for her intact personality, a vague dread of some sort of rudeness. And, naturally, she turned to a man, to the man on whom she had a claim of fascination and homage—the man who could not conceivably fail her at any juncture."

"But," I cried, amazed at this analysis, "if it had been serious, real, I mean—as she thought it was—what could she expect him to do for her?"

X never moved a muscle of her face.

"Goodness knows. I imagine that this charming, generous, and independent creature had never known in her life a single genuine thought; I mean a single thought detached from small human vanities, or whose source was not in some conventional perception. All I know is that after advancing a few steps she extended her hand towards the motionless Sevrin. And that at least was no gesture. It was a natural movement. As to what she expected him to do, who can tell? The impossible. But whatever she expected, it could not have come up, I am safe to say, to what he had made up his mind to do, even before that entreating hand had appealed to him so directly. It had not been necessary. From the moment he had seen her enter that cellar, he had made up his mind to sacrifice his future usefulness, to throw off the impenetrable, solidly fastened mask it had been his pride to wear—"

"What do you mean?" I interrupted, puzzled. "Was it Sevrin, then, who was—"

"He was. The most persistent, the most dangerous, the craftiest, the most systematic of informers. A genius amongst betrayers. Fortunately for us, he was unique. The man was a fanatic, I have told you. Fortunately, again, for us, he had fallen in love with the accomplished and innocent gestures of that girl. An actor in desperate earnest himself, he must have believed in the absolute value of conventional signs. As to the grossness of the trap into which he fell, the explanation must be that two sentiments of such absorbing magnitude cannot exist simultaneously in one heart. The danger of that other and unconscious comedian robbed him of his vision, of his perspicacity, of his judgment. Indeed, it did at first rob him of his self-possession. But he regained that through the necessity—as it appeared to him imperiously—to do something at once. To do what? Why, to get her out of the house as quickly as possible. He was desperately anxious to do that. I have told you he was terrified. It could not be about himself. He had been surprised and annoyed at a move quite unforeseen and premature. I may even say he had been furious. He was accustomed to arrange the last scene of his betrayals with a deep, subtle art which left his revolutionist reputation untouched. But it seems clear to me that at the same time he had resolved to make the best of it, to keep his mask resolutely on. It was only with the discovery of her being in the house that everything—the

forced calm, the restraint of his fanaticism, the mask—all
came off together in a kind of panic. Why panic, do you
ask? The answer is very simple. He remembered—or, I
dare say, he had never forgotten—the Professor alone at
the top of the house, pursuing his researches, surrounded
by tins upon tins of Stone's Dried Soup. There was
enough in some few of them to bury us all where we stood
under a heap of bricks. Sevrin, of course, was aware of
that. And we must believe, also, that he knew the exact
character of the man. He had gauged so many such characters! Or perhaps he only gave the Professor credit for
what he himself was capable of. But, in any case, the effect was produced. And suddenly he raised his voice in
authority.

" 'Get the lady away at once.'

"It turned out that he was as hoarse as a crow; result, no
doubt, of the intense emotion. It passed off in a moment.
But these fateful words issued forth from his contracted
throat in a discordant, ridiculous croak. They required no
answer. The thing was done. However, the man personating the inspector judged it expedient to say roughly:

" 'She shall go soon enough, together with the rest of
you.'

"These were the last words belonging to the comedy
part of this affair.

"Oblivious of everything and everybody, Sevrin strode
towards him and seized the lapels of his coat. Under his
thin bluish cheeks one could see his jaws working with
passion.

" 'You have men posted outside. Get the lady taken
home at once. Do you hear? Now. Before you try to get
hold of the man upstairs.'

" 'Oh! There is a man upstairs,' scoffed the other,
openly. 'Well, he shall be brought down in time to see the
end of this.'

"But Sevrin, beside himself, took no need of the tone.
" 'Who's the imbecile meddler who sent you blun-

dering here? Didn't you understand your instructions? Don't you know anything? It's incredible. Here—'

"He dropped the lapels of the coat and, plunging his hand into his breast, jerked feverishly at something under his shirt. At last he produced a small square pocket of soft leather, which must have been hanging like a scapulary from his neck by the tape whose broken ends dangled from his fist.

" 'Look inside,' he spluttered, flinging it in the other's face. And instantly he turned round towards the girl. She stood just behind him, perfectly still and silent. Her set, white face gave an illusion of placidity. Only her staring eyes seemed bigger and darker.

"He spoke rapidly, with nervous assurance. I heard him distinctly promise her to make everything as clear as day-light presently. But that was all I caught. He stood close to her, never attempting to touch her even with the tip of his little finger—and she stared at him stupidly. For a moment, however, her eyelids descended slowly, patheti-cally, and then, with the long black eyelashes lying on her white cheeks, she looked ready to fall down in a swoon. But she never even swayed where she stood. He urged her loudly to follow him at once, and walked towards the door at the bottom of the cellar stairs without looking behind him. And, as a matter of fact, she did move after him a pace or two. But, of course, he was not allowed to reach the door. There were angry exclamations, a short, fierce scuffle. Flung away violently, he came flying backwards upon her, and fell. She threw out her arms in a gesture of dismay and stepped aside, just clear of his head, which struck the ground heavily near her shoe.

"He grunted with the shock. By the time he had picked himself up, slowly, dazedly, he was awake to the reality of things. The man into whose hands he had thrust the leather case had extracted therefrom a narrow strip of blu-ish paper. He held it up above his head, and, as after the scuffle an expectant uneasy stillness reigned once more, he threw it down disdainfully with the words, 'I think, comrades, that this proof was hardly necessary.'

"Quick as thought, the girl stooped after the fluttering slip. Holding it spread out in both hands, she looked at it; then, without raising her eyes, opened her fingers slowly and let it fall.

"I examined that curious document afterwards. It was signed by a very high personage, and stamped and countersigned by other high officials in various countries of Europe. In his trade—or shall I say, in his mission?—that sort of talisman might have been necessary, no doubt. Even to the police itself—all but the heads—he had been known only as Sevrin the noted anarchist.

"He hung his head, biting his lower lip. A change had come over him, a sort of thoughtful, absorbed calmness. Nevertheless, he panted. His sides worked visibly, and his nostrils expanded and collapsed in weird contrast with his sombre aspect of a fanatical monk in a meditative attitude, but with something, too, in his face of an actor intent upon the terrible exigencies of his part. Before him Horne declaimed, haggard and bearded, like an inspired denunciatory prophet from a wilderness. Two fanatics. They were made to understand each other. Does this surprise you? I suppose you think that such people would be foaming at the mouth and snarling at each other?"

I protested hastily that I was not surprised in the least; that I thought nothing of the kind; that anarchists in general were simply inconceivable to me mentally, morally, logically, sentimentally, and even physically. X received this declaration with his usual woodenness and went on.

"Horne had burst out into eloquence. While pouring out scornful invective, he let tears escape from his eyes and roll down his black beard unheeded. Sevrin panted quicker and quicker. When he opened his mouth to speak, everyone hung on his words.

" 'Don't be a fool, Horne,' he began. 'You know very well that I have done this for none of the reasons you are throwing at me.' And in a moment he became outwardly as steady as a rock under the other's lurid stare. 'I have been thwarting, deceiving, and betraying you—from conviction.'

"He turned his back on Horne, and addressing the girl, repeated the words: 'From conviction.'

"It's extraordinary how cold she looked. I suppose she could not think of any appropriate gesture. There can have been few precedents indeed for such a situation.

" 'Clear as daylight,' he added. 'Do you understand what that means? From conviction.'

"And still she did not stir. She did not know what to do. But the luckless wretch was about to give her the opportunity for a beautiful and correct gesture.

" 'I have felt in me the power to make you share this conviction,' he protested, ardently. He had forgotten himself; he made a step towards her—perhaps he stumbled. To me he seemed to be stooping low as if to touch the hem of her garment. And then the appropriate gesture came. She snatched her skirt away from his polluting contact and averted her head with an upward tilt. It was magnificently done, this gesture of conventionally unstained honour, of an unblemished high-minded amateur.

"Nothing could have been better. And he seemed to think so, too, for once more he turned away. But this time he faced no one. He was again panting frightfully, while he fumbled hurriedly in his waistcoat pocket, and then raised his hand to his lips. There was something furtive in this movement, but directly afterwards his bearing changed. His laboured breathing gave him a resemblance to a man who had just run a desperate race; but a curious air of detachment, of sudden and profound indifference, replaced the strain of the striving effort. The race was over. I did not want to see what would happen next. I was only too well aware. I tucked the young lady's arm under mine without a word, and made my way with her to the stairs.

"Her brother walked behind us. Half-way up the short flight she seemed unable to lift her feet high enough for the steps, and we had to pull and push to get her to the top. In the passage she dragged herself along, hanging on my arm, helplessly bent like an old woman. We issued into an empty street through a half-open door, staggering like besotted revellers. At the corner we stopped a four-wheeler, and the ancient driver looked round from his box with morose scorn at our efforts to get her in. Twice during the drive I felt her collapse on my shoulder in a half faint. Facing us, the youth in knickerbockers remained as mute as a fish, and, till he jumped out with the latch-key, sat more still than I would have believed it possible.

"At the door of their drawing-room she left my arm and walked in first, catching at the chairs and tables. She unpinned her hat, then, exhausted with the effort, her cloak still hanging from her shoulders, flung herself into a deep armchair, sideways, her face half buried in a cushion. The good brother appeared silently before her with a glass of water. She motioned it away. He drank it himself and walked off to a distant corner—behind the grand piano, somewhere. All was still in this room where I had seen, for the first time, Sevrin, the anti-anarchist, captivated and spellbound by the consummate and hereditary grimaces that in a certain sphere of life take the place of feelings with an excellent effect. I suppose her thoughts were busy with the same memory. Her shoulders shook violently. A pure attack of nerves. When it quieted down she affected firmness, 'What is done to a man of that sort? What will they do to him?'

" 'Nothing. They can do nothing to him,' I assured her, with perfect truth. I was pretty certain he had died in less than twenty minutes from the moment his hand had gone to his lips. For if his fanatical anti-anarchism went even as far as carrying poison in his pocket, only to rob his adversaries of legitimate vengeance, I knew he would take care to provide something that would not fail him when required.

"She drew an angry breath. There were red spots on her cheeks and a feverish brilliance in her eyes.

" 'Has ever any one been exposed to such a terrible experience? To think that he had held my hand! That man!' Her face twitched, she gulped down a pathetic sob. 'If I ever felt sure of anything, it was of Sevrin's high-minded motives.'

"Then she began to weep quietly, which was good for her. Then through her flood of tears, half resentful, 'What was it he said to me?—"From conviction!" It seemed a vile mockery. What could he mean by it?'

" 'That, my dear young lady,' I said, gently, 'is more than I or anybody else can ever explain to you.' "

Mr. X flicked a crumb off the front of his coat.

"And that was strictly true as to her. Though Horne, for instance, understood very well; and so did I, especially after we had been to Sevrin's lodging in a dismal back street of an intensely respectable quarter. Horne was known there as a friend, and we had no difficulty in being admitted, the slatternly maid merely remarking, as she let us in, that 'Mr. Sevrin had not been home that night.' We forced open a couple of drawers in the way of duty, and found a little useful information. The most interesting part was his diary; for this man, engaged in such deadly work, had the weakness to keep a record of the most damnatory kind. There were his acts and also his thoughts laid bare to us. But the dead don't mind that. They don't mind anything.

" 'From conviction.' Yes. A vague but ardent humanitarianism had urged him in his first youth into the bitterest extremity of negation and revolt. Afterwards his optimism flinched. He doubted and became lost. You have heard of converted atheists. These turn often into dangerous fanatics, but the soul remains the same. After he had got acquainted with the girl, there are to be met in that diary of his very queer politico-amorous rhapsodies. He took her sovereign grimaces with deadly seriousness. He longed to convert her. But all this cannot interest you. For the rest, I don't know if you remember—it is a good many years ago now—the journalistic sensation of the 'Hermione Street Mystery'; the finding of a man's body in the cellar of an empty house; the inquest; some arrests; many surmises—then silence—the usual end for many obscure martyrs and confessors. The fact is, he was not enough of an optimist. You must be a savage, tyrannical, pitiless, thick-and-thin optimist, like Horne, for instance, to make a good social rebel of the extreme type."

He rose from the table. A waiter hurried up with his overcoat; another held his hat in readiness.

"But what became of the young lady?" I asked.

"Do you really want to know?" he said, buttoning himself in his fur coat carefully. "I confess to the small malice of sending her Sevrin's diary. She went into retirement; then she went to Florence; then she went into retreat in a convent. I can't tell where she will go next. What does it matter? Gestures! Gestures! Mere gestures of her class."

He fitted on his glossy high hat with extreme precision, and casting a rapid glance round the room, full of well-dressed people, innocently dining, muttered between his teeth:

"And nothing else! That is why their kind is fated to perish."

I never met Mr. X again after that evening. I took to dining at my club. On my next visit to Paris I found my friend all impatience to hear of the effect produced on me by this rare item of his collection. I told him all the story, and he beamed on me with the pride of his distinguished specimen.

"Isn't X well worth knowing?" he bubbled over in great delight. "He's unique, amazing, absolutely terrific."

His enthusiasm grated upon my finer feelings. I told

him curtly that the man's cynicism was simply abominable.

"Oh, abominable! abominable!" assented my friend, effusively. "And then, you know, he likes to have his little joke sometimes," he added in a confidential tone.

I fail to understand the connection of this last remark. I have been utterly unable to discover where in all this the joke comes in.

THE MOTHER HIVE
Rudyard Kipling

Society is nurtured by a beneficent myth, Rudyard Kipling tells us in this twentieth-century fable of the bees, "The Mother Hive" (included in *Actions and Reactions*, London, 1909). And like other myths, this myth of the hive is true in essence. To the bees, the gods of the copybook headings with fire and slaughter return.

If the stock had not been old and overcrowded, the Waxmoth would never have entered; but where bees are too thick on the comb there must be sickness or parasites. The heat of the hive had risen with the June honey-flow, and though the fanners worked, until their wings ached, to keep people cool, everybody suffered.

A young bee crawled up the greasy, trampled alighting-board. 'Excuse me,' she began, 'but it's my first honey-flight. Could you kindly tell me if this is my—'

'—own hive?' the Guard snapped. 'Yes! Buzz in, and be foul-brooded to you! Next!'

'Shame!' cried half-a-dozen old workers with worn wings and nerves, and there was a scuffle and a hum.

The little grey Wax-moth, pressed close in a crack in the alighting-board, had waited this chance all day. She scuttled in like a ghost, and, knowing the senior bees would turn her out at once, dodged into a brood-frame, where youngsters who had not yet seen the winds blow or the flowers nod discussed life. Here she was safe, for young bees will tolerate any sort of stranger. Behind her came the bee who had been slanged by the Guard.

'What is the world like, Melissa?' said a companion.

'Cruel! I brought in a full load of first-class stuff, and the Guard told me to go and be foul-brooded!' She sat down in the cool draught across the combs.

'If you'd only heard,' said the Wax-moth silkily, 'the insolence of the Guard's tone when she cursed our sister! It aroused the Entire Community.' She laid an egg. She had stolen in for that purpose.

'There *was* a bit of a fuss on the Gate,' Melissa chuckled. 'You were there, Miss—?' She did not know how to address the slim stranger.

'Don't call me "Miss." I'm a sister to all in affliction—just a working-sister. My heart bled for you beneath your burden.' The Wax-moth caressed Melissa with her soft feelers and laid another egg.

'You mustn't lay here,' cried Melissa. 'You aren't a Queen.'

'My dear child, I give you my most solemn word of honour those aren't eggs. Those are my principles, and I am ready to die for them. She raised her voice a little above the rustle and tramp round her. 'If you'd like to kill me, pray do.'

'Don't be unkind, Melissa,' said a young bee, impressed by the chaste folds of the Wax-moth's wing, which hid her ceaseless egg-dropping.

'*I* haven't done anything,' Melissa answered. 'She's doing it all.'

'Ah, don't let your conscience reproach you later, but

when you've killed me, write me, at least, as one that loved her fellow-workers.'

Laying at every sob, the Wax-moth backed into a crowd of young bees, and left Melissa bewildered and annoyed. So she lifted up her little voice in the darkness and cried, 'Stores!' till a gang of cell-fillers hailed her, and she left her load with them.

'I'm afraid I foul-brooded you just now,' said a voice over her shoulder. 'I'd been on the Gate for three hours, and one would foul-brood the Queen herself after that. No offence meant.'

'None taken,' Melissa answered cheerily. 'I shall be on guard myself, some day. What's next to do?'

'There's a rumour of Death's Head Moths about. Send a gang of youngsters to the Gate, and tell them to narrow it in with a couple of stout scrap-wax pillars. It'll make the Hive hot, but we can't have Death's Headers in the middle of our honey-flow.'

'My Only Wings! I should think not!' Melissa had all a sound bee's hereditary hatred against the big, squeaking, feathery Thief of the Hives. 'Tumble out!' she called across the youngsters' quarters. 'All you who aren't feeding babies, show a leg. Scrap-wax pillars for the Ga-ate!' She chanted the order at length.

'That's nonsense,' a downy, day-old bee answered. 'In the first place, I never heard of a Death's Header coming into a hive. People don't *do* such things. In the second, building pillars to keep 'em out is purely a Cypriote trick, unworthy of British bees. In the third, if you trust a Death's Head, he will trust you. Pillar-building shows lack of confidence. Our dear sister in grey says so.'

'Yes. Pillars are un-English and provocative, and a waste of wax that is needed for higher and more practical ends,' said the Wax-moth from an empty store-cell.

'The safety of the Hive is the highest thing I've ever heard of. You mustn't teach us to refuse work,' Melissa began.

'You misunderstand me as usual, love. Work's the essence of life; but to expend precious unreturning vitality and real labour against imaginary danger, *that* is heartbreakingly absurd! If I can only teach a—a little toleration—a little ordinary kindness here towards that absurd old bogey you call the Death's Header, I shan't have lived in vain.'

'She *hasn't* lived in vain, the darling!' cried twenty bees together. 'You should see her saintly life, Melissa! She just devotes herself to spreading her principles, and—and—she looks lovely!'

An old, baldish bee came up the comb.

'Pillar-workers for the Gate! Get out and chew scraps. Buzz off!' she said. The Wax-moth slipped aside.

The young bees trooped down the frame, whispering.

'What's the matter with 'em?' said the oldster. 'Why do they call each other "ducky" and "darling." 'Must be the weather.' She sniffed suspiciously. 'Horrid stuffy smell here. Like stale quilts. Not Wax-moth, I hope, Melissa?'

'Not to my knowledge,' said Melissa, who, of course, only knew the Wax-moth as a lady with principles, and had never thought to report her presence. She had always imagined Wax-moths to be like blood-red dragon-flies.

'You had better fan out this corner for a little,' said the old bee and passed on. Melissa dropped her head at once, took firm hold with her fore-feet, and fanned obediently at the regulation stroke—three hundred beats to the second. Fanning tries a bee's temper, because she must always keep in the same place where she never seems to be doing any good, and, all the while, she is wearing out her only wings. When a bee cannot fly, a bee must not live; and a bee knows it. The Wax-moth crept forth, and caressed Melissa again.

'I see,' she murmured, 'that at heart you are one of Us.'

'I work with the Hive,' Melissa answered briefly.

'It's the same thing. We and the Hive are one.'

'Then why are your feelers different from ours? Don't cuddle so.'

'Don't be provincial, *carissima*. You can't have all the world alike—yet.'

'But why do you lay eggs?' Melissa insisted. 'You lay 'em like a Queen—only you drop them in patches all over the place. I've watched you.'

'Ah, Brighteyes, so you've pierced my little subterfuge? Yes, they are eggs. By and by they'll spread our principles. Aren't you glad?'

'You gave me your most solemn word of honour that they were not eggs.'

'That was my little subterfuge, dearest—for the sake of the Cause. Now I must reach the young.' The Wax-moth tripped towards the fourth brood-frame where the young bees were busy feeding the babies.

It takes some time for a sound bee to realise a malignant and continuous lie. 'She's very sweet and feathery,' was all that Melissa thought, 'but her talk sounds like ivy honey tastes. I'd better get to my field-work again.'

She found the Gate in a sulky uproar. The youngsters told off to the pillars had refused to chew scrap-wax because it made their jaws ache and were clamouring for virgin stuff.

'Anything to finish the job!' said the badgered Guards. 'Hang up, some of you, and make wax for these slack-jawed sisters.'

Before a bee can make wax she must fill herself with honey. Then she climbs to safe foothold and hangs, while other gorged bees hang on to her in a cluster. There they wait in silence till the wax comes. The scales are either taken out of the maker's pockets by the workers, or tinkle down on the workers while they wait. The workers chew them (they are useless unchewed) into the all-supporting, all-embracing Wax of the Hive.

But now, no sooner was the wax cluster in position than the workers below broke out again.

'Come down!' they cried. 'Come down and work! Come on, you Levantine parasites! don't think to enjoy yourselves up there while we're sweating down here!'

The cluster shivered, as from hooked fore-foot to hooked hind-foot it telegraphed uneasiness. At last a worker sprang up, grabbed the lowest wax-maker, and swung, kicking, above her companions.

'I can make wax too!' she bawled. 'Give me a full gorge and I'll make tons of it.'

'Make it, then,' said the bee she had grappled. The spoken word snapped the current through the cluster. It shook and glistened like a cat's fur in the dark. 'Unhook!' it murmured. 'No wax for any one to-day.'

'You lazy thieves! Hang up at once and produce our wax,' said the bees below.

'Impossible! The sweat's gone. To make your wax we must have stillness, warmth, and food. Unhook! Unhook!'

They broke up as they murmured, and disappeared among the other bees, from whom, of course, they were undistinguishable.

' 'Seems as if we'd have to chew scrap-wax for these pillars, after all,' said a worker.

'Not by a whole comb,' cried the young bee who had broken the cluster. 'Listen here! I've studied the question more than twenty minutes. It's as simple as falling off a daisy. You've heard of Cheshire, Root and Langstroth?'

They had not, but they shouted 'Good old Langstroth!' just the same.

'Those three know all that there is to be known about making hives. One or t'other of 'em must have made ours, and if they've made it, they're bound to look after it. Ours is a "Guaranteed Patent Hive." You can see it on the label behind.'

'Good old guarantee! Hurrah for the label behind!' roared the bees.

'Well, such being the case, *I* say that when we find

they've betrayed us, we can exact from them a terrible vengeance.'

'Good old vengeance! Good old Root! 'Nuff said! Chuck it!' The crowd cheered and broke away as Melissa dived through.

'D'you know where Langstroth, Root and Cheshire live if you happen to want 'em?' she asked of the proud and panting orator.

'Gum me if I know they ever lived at all! But aren't they beautiful names to buzz about? Did you see how it worked up the sisterhood?'

'Yes, but it didn't defend the Gate,' she replied.

'Ah, perhaps that's true, but think how delicate *my* position is, sister. I've a magnificent appetite, and I don't like working. It's bad for the mind. My instinct tells me that I can act as a restraining influence on others. They would have been worse, but for me.'

But Melissa had already risen clear, and was heading for a breadth of virgin white clover, which to an overtired bee is as soothing as plain knitting to a woman.

'I think I'll take this load to the nurseries,' she said, when she had finished. 'It was always quiet there in my day,' and she topped off with two little pats of pollen for the babies.

She was met on the fourth brood-comb by a rush of excited sisters all buzzing together.

'One at a time! Let me put down my load. Now, what is it, Sacharissa?' she said.

'Grey Sister—that fluffy one, I mean—she came and said we ought to be out in the sunshine gathering honey, because life was short. She said any old bee could attend to our babies, and some day old bees would. That isn't true, Melissa, is it? No old bees can take us away from our babies, can they?'

'Of course not. You feed the babies while your heads are soft. When your heads harden, you go on to field-work. Any one knows that.'

'We told her so! We *told* her so; but she only waved her feelers, and said we could all lay eggs like Queens if we chose. And I'm afraid lots of the weaker sisters believe her, and are trying to do it. *So* unsettling!'

Sacharissa sped to a sealed worker-cell whose lid pulsated, as the bee within began to cut its way out.

'Come along, precious!' she murmured, and thinned the frail top from the other side. A pale, damp, creased thing hoisted itself feebly on to the comb. Sacharissa's note changed at once. 'No time to waste! Go up the frame and preen yourself!' she said. 'Report for nursing-duty in my ward to-morrow evening at six. Stop a minute. What's the matter with your third right leg?'

The young bee held it out in silence—unmistakably a drone leg incapable of packing pollen.

'Thank you. You needn't report till the day after to-morrow.' Sacharissa turned to her companion. 'That's the fifth oddity hatched in my ward since noon. I don't like it.'

'There's always a certain number of 'em,' said Melissa. 'You can't stop a few working sisters from laying, now and then, when they overfeed themselves. They only raise dwarf drones.'

'But we're hatching out drones with workers' stomachs; workers with drones' stomachs; and albinoes and mixed-leggers who can't pack pollen—like that poor little beast yonder. I don't mind dwarf drones any more than you do (they all die in July), but this steady hatch of oddities frightens me, Melissa!'

'How narrow of you! They are all so delightfully clever and unusual and interesting,' piped the Wax-moth from a crack above them. 'Come here, you dear, downy duck, and tell us all about your feelings.'

'I wish she'd go!' Sacharissa lowered her voice. 'She meets these—er—oddities as they dry out, and cuddles 'em in corners.'

'I suppose the truth is that we're over-stocked and too well fed to swarm,' said Melissa.

'That *is* the truth,' said the Queen's voice behind them. They had not heard the heavy royal footfall which sets empty cells vibrating. Sacharissa offered her food at once. She ate and dragged her weary body forward. 'Can you suggest a remedy?' she said.

'New principles!' cried the Wax-moth from her crevice. 'We'll apply them quietly—later.'

'Suppose we sent out a swarm?' Melissa suggested. 'It's a little late, but it might ease us off.'

'It would save us, but—I know the Hive! You shall see for yourself.' The old Queen cried the Swarming Cry, which to a bee of good blood should be what the trumpet was to Job's war-horse. In spite of her immense age (three years), it rang between the cañon-like frames as a pibroch rings in a mountain pass; the fanners changed their note, and repeated it up in every gallery; and the broad-winged drones, burly and eager, ended it on one nerve-thrilling outbreak of bugles: '*La Reine le veult!*[1] Swarm! Swar-rm! Swar-r-rm!*'

But the roar which should follow the Call was wanting. They heard a broken grumble like the murmur of a falling tide.

'Swarm? What for? Catch me leaving a good bar-frame Hive, with fixed foundations, for a rotten old oak out in the open where it may rain any minute! *We're* all right! It's a "Patent Guaranteed Hive." Why do they want to turn us out? Swarming be gummed! Swarming was invented to cheat a worker out of her proper comforts. Come on off to bed!'

The noise died out as the bees settled in empty cells for the night.

'You hear?' said the Queen. 'I know the Hive!'

'Quite between ourselves, *I* taught them that,' cried the Wax-moth. 'Wait till my principles develop, and you'll see the light from a new quarter.'

"The Queen wills it." [R.K.]

'You speak truth for once,' the Queen said suddenly, for she recognised the Wax-moth. 'That Light will break into the top of the Hive. A Hot Smoke will follow it, and your children will not be able to hide in any crevice.'

'Is it possible?' Melissa whispered. 'I—we have sometimes heard a legend like it.'

'It is no legend,' the old Queen answered. 'I had it from my mother, and she had it from hers. After the Wax-moth has grown strong, a Shadow will fall across the gate; a Voice will speak from behind a Veil; there will be Light, and Hot Smoke, and earthquakes, and those who live will see everything that they have done, all together in one place, burned up in one great Fire.' The old Queen was trying to tell what she had been told of the Bee Master's dealings with an infected hive in the apiary, two or three seasons ago; and, of course, from her point of view the affair was as important as the Day of Judgment.

'And then?' asked horrified Sacharissa.

'Then, I have heard that a little light will burn in a great darkness, and perhaps the world will begin again. Myself, I think not.'

'Tut! Tut!' the Wax-moth cried. 'You good, fat people always prophesy ruin if things don't go exactly your way. But I grant you there will be changes.'

There were. When her eggs hatched, the wax was riddled with little tunnels, coated with the dirty clothes of the caterpillars. Flannelly lines ran through the honey-stores, the pollen-larders, the foundations, and worst of all, through the babies in their cradles, till the Sweeper Guards spent half their time tossing out useless little corpses. The lines ended in a maze of sticky webbing on the face of the comb. The caterpillars could not stop spinning as they walked, and as they walked everywhere, they smarmed and garmed everything. Even where it did not hamper the bees' feet, the stale, sour smell of the stuff put them off their work; though some of the bees who had taken to egg-laying said it encouraged them to be mothers and maintain a vital interest in life.

When the caterpillars became moths, they made friends with the ever-increasing Oddities—albinos, mixed-leggers, single-eyed composites, faceless drones, half-queens and laying sisters; and the ever-dwindling band of the old stock worked themselves bald and fray-winged to feed their queer charges. Most of the Oddities would not, and many, on account of their malformations, could not, go through a day's field work; but the Wax-moths, who were always busy on the brood-comb, found pleasant home occupations for them. One albino, for instance, divided the number of pounds of honey in stock by the number of bees in the Hive, and proved that if every bee only gathered honey for seven and three-quarter minutes a day, she would have the rest of the time to herself, and could accompany the drones on their mating flights. The drones were not at all pleased.

Another, an eyeless drone with no feelers, said that all brood-cells should be perfect circles, so as not to interfere with the grub or the workers. He proved that the old six-sided cell was solely due to the workers building against each other on opposite sides of the wall, and that if there were no interference, there would be no angles. Some bees tried the new plan for a while, and found it cost eight times more wax than the old six-sided specification; and, as they never allowed a cluster to hang up and make wax in peace, real wax was scarce. However, they eked out their task with varnish stolen from new coffins at funerals, and it made them rather sick. Then they took to cadging round sugar-factories and breweries, because it was easier to get their material from those places, and the mixture of glucose and beer naturally fermented in store and blew the store-cells out of shape, besides smelling abominably. Some of the sound bees warned them that ill-gotten gains never prosper, but the Oddities at once surrounded them and balled them to death. That was a punishment they were almost as fond of as they were of eating, and they expected the sound bees to feed them. Curiously enough the age-old instinct of loyalty and devotion towards the Hive made the sound bees do this, though their reason told them they ought to slip away and unite with some other healthy stock in the apiary.

'What about seven and three-quarter minutes' work now?' said Melissa one day as she came in. 'I've been at it for five hours, and I've only half a load.'

'Oh, the Hive subsists on the Hival Honey which the Hive produces,' said a blind Oddity squatting in a store-cell.

'But honey is gathered from flowers outside—two miles away sometimes,' cried Melissa.

'Pardon me,' said the blind thing, sucking hard. 'But this is the Hive, is it not?'

'It was. Worse luck, it is.'

'And the Hival Honey is here, is it not?' It opened a fresh store-cell to prove it.

'Ye—es, but it won't be long at this rate,' said Melissa.

'The rates have nothing to do with it. This Hive produces the Hival Honey. You people never seem to grasp the economic simplicity that underlies all life.'

'Oh me!' said poor Melissa, 'Haven't you ever been beyond the Gate?'

'Certainly not. A fool's eyes are in the ends of the earth. Mine are in my head.' It gorged till it bloated.

Melissa took refuge in her poorly-paid field-work and told Sacharissa the story.

'Hut!' said that wise bee, fretting with an old maid of a thistle. 'Tell us something new. The Hive's full of such as him—it, I mean.'

'What's the end to be? All the honey going out and none coming in. Things *can't* last this way!' said Melissa.

'Who cares?' said Sacharissa. 'I know now how drones

feel the day before they're killed. A short life and a merry one for me!'

'If it only were merry! But think of those awful, solemn, lop-sided Oddities waiting for us at home—crawling and clambering and preaching—and dirtying things in the dark.'

'I don't mind that so much as their silly songs, after we've fed 'em, all about "work among the merry, merry blossoms," ' said Sacharissa from the deeps of a stale Canterbury bell.

'I do. How's our Queen?' said Melissa.

'Cheerfully hopeless, as usual. But she lays an egg now and then.'

'Does she so?' Melissa backed out of the next bell with a jerk. 'Suppose, now, we sound workers tried to raise a Princess in some clean corner?'

'You'd be put to it to find one. The Hive's all wax-moth and muckings. But— Well?'

'A Princess might help us in the time of the Voice behind the Veil that the Queen talks of. And anything is better than working for Oddities that chirrup about work that they can't do, and waste what we bring home.'

'Who cares?' said Sacharissa. 'I'm with you, for the fun of it. The Oddities would ball us to death, if they knew. Come home, and we'll begin.'

There is no room to tell how the experienced Melissa found a far-off frame so messed and mishandled by abandoned cell-building experiments that, for very shame, the bees never went there. How in that ruin she blocked out a Royal Cell of sound wax, but disguised by rubbish till it looked like a kopje among deserted kopjes. How she prevailed upon the hopeless Queen to make one last effort and lay a worthy egg. How the Queen obeyed and died. How her spent carcass was flung out on the rubbish heap, and how a multitude of laying sisters went about dropping

drone-eggs where they listed, and said there was no more
need of Queens. How, covered by this confusion, Sacharissa educated certain young bees to educate certain
new-born bees in the almost lost art of making Royal
Jelly. How the nectar for it was won out of hours in the
teeth of chill winds. How the hidden egg hatched true—
no drone, but Blood Royal. How it was capped, and how
desperately they worked to feed and double-feed the now
swarming Oddities, lest any break in the food-supplies
should set them to instituting inquiries, which, with songs
about work, was their favourite amusement. How in an
auspicious hour, on a moonless night, the Princess came
forth—a Princess indeed,—and how Melissa smuggled her
into a dark empty honey-magazine, to bide her time; and
how the drones, knowing she was there, went about singing the deep disreputable love-songs of the old days—to
the scandal of the laying-sisters, who do not think well of
drones. These things are written in the Book of Queens,
which is laid up in the hollow of the Great Ash Ygdrasil.

After a few days the weather changed again and became
glorious. Even the Oddities would now join the crowd
that hung out on the alighting-board, and would sing of
work among the merry, merry blossoms till an untrained
ear might have received it for the hum of a working hive.
Yet, in truth, their store-honey had been eaten long ago.
They lived from day to day on the efforts of the few sound
bees, whiile the Wax-moth fretted and consumed again
their already ruined wax. But the sound bees never mentioned these matters. They knew, if they did, the Oddities
would hold a meeting and ball them to death.

'Now you see what we have done,' said the Wax-moths.
'We have created New Material, a New Convention, a
New Type, as we said we would.'

'And new possibilities for us,' said the laying-sisters
gratefully. 'You have given us a new life's work, vital and
paramount.'

'More than that,' chanted the Oddities in the sunshine;

'you have created a new heaven and a new earth. Heaven, cloudless and accessible' (it was a perfect August evening) 'and Earth teeming with the merry, merry blossoms, waiting only our honest toil to turn them all to good. The—er—Aster, and the Crocus, and the—er—Ladies' Smock in her season, the Chrysanthemum after her kind, and the Guelder Rose bringing forth abundantly withal.'

'Oh, Holy Hymettus!' said Melissa, awestruck. 'I knew they didn't know how honey was made, but they've forgotten the Order of the Flowers! What will become of them?'

A Shadow fell across the alighting-board as the Bee Master and his son came by. The Oddities crawled in and a Voice behind a Veil said: 'I've neglected the old Hive too long. Give me the smoker.'

Melissa heard and darted through the gate. 'Come, oh come!' she cried. 'It is the destruction the Old Queen foretold. Princess, come!'

'Really, you are too archaic for words,' said an Oddity in an alley-way. 'A cloud, I admit, may have crossed the sun; but why hysterics? Above all, why princesses so late in the day? Are you aware it's the Hival Tea-time? Let's sing grace.'

Melissa clawed past him with all six legs. Sacharissa had run to what was left of the fertile brood-comb. 'Down and out!' she called across the brown breadth of it. 'Nurses, guards, fanners, sweepers—out! Never mind the babies. They're better dead. Out, before the Light and the Hot Smoke!'

The Princess's first clear fearless call (Melissa had found her) rose and drummed through all the frames. *'La Reine le veult! Swarm! Swar-rm! Swar-r-rm!'*

The Hive shook beneath the shattering thunder of a stuck-down quilt being torn back.

'Don't be alarmed, dears,' said the Wax-moths. 'That's our work. Look up, and you'll see the dawn of the New Day.'

Light broke in the top of the hive as the Queen had prophesied—naked light on the boiling, bewildered bees.

Sacharissa rounded up her rearguard, which dropped headlong off the frame, and joined the Princess's detachment thrusting toward the Gate. Now panic was in full blast, and each sound bee found herself embraced by at least three Oddities. The first instinct of a frightened bee is to break into the store and gorge herself with honey; but there were no stores left, so the Oddities fought the sound bees.

'You must feed us, or we shall die!' they cried, holding and clutching and slipping, while the silent scared earwigs and little spiders twisted between their legs. 'Think of the Hive, traitors! The Holy Hive!'

'You should have thought before!' cried the sound bees. 'Stay and see the dawn of your New Day.'

They reached the Gate at last over the soft bodies of many to whom they had ministered.

'On! Out! Up!' roared Melissa in the Princess's ear. 'For the Hive's sake! To the Old Oak!'

The Princess left the alighting-board, circled once, flung herself at the lowest branch of the Old Oak, and her little loyal swarm—you could have covered it with a pint mug—followed, hooked, and hung.

'Hold close!' Melissa gasped. 'The old legends have come true! Look!'

The Hive was half hidden by smoke, and Figures moved through the smoke. They heard a frame crack stickily, saw it heaved high and twirled round between enormous hands—a blotched, bulged, and perished horror of grey wax, corrupt brood, and small drone-cells, all covered with crawling Oddities, strange to the sun.

'Why, this isn't a hive! This is a museum of curiosities,' said the Voice behind the Veil. It was only the Bee Master talking to his son.

'Can you blame 'em, father?' said a second voice. 'It's rotten with Wax-moth. See here!'

Another frame came up. A finger poked through it, and it broke away in rustling flakes of ashy rottenness.

'Number Four Frame! That was your mother's pet comb once,' whispered Melissa to the Princess. 'Many's the good egg I've watched her lay there.'

'Aren't you confusing *post hoc* with *propter hoc?*' said the Bee Master. 'Wax-moth only succeed when weak bees let them in.' A third frame crackled and rose into the light. 'All this is full of laying workers' brood. That never happens till the stock's weakened. Phew!'

He beat it on his knee like a tambourine, and it also crumbled to pieces.

The little swarm shivered as they watched the dwarf drone-grubs squirm feebly on the grass. Many sound bees had nursed on that frame, well knowing their work was useless; but the actual sight of even useless work destroyed disheartens a good worker.

'No, they have some recuperative power left,' said the second voice. 'Here's a Queen cell!'

'But it's tucked away among—— What on earth *has* come to the little wretches? They seem to have lost the instinct of cell-building.' The father held up the frame where the bees had experimented in circular cell-work. It looked like the pitted head of a decaying toadstool.

'Not altogether,' the son corrected. 'There's one line, at least, of perfectly good cells.'

'My work,' said Sacharissa to herself. 'I'm glad Man does me justice before——'

That frame, too, was smashed out and thrown atop of the others and the foul earwiggy quilts.

As frame after frame followed it, the swarm beheld the upheaval, exposure, and destruction of all that had been well or ill done in every cranny of their Hive for generations past. There was black comb so old that they had forgotten where it hung; orange, buff, and ochre-varnished store-comb, built as bees were used to build before the days of artificial foundations; and there was a little white,

frail new work. There were sheets on sheets of level, even
brood-comb that had held in its time unnumbered thousands of unnamed workers; patches of obsolete drone-
comb, broad and high-shouldered, showing to what marks
the male grub was expected to grow; and two inch deep
honey-magazines, empty, but still magnificent: the whole
gummed and glued into twisted scrap-work, awry on the
wires, half-cells, beginnings abandoned, or grandiose,
weak-walled, composite cells pieced out with rubbish and
capped with dirt.

Good or bad, every inch of it was so riddled by the tunnels of the Wax-moth that it broke in clouds of dust as it
was flung on the heap.

'Oh, see!' cried Sacharissa. 'The Great Burning that
Our Queen foretold. Who can bear to look?'

A flame crawled up the pile of rubbish, and they smelt
singeing wax.

The Figures stooped, lifted the Hive and shook it upside down over the pyre. A cascade of Oddities, chips of
broken comb, scale, fluff, and grubs slid out, crackled, siz-
zled, popped a little, and then the flames roared up and
consumed all that fuel.

'We must disinfect,' said a Voice. 'Get me a sulphur-
candle, please.'

The shell of the Hive was returned to its place, a light
was set in its sticky emptiness, tier by tier the Figures
built it up, closed the entrance, and went away. The
swarm watched the light leaking through the cracks all the
long night. At dawn one Wax-moth came by, fluttering
impudently.

'There has been a miscalculation about the New Day,
my dears,' she began; 'one can't expect people to be perfect all at once. That was our mistake.'

'No, the mistake was entirely ours,' said the Princess.

'Pardon me,' said the Wax-moth. 'When you think of
the enormous upheaval—call is good or bad—which our

influence brought about, you will admit that we, and we alone——'

'You?' said the Princess. 'Our stock was not strong. So *you* came—as any other disease might have come. Hang close, all my people.'

When the sun rose, Veiled Figures came down, and saw their swarm at the bough's end waiting patiently within sight of the old Hive—a handful, but prepared to go on.

Part Twelve

~~~~~~~~~~~~~~~~~~~~~~~~~~~~~~~~

CRITICAL CONSERVATISM

Three American philosophical men of letters—if the
cosmopolitan Santayana may be counted as an
American—maintained the conservative intellectual
tradition during the 1920s and 1930s. Paul Elmer
More (1864–1937), Irving Babbitt (1865–1933), and
George Santayana (1863–1952) never dabbled in
practical politics; but their critical talents still are
quick among conservatives.

PROPERTY AND LAW
Paul Elmer More

Paul Elmer More, for many years editor of *The Nation*, accomplished the most extensive work of American literary criticism in the eleven volumes of *The Shelburne Essays* and the three volumes of *The New Shelburne Essays*. This bold essay on "Property and Law" is from a volume of the former series titled *Aristocracy and Justice* (Boston, 1915), pp. 127–48.

There has been, as every one knows, a long strike in the mines of Colorado, with violence on both sides and bitter recriminations. On the 27th of April, 1914, there was a meeting of some two thousand persons in Carnegie Hall, of New York, before whom Morris Hillquit made this savage statement:

> The investment of the Rockefellers in the coal fields of Colorado is largely for the hiring of criminals and thugs to shoot the strikers, and the pious son of America's money king knows and sanctions the object. When it was alleged of ex-Lieutenant Becker [the convicted police officer of New York] that he had hired four gunmen to kill one gambler, he was indicted on the charge of murder in the first degree. Why not indict the man who has admittedly hired whole bands of gunmen to kill scores of workers?

In sympathy with this idea that in hiring men to protect his property a mine owner is in the same class with a sordid murderer, it will be recalled that a number of men and women paraded before the office of Mr. John D. Rockefeller, Jr., wearing bands of crêpe. On April 28 Mr. Rockefeller issued an official reply, of which the gist was contained in the following paragraph:

> Are the labor unions, representing a small minority of the workers of the country, to be sustained in their disregard of the inalienable right of every American citizen to work without interference, whether he be a union or a non-union man? Surely the vast majority of American citizens will, without fear or favor, stand for evenhanded justice under the Constitution, and equal rights for every citizen.

To this appeal the United Mine Workers responded the next day:

> Of course the right to work is inherent. If, however, the miners exercise their rights as guaranteed by the Constitution and the laws of our country to have a collective voice in establishing the conditions under which they shall work or shall not work, it ought not and cannot be denied by Mr. Rockefeller.

In the same issue in which this response was published, the New York *Sun* printed a brief and pungent editorial, to this effect:

> Whatever the demagogues prate, an elementary and indispensable and indefeasible right is at stake in Colorado. In defending that right to labor, in refusing to yield to timorous counsels from Washington, Mr. Rockefeller has shown civic courage and a just sense of the equal claim of all to liberty and protection.

Now in regard to the truth of the charges of violence and other misconduct urged alternately by the strikers and the owners and by their sympathizers, one may be unable to decide on the evidence; nor is that the question here considered. The remarkable point is that not a single word was uttered on either side for property itself, as at least a substantial element of civilization. Such a silence was no doubt natural on the part of the strikers; but what of the owners? One suspects that Mr. Rockefeller, away from the Sunday school, and in his private office, thinks a good deal about the privileges of property, and one knows that the *Sun* is interested in those privileges. Yet for these neither Mr. Rockefeller nor the *Sun* would appear to have the slightest concern; they are only voluble in behalf of the independent labouring man and on the indefeasible rights of labour! Is this self-deception, or hypocrisy, or merely the policy of men who understand the feelings of a democratic populace, and desire to present their case in the most plausible light? A hundred years ago, in England or America at least, their present attitude would have been impossible; they would have appealed boldly to the public, their public, on the basis of sheer property rights. Twenty years ago such a position as they now assume could scarcely have been anything but ignoble hypocrisy. To-day their motives cannot be classified in any such simple fashion. It is not improbable that, along with the transparent motive of policy, they are a little troubled to know whether their instinctive feelings as property owners are not in some way unethical. At least we can say with entire confidence that such, under such circumstances, would be the complex state of mind of a considerable, certainly also a growing, body of men.

Now what is the meaning of all this? What is the origin of this state of mind which is so manifestly illogical and self-contradictory?

We shall perhaps discover the first plain enunciation of such a growing view of property in the writings of that master of truth and sophistry, Jean-Jacques Rousseau, especially in the *Discours sur l'origine de l'inégalité* and the *Contrat social.* According to the theory there developed, the most blessed stage of human existence was that exemplified by our North American Indians, who, as Rousseau pictured them from certain travellers' fairy tales, had risen to the beginning of social life, but possessed no property beyond the most rudimentary sort—none at all in our sense of the word. Happy indeed was such a state, if innocence is happiness: for, as the all-knowing Locke had observed, there can be no wrong-doing where there is no property. "It was," adds Rousseau sententiously, "the discovery of iron and grain that civilized men, and ruined the human race." Two consequences followed the creation of property: civilization and injustice. There is, Rousseau admits, a natural inequality of faculties among men, but this is of little moment until fixed and reinforced by extrinsic advantages. An unnatural inequality, or injustice, arises as soon as those who are the stronger by nature acquire increase of strength by the aid of superior possessions. And this injustice is fixed by a clever ruse. The few whose natural strength has been enhanced by property, seeing that they should still be at the mercy of the united mass of the poor and weak, delude the mass into binding themselves by passing laws in defence of property. Law is thus the support at once of civilization and of injustice.

The syllogism is rigid, and the inevitable conclusion would be: abolish law, and let mankind return to the happier condition of barbarism. But such a conclusion forces us to reconsider our premises, and we immediately see that the argument rests on two assumptions, one true and the other false. It is a fact that property has been the basis of civilization, and that with property there has come a change from natural inequality to what is assumed to be unnatural injustice. But it is not a fact that barbarism is in general a state of innocence and happiness. Rousseau himself really knew this, and he felt also, when his words began to be taken seriously by men of affairs, that he should be merely stultifying himself if he called on them to abolish what he recognized as the basis of civilized society: under no glamour of a remote paradise would men go to work deliberately to destroy civilization, whatever might be the evils it embraces.

Hence Rousseau proceeds to develop a theory of the State which shall retain the civilization created by property, while avoiding the injustice inherent in it. To this end he would make *tabula rasa* of the existing forms of authority in government, and in their place introduce, as sole sovereign, a power which he describes as the *volonté générale*. By this he does not precisely mean socialism: for still regarding private ownership as the basis of civilization, he cannot admit collective ownership. His notion is that a government by means of the "general will," while acknowledging the need of private ownership, would do away with injustice, because, in such a State, "the sovereign, being formed only of the individuals which compose it, neither has nor can have any interest contrary to theirs." This may be a true proposition metaphysically, if, in the manner of the medieval realists, we regard the general idea of humanity as an active entity, and the individual men as mere accidents. But what does the "general will," when stripped of its metaphysical disguises, mean for Rousseau? Nothing but the unrestricted desire of the majority at any given moment. Now we, who are the inheritors of the French Revolution and the humble audience of socialistic oratory, have seen the operation of a government, or at least have heard the demands of much applauded demagogues, close enough to the spirit of Rousseau's philosophy, to know what the immediate and unrestricted will of the majority means in practice. Whether it means justice to you or not, may depend on your particular sympathies and interests; it manifestly does not mean a careful regard for the rights of property.

Rousseau's scheme, in fact, involves a self-contradiction: by a juggling of words it supposes that the innocence of man in a state of nature, itself an assumption contrary to fact, can somehow be made to continue in a society which has built itself up on what he regards as the cause of injustice. In simple truth, property may rightly be called the cause of civilization, but, strictly speaking, it is only the occasion of injustice: injustice is inherent in the imperfection of man, and the development of the means of living merely brings into greater prominence what is an unavoidable feature of existence, not for man only but for the whole range of creation, in this puzzlinig world of ours. Rousseau, by inflaming the passions of men against the wrongs of society which by his own hypothesis are inevitable, was, and still is, the father of frightful confusions and catastrophes; but he performed a real service to philosophy by stating so sharply the bare truth that *property is the basis of civilization.*

The socialistic theories of communal ownership give the argument, I admit, a new turn. Socialism rests on two assumptions. First, that community of ownership will, for practical purposes, eliminate the greed and injustice of civilized life. This I deny, believing it to be demonstrably false in view of the present nature of most men, and, I might add, in view of the notorious quarrelsomeness of the socialists among themselves. Secondly, that under community of control the material productivity of society will not be seriously diminished. This question I leave to the economists, though here too it would appear to follow demonstrably from the nature of man that the capacity to manage and the readiness to be managed are necessary to efficient production. Certainly, there has been a convincing uniformity in the way in which wealth and civilization have always gone together, and in the fact that wealth has accumulated only when private property was secure. So far as experience or any intelligent outlook goes, there is no sufficient motive for the creation of property but personal ownership, at least in a share of that joint property.

The burden of proof is entirely on those who assert the sufficiency of communal property; their theory has never been proved, but in innumerable experiments has always failed. And, in fact, the real strength of socialism, the force that some think is driving us along the edge of revolution, is in no sense a reasoned conviction that public ownership is better than private ownership, but rather a profound emotional protest against the inequalities of ownership. The serious question is not in regard to the importance of property, but in regard to the justice of its present distribution. Despite all the chatter about the economic interpretation of history, we are to-day driven along by a sentiment, and by no consideration of economics.

Not even a Rousseau could cover up the fact of the initial inequality of men by the decree of that great Ruler, or Law, call it what you will, which makes one vessel for dishonour and another for honour. That is the so-called injustice of Nature. And it is equally a fact that property means the magnifying of that natural injustice into that which you may deplore as unnatural injustice, but which is a fatal necessity, nevertheless. This is the truth, hideous if you choose to make it so to yourself, not without its benevolent aspect to those, whether the favorites of fortune or not, who are themselves true—ineluctable at least. Unless we are willing to pronounce civilization a grand mistake, as, indeed, religious enthusiasts have ever been prone to do (and humanitarianism is more a perverted religion than a false economics), unless our material progress is all a grand mistake, we must admit, sadly or cheerfully, that any attempt by government or institution to ignore that inequality, may stop the wheels of progress or throw the world back into temporary barbarism, but will surely not be the cause of wider and greater happiness. It is not heartlessness, therefore, to reject the sentiment of the humanitarian, and to avow that the security of property is the first and all-essential duty of a civilized community. And we may assert this truth more bluntly, or, if you

please, more paradoxically. Although, probably, the rude
government of barbarous chiefs, when life was precarious
and property unimportant, may have dealt principally
with wrongs to person, yet the main care of advancing civilization has been for property. After all, life is a very
primitive thing. Nearly all that makes it more significant
to us than to the beast is associated with our possessions—with property, all the way from the food we share
with the beasts, to the most refined products of the human
imagination. To the civilized man *the rights of property
are more important than the right to life.*

In our private dealings with men, we may, if we choose,
ignore these claims of civilization with no harm resulting
to society; but it is different when we undertake to lay
down general rules of practice. In allowing our emotions
and our sense of abstract right to oversway us in our attitude towards politics and government, we forget that it is
not ours to determine the fundamental relation of things,
or to define justice, but to make rules of action in accordance with the decrees, immutable so far as we can see, of a
superior power. We are, essentially, not legislators but
judges.

And what then, you ask, of human laws? In sober sooth
it is not we who create laws; we are rather finders and in-
terpreters of laws registered in a court beyond our control,
and our decrees are merely the application of our knowledge, or ignorance, of the law to particular conditions.
When our decrees are counter to the law of fact, they become at best dead letters, and at worst, agents of trouble
and destruction. The office of the legislator in general is
not unlike that of the jurisconsults of the Roman Empire,
upon whom was bestowed the right of giving binding responses to a judge when he was not clear in a question of
equity or interpretation, and who thus helped to mould
the law into the form in which it was finally codified and
handed down to the modern world. And in a more special

sense, the spirit that guided the trend of their opinions is worthy of scrutiny to-day, as its influence is still vastly stronger than is commonly understood. The expansion of Roman affairs had already begun to force the courts to substitute in general practice the *jus gentium*, or principles of law which seemed to be in effect among all peoples, for the old *jus civile*, or custom which prevailed among Roman citizens when these were a small and comparatively homogeneous body. The responses of the jurisconsults inevitably followed and emphasized this tendency, and, under the influence of late Greek philosophy, went even further in generalization. On the conception of a *jus gentium* these Stoic legalists superimposed the conception of a *jus naturale*, or law implanted by Nature in the heart of man, to which custom and statute should, so far as possible, be made to conform. It is not too much to say that this is one of the profoundest conceptions of the human mind; but it was as dangerous as it was profound. It brought into legislation the idea conveyed by the word *nature*, which is, perhaps, the most treacherous that ever slipped from the tongue of man. The ambiguity came from the philosophers themselves, especially from the Stoics, who used the word at one time to signify the forces and material of the world as they actually are, and at another time to signify the world as it ought to be. There might be no great harm in this ambiguity, were it not for the resulting confusion in ideas and practice. When we repeat the Stoic command to *Follow nature*, we really mean, as the Stoic meant, to follow our ideal of nature. We do not mean that a man should imitate the conduct of a tiger, which is yet entirely natural, nor of men as we see them daily acting, but that he should imitate his ideal of what a man should be. The command is unmeaning enough, and has force only because it seems to render the ideal concrete by confounding it with the actual. And there is its peril. We are prone to laziness and self-flattery, and so we are constantly justifying ourselves in imitating the baser actions of men, under cover of the command to follow human nature. Is not nature what all men are doing? It would, in fact, be easy to show that in the sphere of private morals this command has resulted in a curious mixture of good and evil, by clothing custom in the garb of the ideal.

But the peril for law, as law is what we propose for other men in the mass rather than for ourselves, is of the contrary sort. Law is not a code of ideal virtues nor a guide to individual perfection, but a rule for regulating the relations of society for practical purposes. Just so soon as, in any large measure, it fails to recognize the actuality of human nature, or pronounces in conformity with an ideal of human nature, it becomes inoperative or mischievous. If law supposed that all men were honest, what would be the consequence? Or, if law demanded that all men should be kind-hearted, what would be the consequence? These are absurd extremes, but an error of really the same character has obtained a kind of philosophical excuse through the treachery of such a phrase as *jus naturale*. The experience and hard-headedness of the earlier jurisconsults saved the Roman law from falling a prey to an undue idealism, although it is a fact that in Byzantine times there was introduced a certain degree of humanitarianism corresponding with the decay of civilization.

But for reasons which lie deeply imbedded in the sources of our modern life, we are in great and continual peril of a humanitarianism springing from a mistaken conception of the *jus naturale*. The whole impetus of Rousseau's revolutionary philosophy is really derived from his reassumption and eloquent expansion of that conception. We are bound, in any clear-sighted view of the larger exigencies of the relations of man with man, to fortify ourselves against such a perversion of the institutions of government as would adapt them to the nature of man as he ought to be, instead of the nature of man as he actually is, and would relax the rigour of law, in pity for the degree of injustice inherent in earthly life. If our laws, as we call them, being indeed but attempts to copy a code we have not made and cannot repeal, are to work for progress rather than for retrogression, they must recognize property as the basis of civilization, and must admit the consequent inequality of conditions among men. They will have little or no regard for labour in itself or for the labourer in himself, but they will provide rigidly that labour shall receive the recompense it has bargained for, and that the labourer, as every other man, shall be secure in the possession of what he has received. We may try to teach him to produce more and to bargain better, but in face of all appeals of sentiment and all reasonings of abstract justice, society must learn again to-day that it cannot legislate contrary to the decrees of Fate. In this way, looking at the larger good of society, we may say that the dollar is more than the man, and that *the rights of property are more important than the right to life.*

So directly is the maintenance of civilization and peace and all our welfare dependent on this truth, that it is safer, in the utterance of law, to err on the side of natural inequality than on the side of ideal justice. We can go a little way, very slowly, in the endeavour to equalize conditions by the regulation of property, but the elements of danger are always near at hand and insidious; and undoubtedly any legislation which deliberately releases labour from the obligations of contract, and permits it to make war on property with impunity, must be regarded as running counter to the first demands of society. It is an ugly fact, as the world has always seen, that, under cover of the natural inequality of property, evil and greedy men will act in a way that can only be characterized as legal robbery. It is strictly within the province of the State to prevent such action so far as it safely can. Yet even here, in view of the magnitude of the interests involved, *it is better that legal robbery should exist along with the maintenance of law, than that legal robbery should be suppressed at the expense of law.*

No doubt there is a certain cruelty in such a principle, as there is a factor of cruelty in life itself. But it does not, in any proper sense of the word, involve the so-called economic intepretation of history. On the contrary, this principle recognizes, far more completely than does any humanitarian creed, that there is a large portion of human activity lying quite outside of the domain of physical constraint and legislation, and it is supremely jealous that the arms of government should not extend beyond their true province. All our religious feelings, our aspiring hopes, our personal morality, our conscience, our intellectual pursuits, all these things, and all they mean, lie beyond the law—all our individual life, as distinguished from the material relations of man with man, reaches far beyond the law's proper comprehension.

Our most precious heritage of liberty depends on the safeguarding of that realm of the individual against the encroachments of a legal equalitarianism. For there is nothing surer than that liberty of the spirit, if I may use that dubious word, is bound up with the inequality of men in their natural relations; and every movement in history to deny the inequalities of nature has been attended, and by a fatal necessity always will be attended, with an effort to crush the liberty of distinction in the ideal sphere.

As the rights of property do not involve the economic interpretation of history, so neither do they result in materialism. The very contrary. For in this matter, as in all other questions of human conduct and natural forces, you may to a certain degree control a fact, but if you deny a fact it will control you. This is the plain paradox of life, and its application is everywhere. Just so sure as you see a feministic movement undertaking to deny the peculiar characteristics and limitations of the female sex, you will see this sex element overriding all bounds—you will, to take an obvious illustration, see women dressing in a manner to exaggerate their relative physical disability and their appeal to the other sex. I do not say that the feministic denial of facts is the only cause that may bring about this exaggeration; but it is indisputably one such cause. So, in a more general way, the denial of the body, or the romantic idealization of love, will end by producing a state of morbid eroticism, as history abundantly testifies. And, in another direction, the encouraging of a false sentimentality in the idea of marriage, and the slurring over of its importance as a social institution and as the basis of the family, is one of the sure ways of degrading that natural relation into something we do not like to consider.

Again, if you hear a man talking overmuch of brotherly love and that sort of thing—I do not mean the hypocrite, but the sincere humanitarian whom you and I have met and had dealings with and could name—if you hear such a man talking overmuch of serving his fellows, you are pretty sure that here is a man who will be slippery or dishonourable in his personal transactions. I do not say that there are no exceptions; but the "reformer" is a type well known. And societies are much like individual men. As soon as a nation begins to deny officially the inherent combativeness of human nature, it is in a fair way to be hurried into war. We have seen a group of obstinate humanitarians in Washington, by denying the facts of the Mexican situation, drag this country at Vera Cruz into the hypocritical but fortunately short-lived pretence of waging a "war for service." What is the cause of the evils, physical and moral, that have perplexed our Southern States since the era of Reconstruction? Certainly in large measure the humanitarian ideas of justice and equality which were in flagrant disregard of the facts of a particular stage of civilization, and made a cover for every kind of rascality and stupidity. We are seeing something of the same sort beginning to happen in Turkey and Persia and China, and are like to see it in many other places. Again, of course, I do not say that humanitarian denial of the facts is the only cause of war and national dissolution—would to heaven it were!—but it is just as certainly one such cause, or contributing cause, as it is certain that we shall hurt our fingers if we grasp a burning coal under the notion that it is not hot.

And the same paradox holds true of property. You may to a certain extent control it and make it subservient to the ideal nature of man; but the moment you deny its rights, or undertake to legislate in defiance of them, you may for a time unsettle the very foundations of society, you will certainly in the end render property your despot instead of your servant, and so produce a materialized and debased civilization. Let me illustrate what I mean by a single example of the practical working of humanitarianism. I quote from a striking article on *The Law's Delays*, by Professor Tyrrell Williams:

The apotheosis of debtors in America began about a hundred years ago, and has continued to the present time. In its origin the movement was humanitarian and praiseworthy. Imprisonment for debt was a reality in those days. But has not the movement gone too far, and become ridiculous? The traditional debtor is a hard-working farmer or mechanic struggling to keep the wolf from the door. Is that a true picture of the twentieth-century debtor, who glories in delay of justice? Most certainly not. The typical debtor of the twentieth century is a corporation organized along the lines that were so popular in New Jersey before Woodrow Wilson was elected Governor. The transportation and other public-service corporations are the champion debtors of America. They have been very clever. They have capitalized the ordinary American's sentimental affection for debtors. These corporate debtors are the chief beneficiaries of delay of justice in America, and they know it. That is why directly and indirectly they oppose all serious efforts to reform judicial procedure, and why they employ attorneys who are experts at "filling the record full of error."

This is but a single instance of a false sentiment opening the door to the prowling thieves of the highway. More generally, it is in accordance with the law of human nature that the sure way to foster the spirit of materialism is to unsettle the material basis of social life. Manifestly, the mind will be free to enlarge itself in immaterial interests only when that material basis is secure, and without a certain degree of such security a man must be anxious over material things and preponderantly concerned with them. And, manifestly, if this security is dependent on the rights of property, and these rights are denied or belittled in the name of some impossible ideal, it follows that the demands of intellectual leisure will be regarded as abnormal and anti-social, and that he who turns to the still and quiet life will be despised as a drone, if not hated as an enemy of the serious part of the community. There is something at once comical and vicious in the spectacle of those men of property who take advantage of their leisure to dream out vast benevolent schemes which would render their own self-satisfied career impossible.

No doubt the ideal society would be that in which every man should be filled with noble aspirations, and should have the opportunity to pursue them. But I am not here concerned with such Utopian visions, nor, as I have said, am I arguing with those who are honestly persuaded that a socialistic régime is, in our day, or any day, economically or psychologically feasible. My desire is rather to confirm in the dictates of their own reason those who believe that the private ownership of property, including its production and distribution, is, with very limited reservations, essential to the material stability and progress of society. We who have this conviction need very much to-day to strengthen ourselves against the insidious charms of a misapplied idealism; we need to remind ourselves that laws which would render capital insecure and, by a heavy income tax or other discrimination in favour of labour, would deprive property of its power of easy self-perpetuation, though they speak loudly in the name of humanity, will in the end be subversive of those conditions under which alone any true value of human life can be realized.

This, I take it, is the reason that the Church and the University as institutions have almost invariably stood as strongly reactionary against any innovations which threaten the intrenched rights of property. It is not at bottom the greed of possession that moves them—though this motive also may have entered into the attitude of their governors, as into all the theories and practices of men—nor are we justified in casting into their teeth the reproach that they who profess to stand for spiritual things are in their corporate capacity the most tenacious upholders of worldly privilege. They are guided by an instinctive feeling that in this mixed and mortal state of our existence, the safety and usefulness of the institutions they control are finally bound up with the inviolability of property which has been devoted to unworldly pursuits, and removed from the control of popular passions and hasty legislation. They are the jealous guardians of that respite from material labour which they hold in fee for those who are by character destined more specifically to be the creators and transmitters of the world's intellectual and spiritual heritage. Nor does the need of privilege end with institutions. One shudders to think of the bleak pall of anxiety and the rage of internecine materialism that would fall upon society were the laws so altered as to transfer the predominant rights from property acquired to the labour by which it is produced. For *if property is secure,*

*it may be the means to an end, whereas if it is in-
secure it will be the end itself.*

BURKE AND THE MORAL
IMAGINATION
Irving Babbitt

Irving Babbitt, professor of French literature at Harvard (where T. S. Eliot learned much from him),
was also a scholar in Indic studies. Of his several influential books, one, *Democracy and Leadership*
(Boston, 1924), is a work of reflection on the literature of politics. This essay on Burke's mind, from
that volume (pp. 121–40 in the Liberty Classics edition, 1979), sets the first great conservative in the
perspective of twentieth-century discontents.

"Everybody knows," Burke writes of the members of the
French National Assembly, "that there is a great dispute
amongst their leaders, which of them is the best resemblance of Rousseau. In truth, they all resemble him. His
blood they transfuse into their minds and into their manners. Him they study; him they meditate; him they turn
over in all the time they can spare from the laborious mischief of the day, or the debauches of the night. Rousseau is
their canon of holy writ; in his life he is their canon of
Polycletus; he is their standard figure of perfection. To
this man and this writer, as a pattern to authors and to
Frenchmen, the founderies of Paris are now running for
statues, with the kettles of their poor and the bells of their
churches."

I have presented Rousseau in his essential influence as

the extremist and foe of compromise. In contrast to Rousseau, Burke is usually and rightly supposed to embody the spirit of moderation. Many of his utterances on the French Revolution, however (the passage I have just quoted may serve as a sample), are scarcely suggestive of moderation, and towards the end he becomes positively violent. There is at least this much to be said in justification of Burke, that in his writings on the Revolution, he is for the most part debating first principles, and when it comes to first principles, the issue raised is not one of moderation, but of truth or error. Burke was no mere partisan of the *status quo*. He was not opposed on principle to revolutions. He is perhaps open to the charge of pushing too far his admiration for the Revolution of 1688. His attitude towards the American Revolution was consistently one of compromise and in many respects of sympathy. He did not stand in any undue awe of those in authority. No one could on occasion call them to a stricter accounting or show himself a more disinterested champion of the victims of unjust power. He recognized specifically the abuses of the Old Régime in France, and was ready to admit the application to these abuses of fairly drastic remedies. If he refused, therefore, to compromise with the French Revolution, the reason is to be sought less in the field of politics than in that of general philosophy, and even of religion. He saw that the Revolution did not, like other revolutions, seek to redress certain specific grievances, but had universal pretensions. France was to become the "Christ of nations" and conduct a crusade for the political regeneration of mankind. This particular mixture of the things of God and the things of Caesar seemed to him psychologically unsound, and in any case subversive of the existing social order of Europe. The new revolutionary evangel was the final outcome of the speculations that had been going on for generations about a state of nature, natural rights, the social contract, and abstract and unlimited sovereignty. Burke is the chief opponent of this tendency towards what one may term metaphysical politics, especially as embodied in the doctrine of the rights of man. "They are so taken up with the rights of man," he says of the members of this school, "that they have totally forgotten his nature." Under cover of getting rid of prejudice they would strip man of all the habits and concrete relationships and network of historical circumstance in which he is actually implicated and finally leave him shivering "in all the nakedness and solitude of metaphysical abstraction." They leave no limit to logic save despotism. In his attack on the enemies of prejudice, by which was meant practically everything that is traditional and prescriptive, Burke has perhaps neglected unduly certain minor though still important distinctions, especially the distinction between those who were for getting rid of prejudice in the name of reason, and those who, like Rousseau, were for getting rid of it in the name of feeling. The rationalists and the Rousseauists were actually ready to guillotine one another in the Revolution, an opposition prefigured in the feud between Rousseau and various "philosophers," notably Voltaire. Rousseau was as ready as Burke, though on different grounds, as I shall try to show presently, to protest against the "solid darkness of this enlightened age."

By the dismissal as mere prejudice of the traditional forms that are in no small measure the funded experience of any particular community, the State loses its historical continuity, its permanent self, as it were, that unites its present with its past and future. By an unprincipled facility in changing the State such as is encouraged by Rousseau's impressionistic notion of the general will, the generations of men can no more link with one another than the flies of a summer. They are disconnected into the dust and powder of individuality. In point of fact, any political philosophy, whether that of Hobbes or of Rousseau, which starts from the supposition that men are naturally isolated units, and achieve society only as the result of an artifice, is in its essence violently individualistic. For this atomistic, mechanical view of the State, Burke is usually supposed to have substituted an organic, historical conception. Much of his actual influence, in Germany and elsewhere, has certainly been along these lines. Yet this is far from being the whole truth about Burke. A one-sided devotion to the organic, historical conception is itself an outcome of the naturalistic movement. It may lead to fatalistic acquiescence in traditional forms, and discourage, not merely abstract rationalism, but a reasonable adjustment of these forms to shifting circumstance. It relates itself very readily to that side of the romantic movement that exalts the unconscious at the expense of moral choice and conscious deliberation. Once obscure this capacity in the individual, which alone raises him above phenomenal nature, and it will not be easy in the long run to preserve his autonomy; he will tend, as so often in German theory, to lose his independent will and become a mere organ of the all-powerful State. Though Taine, again, often professes to speak as a disciple of Burke in his attacks on the French Revolution, it is not easy to see a true follower in a philosopher who proclaimed that "vice and virtue are products like sugar and vitriol."

The truth is that Burke is in no sense a collectivist, and still less, if possible, a determinist. If he had been either, he would not have attained to that profound perception of true liberty in which he surpasses perhaps any other political thinker, ancient or modern. For one who believes in personal liberty in Burke's sense, the final emphasis is necessarily not on the State but on the individual. His individualism, however, is not, like that of Rousseau, naturalistic, but humanistic and religious. Only, in getting the standards by which the individual may hope to surpass his ordinary self, and achieve humanism or religion, he would have him lean heavily on prescription. Burke is anti-individualistic in that he would not set the individual to trading on his own private stock of wit. He would have him respect the general sense, the accumulated experience of the past that has become embodied in the habits and usages that the superficial rationalist would dismiss as prejudice. If the individual condemns the general sense, and trusts unduly his private self, he will have no model; and a man's first need is to look up to a sound model and imitate it. He may thus become exemplary in his turn. The principle of homage and service to what is above one has its culmination and final justification in fealty to God, the true sovereign and supreme exemplar. Burke's conception of the State may be described as a free and flexible adaptation of genuinely Platonic and Christian elements. "We know, and what is better, we feel inwardly, that religion is the basis of civil society, and the source of all good and all comfort." "God willed the State." (Thus to conceive the highest in terms of will is Christian.) "He willed its connection with the source and original archetype of all perfection." (The language is here Platonic.) Not merely religion but the actual church establishment is held by Englishmen to be essential to their State, as being indeed the very foundation of their constitution.

"Society is indeed a contract," though the basis of the contract is not mere utility. The State is not to be regarded as a partnership agreement in a trade of pepper and coffee. It is not, as a contemporary pacifist has maintained, the "pooled self-esteem" of the community, but rather its permanent ethical self. It is, therefore, a partnership in all science and art and in every virtue and perfection. "As the ends of such a partnership cannot be obtained in many generations, it becomes a partnership not only between those who are living, but between those who are living, those who are dead, and those who are to be born."

Though Burke thus uses the language of contract, it is plain that he moves in a different world from all those, including Locke, for whom the idea of contract meant that man has certain rights as a free gift of nature and anterior to the performance of his duties. Talk to the child, says Rousseau, of something that will interest him—talk to him of his rights, and not of his duties.[1] To assert, as Burke does in the main, that one has only concrete historical rights, acquired as the result of the fulfilment of definite obligations, is evidently remote from Rousseau's assertion that a man enjoys certain abstract rights simply because he has taken the trouble to be born. The difference here is not merely beween Burke and Rousseau, but also between Burke and Locke. The final superficiality of Locke is that he granted man abstract natural rights anterior to his duties, and then hoped that it would be possible to apply this doctrine moderately. But it has been justly said that doctrines of this kind are most effective in their extreme logical form because it is in this form that they capture the imagination. Now if the out-and-out radical is often highly imaginative in the fashion that I have attributed to Rousseau, the Whigs and the liberals who follow the Whig tradition are rather open to the suspicion of being deficient on the side of imagination. One cannot help feeling, for instance, that if Macaulay had been more imaginative, he would have shown less humanitarian complacency in his essay on Bacon. Disraeli again is said to have looked with disdain on J. S. Mill because of his failure to perceive the rôle of the imagination in human affairs, a lack that can scarcely be charged against Disraeli himself, whatever one may think of the quality of his imagination.

Now Burke is the exceptional Whig, in that he is not only splendidly imaginative, but admits the supreme rôle of the imagination rather more explicitly than is common among either Christians or Platonists with whom I have associated him. He saw how much of the wisdom of life consists in an imaginative assumption of the experience of the past in such fashion as to bring it to bear as a living force upon the present. The very model that one looks up to and imitates is an imaginative creation. A man's imagination may realize in his ancestors a standard of virtue and

---

1. *Emile*, liv. II.

wisdom beyond the vulgar practice of the hour; so that he may be enabled to rise with the example to whose imitation he has aspired. The forms of the past and the persons who administer them count in Burke's eyes chiefly as imaginative symbols. In the famous passage on Marie Antoinette one almost forgets the living and suffering woman to see in her with Burke a gorgeous symbol of the age of chivalry yielding to the age of "sophisters, economists, and calculators." There is in this sense truth in the taunt of Tom Paine that Burke pities the plumage and forgets the dying bird. All the decent drapery of life, Burke complains of the new philosophy, is to be rudely torn off. "All the super-added ideas, furnished from the wardrobe of a moral imagination, . . . are to be exploded as a ridiculous, absurd, and antiquated fashion."

The apostles of the rights of man were, according to Burke, undermining the two principles on which everything that was truly civilized in the European order had for ages depended: the spirit of religion and the spirit of a gentleman. The nobility and the clergy, who were the custodians of these principles and of the symbols that embodied them and ministered to the moral imagination, had received in turn the support of the learned. Burke warns the learned that in deserting their natural protectors for Demos, they run the risk of being "cast into the mire, and trodden under the hoofs of a swinish multitude."

Burke is in short a frank champion of aristocracy. It is here especially, however, that he applies flexibly his Christian-Platonic, and humanistic principles. He combines a soundly individualistic element with his cult of the traditional order. He does not wish any static hierarchy. He disapproves of any tendency to deal with men in classes and groups, a tendency that the extreme radical shares with the extreme reactionary. He would have us estimate men, not by their hereditary rank, but by their personal achievement. "There is," he says, "no qualification for government but virtue or wisdom, actual or presumptive. Wherever they are actually found, they have in whatever state, condition, profession or trade, the passport of Heaven to human place and honor." He recognizes, to be sure, that it is hard for the manual worker to acquire such virtue and wisdom for the reason that he lacks the necessary leisure. The ascent of rare merit from the lower to the higher levels of society should, however, always be left open, even though this merit be required to pass through a severe probation.

In the same fashion, Burke would admit innovations in the existing social order only after a period of severe probation. He is no partisan of an inert traditionalism. His true leader or natural aristocrat, as he terms him, has, in his adjustment of the contending claims of new and old, much of the character of the "trimmer" as Halifax has described him. "By preserving the method of nature in the conduct of the state, in what we improve we are never wholly new; in what we retain, we are never wholly obsolete." "The disposition to preserve, and ability to improve, taken together, would be my standard of a statesman." In such utterances Burke is of course simply giving the theory of English liberty at its best, a theory almost too familiar for restatement. In his imaginative grasp of all that is involved in the task of mediating between the permanent and the fluctuating element in life, the Platonic art, as one may say, of seeing the One in the Many, he has had few equals in the field of political thinking.

Burke is, however, in one important respect highly un-Platonic, and that is in his attitude towards the intellect. His distrust of what we should call nowadays the intellectual may be variously explained. It is related in some respects to one side, the weak side, one is bound to add, of Christianity. "A certain intemperance of intellect," he writes, "is the disease of the time, and the source of all its other diseases." He saw so clearly the dangers of this abuse that he was led at times, as the Christian has at times been led, to look with suspicion on intellect itself.

And then he was familiar, as we are all familiar, with persons who give no reasons at all, or the wrong reasons, for doing the right thing, and with other persons who give the most logical and ingenious reasons for doing the wrong thing. The basis for right conduct is not reasoning but experience, and experience much wider than that of the individual, the secure possession of which can result only from the early acquisition of right habits. Then, too, there is something specifically English in Burke's disparagement of the intellect. The Englishman, noting the results of the proneness of a certain type of Frenchman to reason rigorously from false or incomplete premises, comes to prefer his own piecemeal good sense and proclivity for "muddling through." As Disraeli told a foreign visitor, the country is governed not by logic but by Parliament. In much the same way Bagehot in the course of a comparison between the Englishman and the Frenchman in politics, reaches the semi-humorous conclusion that "in real sound stupidity the English are unrivalled."

The anti-intellectual side of Burke reminds one at times of the anti-intellectual side of Rousseau: when, for instance, he speaks of "the happy effect of following nature, which is wisdom without reflection and above it." The resemblance, is, however, only superficial. The wisdom that Rousseau proclaimed was not *above* reflection but *below* it. A distinction of this kind is rather meaningless unless supported by careful psychological analysis. Perhaps the first contrast between the superrational and the subrational is that between awe and wonder.[2] Rousseau is plainly an apostle of wonder, so much so that he is probably the chief single influence in the "renascence of wonder" that has resulted from the romantic movement. The romantic objection to intellect is that by its precise analysis and tracing of cause and effect, it diminishes wonder. Burke, on the other hand, is fearful lest an indiscreet in-

---

2. Cf. *Rousseau and Romanticism.*

tellectual activity may undermine awe and reverence.
"We ought," he says, "to venerate where we are unable
presently to understand." As the best means of securing
veneration, Burke leans heavily upon habit, whereas the
romantics, from Rousseau to Walter Pater, are no less
clearly hostile to habit because it seems to lead to a stereo-
typed world, a world without vividness and surprise. To
lay stress on veneration meant for Burke, at least in the
secular order, to lay stress on rank and degree; whereas the
outstanding trait perhaps of the state of nature projected
by Rousseau's imagination, in defiance of the actual facts
of primitive life so far as we know them, is that it is equa-
litarian. This trait is common to his no-state and his all-
state, his anarchistic and his collectivistic Utopia. The
world of the "Social Contract," no less than that of the
"Second Discourse," is a world without degree and subordination; a world in which no one looks up to any one else
or expects any one to look up to him; a world in which no
one (and this seems to Rousseau very desirable) has
either to command or to obey. In his predominant emphasis on equality,[3] Rousseau speaks, to some extent at
least, not merely for himself but for France, especially the
France of the last two centuries. "Liberty," says Mallet du
Pan, "a thing forever unintelligible to Frenchmen."[4] Perhaps liberty has not been intelligible in its true essence to

---

3. It would not be easy to find in an English author of anything like
the same intellectual distinction the equivalent of the following passage from Proudhon (*Oeuvres*, II, p. 91): "*L'enthousiasme qui nous
possède, l'enthousiasme de l'égalité, . . . est une ivresse plus forte que
le vin, plus pénétrante que l'amour: passion ou fureur divine que le
délire des Léonidas, des Saint Bernard et des Michel-Ange n'égala
jamais.*" [The enthusiasm which possesses us, the enthusiasm for
equality . . . is a drunkenness stronger than wine, more penetrating
than love; a passion or divine furor which the frenzy of Leonardo, of
Saint Bernard, and of Michaelangelo never equalled.]
4. Cf. E. Faguet, *Politiques et moralistes*, vol. I, p. 117: "*Il est à peu
près impossible à un Français d'être libéral, et le libéralisme n'est
pas français.*" [It is almost impossible for a Frenchman to be liberal,
and liberalism is not French.] See also *ibid.*, III, p. 95.

many persons anywhere. "The love, and even the very idea, of genuine liberty," Burke himself admits, "is extremely rare." If the basis of this genuine liberty is, as Burke affirms, an act of subordination, it is simply incompatible with Rousseauistic equality.

The act of subordination to any earthly authority is justified only in case this authority is looking up to something still higher; so that genuine liberty is rooted in the virtue that also underlies genuine Christianity. "True humility, the basis of the Christian system, is the low, but deep and firm foundation of all real virtue. But this, as very painful in the practice and little imposing in the appearance," he goes on to say of the French revolutionists, "they have totally discarded." They have preferred to follow Rousseau, the great "professor and founder of the philosophy of vanity." Rousseau himself said that he based his position on the "noblest pride," and pride is, even more than vanity, the significant opposite of humility. I have already spoken of Rousseau's depreciation of humility in favor of patriotic pride. The problem of pride versus humility is, of course, not primarily political at all. It is a problem of the inner life. Rousseau undermined humility in the individual by substituting the doctrine of natural goodness for the older doctrine of man's sinfulness and fallibility. The forms and traditions, religious and political, that Burke on the other hand defends, on the ground that they are not arbitrary but are convenient summings up of a vast body of past experience, give support to the imagination of the individual; the imagination, thus drawn back as it were to an ethical centre, supplies in turn a standard with reference to which the individual may set bounds to the lawless expansion of his natural self (which includes his intellect as well as his emotions). From a purely psychological point of view, Burke's emphasis on humility and on the imaginative symbols that he deems necessary to secure it, reduces itself to an emphasis on what one may term the centripetal element in liberty.

Rousseau, at least the Rousseau that has influenced the world, practically denies the need of any such centripetal element in liberty, inasmuch as what will emerge spontaneously on the disappearance of the traditional controls is an expansive will to brotherhood. If one rejects like Burke this gospel of "universal benevolence," it is hard not to conceive of liberty in Burke's fashion—namely, as a nice adjustment between the taking on of inner control and the throwing off of outer control. "Society," he says, "cannot exist unless a controlling power upon will and appetite be placed somewhere, and the less of it there is within, the more there must be without." This adjustment between inner and outer control, which concerns primarily the individual, is thus seen to determine at last the degree to which any community is capable of political liberty. True statesmanship is in this sense a humanistic mediation and not an indolent oscillation between extremes. "To make a government requires no great prudence. Settle the seat of power; teach obedience: and the work is done. To give freedom is still more easy. It is not necessary to guide; it only requires to let go the rein. But to form a *free government*—that is, to temper together these opposite elements of liberty and restraint in one consistent work, requires much thought, deep reflection, a sagacious, powerful, and combining mind."

I have already said that Burke is very exceptional in that he is a splendidly imaginative Whig. As a matter of fact, most of the typical Whigs and liberals in the Whig tradition, are, like Burke, partisans of liberty in the sense of personal liberty and of moderation. They do not, however, give their personal liberty and moderation the same basis of religion and humanistic control. On the contrary, they incline to be either rationalists or emotionalists, which means practically that they found their ethics either on the principle of utility, or else on the new spirit of sympathy and service, or more commonly on some compound of these main ingredients of humanitarianism.

The liberty of Burke, I have tried to show, is not only religiously grounded, but involves in its political application a genuine humanistic mediation. The Whig compromise, on the other hand, is only too often an attempt to compromise between views of life, namely, the religious-humanistic and the utilitarian-sentimental, which are in their essence incompatible. Thus the liberalism of J. S. Mill is, compared with the liberalism of Burke, open to the charge of being unimaginative. Furthermore, from a strictly modern point of view, it is open to the charge of being insufficiently critical. For the liberty Mill desires is of the kind that will result only from the traditional spiritual controls, or from some adequate substitute, and his philosophy, as I shall try to show more fully later, supplies neither.

Burke can scarcely be charged with the form of superficiality that consists in an attempt to mediate between incompatible first principles. One may, however, feel that he failed to recognize the full extent and gravity of the clash between the new principles and the old; and one may also find it hard to justify the obscurantist element that enters into his defence of his own religious and humanistic position. One might gather from Burke that England was almost entirely made up of Christian gentlemen ready to rally to the support of the majestic edifice of traditional civilization, to all the decencies of life based finally on the moral imagination, whereas the "sophisters, economists, and calculators" who were destroying this edifice by their substitution for the moral imagination of an abstract metaphysical reason were almost entirely French. He does indeed refer to the English deists, but only to dismiss them as obscure eccentrics. The English intellectuals and radical thinkers of his own time he waves aside with the utmost contempt, opposing to them not those who think more keenly, but those who do not think at all. "Because half a dozen grasshoppers under a fern make the field ring with their importunate chink, whilst thousands of great cattle, reposed beneath the shadow of the British oak,

chew the cud and are silent, pray do not imagine that
those who make the noise are the only inhabitants of the
field; that, of course, they are many in number; or that,
after all, they are other than the little, shrivelled, meagre,
hopping, though loud and troublesome, insects of the
hour."

In this passage we have the obscurantist Burke at his
weakest. The truth is that the little, meagre, hopping insects of the hour were representatives of an international
movement of vast scope, a movement destined finally to
prevail over the prejudice and prescription that Burke was
defending. Moreover, this movement was largely, if not
indeed primarily, of English origin. "It is from England,"
says Joubert, "that have issued forth, like fogs, the metaphysical and political ideas which have darkened everything." It is hard to trace the main currents of European
life and thought from the Renaissance, especially the rise
of humanitarianism in both its utilitarian and its sentimental aspects, and not assent in large measure to the assertion of Joubert. Burke's conception of man and of the
State with its strong tinge of Platonic realism (in the older
sense of the word) and its final emphasis on humility, or
submission to the will of God, has important points of
contact with the mediaeval conception. Now, even before
Francis Bacon, men from the British Islands played an
important part in breaking down this realism. Duns
Scotus discredited reason in theology in favor of an arbitrary divine will, and so released reason for use in the secular order. William of Occam asserted a nominalism that
looks forward to our type of realism, a realism, that is, not
of the One but of the Many, and, therefore, at the opposite
pole from the mediaeval variety. Roger Bacon is significant for the future both by his interest in the physical
order and by the experimental temper that he displays in
dealing with this order.

To come to a later period, the upshot of the civil convulsions of seventeenth-century England was to diminish

imaginative allegiance to the past. The main achievement of Cromwell himself was, as his admirer Marvell avowed, to "ruin the great work of Time." As loyalty to the great traditions declined, England concentrated on the utilitarian effort of which Francis Bacon is the prophet, and thus did more than any other country to prepare and carry through the industrial revolution, compared with which the French Revolution is only a melodramatic incident.

If the Christian classical England that Burke took to be truly representative has survived in a place like Oxford, utilitarian England has got itself embodied in cities like Birmingham, so that the opposition between the two Englands, an opposition that is one of first principles, has come to be written on the very face of the landscape. The Englishman, however, does not proceed by logical exclusions, and is capable of maintaining in more or less friendly juxtaposition things that are ultimately incompatible. Thus a young man receives a religious-humanistic training at Oxford as a preparation for helping to administer the British Empire in India, an empire which is, in its origins, chiefly an outcome of the utilitarian and commercially expansive England. The kind of leadership that Burke desired, the leadership of the true gentleman, still plays no small part in the affairs of England and of the world. The Englishman whom he conceives to be typical, who "fears God, looks up with awe to kings, with affection to parliaments, with duty to magistrates, with reverence to priests, and with respect to nobility," is still extant, but is considerably less typical. Above all, his psychology is not that of the great urban masses that owe their existence to the industrial revolution. What Birmingham stands for has been gaining steadily on what Oxford stands for, and that even at Oxford itself. I have said that the only effective conservatism is an imaginative conservatism. Now it has not only become increasingly difficult to enter imaginatively into certain traditional symbols, but in general the imagination has been drawn away more and more from the element of unity in things to the element of diversity. As a result of the type of progress that has been proclaimed, everything good has come to be associated with novelty and change, with the piling up of discovery on discovery. Life, thus viewed, no longer involves any reverence for some centre or oneness, but is conceived as an infinite and indefinite expansion of wonder and curiosity. As a result of all this intoxication with change, the world is moving, we are asked to believe, towards some "far-off divine event." It is at this point that the affinity appears between the utilitarian or Baconian, and the emotional or Rousseauistic side of the humanitarian movement. The far-off divine event is, no less than Rousseau's state of nature, a projection of the idyllic imagination. The felicity of the divine event, like that of the state of nature, is a felicity that can be shown to involve no serious moral effort or self-discipline on the part of the individual. Rousseau himself put his golden age in the past, but nothing is easier than to be a Rousseauist, and at the same time, like the Baconian, put one's golden age in the future. The differences between Baconian and Rousseauist, and they are numerous, are, compared with this underlying similarity in the quality of their "vision," unimportant. I remarked at the outset that the modern political movement may be regarded in its most significant aspect as a battle between the spirit of Rousseau and that of Burke. Whatever the explanation, it is an indubitable fact that this movement has been away from Burke and towards Rousseau. "The star of Burke is manifestly fading," Lecky was able to write a number of years ago, "and a great part of the teaching of the 'Contrat Social' is passing into English politics." Professor Vaughan, again, the editor of the recent standard edition of Rousseau's political writings, remarked in his introduction, apparently without awakening any special contradiction or surprise, that in the essentials of political wisdom Burke is "immeasurably inferior to the man of whom he never speaks but with scorn and loathing; to the despised theorist, the metaphysical madman of Geneva."

Burke will be cherished as long as any one survives in the world who has a perception of the nature of true liberty. It is evident, however, that if a true liberalism is to be successfully defended under present circumstances, it will not be altogether by Burke's method. The battle for prejudice and prescription and a "wisdom above reflection" has already been lost. It is no longer possible to wave aside the modernists as the mere noisy insects of an hour, or to oppose to an unsound activity of intellect mere stolidity and imperviousness to thought—the great cattle chewing their cud in the shadow of the British oak. But before coming to the question of method, we need to consider what the triumph of Rousseau has actually meant in the history of modern Europe, during and since the Great Revolution. A survey of this kind will be found to involve a consideration of the two chief political problems of the present time, the problem of democracy and the problem of imperialism, both in themselves and in their relation to one another.

THE IRONY OF LIBERALISM
George Santayana

The urbane Santayana, in the United States, England, Spain, or Italy, wrote with a beautiful dispassion. "The Irony of Liberalism," taken from *Soliloquies in England and Later Soliloquies* (New York, 1922), pp. 178–89, regards liberalism as an evanescent phase.

To the mind of the ancients, who knew something of such matters, liberty and prosperity seemed hardly compatible, yet modern liberalism wants them together. Liberals believe that free inquiry, free invention, free association, and free trade are sure to produce prosperity. I have no doubt they are right in this; the nineteenth century, that golden age of liberalism, certainly saw a great increase in wealth, in science, and in comforts. What the ancients had before them was a different side of the question; they had no experience of liberalism; they expected to be state-ridden in their religion, their customs, and their military service; even in their personal and family morals they did not begrudge the strictest discipline; their states needed to be intensely unified, being small and in constant danger of total destruction. Under these circumstances it seemed clear to them that prosperity, however it might have been produced, was dangerous to liberty. Prosperity brought power; and when a people exercises control over other peoples its government becomes ponderous even at home; its elaborate machinery cannot be stopped, and can hardly be mended; the imperial people becomes the slave of its commitment. Moreover, prosperity requires inequalities of function and creates inequalities of fortune; and both too much work and too much wealth kill liberty in the individual. They involve subjection to *things;* and this is contrary to what the ancients, who had the pride of noble animals, called freedom. Prosperity, both for individuals and for states, means possessions; and possessions mean burdens and harness and slavery; and slavery for the mind, too, because it is not only the rich man's time that is pre-empted, but his affections, his judgement, and the range of his thoughts.

I often wonder, looking at my rich friends, how far their possessions are facilities and how far they are impediments. The telephone, for instance, is a facility if you wish to be in many places at once and to attend to anything that may turn up; it is an impediment if you are happy where you are and in what you are doing. Public motor-vehicles, public libraries, and public attendants (such as waiters in hotels, when they wait) are a convenience, which even the impecunious may enjoy; but private automobiles, private collections of books or pictures, and private servants are, to my thinking, an encumbrance: but then I am an old fogy and almost an ancient philosopher, and I don't count. I prize civilization, being bred in towns and liking to hear and to see what new things people are up to. I like to walk about amidst the beautiful things that adorn the world; but private wealth I should decline, or any sort of personal possessions, because they would take away my liberty.

Perhaps what liberalism aspires to marry with liberty is not so much prosperity as progress. Progress means continued change for the better; and it is obvious that liberty will conduce to progress in all those things, such as writing poetry, which a man can pursue without aid or interference from others: where aid is requisite and interference probable, as in politics, liberty conduces to progress only in so far as people are unanimous, and spontaneously wish to move in the same direction. Now what is the direction of change which seems progress to liberals? A pure liberal might reply, The direction of liberty itself: the ideal is that every man should move in whatever direction he likes, with the aid of such as agree with him, and without interfering with those who disagree. Liberty so conceived would be identical with happiness, with spontaneous life, blamelessly and safely lived; and the impulse of liberalism, to give everybody what he wants, in so far as that is possible, would be identical with simple kindness. Benevolence was one of the chief motives in liberalism in the beginning, and many a liberal is still full of kindness in his private capacity; but politically, as a liberal, he is something more than kind. The direction in which many, or even most, people would like to move fills him with disgust and indignation; he does not at all wish them to be happy, unless they can be happy on his own diet; and being a reformer and a philanthropist, he exerts himself to turn all men into the sort of men he likes, so as to be able to like them. It would be selfish, he thinks, to let people alone. They must be helped, and not merely helped to what they desire—that might really be very bad for them—but helped onwards, upwards, in the *right* direction. Progress could not be rightly placed in a smaller population, a simpler economy, more moral diversity between nations, and stricter moral discipline in each of them. That would be progress backwards, and if it made people happier, it would not make the liberal so. Progress, if it is to please him, must continue in the direction in which the nineteenth century progressed, towards vast numbers, material complexity, moral uniformity, and economic interdependence. The best little boy, for instance, according to the liberal ideal, desires to be washed, to go to school, to do Swedish exercises, and to learn everything out of books. But perhaps the individual little boy (and according to the liberal philosophy his individuality is sacred, and the only judge of what is good or true for him is his own consciousness) desires to go dirty, to make mudpies in the street, and to learn everything by experience or by report from older boys. When the philanthropist runs up to the rescue, this little ingrate snivels at him the very principle of liberal liberty, "Let me alone." To inform such an urchin that he does not know what is good for him, that he is a slave to bad habits and devilish instincts, that true freedom for him can only come of correcting himself, until he has learned to find happiness in virtue— plainly that would be to abandon liberalism, and to preach the classical doctrine that the good is not liberty but wisdom. Liberalism was a protest against just such assumptions of authority. It emphatically refused to pursue an eventual stoical freedom, absurdly so called, which was to come when we had given up everything we really wanted—the mock freedom of service. In the presence of the little boy liberal philosophy takes a middle course. It is convinced—though it would not do to tell him so prematurely—that he must be allowed to go dirty for a time, until sufficient experience of filth teaches him how much more comfortable it is to be clean; also that he will go to school of his own accord if the books have pictures enough in them, and if the teacher begins by showing him how to make superior mud-pies. As to morals and religion, the boy and his companions will evolve the appropriate ones in time out of their own experience, and no others would be genuine.

Liberal philosophy, at this point, ceases to be empirical and British in order to become German and transcendental. Moral life, it now believes, is not the pursuit of liberty and happiness of all sorts by all sorts of different creatures; it is the development of a single spirit in all life through a series of necessary phases, each higher than the preceding one. No man, accordingly, can really or ultimately desire anything but what the best people desire. This is the principle of the higher snobbery; and in fact, all earnest liberals are higher snobs. If you refuse to move in the precribed direction, you are not simply different, you are arrested and perverse. The savage must not remain a savage, nor the nun a nun, and China must not keep its wall. If the animals remain animals it is somehow through a failure of the will in them, and very sad. Classic liberty, though only a name for stubborn independence, and obedience to one's own nature, was too free, in one way, for the modern liberal. It accepted all sorts of perfections, animal, human, and divine, as final after their kind, each the seat of a sufficient virtue and happiness. It was polytheistic. Between master and slave, between man and woman, it admitted no moral advance or development; they were, or might be, equally perfect. Inequality was honourable; amongst the humblest there could be dignity and sweetness; the higher snobbery would have been absurd, because if you were not content to be what you were now, how could you ever be content with anything? But the transcendental principle of progress is pantheistic. It requires everything to be ill at ease in its own house; no one can be really free or happy but all must be tossed, like herded emigrants, on the same compulsory voyage, to the same unhomely destination. The world came from a nebula, and to a nebula it returns. In the interval, happiness is not to be found in being a fixed star, as bright and pure as possible, even if only for a season; happiness is to flow and dissolve in sympathy with one's higher destiny.

The notion of progress is thus merged with that of universal evolution, dropping the element of liberty and even of improvement. Nevertheless, in the political expression of liberalism, liberty took the first innings. Protestants began by asserting the right of private judgement in interpreting scripture; transcendentalists ended by asserting the divine right of the individual to impose his own spirit on everything he touched. His duty to himself, which was also his deepest instinct, was to suck in from the widest possible field all that was congenial to him, and to reject, down to his very centre, whatever might thwart or offend. Sometimes he carried his consistency in egotism to the length of denying that anything he could not digest could possibly exist, or that the material world and foreign nations were more than ideal pawns in the game he played with himself for his self-development. Even when not initiated into these transcendental mysteries, he was filled with practical self-trust, the desire to give himself freedom, and the belief that he deserved it. There was no need of exploring anything he was not tempted to explore; he had an equal right to his opinion, whatever the limits of his knowledge; and he should be coerced as little as possible in his action. In specific matters, for the sake of expediency, he might be willing to yield to the majority; but only when his vote had been counted, and as a sort of insurance against being disturbed in his residual liberty.

There was a general conviction behind all these maxims, that tradition corrupts experience. All sensation—which is the test of matters of fact—is somebody's sensation; all reasoning is somebody's reasoning, and vitally persuasive as it first comes; but when transmitted the evidence loses its edge, words drop their full meaning, and inert conventions falsify the insights of those who had instituted them. Therefore, reform, revision, restatement are perpetually required: any individual, according to this view, who honestly corrected tradition was sure to improve upon it. Whatsoever was not the fresh handiwork of the soul and true to its present demand was bad for that soul. A man without traditions, if he could only be materially well equipped, would be purer, more rational, more virtuous than if he had been an heir to anything. *Weh dir, dass du ein Enkel bist!*[1] Blessed are the orphans, for they shall deserve to have children; blessed the American! Philosophy should be transcendental, history romantic and focussed in one's own country, politics democratic, and art individual and above convention. Variety in religious dogma would only prove the truth—that is, the inwardness—of inspiration.

Yet if this transcendental freedom had been the whole of liberalism, would not the animals, such of them at least as are not gregarious, have been the most perfect liberals? Are they not ruled wholly from within? Do they not enjoy complete freedom of conscience and of expression? Does Mrs. Grundy interfere with their spontaneous actions? Are they ever compelled to fight except by their own impulse and in their private interest? Yet it was not the ideal of liberalism to return to nature; far from it. It admonished the dogs not to bark and bite, even if, in the words of the sacred poet, "it is their nature to." Dogs, according to transcendental philosophy, ought to improve their nature, and to behave better. A chief part of the liberal inspiration was the love of peace, safety, comfort, and general information; it aimed at stable wealth, it insisted

---

1. "Woe to you, that you are a grandchild!" [R.K.]

on education, it venerated culture. It was wholly out of sympathy with the wilder instincts of man, with the love of foraging, of hunting, of fighting, of plotting, of carousing, or of doing penance. It had an acute, a sickening horror of suffering; to be cruel was devilish and to be hardened to pain was brutal. I am afraid liberalism was hopelessly pre-Nietzschean; it was Victorian; it was tame. In inviting every man to be free and autonomous it assumed that, once free, he would wish to be rich, to be educated, and to be demure. How could he possibly fail to covet a way of life which, in the eyes of liberals, was so obviously the best? It must have been a painful surprise to them, and most inexplicable, that hardly anybody who has had a taste of the liberal system has ever liked it.

What about liberty in love? If there is one ingenuous and winged creature among the immortals, it is Eros; the freer and more innocent love is, the more it will flutter, the farther it will range, and the higher it will soar. But at the touch of matter, of conditions, of consequences, how all its freedom shrivels, or turns into tragedy! What prohibitions, what hypocrisies, what responsibilities, what sorrows! The progress of civilization compels love to respect the limits set to it by earlier vows, by age, sex, class, race, religion, blood relationship, and even fictitious relationship; bounds of which the impertinent Eros himself knows nothing. Society smothers the imp altogether in the long christening-clothes of domestic affection and religious duty. What was once a sensuous intoxication, a mystic rapture, an enchanted friendship, becomes all a question of money, of habit, of children. British liberalism has been particularly cruel to love; in the Victorian era all its amiable impulses were reputed indecent, until a marriage certificate suddenly rendered them godly, though still unmentionable. And what liberty does even the latest radicalism offer to the heart? Liberty to be divorced; divorced at great expense, with shabby perjuries and public scandal, probably in order to be at once married again, until the next divorce. Was it not franker and nobler to leave love, as in Spain, to the poets; to let the stripling play the guitar as much as he liked in the moonlight, exchange passionate glances, whisper daily at the lattice, and then, dressing the bride in black, to dismiss free fancy at the church door, saying: Henceforth let thy names be charity and fidelity and obedience?

It is not politics that can bring true liberty to the soul; that must be achieved, if at all, by philosophy; but liberalism may bring large opportunities for achievement in a man's outward life. It intensifies—because it renders attainable—the lure of public distinction, of luxury, of love surrounded by refined pleasures. The liberal state stimulates the imagination of an ambitious man in the highest degree. Those who have a good start in the universal competition, or sharp wits, or audacity, will find plenty of prizes awaiting them. With the pride of wealth, when it is great, there comes the pride of munificence; in the suburbs of wealth there is culture, and in its service there is science. When science can minister to wealth and intelligence to dominion, both can be carried on the shoulders of the plutocracy which dominates the liberal state; and they can fill it with innumerable comforts and marvellous inventions. At the same time, nothing will hinder the weaker members of rich families from becoming clergymen or even scholars or artists; or they may range over the five continents, hunt whatever wild beasts remain in the jungle, and write books about savages.

Whether these prizes offered by liberal society are worth winning, I cannot say from experience, never having desired them; but the aspects of modern life which any one may observe, and the analytic picture of it which the novelists supply, are not very attractive. Wealth is always, even when most secure, full of itch and fear; worry about health, children, religion, marriage, servants; and the awful question of where to live, when one may live anywhere, and yet all seems to depend on the choice. For the

politician, politics are less important than his private affairs, and less interesting than bridge; and he has always a
party, or a wicked opposition, on which to throw the
blame if his careless measures turn out badly. No one in
office can be a true statesman, because a true statesman is
consistent, and public opinion will never long support any
consistent course. What the successful man in modern society really most cares about is love; love for him in a curious mixture of sensuality, vanity, and friendship; it lights
up all the world of his thought and action with its secret
and unsteady flame. Even when mutual and legal, it seems
to be three-quarters anxiety and sorrow; for if nothing
worse happens to lovers, they grow old. I hear no laughter
among the rich which is not forced and nervous. I find no
sense of moral security amongst them, no happy freedom,
no mastery over anything. Yet this is the very cream of
liberal life, the brilliant success for the sake of which
Christendom was overturned, and the dull peasantry elevated into factory-hands, shopkeepers, and chauffeurs.

When the lists are open to all, and the one aim of life is
to live as much as possible like the rich, the majority must
needs be discouraged. The same task is proposed to unequal strengths, and the competition emphasizes the inequality. There was more encouragement for mediocre
people when happiness was set before them in mediocrity,
or in excellence in some special craft. Now the mass,
hopelessly out of the running in the race for wealth, falls
out and drifts into squalor. Since there is liberty, the listless man will work as little and drink as much as he can; he
will crawl into whatever tenement he can get cheapest,
seek the society in which least effort is demanded and least
shame is felt, have as many children as improvidence
sends him, let himself out, at a pinch, for whatever service
and whatever wages he can obtain, drift into some syndi-
cated servitude or some great migration, or sink in solitude
into the deepest misery. He then becomes a denizen of
those slimy quarters, under the shadow of railway

bridges, breweries, and gas-works, where the blear lights of a public-house peer through the rain at every corner, and offer him the one joy remaining in life; for joy is not to be mentioned in the same breath as the female prowling by the door, hardly less befuddled and bedraggled than the lurching idlers whom she endeavours to entice; but perhaps God does not see all this, because a pall hangs over it perpetually of impenetrable smoke. The liberal system, which sought to raise the individual, has degraded the masses; and this on so vast a scale and to so pitiable a degree, that the other element in liberalism, philanthropic zeal, has come again to the fore. Liberty go hang, say the new radicals; let us save the people. Liberal legislation, which was to have reduced government to the minimum of police control, now has undertaken public education, social reform, and even the management of industry.

This happy people can read. It supports a press conforming to the tastes of the common man, or rather to such tastes as common men can have in common; for the best in each is not diffused enough to be catered for in public. Moreover, this press is audaciously managed by some adventitious power, which guides it for its own purposes, commercial or sectarian. Superstitions old and new thrive in this infected atmosphere; they are now all treated with a curious respect, as if nobody could have anything to object to them. It is all a scramble of prejudices and rumours; whatever first catches the ear becomes a nucleus for all further presumptions and sympathies. Advertising is the modern substitute for argument, its function is to make the worse appear the better article. A confused competition of all propagandas—those insults to human nature—is carried on by the most expert psychological methods, which the art of advertising has discovered; for instance, by always repeating a lie, when it has been exposed, instead of retracting it. The world at large is deafened; but each propaganda makes its little knot of proselytes, and inspires them with a new readiness to persecute and to suffer in the sacred cause. The only question is, which propaganda can first materially reach the greatest number of persons, and can most efficaciously quench all the others. At present, it looks as if the German, the Catholic, and the communist propaganda had the best chances; but these three are divergent essentially (though against a common enemy they may work for a while together, as they did during this war), and they appeal to different weaknesses of human nature; they are alike, however, in being equally illiberal, equally *"rücksichtlos"* and *"böse,"*[2] equally regardless of the harm they may do, and accounting it all an added glory, like baiting the devil. By giving a free rein to such propagandas, and by disgusting the people with too much optimism, toleration, and neutrality, liberalism has introduced a new reign of unqualified ill-will. Hatred and wilfulness are everywhere; nations and classes are called to life on purpose to embody them; they are summoned by their leaders to shake off the lethargy of contentment and to become conscious of their existence and of their terrible wrongs. These propagandas have taken shape in the blue sky of liberalism, like so many summer clouds; they seem airships sailing under a flag of truce; but they are engines of war, and on the first occasion they will hoist their true colours, and break the peace which allowed them to cruise over us so leisurely. Each will try to establish its universal ascendancy by force, in contempt of personal freedom, or the voice of majorities. It will rely, against the apathy and vagueness of the million, on concentrated zeal in its adepts. Minorities everywhere have their way; and majorities, grown familiar with projects that at first shocked them, decide one fine morning that there may be no harm in them after all, and follow like sheep. Every trade, sect, private company, and aspiring nation, finding some one to lead it, asserts itself *"ruthlessly"* against every other. Incipient formations

---

2. *Rücksichtlos:* ruthless. *Böse:* malicious. [R.K.]

in the body politic, cutting across and subverting its old
constitution, eat one another up, like different species of
animals; and the combat can never cease except some day,
perhaps, for lack of combatants. Liberalism has merely
cleared a field in which every soul and every corporate interest may fight with every other for domination. Whoever is victorious in this struggle will make an end of
liberalism; and the new order, which will deem itself
saved, will have to defend itself in the following age
against a new crop of rebels.

For myself, even if I could live to see it, I should not be
afraid of the future domination, whatever it may be. One
has to live in some age, under some fashion; I have found,
in different times and places, the liberal, the Catholic, and
the German air quite possible to breathe; nor, I am sure,
would communism be without its advantages to a free
mind, and its splendid emotions. Fanatics, as Tacitus said
of the Jews or Christians, are consumed with hatred of
the human race, which offends them; yet they are themselves human; and nature in them take its revenge, and
something reasonable and sweet bubbles up out of the
very fountain of their madness. Once established in the
world the new dispensation forms a ruling caste, a conventional morality, a standard of honour; safety and happiness soften the heart of the tyrant. Aristocracy knows
how to kiss the ruddy cheeks of its tenants' children; and
before mounting its thoroughbred horse at the park gates,
it pats him with a gloved hand, and gives him a lump of
sugar; nor does it forget to ask the groom, with a kindly interest, when he is setting out for the war. Poor flunkey!
The demagogues will tell him he is a fool, to let himself be
dragooned into a regiment, and marched off to endure untold privations, death, or ghastly wounds, all for some
fantastic reason which is nothing to him. It is a hard fate;
but can this world promise anybody anything better? For
the moment he will have a smart uniform, beers and lasses
will be obtainable; many comrades will march by his side;

and he may return, if he is lucky, to work again in his master's stables, lounge at the public-house, and bounce his children on his knee amongst the hollyhocks before his cottage. Would the demagogues give him better prospects, or prove better masters? Would he be happier with no masters at all? Consider the demagogues themselves, and their history. They found themselves in the extreme of misery; but even this is a sort of distinction, and marks off a new species, seizing new weapons in the struggle for existence. The scum of the earth gathers itself together, becomes a criminal or a revolutionary society, finds some visionary or some cosmopolitan agitator to lead it, establishes its own code of ethics, imposes the desperate discipline of outlaws upon its members, and prepares to rend the free society that allowed it to exist. It is astonishing with what docility masses of Englishmen, supposed to be jealous of their personal liberty, will obey such a revolutionary junta, that taxes and commands them, and decrees when they starve and when they shall fight. I suspect that the working-people of the towns no longer have what was called the British character. Their forced unanimity in action and passion is like that of the ages of faith; its inspiration, like that of early Christianity, comes from a few apostles, perhaps foreign Jews, men who in the beginning had visions of some millennium; and the cohesion of the faithful is maintained afterwards by preaching, by custom, by persecution, and by murder. Yet it is intelligible that the most earnest liberals, who in so far as they were advocates of liberty fostered these conspiracies, in so far as they are philanthropists should applaud them, and feel the need of this new tyranny. They save liberal principles by saying that they applaud it only provisionally as a necessary means of freeing the people. But of freeing the people from what? From the consequences of freedom.

Part Thirteen

~~~~~~~~~~~~~~~~~~~~~~~~~~~~~~~~~~~~~

CONSERVATISM BETWEEN TWO WARS

The First and Second World Wars dealt the conservative interest and conservative institutions, either side of the Atlantic, terrible blows from which the old order never will recover wholly. Amid the crash of empires, and the practical triumph of the Communist, Fascist, and Nazi ideologies, some men of intellect sought to shore up order and justice and freedom. Here we consider the ideas of Christopher Dawson (1889–1970) and T. S. Eliot (1888–1965).

RELIGION AND THE TOTALITARIAN STATE
Christopher Dawson

What we call "culture" arises from the religious cult, the historian Christopher Dawson pointed out in several of his books. It is religion, rather than some counter-ideology or economic scheme, which may restrain the totalist powers, Dawson makes clear in "Religion and the Totalitarian State." This essay was published first in Eliot's quarterly *The Criterion* (Vol. XIV, No. LIV, October, 1934, pp. 1–16), and included in Dawson's *Religion and the Modern State* (London, 1935), in substance.

One of the most striking features of modern society is the increasing claims of the State on the individual. The sphere of action of the State has grown steadily larger until it now threatens to embrace the whole of human life and to leave nothing whatsoever outside its competence.

As I have written elsewhere, the modern state is daily extending its control over a wider area of social life and is taking over functions that were formerly regarded as the province of independent social units such as the family and the church, or as a sphere for the voluntary activities of private individuals. It is not merely that the state is becoming more centralized, but that society and culture are becoming *politicized*. In the old days the statesman was responsible for the preservation of internal order and the defence of the state against its enemies. To-day he is called upon to deal more and more with questions of a purely sociological character and he may even be expected to transform the whole structure of society and refashion the cultural traditions of the people. The abolition of war, the destruction of poverty, the control of the birth-rate, the elimination of the unfit—these are questions which the statesmen of the past would no more have dared to meddle with than the course of the seasons or the movements of the stars; yet they are all vital political issues today and some of them figure in the agenda of our political parties.

The most important step in this advance was undoubtedly the introduction of universal compulsory education for that put into the hands of the State the power and responsibility of forming the minds of the youth of the nation. But even before this the State on the Continent had made another advance that was almost as important, namely the institution of universal military service. The absence of this in the British Empire and America is one of the main dividing lines between the civilization of the Anglo-Saxon peoples and that of the rest of the world. It is a division which cuts across the division between East and West and between Fascist and Communist: for conscription is found equally in Russia and Italy, in Germany and Japan, in Turkey and Holland. And it is a distinction that rests at least to some extent on religious causes. For there can be no doubt that the attitude of the Free Churches, or some of them, would have made it very difficult for any British government to introduce permanent conscription in the nineteenth century, even if circumstances had demanded it.

Thirdly, we have the extension of economic control by the state, which is now perhaps the most important factor of all. It is due in part to Socialism, in part to the inherent needs of a highly organized industrial society, and in part to the humanitarian movement for social reform, which in this country, at least, is responsible for a great deal of modern social legislation.

It is interesting to note the diverse elements and person-alities that have contributed to this result. In England we have the influence of an Evangelical individualist like Shaftesbury, alongside of the trade union movement, both currents finally merging in the Parliamentary social re-form of the early twentieth century. In Germany we have the influence of the Social Democratic Party as well as the anti-socialist social legislation of Bismarck; and finally in Russia there is the anti-Christian communism of the So-viets and in Italy the anti-communist and anti-liberal cor-porativism of the Fascists.

I think it is difficult to avoid the conclusion that the movement towards state control in every department of life is a universal one and is not to be confused with the political tenets of a party, whether Communist or Fascist. (The essential principle of the Totalitarian State was, in fact, asserted by Liberalism before Fascism was ever heard of.) What is happening to-day is that the movement towards state-control and state-organization has reached a point at which it comes into conflict with the older forms of parliamentary democracy. The vast increase in the numbers of the electorate, the multiplication of political parties and the fundamental character of the points at issue all tend to produce a state of political deadlock which in turn leads parties to look to extra-parliamentary action in order to gain their ends. In practice this may mean gen-eral strikes, dictatorships, revolutions and every kind of violence. Nevertheless it rests fundamentally in a per-fectly healthy and reasonable desire to put the state and the government of the state above party, and to ensure that the power which has so immense an influence for good or evil on the lives of every citizen shall not be at the mercy of a political clique or the servant of class interests. It is moreover difficult to deny that the old political ideal of individual liberty corresponded to the old ideals of eco-nomic individualism and *laisser faire*, and that the super-session of the latter by state economic control and a planned economy involves some limitation of individual liberty in the political sphere and some increase in the authority of the government.

Now in fact we do find in every state, and not least in our own, such a limitation of freedom and increase of state authority taking place owing to the extension of bureaucratic government. In the Totalitarian State, however, we find in addition to this a new principle of political authority. This is not simply dictatorship. Indeed the pure type of dictatorship is to be found rather in the Spain of Primo da Rivera than in either Russia or Germany. The new type of political authority is the dictatorship not of a man but of a party. But it is something very different from the political parties that we know in democratic countries. It is organized in an hierarchical fashion. That is to say, it is based on authority, discipline and subordination. It demands complete obedience and unlimited devotion from its members, who may have to undergo a period of probation before their admission and who may be degraded in rank, or expelled from the party altogether, if they show any signs of disloyalty or inefficiency. In short it resembles a religious or military order rather than a political party of the old type, and it tends to foster the same strong *esprit de corps* as they do.

There is no doubt that the type of political organization has shown its effectiveness both in the Communist and Fascist States. It is in fact the one element in the Totalitarian State that is an undisputed success.[1] It combines the

---

1. Since this was written events in Germany have shown the existence of a serious conflict between the principle of State authority and that of Party Dictatorship. The Reichswehr is not like the Red Army, the passive instrument of the dominant party, it is a quasi-independent power which recognizes the Nazi Party only in so far as the party recognizes the paramount authority of the State. Thus there is a certain dualism in the present régime in Germany, which has been resolved, in so far as it has been resolved by the subordination of the Party to the State rather than vice versa.

aristocratic principle of government by a privileged elite with a democratic width in the basis of selection. But at the same time it can be a most formidable instrument of tyranny, for the very strength of its corporate spirit is apt to generate intolerance and fanaticism. Yet on the other hand it may be argued that a Totalitarian State without this element would be a soulless bureaucracy which would leave no room for any free initiative and would reduce the whole society to a dead level of mechanical uniformity.

What then is the position of the religious man and the religious society under these new political circumstances? How far does this new political development threaten the spiritual liberty which is essential to religion? Ought the Church to condemn the Totalitarian State in itself and prepare itself for resistance to the secular power and for persecution? Should the Church ally itself with the political and social forces that are hostile to the new state? Or should it limit its resistance to cases of state interference in ecclesiastical matters or in theological questions? Or finally are the new forms of authority and political organization reconcilable in principle with Christian ideas and are the issues that divide Church and State accidental and temporary ones which are extraneous to the essential nature of the new political development? It is impossible to answer these questions offhand and in the lump. We must first clear the ground by a closer definition of the issues and by making a number of necessary distinctions.

1. In the first place we must distinguish between spiritual freedom and political and economic liberty. It is one of the great classical commonplaces of religion and of ancient philosophy that the two are not the same: that a man may possess citizenship and wealth and yet be without spiritual freedom and that a man may be poor and a slave, like Epictetus and yet enjoy the good of spiritual freedom. To-day there are many who would question this. But whether it be true or no there can be no question that the

two kinds of freedom are distinct and that they do not always co-exist with one another.

Now the great age of liberalism and individualism was not in fact approved by the religious conscience of the age. On the Continent the advance of political liberty was accompanied almost everywhere by an anti-religious movement which did much to secularize European civilization. And at the same time, the economic individualism of the Liberal economists was condemned as being inconsistent with Christian morals by religious leaders such as Leo XIII and Bishop von Ketteler of Mainz.

In England Liberalism on the whole had not this irreligious character. Nevertheless it was far from meeting with the unrestricted approval of religious men. The Oxford Movement, for instance, was definitely opposed to political liberalism, while F. D. Maurice, the leading social thinker in the Church of England, was as outspoken in his condemnation of democracy as in his opposition to economic individualism. In these respects he was the disciple of Coleridge and Carlyle, and though the latter cannot perhaps be regarded as a Christian thinker he certainly exercised a very strong influence on religious thought in nineteenth century England.

I think we may conclude that there is no essential connection between Christianity on the one hand and the parliamentary democracy and economic liberalism of the nineteenth century on the other. Undoubtedly a fusion between the two did take place in the later nineteenth century in England, the age of Gladstonian liberalism, but this was a local and temporary phenomenon which has little bearing on the fundamental character of the forces involved.

Consequently there is no fundamental reason why the passing of parliamentary democracy and economic individualism should be opposed to Christian principles or sentiment. It is at least theoretically possible that the limitation of political and economic freedom by the extension of social control should be actually favourable to the cause of spiritual freedom. In practice, however, we have got to consider the spiritual tendency of the new political forces, before we can decide whether their influence is favourable or hostile to Christianity.

2. Here we must distinguish between the various forms of the totalitarian State. It is obvious that the totalitarian State is not a uniform phenomenon. There is obviously not only a difference but an opposition between the Fascist and Communist types. While within Fascism there is a considerable difference in the character and principles of the Fascist regime in its Italian and German forms.

Now in the case of Communism, there is an obvious and apparently irreducible opposition between Communism and Christianity. The Soviet state has gone further to eliminate religion from society than any state that has ever existed. And no doubt it is the spectacle of this vast system of organized secularism that has alarmed Christian opinion more than anything else. We feel that the modern Totalitarian State has a power of control over the lives and thoughts of its members which no ancient state ever possessed and consequently we are doubtful of the power of Christianity to face this new power as it faced its persecutors in the past.

Nevertheless Communism is not simply a form of political organization; it is an economy, a philosophy and a creed. And its hostility to Christianity is due not to its political form, but to the philosophy that lies behind it. Communism, in fact, challenges Christianity on its own ground by offering mankind a *rival way of salvation*. In the words of a Communist poster: 'Jesus promised the people Paradise after death, but Lenin offers them Paradise on earth'. Consequently the opposition of Communism to Christianity rests not on the Totalitarian character of the Communist state, but on the religious exclusivism of the Communist philosophy, and though these phenomena are not unrelated they are by no means iden-

tical. After all, Marx himself was no believer in the Totalitarian State. He believed that Communism involved the
'withering away' of the state and the complete supersession of all forms of political authority. Yet his state-less
society, if it could be realized, would be even more anti-
religious than the most secularized type of Totalitarian
State. It would be, so to speak, the Church of the Godless
Triumphant, whereas the Communist state under the
Proletarian Dictatorship is only the Godless Church Militant.

Hence if we wish to study the Totalitarian State in its
essential character, we shall do better to look to Fascism
rather than to Communism, for it was, after all, the Fascists who first coined the expression, and with them the
new state stands on its own rights and its own principles
and is not merely, as with the Communists, the vehicle of
a philosophy and a temporary instrument for the carrying
out of an economic revolution.

Now the Fascist State is not consciously or intention-
ally hostile to religion. In Italy and Austria it has given a
much fuller recognition to the place of religion in national
life than did the democratic regime that it replaced. In
Italy the attitude of the Fascist State is objective and real-
istic. It takes account of the Church as a living element in
the national being, as a cultural and social asset which
must be incorporated in the new system. Moreover Mussolini, at least, has increasingly recognized the ethical
basis of the state and of political authority, a conception
on which the traditional concordance or alliance of the
temporal and spiritual powers has always been based.

In Germany however the situation is different. There is
a strong strain of racial and political mysticism in National Socialism which involves a serious danger of conflict between Church and State. It is not that the Nazi
movement is anti-religious. The danger is rather that it
has a religion of its own which is not that of Christian orthodoxy. This religion has not the dogmatic character of

the Communist creed, it is a fluid and incoherent thing which expresses itself in several different forms. There is the neo-paganism of the extreme Pan-German element, there is the Aryanized and nationalized Christianity of the German Christians, and there is the racial and nationalist idealism which is characteristic of the movement as a whole, and which, if not religious in the strict sense, tends to develop a mythology and ethic of its own that may easily take the place of Christian theology and Christian ethics.

At the same time it would be a mistake to suppose that National Socialism is generally regarded in Germany as hostile to Christianity. The coming of the new regime means the abandonment of the religious neutrality or indifferentism of the liberal state, and this cannot but meet with the approval of those who still accept the traditional Lutheran ideal of the relations of Church and State. German Protestants, or at least Lutherans, cannot but sympathize with the ideal of a National Church which would be organically related to the new national state and would restore the spiritual unity of the German people. There are however grave objections even to this ideal. For in the first place, such a union could only embrace the Protestant part of the nation, and consequently it would only accentuate the religious divisions of Germany and would thus increase rather than diminish the danger of religious strife. Moreover, in the second place, the relation of the State to the National Church would be fundamentally different from that which existed in earlier centuries. In the past the Church and State were bound together, because the people was consciously Christian. The same individuals were members of both societies, and even when the prince asserted his supremacy in ecclesiastical matters, he did so as a member of the Church who accepted its moral and theological teachings.

But this state of things no longer exists in the world today. In Protestant Germany, above all, only a small part of the population consists of practising Christians and there is no reason to suppose that the rulers of the state should be more Christian than the rest of the nation. If the National Socialists create a national church and give it a privileged position, it will not be because they believe that the Christian faith is necessary for salvation, but because they think that such a church would be a valuable support to them in their work of national reorganization and education. In other words, the national church will be the servant of the national state and the organ of its moral and social propaganda.

Now it is easy for us to condemn such a development because we as Englishmen have no political sympathy with the Nazi propaganda or with the German type of Totalitarian State. But what would our attitude be towards a similar development which had a different political movement and a different set of ideas behind it? We may not have a Totalitarian State in this country of the same kind that we find in Germany or in Italy. Nevertheless, as I have already pointed out, the same forces that make for governmental control and social uniformity are at work here also and in the U.S.A., and it seems to me highly probable that these forces will result in the formation of a type of Totalitarian State which bears the same relation to Anglo-Saxon political and social traditions, as the Nazi State bears to the traditions of Prussia and Central Europe. Such a state might be nominally Socialist, but it would not be the Socialism of the Third International; it might be Nationalist, but it would not be the militant racial nationalism of the Nazis. Its ideals would probably be humanitarian, democratic and pacific. Nevertheless it will make the same universal claims as the Totalitarian State in Russia and Germany and it will be equally unwilling to tolerate any division of spiritual allegiance.

What attitude will such a state adopt towards Christianity and the Christian Churches? I do not believe that it will be anti-Christian in the Russian sense, or that it will be inspired by any conscious hostility to religion. On the other hand, it will have very little in common with the old liberal state which claimed to be no more than a policeman and left men free to guide their lives by whatever religious or moral standard they chose to adopt. The new state will be universal and omnicompetent. It will mould the mind and guide the life of its citizens from the cradle to the grave. It will not tolerate any interference with its educational functions by any sectarian organization, even though the latter is based on religious convictions. And this is the more serious, since the introduction of psychology into education has made the schoolmaster a spiritual guide as well as a trainer of the mind. In fact it seems as though the school of the future must increasingly usurp the functions that the Church exercised in the past, and that the teaching profession will take the place of the clergy as the spiritual power of the future.

Nor will the state confine its educational activities to the training of the young. It will more and more tend to control public opinion in general by its organs of instruction and propaganda in this country. We have already secured the nationalization and public control of Broadcasting, and I believe the time is not far distant when similar methods will be applied to the control of the Press, and the Cinema. It is obvious that a Totalitarian State, whether of the Fascist or the democratic type, cannot afford to leave so great a power of influencing public opinion in private hands, and the fact that the control of the popular Press and of the film industry is often in unworthy hands gives the state a legitimate excuse to intervene. The whole tendency of modern civilization is, in fact, to concentrate the control of opinion in a few hands. For example, Hollywood to-day forms the taste and influences the thought of millions all over the world. As our civilization becomes more completely mechanized, it becomes easier to control, and the organs of control become more centralized. It is true that these things are not usually regarded as having much relevance to the religious issue. But we may ask ourselves—do people go to the cinema or to church? Does not the cinema take the place that was formerly occupied by church and chapel? Has not Hollywood got a distinct ethic of its own which influences the minds of its audiences? Is this ethic in any sense Christian?

Now the centralized control which will be characteristic of the new state will doubtless stand on a higher moral level than that of Hollywood, but there is no reason to suppose that it will be Christian in any real sense. Its moral standards will no doubt be higher than the commercialized morality of the press and cinema, but they will be essentially secular standards and consequently more akin to the latter than to the traditional Christian ethics of the Church. But whether these standards are high or low, whether they represent the bourgeois idealism of the Rotarians, or the racial idealism of the Nazis or the proletarian idealism of the Communists, they will be the only standards recognized and tolerated. They will govern the whole of life. It will be impossible to go one's own way, as in the old days, and leave the state in control of politics. For there will be no department of life in which the state will not intervene and which will not be obliged to conform to the mechanized order of the new society.

This is the situation that Christians have got to face. The great danger that we have to meet is not the danger of violent persecution but rather that of the crushing out of religion from modern life by the sheer weight of a state-inspired public opinion and by the mass organization of society on a purely secular basis. Such a state of things has never occurred before because the state has never been powerful enough to control every side of social life. It has been a state with limited functions, not a Totalitarian State. Moreover, in the past, public opinion recognized the validity of the religious category and the autonomy of the religious life, even when it opposed and persecuted particular forms of religion. To-day the conflict is a deeper and a wider one. It goes to the very roots of life and affects every aspect of human thought and action. One might even say that the very existence of religion itself is at stake, were it not that there are some who hold that religion is no longer to be identified with Christianity and the other historic religions but is finding a new social expression in the movements that are creating the new state: Communism, National Socialism and Liberal Humanitarianism. If this is the case, we must alter our terminology and say, as Professor Julian Huxley said the other day, that the coming conflict is not one between religion and secular civilization but rather 'between the God-religious and the social-religious'—in other words between the worship of God and the cult of the state or of the race or of humanity. I do not myself believe that man will ever find a true religious satisfaction in the worship of himself, or even of some magnified and idealized reflection of himself in the race or in humanity at large. Nevertheless it is impossible to deny that Russian Communism, for example, resembles a religion in many respects. Its attitude to the Marxian doctrines is not the attitude of an economist or a historian towards a scientific theory, it is the attitude of a believer to the gospel of salvation; Lenin is more than a political hero, he is the canonized saint of Communism with a highly developed cultus of his own; and the Communist ethic is religious in its absoluteness and its unlimited claims to the spiritual allegiance of its followers. This, however, is an extreme case. Outside Russia I do not think we are likely to find a state religion of so exclusive and uncompromising a kind. Everywhere, however, the new state will make for spiritual uniformity, and this uniformity will not be based on Christian principles and will hardly admit of the continued existence of autonomous spiritual societies.

Now it is clear that we cannot meet this development

on its own ground—the ground of politics. We cannot demand that the state should return to nineteenth century principles of non-intervention and individual liberty, because these conditions are favourable to the free development of the Christian churches or sects. Still less can we hope to see the creation of a definitely Christian social and political order, such as a truly Christian people might achieve. We cannot expect the world to accept Christian political or economic principles when it does not accept the Christian faith or Christian moral principles. We must recognize our material weakness before we can realize the sources of our spiritual strength. As I have said elsewhere, there has seldom been a time when the People of God seemed weaker and more scattered and more at the mercy of its enemies than it seems today. As Karl Barth has said in his remarkable reply to the German Christians, this is not a time for political or ecclesiastical-political movements, but for the creation of a spiritual centre of resistance, a return to the real sources of spiritual vitality. It is important for us to remember that the religious solution of the spiritual problems of an age does not arise out of the political situation; it arises out of the religious situation as a religious answer to a religious need. Consequently it often arises from some quarter which the publicists and the leaders of public opinion entirely ignore.

The ancient world in the first century B.C. was in dire need of a religious solution, and the wise men of the age provided one in the religious revival of the Augustan age. But since their solution arose directly from the political situation, it provided merely a political remedy. The true solution came from an entirely unsuspected quarter— from an unknown sect and a despised people. But it arose directly out of the religious situation: it was not an answer to the political needs of the Roman world, but the fulfilment of the hope of Israel. The same principle holds good in every age. Nothing could have been more discouraging than the religious situation in England in the early part of the eighteenth century. It was threatened by the rationalism of the Deists, by the secularism of the Whig state and by popular materialism and the brutalization of the masses. The wise men attempted to find their solution in a rational Christianity purged of enthusiasm which would be indispensable to the state as a bulwark of law and order and morality. Then there arose a prophet in Israel, John Wesley, and the whole situation was altered. The solution of Hoadley and Warburton did not ever gain the respect of those whom it was intended to conciliate, while the solution of Wesley transformed the whole spiritual climate of eighteenth century England. Of course this was not simply the result of Wesley's personal genius. It meant that English religion possessed spiritual resources which the intellectual and ecclesiastical leaders of the age had not discovered and Wesley was the man who released these reserves of spiritual energy.

The essential duty of the Church towards the State and the world is to bear witness to the truth that is in her. If the light is hidden, we cannot blame the world outside for ignoring it. It is of course possible that men may know Christianity and still reject it, but in the great majority of cases the men who follow the new secularist ideals of life and regard Christianity as discredited are men who have never known it as a living reality, but have been acquainted with it only at second-hand or in distorted forms. Here sectarianism has much to answer for. We can see, for example, from Edmund Gosse's story of his early life how a really sincere and pious Christian can make religion hateful to those he knows best owing to the narrow and unlovely forms with which he identifies it.

Nevertheless sectarianism is by no means solely responsible for the failure of religion in the modern world. An even more widely spread cause is the indifference and apathy which spring from a mechanical and lifeless acceptance of religion as a matter of course. When the practice of religion becomes a matter of social conformity, it is powerless to change the world. Indeed the men who are religious because society expects them to be, will be irreligious for the same reason in a secular society. It is impossible to deny that there has been an immense amount of this social conformity in English religion and the drastic secularization of state and culture will not have been an unmixed evil if it produces in reaction a thorough desecularization of the church and of religion.

It is very noticeable that this process of secularization is most violent in the countries such as Russia where the Church has been most closely associated with the state and where social conformity played the largest part in religion. Of course there are fundamental differences between the type of social conformity that was typical of Russian religion and that which is characteristic of England. The former was conspicuously non-ethical, whereas the latter usually takes the form of an identification of Christianity with social ethics. Nevertheless each of these types is equally compromised by the new situation; neither of them can survive in the atmosphere of the new state. The ethical idealism which was characteristic of nineteenth century culture is passing away with the culture that gave it birth. As Karl Barth has written: 'All that was called Liberty, Justice, Spirit, only a year ago and for a hundred years farther back, where has it all gone? Now these are all temporal, material, earthly goods. All flesh is as grass. . . .' It is harder for us to realize this here in England than for Christians in Germany, just as it was easier for the Russians to realize it than for the Germans. The sun sets later in the West, but it must set at last. The state is steadily annexing all that territory that was formerly the domain of individual freedom; it has already taken more than anyone would have conceived possible a century ago. It has taken economics, it has taken science, it has taken ethics. But there is one thing it can never take, because to quote Karl Barth once more, 'Theology and the

Church are the natural frontiers of everything—even of the Totalitarian State.' Only it is necessary that Christians should themselves recognize this frontier: that they should remember that it is not the business of the Church to do the same thing as the State—to build a Kingdom like the other kingdoms of men, only better; nor to create a reign of earthly peace and justice. The Church exists to be the light of the world, and if it fulfils its function, the world is transformed in spite of all the obstacles that human powers place in the way. A secularist culture can only exist, so to speak, in the dark. It is a prison in which the human spirit confines itself when it is shut out of the wider world of reality. But as soon as the light comes, all the elaborate mechanism that has been constructed for living in the dark becomes useless. The recovery of spiritual vision gives man back his spiritual freedom. And hence the freedom of the Church is in the faith of the Church and the freedom of man is in the knowledge of God.

MARXIST LITERARY CRITICISM
T. S. Eliot

Probably future historians of literature will call several decades of the twentieth century "the age of Eliot." In T. S. Eliot the political beliefs of Tory England unite with the principles of Eliot's Adams ancestors in New England. Eliot's good-natured dissection of Trotsky and lesser Marxist critics, here reprinted for the first time, appeared as his editorial commentary in *The Criterion*, Vol. XII (January, 1933), pp. 244–49.

Writing from a country in which communistic theories appear to have more vogue among men of letters than they have yet reached in England, I have recently looked at two books which discuss the relation of literature to social affairs. One is not very new; Trotsky's *Literature and Revolution* was first published in translation in 1925, and has since become a text-book for revolutionary litterateurs. The other, Mr. Calverton's *Liberation of American Literature*, is pretty fresh from the mint. The former is much shorter and of course more important. It is natural, and not necessarily convincing, to find young intellectuals in New York turning to communism, and turning their communism to literary account. The literary profession is not only, in all countries, overcrowded and underpaid (the few overpaid being chiefly persons who have outlived their influence, if they ever had any); it is embarrassed by such a number of ill-trained people doing such a number of unnecessary jobs; and writing so many unnecessary books and unnecessary reviews of unnecessary books, that it has much ado to maintain its dignity as a profession at all. One is almost tempted to form the opinion that the world is at a stage at which men of letters are a superfluity. To be able therefore to envisage literature under a new aspect, to take part in the creation of a new art and new standards of literary criticism, to be provided with a whole stock of ideas and of words, that is for a writer in such circumstances to be given a new lease of life. It is not always easy, of course, in the ebullitions of a new movement, to distinguish the man who has received the living word from the man whose access of energy is the result of being relieved of the necessity of thinking for himself. Men who have stopped thinking make a powerful force. There are obvious inducements, beside that—never wholly absent—of simple conversion, to entice the man of letters into political and social theory which he then employs to revive his sinking fires and rehabilitate his profession.

There is no such obvious reason why a man like Trotsky should take the trouble to pronounce upon the literature of revolution and the literature of the future; the only reason that occurs to me in reading his book is that he may have been exasperated by the futilities of previous Russian writers upon the subject. He is certainly a man of first-rate intelligence, expressing himself in a rough and ready metaphorical style, and he utters a good deal of sound sense. Most of his book is devoted to the criticism of authors whom I have not read, and who I imagine have not been translated and never will be; but as an antidote to the false art of revolution his treatise is admirable.

The faith of Trotsky, however, in the possibilities of Marxian literature, has about it something very touching —still more touching than that of Mr. Calverton. The early champions of the Christian Faith, one remembers, often adopted a very different attitude towards literature and art in general. No attempt was made to conciliate or to seduce the literary world. Eminent literary conversions were not then received with a burst of applause because of their advertisement value. Classical authors fared more hardly than any dead writers are likely to fare in reputation under the rule of Marxian criticism; and the fathers of the young Church did not feel any pressing need for literature and art as evidence of the truth of Christianity. Those manifestations followed in due course. They are never likely to reappear any more quickly than they did then. Trotsky is quite aware—more aware than his compatriots seem to have been before he wrote his book—of the difference between literature written in and for a period of revolution, and literature produced by a people which has gone through a revolution, and he seems to understand that the first is unlikely to have any permanent value; but he seems to feel, in common with other communists, an impatience for the latter to appear.

I can agree with Mr. Trotsky up to a point. 'The proletarian,' he says, 'has to have in art the expression of the new spiritual[1] point of view which is just beginning to be formulated within him, and to which art must help him to give form.' If we assume for the moment that the revolution is to take place, and that the final classless society will appear, then I concede the possibility that great works of art in new forms will subsequently appear too; I disbelieve, not only that the new art will be any better than the art of all the past, but that the new art will owe its life to communism. The chances for art are no better than out of any other possible development of society, and are not improved by a flood of anticipatory criticism. I certainly prefer the greatest Christian art to the greatest art of pagan times, before or since, but I do not believe that because it is Christian art it is greater art. What would happen, at best, under a wholly new dispensation, would be that the artist would have his material given him, and would be so inoculated with communism as to be able to ignore it. Christian apologists have not, those who have been serious and qualified, cited Christian art as an apology for Christianity. From the point of view of art, if there is such a point of view, Christianity was merely a change, a provision of a new world with new material; from the point of view of communism as of Christianity, art and literature are strictly irrelevant.

There is a great deal more to the difference, however, than a mere change of mental categories. Both Mr. Trotsky and Mr. Calverton speak as if you had only to adopt the categories of communism, and after that, if you were an artist, you would be able to devote your attention to questions of 'form.' Mr. Trotsky says:

It is unquestionably true that the need for art is not created by economic conditions. But neither is the need for food created by economic conditions. On

1. One would like to penetrate Mr. Trotsky's conception of 'the spiritual'.

the contrary, the need for food and warmth creates economics. It is very true that one cannot always go by the principles of Marxism in deciding whether to reject or to accept a work of art. A work of art should, in the first place, be judged by its own law, that is, by the law of art. But Marxism alone can explain why and how a given tendency in art has originated in a given period of history; in other words, who it was who made a demand for such an artistic form and not for another, and why. . . . Materialism does not deny the significance of form, either in logic, jurisprudence, or art.

And Mr. Calverton:

The revolutionary proletarian critic does not aim to underestimate literary craftsmanship. What he contends is simply that literary craftsmanship is not enough. The craftsmanship must be utilized to create objects of revolutionary meaning.

Now, this is all quite praiseworthy, so far as it goes, but I find it difficult to apply in comprehensive criticism of any great piece of literature of the past: what was the 'meaning' of a play of Shakespeare which corresponds to the 'revolutionary meaning' of the art of the future? the 'meaning' which it must have or must have had, if we are to regard it as anything more than the 'literary craftsmanship' which is not enough? If Marxism explains why and how a given tendency in history originated, such as the tendency for Shakespeare's plays to be written, and who it was who made a demand for such an artistic form as that of *Antony and Cleopatra*, and if everything else is 'literary craftsmanship' (an accomplishment in which Mr. Calverton is not notably proficient), then there seems to me to be a good deal left to explain. Mr. Calverton, in fact, does leave a great deal, for throughout his book on American literature everything is explained except the genius of the greater men of letters, who do not, on the whole, receive very much of his attention. They are 'explained' by their environment, and their genius, apparently, is just a genius for literary craftsmanship.

I should suppose it to be desirable that every country shall provide an environment in which its best minds can flourish; it also seems desirable that these best minds should come to terms with their environment; but it is possible also that some amount of maladaptation is desirable. Hawthorne was apparently adapted to the past of America rather than to its future; but it is just possible that this retrospective inclination suited Hawthorne's peculiar spiritual qualities. If Mr. Calverton had treated Poe as a case of maladaptation, and Emerson as a case of excessive adaptation, the results might have been interesting. But the spectacle of the individual in conflict with the dominant tendencies and prejudices of his time, and consequently that of the individual in conflict with the dominant prejudices and tendencies of the coming time, does not influence critics like Mr. Calverton in favour of the individual.

There are also people who, while recognizing the interest of the work of literature as a document upon the ideas and the sensibility of its epoch, and recognizing even that the permanent work of literature is one which does not lack this interest, yet cannot help valuing literary work, like philosophical work, in the end by its transcendence of the limits of its age; by its breaking through the categories of thought and sensibility of its age; by its speaking, in the language of its time and in the imagery of its own tradition, the word which belongs to no time. Art, we feel, aspires to the condition of the timeless; and communist art, according to the sentence of those who would foretell what it is to be, is bound to the temporal.

It is the decay of the whole middle class way of existence, that of the upper bourgeoisie as well as the

petty bourgeoisie, which has robbed the contemporary writer in Europe as well as in America of his
faith in life, and left him without beliefs or convictions.

(What faith in life may be I know not; I might inform Mr.
Calverton that, for the Christian, faith in death is what
matters.) He continues:

The sickness and sham which underlay the nature
of middle-class life is no longer concealed from him.

It was no doubt the sickness and sham which underlay the
nature of Pharisee and Sadducee life that, being no longer
concealed from the writers of the Gospels, left them without beliefs or convictions, and with a less polished prose
style than that of Mr. Calverton or that of Mr. Murry. And
yet we persist in believing that Confucius and Plato,
Homer and Shakespeare, even though 'their faith was
founded upon a false premise; fitting and persuasive
enough in their generation,' have yet something to say to
every future generation if it will listen, no matter how
many future generations there may be to come.

In matters of æsthetics the Christian theorist is in a position of unfair terms with the communist, of which he is
not slow to take advantage. He is able to recognize an in-
consistency in the affairs of this world, even to admitting
the possibility that a man might be a communist, an orthodox Marxian dialectician, in our time, in this very year
and month, and yet write decent English prose; even that
such a one might be a great poet. He might even derive
pleasure and instruction from the man's poetry. But the
Marxian is compelled to scorn delights, even such moderate ecstasies as may be provoked by the reading of Emerson's Essays, and live laborious days in deciding what art
ought to be. For this knowledge of literature he is obliged
to apply himself, not to the furtive and facile pleasures of
Homer and Virgil—the former a person of doubtful iden-

tity and citizenship, the latter a sycophantic supporter of a middle-class imperialist dynasty—but to the arduous study of Ernest Hemingway and John Dos Passos; and the end of his precipitous ascent will be an appreciation of the accomplishment of Sam Ornitz, Lester Cohen, and Granville Hicks.[2]

---

2. *The Liberation of American Literature*, p. 479. By V. F. Calverton, author of *Sex Expression in Literature* and *Bankruptcy of Marriage* which has been translated into eight languages and used in leading universities in London (ask Mr. Laski), Berlin and Tokyo. Scribners.

Part Fourteen

~~~~~~~~~~~~~~~~~~~~~~~~~~~~~~~~

A BENT WORLD

By the end of the Second World War, civilization had descended deep into what Arnold Toynbee called "a time of troubles." Much of the world had been subjugated by a ferocious and sterile collectivism. Conservative writers, of whom we represent four here, labored during the 1950s to remind postwar folk of what had been and what might be again.

THE POISON OF SUBJECTIVISM

C. S. Lewis

C. S. Lewis' books have become a major intellectual influence since the Second World War. Lewis (1898–1963) was politically conservative, but his writings are more concerned with the moral order than with the social order. "The Poison of Subjectivism," a subject treated more fully in his tiny volume *The Abolition of Man,* first appeared in the periodical *Religion in Life,* Vol. XII (summer, 1943); it is included in the Lewis collection *Christian Reflections* (Grand Rapids, Mich., 1967), pp. 72–81.

One cause of misery and vice is always present with us in the greed and pride of men, but at certain periods in history this is greatly increased by the temporary prevalence of some false philosophy. Correct thinking will not make good men of bad ones; but a purely theoretical error may remove ordinary checks to evil and deprive good intentions of their natural support. An error of this sort is abroad at present. I am not referring to the Power philosophies of the Totalitarian states, but to something that goes deeper and spreads wider and which, indeed, has given these Power philosophies their golden opportunity. I am referring to Subjectivism.

After studying his environment man has begun to study himself. Up to that point, he had assumed his own reason and through it seen all other things. Now, his own reason has become the object: it is as if we took out our eyes to look at them. Thus studied, his own reason appears to him as the epiphenomenon which accompanies chemical or electrical events in a cortex which is itself the by-product of a blind evolutionary process. His own logic, hitherto the king whom events in all possible worlds must obey, becomes merely subjective. There is no reason for supposing that it yields truth.

As long as this dethronement refers only to the theoretical reason, it cannot be wholehearted. The scientist has to assume the validity of his own logic (in the stout old fashion of Plato or Spinoza) even in order to prove that it is merely subjective, and therefore he can only flirt with subjectivism. It is true that this flirtation sometimes goes pretty far. There are modern scientists, I am told, who have dropped the words *truth* and *reality* out of their vocabulary and who hold that the end of their work is not to know what is there but simply to get practical results. This is, no doubt, a bad symptom. But, in the main, subjectivism is such an uncomfortable yokefellow for research that the danger, in this quarter, is continually counteracted.

But when we turn to practical reason the ruinous effects are found operating in full force. By practical reason I mean our judgement of good and evil. If you are surprised that I include this under the heading of reason at all, let me remind you that your surprise is itself one result of the subjectivism I am discussing. Until modern times no thinker of the first rank ever doubted that our judgements of value were rational judgements or that what they discovered was objective. It was taken for granted that in temptation passion was opposed, not to some sentiment, but to reason. Thus Plato thought, thus Aristotle, thus Hooker, Butler and Doctor Johnson. The modern view is very different. It does not believe that value judgements are really judgements at all. They are sentiments, or complexes, or attitudes, produced in a community by the pressure of its environment and its traditions, and differing from one community to another. To say that a thing is good is merely to express our feeling about it; and our feeling about it is the feeling we have been socially conditioned to have.

But if this is so, then we might have been conditioned to feel otherwise. 'Perhaps,' thinks the reformer or the educational expert, 'it would be better if we were. Let us improve our morality.' Out of this apparently innocent idea comes the disease that will certainly end our species (and, in my view, damn our souls) if it is not crushed; the fatal superstition that men can create values, that a community can choose its 'ideology' as men choose their clothes. Everyone is indignant when he hears the Germans define justice as that which is to the interest of the Third Reich. But it is not always remembered that this indignation is perfectly groundless if we ourselves regard morality as a subjective sentiment to be altered at will. Unless there is some objective standard of good, over-arching Germans, Japanese and ourselves alike whether any of us obey it or no, then of course the Germans are as competent to create their ideology as we are to create ours. If 'good' and 'better' are terms deriving their sole meaning from the ideology of each people, then of course ideologies themselves cannot be better or worse than one another. Unless the measuring rod is independent of the things measured, we can do no measuring. For the same reason it is useless to compare the moral ideas of one age with those of another: progress and decadence are alike meaningless words.

All this is so obvious that it amounts to an identical proposition. But how little it is now understood can be gauged from the procedure of the moral reformer who, after saying that 'good' means 'what we are conditioned to like' goes on cheerfully to consider whether it might be 'better' that we should be conditioned to like something else. What in Heaven's names does he mean by 'better'?

He usually has at the back of his mind the notion that if he throws over traditional judgement of value, he will find something else, something more 'real' or 'solid' on which

to base a new scheme of values. He will say, for example,
'We must abandon irrational taboos and base our values
on the good of the community'—as if the maxim 'Thou
shalt promote the good of the community' were anything
more than a polysyllabic variant of 'Do as you would be
done by' which has itself no other basis than the old universal value judgement he claims to be rejecting. Or he
will endeavour to base his values on biology and tell us
that we must act thus and thus for the preservation of our
species. Apparently he does not anticipate the question,
'Why should the species be preserved?' He takes it for
granted that it should, because he is really relying on traditional judgements of value. If he were starting, as he
pretends, with a clean slate, he could never reach this
principle. Sometimes he tries to do so by falling back on
'instinct.' 'We have an instinct to preserve our species,' he
may say. But have we? And if we have, who told us that
we must obey our instincts? And why should we obey
this instinct in the teeth of many others which conflict
with the preservation of the species? The reformer knows
that some instincts are to be obeyed more than others only
because he is judging instincts by a standard, and the
standard is, once more, the traditional morality which he
claims to be superseding. The instincts themselves obviously cannot furnish us with grounds for grading the
instincts in a hierarchy. If you do not bring a knowledge
of their comparative respectability *to* your study of them,
you can never derive it *from* them.

This whole attempt to jettison traditional values as
something subjective and to substitute a new scheme of
values for them is wrong. It is like trying to lift yourself
by your own coat collar. Let us get two propositions written into our minds with indelible ink.

(1) The human mind has no more power of inventing a
new value than of planting a new sun in the sky or a new
primary colour in the spectrum.

(2) Every attempt to do so consists in arbitrarily se-

lecting some one maxim of traditional morality, isolating it from the rest, and erecting it into an *unum necessarium*.[1]

The second proposition will bear a little illustration. Ordinary morality tells us to honour our parents and cherish our children. By taking the second precept alone you construct a Futurist Ethic in which the claims of 'posterity' are the sole criterion. Ordinary morality tells us to keep promises and also to feed the hungry. By taking the second precept alone you get a Communist Ethic in which 'production', and distribution of the products to the people, are the sole criteria. Ordinary morality tells us, *ceteris paribus*,[2] to love our kindred and fellow-citizens more than strangers. By isolating this precept you can get either an Aristocratic Ethic with the claims of our class a sole criterion, or a Racialist Ethic where no claims but those of blood are acknowledged. These monomaniac systems are then used as a ground from which to attack traditional morality; but absurdly, since it is from traditional morality alone that they derive such semblance of validity as they possess. Starting from scratch, with no assumptions about value, we could reach none of them. If reverence for parents or promises is a mere subjective by-product of physical nature, so is reverence for race or posterity. The trunk to whose root the reformer would lay the axe is the only support of the particular branch he wishes to retain.

All idea of 'new' or 'scientific' or 'modern' moralities must therefore be dismissed as mere confusion of thought. We have only two alternatives. Either the maxims of traditional morality must be accepted as axioms of practical reason which neither admit nor require argument to support them and not to 'see' which is to have lost human status; or else there are no values at all, what we mistook for values being 'projections' of irrational emotions. It is perfectly futile, after having dismissed traditional morality

---

1. The one necessary thing. [R.K.]
2. Other things being equal. [R.K.]

with the question, 'Why should we obey it?' then to attempt the reintroduction of value at some later stage in our philosophy. Any value we reintroduce can be countered in just the same way. Every argument used to support it will be an attempt to derive from premises in the indicative mood a conclusion in the imperative. And this is impossible.

Against this view the modern mind has two lines of defence. The first claims that traditional morality is different in different times and places—in fact, that there is not one morality but a thousand. The second exclaims that to tie ourselves to an immutable moral code is to cut off all progress and acquiesce in 'stagnation.' Both are unsound.

Let us take the second one first. And let us strip it of the illegitimate emotional power it derives from the word 'stagnation' with its suggestion of puddles and mantled pools. If water stands too long it stinks. To infer thence that whatever stands long must be unwholesome is to be the victim of metaphor. Space does not stink because it has preserved its three dimensions from the beginning. The square on the hypotenuse has not gone mouldy by continuing to equal the sum of the squares on the other two side. Love is not dishonoured by constancy, and when we wash our hands we are seeking stagnation and 'putting the clock back,' artificially restoring our hands to the *status quo* in which they began the day and resisting the natural trend of events which would increase their dirtiness steadily from our birth to our death. For the emotive term 'stagnant' let us substitute the descriptive term 'permanent.' Does a permanent moral standard preclude progress? On the contrary, except on the supposition of a changeless standard, progress is impossible. If good is a fixed point, it is at least possible that we should get nearer and nearer to it; but if the terminus is as mobile as the train, how can the train progress towards it? Our ideas of the good may change, but they cannot change either for the better or the worse if there is no absolute and immutable good to which they can approximate or from which they can recede. We can go on getting a sum more and more nearly right only if the one perfectly right answer is 'stagnant.'

And yet it will be said, I have just admitted that our ideas of good may improve. How is this to be reconciled with the view that 'traditional morality' is a *depositum fidei*[3] which cannot be deserted? The answer can be understood if we compare a real moral advance with a mere innovation. From the Stoic and Confucian, 'Do not do to others what you would not like them to do to you'; to the Christian, 'Do as you would be done by' is a real advance. The morality of Nietzsche is a mere innovation. The first is an advance because no one who did not admit the validity of the old maxim could see reason for accepting the new one, and anyone who accepted the old would at once recognize the new as an extension of the same principle. If he rejected it, he would have to reject it as a superfluity, something that went too far, not as something simply heterogeneous from his own ideas of value. But the Nietzschean ethic can be accepted only if we are ready to scrap traditional morals as a mere error and then to put ourselves in a position where we can find no ground for any value judgments at all. It is the difference between a man who says to us: 'You like your vegetables moderately fresh; why not grow your own and have them perfectly fresh? and a man who says, 'Throw away that loaf and try eating bricks and centipedes instead.' Real moral advances, in fine, are made *from within* the existing moral tradition and in the spirit of that tradition and can be understood only in the light of that tradition. The outsider who has rejected the tradition cannot judge them. He has, as Aristotle said, no *ache*, no premises.

And what of the second modern objection—that the ethical standards of different cultures differ so widely that

---

3. Deposit of the faith. [R.K.]

there is no common tradition at all? The answer is that this is a lie—a good, solid, resounding lie. If a man will go into a library and spend a few days with the *Encyclopedia of Religion and Ethics* he will soon discover the massive unanimity of the practical reason in man. From the Babylonian *Hymn to Samos*, from the Laws of Manu, the *Book of the Dead*, the Analects, the Stoics, the Platonists, from Australian aborigines and Redskins, he will collect the same triumphantly monotonous denunciations of oppression, murder, treachery and falsehood, the same injunctions of kindness to the aged, the young, and the weak, of almsgiving and impartiality and honesty. He may be a little surprised (I certainly was) to find that precepts of mercy are more frequent than precepts of justice; but he will no longer doubt that there is such a thing as the Law of Nature. There are, of course, differences. There are even blindnesses in particular cultures—just as there are savages who cannot count up to twenty. But the pretence that we are presented with a mere chaos—though no outline of universally accepted value shows through—is simply false and should be contradicted in season and out of season wherever it is met. Far from finding a chaos, we find exactly what we should expect if good is indeed something objective and reason the organ whereby it is apprehended—that is, a substantial agreement with considerable local differences of emphasis and, perhaps, no one code that includes everything.

The two grand methods of obscuring this agreement are these: First, you can concentrate on those divergences about sexual morality which most serious moralists regard as belonging to positive rather than to Natural Law, but which rouse strong emotions. Differences about the definition of incest or between polygamy and monogomy come under this head. (It is untrue to say that the Greeks thought sexual perversion innocent. The continual tittering of Plato is really more evidential than the stern prohibition of Aristotle. Men titter thus only about what they regard as, at least, a *peccadillo:* the jokes about drunkenness in *Pickwick,* far from proving that the nineteenth-century English thought it innocent, prove the reverse. There is an enormous difference of *degree* between the Greek view of perversion and the Christian, but there is not opposition.) The second method is to treat as differences in the judgement of value what are really differences in belief about fact. Thus human sacrifice, or persecution of witches, are cited as evidence of a radically different morality. But the real difference lies elsewhere. We do not hunt witches because we disbelieve in their existence. We do not kill men to avert pestilence because we do not think petilence can thus be averted. We do 'sacrifice' men in war, and we do hunt spies and traitors.

So far I have been considering the objections which unbelievers bring against the doctrine of objective value, or the Law of Nature. But in our days we must be prepared to meet objections from Christians too. 'Humanism' and 'liberalism' are coming to be used simply as terms of disapprobation, and both are likely to be so used of the position I am taking up. Behind them lurks a real theological problem. If we accept the primary platitudes of practical reason as the unquestioned premises of all action, are we thereby trusting our own reason so far that we ignore the Fall, and are we retrogressively turning our absolute allegiance away from a person to an abstraction?

As regards the Fall, I submit that the general tenor of scripture does not encourage us to believe that our knowledge of the Law has been depraved in the same degree as our power to fulfil it. He would be a brave man who claimed to realize the fallen condition of man more clearly than St Paul. In that very chapter (Romans 7) where he asserts most strongly our inability to keep the moral law he also asserts most confidently that we perceive the Law's goodness and rejoice in it according to the inward man. Our righteousness may be filthy and ragged; but Christianity gives us no ground for holding that our perceptions of right are in the same condition. They may, no doubt, be impaired; but there is a difference between imperfect sight and blindness. A theology which goes about to represent our practical reason as radically unsound is heading for disaster. If we once admit that what God means by 'goodness' is sheerly different from what we judge to be good, there is no difference left between pure religion and devil worship.

The other objection is much more formidable. If we once grant that our practical reason is really reason and that its fundamental imperatives are as absolute and categorical as they claim to be, then unconditional allegiance to them is the duty of man. So is absolute allegiance to God. And these two allegiances must, somehow, be the same. But how is the relation between God and the moral law to be represented? To say that the moral law is God's law is no final solution. Are these things right because God commands them or does God command them because they are right? If the first, if good is to be *defined* as what God commands, then the goodness of God Himself is emptied of meaning and the commands of an omnipotent fiend would have the same claim on us as those of the 'righteous Lord.' If the second, then we seem to be admitting a cosmic dyarchy, or even making God Himself the mere executor of a law somehow external and antecedent to His own being. Both views are intolerable.

At this point we must remind ourselves that Christian theology does not believe God to be a person. It believes Him to be such that in Him a trinity of persons is consistent with a unity of Deity. In that sense it believes Him to be something very different from a person, just as a cube, in which six squares are consistent with unity of the body, is different from a square. (Flatlanders, attempting to imagine a cube, would either imagine the six squares coinciding, and thus destroy their distinctness, or else imagine them set out side by side, and thus destroy the unity. Our difficulties about the Trinity are of much the same kind.) It is therefore possible that the duality which seems to force itself upon us when we think, first, of our Father in Heaven, and, secondly, of the self-evident imperatives of the moral law, is not a mere error but a real (though inadequate and creaturely) perception of things that would necessarily be two in any mode of being which enters our experience, but which are not so divided in the absolute being of the superpersonal God. When we attempt to think of a person and a law, we are compelled to think of this person either as obeying the law or as making it. And when we think of Him as making it we are compelled to think of Him either as making it in conformity to some yet more ultimate pattern of goodness (in which case that pattern, and not He, would be supreme) or else as making it arbitrarily by a *sic volo, sic jubeo*[4] (in which case He would be neither good nor wise). But it is probably just here that our categories betray us. It would be idle, with our merely mortal resources, to attempt a positive correction of our categories—*ambulavi in mirabilibus supra me.*[5] But it might be permissible to lay down two negations: that God neither *obeys* nor *creates* the moral law. The good is uncreated; it never could have been otherwise; it has in it no shadow of contingency; it lies, as Plato said, on the other side of existence. It is the *Rita* of the Hindus by which the gods themselves are divine, the *Tao* of the Chinese from which all realities proceed. But we, favoured beyond the wisest pagans, know what lies beyond existence, what admits no contingency, what lends divinity to all else, what is the ground of all existence, is not simply a law but also a begetting love, a love begotten, and the love which, being between these two, is also imminent in all those who are caught up to share the unity of their self-caused life. God is not merely

---

4. "As I wish, so I command." [R.K.]
5. "I have occupied myself with things too wondrous for me." (Cp. Psalm 131.1) [R.K.]

good, but goodness; goodness is not merely divine, but God.

These may seem fine-spun speculations: yet I believe that nothing short of this can save us. A Christianity which does not see moral and religious experience converging to meet at infinity, not at a negative infinity, but in the positive infinity of the living yet superpersonal God, has nothing, in the long run, to divide it from devil worship; and a philosophy which does not accept value as eternal and objective can lead us only to ruin. Nor is the matter of merely speculative importance. Many a popular 'planner' on a democratic platform, many a mild-eyed scientist in a democratic laboratory means, in the last resort, just what the Fascist means. He believes that 'good' means whatever men are conditioned to approve. He believes that it is the function of him and his kind to condition men; to create consciences by eugenics, psychological manipulation of infants, state education and mass propaganda. Because he is confused, he does not yet fully realize that those who create conscience cannot be subject to conscience themselves. But he must awake to the logic of his position sooner or later; and when he does, what barrier remains between us and the final division of the race into a few conditioners who stand themselves outside morality and the many conditioned in whom such morality as the experts choose is produced at the experts' pleasure? If 'good' means only the local ideology, how can those who invent the local ideology be guided by any idea of good themselves? The very idea of freedom presupposes some objective moral law which overarches rulers and ruled alike. Subjectivism about values is eternally incompatible with democracy. We and our rulers are of one kind only so long as we subject to one law. But if there is no Law of Nature, the *ethos* of any society is the creation of its rulers, educators and conditioners; and every creator stands above and outside his own creation.

Unless we return to the crude and nursery-like belief in

objective values, we perish. If we do, we may live, and such a return might have one minor advantage. If we believed in the absolute reality of elementary moral platitudes, we should value those who solicit our votes by other standards than have recently been in fashion. While we believe that good is something to be invented, we demand of our rulers such qualities as 'vision,' 'dynamism,' 'creativity,' and the like. If we returned to the objective view we should demand qualities much rarer, and much more beneficial—virtue, knowledge, diligence and skill. 'Vision' is for sale, or claims to be for sale, everywhere. But give me a man who will do a day's work for a day's pay, who will refuse bribes, who will not make up his facts, and who has learned his job.

SOME DAY, IN OLD CHARLESTON
Donald Davidson

The most consistent and unyielding of the "Southern Agrarians" who opposed centralization and industrial "progress" during the 1930s and 1940s, Donald Davidson (1893–1968) published in 1938 an important political study that few have read: *The Attack on Leviathan: Regionalism and Nationalism in the United States.* Davidson's poetry, too, has been neglected. "Some Day, in Old Charleston," from his collection *Still Rebels, Still Yankees* (Baton Rouge, 1957), pp. 213–27, is a reassertion of the South's conservative tradition.

On Wednesay last, said the South Carolina Gazette, *four large transport ships sailed up Cooper River for Straw-*

*berry with the heavy baggage of His Majesty's troops,
which are to be employed (in conjunction with the forces
of this Province) under the command of Lieutenant Colonel James Grant in the approaching campaign against
the Cherokees.*

Outside, on King Street, a distant rhythmic clangor in-
truded among the ordinary traffic noises. We ignored it,
for we were trying to hear, within the sheltering walls of
the Charleston Library Society, the noise of "waggons"
carrying heavy baggage from Cooper River to Strawberry, and thence to Monck's Corner, where the Highland
Scottish troops of Grant's command were assembled, and
the bagpipes doubtless were playing. The large bound
volumes of the *South Carolina Gazette* for 1760 and 1761
were open before us, and we were both taking notes. For
that was the trade between us, between husband and
wife, that if I would go with her to the various gardens at
certain times, she would go with me to the Charleston Library Society at certain other times.

Right now it might be April 6, 1948, in the United
States in general, and even on King Street, but inside the
Charleston Library Society building it was March 21,
1761. The *South Carolina Gazette* said so. We did not
want to be interrupted.

Yesterday morning—now that must have been March
20, 1761—*the troops began their march from Monck's
Corner to Fort Prince George on the Keowee River.*

From the fort as advanced base Grant would raid the
Cherokee towns hidden among the mountains. Grant was
a Scot, probably of an ex-Jacobite family, but like most
British officers he believed that Indians armed with rifles
could be defeated by regulars armed with muskets, if the
regulars kept formation and volleyed by platoons upon
command of an officer waving a sword. . . .

The noise on King Street was getting louder. There was
a lot of thumping in it, which we tried to tell ourselves
was the drums of Grant's expedition, moving up from the

Congarees to Ninety-Six. "The behavior of the troops during their stay in Charles-Town has given the greatest satisfaction to the inhabitants," said the *South Carolina Gazette*. The officers of the army had given a theatrical entertainment the week before—had put on a comedy and a farce, in the Council Chamber.

But everybody was leaving the reading rooms and going to the door. Even the librarians were going—even Miss Mazyck and Miss Bull. Then how could we forbear?

So we came out into the fine spring sunshine of present-day Charleston, and from the lofty stone porch of the Charleston Library Society we looked down as from a reviewing stand upon the approaching military parade. Recalled from March 21, 1761, and not unmindful of April 12, 1861, we entered without any great jolt into the concerns of April 6, 1917—no, April 6, 1948—and looked down upon King Street, feeling very proper, safe, relaxed, and patriotic, in the company of the lady who was looking up genealogies, the boy who was reading romances, a casual tourist or two, and Miss Mazyck and Miss Bull. It was (we at last remembered) a day called "Army Day." We had read about it in the *South Carolina Gazette*—no, the Charleston *News and Courier*—while we were eating breakfast at a grill recommended by Duncan Hines. There would be a parade of army and navy units, and airplanes overhead, including jets, and after the parade there would be a patriotic address by the inevitable successor of Lieutenant Colonel Grant.

It was a good parade, and we thoroughly enjoyed it, at least the military part of it, and no doubt we enjoyed it the more because of the amiable confusion that always comes over the visitor to Charleston, who can never be quite certain whether at a given moment he is participating in the ardors and pleaures of the seventeenth, the eighteenth, the nineteenth, or the twentieth century. After all, troops had been marching along King Street and other Charleston streets for a long, long time—say about 250 years, to get a round number. It was so easy to get mixed up and see redcoats, or kilts, or blue-and-buff, or Confederate gray where the uniform of the day was actually khaki. One had to make an effort to remember that the column obeyed the orders of someone whose name was in the morning newspaper, and not of Craven, Chicken, Cornwallis, Tarleton, Moultrie, Nathanael Greene, Beauregard, Hampton, or Sherman.

The column of 1948, if the evidence of the eyes could be believed, was mostly in khaki, mostly in the undistinguished drab that properly belongs to the mechanical twentieth century. Its weapons were modern, and it had no horses or horse-drawn "waggons," but only the self-propelled, often fantastically odd vehicles of up-to-date mobile warfare. And far above the column—far above the Georgian façades and West Indian verandas of Charleston—whizzed the bomber groups and jet planes of the war in the air. But in its fundamental aspects it was like all military parades from Julius Caesar to Eisenhower. It was a ceremonious procession stepping to martial music, carrying flags and deadly weapons—a reminder, cast into a form as ritualistic and devotional as the ceremonies of a church, that the processes of government, laboratory science, liberalism, and expertism must be depended upon sometime, somewhere, to reach a breaking point, at which breaking point the army takes over and the ancient battle begins once more. For this reason a military parade has a certain order and decorum that are traditional and unalterable.

This one was traditional up to a point. It was led by a company of paratroopers in helmets and half-boots. Soon came the Marines, in red and blue, and a unit of sailors who looked unhappy as sailors always do when marching as infantry. The thin crowd that fringed the street looked on in silence.

But now the crowd stirred, as another band rolled its drums and burst into music, and another column of infantry appeared. At its head, floating beside the Stars and Stripes, was the blue flag of South Carolina, with its palmetto tree and crescent moon. What was the regiment? The folds of the flag, drooping in the quiet air, hid part of the numerals. It was the One Hundred and—something—Infantry. From the back of the porch, near the door where the librarians stood, a Charleston voice spoke softly but firmly, and also, I thought, a little correctively: "The Washington Light Infantry." An old regiment, then, disguised in modern numerals, modern khaki. A regiment that had fought in the Revolution, at the Cowpens with Morgan, at Eutaw with Greene. But now—absorbed into anonymity—it was the One Hundred and—something—Infantry. The crowd handclapped merrily; a few cheers drifted up, half-apologetic.

Then here came another palmetto flag, and another South Carolina regiment, another One Hundred and Something. More cheers, that threatened to become yells, louder hand-clapping, a little tumult of excitement, amid which I thought I heard the corrective voice say: "The Sumter Guards." The names and even the old numerals (where there were numerals) of the old state regiments were wiped out, I remembered, during World War I, when it seemed safer for democracy to revise the old system and merge everything into the national lump. The regular regiments and divisions got the lowest numbers; the state or "national guard" regiments were renumbered in the hundreds; and the "national army" or drafted regiments were numbered in the three hundreds.

And now came the miscellaneous units of reservists, and after them the Citadel band, and after the Citadel band, the young cadets of Porter Military Academy. These were Charleston's own, and they were well received by the crowd. It was not until later that we learned why the Citadel cadets did not march, but sent only a band. They were having term examinations at Citadel, and only the band was allowed to join this parade.

Thus far, all had been traditional, all was in order, and just about what one would expect in a military parade in Charleston—a certain spirited smartness of appearance, combined with due restraint; a notion of doing well once more what had been done well many times in the past; a sense of a present occasion moved not only by its own energy but by the merging and supporting energies of all that had gone before.

But now, suddenly, there was more music, with a saucy blare in its horns and drums and a continuance of the parade that almost amounted to an interruption.

It was a band of youngsters not in uniform but in civilian dress. At the head of the band a girl dressed up in the stage costume of a blue devil turned dizzying cartwheels on the pavement of King Street. Up went the little devil's heels and around she went cleverly on feet and hands. And behind her pranced a whole squad of drum majorettes. They threw their knees high to the beat of the drums. They tossed and swung their batons, twisted hips and bodies, nodded their heads under their grotesque shakos. They simpered brassily, their girlish features frozen in a Hollywood smile. With them, not far behind the comely blue devil, trudged a youth carrying a large sign with the legend: NORTH CHARLESTON HIGH SCHOOL. They were received in silence, though eyes followed them and the agile blue devil as they passed on. There were a few half-suppressed titters, a few remarks in undertone along the sidewalk, and soon we drifted away as the end of the column came in sight. It was over, and we could go back to the files of the *South Carolina Gazette*, or we could adjourn to Middleton Gardens. Middleton Gardens seemed the better choice. We felt an urgent need to return to the seventeenth century and get our bearings once more. We had not counted on seeing the naked legs of drum majorettes on King Street in old Charleston. Pathetic they might be in their juvenile insolence, in their parading of a new American convention that was not

Charleston's, that could not possibly have been thought up in Charleston. But they were formidable, too.

Later on we brought our problem of disorientation to the attention of a Charleston friend. His family name is not Pinckney or Huger or Rutledge, but it is a Charleston name. For convenience let him be known here as Mr. Charles.

Out of deference to us, Mrs. Charles had moved the dinner hour up from the regular 2 P.M. to 1:30. It was dinner, not lunch, and we had ample time to talk before Mr. Charles had to return to his office on Broad Street and we to the Library Society.

There is no really proper moment for introducing a question about North Charleston into an after-dinner conversation in an old Charleston home, and we never would have succeeded in introducing it if Mr. Charles himself had not prepared the way. The conversation somehow turned to the Carolina Yacht Club, of which I knew he had long been a member. Did he still go boating as of old? Well, he still was a member, still had a boat—he said "bo't" in the Charleston English that is so odd and so charming to non-Charleston ears. Mr. Charles still had a "bo't," but he went sailing less often than of old. Formerly you just went to the bo't-yard, hoisted sail, and put right out with no delay. Now you had to go to the "yacht basin" and work your "bo't" slowly out through a lot of congestion, by a devious route, before you could do any sailing. It was too much trouble.

Things were not exactly what they used to be. For years and years Mr. Charles and his family had moved out to Sullivan's Island during the hot season, to get the sea breeze. It was very nice there, and they, like other Charlestonians, had always enjoyed their simple cottage and the relative seclusion of that summer colony. Now a large tract on Sullivan's Island was about to become a "state project," and their ancient privacy was threatened with invasion by the multitude.

The portraits of Mrs. Charles's Colonial and Revolutionary ancestors were there on the wall. In particular there was a gentleman in a stock, with excellently powdered hair, who might have been Mr. Charles himself dressed up for a masquerade. In times past this gentleman and others like him had faced and solved, over and over again, the problem of the invasion of privacy, and still worse problems. They had known what to do about "state projects." They had a theory about such matters and had applied it with astonishing skill. Old Charleston was the physical evidence of their success. I looked this gentleman in the eye and put my question: "What about North Charleston?"

The gentleman in the stock did not change countenance. Neither did Mr. Charles. When you have been fighting intrusions with considerable success for nearly three hundred years, you do not quail before a North Charleston. Mr. Charles, smiling a little, explained the situation carefully, without the least air of irritation or patronage, as if my question were the most natural question that could arise in after-dinner talk.

During World War II there had been, he said, a vast development in connection with the Navy Yards and such things. A lot of people came in. They brought their families and settled down. So a small new city grew up over there in the direction of Cooper River. The Charleton Chamber of Commerce thought all that development a good thing because it brought new business to Charleston.

And that was the kind of thing Mr. Charles had believed in, too, in his younger days. But he had found out, long ago, that although business expansion looked good on paper, in practice it didn't mean that Charleston folks like himself were any better off. There would be more business, yes, but there would be more competition. So what happened was that you just worked harder than ever— harder than you ought—without getting any real increase of benefits.

As to North Charleston, he had expected it would more or less fade out after the war was over. But a lot of those people had stayed on. They didn't have war jobs any longer, but they got up things to do—dry-cleaning shops, garages, all sorts of little makeshift establishments. Perhaps some of them just lived off the government. And now it looked as if North Charleston were going to be a permanent thing. They had a population of some thousands, and yes, they had a high school. People had come from all around—not from South Carolina so much, not even from the South maybe, but from all over the United States. They hustled and made a lot of noise. They had begun to say that the future belonged to them, not to Old Charleston. They had even been known to say that they of North Charleston had the better right to the name *Charleston*. They wanted to assume the name—to drop the "North" part—and to let Old Charleston slide into a subordinate role, let it be the decaying suburb of a new city.

At this point Mr. Charles smiled again, as if to say that all occasion for gravity had passed, once the claims of North Charleston had been actually stated. He neither refuted nor supported the claims. He just stated them. There they stood in all their nakedness. That was what one noticed about them mainly, in Mr. Charles's sitting-room, as it was what one noticed about the drum majorettes during the parade. The flesh and the devil are doubtless ineradicable elements of human life, but when they suddenly appear as an accent in a parade or program, one can see how stripped they are of any but the crudest meaning. Their inappropriateness is the signal of the power they propose to exercise—if they can gain power.

Back at the Charleston Library Society, or walking in Middleton Gardens, or elsewhere in Old Charleston, it was hard to have much faith in the boldly asserted claims of any other Charleston. If anything were going to swallow Old Charleston, it would have to display more capacity for destruction than any other natural or human force had yet been able to exert upon the ancient city. For from the beginning, through storm, siege, revolution, earthquake, flood and fire, and drastic social and economic changes, Charleston had remained distinctly Charleston, and nobody had ever found a way to nickname it or advertise it as anything but Charleston.

Its Library Society, its colleges, schools, churches, orphanages, its St. Cecilia Society and other organizations had histories that reached back continuously into its remote past. The names on the rosters and at the heads of its organizations were the names that had been in such places since colonial days. Continuity of family, of family life, and family position—irrespective of economic status— was in fact a great distinction of Charleston among old American cities; for elsewhere that continuity had been generally broken by one cause or another.

With this continuity Charleston had a stability that expressed itself in the pattern of its streets and the conservatism of its architecture. The map of Charleston in 1948 was not substantially different from the map of Charleston two centuries before. If John Stuart, whom George III in 1763 appointed superintendent of Indian affairs for the South, could have returned in 1948 to seek his home, he would have found it at 106 Tradd Street, just where he built it in 1772—for a brief occupancy, as it happened, since the Revolution ejected him, as a Tory, rather speedily from his new house.

Not that Charleston had not changed from time to time in its own way. It had changed, but generally only by some mysterious process of adaptation that kept it still Charleston. Some might argue that this was all accident— might say that it was due to Charleston's unfavorable position as a seaport, or that kind of thing. But there must have been, surely, a strong element of deliberate choice in Charleston's process of adaptation to the new. As a seaport city, Charleston was necessarily an entrepreneur that had to give a great deal of consideration to its material concerns. In process of looking after its material concerns, if it had chosen to do so, Charleston at any time could have wrecked its Georgian houses, torn down its enclosed yards, junked its handsome iron gates, and gone in for Victorian gingerbread, bungalows, imitation Greek revival, imitation English cottage types, functional architecture, or whatever might happen along. But it had not done so. Eighteenth-century Charleston had made just enough concessions to take advantage of the more desirable modern improvements. No more. And there it was. Among older American cities only its neighbor, Savannah in Georgia, approached that condition.

The secret of Charleston's stability, if it was any secret, was only the old Southern principle that material considerations, however important, are means not ends, and should always be subdued to the ends they are supposed to serve, should never be allowed to dominate, never be mistaken for ends in themselves. If they are mistaken for ends, they dominate everthing, and then you get instability. You get the average modern city, you get New York and Detroit, you get industrial civilization, world wars, Marxist communism, the New Deal.

Historians, noting that the ante-bellum South was in a sense materialistic, in that it found ways of prospering from the sale of cotton and tobacco, and relied heavily upon slave labor, have had the problem of explaining why that same South developed a chivalrous, courteous, religious, conservative, and stable society quite different from that which obtained in the also materialistic, but more industrialized, rational, idealistic, progressive North. Frequently they have explained the paradox of Southern society by saying that the "aristocratic" planter was somehow able to dominate the coarser, more acquisitive elements of Southern life and, through some mysterious exercise of prestige, to persuade these elements to accept his "code" of chivalry, courtesy, religion, conservatism. But the historians have mistaken effect for cause. The planter's "aristocratic" leadership was the result, not the cause, of a general diffusion of standards of judgment that all the South, even the Negro slaves, accepted as a basic principle of life. Mr. Francis Butler Simkins, in his book *The South Old and New*, has taken securer ground than the average historian when he notes that the South at the outbreak of the Civil War was almost the only truly religious society left in the Western world.

That old, religious South set the good life above any material means to life and consistently preferred the kind of material concerns that would least interfere with and best contribute to the good life. Its preferred occupations were agriculture, law, the church, and politics—pursuits which develop the whole man rather than the specialist, the free-willed individual rather than the anonymous unit of the organized mass. It had other preferences which, like those named, represented the metaphysical choices of a traditional society. Books could be, and have been, and ought still to be written about these metaphysical choices; but with reference to material means of existence, such as money, one could clinch the discourse by pointing out the traditional attitude of the Southern Negro toward work and wages. If you paid the Negro twice the normal wage for a day's work, you did not get more work from him— that is to say, more devotion to work within a given period, with increased production as the result. Not at all. The Negro simply and ingenuously worked only *half* as many days or hours as before—and spent the rest of the time in following his conception of the good life: in hunting, dancing, singing, social conversation, eating, religion, and love. This well-known habit of the Negro's, disconcerting to employers and statisticians, was absolutely correct according to Southern principles. The Negro, so far as he had not been corrupted into heresy by modern education, was the most traditional of Southerners, the mirror which faithfully and lovingly reflected the traits that Southerners once all but unanimously professed.

That had been the idea in Charleston too. It was what Mr. Simkins in his book, perhaps being misled by his historical predecessors, had called the "country gentleman" idea. But Charleston, which had always been urban, always a town or a city of counting-houses, warehouses, factors, bankers, financial agents, and the like, was not a city of country gentlemen, exactly. It had agreed with the country gentlemen and with others of every sort, including the Negro, on letting the relationship between work, wages, and life be determined by the metaphysical judgment indicated above. That was what made Charleston Charleston and not "The Indigo City" or something of the kind.

But now here were the drum majorettes, representing North Charleston.

Perhaps they were, after all, the most formidable invaders that Charleston ever had to face.

What is a drum majorette? The word is not in my copy of *Webster's Collegiate Dictionary*.

A drum major, however, can easily be defined. A drum major is the leader of a band of music. Not its leader in a musical sense, not its musical director. The drum major is the leader of the band for the purposes of marching and parading while band music is being played. As such he fills a utilitarian as well as an ornamental role. He marches in front and center of the band as it marches and plays, and with his baton he marks the time and signals for the marching evolutions like "column right," "column left," "countermarch," "halt," "forward, march." His baton is not a mere foolish ornament; it is an instrument of direction. Formerly the drum majors of military and quasi-military bands were always as tall as could be obtained, no doubt because drum majors might be better seen and followed as they wielded their batons. Tradition also prescribed that they should be of tremendously military aspect, however ornately uniformed; and severity and precision, rather than drollery, were the essential thing. But, since a band of music is itself a kind of flourish, a gallant addition to the busines of systemized killing and being killed, the drum major was permitted his individual flourishes even in strictly military bands. He could exhibit a certain amount of skill at twirling and tossing his baton if he did not abuse his official military capacity in doing so.

Now a drum majorette is or ought to be a female drum major. It must be allowed that such a role *can* be undertaken by a girl or woman, provided the drum majorette performs the useful as well as the ornamental duties of a drum major. It would be supposed that a drum majorette would be uniformed like the members of the band.

When a drum majorette is not so uniformed, is in fact largely without clothes, a new element has entered, and it is time to ask what is happening. When a band is led not by one but by a squad of drum majorettes, all equipped with batons and all equally unclad, you know exactly what is happening. The real function and use of the drum major have been ignored in favor of an exciting display which has nothing to do with music or marching or ceremony. An occasion has been exploited for purposes that will not bear examination. The drum major has turned into a follies girl, a bathing beauty, a strip-tease dancer. The baton, once used to give commands to the band, becomes the ornament by which the drum majorette attracts attention to her charms. The band, less and less important, gets along the best it can and becomes, in fact, a jazz orchestra accompanying the drum majorette dance.

To put it in other terms, the modern regime has performed one of the abstractions typical of its sway. It has abstracted the spectacular and ornamental features of the drum major from his complete role, and made that abstraction dominant to the point of extinction of all other features. The next logical step would be to abandon the band and to substitute a sound-truck playing phonograph records—a sound-truck which could be preceded by and followed by and covered with a large company of drum majorettes, all twirling batons, all as little clothed as the censor would allow.

The abstraction is so alluring that even college presidents, to say nothing of the public, do not perceive its meaning, which is as completely immoral and ruthless as can be. But it is not the bare flesh of drum majorettes in their quasi-march—really a dance—that is per se immoral. It is the misuse of the ceremony of gallantry, implied in all march music, that is immoral in itself and that is symptomatic of a deeper immorality. Drum majorettes came into style, I believe, in high schools and colleges that had become addicted to professionalized athletics of the modern kind. The old amateur athletics, particularly football, was an exhibition of valor that once naturally deserved the kind of encouragement supplied by band music, especially martial band music. The new athletics systematically exploits the gallantry of youth for purposes confessedly material. It has put the schools and colleges in the business of commercial entertainment. The drum majorettes are an advertisement of that entertainment, a lure to the admission gate.

Communities that accept such perversions of the beautiful and the gallant are no longer communities in any true sense. They have passed into a state of disequilibrium and social instability that makes them extremely dangerous. If they do not know what use ought to be made of beauty and gallantry and, still worse, do not care what use is made of these so long as impressive material results are obtained, there is nothing to stop them from perverting and using as an instrument of power anything that can be so perverted and used. They are mobs, made vastly more dangerous than the ordinary spontaneous mob because, though spiritually mobs, they retain the rational organization supplied to them by science and education, and can thus use chaos itself as a form of power. The mob leaders always excuse the mob acts, of course, by proclaiming wondrous distant goals some day to be attained. Their proclamations are to be found in such documents as the Communist Manifesto, the Atlantic Charter, and the reports of the President's committees on education, civil rights, and the like. But always, inevitably, these mob leaders and mobs are so preoccupied with and dominated by the abstractions they create as means to an end that they never reach or even approximate the distant goal. They merely exert the power derived from the original abstraction, which becomes an end in itself.

The terrible results of this process are visible throughout the world. Everywhere one looks there are ruins—the ruins of societies no less than the ruins of cities. Over the ruins stream mobs led by creatures no longer really human—creatures who, whether they make shift to pass as educators, planners, editors, commissars, or presidents, wield batons, dance dances, and flaunt their naked abstractions with exactly the same inappropriateness and destructiveness as does the drum majorette.

Is Charleston gulled by the drum majorette and her parallels? I have no way of knowing. But things move very rapidly in our time, and doubtless we shall soon know the event. If any agent of abstraction rolls over and possesses Old Charleston, then something will be gone that money could not buy and that money can never restore, either through private philanthropy or Federal subsidy. And if Charleston should perish, strong and subtle in resistance though it has been in the past, can other communities which with varying success have fought the same fight continue to stand? All face the same foe, and the foe is stronger, is pressing harder than ever.

WHAT MUST BE DEVELOPED?
James McAuley

James McAuley (1917–1977), Australian poet, critic, and social thinker, was the editor of the periodical *Quadrant*, published by the Australian Congress for Cultural Freedom. The development of mind and spirit, McAuley contends, is far more important than the programs of economic change for "underdeveloped countries" popular after the Second World War. "What Must Be Developed?" is from McAuley's collection *The End of Modernity: Essays on Literature, Art, and Culture* (Sydney, 1959), pp. 22–29.

Pascal said that all the generations of men should be regarded as one man, growing up through the course of history. Yet in the past the human race could be seen as forming an actual unity only from the highest and the lowest standpoints, that is, theologically and biologically. From the intermediate standpoint of social existence there was not one human body with a common life and history, but many communities more or less sealed off from one another within different civilizational areas, each with its own principles of order and its own history. The most that could be claimed was a certain *family likeness* between these cultures, an analogical unity. For instance, they were all "traditional" cultures, centred upon a particular sacred doctrine; and between these traditional doctrines analogies could, within limits, be discerned.

Only in modern times has it become possible to envisage the formation of a world community in which mankind will have a common history. One can now imagine the building of a world house, whose inhabitants will doubtless occupy different suites of rooms with different aspects, but will nevertheless participate in a common life, within an inclusive economic, legal, political and intellectual structure. Failing this, the modern nations, lacking "the tranquillity of order," may come close to destroying civilized life by the violence of modern warfare.

This possibility of creating an ecumenical order has come about because modern Western civilization, diverging from that analogical unity or family resemblance of the traditional civilizations, developed in a novel and anomalous way, until it could truly say, in the words of one of its culture-heroes, J. J. Rousseau at the beginning of his *Confessions:* "I am not as others I have seen.... If I am not of higher worth, at least I am different." Features that were absent from other civilizations, or present only as subordinate, undeveloped and to some extent heretical tendencies became in the West dominant themes. These features were: commercialization and industrialization; empirical science and technology; anti-metaphysical scepticism and an activist mentality; secularism and nationalism. Whether these features hang necessarily together, as inseparable aspects of a single movement, or whether their connections are to some extent rather historical and accidental, is an arguable question; but they do in fact appear as a complex which can be called Western modernism and which is the most revolutionary force the world has seen. It is this Western modernism that has raised the possibility of achieving an inclusive world order. Its devoted adherents are convinced that it has not only raised the possibility but also offers the means, practical and theoretical, of actualizing it. Others, however, are very uneasy on this score, or even convinced that along the line of modernist progress lies not a new order but catastrophe.

During the first century of triumphant progressivism, 1750 to 1850, reforming zeal was centred upon political change. In the non-Western world this intense expectation of benefits from political change was prolonged by the existence of colonial regimes, which evoked a militant colonial nationalism. In the second century of triumphant modernism, 1850 to 1950, hopes were more and more centred upon economic change, and this phase has now hit the non-Western countries with full force in the form of great expectations from development programmes for "underdeveloped" areas. (Is a third phase now beginning, in which hopes will be focused above all on cultural change—ideological adaptation—as the clue to progress? It may be so.) The expectations being encouraged are rather extreme. Are millions in poverty? Development brings welfare. Are some territories still politically dependent? Development creates the conditions for independence. Is there social unrest and the threat of revolution? Development allays discontent. Are democratic liberties desired? Development promotes democracy. Is peace threatened by inequalities between nations? Convert have-nots into haves by development. These are exceedingly perilous generalizations, which few informed minds would accept without great reservations, but they form the present climate of popular opinion on the subject. Thus the Institute of Ethnic Affairs in its *Newsletter* hailed President Truman's enunciation of Point Four as a promise that: "human resources, technical and spiritual, now in the main latent within the 1,600,000,000 non-industrial people, will emerge into a world-wide springtime. A new World's Great Age will have begun."

This enraptured prophecy assumes that in the already industrialized parts of the world not only the technical but also the spiritual resources of the population are enjoying a springtime efflorescence, towards which the unindustrialized civilizations might gladly aspire; and that industrialization is precisely the means whereby these latent spiritual resources are liberated. But the truth is that a terrible price is exacted for development along the lines of

Western modernism. It is necessary to insist on this in spite of the fact that whoever insists on it is at once accused of indifference to the physical wretchedness of millions of people who need food, housing, clothing, hygiene, medicine and other basic necessities.

The result of Western modernism is regularly a psychic bewilderment and impoverishment, which literacy, schooling and training do not prevent but may rather increase. Corresponding to "the reign of quantity" inaugurated by economic development is a loss of quality. Life loses its metaphysical support, its meaningful pattern, its inwardness. The world of industrial progress is a world of disinherited beings, cut off from the deepest sources of human satisfaction, restless and jangled, driven by unstilled cravings through a course of life without meaning or direction. Ritual and art and symbolism no longer feed such lives. Women become estranged from their own natures and lead disoriented existences. Work is drained of its normal interest and satisfaction; leisure is given over not to recreation but to commercialized distraction. Elton Mayo found that the logic of industrial production gives rise to a "sense of human defeat," and "an experience of personal futility." The indices for personal disorganization show how closely the rise of industrial civilization is correlated with suicide, mental illness, psychosomatic disorders, criminality, drug addiction. "For the individual," says Robert Lynd, "it is a pattern of extreme complexity, contradictoriness and insecurity." "The life of man," says Werner Sombart, "has become meaningless. Cut off from transcendental relations, man recoils upon himself, seeks the realization of his ideas within himself, and finds it not."

Personal disorganization and deprivation occur within the context of a disintegrating society. Discord and instability reach far into family life, the bonds of neighbourhood and community decay, social controls are weakened.

The unanimity about fundamentals which characterizes a traditional society gives way to a chaos of irreconcilable conceptions and deceptions concerning the nature of man and society, the proper ends and means to be adopted. The more society loses it organic cohesion and spontaneous self-discipline, the greater the need for the application of external and mechanical forms of organization which dispose the rootless masses into categories according to the needs of production and administration under the sign of some openly or covertly materialist ideology. Thus totalitarianism lurks as the nemesis of triumphant industrialism. The masses become a prey to visions of an earthly paradise, and these visions are used as the means of imposing some kind of order on what Durkheim called the *anomie* of modern society. Yet that totalitarian order is deceptive and self-defeating, since its methods still further weaken all genuine communal bonds.

"Greater production," said President Truman, outlining his Point Four, "is the key to prosperity and peace." Alas, Aristotle knew better: "The fact is that the greatest crimes are caused by excess and not by necessity." The era of greatest production has been the most bloody, violent, disordered, hysterical and tormented era that mankind has endured. "No half-century," said Mr. Justice Jackson at the Nuremberg trials, "has ever witnessed such slaughter on such a scale, such cruelties, such annihilations, such wholesale deportations and annihilations of minorities." Just as the loss of any metaphysical orientation has deprived modernized individuals and societies of principles of order, so it has rendered impossible an international order based on law and justice. The contending nationalisms of the modern world thresh about in a nihilistic darkness, armed with the weapons of total destruction, mouthing debased slogans and imbecilic passwords.

And what if, after all, the programme of development for underdeveloped territories fails to create the economic prosperity demanded? There is no place for dogmatic affirmations or denials on this score, since the relevant factors are shifting and uncertain and only partly understood. It is true that development of the Western type has raised levels of material existence in some communities. It is not certain how successful it will be in other communities. I do not wish to develop the doubts that occur on this point, but amongst them must be reckoned three considerations. Firstly, nations poorly endowed with natural resources cannot expect to achieve the results obtained by nations in more favourable circumstances. Secondly, even if it prove possible to raise the level of material well-being to some extent, a *relative poverty* may be created because desires are increased faster than means of satisfying them, and the greater prosperity of more favoured peoples becomes a source of dissatisfaction. Thirdly, it seems possible, on the example of Communist countries, to increase production and thus increase national power, without raising the real income levels of the mass of the people. Under certain circumstances the result of world economic development might be a vast industrial slum.

In spite, however, of these gloomy perspectives, there still remains the hope that somehow modern techniques can be successfully applied to the task of giving all men the physical means for a decent existence, and that somehow this can be done without such unfavourable consequences in the sphere of individual and social and political life as will nullify the progress made. Development, of some sort, is a moral necessity. What then must be developed?

My contention is that there must be concurrent development of the intellectual resources of mankind if we are to have any hope of achieving forms of commerce and industry, and institutions of national and international life, which are durable and tolerable.

The first need is to overcome the conscious or unconscious anti-intellectualism that lies at the base of much thinking about progress and development. It is an illusion to think that economic means will suffice to solve problems that transcend the economic sphere, such as the problems of personal welfare, social harmony or international peace. Economic change is in itself an unsettling influence and needs to be guided and contained by supra-economic considerations. There is no substitute, if we want principles of order, for intellectual truth as a basis of agreement. Unless we can establish rational ends as the principles of common action we are left with the blind concurrences and oppositions of feeling and interest from which nothing stable, nothing fit for humans, can be built. It is the loss of intellectuality that is the self-defeating feature of Western modernism. This may sound paradoxical, for Westernism is notable for its concentration on certain kinds of cerebral activity, namely the specialized pursuit of empirical science, technology, and social studies, and is often accused of being over-cerebral; yet it has lost the light of metaphysical and theological truth and rational philosophy. Towards the resources possessed by Aristotle and St. Thomas in the West, or Sankara and Ramanuja and others in the East the modern attitude is one of ignorance if not spiteful animosity. It seems to be regarded as a qualification for social scientists who study the traditions of other cultures to have an opinionated ignorance in respect of their own. Positivism has broken down the framework within which the sciences are properly ordered and excludes from the sphere of verifiable truth every question concerning the meaning of existence, questions for which intelligible answers must nevertheless be found if government, authority, and social life are not to be handed over to the play of irrational forces. Confidence in the ability of the mind to attain rational truth has been seriously impaired, and with it the capacity for intellectual contemplation.

It will not do to use the fact that at the metaphysical

and religious level a number of irreconcilable doctrines are in existence as a reason for abandoning the field and seeking unity where it is quite impossible to find it, namely, at the level of material interests or of sentiment. I am far from suggesting that the oppositions between different metaphysical and religious traditions are unreal or in any way reducible to unity. Such procedures falsify the situation and stultify inquiry. For the present, there is a need, not for any sort of syncretism or equivalentism, but for the loyal development from within of the wealth of these different traditions, a development which will proceed all the more effectively in the light of a real knowledge of and respect for other traditions. In this way it may be found that, pending the complete prevalence of a single truth which all desire, a degree of practical unity can be achieved, sufficient for effective common work on the principles of international law, of economic life, of human rights, and other pressing problems. This practical unity may be at best partial and precarious, since it represents the approximate convergence in limited fields of very different world-views. But to seek practical unity along the lines of positivism and activism by disregarding the claims of intellectual truth is not a practical policy at all but a counsel of despair.

THE PLANSTER'S VISION
Sir John Betjeman

Zealous in the cause of architectural preservation in England, Sir John Betjeman (1906–   ) has enjoyed a success as a comic poet scarcely equalled since Victorian days. With occasional successes, he has been a leader in resistance to bad town-and-country planning in Britain. "The Planster's

Vision" (from *John Betjeman's Collected Poems*, London, 1958, p. 128) illustrates his attachment to a society with old roots.

Cut down that timber! Bells, too many and strong,
   Pouring their music through the branches bare,
   From moon-white church-towers down the windy air
Have pealed the centuries out with Evensong.
Remove those cottages, a huddled throng!
   Too many babies have been born in there,
   Too many coffins, bumping down the stair,
Carried the old their garden paths along.

I have a Vision of The Future, chum,
   The workers' flats in fields of soya beans
      Tower up like silver pencils, score on score:
And Surging Millions hear the Challenge come
   From microphones in communal canteens
      "No Right! No Wrong! All's perfect, evermore."

Part Fifteen

WOMEN'S CONSERVATIVE VISION

George Bernard Shaw's *Intelligent Woman's Guide to Socialism and Capitalism* notwithstanding, in all ages women generally have exerted a power socially conservative. In the era following the Second World War, several remarkable women of letters sensitively employed their conservative imagination. Here are three of them: Freya Stark (1893–   ); Phyllis McGinley (1905–1978); and Jacquetta Hawkes (Mrs. J. B. Priestley) (1910–   ).

CHOICE AND TOLERATION
Freya Stark

Famous traveler and serious historian, Freya Stark is
one of the most moving of twentieth-century writers.
"Choice and Toleration" reminds us of the perils latent in what Burke (an advocate of religious toleration) called "a licentious toleration." This essay is
taken from her collection *Perseus in the Wind* (London, 1948), pp. 143–49.

The man who weeds is usually looked upon as innocent,
mild and harmless, an avoider of complexity, a lover of
peace, to whom the gentleness of nature opens when the
soil is moist and yielding and neither powdered with
drought nor sodden with rain. On such days, when the
sun finds woolly leaves that hold dew in shady corners,
the traveling bees and thin flies with strait-laced figures,
and beetles with hard metal business wings, and butter-
flies uncertain of their way come wandering through the
garden, each with an idea of his own as to what the defect
may be that divides the weeds and flowers. The true gar-
dener then brushes over the ground with slow and gentle
hand, to liberate a space for breath round some favorite;
but he is not thinking about destruction except inciden-
tally. It is only the amateur like myself who becomes obsessed and rejoices with a sadistic pleasure in weeds that
are big and bad enough to pull, and at last, almost forgetting the flowers altogether, turns into a Reformer.

Reformers are tiresome people, but what is one to do?

Tolerance, too, makes the home unfit to live in. My god-
father used to say that an Englishman considers himself
broad-minded only when he is upholding convictions the
opposite of his own. I remember one such during the war.
He was a colonel commanding a camp for Italian internees
in whom I was interested: our friends among the prisoners
were browbeaten by the Fascists, flogged when they read
the newspaper provided by us at great expense, and forced
to sing the Mussolini hymn at mealtimes: the Colonel left
them to it, refusing to interfere, on the ground that "Fascists, too, must be allowed to be patriotic."

The most disastrous scene of tolerance I have witnessed
was not an affair of human beings at all, but a drama of the
mineral and vegetable worlds, a war between trees and
ruins in the deserted city of Mandu. Here, in central
India, on a wooded ridge like a moraine that overhangs the
endless plain, one of those small and swift Muhammedan
dynasties of Mogul times sprang up and died: and before
it did so, built stone memorials of its gaiety and beauty
that still survive, lovely and derelict islands, among the
glades of the jungle.

We drove up here one day, when the hot weather had
already begun and the rain bird had uttered its yelling
brainless cry; when the leaves of trees drooped through
noon over the fainting fields. In the Arab summer there is,
as it were, a mineral endurance: strength withdraws itself
into the veins of the rocks and secret chasms of water, and
leaves no vulnerable surface open to the sun. But in these
parklands of central India the strong soil wrestles with the
heat and holds it in its arms and drinks it in, and lies vanquished as in a lassitude of love, transfused, and alive in its
stillness. And the dawn, transparent as a seashell washed
up on the wet sand, finds no quick response—as it does in
Arabia, flushing upon the brows of naked cliffs—but
spreads its pageant remote in the wide sky, above the
quiet unresponsive trees. The grey monkeys wake and
slide from wayside branches into the warming dust, and

flocks of green parrots fly to forage in the fields. Here, as
the light strengthens, the sun cuts its way with sudden
crescents and bright scimitars into the well-spaced avenues that line the Indian roads; and swiftly, as into an
open sea, we push out to the fullness of the day.

A Hindu village had lingered on beside the deserted
halls of Mandu, and was celebrating its annual fair. Carts
filled with bright *saris*, and women's gay talkative faces,
and a tumult of anklets and bangles and heavy black coiled
hair, creaked and swayed up the ridge, drawn by dust-
colored oxen, nonchalant and slow, on whose backs lay the
branching shadows of the jungle. Towards walls hidden
and overgrown and a crumbling gate that pierced them,
thin-legged countrymen were climbing by a stone-flagged
way. To them Mandu is but a village of the numberless
villages that appear monotonous in central India as stationary waves upon a sea. Beside its palace walls they un-
harnessed their cattle and tilted their booths and stretched
their crazy awnings against the sun, and laid out the various grains and nuts of their fields and spicy cooked things
wrapped in leaves, and colored pedlars' wares. They
bathed in the tank whose springs no doubt decided the
choice of this height for the building of the city in its day.
The women's secluded harems in the palaces are now
ruined and forgotten: men and women splashed in the
same water, cool and green in the shadow of the masonry;
the wet *saris* clung to slim bodies, dusky as ripe grapes;
the young girls wrung out their smoothly parted hair and
coiled it up again, and slipped the new dress for the feast
out of its cotton wrapping and donned it at the water's
edge. They played there, gay and vivid as dragonflies in
the shortness of their day; and when the sun began to etch
the branches of the trees, the carts were loaded and departed down the slanting road that cuts the jungle.

Then the modern life shrank back into its hovels and
small fields, and rested in apparent peace under the evening light, while around it a siege continued uninter-

rupted and unobserved—the slow eating of the ruins by the trees.

They have already swallowed the undistinguished quarters of the city; their glades have covered the traces of streets and squares. The mosque stands, with smooth walls, and aisles on rough-hewn piers, one of the noblest mosques in India: and so do the royal tombs built square on platforms. The shorn water palace dreams between its artificial sheets of water, whose stone edges the forest has broken down. Here flying steps, unbanistered, soar up to terraces and jutting windows and pagodas—volatile thoughts chiseled and made safe, as they hoped, in stone. All this is preserved and stands, though, even here, the forest roots have buckled the courtyard paving stones, and it is but a truce. The city must once have been extended widely on its height: its walls on the jungle slopes are made visible by the high crowns of the trees they feed. And the tombs of its forgotten inhabitants, square and dome-surmounted Mogul tombs, are spread a great way down the road as one descends.

Many have already sunk into heaps, sucked shapeless by the roots in which they are entwined; some fissured and lopsided, carry whole trees fattened and relentless into the sunlight. The random seeds that were harbored and throve on the lime of the masonry, and pushed their threadlike fingers unresisted into cracks of stone or rubble, have now become monsters with swollen necks that feed on these defeated pieties of men; and the unrecognizable mounds, the cracked and blistered plaster, the fragments of ornament and marble show every step in the long stairway whose beginning is tolerance and whose end is decay.

Tolerance cannot afford to have anything to do with the fallacy that evil may convert itself to good.

In the dark central crisis of his life Shakespeare came to realize that goodness cannot *convert*. This is the secret, I believe, of his greatest plays. In *King Lear*, the Duke of Albany declares to Goneril that "wisdom and goodness to the vile seem vile." The New Testament does likewise. The seed that falls on stony ground must die, and there is never a hope for the goats (though it seems a pity that sheep are chosen as emblems of the virtuous). To call upon sinners is different; they are mixed, and the best in us answers: for goodness is loved at sight. If evil could *see*, it would cease. But evil is by its nature incapable of sight, and unable to understand what goodness is; and the whole art of corruption therefore begins by training the victims to be *incapable of comprehending good.* "The heart's division divideth. . . ." The simply virtuous are unaware of division, and their unawareness—a state of rubble and plaster like the tombs of Mandu—is the stuff of tragedy: it causes an exasperation, an encouragement, an excitement of evil.

This happens over and over again in Shakespeare's tragedies. The goodness, the generosity, the innocence of Prospero, Cordelia, Troilus, Duncan, Desdemona are the door by which all horror enters. In *King Lear,* a justification is given to Nemesis by the old man's foibles: it is carefully contradicted by the character of Gloucester, who has no other reason for prominence in the play, who suffers equally with his king, and for such slight offense. In *Timon of Athens* the problem is crudely shown and our sense of proportion revolts, perhaps because even now we are not as inured to injustice as was the Tudor world: but the play is one of the most interesting because, so nakedly presented, it has probably preserved the first form in which it held the poet's thoughts. The theme, often repeated, must have been strongly present in the author's mind.

Where the idea of conversion does not exist, virtue is regarded as a state of detachment. It is strong as a tower is strong, in a defensive way, secure on its foundations, but static, and not mobile for attack. It triumphs at last, because it is unassailable in itself, a shelter and a bulwark for its adherents. It minds its own business, and toleration, in the sense only of non-interference, follows as a matter of course.

Conversion is recognized to be impossible in advertisement or war, where mistakes are either visible or deadly: no business firm or commanding general would think to succeed by concentrating on the shoddiness of others rather than on the excellence of his own. But in preaching and in propaganda, we still think to convert, and this fallacy makes us either wholeheartedly interfering or modestly ashamed, and anyway robs us of warmth and passion, making a dowdiness of our idea of good.

The true secret of persuasiveness is that it *never* converts: it speaks to its own only, and discovers to them the unexpected secrets of their hearts.

For seven years, during the war and after, I was engaged in one way or another in the art of persuasion, which I would call propaganda if that unfortunate word were not doomed to swing with opposite meanings between Herr Goebbels and St. Paul. In all that time we never troubled about what our adversaries said, but stuck to our own story, which was good enough.

Our Ministry, we hoped, felt apostolic too, but was surprisingly apologetic towards its own gospels, and reluctant to prod the lions in its path with anything sharp enough for a lion to mind. There was an assumption that efficient propaganda is indecent; only bungling could make it excusable.

How different is this from the gift of tongues—how timid and how base. The right way if we have something to say is to say it plainly—not for conversion, but for such as may be waiting for our voice.

From their high Olympus, as the last of their gifts, the Gods gave free will to man, and with it laid upon him the burden of choice, and made everything in all his worlds depend on the choice that he made. Out of the humility of his choice is his tolerance born: for he sees his brothers taking paths different from his own, and finds it hard to think himself better than they: until in his perplexity he comes to surmise that there may be freedom only, and never a choice at all. This is the very wilderness of toleration.

Let him choose for himself with such care that he may not fear to give his reasons, but be ready, like some honest countryman, to point out a direction to those who wish to travel in the region that he knows: and then he will find himself in a company larger than he had ever thought, of such as like the roughness and adventure of his way. And let this be his tolerance, that he knows those who travel by other paths to be out of hearing, and that the variety of choice was infinite at the start: therefore he will not trouble them to join him, but out of his confidence in his own way will cast his eye over the open landscape and watch their progress, with a detached and friendly and interested mind: and not call it tolerance to be afraid of his own choice, or afraid to give the reasons of its making, but let his humility lie rather in remembering how hard in its time it was to make. And if he is inclined to missionary undertakings, let him remember that his knowledge of the country is useful only to those who wish to travel in his path.

THE ANGRY MAN
Phyllis McGinley

The author of several volumes of comic verse, an amusing book about saints, and the essays of *The Province of the Heart*, the wise Mrs. McGinley here examines another aspect of professed toleration. This poem is in *The Love Letters of Phyllis McGinley* (New York, 1954), p. 114.

The other day I chanced to meet
An angry man upon the street—
A man of wrath, a man of war,
A man who truculently bore
Over his shoulder, like a lance,
A banner labeled "Tolerance."

And when I asked him why he strode
Thus scowling down the human road,
Scowling, he answered, "I am he
Who champions total liberty—
Intolerance being, ma'am, a state
No tolerant man can tolerate.

"When I meet rogues," he cried, "who choose
To cherish oppositional views,
Lady, like this, and in this manner,
I lay about me with my banner
Till they cry mercy, ma'am." His blows
Rained proudly on prospective foes.

Fearful, I turned and left him there
Still muttering, as he thrashed the air,
"Let the Intolerant beware!"

THE WOODPECKERS AND THE STARLINGS
Jacquetta Hawkes

Jacquetta Hawkes, archeologist, supplied the theme, "A Land," for the Festival of Britain after the Second World War. In this short parable of hers the reader will not find it difficult to recognize what George Orwell called "the naked democracy of the public swimming-baths" in post-war Britain. This recent specimen of what Burke called "the wardrobe of a moral imagination" is from her *Fables* (London, 1953), pp. 58–65.

The pair of woodpeckers were easily the most splendid birds in the Plantation. In spring and summer their green plumage glinted with brassy lights, setting off to perfection the crimson crowns which were their proud insignia. No other birds in the island, except the kingfishers, had these tropical, metallic feathers; when the sun's rays struck them they glowed and flashed as though the yaffles carried rubies on their brows.

The other birds took pride in this princely pair; in particular the garrulous nuthatches, who had been talking ceaselessly ever since they told Sigurd of the Treasure of the Volsungs, regarded themselves as the retainers of the larger birds whose habits and tastes their own resembled. Even the wrens liked to have them in the Plantation, though often when the yaffles flew laughing back into the wood, the cock would whizz from an ivy-covered stump and pour out more abuse than it seemed possible for his morsel of body to contain.

As for the nightingales, they were confident enough of their infinitely superior genius to feel an untroubled appreciation of the yaffles. Returning from the South where they had seen flamingoes, bee-eaters, hoopoes and many other birds far more powerful, handsome or brilliant, these musicians moving softly among the thorn trees enjoyed the bold eye and arrogant carriage of the head, the showy plumage and even the strange harsh voices of the natural lords of the Plantation. When the male bird sang among the hawthorn blossom, whose pale flowers answered the addresses of the moon, he was conscious of the crimson crowns now somewhere muted in the darkness, and added his thought of them, as he would have added a moss frond to his nest, to the shape of the song which he built in the spaces of the night.

All the birds admired the woodpeckers not only for their appearance and lordly ways, but also for their unique skill as carpenters. It was a commonplace ability to be deft in the weaving of twigs, moss, horsehair or cobwebs, even if it were performed with the virtuosity of the long-tailed tits, but it was a mark of extraordinary strength and cunning to be able to carve a shapely chamber in the heart of branch or trunk. By what means nature could at once instil the idea of carving such a chamber and slowly strengthen the bill to enable it to perform the operation, no evolutionist has been able to explain. But the thing had happened; with mathematical precision the yaffles could drive a circular hole through bark and outer skin, hollow a smooth cupola above it, and then drive downwards to make an oval cyst with a couch of wood chips to receive the eggs.

The first year they came to the Plantation the season had been already far advanced, and the woodpeckers had taken over an old, long-abandoned nesting-hole, cleaned out the cobwebs, made a small meal of the insect population, and succeeded in rearing a brood of four. Now, however, they were dissatisfied with this unworthy nest and resolved to cut a new one. The cock knew that some of his kind, ageing or decadent birds, were ready to work in rotten wood even though it inevitably resulted in a damp chamber and a ragged, unsightly hole. He would not imitate them; being at the height of his powers he decided to select the hardest wood which it was possible for any woodpecker to penetrate. He found an oak which, while it was outwardly quite sound, returned a note to his tapping that proved it to be slightly decayed at the core. The hen approved his choice and they began their exacting task.

For several days the Plantation echoed with their hammering, while a drift of chippings formed against the roots of the oak. When the work was finished all the birds rejoiced with the woodpeckers; blackbirds, warblers and finches, as well as the faithful nuthatches, flew beside them as an escort when they went to the largest and most populous anthill and there celebrated the end of their labour by devouring thousands of the piquant insects which swarmed on to their probing tongues. The nightingales did not join in this flight, but the cock sang one of his daylight songs, perched below the canopy of a young hazel leaf and with his eyes fixed on the perfectly round hole in the trunk above him.

It was while the hen woodpecker, now grown as serious and dedicated as a nun, was daily laying an egg on the sweet-smelling chips of her nest, that the starlings began to visit the Plantation. They came from the direction where a housing-estate for humans was spreading out from a small industrial town. At first a single pair, then three or four pairs together with a riff-raff of unmated birds roosted in the line of elms bordering the road. They were sleek and shiny as though wearing brilliantine, and they were always chattering together and imitating other birds or the noises they heard when picking up scraps round the human houses. One of them had accurately mastered the whistle made by local youths at the sight of smartly dressed young women. The woodpeckers ignored the newcomers, but they were aware that this particularly odious bird kept his loudest whistle for the occasions when they were flying past.

Their clutch was complete, and both the yaffles were as delighted and proud as the simplest minded chiff-chaff. Each of them in turn looked in through the hole to enjoy the white eggs gleaming dully in the gloom, faintly touched by such light as could make its way round their peering heads. Again the Plantation birds shared in the woodpeckers' satisfaction; surely now all was auspicious for their own nesting.

That same day when the cock passed their old nest he noticed straw sticking out of the hole and a dirty apron of droppings below it. Alighting on a nearby branch, he could hear an unpleasant din coming from inside and then, in response to his own angry cries, the squawking ceased, there was a scuffle and a dark head appeared in the opening. It was a starling. This bird looked into the fierce yellow eye of the woodpecker and made obsequious noises in his throat while at the same time uttering some shrill calls. Just as the woodpecker was about to launch himself at the intruder and split open his papery skull, a little flock of starlings arrived and settled on twigs and branches all round the hole. They chattered, squawked and stuck out their upper breast feathers in the fashion peculiar to starlings. Filled with disgust the great bird judged he could not engage in a dispute with such a rabble, and flew away feeling both scorn and humiliation. Admittedly he did not need the old nest and the starlings were acutely short of accommodation. Nevertheless, it was a defeat—a defeat by force of numbers.

Day after day the hen brooded the eggs, sitting in the narrow cell with her long tail folded above her head, while her mate, grown humble in the presence of maternity, fed her through the hole. When at last in place of the smooth convexities of the eggs she felt squirming soft bodies pressing through her breast-feathers her vigil was over and her hardest work about to begin. From soon after the hour of the dawn chorus until the owls began to call, the woodpeckers were the slaves of their young, whose funnel-mouths supplied insatiable bellies. On all their food-hunting journeys they avoided the distasteful spectacle of their old nest, but they did not suspect further aggression even though occasionally they noticed a starling or two hanging about near their oak.

The cock bird was weary and bored by the ceaseless hunt for food, by the monotonous to-and-fro; his plumage and his sacred crown were growing dull from too much toil. How could the other birds be strengthened and inspired by his presence if he allowed himself to become dowdy and jaded? It was his duty to rest. He lingered for hours at the most appetizing of the anthills, shaking out and combing his feathers, feasting, and assuring himself that the sun was renewing the fire of his crown.

The hen too was tired; the vigil in the dark chamber had been a strain, and since their young hatched she had worked even harder than her mate. Searching for insects in a plantation of firs, she found the sun hot, the air resinous and soothing; after one or two journeys she settled herself on a comfortable branch. There she was lulled into a daydream, imagining the splendid future possible for their fledgelings (their quills were sprouting already) and rehearsing scenes in which she saved them from hawks by her bravery and cunning. The pine cones popped like passing minutes, but she did not count them.

The cock and the hen returned almost simultaneously to the Plantation, which by now had lapsed into the disillusioned melancholy of a summer afternoon. It was not peaceful, however. Both blackbirds from the nest in the hedge were flying up and down uttering their distraught ejaculations, the wrens were consuming themselves with angry song, and the whole wood sounded with the urgent speech of the nuthatches. With their heavy, looping flight the woodpeckers converged on their nest.

At their approach two starlings squeezed their heads out of the hole; a score of unmated loafers from the housing-estate stationed on neighbouring branches raised their usual hostile din. Scattered over the moss-grown roots of the oak were the bodies of the five fledgelings, their hopeful feathers showing through the down as ugly black stumps. One, lying apart from the rest, had been partly eaten and the flies were already massing. All five of the beaks, whose gaping greed seemed now so dear, were open in death.

The cock woodpecker hurled himself at the two silly heads in the opening, split one open instantly with his bill, and killed the second bird after a moment's struggle inside the hole. Meanwhile the other starlings gathered round outside, determined to mob him as he came out. There was pandemonium. The blackbirds and wrens were still shrieking and swearing, several woodpigeons dropped from the treetops clapping their wings, the nuthatches fearlessly attacked the starlings and found unexpected support from a pair of passing jackdaws hopeful of carrion. The hen bird did nothing but leap up and down in agony on a branch, alternately driving in and retracting her claws and uttering grotesque cries.

With the diversion made by the nuthatches and jackdaws the cock escaped and joined his mate, and the two great birds flew away together, their flight rising and falling in mournful unison. Their laughter, which sometimes had been mocking, sometimes triumphant, now, as it sounded through the wood for the last time, was harsh and despairing. Yet the clever whistling lout sent after them a shrill imitation of their cry. The bloody bodies of the dead marauders now lay with those of the young woodpeckers, and three other pairs of starlings, egged on by the loafers, were fighting for the hole.

It cannot be said that anything was at once outwardly changed by the going of the woodpeckers, yet the other birds were aware of some lessening of enjoyment in their affairs, some sense of a falling apart of the life of the Plantation. The nuthatches, the most deeply affected, plastered more mud round their hole for security and early fell silent. Even the starlings were annoyed when they realized that there was now nobody left who could make holes for their occupation. To justify themselves they babbled about equality and the evils of privilege. 'What was there, after all, in the least remarkable in the yaffles? They were large, and had bright feathers and red heads and a good deal of self-importance, all the rest was your imagination.'

'Of course it was,' replied the nightingale, 'that was the whole point.' And he sang his last lament, for the next season he and his mate did not return to the Plantation.

Part Sixteen

THE WISDOM OF OUR ANCESTORS

By the 1960s, the renewal of conservative thought could not be ignored in either America or Britain. By the 1970s, this resurrection of immemorial consensus that G. K. Chesterton called "the democracy of the dead" began to affect elections and public policies occasionally. Among the renewers were Michael Oakeshott (1901–   ), of the London School of Economics, and Malcolm Muggeridge (1903–   ), the century's most entertaining and mordant journalist.

ON BEING CONSERVATIVE
Michael Oakeshott

Succeeding to the chair at the London School of Economics previously occupied by the socialist Harold Laski, Michael Oakeshott has taught politics to the turbulent rising generation. His writings are few but persuasive. This essay in definition is taken from his *Rationalism in Politics and Other Essays* (New York, 1962), pp. 168–96.

The common belief that it is impossible (or, if not impossible, then so unpromising as to be not worth while attempting) to elicit explanatory general principles from what is recognized to be conservative conduct is not one that I share. It may be true that conservative conduct does not readily provoke articulation in the idiom of general ideas, and that consequently there has been a certain reluctance to undertake this kind of elucidation; but it is not to be presumed that conservative conduct is less eligible than any other for this sort of interpretation, for what it is worth. Nevertheless, this is not the enterprise I propose to engage in here. My theme is not a creed or a doctrine, but a disposition. To be conservative is to be disposed to think and behave in certain manners; it is to prefer certain kinds of conduct and certain conditions of human circumstances to others; it is to be disposed to make certain kinds of choices. And my design here is to construe this disposition as it appears in contemporary character, rather than to transpose it into the idiom of general principles.

The general characteristics of this disposition are not difficult to discern, although they have often been mistaken. They centre upon a propensity to use and to enjoy what is available rather than to wish for or to look for something else; to delight in what is present rather than what was or what may be. Reflection may bring to light an appropriate gratefulness for what is available, and consequently the acknowledgment of a gift or an inheritance from the past; but there is no mere idolizing of what is past and gone. What is esteemed is the present; and it is esteemed not on account of its connections with a remote antiquity, nor because it is recognized to be more admirable than any possible alternative, but on account of its familiarity: not, *Verweile doch, du bist so schön,*[1] but, *Stay with me because I am attached to you.*

If the present is arid, offering little or nothing to be used or enjoyed, then this inclination will be weak or absent; if the present is remarkably unsettled, it will display itself in a search for a firmer foothold and consequently in a recourse to and an exploration of the past; but it asserts itself characteristically when there is much to be enjoyed, and it will be strongest when this is combined with evident risk of loss. In short, it is a disposition appropriate to a man who is acutely aware of having something to lose which he has learned to care for; a man in some degree rich in opportunities for enjoyment, but not so rich that he can afford to be indifferent to loss. It will appear more naturally in the old than in the young, not because the old are more sensitive to loss but because they are apt to be more fully aware of the resources of their world and therefore less likely to find them inadequate. In some people this disposition is weak merely because they are ignorant of what their world has to offer them: the present appears to them only as a residue of inopportunities.

---

1. "Stay with me, you are so beautiful." (Goethe, *Faust,* Part I, 1700.) [R.K.]

To be conservative, then, is to prefer the familiar to the unknown, to prefer the tried to the untried, fact to mystery, the actual to the possible, the limited to the unbounded, the near to the distant, the sufficient to the superabundant, the convenient to the perfect, present laughter to utopian bliss. Familiar relationships and loyalties will be preferred to the allure of more profitable attachments; to acquire and to enlarge will be less important than to keep, to cultivate and to enjoy; the grief of loss will be more acute than the excitement of novelty or promise. It is to be equal to one's own fortune, to live at the level of one's own means, to be content with the want of greater perfection which belongs alike to oneself and one's circumstances. With some people this is itself a choice; in others it is a disposition which appears, frequently or less frequently, in their preferences and aversions, and is not itself chosen or specifically cultivated.

Now, all this is represented in a certain attitude towards change and innovation; change denoting alterations we have to suffer and innovation those we design and execute.

Changes are circumstances to which we have to accommodate ourselves, and the disposition to be conservative is both the emblem of our difficulty in doing so and our resort in the attempts we make to do so. Changes are without effect only upon those who notice nothing, who are ignorant of what they possess and apathetic to their circumstances; and they can be welcomed indiscriminately only by those who esteem nothing, whose attachments are fleeting and who are strangers to love and affection. The conservative disposition provokes neither of these conditions: the inclination to enjoy what is present and available is the opposite of ignorance and apathy and it breeds attachment and affection. Consequently, it is averse from change, which appears always, in the first place, as deprivation. A storm which sweeps away a copse and transforms a favourite view, the death of friends, the sleep of friendship, the desuetude of customs of behaviour, the retirement of a favourite clown, involuntary exile, reversals of fortune, the loss of abilities enjoyed and their replacement by others—these are changes, none perhaps without its compensations, which the man of conservative temperament unavoidably regrets. But he has difficulty in reconciling himself to them, not because what he has lost in them was intrinsically better than any alternative might have been or was incapable of improvement, nor because what takes its place is inherently incapable of being enjoyed, but because what he has lost was something he actually enjoyed and had learned how to enjoy and what takes its place is something to which he has acquired no attachment. Consequently, he will find small and slow changes more tolerable than large and sudden; and he will value highly every appearance of continuity. Some changes, indeed, will present no difficulty; but, again, this is not because they are manifest improvements but merely because they are easily assimilated: the changes of the seasons are mediated by their recurrence and the growing up of children by its continuousness. And, in general, he will accommodate himself more readily to changes which do not offend expectation than to the destruction of what seems to have no ground of dissolution within itself.

Moreover, to be conservative is not merely to be averse from change (which may be an idiosyncrasy); it is also a manner of accommodating ourselves to changes, an activity imposed upon all men. For, change is a threat to identity, and every change is an emblem of extinction. But a man's identity (or that of a community) is nothing more than an unbroken rehearsal of contingencies, each at the mercy of circumstance and each significant in proportion to its familiarity. It is not a fortress into which we may retire, and the only means we have of defending it (that is, ourselves) against the hostile forces of change is in the open field of our experience; by throwing our weight upon the foot which for the time being is most firmly placed, by cleaving to whatever familiarities are not immediately threatened and thus assimilating what is new without becoming unrecognizable to ourselves. The Masai, when they were moved from their old country to the present Masai reserve in Kenya, took with them the names of their hills and plains and rivers and gave them to the hills and plains and rivers of the new country. And it is by some such subterfuge of conservatism that every man or people compelled to suffer a notable change avoids the shame of extinction.

Changes, then, have to be suffered; and a man of conservative temperament (that is, one strongly disposed to preserve his identity) cannot be indifferent to them. In the main, he judges them by the disturbance they entail and, like everyone else, deploys his resources to meet them. The idea of innovation, on the other hand, is improvement. Nevertheless, a man of this temperament will not himself be an ardent innovator. In the first place, he is not inclined to think that nothing is happening unless great changes are afoot and therefore he is not worried by the absence of innovation: the use and enjoyment of things as they are occupies most of his attention. Further, he is aware that not all innovation is, in fact, improvement; and he will think that to innovate without improving is either designed or inadvertent folly. Moreover, even when an innovation commends itself as a convincing improvement, he will look twice at its claims before accepting them. From his point of view, because every improvement involves change, the disruption entailed has always to be set against the benefit anticipated. But when he has satisfied himself about this, there will be other considerations to be taken into the account. Innovating is always an equivocal enterprise, in which gain and loss (even excluding the loss of familiarity) are so closely interwoven that it is exceedingly difficult to forecast the final up-shot: there is no such thing as an unqualified improvement. For, innovating is an activity which generates not only the 'improvement' sought, but a new and complex situation of which this is only one of the components. The total change is always more extensive than the change designed; and the whole of what is entailed can neither be foreseen nor circumscribed. Thus, whenever there is innovation there is the certainty that the change will be greater than was intended, that there will be loss as well as gain and that the loss and the gain will not be equally distributed among the people affected; there is the chance that the benefits derived will be greater than those which were designed; and there is the risk that they will be off-set by changes for the worse.

From all this the man of conservative temperament draws some appropriate conclusions. First, innovation entails certain loss and possible gain, therefore, the onus of proof, to show that the proposed change may be expected to be on the whole beneficial, rests with the would-be innovator. Secondly, he believes that the more closely an innovation resembles growth (that is, the more clearly it is intimated in and not merely imposed upon the situation) the less likely it is to result in a preponderance of loss. Thirdly, he thinks that an innovation which is a response to some specific defect, one designed to redress some specific disequilibrium, is more desirable than one which springs from a notion of a generally improved condition of human circumstances, and is far more desirable than one generated by a vision of perfection. Consequently, he prefers small and limited innovations to large and indefinite. Fourthly, he favours a slow rather than a rapid pace, and pauses to observe current consequences and make appropriate adjustments. And lastly, he believes the occasion to be important; and, other things being equal, he considers the most favourable occasion for innovation to be when the projected change is most likely to be limited to what is intended and least likely to be corrupted by undesired and unmanageable consequences.

The disposition to be conservative is, then, warm and positive in respect of enjoyment, and correspondingly cool and critical in respect of change and innovation: these two inclinations support and elucidate one another. The man of conservative temperament believes that a known good is not lightly to be surrendered for an unknown better. He is not in love with what is dangerous and difficult; he is unadventurous; he has no impulse to sail uncharted seas; for him there is no magic in being lost, bewildered or shipwrecked. If he is forced to navigate the unknown, he sees virtue in heaving the lead every inch of the way. What others plausibly identify as timidity, he recognizes in himself as rational prudence; what others interpret as inactivity, he recognizes as a disposition to enjoy rather than to exploit. He is cautious, and he is disposed to indicate his assent or dissent, not in absolute, but in graduated terms. He eyes the situation in terms of its propensity to disrupt the familiarity of the features of his world.

It is commonly believed that this conservative disposition is pretty deeply rooted in what is called 'human nature.' Change is tiring, innovation calls for effort, and human beings (it is said) are more apt to be lazy than energetic. If they have found a not unsatisfactory way of getting along in the world, they are not disposed to go looking for trouble. They are naturally apprehensive of the unknown and prefer safety to danger. They are reluctant innovators, and they accept change not because they like it but (as Rochefoucauld says they accept death) because it is inescapable. Change generates sadness rather than exhilaration: heaven is the dream of a changeless no less than of a perfect world. Of course, those who read 'human nature' in this way agree that this disposition does not stand alone; they merely contend that it is an exceedingly strong, perhaps the strongest, of human propensities. And, so far as it goes, there is something to be said for this belief: human circumstances would certainly be very different from what they are if there were not a large ingredient of conservatism in human preferences. Primitive peoples are said to cling to what is familiar and to be averse from change; ancient myth is full of warnings against innovation; our folklore and proverbial wisdom about the conduct of life abounds in conservative precepts; and how many tears are shed by children in their unwilling accommodation to change. Indeed, wherever a firm identity has been achieved, and wherever identity is felt to be precariously balanced, a conservative disposition is likely to prevail. On the other hand, the disposition of adolescence is often predominantly adventurous and experimental: when we are young, nothing seems more desirable than to take a chance; *pas de risque, pas de plaisir*. And while some peoples, over long stretches of time, appear successfully to have avoided change, the history of others displays periods of intense and intrepid innovation. There is, indeed, not much profit to be had from general speculation about 'human nature,' which is no steadier than anything else in our acquaintance. What is more to the point is to consider current human nature, to consider ourselves.

With us, I think, the disposition to be conservative is far from being notably strong. Indeed, if he were to judge by our conduct during the last five centuries or so, an unprejudiced stranger might plausibly suppose us to be in love with change, to have an appetite only for innovation and to be either so out of sympathy with ourselves or so careless of our identity as not to be disposed to give it any consideration. In general, the fascination of what is new is felt far more keenly than the comfort of what is familiar. We are disposed to think that nothing important is happening unless great innovations are afoot, and that what is not being improved must be deteriorating. There is a positive prejudice in favour of the yet untried. We readily presume that all change is, somehow, for the better, and we are easily persuaded that all the consequences of our innovating activity are either themselves improvements or at least a reasonable price to pay for getting what we want. While the conservative, if he were forced to gamble, would bet on the field, we are disposed to back our individual fancies with little calculation and no apprehension of loss. We are acquisitive to the point of greed; ready to drop the bone we have for its reflection magnified in the mirror of the future. Nothing is made to outlast probable improvement in a world where everything is undergoing incessant improvement: the expectation of life of everything except human beings themselves continuously declines. Pieties are fleeting, loyalties evanescent, and the pace of change warns us against too deep attachments. We are willing to try anything once, regardless of the consequences. One activity vies with another in being 'up-to-date': discarded motor-cars and television sets have their counterparts in discarded moral and religious beliefs: the eye is ever on the new model. To see is to imagine what might be in the place of what is; to touch is to transform. Whatever the shape or quality of the world, it is not for as long as we want it. And those in the van of movement infect those behind with their energy and enterprise. *Omnes eodem cogemur:* when we are no longer light-footed we find a place for ourselves in the band.[2]

Of course, our character has other ingredients besides this lust for change (we are not devoid of the impulse to cherish and preserve), but there can be little doubt about its pre-eminence. And, in these circumstances, it seems appropriate that a conservative disposition should appear, not as an intelligible (or even plausible) alternative to our mainly 'progressive' habit of mind, but either as an unfortunate hindrance to the movement afoot, or as the custodian of the museum in which quaint examples of superseded achievement are preserved for children to gape at, and as the guardian of what from time to time is con-

---

2. 'Which of us,' asks a contemporary (not without some equivocation), 'would not settle, at whatever cost in nervous anxiety, for a febrile and creative rather than a static society?'

sidered not yet ripe for destruction, which we call (ironically enough) the amenities of life.

Here our account of the disposition to be conservative and its current fortunes might be expected to end, with the man in whom this disposition is strong last seen swimming against the tide, disregarded not because what he has to say is necessarily false but because it has become irrelevant; outmanoeuvred, not on account of any intrinsic demerit but merely by the flow of circumstance; a faded, timid, nostalgic character, provoking pity as an outcast and contempt as a reactionary. Nevertheless, I think there is something more to be said. Even in these circumstances, when a conservative disposition in respect of things in general is unmistakably at a discount, there are occasions when this disposition remains not only appropriate, but supremely so; and there are connections in which we are unavoidably disposed in a conservative direction.

In the first place, there is a certain kind of activity (not yet extinct) which can be engaged in only in virtue of a disposition to be conservative, namely, activities where what is sought is present enjoyment and not a profit, a reward, a prize or a result in addition to the experience itself. And when these activities are recognized as the emblems of this disposition, to be conservative is disclosed, not as prejudiced hostility to a 'progressive' attitude capable of embracing the whole range of human conduct, but as a disposition exclusively appropriate in a large and significant field of human activity. And the man in whom this disposition is pre-eminent appears as one who prefers to engage in activities where to be conservative is uniquely appropriate, and not as a man inclined to impose his conservatism indiscriminately upon all human activity. In short, if we find ourselves (as most of us do) inclined to reject conservatism as a disposition appropriate in respect of human conduct in general, there still remains a certain kind of human conduct for which this disposition is not merely appropriate but a necessary condition.

There are, of course, numerous human relationships in which a disposition to be conservative, a disposition merely to enjoy what they offer for its own sake, is not particularly appropriate: master and servant, owner and bailiff, buyer and seller, principal and agent. In these, each participant seeks some service or some recompense for service. A customer who finds a shopkeeper unable to supply his wants either persuades him to enlarge his stock or goes elsewhere; and a shopkeeper unable to meet the desires of a customer tries to impose upon him others which he can satisfy. A principal ill-served by his agent, looks for another. A servant ill-recompensed for his service, asks for a rise; and one dissatisfied with his conditions of work, seeks a change. In short, these are all relationships in which some result is sought; each party is concerned with the ability of the other to provide it. If what is sought is lacking, it is to be expected that the relationship will lapse or be terminated. To be conservative in such relationships, to enjoy what is present and available regardless of its failure to satisfy any want and merely because it has struck our fancy and become familiar, is conduct which discloses a *jusqu'auboutiste*[3] conservatism, an irrational inclination to refuse all relationships which call for the exercise of any other disposition. Though even these relationships seem to lack something appropriate to them when they are confined to a nexus of supply and demand and allow no room for the intrusion of the loyalties and attachments which spring from familiarity.

But there are relationships of another kind in which no result is sought and which are engaged in for their own sake and enjoyed for what they are and not for what they provide. This is so of friendship. Here, attachment springs from an intimation of familiarity and subsists in a mutual sharing of personalities. To go on changing one's butcher until one gets the meat one likes, to go on educating one's

---

3. Diehard. [R.K.]

agent until he does what is required of him, is conduct not inappropriate to the relationship concerned; but to discard friends because they do not behave as we expected and refuse to be educated to our requirements is the conduct of a man who has altogether mistaken the character of friendship. Friends are not concerned with what might be made of one another, but only with the enjoyment of one another; and the condition of this enjoyment is a ready acceptance of what is and the absence of any desire to change or to improve. A friend is not somebody one trusts to behave in a certain manner, who supplies certain wants, who has certain useful abilities, who possesses certain merely agreeable qualities, or who holds certain acceptable opinions; he is somebody who engages the imagination, who excites contemplation, who provokes interest, sympathy, delight and loyalty simply on account of the relationship entered into. One friend cannot replace another; there is all the difference in the world between the death of a friend and the retirement of one's tailor from business. The relationship of friend to friend is dramatic, not utilitarian; the tie is one of familiarity, not usefulness; the disposition engaged is conservative, not 'progressive'. And what is true of friendship is not less true of other experiences—of patriotism, for example, and of conversation—each of which demands a conservative disposition as a condition of its enjoyment.

But further, there are activities, not involving human relationships, that may be engaged in, not for a prize, but for the enjoyment they generate, and for which the only appropriate disposition is the disposition to be conservative. Consider fishing. If your project is merely to catch fish it would be foolish to be unduly conservative. You will seek out the best tackle, you will discard practices which prove unsuccessful, you will not be bound by unprofitable attachments to particular localities, pieties will be fleeting, loyalties evanescent; you may even be wise to try anything once in hope of improvement. But fishing is an activity that may be engaged in, not for the profit of a catch, but for its own sake; and the fisherman may return home in the evening not less content for being empty-handed. Where this is so, the activity has become a ritual and a conservative disposition is appropriate. Why worry about the best gear if you do not care whether or not you make a catch? What matters is the enjoyment of exercising skill (or, perhaps, merely passing the time),[4] and this is to be had with any tackle, so long as it is familiar and is not grotesquely inappropriate.

All activities, then, where what is sought is enjoyment springing, not from the success of the enterprise but from the familiarity of the engagement, are emblems of the disposition to be conservative. And there are many of them. Fox placed gambling among them when he said that it gave two supreme pleasures, the pleasure of winning and the pleasure of losing. Indeed, I can think of only one activity of this kind which seems to call for a disposition other than conservative: the love of fashion, that is, wanton delight in change for its own sake no matter what it generates.

But, besides the not inconsiderable class of activities which we can engage in only in virtue of a disposition to be conservative, there are occasions in the conduct of other activities when this is the most appropriate disposition; indeed there are few activities which do not, at some point or other, make a call upon it. Whenever stability is more profitable than improvement, whenever certainty is more valuable than speculation, whenever familiarity is more desirable than perfection, whenever agreed error is

---

4. When Prince Wen Wang was on a tour of inspection in Tsang, he saw an old man fishing. But his fishing was not real fishing, for he did not fish in order to catch fish, but to amuse himself. So Wen Wang wished to employ him in the administration of government, but he feared his own ministers, uncles and brothers might object. On the other hand, if he let the old man go, he could not bear to think of the people being deprived of his influence. *Chuang Tzu.*

superior to controversial truth, whenever the disease is
more sufferable than the cure, whenever the satisfaction of
expectations is more important that the 'justice' of the expectations themselves, whenever a rule of some sort is
better than the risk of having no rule at all, a disposition to
be conservative will be more appropriate than any other;
and on any reading of human conduct these cover a not
negligible range of circumstances. Those who see the man
of conservative disposition (even in what is vulgarly
called a 'progressive' society) as a lonely swimmer bat-
tling against the overwhelming current of circumstance
must be thought to have adjusted their binoculars to exclude a large field of human occasion.

In most activities not engaged in for their own sake a
distinction appears, at a certain level of observation, between the project undertaken and the means employed,
between the enterprise and the tools used for its achievement. This is not, of course, an absolute distinction; projects are often provoked and governed by the tools
available, and on rarer occasions the tools are designed to
fit a particular project. And what on one occasion is a
project, on another is a tool. Moreover there is at least one
significant exception: the activity of being a poet. It is,
however, a relative distinction of some usefulness because
it calls our attention to an appropriate difference of attitude towards the two components of the situation.

In general, it may be said that our disposition in respect
of tools is appropriately more conservative than our attitude towards projects; or, in other words, tools are less
subject to innovation than projects because, except on rare
occasions, tools are not designed to fit a particular project
and then thrown aside, they are designed to fit a whole
class of projects. And this is intelligible because most tools
call for skill in use and skill is inseparable from practice
and familiarity: a skilled man, whether he is a sailor, a
cook or an accountant, is a man familiar with a certain
stock of tools. Indeed, a carpenter is usually more skilful

in handling his own tools than in handling other examples of the kind of tools commonly used by carpenters; and the solicitor can use his own (annotated) copy of Pollock on *Partnership* or Jarman on *Wills* more readily than any other. Familiarity is the essence of tool using; and in so far as man is a tool using animal he is disposed to be conservative.

Many of the tools in common use have remained unchanged for generations; the design of others has undergone considerable modification; and our stock of tools is always being enlarged by new inventions and improved by new designs. Kitchens, factories, workshops, building sites and offices disclose a characteristic mixture of long-tried and newly invented equuipment. But, be that how it may, when business of any kind is afoot, when a particular project has been engaged in—whether it is baking a pie or shoeing a horse, floating a loan or a company, selling fish or insurance to a customer, building a ship or a suit of clothes, sowing wheat or lifting potatoes, laying down port or putting up a barrage—we recognize it to be an occasion when it is particularly appropriate to be conservative about the tools we employ. If it is a large project, we put it in charge of a man who has the requisite knowledge, and we expect him to engage subordinates who know their own business and are skilled in the use of certain stocks of tools. At some point in this hierarchy of tool-users the suggestion may be made that in order to do this particular job an addition or modification is required in the available stock of tools. Such a suggestion is likely to come from somewhere about the middle of the hierarchy: we do not expect a designer to say 'I must go away and do some fundamental research which will take me five years before I can go on with the job' (his bag of tools is a body of knowledge and we expect him to have it handy and to know his way about it); and we do not expect the man at the bottom to have a stock of tools inadequate for the needs of his particular part. But even if such a suggestion is made and is followed up, it will not disrupt the appropriateness of a conservative disposition in respect of the whole stock of tools being used. Indeed, it is clear enough that no job would ever get done, no piece of business could ever be transacted if, on the occasion, our disposition in respect of our tools were not, generally speaking, conservative. And since doing business of one sort or another occupies most of our time and little can be done without tools of some kind, the disposition to be conservative occupies an unavoidably large place in our character.

The carpenter comes to do a job, perhaps one the exact like of which he has never before tackled; but he comes with his bag of familiar tools and his only chance of doing the job lies in the skill with which he uses what he has at his disposal. When the plumber goes to fetch his tools he would be away even longer than is usually the case if his purpose were to invent new or to improve old ones. Nobody questions the value of money in the market place. No business would ever get done if, before a pound of cheese were weighed or a pint of beer drawn, the relative usefulness of these particular scales of weight and measurement as compared with others were threshed out. The surgeon does not pause in the middle of an operation to redesign his instruments. The MCC does not authorize a new width of bat, a new weight of ball or a new length of wicket in the middle of a Test Match, or even in the middle of a cricket season. When your house is on fire you do not get in touch with a fire-prevention research station to design a new appliance; as Disraeli pointed out, unless you are a lunatic, you send for the parish fire-engine. A musician may improvise music, but he would think himself hardly done-by if, at the same time, he were expected to improvise an instrument. Indeed, when a particularly tricky job is to be done, the workman will often prefer to use a tool that he is thoroughly familiar with rather than another he has in his bag, of new design, but which he has not yet mastered the use of. No doubt there is a time and a place to be radical about such things, for promoting innovation and carrying out improvements in the tools we employ, but these are clearly occasions for the exercise of a conservative disposition.

Now, what is true about tools in general, as distinct from projects, is even more obviously true about a certain kind to tool in common use, namely, general rules of conduct. If the familiarity that springs from relative immunity from change is appropriate to hammers and pincers and to bats and balls, it is supremely appropriate, for example, to an office routine. Routines, no doubt, are susceptible of improvement; but the more familiar they become, the more useful they are. Not to have a conservative disposition in respect of a routine is obvious folly. Of course, exceptional occasions occur which may call for a dispensation; but an inclination to be conservative rather than reformist about a routine is unquestionably appropriate. Consider the conduct of a public meeting, the rules of debate in the House of Commons or the procedure of a court of law. The chief virtue of these arrangements is that they are fixed and familiar; they establish and satisfy certain expectations, they allow to be said in a convenient order whatever is relevant, they prevent extraneous collisions and they conserve human energy. They are typical tools—instruments eligible for use in a variety of different but similar jobs. They are the product of reflection and choice, there is nothing sacrosanct about them, they are susceptible of change and improvement; but if our disposition in respect of them were not, generally speaking conservative, if we were disposed to argue about them and change them on every occasion, they would rapidly lose their value. And while there may be rare occasions when it is useful to suspend them, it is pre-eminently appropriate that they should not be innovated upon or improved while they are in operation. Or again, consider the rules of a game. These, also, are the product of reflection and choice, and there are occasions when it is appropriate to reconsider them in the light of current experience; but it is inappropriate to have anything but a conservative disposition towards them or to consider putting them all together at one time into the melting-pot; and it is supremely inappropriate to change or improve upon them in the heat and confusion of play. Indeed, the more eager each side is to win, the more valuable is an inflexible set of rules. Players in the course of play may devise new tactics, they may improvise new methods of attack and defence, they may do anything they choose to defeat the expectations of their opponents, except invent new rules. That is an activity to be indulged sparingly and then only in the off-season.

There is much more that might be said about the relevance of the disposition to be conservative and its appropriateness even in a character, such as ours, chiefly disposed in the opposite direction. I have said nothing of morals, nothing of religion; but perhaps I have said enough to show that, even if to be conservative on all occasions and in all connections is so remote from our habit of thought as to be almost unintelligible, there are, nevertheless, few of our activities which do not on all occasions call into partnership a disposition to be conservative and on some occasions recognize it as the senior partner; and there are some activities where it is properly master.

How, then, are we to construe the disposition to be conservative in respect of politics? And in making this inquiry what I am interested in is not merely the intelligibility of this disposition in any set of circumstances, but its intelligibility in our own contemporary circumstances.

Writers who have considered this question commonly direct our attention to beliefs about the world in general, about human beings in general, about associations in general and even about the universe; and they tell us that a conservative disposition in politics can be correctly construed only when we understand it as a reflection of certain beliefs of these kinds. It is said, for example, that conservatism in politics is the appropriate counterpart of a generally conservative disposition in respect of human conduct: to be reformist in business, in morals or in religion and to be conservative in politics is represented as being inconsistent. It is said that the conservative in politics is so by virtue of holding certain religious beliefs; a belief, for example, in a natural law to be gathered from human experience, and in a providential order reflecting a divine purpose in nature and in human history to which it is the duty of mankind to conform its conduct and departure from which spells injustice and calamity. Further, it is said that a disposition to be conservative in politics reflects what is called an 'organic' theory of human society; that it is tied up with a belief in the absolute value of human personality, and with a belief in a primordial propensity of human beings to sin. And the 'conservatism' of an Englishman has even been connected with Royalism and Anglicanism.

Now, setting aside the minor complaints one might be moved to make about this account of the situation, it seems to me to suffer from one large defect. It is true that many of these beliefs have been held by people disposed to be conservative in political activity, and it may be true that these people have also believed their disposition to be in some way confirmed by them, or even to be founded upon them; but, as I understand it, a disposition to be conservative in politics does not entail either that we should hold these beliefs to be true or even that we should suppose them to be true. Indeed, I do not think it is necessarily connected with any particular beliefs about the universe, about the world in general or about human conduct in general. What it is tied to is certain beliefs about the activity of governing and the instruments of government, and it is in terms of beliefs on these topics, and not on others, that it can be made to appear intelligible. And, to state my view briefly before elaborating it, what makes a conservative disposition in politics intelligible is nothing to do with a natural law or a providential order, nothing to do with morals or religion; it is the observation of our current manner of living combined with the belief (which from our point of view need be regarded as no more than an hypothesis) that governing is a specific and limited activity, namely the provision and custody of general rules of conduct, which are understood, not as plans for imposing substantive activities, but as instruments enabling people to pursue the activities of their own choice with the minimum frustration, and therefore something which it is appropriate to be conservative about.

Let us begin at what I believe to be the proper starting-place; not in the empyrean, but with ourselves as we have come to be. I and my neighbours, my associates, my compatriots, my friends, my enemies and those who I am indifferent about, are people engaged in a great variety of activities. We are apt to entertain a multiplicity of opinions on every conceivable subject and are disposed to change these beliefs as we grow tired of them or as they prove unserviceable. Each of us is pursuing a course of his own; and there is no project so unlikely that somebody will not be found to engage in it, no enterprise so foolish that somebody will not undertake it. There are those who spend their lives trying to sell copies of the Anglican Catechism to the Jews. And one half of the world is engaged in trying to make the other half want what it has hitherto never felt the lack of. We are all inclined to be passionate about our own concerns, whether it is making things or selling them, whether it is business or sport, religion or learning, poetry, drink or drugs. Each of us has preferences of his own. For some, the opportunities of making choices (which are numerous) are invitations readily accepted; others welcome them less eagerly or even find them burdensome. Some dream dreams of new and better worlds: others are more inclined to move in familiar paths or even to be idle. Some are apt to deplore the rapidity of change, others delight in it; all recognize it. At times we grow tired and fall asleep: it is a blessed relief to gaze in a shop window and see nothing we want; we are grateful for ugliness merely because it repels attention. But, for the most part, we pursue happiness by seeking the satisfaction of desires which spring from one another inexhaustably. We enter into relationships of interest and of emotion, of competition, partnership, guardianship, love, friendship, jealousy and hatred, some of which are more durable than others. We make agreements with one another; we have expectations about one another's conduct; we approve, we are indifferent and we disapprove. This multiplicity of activity and variety of opinion is apt to produce collisions: we pursue courses which cut across those of others, and we do not all approve the same sort of conduct. But, in the main, we get along with one another, sometimes by giving way, sometimes by standing fast, sometimes in a compromise. Our conduct consists of activity assimilated to that of others in small, and for the most part unconsidered and unobtrusive, adjustments.

Why all this should be so, does not matter. It is not necessarily so. A different condition of human circumstance can easily be imagined, and we know that elsewhere and at other times activity is, or has been, far less multifarious and changeful and opinion far less diverse and far less likely to provoke collision; but, by and large, we recognize this to be our condition. It is an acquired condition, though nobody designed or specifically chose it in preference to all others. It is the product, not of 'human nature' let loose, but of human beings impelled by an acquired love of making choices for themselves. And we know as little and as much about where it is leading us as we know about the fashion in hats of twenty years' time or the design of motor-cars.

Surveying the scene, some people are provoked by the

absence of order and coherence which appears to them to be its dominant feature; its wastefulness, its frustration, its dissipation of human energy, its lack not merely of a pre-meditated destination but even of any discernible direction of movement. It provides an excitement similar to that of a stock-car race; but it has none of the satisfaction of a well-conducted business enterprise. Such people are apt to exaggerate the current disorder; the absence of plan is so conspicuous that the small adjustments, and even the more massive arrangements, which restrain the chaos seem to them nugatory; they have no feeling for the warmth of untidiness but only for its inconvenience. But what is significant is not the limitations of their powers of observation, but the turn of their thoughts. They feel that there ought to be something that ought to be done to con-vert this so-called chaos into order, for this is no way for rational human beings to be spending their lives. Like Apollo when he saw Daphne with her hair hung carelessly about her neck, they sigh and say to themselves: 'What if it were properly arranged.' Moreover, they tell us that they have seen in a dream the glorious, collisionless man-ner of living proper to all mankind, and this dream they understand as their warrant for seeking to remove the di-versities and occasions of conflict which distinguish our current manner of living. Of course, their dreams are not all exactly alike; but they have this in common: each is a vision of a condition of human circumstance from which the occasion of conflict has been removed, a vision of human activity co-ordinated and set going in a single di-rection and of every resource being used to the full. And such people appropriately understand the office of govern-ment to be the imposition upon its subjects of the condi-tion of human circumstances of their dream. To govern is to turn a private dream into a public and compulsory manner of living. Thus, politics becomes an encounter of dreams and the activity in which government is held to this understanding of its office and provided with the appropriate instruments.

I do not propose to criticize this jump to glory style of politics in which governing is understood as a perpetual take-over bid for the purchase of the resources of human energy in order to concentrate them in a single direction; it is not at all unintelligible, and there is much in our circumstances to provoke it. My purpose is merely to point out that there is another quite different understanding of government, and that it is no less intelligible and in some respects perhaps more appropriate to our circumstances.

The spring of this other disposition in respect of governing and the instruments of government—a conservative disposition—is to be found in the acceptance of the current condition of human circumstances as I have described it: the propensity to make our own choices and to find happiness in doing so, the variety of enterprises each pursued with passion, the diversity of beliefs each held with the conviction of its exclusive truth; the inventiveness, the changefulness and the absence of any large design; the excess, the over-activity and the informal compromise. And the office of government is not to impose other beliefs and activities upon its subjects, not to tutor or to educate them, not to make them better or happier in another way, not to direct them, to galvanize them into action, to lead them or to coordinate their activities so that no occasion of conflict shall occur; the office of government is merely to rule. This is a specific and limited activity, easily corrupted when it is combined with any other, and, in the circumstances, indispensable. The image of the ruler is the umpire whose business is to administer the rules of the game, or the chairman who governs the debate according to known rules but does not himself participate in it.

Now people of this disposition commonly defend their belief that the proper attitude of government towards the current condition of human circumstance is one of acceptance by appealing to certain general ideas. They contend that there is absolute value in the free play of human choice, that private property (the emblem of choice) is a natural right, that it is only in the enjoyment of diversity of opinion and activity that true belief and good conduct can be expected to disclose themselves. But I do not think that this disposition requires these or any similar beliefs in order to make it intelligible. Something much smaller and less pretentious will do: the observation that this condition of human circumstance is, in fact, current, and that we have learned to enjoy it and how to manage it; that we are not children *in statu pupillari* but adults who do not consider themselves under any obligation to justify their preference for making their own choices; and that it is beyond human experience to suppose that those who rule are endowed with a superior wisdom which discloses to them a better range of beliefs and activities and which gives them authority to impose upon their subjects a quite different manner of life. In short, if the man of this disposition is asked: Why ought governments to accept the current diversity of opinion and activity in preference to imposing upon their subjects a dream of their own? it is enough for him to reply: Why not? Their dreams are no different from those of anyone else; and if it is boring to have to listen to dreams of others being recounted, it is insufferable to be forced to re-enact them. We tolerate monomaniacs, it is our habit to do so; but why should we be *ruled* by them? Is it not (the man of conservative disposition asks) an intelligible task for a government to protect its subjects against the nuisance of those who spend their energy and their wealth in the service of some pet indignation, endeavouring to impose it upon everybody, not by suppressing their activities in favour of others of a similar kind, but by setting a limit to the amount of noise anyone may emit?

Nevertheless, if this acceptance is the spring of the conservative's disposition in respect of government, he does not suppose that the office of government is to do nothing. As he understands it, there is work to be done which can be done only in virtue of a genuine acceptance of current beliefs simply because they are current and current activities simply because they are afoot. And, briefly, the office he attributes to government is to resolve some of the collisions which this variety of beliefs and activities generates; to preserve peace, not by placing an interdict upon choice and upon the diversity that springs from the exercise of preference, not by imposing substantive uniformity, but by enforcing general rules of procedure upon all subjects alike.

Government, then, as the conservative in this matter understands it, does not begin with a vision of another, different and better world, but with the observation of the self-government practised even by men of passion in the conduct of their enterprises; it begins in the informal adjustment of interests to one another which are designed to release those who are apt to collide from the mutual frustration of a collision. Sometimes these adjustments are no more than agreements between two parties to keep out of each other's way; sometimes they are of wider application and more durable character, such as the International Rules for the prevention of collisions at sea. In short, the intimations of government are to be found in ritual, not in religion or philosophy; in the enjoyment of orderly and peaceable behaviour, not in the search for truth or perfection.

But the self-government of men of passionate belief and enterprise is apt to break down when it is most needed. It often suffices to resolve minor collisions of interest, but beyond these it is not to be relied upon. A more precise and a less easily corrupted ritual is required to resolve the massive collisions which our manner of living is apt to generate and to release us from the massive frustrations in which we are apt to become locked. The custodian of this ritual is 'the government', and the rules it imposes are 'the law'. One may imagine a government engaged in the activity of an arbiter in cases of collisions of interest but doing its business without the aid of laws, just as one may imagine a game without rules and an umpire who was appealed to in cases of dispute and who on each occasion merely used his judgment to devise *ad hoc* a way of releasing the disputants from their mutual frustration. But the diseconomy of such an arrangement is so obvious that it could only be expected to occur to those inclined to believe the ruler to be supernaturally inspired and to those disposed to attribute to him a quite different office—that of leader, or tutor, or manager. At all events the disposition to be conservative in respect of government is rooted in the belief that where government rests upon the acceptance of the current activities and beliefs of its subjects, the only appropriate manner of ruling is by making and enforcing rules of conduct. In short, to be conservative about government is a reflection of the conservatism we have recognized to be appropriate in respect of rules of conduct.

To govern, then, as the conservative understands it, is to provide a *vinculum juris*[5] for those manners of conduct which, in the circumstances, are least likely to result in a frustrating collision of interests; to provide redress and means of compensation for those who suffer from others behaving in a contrary manner; sometimes to provide punishment for those who pursue their own interests regardless of the rules; and, of course, to provide a sufficient force to maintain the authority of an arbiter of this kind. Thus, governing is recognized as a specific and limited activity; not the management of an enterprise, but the rule of those engaged in a great diversity of self-chosen enterprises. It is not concerned with concrete persons, but with activities; and with activities only in respect of their propensity to collide with one another. It is not concerned

---

5. Bond of law.[R.K.]

with moral right and wrong, it is not designed to make men good or even better; it is not indispensable on account of 'the natural depravity of mankind' but merely because of their current disposition to be extravagant; its business is to keep its subjects at peace with one another in the activities in which they have chosen to seek their happiness. And if there is any general idea entailed in this view, it is, perhaps, that a government which does not sustain the loyalty of its subjects is worthless; and that while one which (in the old puritan phrase) 'commands for truth' is incapable of doing so (because some of its subjects will believe its 'truth' to be error), one which is indifferent to 'truth' and 'error' alike, and merely pursues peace, presents no obstacle to the necessary loyalty.

Now, it is intelligible enough that any man who thinks in this manner about government should be averse from innovation: government is providing rules of conduct, and familiarity is a supremely important virtue in a rule. Nevertheless, he has room for other thoughts. The current condition of human circumstances is one in which new activities (often springing from new inventions) are constantly appearing and rapidly extend themselves, and in which beliefs are perpetually being modified or discarded; and for the rules to be inappropriate to the current activities and beliefs is as unprofitable as for them to be unfamiliar. For example, a variety of inventions and considerable changes in the conduct of business, seem now to have made the current law of copyright inadequate. And it may be though that neither the newspaper nor the motor-car nor the aeroplane have yet received proper recognition in the law of England; they have all created nuisances that call out to be abated. Or again, at the end of the last century our governments engaged in an extensive codification of large parts of our law and in this manner both brought it into closer relationship with current beliefs and manners of activity and insulated it from the small adjustments to circumstances which are characteristic of the operation of our common law. But many of these Statues are now hopelessly out of date. And there are older Acts of Parliament (such as the Merchant Shipping Act), governing large and important departments of activity, which are even more inappropriate to current circumstances. Innovation, then, is called for if the rules are to remain appropriate to the activities they govern. But, as the conservative understands it, modification of the rules should always reflect, and never impose, a change in the activities and beliefs of those who are subject to them, and should never on any occasion be so great as to destroy the *ensemble*. Consequently, the conservative will have nothing to do with innovations designed to meet merely hypothetical situations; he will prefer to enforce a rule he has got rather than invent a new one; he will think it appropriate to delay a modification of the rules until it is clear that the change of circumstance it is designed to reflect has come to stay for a while; he will be suspicious of proposals for change in excess of what the situation calls for, of rulers who demand extra-ordinary powers in order to make great changes and whose utterances are tied to generalities like 'the public good' or 'social justice', and of Saviours of Society who buckle on armour and seek dragons to slay; he will think it proper to consider the occasion of the innovation with care; in short, he will be disposed to regard politics as an activity in which a valuable set of tools is renovated from time to time and kept in trim rather than as an opportunity for perpetual re-equipment.

All this may help to make intelligible the disposition to be conservative in respect of government; and the detail might be elaborated to show, for example, how a man of this disposition understands the other great business of a government, the conduct of a foreign policy; to show why he places so high a value upon the complicated set of arrangements we call 'the institution of private property'; to show the appropriateness of his rejection of the view that politics is a shadow thrown by economics; to show why he believes that the main (perhaps the only) specifically economic activity appropriate to government is the maintenance of a stable currency. But, on this occasion, I think there is something else to be said.

To some people, 'government' appears as a vast reservoir of power which inspires them to dream of what use might be made of it. They have favourite projects, of various dimensions, which they sincerely believe are for the benefit of mankind, and to capture this source of power, if necessary to increase it, and to use it for imposing their favourite projects upon their fellows is what they understand as the adventure of governing men. They are, thus, disposed to recognize government as an instrument of passion; the art of politics is to inflame and direct desire. In short, governing is understood to be just like any other activity—making and selling a brand of soap, exploiting the resources of a locality, or developing a housing estate—only the power here is (for the most part) already mobilized, and the enterprise is remarkable only because it aims at monopoly and because of its promise of success once the source of power has been captured. Of course a private enterprise politician of this sort would get nowhere in these days unless there were people with wants so vague that they can be prompted to ask for what he has to offer, or with wants so servile that they prefer the promise of a provided abundance to the opportunity of choice and activity on their own account. And it is not all as plain sailing as it might appear: often a politician of this sort misjudges the situation; and then, briefly, even in democratic politics, we become aware of what the camel thinks of the camel driver.

Now, the disposition to be conservative in respect of politics reflects a quite different view of the activity of governing. The man of this disposition understands it to be the business of a government not to inflame passion and give it new objects to feed upon, but to inject into the activities of already too passionate men an ingredient of moderation; to restrain, to deflate, to pacify and to reconcile; not to stoke the fires of desire, but to damp them down. And all this, not because passion is vice and moderation virtue, but because moderation is indispensable if passionate men are to escape being locked in an encounter of mutual frustration. A government of this sort does not need to be regarded as the agent of a benign providence, as the custodian of a moral law, or as the emblem of a divine order. What it provides is something that its subjects (if they are such people as we are) can easily recognize to be valuable; indeed, it is something that, to some extent, they do for themselves in the ordinary course of business or pleasure. They scarcely need to be reminded of its indispensability, as Sextus Empiricus tells us the ancient Persians were accustomed periodically to remind themselves by setting aside all laws for five hair-raising days on the death of a king. Generally speaking, they are not averse from paying the modest cost of this service; and they recognize that the appropriate attitude to a government of this sort is loyalty (sometimes a confident loyalty, at others perhaps the heavy-hearted loyalty of Sidney Godolphin), respect and some suspicion, not love or devotion or affection. Thus, governing is understood to be a secondary activity; but it is recognized also to be a specific activity, not easily to be combined with any other, because all other activities (except the mere contemplation of the scent) entail taking sides and the surrender of the indifference appropriate (on this view of things) not only to the judge but also to the legislator, who is understood to occupy a judicial office. The subjects of such a government require that it shall be strong, alert, resolute, economical and neither capricious nor over-active: they have no use for a referee who does not govern the game according to the rules, who takes sides, who plays a game of his own, or who is always blowing his whistle; after all, the game's the thing, and in playing the game we neither need to be, nor at present are disposed to be, conservative.

But there is something more to be observed in this style of governing than merely the restraint imposed by familiar and appropriate rules. Of course, it will not countenance government by suggestion or cajolery or by any other means than by law; an avuncular Home Secretary or a threatening Chancellor of the Exchequer. But the spectacle of its indifference to the beliefs and substantive activities of its subjects may itself be expected to provoke a habit of restraint. Into the heat of our engagements, into the passionate clash of beliefs, into our enthusiasm for saving the souls of our neighbours or of all mankind, a government of this sort injects an ingredient, not of reason (how should we expect that?) but of the irony that is prepared to counteract one vice by another, of the raillery that deflates extravagance without itself pretending to wisdom, of the mockery that disperses tension, of inertia and of scepticism: indeed, it might be said that we keep a government of this sort to do for us the scepticism we have neither the time nor the inclination to do for ourselves. It is like the cool touch of the mountain that one feels in the plain even on the hottest summer day. Or, to leave metaphor behind, it is like the 'governor' which, by controlling the speed at which its parts move, keeps an engine from racketing itself to pieces.

It is not, then, mere stupid prejudice which disposes a conservative to take this view of the activity of governing; nor are any highfalutin metaphysical beliefs necessary to provoke it or make it intelligible. It is connected merely with the observation that where activity is bent upon enterprise the indispensable counterpart is another order of activity, bent upon restraint, which is unavoidably corrupted (indeed, altogether abrogated) when the power assigned to it is used for advancing favourite projects. An 'umpire' who at the same time is one of the players is no umpire; 'rules' about which we are not disposed to be conservative are not rules but incitements to disorder; the conjunction of dreaming and ruling generates tyranny.

* * *

Political conservatism is, then, not at all unintelligible in a people disposed to be adventurous and enterprising, a people in love with change and apt to rationalize their affections in terms of 'progress'.[6] And one does not need to think that the belief in 'progress' is the most cruel and unprofitable of all beliefs, arousing cupidity without satisfying it, in order to think it inappropriate for a government to be conspicuously 'progressive'. Indeed, a disposition to be conservative in respect of government would seem to be pre-eminently appropriate to men who have something to do and something to think about on their own account, who have a skill to practise or an intellectual fortune to make, to people whose passions do not need to be inflamed, whose desires do not need to be provoked and whose dreams of a better world need no prompting. Such people know the value of a rule which imposes orderliness without directing enterprise, a rule which concentrates duty so that room is left for delight. They might even be prepared to suffer a legally established ecclesiastical order; but it would not be because they believed it to represent some unassailable religious truth, but merely because it restrained the indecent competition of sects and (as Hume said) moderated 'the plague of a too diligent clergy.'

Now, whether or not these beliefs recommend themselves as reasonable and appropriate to our circumstances and to the abilities we are likely to find in those who rule us, they and their like are in my view what make intelligible a conservative disposition in respect of politics. What would be the appropriateness of this disposition in circumstances other than our own, whether to be conservative in respect of government would have the same

---

6. I have not forgotten to ask myself the question: Why, then, have we so neglected what is appropriate to our circumstances as to make the activist dreamer the stereotype of the modern politician? And I have tried to answer it elsewhere.

relevance in the circumstances of an unadventurous, a slothful or a spiritless people, is a question we need not try to answer: we are concerned with ourselves as we are. I myself think that it would occupy an important place in any set of circumstances. But what I hope I have made clear is that it is not at all inconsistent to be conservative in respect of government and radical in respect of almost every other activity. And, in my opinion, there is more to be learnt about this disposition from Montaigne, Pascal, Hobbes and Hume than from Burke or Bentham.

Of the many entailments of this view of things that might be pointed to, I will notice one, namely, that politics is an activity unsuited to the young, not on account of their vices but on account of what I at least consider to be their virtues.

Nobody pretends that it is easy to acquire or to sustain the mood of indifference which this manner of politics calls for. To rein-in one's own beliefs and desires, to acknowledge the current shape of things, to feel the balance of things in one's hand, to tolerate what is abominable, to distinguish between crime and sin, to respect formality even when it appears to be leading to error, these are difficult achievements; and they are achievements not to be looked for in the young.

Everybody's young days are a dream, a delightful insanity, a sweet solipsism. Nothing in them has a fixed shape, nothing a fixed price; everything is a possibility, and we live happily on credit. There are no obligations to be observed; there are no accounts to be kept. Nothing is specified in advance; everything is what can be made of it. The world is a mirror in which we seek the reflection of our own desires. The allure of violent emotions is irresistible. When we are young we are not disposed to make concessions to the world; we never feel the balance of a thing in our hands—unless it be a cricket bat. We are not apt to distinguish between our liking and our esteem; urgency is our criterion of importance; and we do not easily understand that what is humdrum need not be despicable. We are impatient of restraint; and we readily believe, like Shelley, that to have contracted a habit is to have failed. These, in my opinion, are among our virtues when we are young; but how remote they are from the disposition appropriate for participating in the style of government I have been describing. Since life is a dream, we argue (with plausible but erroneous logic) that politics must be an encounter of dreams, in which we hope to impose our own. Some unfortunate people, like Pitt (laughably called 'the Younger'), are born old, and are eligible to engage in politics almost in their cradles; others, perhaps more fortunate, belie the saying that one is young only once, they never grow up. But these are exceptions. For most there is what Conrad called the 'shadow line' which, when we pass it, discloses a solid world of things, each with its fixed shape, each with its own point of balance, each with its price; a world of fact, not poetic image, in which what we have spent on one thing we cannot spend on another; a world inhabited by others besides ourselves who cannot be reduced to mere reflections of our own emotions. And coming to be at home in this commonplace world qualifies us (as no knowledge of 'political science' can ever qualify us), if we are so inclined and have nothing better to think about, to engage in what the man of conservative disposition understands to be political activity.

THE GREAT LIBERAL
DEATH WISH
Malcolm Muggeridge

Journalist in Soviet Russia, British espionage agent in Mozambique, editor of *Punch*, Christian lay preacher late in life, the often iconoclastic Malcolm Muggeridge is the author of a marvelous autobiography, *Chronicles of Wasted Time.* The present form of this unsparing essay (which Muggeridge has published in various versions at various times) occurs in the collection of his pieces entitled *Things Past* (New York, 1979), pp. 220–38. The progress of liberalism, Muggeridge declares, has been a progress into ruinous decadence.

Searching in my mind for an appropriate name for the seventies, I settle for The Decade of The Great Liberal Death Wish. It seems to me that this process of death-wishing, in the guise of liberalism, has been eroding the civilization of the West for a century and more, and is now about to reach its apogee. The liberal mind, effective everywhere, whether in power or in opposition, particularly so during the present period of American world domination, has provided the perfect instrument. Systematically, stage by stage, dismantling our Western way of life, depreciating and deprecating all its values so that the whole social structure is now tumbling down, dethroning its God, undermining all its certainties, and finally mobilizing a Praetorian Guard of ribald students, maintained at the public expense, and ready at the drop of a hat to go into action, not only against their own weak-kneed, bemused academic authorities, but also against any institution or organ for the maintenance of law and order still capable of functioning, especially the police. And all this, wonderfully enough, in the name of the health, wealth and happiness of all mankind.

Previous civilizations have been overthrown from without by the incursion of barbarian hordes; ours has dreamed up its own dissolution in the minds of its own intellectual élite. It has carefully nurtured its own barbarians—all reared on the best Dr. Spock lines, sent to progressive schools and colleges, fitted with contraceptives or fed birth pills at puberty; mixing D. H. Lawrence with their Coca-Cola, and imbibing the headier stuff (Marcuse, Chairman Mao, Malcolm X) in evening libations of hot chocolate. Not Bolshevism, which Stalin liquidated along with all the old Bolsheviks; not Nazism, which perished with Hitler in his Berlin bunker; not Fascism, which was left hanging upside down, along with Mussolini and his mistress, from a lamp-post—none of these, history will record, was responsible for bringing down the darkness on our civilization, but liberalism. A solvent rather than a precipitate, a sedative rather than a stimulant, a slough rather than a precipice; blurring the edges of truth, the definition of virtue, the shape of beauty; a cracked bell, a mist, a death wish.

I was fortunate enough myself, while still in my late twenties, to be presented with a demonstration of the great liberal death wish at work, so manifest, so incontestable in its implications, and, at the same time, so hilariously funny, that I have never subsequently felt the smallest doubt that here lay the key to the tragicomedy of our time. It happened in Moscow, in the autumn of 1932 and spring of 1933, when I was working there as correspondent for the, then, *Manchester Guardian.* In those days, Moscow was the Mecca for every liberal mind, whatever its particular complexion. They flocked there in an unending procession, from the great ones like Shaw and Gide and Barbusse and Julian Huxley and Harold Laski and the Webbs, down to poor little teachers, crazed clergymen and millionaires, and drivelling dons; all utterly convinced that, under the aegis of the great Stalin, a new dawn was breaking in which the human race would at last be united in liberty, equality and fraternity for evermore.

Stalin himself, to do him justice, never troubled to hide his contempt for them and everything they stood for, and mercilessly suppressed any like tendencies among his own people. This, however, in no way deterred them. They were prepared to believe anything, however preposterous; to overlook anything, however villainous; to approve anything, however obscurantist and brutally authoritarian, in order to be able to preserve intact the confident expectation that one of the most thoroughgoing, ruthless and bloody tyrannies ever to exist on earth could be relied on to champion human freedom, the brotherhood of man, and all the other good liberal causes to which they had dedicated their lives. It is true that many of them subsequently retracted; that incidents like the Stalinist purges, the Nazi-Soviet Pact, the debunking of Stalin at the Twentieth Party Congress, the Hungarian and Czech risings, each caused a certain leakage among liberal well-wishers. Yet when the dust settles, the same old bias is clearly discernible. It is an addiction, like alcoholism, to which the liberal mind is intrinsically susceptible—to grovel before any Beelzebub who claims, however implausibly, to be a prince of liberals.

Why? After all, the individuals concerned are ostensibly the shining lights of the Western world; scholars, philosophers, artists, scientists and the like; the favoured children of a troubled time. Held in respect as being sages who know all the answers; sought after by governments and international agencies; holding forth in the press and on the air. The glory of faculties and campuses; beating a path between Harvard and Princeton, and Washington, D.C.; swarming like migrant birds from the London School of Economics, Oxford and Cambridge into Whitehall. Yet I have seen their prototypes—and I can never forget it—in the role of credulous buffoons capable of being taken in by grotesquely obvious deceptions. Swallowing unquestioningly statistics and other purported data whose falsity was immediately evident to the meanest intelligence. Full of idiot delight when Stalin or one of his henchmen yet again denounced the corrupt, cowardly intelligentsia of the capitalist West—viz., themselves. I detect in their like today the same impulse. They pass on from one to another, like a torch held upside down, the same death wish. Editors come and go, newspapers decline and fold, Labour Governments form and unform; after Roosevelt, Truman and then Eisenhower; after Kennedy, Johnson and then Nixon; but the great liberal death wish goes marching on.

In those far-off days in Moscow it was possible to discuss matters like distinguished visiting intellectuals with officials of the Press Department of the Soviet Foreign Office, with whom, of course, we foreign journalists were in constant contact. Most of them were Russian Jews who had lived abroad before the Revolution. Unlike the usual sort of wooden-face Soviet functionary, they had a sense of humour and a taste for irony. One and all, as it happened, were fated to be shot when, later on, Stalin swung the regime back to traditional Russian anti-Semitism. Yes, of course, they said, people like Shaw and the Webbs were natural stool pigeons, historically destined to play a Judas part and betray—admittedly, rather out of vanity than cupidity—their own phony liberal principles to a triumphant Marxist revolutionary movement in whose eyes they were, and must always be, anathema. Meanwhile, they had their usefulness, if only in reassuring the Soviet authorities that, whatever they might feel bound to do in the way of terrorism and dictatorial practices, they never need worry their heads about hostile reactions in enlightened circles and newspapers in the West. The Foreign Office men told me that they even on occasion amused themselves by seeing how far they could go in gulling distinguished visitors, fabricating production statistics and Stakhanovite feats at the factory bench which could not possibly be true. However tall their stories, they were invariably believed, and often quoted in learned publications abroad; the credulity of their visitors was, it seemed, fathomless.

To the fevered mind of a Senator Joseph McCarthy, or the more sedate, but still irascible one of a Vice-President

Spiro Agnew; even to so erudite and responsible a citizen as Enoch Powell, it all smells unmistakably of conspiracy. How otherwise to account for the fact that the liberal mind, like deathwatch beetles, seems to be active in all the rafters and foundations of the State? So, they imagine suborned men, and hurl wild accusations and denunciations. Ah, if only it were a conspiracy! How easy, then, to apprehend the principals and subdue their dupes! But a death wish subconsciously entertained in newspaper offices and college faculties, in television and radio studios, in churches of all denominations, wherever two or more illuminati are gathered together—that is something else. To suppress a death wish it is necessary to proclaim a corresponding life wish—which is just what a Senator McCarthy, a Vice-President Agnew, an Enoch Powell cannot do; with the result that their wild accusations only serve to advance the very thing they believe they are attacking. They remind me of an old evangelical missionary I came across years ago in South India when I was living there. This good man had got in the way of appearing each year at a local Hindu festival and denouncing the God Shiva, before whom devotees were prostrating themselves. At first he was stoned, then just cursed and insulted, and finally taken for granted. When the time came for him to retire, the organizers of the festival petitioned his missionary society to send a replacement. He had become part of the show.

Recalling, in the light of these experiences, my time as an editorial writer on the *Guardian* before going to Moscow, I realized that there, in that citadel of liberalism, we were engaged in spelling out the essential terms of the great liberal death wish. All our protestations and prognostications were governed by its exigencies. Thus, in our editorials, it was a basic principle that our enemies were always in the right and our friends in the wrong. If, for instance, a British soldier was killed anywhere, it was an unfortunate consequence of the brutal and crooked policies the poor fellow was required to implement; if, on the other hand, a British soldier killed someone, the victim was automatically a blessed martyr, to be mourned, and possibly made the subject of a demonstration, by all decent liberal people. Likewise, any Indians who were misguided enough to be our friends became thereby worthless and despicable figures in our eyes—with the exception, curiously enough, of the Aga Khan, who really was worthless. The repute in which he was held, however, was not due to any appreciation of his political views, but rather to his eminence on the racetrack; something so esteemed by the English that it covers even being on our side. Other Indians, like Nehru, who specialized in holding us up to hatred and contempt, were treated with the utmost consideration. I note that a similar role has come to be adopted by *The New York Times*, *The Washington Post*, and other high-toned American newspapers, as well as by the more eminent radio and television commentators, who pour out their wrath and derision on any poor sucker who is fool enough to support the American side anywhere, but are quick to offer sympathetic treatment to a Castro, a Ho Chi Minh, a Che Guevara, none of whom can be regarded as exactly Americanophil. As far as the death wish or Gadarene stakes are concerned, I calculate that America is running a shade behind us, but is going hard in the direction of the same cliff.

In the view we propounded of Europe in the *Guardian*'s columns in those just pre-Hitler years, the villain was France, armed to the teeth, and, we insisted, ruthlessly pursuing selfish national ends: the hero, a much-wronged Germany, disarmed, bankrupted, victimized by the greedy, revengeful victors of the 1914–18 War. No view could have better pleased the then emerging Dr. Goebbels, or have been more conducive to the disaster of September 1939; more especially as it was combined with an unwavering, sanctimonious refusal to countenance anything in the nature of rearming, and a naïve, obstinately held faith in the ramshackle League of Nations as a peace-keeping instrument. In this way our national interests were damaged far more drastically than by anything a specifically conspiratorial body like the Comintern could hope to achieve. We were led into a war we had little chance of winning, and whose outcome, whether we were on the winning or the losing side, was bound to be, as far as we were concerned, ruinous. A bull's eye for the great liberal death wish.

In the same sort of way, today's version of the liberal mind makes America the universal villain. Sinister American pressures and stratagems are detected behind every financial and economic crisis anywhere in the world; as are the machinations of the CIA behind every reactionary regime or take-over. America is seen as the watchdog of a capitalist-imperialist *status quo,* just as France was in the post 1914–18 War years. No doubt, in due course there will be a similar awakening. Such an attitude, contradictorily enough, is combined with an eager acceptance of current American styles and practices. Veterans of American campus fighting are to the fore in student disorders in London, Paris and Berlin; American pot, pornography, Andy Warhol films, and other intimations of decadence and decay find a ready market across the Atlantic. The demonstrators who advance on London policemen guarding the United States Embassy in Grosvenor Square are mostly jeans-clad, infantile slogan-chanting, obscenities-mouthing, tousled, tangled bearded baboons, who yell 'Pigs!' and 'Fuzz!' in the true Berkeley manner. In other words, what is objected to is the, now waning, American endeavour to underpin crumbling West European economies, and reinforce such defences as can be mustered there against an attack from the East. The incursions of American decadence are as eagerly welcomed as these efforts are abhorred—a characteristic death-wishing stance.

Again, when the final decomposition of the British Empire took place, the death wish, operating through the liberal mind, ensured that, having shed a real empire, we should have a phantom one on our hands in the shape of the so-called British Commonwealth—the most ephemeral setup of the kind since the Holy Roman Empire—involving us in the cares and expense of an empire with none of the compensations. Thus, we have been forced to finance, and sometimes defend, demagogue-dictators of the most unedifying kind, who have ridden to power on the one-man-one-vote principle so dear to liberal hearts. It is a case of responsibility without power—the opposite of the prerogative of the harlot. A similar process may be detected at work in America, whereby the liberal mind's proneness to excessive guilt feelings has induced so fawning and sycophantic an attitude towards Negro discontent and subversion that lifelong white agitators for civil rights, inveterate freedom-marchers and admirers of Martin Luther King, integrationists who have squatted and howled and been carried screaming away by the police for years past, nowadays find themselves being kicked in the teeth by Black Panthers and other Negro militants with a ferocity which might seem excessive directed against the reddest of red-necks.

I ask myself how this predilection for enemies and distaste for friends came to pass in what many of us have been brought up to regard as the most cultivated and enlightened minds of our time. Why it has seemed so obvious to them that whatever commends itself to our well-wishers must be despicable, and whatever serves the interest of our ill-wishes must be beneficial. Why, for instance, there should be so unanimous a feeling in such circles in the United States that the discrediting of American policies and the defeat of American arms in Vietnam represents a progressive aspiration, and the converse a reactionary one. Why, in a world full of oppressive regimes and terrorist practices, in England the venom and fury of the liberal mind should pick on the white South Africans with particular spleen when their oligarchic rule only differs from that of a dozen others—Tito's, Franco's, Ulbricht's, Castro's, etc., etc.—in that they happen to be anxious to be on good terms with the English.

What but a death wish could bring about so complete a reversal of all the normal worldly considerations of good sense, self-interest and a desire to survive? I remember reading in Taine's *Origines de la France Contemporaine* of how, shortly before the Revolution, a party of affluent liberal intellectuals were discussing over their after-dinner cognac all the wonderful things that were going to happen when the Bourbon regime was abolished, and freedom à la Voltaire and Jean-Jacques Rousseau reigned supreme. One of the guests, hitherto silent, suddenly spoke up. Yes, he said, the Bourbon regime would indeed be overthrown, and in the process—pointing round—you and you and you will be carried screaming to the guillotine; you and you and you go into penurious exile, and—now pointing in the direction of some of the elegant ladies present—you and you and you will hawk your bodies round from sansculotte to sansculotte. There was a moment of silence while this, as it turned out, all too exact prophecy sank in, and then the previous conversation was resumed. I know several fashionable and affluent households in London and Washington and Paris where similar conversations take place, and where similarly exact prophecies might be made, without, as on the occasion Taine so appositely described, having the slightest impact.

It would seem to be clear, then, that the great liberal death wish arises out of a historical, or maybe biological, necessity, rather than out of any rational, or even irrational, considerations. Civilizations, like classes and families and regimes, degenerate, and so must be wound up. Just as the great-grandson of some famous ducal figure or billionaire may have thrust upon him the disagreeable fate of ending his line, and, drooling and dissolute, duly ends it, so the liberal mind, likewise drooling, has been entrusted with the historic task of bringing to an end what we are supposed to be defending with might and main—I mean what we still like to call our free way of life and the free institutions which have sustained it. On such a basis, all the views, attitudes, values and recommendations of the liberal mind today make complete sense. Going back to my Moscow experience, those eminent intellectuals abasing themselves before Stalin, and so fatuously accepting his bona fides as a lover of human freedom and enlightenment, were simply fulfilling a manifest destiny to abolish themselves, their culture and their world.

Suppose that somehow or other a lot of contemporary pabulum—video tape of television programmes with accompanying advertisements, news footage, copies of newspapers and magazines, stereo tapes of pop groups and other cacophonies, best-selling novels, films, and other such material—gets preserved, like the Dead Sea Scrolls, in some remote salt cave. Then, some centuries, or maybe millennia, later, when our civilization will long since have joined all the others that once were, and now can only be patiently reconstructed out of dusty ruins, incomprehensible hieroglyphics and other residuary relics, archaeologists discover the cave, and set about sorting out its contents and trying to deduce from them what we were like and how we lived. (This is assuming, of course, that we do not, in the process of working out the great liberal death wish, blow ourselves and our earth to smithereens—a large assumption.) What will they make of us? I wonder. Materially, so rich and so powerful; spiritually, so impoverished and fear-ridden. Having made such remarkable inroads into the secrets of nature; beginning to explore, and perhaps to colonize, the universe itself; developing the means to produce in more or less unlimited quantities everything we could possibly need or desire, and to transmit swifter than light every thought, smile or word that could possibly delight, entertain or instruct us. Disposing of treasure beyond calculation, opening up possibilities beyond conception. Yet haunted and obsessed by the fear that we are too numerous; that soon, as our numbers go on increasing, there will be no room or food for us. On the one hand a neurotic passion to increase consumption, sustained by every sort of imbecile persuasion; on the other, ever-increasing hunger and penury among the so-called backward or underdeveloped peoples. Never, our archaeologists will surely conclude, was any generation of men intent upon the pursuit of happiness more advantageously placed to attain it, who yet, with seeming deliberation, took the opposite course—towards chaos, not order; towards breakdown, not stability; towards death, destruction and darkness, not life, creativity and light. An ascent that ran downhill; plenty that turned into a wasteland; a cornucopia whose abundance made hungry; a death wish inexorably unfolding.

Searching about in their minds for some explanation of this pursuit of happiness that became a death wish, the archaeologists, it seems to me, would be bound to hit upon the doctrine of progress; probably the most ludicrous, certainly the most deleterious, fancy ever to take possession of the human heart; the liberal mind's basic dogma. The notion that human beings, as individuals, must necessarily get better and better is even now considered by most people to be untenable in the light of their indubitably outrageous behaviour towards one another; but the equivalent collective concept—that their social circumstances and conduct must necessarily improve—has come to seem almost axiomatic. On this basis, all change represents progress, and is therefore good; to change anything is, *per se*, to improve or reform it.

For instance, to dilute the marriage tie to the point that it no longer impedes virtually unrestrained promiscuity, or provides the possibility of a stable home to bring up children in, is a reform; to oppose this, reactionary. Likewise, to abolish all restrictions on what may be published, or publicly shown as entertainment, is a reform, even though it opens the way for an avalanche of pornography, and gives full freedom to operate to the sinister individuals and interests engaging in this unsavoury trade. Again, the legalization of abortion is a reform, as, we may be sure, will be claimed in due course for the legalization of euthanasia. In Germany, under the Nazi regime—a decidedly liberal one in this field—sterilization of the allegedly unfit was practised with a zeal and expedition that must be the envy of our eugenists, forced as they are, to adopt such paltry devices as offering transistor radio sets to putative Indian sterilees. The Nazis were able, too, to dispose painlessly and expeditiously of unproductive citizens— what the French, with their usual brutal realism, call 'useless mouths'—without any questions being asked, and to conduct experiments in transplant surgery that would have uplifted Dr. Christiaan Barnard himself. All this Nazi-sponsored progress was summarily interrupted by Germany's military defeat in 1945, but after a decent interval has been resumed in the victor countries. It will surely lead to a decision—which I have an uneasy feeling has already been taken, at any rate subconsciously—not to go on much longer bearing the burden of caring for the senile and incurable mentally sick. Hence the starving of these services for funds and personnel, the noticeable reluctance to build new accommodation, when expenditure on public health generally has been soaring. I anticipate quite soon a campaign, conducted at the most elevated moral level, to dispose painlessly of incurables in gerontological and psychiatric wards, no doubt acquiring a useful reserve of transplantable organs in the process. It will represent an important advance for the liberal mind—and for the great liberal death wish.

It was, of course, Darwin's theory of natural selection which first popularized the notion that Man and his environment are involved in an endless and automatic process of improvement. Who can measure the consequences of this naïve assumption? What secret subversive organization, endowed with unlimited funds and resources, could hope to achieve a thousandth part of what it achieved in the way of discrediting the then prevailing moral values and assumptions, putting in their place nothing more than vague, sentimental hopes of collective human betterment, and the liberal mind to entertain them? It is interesting to reflect that now, in the light of all that has happened, the early obscurantist opponents of Darwinian evolution seem vastly more sagacious and far-seeing than its early excited champions. There must be quite a number today who, like myself, would rather go down to history even as a puffing, portentous Bishop Wilberforce than, say, a Herbert Spencer, or a poor, squeaky H. G. Wells, ardent evolutionist and disciple of Huxley, with his vision of an earthly paradise achieved through science and technology; those twin monsters which have laid waste a whole world, polluting its seas and rivers and lakes with poisons, infecting its very earth and all its creatures, reaching into Man's mind and inner consciousness to control and condition him, at the same time entrusting to irresponsible, irresolute human hands the instruments of universal destruction. It must be added that, confronted with this prospect when, at the very end of his life, the first nuclear explosion was announced, Wells turned his face to the wall, letting off in *Mind at the End of its Tether* one last, despairing, whimpering cry which unsaid everything he had ever thought or hoped. Belatedly, he understood that what he had followed as a life-force was, in point of fact, a death wish, into which he was glad to sink the little that remained of his own life in the confident expectation of total and final obliteration.

The enthronement of the gospel of progress necessarily required the final discrediting of the gospel of Christ, and the destruction of the whole edifice of ethics, law, culture, human relationships and human behaviour constructed upon it. Our civilization, after all, began with the Christian revelation, not the theory of evolution, and, we may be sure, will perish with it, too—if it has not already. Jesus of Nazareth was its founding father, not Charles Darwin; it was Paul of Tarsus who first carried its message to Europe, not Karl Marx, or even Lenin. Jesus, by dying on the Cross, abolished death-wishing; dying became thenceforth life's glory and fulfilment. So, when Jesus called on his followers to die in order to live, he created a tidal wave of joy and hope on which they have ridden for two thousand years. The gospel of progress represents the exact antithesis. It plays the Crucifixion backwards, as it were; in the beginning was the flesh, and the flesh became Word. In the light of this Logos in reverse, the quest for hope is the ultimate hopelessness; the pursuit of happiness, the certitude of despair; the lust for life, the embrace of death.

The liberal assault on Christianity has been undertaken with a fury and fervour which today, when the battle seems to have been conclusively won, is difficult to comprehend. I well remember my surprise, in a television encounter with Bertrand Russell, at discovering in him an almost demented hatred of Christ and Christianity, to which he attributed all the horrors and misfortunes mankind has had to endure since the fall of the Roman Empire. As I attempted to confute this view, I found myself watching with fascination a red flush which rose steadily up his thin stringy neck and spread to his face. The receding chin, the pasty flesh, the simian features struck me then as suggestive of a physical degeneracy (doubtless to be expected in view of his family history) matching the moral degeneracy he had done so much to promote. It was a cruel, and doubtless unfair, light in which to see him; a product, I daresay, of the passionate and physically agonizing conflict in which I found myself involved. At the time, however, the impression was particularly vivid and convincing, and abides with me still.

The script of this strange encounter is still extant, and reveals the philosopher in a most unphilosophic mood; roaring and bellowing like any atheist orator at Hyde Park

Corner. In the light of it, I derived a lot of quiet amusement from the tributes paid to Russell by eminent churchmen when he died. To the best of my knowledge, there was not one single ecclesiastical or clerical voice raised to point out that the great influence Russell undoubtedly exerted was inimical to the Christian faith and the moral standards derived therefrom. It is rather as though one were to find in the literature of the Royal Society for Prevention of Cruelty to Animals a panegyric of bullfighting or fox hunting, or to fall in with a party of total abstainers on their way to a wine festival in Provence. Yet even these comparisons pale into insignificance when we have clergymen who find an echo of the Gospels in the brutal materialism of Marx and Engels; who lay wreaths on shrines to Lady Chatterley, or even to *Playboy* magazine. Or—what must surely be the final *reductio ad absurdum*—a sometime lecturer in biblical studies at Manchester University who detects in the New Testament the encoded version of a phallic-narcotic cult based on the consumption of particular mushrooms.

It is, indeed, among Christians themselves that the final decisive assault on Christianity has been mounted; led by the Protestant churches, but with Roman Catholics eagerly, if belatedly, joining in the fray. All they had to show was that when Jesus said that His kingdom was not of this world, He meant that it was. Then, moving on from there, to stand the other basic Christian propositions similarly on their heads. As, that to be carnally minded is life; that it is essential to lay up treasure on earth in the shape of a constantly expanding Gross National Product; that the flesh lusts with the spirit and the spirit with the flesh, so that we can do whatever we have a mind to; that he that loveth his life in this world shall keep it unto life eternal. And so on. One recalls a like adjustment of the rules in Orwell's *Animal Farm*. A whole series of new interpretative 'translations' of the Bible have appeared supporting the new view, and in case there should be any anxiety about the reception of these adjustments in Heaven, God, we are told on the best theological authority, has died.

To counteract any anxiety on earth, there is the concept of situational ethics, whereby our moral obligations are governed, not by a moral law or moral order underlying all earthly ones, but by the circumstances in which we happen to find ourselves. Thus, the Ten Commandments have only a conditional validity; it may, in particular circumstances, be positively virtuous to covet a neighbour's goods or seduce his wife. Reacting accordingly, Roman Catholic priests and religious are walking out in shoals to resume the material and sensual preoccupations they once thought it proper to renounce, or from within demand the right to follow Demas and love this present world. As for the congregations—not surprisingly, they are dwindling fast. Situational ethics prepares the way for situational worship—a state of affairs not remedied by introducing pop groups, folk singers, and I daresay in time LSD and striptease to enliven divine service. The new enlightened clergy positively revel in the decline in church attendance, gleefully recommending selling off redundant churches and their contents, and looking forward to the time when institutional Christianity, like the State in Marxist mythology, will have withered away. In this aspiration, at any rate, they are unlikely to be disappointed.

In the moral vacuum left by thus emptying Christianity of its spiritual or transcendental content, the great liberal death wish has been able to flourish and luxuriate; the more so because it can plausibly masquerade as aiming at its opposite—life enhancement. Thus, our wars, each more ferocious and destructive than the last, are to establish once and for all the everlasting reign of peace. As the media spout better and bigger lies, their dedication to truth is the more insistently proclaimed. One thinks again of Orwell, and the Ministries of Truth and Peace in *Nineteen Eighty-Four*, the former, as he told me himself, being based on the BBC, where he worked for a while during the 1939–45 War. Again, in a frenzied quest for the physical and mental well-being which should accompany the pursuit of happiness as naturally as a tan comes from lying in the Mediterranean sun, resort to drugs steadily increases, as does the variety available; while medicine men (doctors, psychiatrists and the like) are in ever greater demand, assuming the role of priests, advising and moulding their flock, uplifting and depressing them, keeping them alive and killing them off as they think fit. Just where happiness seems most accessible—in the happy lands, the Scandinavias and Californias—many jump after it from upstairs windows, or gulp it down in coloured barbiturates, or try to tear it out of one another's bodies, or scatter it in blood and bone about the highways, along which, with six lanes a side and Muzak endlessly playing, automobiles roll on from nowhere to nowhere.

Pascal says that when men become separated from God, two courses present themselves; to imagine that they are gods themselves, and try to behave as such, or, alternatively, to seek for enduring satisfaction in the transitory pleasures of the senses. The one sends them, like Icarus, flying into the bright furnace of the sun, there to perish; the other reduces them to far below the level of the farmyard, where the cows with their soft eyes, and the hens with their shrill cries, and the strutting peacocks and the grunting pigs, down to the tiny darting flies and wasps and insects, all live out whatever span of animal existence is vouchsafed them, under God's kindly gaze. Men are denied this satisfaction. If they set up as a farmyard, it is a place of dark fantasies and weird imaginings—Prometheus, unbound, chaining himself to the rock, and there, day by day, gorging his own entrails.

Both these recourses have played their part in the unfolding of the great liberal death wish. In their laboratories, men like gods are working on our genes, to remake them after their own image; with computers for minds, and all our procreation done in test tubes, leaving us free to frolic with our sterilized bodies as we please in unconstrained and perfect bliss. Other men like gods build Towers of Babel in glass and chromium, reaching higher and higher into the sky. Yet others prepare the broiler houses and factory farms for men, not fowl and beasts; even designing for us, as gods should, a kind of immortality; keeping us on the road indefinitely, like vintage cars, by replacing our organs as they wear out—kidney, heart, lungs, genitals, brain even—with spare parts from newer models. Young heads on old shoulders; new ballocks on old crotches.

As for the farmyard—what a gilded sty has been devised! What ambrosial fodder! What perfumed rutting, melodious orgasmic grunts, downy straw and succulent swill! If the purpose of life is, indeed, to pursue happiness here and now, on this earth, then, clearly, it can only be realized in terms of what this earth provides—that is, of goods and toys, of egotistic success or celebrity, of diversions like speed and travel and narcotic fantasies; above all, of sexual pleasure and excitement which alone offers an additional illusory sense of transcendental satisfaction notably lacking in another Cadillac, a trip to Tibet or to the moon, or a press of autograph hunters.

Sex is the only mysticism materialism offers, and so to sex the pursuers of happiness address themselves with an avidity and dedication seldom, if ever, surpassed. Who among posterity will ever be able to reconstruct the resultant scene? Who for that matter can convey it today? The vast, obsessive outpouring of erotica in every shape and form; in book and film and play and entertainment, in body and word and deed, so that there is no escape for anyone. The lame and the halt, the doddering and the infirm, equally called upon somehow to squeeze out of their frail flesh the requisite response. It is the flesh that quickeneth, the spirit profiteth nothing; *copulo ergo sum*, I screw, therefore I am—the new version of Descartes's famous axiom. All possible impediments swept away; no moral taboos, no legal ones, either. An orgasm a day, however procured, keeps the doctor away. Pornography, like Guinness, is good for us, as numerous learned doctors and professors have been at great pains to establish. For instance, a Dr. O. Elthammer of the Stockholm Child Psychiatric Department, who, I read in a letter to the *New Statesman*—that faithful chronicler of the liberal mind through every twist and turn and tergiversation for half a century past—has 'proved conclusively' that pornography does not have a corrupting effect, by showing to some children between the ages of eleven and eighteen a film of a woman being raped by a group of intoxicated louts and then forced to have intercourse with a dog. 'None of the children,' the doctor triumphantly concluded 'was frightened during or after the film, but a proportion of the older girls did admit to being shocked,' while two adults also present 'needed psychological treatment for a month afterward'. One idly wonders what, if anything, happened to the dog.

Each seeming impediment provides an occasion for another spurt. If one Cadillac fails to produce the requisite yield of happiness, then two assuredly will; if not two, then three, or four, or five. If going to bed with one particular woman proves wearisome, then try another. Or two at a time. Or an orgy. Or jumping from a candelabrum. Or any other device or combination. For fuel to keep this fire going, the pornography of the ages is dredged and dredged again, as are the sick memories and imaginings of popular novelists. The fire's extinction would spell, not just impotence, but exclusion from life itself; like those poor souls in Dante's *Inferno* without a place in either Heaven or Hell. Whatever else may be the case, the magic formula itself cannot be wrong. It must, it must work. So try again! The psychiatric wards fill to overflowing with

deluded pursuers of happiness whose quest has proved
abortive; guiltily conscious that happiness has eluded
them in a society in which it is the only good. There, the
children of affluence wail and fret over their broken toys
and broken hopes and unresponding flesh. No matter;
press on, grasping after new toys, new hopes and new
flesh.

In the birth pill, quasi-divine invention, a little death
wish in itself, may be seen the crowning glory of the pursuit of happiness through sex. Adapting Voltaire's famous
saying, if the pill had not been invented it would have
been necessary for it to exist. What laborious days and
nights to bring it into existence! What ingenuity and
concentration of purpose on the single objective—the
achievement of unprocreative procreation, of *coitus non
interruptus* that is guaranteed also to be *non fecundus!*
What armies of mice and rats and rabbits and other such
small deer to be experimented upon, until—oh! glory hal-
lelujah!—their tiny wombs, minutely dissected out, are
seen to be blessedly vacant despite prior coupling, holding
out to all mankind the sublime prospect—the converse of
what was vouchsafed the Virgin Mary—of likewise being
able to couple without conceiving. A Minificat rather than
a Magnificat.

With the pill, the procreative process has at last been
sanctified with sterility. Aphrodite sinking into the sea,
unmenstrual, and forever sterile; unending, infertile orgasm—a death-wish formula if ever there was one. Is it
not remarkable?—millions upon millions of women dedicated to the pursuit of happiness, all pummelled and
perfumed and pomaded, all coiffured and clothed and
contained in accordance with the best television and
glossy-page recommendations; stuffed full of vitamins,
fruit juice and rare steaks, with svelte, sun-tanned, agile
bodies; their hands beseechingly outstretched, insistently
demanding a specific against conception. Ready to run

any risk, make any sacrifice, suffer any disability—loss of appetite, if not of wits growing sick and languid, sexless even, and fat—provided only they can be guaranteed fool and accident-proof sterility.

This neat compact death wish, so easily swallowed, is for export as well as home consumption. Under the auspices of the World Health Organization and other enlightened agencies, earnest colporteurs of contraception carry the good news to darkest Africa; awesome lady missionaries of family planning take their coils and caps and pills, as traders once did coloured beads, to the teeming populations of Asia and Latin America. Only among the Western educated, however, do they find any appreciable number of clients. In the countryside their product has few takers. The result is that it is the new bourgeoisie, admirers of *Oh! Calcutta!* rather than residents of Calcutta proper, who take to the pill. The others continue to procreate regardless, leaving the apostles of the liberal mind to the self-genocide they have chosen.

If sex provides the mysticism of the great liberal death wish, it needs, as well, its own special mumbo-jumbo and brainwashing device; a moral equivalent of conversion, whereby the old Adam is put aside, and the new liberal man is born—enlightened, erudite, cultivated. This is readily to hand in education in all its many branches and affiliations. To the liberal mind, education provides the universal panacea. Whatever the problem, education will solve it. Law and order breaking down?—then yet more statistics chasing yet more education; venereal disease spreading, to the point that girls of ten are found to be infected?—then, for heaven's sake, more sex education, with tiny tots lisping out what happens to mummy's vagina when daddy erects, as once they did the Catechism; drug addiction going up by leaps and bounds, especially in the homes where educational television is looked at, and the whole family marches to protest against the Vietnam war?—surely it's obvious that what the kids need is extra classes under trained psychiatrists to instruct them in the why and the wherefore of narcotics. And so on.

On radio and television panels, on which I have spent more time than I care to remember, to questions such as: What does the panel think should be done about the rising rate of juvenile delinquency? the answer invariably offered is: more education. I can hear the voice ringing out now, as I write these words; the male ones throaty and earnest, with a tinge of indignation, the female ones particularly resonant as they insist that, not only should there be more education, but more and better education. It gives us all a glow of righteousness and high purpose. More and better education—that's the way to get rid of juvenile delinquency, and adult delinquency, for that matter, and all other delinquencies. If we try hard enough, and are prepared to pay enough, we can surely educate ourselves out of all our miseries and troubles, and into the happiness we seek and deserve. If some panel member—as it might be me—ventures to point out that we have been having more, and what purports to be better, education for years past, and that nonetheless juvenile delinquency is still year by year rising, and shows every sign of going on so doing, he gets cold, hostile looks. If he then adds that, in his opinion, education is a stupendous fraud perpetrated by the liberal mind on a bemused public, and calculated, not just not to reduce juvenile delinquency, but positively to increase it, being itself a source of this very thing; that if it goes on following its present course, it will infallibly end by destroying the possibility of anyone having any education at all, the end product of the long, expensive course from kindergarten to postgraduate studies being neo-Stone Age men—why, then, a perceptible shudder goes through the other panelists, and even the studio audience. It is blasphemy.

The bustling campuses multiply and expand, as do their faculties and buildings. More and more professors instruct more and more students in more and more subjects, producing barely articulate graduates, who irresistibly recall to me the *bezprisorny* I remember so vividly from my time in the USSR—those wild children whose parents and guardians had died in the great Russian famines of the early twenties, but who had somehow lived on themselves to race about Moscow and Leningrad and Kiev like wolf packs. Their wild, pinched faces, their bright animal eyes, suddenly glimpsed when they rushed out from under some bridge or embankment—have I not seen them again among our own pampered children, wearing their proletarian fancy dress, on any campus between the Berlin Wall and the California coastline? Here, too, the death-wish cycle completes itself. Pursuing knowledge, we find ignorance, and join hands across the civilized centuries with our own primitive, savage origins. A Picasso, after a lifetime's practice, arrives at the style of the cave drawings in the Pyrenees, and Beethoven is drowned in the insistent beat of jungle drums and jungle cries. The struggle to extricate meaning and order from confusion and chaos is abandoned, and literature itself reverts to total incoherence, in the process disappearing. Fiat Nox!

I see the great liberal death wish driving through the years ahead in triple harness with the gospel of progress and the pursuit of happiness. These our three Horsemen of the Apocalypse—progress, happiness, death. Under their auspices, the quest for total affluence leads to total deprivation; for total peace, to total war; for total education, to total illiteracy; for total sex, to total sterility; for total freedom, to total servitude. Seeking only agreement based on a majority, we find a consensus based on a consensocracy, or oligarchy of the liberal mind, of whose operation an admitted maestro—R. H. S. Crossman, former minister in Harold Wilson's Government and *New Statesman* editor—has written in his inimitable way: 'Better the liberal élitism of the statute book than the reactionary populism of the marketplace.' Seeking only truth supported by facts, we find only fantasy supported by celluloid or video dreams, seen through a camera-eye brightly (the camera, like the pill, a minuscule death wish). All the world compressed into a television screen; seen with, not through, the eye, and so, as Blake tells us, leading us to believe a lie. What lies believed! So many and so varied; from far and near, satellite-carried, earnestly spoken, persuasively whispered, in living colour. The lie, the whole lie, and nothing but the lie.

Demonstrators waiting, bearded men and bra-less girls poised to emit their shrill cries, placards grounded, police standing by, their van discreetly parked, one or two journalists looking at their watches and thinking of editions. Everyone waiting. When, oh when, will they come? At last, patience rewarded; the cameras arrive and are set up. Sound-recordist ready, cameraman ready. Action! And lo! magically, action it is. Beards wag, breasts shake, placards lift, fists clench, slogans chant, police charge, van loads. Screaming, yelling—Pigs! Until—Cut! All is over. Slogans die away, beards and breasts subside, cops and vans drive off. All depart, leaving the street silent. From Action! to Cut!—oh, death wish, where is thy sting?

As the astronauts soar into the vast etenities of space, on earth the garbage piles higher; as the groves of academe extend their domain, their alumni's arms reach lower; as the phallic cult spreads, so does impotence. In great wealth, great poverty; in health, sickness; in numbers, deception. Gorging, left hungry; sedated, left restless; telling all, hiding all; in flesh united, forever separate. So we press on through the valley of abundance that leads to the wasteland of satiety, passing through the gardens of fantasy; seeking happiness ever more ardently, and finding despair ever more surely.

Part Seventeen

RESISTANCE AND HOPE

Practically considered, conservative political and social institutions lost much ground during the seventh decade of the twentieth century. Yet intellectually—despite the evanescent anti-intellectual phenomenon of the "New Left"—conservatives won decisive battles. The number of writers, scholars, and politicians willing to be called "conservative" increased conspicuously. Space remains for three leaders of conservative opinion in recent years, all still scribbling as this volume goes to the printer; Irving Kristol (born 1914); Robert Nisbet (born 1913); Russell Kirk (born 1918).

CAPITALISM, SOCIALISM, AND NIHILISM
Irving Kristol

When Irving Kristol was the first editor of the London magazine *Encounter*, during the years that followed the Second World War, some people curiously mistook him for a liberal. But he never has been that, either in the nineteenth-century signification of the term nor in the twentieth-century sense. Still less is he a socialist or a nihilist. For capitalism he gives two cheers merely; of libertarianism he is goodnaturedly contemptuous. The dread real enemy of a tolerable society, he reasons, is nihilism. This selection first was published in Kristol's periodical *The Public Interest*; it appears as the seventh chapter of his book *Two Cheers for Capitalism* (New York, 1978).

Whenever and wherever defenders of "free enterprise," "individual liberty," and "a free society" assemble these days, one senses a peculiar kind of nostalgia in the air. It is a nostalgia for that time when they were busily engaged in confronting their old and familiar enemies, the avowed proponents of a full-blown "collectivist" economic and social order. In the debate with these traditional enemies, advocates of "a free society" have, indeed, done extraordinarily well. It is therefore a source of considerable puzzlement to them that, though the other side seems to have lost the argument, their side seems somehow not to have won it.

Now, I am aware that within this group itself there are

different ideological and philosophical tendencies. Friedrich Hayek is not Milton Friedman, for instance, nor vice versa, and there are interesting differences between the 19th-century liberal individualism of the one and the 19th-century radical individualism of the other. Still, these twain do meet—and not only in Switzerland. There can be little doubt, for instance, that their thinking has converged into a powerful attack on the traditional socialist notions of central economic planning and a centrally administered economy. And there is absolutely no doubt, in my own mind, that this attack has been enormously successful—far more successful than one would have dreamed possible 25 years ago.

This attack, like so many successful attacks, has taken the form of a pincer movement. On the one hand, Professor Hayek has explored, in *The Counterrevolution of Science*, the ideological origins in the 19th century of the notion of largescale "social engineering," and his critical history of what he calls—and of what we now call, after him—"scientism" is a major contribution to the history of ideas. It is in good part because of Professor Hayek's work in this area, and also because of his profound insights—most notably in *The Constitution of Liberty*—into the connection between a free market, the rule of law, and individual liberty, that you don't hear professors saying today, as they used so glibly to say, that "we are all socialists now." They are far more likely to say that the question of socialism is irrelevant and they would prefer not to discuss it.

Milton Friedman, on the other hand, has launched his main attack on "the planned society" through the jungles of social and economic policy, as distinct from the highlands of theory. No other thinker of our time has so brilliantly exposed and publicized the perversities that can be engendered by governmental intervention in the economic life of a nation. Whereas Hayek demonstrated why large-scale, centralized planning does not have the wonderful results it is supposed to, Friedman shows us how governmental rules and regulations so frequently get results that are the opposite of those intended. In addition, Friedman has instructed us all—including most socialists and neo-socialists—in the unsuspected, creative powers of the market as a mechanism for solving social problem. Indeed, we have now reached the stage where planners will solemnly assemble and contemplate ways of using the powers of government *to create markets* in order to reach their goals.

As a result of the efforts of Hayek, Friedman, and the many others who share their general outlook, the idea of a centrally planned and centrally administered economy, so popular in the 1930s and early 1940s, has been discredited. Even in the socialist nations, economists are more interested in reviving the market than in permanently burying it. Whether they can have a market economy without private property is, of course, an issue they will shortly have to face up to.

The question then naturally arises: If the traditional economics of socialism has been discredited, why has not the traditional economics of capitalism been vindicated? I should say that the reasons behind this state of affairs are quite obvious and easily comprehensible—only they are terribly difficult to explain to economists.

On "Thinking Economically"

The original appeal of the idea of central economic planning—like the traditional appeal of socialism itself—was cast primarily in economic terms. It was felt that such planning was necessary to (a) overcome the recurrent crises—i.e., depressions—of a market economy, and (b) provide for steady economic growth and greater material prosperity for all. This importance which traditional socialism—the Old Left, as we would call it today—ascribed to economics was derived from Marxism, which in turn based itself on the later writings of Marx. But the socialist impulse always had other ideological strands in it, especially a yearning for "fraternity" and "community," and a revulsion against the "alienation" of the individual in liberal-bourgeois society. These ideological strands were prominent among the "utopian socialists," as Engels was to label them, and in the early thought of Karl Marx himself, in which economics received much less attention than religion and political philosophy. They are prominent again today, in the thinking of what is called the "New Left."

The Old Left has been intellectually defeated on its chosen battleground, i.e., economics. But the New Left is now launching an assault on liberal society from quite other directions. One of the most astonishing features of the New Left—astonishing, at least, to a middle-aged observer—is how little interest it really has in economics. I would put it even more strongly: the identifying marks of the New Left are its refusal *to think economically* and its contempt for bourgeois society precisely because this is a society that does think economically.

What do I mean by "thinking economically"? I have found that it is very hard to convey this meaning to economists, who take it for granted that this is the only possible way for *a sensible man to think*—that, indeed, thinking economically is the same as thinking rationally. Economics is the social science *par excellence* of modernity, and economists as a class find it close to impossible to detach themselves from the philosophical presuppositions of modernity. This would not be particularly significant—until recently has not been particularly significant—were it not for the fact that the New Left is in rebellion against these philosophical presuppositions themselves.

Let me give you a simple illustration. One of the keystones of modern economic thought is that it is impossible to have an *a priori* knowledge of what constitutes happiness for other people; that such knowledge is incorporated in an individual's "utility schedules"; and this knowledge, in turn, is revealed by the choices the individual makes in a free market. This is not merely the keystone of modern economic thought; it is also the keystone of modern, liberal, secular society itself. This belief is so deeply ingrained in us that we are inclined to explain any deviation from it as perverse and pathological. Yet it is a fact that for several millennia, until the advent of modernity, people did not believe any such thing and would, indeed, have found such a belief to be itself shockingly pathological and perverse. For all pre-modern thinkers, *a priori* knowledge of what constituted other people's happiness was not only possible, it was a fact. True, such knowledge was the property of a small elite—religious, philosophical, or political. But this was deemed to be altogether proper: such uncommon knowledge could not be expected to be found among common men. So you did not need a free market or a free society to maximize individual happiness; on the contrary, a free market, not being guided by the wisdom of the elite, was bound to be ultimately frustrating, since the common people could not possibly know what they *really* wanted or what would really yield them "true" happiness.

Now, we know from our experience of central economic planning that this pre-modern approach is fallacious—but if, and only if, you define "happiness" and "satisfaction" in terms of the material production and material consumption of commodities. If you do not define "happiness" or "satisfaction" in this way, if you refuse to "think economically," then the pre-modern view is more plausible than not. It is, after all, one thing to say that there is no authentically superior wisdom about people's tastes and preferences in commodities; it is quite another thing to deny that there is a superior wisdom about the spiritual dimensions of a good life. Even today, that last proposition does not sound entirely ridiculous to us. And if you believe that man's spiritual life is infinitely more important than his trivial and transient adventures in the marketplace, then you may tolerate a free market for practical reasons, within narrow limits, but you certainly will have no compunctions about overriding it if you think the free market is interfering with more important things.

The Shamefaced Counterrevolution

Modern economists are for the most part unaware that their habit of "thinking economically" only makes sense within a certain kind of world, based on certain peculiarly modern presuppositions. They insist that economics is a science, which is certainly true, but only if you accept the premises of modern economics. Thus, one of our most distinguished economists, Ludwig von Mises, wrote:

> Economics is a theoretical science and as such abstains from any judgment of value. It is not its task to tell people what ends they should aim at. It is a science of the means to be applied for the attainment of ends chosen, not . . . a science of the choosing of ends.

That statement sounds terribly modest and uncontroversial and platitudinous. But is it? Is it really so easy to separate means from ends? What, for example, if we are members of a monastic community and our end is holy poverty—not just poverty but holy poverty, a poverty suffused with a spiritual intention? Can economics help us attain this end? Or, to take a somewhat less extreme instance: What if we are loyal members of the kind of Orthodox Jewish community that even today is to be found in sections of New York City? In such a community, where most people are engaged in business, there unquestionably is some role for an economist—but only within narrow limits. In the end, the superior purpose of such a community is obedience to sacred Law and meditation on the meaning of this Law. For the maximization of such an end, economics is of little use.

Modern, liberal, secular society is based on the revolutionary premise that there is no superior, authoritative information available about the good life or the true nature of human happiness, that this information is implicit only in individual preferences, and that therefore the individual has to be free to develop and express these preferences. What we are witnessing in Western society today are the beginnings of a counterrevolution against this conception of man and society. It is a shamefaced counterrevolution, full of bad faith and paltry sophistry, because it feels compelled to define itself as some kind of progressive extension of modernity instead of, what it so clearly is, a reactionary revulsion against modernity. It is this failure in self-definition that gives rise to so much irrelevant controversy.

The debate provoked by the writings of John Kenneth Galbraith is, it seems to me, a case in point. Galbraith thinks he is an economist and, if one takes him at his word, it is easy to demonstrate that he is a bad one. But the truth is that Galbraith is not really an economist at all; he can be more accurately described as a reluctant rabbi. His essential thesis is one familiar to pre-modern moralists and theologians: consumption *ought not to be* a constant function of relative income. Implicit in this thesis are the corollaries that (1) Galbraith knows better than any common man what "utility schedule" will provide all common men with enduring and meaningful satisfaction, and (2) if common men were uncorrupted by capitalist propaganda, they would permit Galbraith to prescribe "utility schedules" for them. Some of Galbraith's critics think they have refuted him when they make all this explicit. What they have done, I should say, is to enlighten him as to his own true purpose. That he so stubbornly resists such enlightenment is to be explained by his naive conviction that, because he is attacking bourgeois society, he must be a "progressive" thinker.

The New Left vs. "Economic Man"

A similar confusion, I should say, arises in connection with what we call the "environmentalist" movement. Economists and politicians both—the one with naivety, the other with cunning—have decided to give a literal interpretation to the statements of this movement. And, given this literal interpretation, the thrust of environmentalism is not particularly subversive. If people today are especially concerned about clean air and clean water, then economic analysis can show them different ways—with different costs and benefits—of getting varying degrees of clean air and clean water. But it turns out that your zealous environmentalists do not want to be shown anything of the sort. They are not really interested in clean air or clean water at all. What *does* interest them is modern industrial society and modern technological civilization, toward which they have profoundly hostile sentiments. When they protest against "the quality of life" in this society and this civilization, they are protesting against nothing so trivial as air or water pollution. Rather they are at bottom rejecting a liberal civilization which is given shape through the interaction of a countless sum of individual preferences. Since they do not like the shape of that civilization, they are moved to challenge—however indirectly or slyly—the process that produces this shape. What environmentalists really want is very simple: they want the authority, the power to create an "environment" which pleases them; and this "environment" will be a society where the rulers will not want to "think economically" and the ruled will not be permitted to do so.

Something similar is going on with the "consumers' protection movement," whose true aim is not to "protect" the consumer but rather to circumscribe—and ultimately abolish—his "sovereignty." The objection to such sovereignty is that common people *do* "think economically" when they are liberated from traditional constraints and are encouraged to do whatever they think best for themselves. The "consumers' protection movement," like the "environmentalist" movement, is a revulsion against the kind of civilization that common men create when they are given the power, which a market economy does uniquely give them, to shape the world in which they wish to live.

I think we can summarize our situation as follows: the Old Left accepted the idea of the common good proposed by bourgeois-liberal society. The essential ingredients of this idea were material prosperity and technological progress. Bourgeois liberalism insisted that individual liberty was a precondition of this common good; the Old Left insisted that centralized planning was a precondition but that individual liberty would be an eventual consequence. The experience of the post–World War II decades has revealed that the Old Left simply could not compete with bourgeois liberalism in this ideological debate. The result has been the emergence of a New Left which implicitly rejects both the bourgeois-liberal and the Old Left idea of the common good, and which therefore rejects (again implicitly, for the most part) the ideological presuppositions of modernity itself. This movement, which seeks to end the sovereignty over our civilization of the common man, must begin by seeking the death of "economic man," because it is in the marketplace that this sovereignty is most firmly established. It thinks of itself as a "progressive" movement, whereas its import is regressive. This is one of the reasons why the New Left, every day and in every way, comes more and more to resemble the Old Right, which never did accept the liberal-bourgeois revolution of the 18th and 19th centuries.

The Inadequacies of Liberalism

One is bound to wonder at the inadequacies of bourgeois liberalism that have made it so vulnerable, first to the Old Left and now to the New. These inadequacies do not, in themselves, represent a final judgment upon it; every civilization has its necessary costs and benefits. But it does seem to be the case that, in certain periods, a civilization will have greater difficulty striking an acceptable balance than in others, and that sometimes it arrives at a state of permanent and precarious "tilt" for reasons it cannot quite comprehend. What it is important to realize, and what contemporary social science finds it so hard to perceive, is that such reasons are not necessarily new events or new conditions; they may merely be older inadequacies—long since recognized by some critics—that have achieved so cumulative an effect as to become, suddenly, and seemingly inexplicably, intolerable.

Certainly, one of the key problematic aspects of bourgeois-liberal society has long been known and announced. This is the fact that liberal society is of necessity a secular society, one in which religion is mainly a private affair. Such a disestablishment of religion, it was predicted by Catholic thinkers and others, would gradually lead to a diminution of religious faith and a growing skepticism about the traditional consolations of religion—especially the consolations offered by a life after death. That has unquestionably happened, and with significant consequences. One such consequence is that the demands placed upon liberal society, in the name of temporal "happiness," have become ever more urgent and ever more unreasonable. In every society, the overwhelming majority of the people lead lives of considerable frustration, and if society is to endure, it needs to be able to rely on a goodly measure of stoical resignation. In theory, this could be philosophical rather than religious; in fact, philosophical stoicism has never been found suitable for mass consumption. Philosophical stoicism has always been an aristocratic prerogative; it has never been able to give an acceptable rationale of "one's station and one's duties" to those whose stations are low and whose duties are onerous. So liberal civilization finds itself having spiritually expropriated the masses of its citizenry, whose demands for material compensation gradually become as infinite as the infinity they have lost. All of this was clearly foreseen by many of the anti-modern critics who witnessed the birth of modernity.

Another, and related, consequence of the disestablishment of religion as a publicly sanctioned mythos has been the inability of liberal society ever to come up with a convincing and generally accepted theory of political obligation. Liberal philosophers have proposed many versions of utilitarianism to this end, but these have remained academic exercises and have not had much popular impact. Nor is this surprising: No merely utilitarian definition of civic loyalty is going to convince anyone that it makes sense for him to die for his country. In actual fact, it has been the secular myth of nationalism which, for the past century and a half, has provided this rationale. But this secular myth, though it has evolved hand in hand with bourgeois society, is not intrinsically or necessarily bourgeois. Nationalism ends by establishing "equal sacrifice" as the criterion of justice; and this is no kind of bourgeois criterion. We have seen, in our own day, how the spirit of nationalism can be utterly contemptuous of bourgeois proprieties, and utterly subversive of the bourgeois order itself.

The Depletion of Moral Capital

Even the very principles of individual opportunity and social mobility, which originally made the bourgeois-liberal idea so attractive, end up—once the spirit of religion is weakened—by creating an enormous problem for bourgeois society. This is the problem of publicly establishing an acceptable set of rules of distributive justice. The problem does not arise so long as the bourgeois ethos is closely linked to what we call the Puritan or Protestant ethos, which prescribes a connection between personal merit—as represented by such bourgeois virtues as honesty, sobriety, diligence, and thrift—and worldly success. But from the very beginnings of modern capitalism there has been a different and equally influential definition of distributive justice. This definition, propagated by Mandeville and Hume, is purely positive and secular rather than philosophical or religious. It says that, under capitalism, whatever is, is just—that all the inequalities of liberal-bourgeois society must be necessary, or else the free market would not have created them, and therefore they must be justified. This point of view makes no distinction between the speculator and the bourgeois-entrepreneur: both are selfish creatures who, in the exercise of their private vices (greed, selfishness, avarice), end up creating public benefits.

Let us leave aside the intellectual deficiencies of this conception of justice—I myself believe these deficiencies are radical—and ask ourselves the question which several contemporaries of Mandeville and Hume asked before us: Will this positive idea of distributive justice commend itself to the people? Will they accept it? Will they revere it? Will they defend it against its enemies? The answer, I submit, is as obvious as it is negative. Only a philosopher could be satisfied with an *ex post facto* theory of justice. Ordinary people will see it merely as a self-serving ideology; they insist on a more "metaphysical" justification of social and economic inequalities. In the absence of such a justification, they will see more sense in simple-minded egalitarianism than in the discourses of Mandeville or Hume. And so it has been: As the connection between the Protestant ethic and liberal-bourgeois society has withered away, the egalitarian temper has grown ever more powerful.

For well over a hundred and fifty years now, social critics have been warning us that bourgeois society was living off the accumulated moral capital of traditional religion and traditional moral philosophy, and that once this capital was depleted, bourgeois society would find its legitimacy ever more questionable. These critics were never, in their lifetime, either popular or persuasive. The educated classes of liberal-bourgeois society simply could not bring themselves to believe that religion or philosophy was that important to a polity. *They* could live with religion or morality as a purely private affair, and they could not see why everyone else—after a proper secular education, of course—could not do likewise. Well, I think it is becoming clear that religion, and a moral philosophy associated with religion, is far more important politically than the philosophy of liberal individualism admits. Indeed, I would go further and say that it is becoming clearer every day that even those who thought they were content with a religion that was a private affair are themselves discovering that such a religion is existentially unsatisfactory.

Libertarianism and Libertinism

But if the grave problems that secularization would inevitably produce for liberal-bourgeois society were foreseen, if only in general terms, not all the problems that our liberal society faces today were foreseen. While many critics predicted a dissolution of this society under certain stresses and strains, none predicted—none could have predicted—the blithe and mindless self-destruction of bourgeois society which we are witnessing today. *The enemy of liberal capitalism today is not so much socialism as nihilism.* Only liberal capitalism doesn't see nihilism as an enemy, but rather as just another splendid business opportunity.

One of the most extraordinary features of our civilization today is the way in which the "counterculture" of the New Left is being received and sanctioned as a "modern" culture appropriate to "modern" bourgeois society. Large corporations today happily publish books and magazines, or press and sell records, or make and distribute movies, or sponsor televison shows which celebrate pornography, denounce the institution of the family, revile the "ethics of acquisitiveness," justify civil insurrection, and generally argue in favor of the expropriation of private industry and the "liquidation" of private industrialists. Some leaders of the New Left are sincerely persuaded that this is part of a nefarious conspiracy to emasculate them through "cooptation." In this, as in almost everything else, they are wrong. There is no such conspiracy—one is almost tempted to add, "alas." Our capitalists promote the ethos of the New Left for only one reason: they cannot think of any reason why they should not. For them, it is "business as usual."

And indeed, why shouldn't they seize this business opportunity? The prevailing philosophy of liberal capitalism gives them no argument against it. Though Milton Friedman's writings on this matter are not entirely clear—itself an odd and interesting fact, since he is usually the most pellucid of thinkers—one gathers that he is, in the name of "libertarianism," reluctant to impose any prohibition or inhibition on the libertine tendencies of modern bourgeois society. He seems to assume, as I read him, that one must not interfere with the dynamics of "self-realization" in a free society. He further seems to assume that these dynamics cannot, in the nature of things, be self destructive—that "self-realization" in a free society can only lead to the creation of a self that is compatible with such a society. I don't think it has been sufficiently appreciated that Friedman is the heir, not only to Hume and Mandeville, but to modern romanticism too. In the end, you can maintain the belief that private vices, freely exercised, will lead to public benefits only if you are further persuaded that human nature can never be utterly corrupted by these vices, but rather will always transcend them. The idea of bourgeois virtue has been eliminated from Friedman's conception of bourgeois society, and has been replaced by the idea of individual liberty. The assumption is that, in "the nature of things," the latter will certainly lead to the former. There is much hidden metaphysics here, and of a dubious kind.

And Hayek, too, though obviously hostile in temperament and mood to the new nihilism, has no grounds for opposing it in principle. When Hayek criticizes "scientism," he does indeed write very much like a Burkean Whig, with a great emphasis on the superior wisdom implicit in tradition, and on the need for reverence toward traditional institutions that incorporate this wisdom. But when he turns to a direct contemplation of present-day society, he too has to fall back on a faith in the ultimate benefits of "self-realization"—a phrase he uses as infrequently as possible, but which he is nevertheless forced to use at crucial instances. And what if the "self" that is "realized" under the condition of liberal capitalism is a self that despises liberal capitalism, and uses its liberty to subvert and abolish a free society? To this question, Hayek—like Friedman—has no answer.

And yet this is *the* question we now confront, as our society relentlessly breeds more and more such selves, whose private vices in no way provide public benefits to a bourgeois order. Perhaps one can say that the secular, "libertarian" tradition of capitalism—as distinct from the Protestant-bourgeois tradition—simply had too limited an imagination when it came to vice. It never really could believe that vice, when unconstrained by religion, morality, and law, might lead to viciousness. It never really could believe that self-destructive nihilism was an authen-

tic and permanent possibility that any society had to
guard against. It could refute Marx effectively, but it
never thought it would be called upon to refute the Mar-
quis de Sade and Nietzsche. It could demonstrate that the
Marxist vision was utopian; but it could not demonstrate
that the utopian vision of Fourier—the true ancestor of
our New Left—was wrong. It was, in its own negligent
way, very much a bourgeois tradition in that, while ignoring the bourgeois virtues, it could summon up only a
bourgeois vision of vice.

The Hunger for Legitimacy

Today, the New Left is rushing in to fill the spiritual vacuum at the center of our free and capitalist society. For the
most part, it proclaims itself as "socialist," since that is the
only tradition available to it. It unquestionably feeds upon
the old, socialist yearnings for community—for a pre-indi-
vidualist society—and is therefore, if not collectivist, at
least "communalist" in its economics and politics. But it is
also nihilistic in its insistence that, under capitalism, the
individual must be free to create his own morality. The
New Left is best seen as a socialist heresy, in that it refuses to "think economically" in any serious way. One
might say it is a socialist heresy that corresponds to the
liberal heresy it is confronting: the heresy of a "free society" whose individuals are liberated from the bourgeois
ethos that used to bind them together in a bourgeois-liberal community. And as the "free society" produces material affluence, but also moral and political anarchy, so the
New Left—even as it pushed individual liberty beyond
anarchy itself—longs for a moral and political community
in which "thinking economically" will be left to our
Helots, the machines. In all their imagined utopian communities, the free individual who contracts for "the good
life" has to surrender both his individualism and his freedom.

It is in the nature of heresies to take a part for the whole. Thus, our version of the "free society" is dedicated to the proposition that to be free is to be good. The New Left, though it echoes this proposition when it is convenient for its purposes, is actually dedicated to the counter-belief—which is the pre-liberal proposition—that to be good is to be free. In the first case, the category of goodness is emptied of any specific meaning; in the second case, it is the category of freedom which is emptied of any specific meaning. In the war between these two heresies, the idea of a free society that is in some specific sense virtuous (the older "bourgeois" ideal) and the idea of a good community that is in some specific sense free (the older "socialist" ideal as represented, say, by European social democracy) are both emasculated; and the very possibility of a society that can be simultaneously virtuous and free, i.e., that organically weds order to liberty, becomes ever more remote.

And yet no society that fails to celebrate the union of order and liberty, in some specific and meaningful way, can ever hope to be accepted as legitimate by its citizenry. The hunger for such legitimacy is, I should say, the dominant political fact in the world today—in the "free" nations and among the "socialist" countries as well. It is instructive, and rather sad, to observe the enormous popularity of the recent TV serial, *The Forsyte Saga*, in both capitalist and socialist societies. Obviously, it evoked a profound nostalgia for an order—a society where virtue and freedom were reconciled, however imperfectly—which some of these nations had lost, and which others had never even known. I should say that something of the sort also explains the international popularity of *Fiddler on the Roof*, which gives us a picture of a different kind of legitimate order—a picture that has obvious appeal even to people who do not know the difference between the Talmud and the Code Napoleon.

I find even more pathetic the efforts of the governments

of the "free world" and of the "socialist" nations to achieve some minimum legitimacy by imitating one another. The "free societies" move haltingly toward collectivism, in the hope that this will calm the turbulence that agitates them and threatens to tear them apart. The "socialist" nations take grudging steps toward "liberalization," for the same purpose. The results, in both cases, are perverse. Each such step, so far from pacifying the populace, further provokes them, since each such step appears as a moral justification of the turbulence that caused it.

What medicine does one prescribe for a social order that is sick because it has lost its soul? Our learned doctors, the social scientists, look askance at this kind of "imaginary" illness, which has dramatic physical symptoms but no apparent physical causes. Some, on what we conventionally call the "right," cannot resist the temptation to conclude that the patient is actually in robust health, and that only his symptoms are sick. Others, on what we conventionally call the "left," declare that the patient is indeed sick unto death and assert that it is his symptoms which are the causes of his malady. Such confusion, of course, is exactly what one would expect when both patient and doctors are suffering from the same mysterious disease.

THE RESTORATION OF AUTHORITY
Robert Nisbet

With the publication of his *The Quest for Community* in 1953, the historical sociologist Robert Nisbet acquired a reputation for original scholarship and broad views that was increased by his successive publication of other serious studies of a conservative cast of thought. "The Restoration of Authority" is the fifth chapter of his *Twilight of Authority* (New York, 1975, pp. 230–87). Because Nisbet believes a real restoration of authority and of much else to be quite conceivable, his analysis is a fitting conclusion to an anthology of conservative writing.

Is it possible to arrest, to actually reverse, present accelerating tendencies toward political Leviathan on the one hand and moribundity of the social order on the other? Can the bureaucratization of culture, mind, and spirit which assumes an ever more militant, even military cast in the West be somehow offset by renewal of the social bond and its diverse contexts of authority and freedom?

Nothing about us at the moment offers much encouragement. We live, after all, in a world that becomes constantly more militarized, more power-oriented, and hence more dangerous to America and other Western countries. The mere presence of the great military socialisms which are Russia and China, with their consecration to aggrandizement of one kind or other, is enough to create pessimism so far as our own prospects are concerned. And we have begun to see in the Western world—in Greece, Chile, and Portugal—open rule by the military in the name of one moral or political value after the other. Will this process of militarization of government in the West cease before other countries have been added to the list?

Everything suggests continuation of the trends I have described. After all, if the advancing power of centralized government could not be checked during the age of affluence that for a quarter of a century followed World War II, when Western economies, especially that of the United States, were generally strong, when recession seemed banned forever and inflation was still moderate, what likelihood exists for retreat now amidst fear of depression and inflation alike? Moreover, as I have noted, it was precisely in that period of affluence that the authority of the university, of reason, of objectivity, of language, and of culture underwent its most pronounced decline in modern times. The combination of widespread sense of corruption in society and government and of spreading psychological unease, alienation, and fear of future is in itself an admirable recipe for the spread of power in military form.

Nor is the voice of the political clerisy any less clamant today than in recent times past. To a man the veterans of the New Deal, of Kennedy's Camelot, and of the Johnson administration, those who sat at the right hand of power and relished every moment of it, preach the gospel that was first heard in this country from Woodrow Wilson, especially after America's entry into World War I. That this clerisy and this gospel have an imposing record of big budgets and bureaucracies, of adventures in what is by now a string of foreign wars, and of close total failure in the work either of terminating depression and inflation or of creating the conditions of economic and social prosperity, does not matter in the slightest. For labor, press, the academic and intellectual world, and even increasingly for business and industry, it is this clerisy, with roots deep in the doctrines of Hobbes, Rousseau, and Bentham, that speaks most authoritatively at the present time. The ranks of those still committed to the private sector, to the social sphere, and to the individual liberties within each of these, become progressively thinner, their voices increasingly muted. The worse the conditions become which are the direct spawn of the New Despotism, the greater the cry for its intensification. After all, the huge regulatory agencies, the military, and the numberless laws passed by Congress do represent action of a sort, and in twilight ages action is king.

We are thus obliged to be skeptical in the extreme that any arrest, much less reversal, of the tendencies of political centralization and social disintegration around us is possible. It was one of the prophecies of those like Tocqueville, Burckhardt, and Nietzsche, who a century ago foresaw our time of troubles, that paralysis of the will on the part of peoples and governments would be a part of what lay ahead. Burckhardt's imagined future of military commandos ascendant in the West had no room in it, obviously, for very much of civility and culture. We live, as I have suggested, in one of Saint-Simon's "critical ages," and there is no reason to believe optimistically that we are reaching its end, with something substantially different at hand. If one were to wager, it would be sounder to think in terms of a few decades at least, perhaps another century, of continuation of present tendencies in the direction of a military Leviathan set in circumstances of social erosion and cultural decay.

But having said this, indeed taking it virtually for granted as social analyst and prophet, I would like nevertheless to turn to something very different: to some reflections on what a genuine social regeneration in the West might consist of—either as the consequence of historical factors now only dimly to be seen or foreseen or of direct, enlightened statesmanship. After all, the present scene is not wholly without possible portents. Some of the forces I described at the beginning of this book as challenges to the political community and the political way of life—the upthrust of ethnic nationalism, of fundamentalist religion, of the commune, of kinship and localism, and the still-enigmatic role of the multinational corporation, among others—might from a different point of view be thought of as the faint, still amorphous but potentially decisive harbingers of the next age of civilization, one that will contain renewal of the roots of society and culture alike, much as did that age in the West that followed the decline and disintegration of the Roman military-imperial order.

Who can ever be sure in these matters? Prediction of the future is—despite the pretenses of self-styled futurologists—impossible save as expressions of intuition, guess, and wish-generated or anxiety-inspired fantasy. No matter how inexorable any given trend may seem, the history of mankind teaches us to be respectful of the impacts of the Prophet, the Genius, the Maniac, and the Random Event.

I do not, in short, know any more about what the future does indeed hold than does anyone else. We can only guess and, on the basis of postulated conditions, describe. What I shall do in this final chapter is indicate a few of the fundamental elements which, on history's evidence, are vital to any real liberation from the kind of power that envelops us at the present time.

The Recovery of Pluralism

I begin with the philosophy of pluralism. Everything vital in history reduces itself ultimately to ideas, which are the motive forces. Man *is* what he *thinks!* So might the epigram be restated. He is what he thinks he himself is, what his fellows are, and what the surrounding circumstances are in their deepest reality. Above all, man is what he thinks the transcending moral values are in his life and in the lives of those around him. I know of nothing more absurd than the "realist" position that ideas and ideals do not shape history. What else, in heaven's name, could possibly shape history, lift it above the level of the statistically random or fortuitous? The difference between biological evolution and social evolution consists precisely in the fact that where the former, in its modern scientific statement, is purely statistical, concerned only with "populations" of which we can determine the arithmetic mean and the coefficients of variation from this mean, social evolution is necessarily devoted to the very structures and types which the biological evolutionist is obliged to eschew utterly. Social evolution deals with kinship systems, guilds, communities, churches, schools, universities, economic corporations, political states, and the like. It is inherently and ineradicably "typological" by the standards of the biologist.

Behind each of the structures or types that we deal with in the history of society is, inevitably, a complex pattern of ideas and ideals, for human behavior is nothing if not purposive. They may be ideas based upon cunning, covetousness, avarice, intensification of power and exploitation, or conversely they may be ideas of godliness, redemption, reform, revolution, justice, or freedom; but apart from ideas, however diversely and amorphously, even uncomprehendingly, held, it is absurd to think of either social behavior or social organization.

Insensibly, ideas, ideals, and values form patterns in time, patterns which often, as in the case of religious and philosophical systems, are greater in each case than the sum of the parts. And once human beings become aware more or less directly of these patterns, in whatever sphere, these too operate to inspire and to motivate. Whether it is Buddhism or Islam or Christianity, nationalism, democracy, or socialism, gradualism or revolution, the historical record is plain that human beings do indeed live and die for such things as the "realist" might contemptuously refer to as idealistic abstractions.

Among the greatest needs of our present age is a recrudescence of the whole set of ideas that, for want of better term, we may think of as *pluralism*. It is, as William James wrote, a pluralistic universe we live in, and *that* is the kind of universe one hopes that Margaret Fuller and Thomas Carlyle alike had in mind. And as it is a pluralistic universe, so is it normally a pluralistic society that we inhabit.

One of the most grievous casualties of modern times is the true utopian mentality, the kind of mind we find in Sir Thomas More, Francis Bacon, in dozens of writers in the eighteenth and early nineteenth centuries including Saint-Simon, Fourier, Comte, Proudhon, and others. This is, or was, a mentality that did not hesitate to try, as realistically as possible, to think out, to plan for, to guide toward, the future. Past and present were indeed respected, but one is not conscious in their extraordinary works of any dogmatic conviction of an inexorable trend that must by its nature reduce human thought to the level of handmaiden or worse. It was, I believe, Marxism, above any other single force in the nineteenth century, that led eventually to the death of the utopian mentality, or else to its inversion, as in the works of Aldous Huxley and George Orwell. No dogma or superstition in any religion yet uncovered by anthropologists is more tyrannizing, and also more intellectually absurd, than that of the historically inevitable or necessary. But it is this dogma nevertheless that has had greatest appeal to several generations of intellectuals bereft of religion and driven thereby into the arms of the waiting church of historical necessity.

The worst aspect of this kind of thinking is its division of the present—basically all we have to observe and to cogitate upon—into the "relevant" and the "irrelevant" present. If one is convinced, by his dogma of the *necessary* future, that progress lies only in the uses of political power, in the sterilization of cultural diversity, the extinction of localism, regionalism, and the whole private sector, and the replacement of all this by something euphemistically called the welfare state, the planned state, whatever, then obviously there is a large realm of the manifest present that can be categorically dismissed as fundamentally irrelevant, as wasteful, as a distraction from achievement of the future, as contemplated by the unitary or monistic mentality. The harshest charge the modern intellectual, so often under the influence of one variation or other of the Marxist mind, has been able to hurl at others is not that their ideas are wrong, immoral, or undesirable, but *unrealistic*, conceived in blindness to what is real and objective in the present.

Given this whole habit of mind, conceived in the union of necessity and politics—the two greatest idols of the modern intellectual mind—it will not be easy for a philosophy of pluralism to reassert itself as it has from time to time in other ages of Western history. And yet I am convinced that it will so assert itself, though I do not know when, if only because the ravages of the social and cultural landscape effected by the political clerisy and its works are bound to become so great, and so visible, that there will be no other way for human beings to turn than to some kind of rebirth of a basically pluralist philosophy. What are the central values of pluralism, either as they may be observed in epochs of substantive pluralism or else imagined for our own future? The following seem to me to be the four constitutive elements of the pluralist philosophy.

Functional autonomy. What characterizes the pluralist view of autonomy can best be thought of in terms of the ability of each major function in the social order to work with the maximum possible freedom to achieve its own distinctive ends. What applies to school or university should apply also to economy, to family, to religion, and to each of the other great spheres of society. Everything must be done to avoid intrusion by some one great institution, such as the political state, into the spheres of other institutions. Perfect autonomy is scarcely possible, or even desirable perhaps, given the needs of unity in some degree in a society. But, as Aristotle observed in his criticism of Plato's communism, there is the kind of unity that comes from harmony, that is articulation of diverse sounds or elements, and there is the kind of unity that comes from mere unision. It is harmony that our society needs above anything else—and I use that word precisely as Aristotle did, and as Althusius, Burke, and Tocqueville later did in their different ways—as the bringing into consonance of elements in the social order the diversity of which is recognized as vital to both freedom and creativeness.

Edmund Burke epitomized this element of pluralism with his characteristic pungency and eloquence:

The nature of man is intricate; the objects of society are of the greatest possible complexity; and therefore no simple disposition of direction of power can be suitable either to man's nature or to the quality of his affairs. When I hear the simplicity of contrivance aimed at and boasted of in any new political constitutions, I am at no loss to decide that the artificers are grossly ignorant of their trade, or totally negligent of their duty. The simple governments are fundamentally defective, to say no worse of them.

But for the clerisy of power in the West, since at least the time of Hobbes, such words can seem, and have seemed, but the pious exclamations of an irretrievably archaist mind. The managerial revolutions of the twentieth century have been conceived basically by mentalities for whom unity, simplicity, and above all uniformity are not merely desirable values but inevitable values.

Decentralization is the second major element of pluralism. If the functional autonomy of social units is to be respected, if localism, regionalism, and the whole spirit of voluntary association is to flourish, power wielded by government must be distributed into as many hands as possible—not abstract, desocialized *political* hands but those we actually see in the social order, those of workers, enterprisers, professionals, families, and neighborhoods. Centralization, Lamennais wrote, breeds apoplexy at the center and anemia at the extremities. From Aristotle through Aquinas, Althusius, Bodin, Burke, Tocqueville, Durkheim, and Weber, through the whole succession of minds in the West in which respect for social diversity and individual autonomy is to be seen, there has been a profound stress upon the need for decentralization—not merely in political government alone, though there preeminently, but in all large institutions. Few things have more grievously wounded the political community in our time than the kind of centralization that has become virtually a passion in the political clerisy during most of this century and that is increasingly becoming but another word for the Federal government today. Dispersion, division, loosening, and localization of power: these are all vital needs today, and they can be brought about only when weariness with centralization and sickness of its consequences become so great that the philosophy of decentralization will achieve once again the prestige it had among the Founding Fathers.

Hierarchy. I refer of course to the hierarchy that comes from the very functional requirements of the social bond. There is no form of community that is without some form of stratification of function and role. Wherever two or more people associate, there is bound to be some form of hierarchy, no matter how variable, changing from one actor to the other, or how minor. Hierarchy is unavoidable in some degree. Our gravest problem at the present time, in many respects, is the disrepute into which this word, this unavoidable necessity, has fallen as the consequence of the generalized philosophy of equalitarianism I described in the preceeding chapter. We have seen institution after institution weakened or crippled in the social order as the result of arbitrary power wielded by one or other regulatory agency in the name of a vain and vapid equality. At the present time the ascendant moral philosophy in the West is that which, as I have noted, takes what is in effect leveling as the desired norm of justice. How welcome would be Burke's words today: "Believe me, Sir, those who attempt to level never equalize."

The philosophy of pluralism is, then, rooted not only in the virtues of functional autonomy and localism but also in frank recognition of the value inherent in hierarchy. This in no sense consigns any ethnic, economic, or regional segment to perpetual servitude. Far from it. Again we may quote Burke:

> Woe to the country which would madly and impiously reject the service of the talents and virtues, civil, military, or religious, that are given to grace and to serve it; and would condemn to obscurity every

thing formed to diffuse luster and glory around a state. Woe to that country too, that passing into the opposite extreme considers a low education, a mean contracted view of things, a sordid mercenary occupation, as a preferable title to command. *Everything ought to be open but not indifferently to every man.* [Italics added.]

We have seen, alas, the appearance of *ressentiment* that Tocqueville and Nietzsche, among others after Burke, predicted: the sense of the greater worthiness of the low, the common, and the debased over what is exceptional, distinctive, and rare, and, going hand in hand with this view, the profound sense of guilt—inscribed in the works of the New Equalitarians—at the sight of the latter. Hierarchy in some degree is, as I say, an ineradicable element of the social bond, and, with all respect for equality before the law—which is, of course, utterly vital to free society—it is important that rank, class, and estate in all spheres become once again honored rather than, as is now the case, despised or feared by intellectuals. Certainly, no philosophy of pluralism is conceivable without hierarchy—as open as is humanly possible for it to be but not, in Burke's word, indifferently open.

Tradition is fourth among the central elements of pluralism. I mean reliance upon, in largest possible measure, not formal law, ordinance, or administrative regulation, but use and wont, the uncalculated but effective mechanisms of the social order, custom, folkway, and all the uncountable means of adaptation by which human beings have proved so often to be masters of their destinies in ways governments cannot even comprehend. I shall say more about this adaptational or inventive proclivity shortly. What I have reference to here is the larger matter of maximum possible utilization of tradition in place of law.

At the end of the section on the Romanization of the

West above I spoke of the present increasingly broad and committed effort of intellectuals and reformers to bring as much of the economy and the social order within the purview of law, litigation, and the judiciary as possible. Those of revolutionary disposition have, understandably, abandoned the barricade for the courtroom, seeing the manifold accomplishments of the latter in the whole realm of the New Equalitarianism and the New Despotism that goes with it. Few tendencies in our time are more vivid than that of the conversion of once-traditional, once-autonomous, once-social relationships into those of the law and the courts. The university alone is a superb case history of what I am describing. Within the past quarter of a century we have seen a formerly free and largely autonomous social body reduced in a score of ways to becoming the handmaiden of legislature, law office, regulatory agency, and the courtroom.

Pluralist society is free society exactly in proportion to its ability to protect as large a domain as possible that is governed by the informal, spontaneous, custom-derived, and tradition-sanctioned habits of the mind rather than by the dictates, however rationalized, of government and judiciary. Law is vital—formal, statute law—but when every relationship in society becomes a potentially legal relationship, expressed in adversary fashion, the very juices of the social bond dry up, the social impulse atrophies. The genius of the English common law lies not only in the social and communal roots of this law, as these are to be seen in the history of England during the Middle Ages, but also in its tacit concern, repeatedly expressed in judicial decision, that as little as possible be transferred from the nonlegal, nonpolitical lives of human beings living in a social order to the necessarily legal and political lives of the same human beings conceived as subjects of the sovereign. Nothing, it would seem, so quickly renders a population easy prey for the Watergate mentality of government as the dissolution of those customs and traditions which are the very stuff of morality and, hence, of resistance to oppression and corruption. Again I turn to Burke. What he chose to term prejudice I call here tradition, but the point is the same:

> Prejudice is of ready application in the emergency; it previously engages the mind in a steady course of wisdom and virtue, and does not leave the man hesitating in the moment of decision, skeptical, puzzled, and unresolved. Prejudice renders a man's virtue his habit; and not a series of unconnected acts. Through just prejudice, his duty becomes a part of his nature.

Of all the consequences of the steady politicization of our social order, of the unending centralization of political power, and of the accelerating invasion of the social order by the adversary mentality of the lawyer, the greatest, in many ways, is the weakening and disappearance of traditions in which authority and liberty alike were anchored. I do not happen to regard present feverish bumbling in connection with celebration of the Bicentennial as the worst of our national afflictions, but the whole spectacle of futility in this instance is a perfect image, it seems to me, of the condition in which we find ourselves. What one celebrates—whether in family, religion, or nation—is tradition, or a set of traditions. The sight of literally thousands of bureaucratic bodies struggling to find something to celebrate, some way of celebrating, the Bicentennial, with little if any help to be had, it must be noted, from press, clergy, or the academic world, is sufficient in itself as a commentary on the role of tradition in our society.

The Rediscovery of the Social

If modern life is to be saved from the monolith of power the state has become, from cultural decadence, and from spreading boredom relieved only by war, spectacle, crusade, or riot, means must be found of restoring the kind of social initiative that springs from the groups, neighborhoods, localities, and voluntary associations within which people too plainly wish to live and indeed do live, at least as far as nationalization of modern society permits.

Of all needs in this age the greatest is, I think, a recovery of the *social*, with its implication of the diversity of social membership that in fact exists in human behavior, and the liberation of the idea of the social from the political. I do not doubt that there are functions in modern society which can be met by the political order alone. The great challenge to the contemporary imagination—unlike the imagination that took shape in the Renaissance—is, however, the identification of functions, processes, and memberships which do *not* belong to the state and whose protection from the state and its bureaucracy should be a first order of business. And not least of the results of our lack of attention to the distinctly social, to the *nonpolitical* areas of human experience, and to means whereby the social can be kept strong, is the seeming inability of the state in our time to manage properly what it can best do: maintain order in the towns and cities, for instance!

We are, it would seem, prisoners in the House of Politics. It is a depressing fact that all the great increases in the theory of political power have come from those who gave the appearance of damning it. Rousseau, father of modern political intellectuals, declared all political government iniquitous, ending up, nevertheless, with that indispensable myth of the totalitarian state, the General Will, with its extermination of all forms of community and association which do not proceed directly from it. Bentham, who made a virtual science of the transformation of social authority into monistic power, loathed politics and government as these existed in an England that was witnessing the rise of modern liberal democracy, but he gave the world his infamous Panopticon Principle. Marx, who yielded to no one in hatred of the bourgeois state and whose condemnations of bureaucracy are among the most

eloquent anywhere, yet was the author of that politicization, that totalitarianism indeed, which socialism came increasingly to know thereafter. So it goes: hate politics and
love power—provided only that the cosmetics of humanitarianism, of equality, rights, and freedom are liberally
applied to it.

To identify any act or structure of government, however blatantly bureaucratic it may be, however destruc-
tively it deals with the natural communities of human
beings, however closely it binds the individual to itself at
the expense of older and deeper loyalties, as *social* is, of
course, to endow it with a luster it would not and could
not have were it to be advertised for what it is in fact: political and bureaucratic. The adjective *social* is the tribute
politics pays to those still-remaining wisdoms and apprehensions in the popular mind which recognize and properly fear the never-ending invasion of the political state in
the social sphere. In an earlier chapter I noted the appall-
ing corruption of language in our time, a corruption
caused chiefly, as George Orwell stressed, by the political
mind and, more often than not, the left political mind. Of
all such corruptions none seems to be greater in effect than
that which buries the *social* in the *political;* which, in its
more ignorant and arrogant forms, actually denies any difference between the two, declaring that the political is
simply the summation of all that has ever historically been
involved in the social and moral structures.

But even leaving aside here the practical question of
whether there is any alternative to the nearly total domination of the social and moral orders by the political state,
it is at least disingenuous, at worst dishonest and deceptive, to blur the difference between the political and the
social and also between the separate traditions in Western
thought which express the two.

I offer the guess that 90 percent of what passes for "social thought" in the textbook histories written during the
past century is either political thought in fact or else pre-

sented with a strongly political thrust. The divisions and stages which we create in our history-writing are overwhelmingly political, reflecting the dominance of the West since the Renaissance at least by largely political values. That overweening attention to the political and the military which a few social and cultural historians complained about in the nineteenth century in their efforts to get the social lives of human beings more nearly center stage in historical writing had its full effect upon those who, starting about the end of the nineteenth century, began to deal with the history of social, cultural, and intellectual materials. Such historians took over, and still do in large degree, the categories of Renaissance, Reformation, Age of Reason, Enlightenment, Age of Revolution, Democracy, Welfare State, among others, all originally conceived by minds concerned foremost with political matters.

But this practice is awkward to say the least, often downright delusive. The distinguished historian of science Herbert Butterfield has written that for purposes of the history of science in the West the cherished historiographic categories of Renaissance and Reformation can simply be disregarded. As categories or epochs, Butterfield writes, they contribute nothing of substance to any understanding of either the central periods or central processes involved in the rise of modern science. I would suggest that from the point of view of social, cultural, and intellectual history we would be well advised to abandon, or at least significantly reduce dependence upon, these two, and other constructed time-periods brought into being initially, as I have noted, in the terms of an overwhelmingly political orientation toward Western history.

If we are concerned with periods of rise and fall, of prosperity and depression, in the realm of social institutions such as property, local community, neighborhood, guild, and family, we discover that it is precisely in some of the most celebrated of ages—such as Renaissance and

Enlightenment—that these institutions underwent significant erosion or dislocation. Much the same, it might be observed in passing, holds true in the history of certain notable intellectual areas as well. What Butterfield has pointed out with respect to science is equally true of philosophy. Despite the widespread conviction that the Italian Renaissance was an illustrious age of philosophy, it was in fact as sterile in this regard as it was in science. I know of no other epoch in Western history that has been the beneficiary of historiographic inflation to the degree that the Renaissance has—*the* Renaissance, as we are prone to refer to it, as though there were no other renaissances in Western and also world history.

We may truthfully say that the Renaissance was the period in which worship of political power and of ethically unlimited warfare made its entrance. Within a century after Renaissance humanist writings, overwhelmingly consecrated to political power in their hatred of church, had appeared on the scene, the momentous theory of the modern national, collective state had been brought into existence. Socially, however, the Renaissance was in large degree a time of institutional dislocation, breakdown, and collapse.

There have been two great traditions in Western social and political thought, and these have little to do with conventional distinctions between "liberal" and "absolutist." In the first, which begins with Plato, the political state is given an emphasis that virtually extinguishes other forms of association. Hobbes, Rousseau, Bentham, Michelet, Fichte, Treitschke are among principals in this tradition which includes, of course, the numberless members of the political clerisy of our own day. Distinction between state and society is either denied in this succession of thinkers or else the social sphere is deemed to be so inherently ridden with conflict and corruption that only through the most stringent uses of political power may the individual be saved. Such groups as family, locality, neighborhood, church, and other autonomous associations are almost uniformly reduced to their individual atoms, made into unities dependent upon concession of existence by the state, or in some other way significantly degraded.

The second tradition is far more interesting and also valuable, I would argue, so far as the actual history of Western society is concerned. This tradition begins, really, with Aristotle, in his famous criticisms of Plato's unitary state, and it includes among its most illustrious figures Cicero, Thomas Aquinas, Bodin, Althusius, Burke, Tocqueville, Proudhon, and some of the members of the lamentably short-lived school of modern English and French pluralists. Basic to this tradition is the clear distinction between social institutions and the political state and the insistence that true freedom in any society proceeds less from what the actual constitution of the political order proper may prescribe than from the relationship that exists between political state, whatever its form of government, and the several institutions of the social sphere. A political government may be nominally democratic or republican, but it cannot be a genuinely free government if the powers of the state have reached out to encompass all spheres of social, moral, economic, and intellectual existence. Conversely a government monarchical or oligarchical in structure can be a free government if—as has been the case many times in history—it respects the other institutions of society and permits autonomies accordingly in the social and economic spheres.

I believe this second tradition, stretching, as I say, from Aristotle down to Burke, Tocqueville, Acton, and to some of the anarchists of the nineteenth century, is by far the more relevant to the needs of our own time. No doubt there are ages and societies in which affirmation of the centralized power of the state is valuable, and I do not argue that any utopian abandonment of the sovereignty of the political state is worth much reflection even today. But we live nevertheless in a time of saturation of social order by political power, and I suggest that it would require a great deal of political retreat from the social sphere before anything resembling a crisis in this respect would be likely.

There are two separate and distinctive manifestations in the nineteenth century of this second, social, tradition of Western thought. The first is conservative, the second is radical, but what they have in common is profound belief in the necessity of protection of the social from the political. Whether it is Burke and von Haller among conservatives, or Proudhon and Kropotkin among radicals, there is identical emphasis upon the values of localism, regionalism, voluntary association, decentralization of authority, and also identical fear of the political state, whether monarchical or republican in character.

It was the French Revolution that formed the background of both bodies of thought. Burke's famous attack on revolutionary centralization and collectivization of power is the starting-point. During the quarter-century that followed publication of his *Reflections* a veritable renascence of conservatism took place in the West—to be seen in the works of Bonald and Maistre and the young Lamennais in France; in Haller in Switzerland; Hegel in Germany; Balmes and Donoso y Cortes in Spain; and in Southey and Coleridge in England. The central thrust of each of these minds was, irrespective of base, against the revolutionary-Jacobin conception of a quasi-totalitarian state in which all authority is made the monopoly of political government. It is in this tradition that kinship, guild, locality, region, parish, and voluntary association became once again ascendant in Western thought after the long period of adoration of the sovereign political state that had begun in the Renaissance. However harsh the religious ideas of, say, a Bonald or Maistre might be, there is nevertheless a clear vein of pluralism to be seen in their writings as in those of the other conservatives.

But if the conservative reaction began the rediscovery of

society and of social values, there were other groups, in no way conservative, to continue and to develop the reaction against political monism. Among liberals there were Lacordaire, Montalembert, Tocqueville, Wilhelm von Humboldt, Mill, and Acton, all of whom were manifestly influenced by the conservative recovery of the social, of the local, voluntary, and decentralized, that had begun with Burke.

In many ways the most interesting of all such groups in the nineteenth century is that which has come to be called the anarchist. There is a world of difference between the radicalism of the anarchists, as stated brilliantly by such minds as Proudhon and Bakunin and Kropotkin, and the radicalism of the Marxists and of other elements that made centralization of power, dictatorship of working class, even the national state itself the contexts of their war against capitalism. The hostility that can be seen to this day between Marxists of the main line and radicals of anarchist persuasion has its roots in the bitterness that developed early on between Marx and Proudhon in the late 1840s. For the smaller patriotism of family, guild, parish, and cooperative association Marx and his disciples had only contempt; such groups were consigned by Marxists, in accord with an iron determinism of philosophy of history, into the dustbin of history. But in the works of the anarchists, from Proudhon's day to ours, and nowhere stated more profoundly and encompassingly than in Kropotkin's *Mutual Aid* and *Fields, Factories and Workshops*, it is precisely on the foundation of such groups, each with maximum autonomy of function and authority, that the edifice of the free society is to be built.

· I do not for a moment question the major differences of emphasis which are to be found between nineteenth-century conservatives in the Burke tradition and anarchists molded by Proudhon. But I do not hesitate to say that there is a great deal more in common, so far as fundamental perspective is concerned, between a Burke and a

Proudhon than there is between the former and some of those who today style themselves conservatives and between the latter and the vast majority of radicals, over whelmingly dominated by Marx, in the late nineteenth and the twentieth centuries. In what I here term the recovery of the pluralist and the social, there is as much to be learned at the present time from the classical anarchists as from the classical conservatives.

There are others in the nineteenth and early twentieth centuries from whom there is much to be learned at this juncture in history. I think of the founders of the cooperative movement, consumer and producer, of the labor unions before they chose to enter the political lists, as they have in recent times, and also the guild socialists and the so-called political pluralists, the latter including such illustrious minds as J. N. Figgis, F. W. Maitland, Otto von Gierke, and Léon Duguit. It is one of the tragedies of the twentieth century that, in such large part as the intellectual consequence of World War I and its bizarre but momentous combination of so many creeds from the left, right, and center into the unitary, collectivist nationalism that has been a byword for political thought and planning ever since, we have lost for all practical purposes both the content and the buoyancy of the pluralism and devotion to the social which flourished in so many spheres in the decades following the French Revolution.

It is worth noting here also that what are today called the social sciences had their origins in the same currents of thought I have been writing of. Those minds in the very late eighteenth and the early nineteenth centuries which are by common assent the founders of the social sciences were for the most part extremely skeptical of the role of the state and apprehensive of the centralization its administering of power had already made a dominant fact in Western Europe. Such thinkers as Adam Smith, David Ricardo, Auguste Comte, Haller, Mill, and Maine, down through Le Play, Durkheim, Geddes, Weber, Spencer, and Sumner—one and all concerned with putting the study of social behavior and of institutions on a scientific basis—were far from envisaging social reconstruction and the conduct of society's institutions in the narrow terms of nationalist politics and administration. In reaction to the long tradition, the unitary tradition, that stretched from Renaissance to the bureaucratized monarchies of the eighteenth century, that reached very high apogee in the Jacobin centralization of the Revolution, these minds set themselves to discover the mechanisms, processes, and structures in society that proved that man was *not* dependent upon the political state as the unitary tradition argued—and continues to argue in our own day.

Behold how we have fallen! I mean in the social sciences. There are distinguished exceptions in our day, but for the most part the ideas and proposals of self-styled social scientists should require that the social sciences be termed for what they so largely are: the *political* sciences. It is the national state and its centralized power that is the be-all and end-all in the minds of the vast majority of social scientists in our time. The discovery of the free market and its self-regulating processes in the economy was—though our histories of social thought rarely reveal this fact—matched in the nineteenth century by the discovery of comparable processes in the whole social realm: in kinship, local community, voluntary association, and other forms of social life. Such discovery was, as I say, the overwhelming objective, and triumph, of the titans of social science. However different a Comte may have been from a Spencer, a Morgan from a Tylor, a Wundt from a William James, there was common belief in the reality of social and psychological processes which separated man from the pawn-like, robot-like position in which the philosophy of centralized, unitary sovereignty had put him ever since Hobbes.

For a time just after World War II there seemed to be a reversal of the drive toward politicization of mind that had dominated most of the twentieth century. There was the New Conservatism that had so much to do with restoring both Burke and Tocqueville to rightful place. In sociology and anthropology, and certain other small areas also, the ideas of functionalism were ascendant, ideas which went straight back to classical preoccupations with the nature of the social bond, those of the early and late nineteenth century, those which were mediated by such minds as Weber and Durkheim. In economics the now-historic Chicago school, chiefly under the intellectual leadership of Milton Friedman, flourished—indeed still does—and radiated an influence that had not been dreamed of since Keynes exerted his power over the economic mind in the 1930s. Then came, albeit in very different guise, the New Left, which also spurned, at least in the beginning, the political centralization and bureaucratization which had become hallmarks of the left up to that point. Not Marx but Proudhon was king; or if Marx it was the "humanistic" Marx of the Paris years that the New Left welcomed, not the Marx of *Capital* or *Criticism of the Gotha Program.*

But few if any of these movements would appear to have retained their luster. Emerging conservatism was dealt a possibly fatal hammer blow by the right that culminated in Nixon's Watergate; the new radicalism dissolved into intellectual inanity and vandalism on the campus. And the movements in the social sciences I mentioned above, particularly functionalism, are scarcely to be seen now. None of them has been proof against the political clerisy that governs, in effect, the modern social sciences as it does so many other areas of life and thought.

The Public and Private

I shall be brief here, for the point I wish to stress has already been set forth, though in different perspective and terminology, in the two preceding sections. If there is to be an efflorescence of a truly free and also stable society, there must be a revival of the prestige of the private, as contrasted with the public. Perhaps this revival is under way now in some degree, the result of the horrifying invasions of personal life which we have discovered to be endemic in modern democratic government, especially since Woodrow Wilson's America of World War I, since Roosevelt's New Deal, and most recently since the administrations of Kennedy, Johnson, and Nixon. True, the anguish over such invasions tends to be limited to the invasions of bugging, reading of mail, and other forms of governmental penetration to the innermost of individuals; it is not as often manifest in the kinds of invasion we see in the economy as the result of a host of regulatory agencies, or in the professions and in the universities and schools as the result of HEW's massive and ever-suspicious bureaus and offices. It is, as we know, difficult for the modern liberal to believe that the two kinds of invasion of personal privacy are closely related, that invasion which begins in the name of Plato or Rousseau commonly winds up as invasion in the name of CIA and FBI.

The main point here, though, is reversal, so far as possible, of the whole tendency in political and social philosophy that has, ever since the early nineteenth century, made the "public" ethically superior to the "private." It is Rousseau in the first instance, with his doctrine of the General Will, and then Bentham, with his hatred of all traditional privacies, his veneration of the collective, who are chiefly responsible, I believe, for the conviction that what is public is inherently better in the moral sense than what is private.

Insensibly in the nineteenth century the idea began to spread that what would be justified only in terms of private property, personal reward, economic position, or the like was inherently inferior, from the point of view of ethics, to what could be justified in the name of "public." The immense upsurge of national patriotism that I wrote of in the first chapter was bound, of course, to accelerate veneration for the public in contrast to the private, even though for a long time private enterprise in all spheres managed to prosper.

The result of all this has been that actions by individuals in the realm of the private which have been roundly condemned as immoral or antisocial by our political clerisy have managed until recently to escape censure if only service to the public could somehow be pleaded. To be aggressive and rapacious in the name of one's family, job, or business is by definition evil; but to be aggressive and rapacious in the name, say, of HEW or IRS, or, as we have learned in such nauseating detail, of the White House, carries a different evaluation in the mind of the political intellectual.

This, however, may well be changing. What began as dismay and revulsion over Watergate has possibly acquired a momentum that will come to include those regulatory agencies in Washington—and there are by now dozens of them—which invade every intimate, personal detail of our educational, intellectual, moral, medical, as well as our economic lives. There is no need to repeat here what I said above about the shape of the New Despotism. But it is worthwhile to insist that until the Private has become once again as honorable a concept as the Public— and this in *all* areas—we are not likely to know freedom.

The Renascence of Kinship

As I suggested at the beginning of this book, strange shapes are to be discerned among the mists which envelop the historic political community, among them those of revived religion, ethnicity, kinship, localism, and voluntary association. I shall concern myself here only with the last three.

There is no doubt that family and kindred hold a very different place in both intellectual and popular consciousness from what they held even a generation ago. Then the heritage of the rationalist Enlightenment was almost entirely unchallenged, and there was little place in this heritage for a group as ancient and freighted with traditionalism as the family. A great many minds earlier in this century would have agreed with Rousseau and Bentham that kinship was both obsolete and a barrier to individual freedom. That is plainly not the situation today. A steady succession of studies has made clear the vital place the family holds in individual motivation toward education, reason, and achievement generally. In society in large there would appear to be forces germinating in support of not only the conjugal family but also, more important in some ways, kindred. Very possibly the popularity of "kin groups" among the young is some kind of augury.

The great contributions of kinship to society are, on the one hand, the sense of membership in and continuity of the social order, generation after generation; and on the other, the spur to individual achievement, in all areas, that the intimacy of the family alone seems able to effect. These are the essential psychological functions of family, and may be seen as the sources of the desire for autonomy and freedom of the household and kindred which has for many millennia been the strongest force against the kind of military or political power that atomizes a social order. Between family and state there has been everywhere, throughout history, an inverse relation so far as the influence of each on society is concerned.

More than any other social scientist, it was Frederick Le Play in the last century who first saw clearly and systematically the close relation between what he called the "stem" family—*la famille souche*—and the general creative prosperity of the surrounding social order. The "stem" family Le Play found among the Jews, ancient Greeks, pre-Imperial Romans, and most of the European peoples prior to the advent of the national state and its increasingly atomizing effect upon kindred, clan, and household. It was a type of family, Le Play observed, that combined communality and opportunity for individual expression in a way that avoided the corporatism of the ancient patriarchal type of family on the one hand and the egoistic particularism of modernity on the other. Le Play thought revival of the family, for purposes of both mutual aid and individual enterprise in all spheres, the sovereign need of a Western Europe that was fast becoming stait-jacketed by national centralization and bureaucracy.

Every great age, and every great people, Le Play discovered, is characterized at bottom by the strength of the kinship principle. We can, he argued, use the family as an almost infallible touchstone of the material and cultural prosperity of a people. When it is strong, closely linked with private property, treated as the essential context of education in society, and its sanctity recognized by law and custom, the probability is extremely high that we shall find the rest of the social order characterized by that subtle but puissant fusion of stability and individual mobility which is the hallmark of great ages.

I believe that by common assent the Greeks, Jews, and Chinese are the three most creative peoples in history of whom we have substantial record. There is not much of high quality in Western civilization that is not the product of thought processes emanating within from the first two and from thought processes diffused to the West from China. Naturally, fusion in complex and ofen subtle ways of these thought processes has been a vital aspect of the record. Observe in all three of these peoples, especially during periods of their greatest creative fertility, the immense strength of the family tie. Family has been more than the nidus of cohesion and of continuity; it has been visibly the source of themes in ethics, literature, and art which have been among the very brightest and most durable in the history of civilization. Merely to study the great fifth century B.C. in ancient Greece is to be struck repeatedly by the power that kinship and its multifold themes exerted upon tragedy and comedy alike, upon religion, and also upon philosophy. Nor was the matter very different in England's Age of Elizabeth, not very far in quality and intensity from the Athens of Pericles. Here too we are struck by endemic fascination with family, descent, lineage, and all the vices as well as virtues inseparable from the bond of kinship. It is pretty much the same, I believe, in all the greater ages of culture. Granted, as I shall stress in the next section, that localism is also vital, family yet remains the greatest simple element of a creative culture—that is, so far as social contexts are concerned.

I am aware that more than simple family allegiance is involved in such ages. Using literature as an example, there is almost invariably to be seen the unleashing of passions, emotions, and moral evils which can properly be regarded as signs of disintegration of family, of conflicts often too great to be contained within a single kinship community. But such observation in no way negates the social and psychological importance of the kinship principle. Only the naivest would ever define or conceive of family as a synonym for unadulterated love and tranquility.

Almost certainly it is the form and significance of the family tie rather than racial or genetic stock that explains individual achievement in history. That variations of genetic quality exist among population groups, as among individuals, is scarcely to be denied. But, as Tocqueville declared, almost passionately, in his interchange of views on race with Gobineau, it is unlikely that we shall ever be able to so isolate and hold constant non-genetic factors as to assess usefully the role of the biological—the actual, opational function of the genetic—in the appearance of genius.

It was Sir Francis Galton among modern scholars who first called attention to the striking relationship between individual achievement and family line. He did not err in seeing the whole issue in terms of family—conceived as a unity in time as well as of place. Where Galton unfortunately did err was in his assumption that what is crucial in family is *genetic*. It was to the biological element, basically, that Galton was referring in his notable concept—and it is only a hypothesis, we must remember, in Galton—of "genius." Why are certain individuals great? Because, Galton tells us, of their "genius"; that is, their superior biological aptitude transmitted through the family line.

What Galton neglected in kinship was the important *social* aspect of norms, roles, statuses, and traditions transmitted from generation to generation. That talented individuals so frequently are found to have talented, or at least extraordinary, fathers or mothers, and even more distant forebears and relatives may and probably does argue something in behalf of genetic transmission, but it much more visibly and incontestably argues something in the way of continuity of cultural patterns: patterns of incentive—recorded achievement to serve as example; of the kind of training and instruction that can come only from someone who is emotionally close, indeed persistingly close; and of the discipline, encouragement, and emulation which are so vital in the formation of personalities, good or bad, gifted or sterile.

In his superb *The Art of Teaching*, the classical scholar Gilbert Highet has given special attention to the father as teacher in history. Rightly does Highet write: "It would be interesting to write a book on the fathers of great men: those who educated their sons by neglecting them, those who educated their sons by bullying and thwarting them, those who educated their sons by being their friends." Precisely! Let us have no nonsense about love and unremitting devotion—among the most evanescent and rare of qualities, surely, in the total picture of the family that history reveals; for, paradoxical as it may seem, it is not love—least of all sexual passion—that the family has been built around historically, but, rather, duty and obligation.

And these, obviously, may or may not coexist with love and affection.

This is why, as Durkheim pointed out in several of his lectures and essays on morality, the conjugal family—so single-mindedly stressed in modern culture—is the last important aspect of the kinship institution save only in respect to its procreative function. As we know, not many peoples apparently have allowed even the conjugal tie to rest upon something so fragile as the emotion of love; but even if we assume that in most places at most times a majority of spouses knew something akin to passionate love, however fleetingly, the great strength of the family has everywhere been consanguineal rather than conjugal. And here, not affection, but duty, obligation, honor, mutual aid, and protection have been the key elements.

And yet, all of this kept in mind, we would be blind were we to neglect the countless instances in the biographies of the great where the kindly if not affectionate devotion of a parent or grandparent or collateral relative proved to be the decisive factor in the subsequent development of the individual concerned. Granted, as Highet points out, that Beethoven's father was a drunk and often a bully, with Beethoven's own revolt against his father a paramount aspect of his life, the father yet taught Beethoven at the age of four both violin and clavier. And there is much reason to suppose that the relationships that existed between Mozart and his father, within the Bach family as a whole, or, changing our field of illustration, between Aristotle and his biologist-physician father or St. Augustine and his Christian mother and pagan father, have been by far more characteristic of the emergence of genius or great talent.

Quite as important, though, as the direct relation between two or more family members of different generations is the tradition that can develop within a family line over a succession of generations. No prescription can be infallible in such complex matters as these, but one is almost tempted to recommend a minimum of three sequential generations of cultural quality within a single family line for the production of truly high talent. Heaven knows, exceptions abound of every kind, and the last thing I would claim for this section is the secret of genius, which will no doubt be a well kept one for a long time. And yet the continuity of these intellectual and cultural elements of high quality in a family line in which unity of property has a powerful constraining effect is surely of inestimable value. As I say, Galton did not err in pointing to genealogical continuity, only in assuming that biological stock was alone vital in this. Far more important, it would seem to me, in the eventual emergence of a Charles Darwin was exposure to the legacy of a grandfather like Erasmus, no less fascinated than his grandson with fauna and flora and the complex relations in time and space to be found among them. For such a legacy cannot help but create an ambience of striking value and stimulus. Nor was Charles Darwin without other family relationships, on both sides, which must have had cumulative effect in the creation of a fertile tradition.

Emulation is a most important element of the creative process. The Roman Velleius Paterculus, among the first to speculate on the spasmodic appearance of genius and great talent in history, using the drama as his primary example of thought, concluded that emulation was the vital factor. Naturally, it need not be emulation solely or even at all of a parent or other relative, but clearly kinship is the commonest field of emulation.

There are, of course, surrogate fathers. I mean the kind of teacher or "father" of whom Socrates will always remain the most luminous example in Western thought. Here instruction is vastly more than what is ordinarily conveyed by that word. There is the whole range of ties, from explicit coercion and discipline to affection and devotion, that makes the teaching-learning process almost indistinguishable from what might be found in the kinship context. What Alfred North Whitehead called "the habitual vision of greatness" is without any question crucial in the life of the pupil—be he child of parent or child of great teacher. There could not be very many truly creative minds in history which lacked altogether in their formative periods "the habitual vision of greatness," whether this was experienced in family or, *in loco parentis,* in a Socrates-Plato relation or, as the American educational idiom has it, with Mark Hopkins at one end of a log and a pupil at the other.

Heredity, then, is immensely important to any society that prizes genius and talent. But it is transmitted by the germ plasm. Social and cultural and moral heredity are equally real within any family line.

For a long time it was a cardinal proposition of the democratic dogma—one derived chiefly from Rousseau—that what had been accomplished by kinship for so may millennia in history could be accomplished in equal, if not superior, degree by other structures, such as the public school. Given the stress upon equalitarianism in the Rousseuian and populist traditions of democracy, animus toward the family might be expected. Rousseau, as we have noted, saw the state as the means of saving the children from the prejudices of their parents, and like all others who have made the state the sacred object of their aspirations, he saw it as the indispensable instrument of the kind of equality to which kinship, when active and buoyant, must forever be a barrier.

We have discovered that the school, for all the vast sums of money spent on it in American society, is not, by itself, particularly effective. That it is indispensable to any society such as ours is evident enough; the technical demands of modern society make school and college imperative. But, as countless studies—the most important and exhaustive being the now famous Coleman report—have suggested, the effectiveness of the school is greatest when it is united in a pupil's life with family. We know of great peoples and ages of history where a strong family system, together with deliberately created surrogates for the family and its roles, has existed in the total absence of institutions comparable to our by now almost hopelessly formalized and bureaucratized schools and colleges. But we have not yet seen a great people or great age of history resting on the school or college to the exclusion of those ties and motivations which are inseparable from kinship.

It should be obvious that family, not the individual, is the real molecule of society, the key link of the social chain of being. It is inconceivable to me that either intellectual growth or social order or the roots of liberty can possibly be maintained among a people unless the kinship tie is strong and has both functional significance and symbolic authority. On no single institution has the modern political state rested with more destructive weight than on the family. From Plato's obliteration of the family in his *Republic*, through Hobbes, Rousseau, Bentham, and Marx, hostility to family has been an abiding element of the West's political clerisy.

The Revival of Localism

Along with the apparent beginnings of a renascence of the kinship tie are those of revival of the sense of locality and neighborhood. There is, of course, close affinity between the two types of social attachment, and there has been ever since the local community came into being, with the rise of the agricultural arts, approximately ten thousand years ago. The toll exacted from both social unities by modern forces of collectivization and centralization has been great.

Recent events in both the totalitarian countries and the democracies make evident how deeply rooted the local tie, like kinship, remains in the human spirit. Extreme measures taken during the past several years by the Chinese government suggest how resistant to national collectivization village and regional allegiances remain. In Soviet Russia even after a half century of continuous official assault upon these allegiances, we learn that they continue to exist and, at times, to make difficult the life of the bureaucrat in Moscow.

In the United States conflict between national government and the smaller regional and local ties has been evident from the beginning, with nationalism on the whole winning out. Even so the emotional roots of local loyalties remain strong. The results in this country of the government effort to achieve racial balance in the schools is some indication of how profound are human loyalties to neighborhood and local community. I do not doubt that some of the resistance to busing is racist in origins. But by this time agreement is quite general that the greater part of the opposition to such busing springs directly from pride in and sense of attachment in neighborhood.

Nor are expressions of such attachment confined to opposition to integration quotas. We could have taken some counsel from the bitter reactions beginning in the late 1940s, perhaps even earlier, to urban renewal and to the depredations of what has so well been called "the Federal bulldozer." Jane Jacobs is only the most eloquent of experts on town and city planning to register dismay at the callous destruction in the larger cities of old and tightly constituted communities, some ethnic, some occupational, most merely local, under the spur of Federal programs of urban reconstruction. It would well be that the greatest and most valuable single consequence of such nationalizing programs is the counteracting awareness on the part of individuals of how much locality means in their lives.

The fault is by no means lodged in Federal government alone. Great industries, trade unions, and other elements of American society have not infrequently shown—and often lived to regret—comparable insensitivity to local allegiances. We have seen, during the past two or three decades, small businesses, branches of large business, and union locals react with extreme passion to centralizing, nationalizing programs of great industrial and labor organizations. The situation is hardly different in the university. It would be difficult to list accurately all of the once-small, once-local colleges and schools which, after World War II, were swept into large, unified, centralized systems of university administration in the various states, all in the name of educational progress and efficiency.

Many years ago, in his *School for Dictators*, Ignazio Silone wrote:

> The first test to be applied in judging an alleged democracy is the degree of self-governing of its local institutions. If the master's rule in the factories is absolute, if the trade unions are controlled by bureaucracies, if the province is governed by representatives of the central government, there can be no true and complete democracy. Only local government can accustom men to responsibility and independence, and enable them to take part in the wider life of the state.

Silone gives modern expression to a very old theme in Western writing on freedom. Aristotle knew how important, even with the culmination of social evolution in the political state, the local community and its prosperity were, and his criticisms of Plato's centralized, unitary state rest upon defense of localism as much as any other form of social attachment. Similarly, the names of St. Benedict, Thomas More, Althusius, Burke, Tocqueville, Le Play, W. H. Riehl, and, in our century, Patrick Geddes and Victor Branford in England and Lewis Mumford in this country are properly associated with awareness of the importance of local ties in a genuinely stable and free society.

Unfortunately the tradition they represent has been overshadowed, especially in modern times, by that which is devoted to the homogeneous national state and to centralization of power. Plato had no more affection for local autonomies within his ideal political order than he did for any other distractions from its unity. And from Plato through the Roman Lawyers, Marsiglio, Machiavelli, Hobbes, Rousseau, and Bentham, down to our own clerisy of power today, there has been scant regard for the values of localism and regionalism. Progress was escape from localism. Mumford writes that in the eighteenth century the *philosophes* and others of like devotion to the uses of central power would in drawing a burgomaster commonly give him the head of a donkey. In England Bentham and other Philosophical Radicals, committed as they were to nationalized civil service with power focused in the national capital, did everything in their capacity to weaken the traditional liberties and functions of the villages and towns, in which Bentham saw only the dead hand of the past.

There is no more affection for the values of localism in Marx and Engels. Marx, as I have noted, even endorsed English depredations in India on the ground that these would hasten Indian emancipation from the village. "The idiocy of rural life" is the phrase in the *Manifesto* that faithfully reflects Marx's attitude toward local allegiances, and his own hatred was continued in that of the Bolsheviks for the *mir* and other traditional unities of place in Russia.

Such, however, was the depth of regard in Russia for local attachments that the Bolsheviks were forced, in their bid for power, to support a high degree of local autonomy. Hannah Arendt in *On Revolution* writes that the most popular, and undoubtedly crucial, of all Bolshevik proposals in 1917, second only to bread, was the idea of the *soviet*, which was in principle a local articulation of economic, social, cultural, and political functions. "All power to the soviets" was, as every student of the Russian Revolution knows, one of the most popular slogans, and it was only after several of the peoples' soviets had been put down bloodily by Bolshevik forces in the interests of party rule and communist centralization that it became evident how hollow Lenin's promises regarding the soviets actually were. To this day the use of the word "soviet" in the official name of the Russian nation is some testimony to the continuing appeal of the idea of the soviets. Their existence is, however, purely nominal and has been since the earliest days of the Revolution. It was discovery of that fact, almost above anything else, that turned such previously eager minds as Emma Goldman, Alexander Berkman, and Peter Kropotkin away in deep disillusionment from the Russian Revolution.

It is interesting to discover that prior to about World War I, the principle of localism had become a powerful one in a good many Western circles. In England the first major book of Sidney and Beatrice Webb was on the history of local government in England, and the story of the Webbs' life can be told pretty much in the tragic evolution we see from their early interest in localism and pluralism to their notorious whitewash of Stalinist government in the 1930s. Along with the early Webbs there were the Fabians and the Guild Socialists in England. On the continent the syndicalists and cooperationists were strong. In all of these, under whatever name, there was deep recognition of the vital importance of the local community. In the social philosophy of the great town planning movements associated with Riehl, Le Play, Geddes, and Branford in Europe and with Ralph Adams Cram in this country, the local community and its development was foremost. Socialist thought in this country—never extensive, to be sure—was strongly tinctured by values at once utopian and local. The increasingly nationalized socialism of such a country as Germany was utterly foreign to socialist thought in America.

World War I is, I think the sharp dividing line. Afterward interest in local community did not attain its earlier intensity, flavor, and eloquence. The influence of Woodrow Wilson and his New Freedom in this country and of Lenin in European radical thought had a great deal to do with turning revolutionary and progressive thought away from its concern with locality or, for that matter, any of the smaller unities. The nation, the centralized nation freed of local regional encrustations, seemed to an ever larger number of intellectuals the true repository of the spirit of progress. Suddenly the local community became the symbol of reaction, dullness, mediocrity, and oppression of mind. Sinclair Lewis's *Main Street*, *Babbitt*, and other novels were only the most popular of a literature in the 1920s that satirized, caricatured, and pilloried the village or small town. And such rendering of local roots was in keeping with the increasing nationalism to be seen in the social sciences, in education, and in government policy from World War I on.

Schools and colleges were particularly hurt by it. So much of their genius and effectiveness had been precisely their close relation to locality and region, making possible an unrivaled diversity and opportunity for experiment in American education, as contrasted with European. But increasingly, from one side of the country to the other, national models began to prevail. Universities like Harvard sought to broadcast the image of a "national" rather than local or regional university; and what Harvard began, and managed to do with some distinction, other universities in all parts of the country sought to emulate, often taking Harvard as the model but failing for the most part to achieve comparable distinction—and losing much of what had been distinctive and potentially creative in their regional flavor.

As I say, all that may be about to reverse itself. Certainly, there is a manifest reaffirmation of the tie of neighborhood, whether in city or suburb, some of it—though not all, by any means—in reaction to integration-based busing operations. But there is more, I suspect, to this beginning of local renascence than reaction to busing or to urban renewal projects emanating from Washington. The weakened position of nationalism on the world scene, the growing acceptance of transnational economic and political authorities, bespeak a certain universalism that harmonizes very nicely with localism in any given country. This point needs brief expansion.

Despite a widespread misunderstanding, the era of the national state has been as disruptive of an earlier universalism in the West as it has of an earlier localism. There is nothing paradoxical in the fact that in medieval society, when local roots were strong, one could make his way—as so many traders, merchants, students, and others did regularly—throughout Western society without the slightest thought of passports, visas, or other restrictions upon travel. It was, as only a few historians have adequately realized, the absence then of the national state in any significant form that made possible economic and intellectual universality, as well as the vigorous town and village life of the Middle Ages. Such remarkable instances of universalism as the various leagues of cities—Hanseatic, Rhenish, and other—could only have been present in a society largely free of centralized national sovereignty. And that fact is evidenced strongly by the almost instant disappearance of the leagues of cities and towns during the period when national states were becoming powerful. I think it entirely possible that in the years ahead, if national sovereignty should continue to weaken, if the more universal types of economic and political organization continue to increase on the world scene, that the local community everywhere will flourish. We shall then have a chance to see how constrictive, how suffocating, the modern national state has been in its impact upon regional and local diversity.

It is possible that we shall also see a great recovery of culture, high culture, a possible liberation, or the begin-

ning of it, from the twin forces of triviality and subjectivism which have been so long ascendant in Western imaginative writing and art. It is impossible to be certain in
such matters, but the historic roots of the greater ages
have lain in diverse, varied, relatively small areas rather
than in the atmosphere that goes with bigness, imperson-
ality, and standardization. We refer properly, of course, to
American literature, but looking back on its more resplendent periods of creativity, it is impossible to overlook locality and region. What Van Wyck Brooks and others
have referred to as the flowering of New England took
place in a strikingly small geographic sector; so did those
other efflorescences we identify with New York at the
turn of the century, San Francisco, Chicago, and a few
other places. It has not been different, really, throughout
the history of the creative mind, and this seems to be as
true of the sciences, including technology, as of the arts.
"The glory that was Greece" was really the achievement
of a tiny part of Greece—Athens—in a very short period
of time. Rome was, by modern standards, a small town
when Vergil and Lucretius flourished. The remarkable
developments in the arts and science which we find in the
twelfth and thirteenth centuries are all tied closely to
highly individualized towns; and this role of the locality
remains in substantial degree right down to the present
century. We take nothing away from the vital, indispensable role of the city in the history of creativity and intellectual freedom in noting all this, for, prior to the
metropolitan giants in this century, cities have always
possessed, despite their relative size, a tightness and a
sense of enclosure that, as is only too obvious now, have
disappeared or weakened.

There is also the fact of neighborhood in the city,
seemingly as important to the creative mind as to the rest
of us. Even on present evidence, artists, writers, and
others engaged in analogous pursuits seem to like a certain

degree of propinquity. If the modern city as a whole has become too large to serve as did a medieval Florence, Bologna, Oxford, Paris, or a more modern London, Boston, and New York as the effective context of intellectual labor, there is no reason why, within our swollen cities today, there cannot be local influences, as in neighborhoods. Even in a city like New York, there is far more neighborhood community than we commonly give it credit for in the country at large. The tragedy is the lack of recognition in so much national and state policy of the role of neighborhood. When the local-ethnic sentiment began a few years ago to manifest itself in school matters, reaction against it from school systems, urban government, and the Federal bureaucracy was for the most part very strong. No one aware of what happened, what continues to happen, will deny that mistakes have been made, sometimes with serious lowering of academic standards, but it would be wise policy to encourage, aid, and reinforce such local sentiment. Only when education—and art and thought and leadership—can be seen and understood in genuinely local terms is efflorescence likely. It has always been this way.

By comparison the tie of nationalism in the modern West has been singularly ineffective in promoting intellectual works of high order. I think it is possible to see a certain impetus in the beginning when nationalization takes command, as in England and France in the sixteenth and seventeenth centuries, in Germany in the late nineteenth, and in the United States after the Revolutionary War. I have noted above the coincidence of creative ages and a high degree of politicization, but this coincidence is almost always of very short duration. Alas, what happens after the scintillating presence of a Pericles, Julius Caesar, Frederick II, or like figure in political history is the routinization of politics and a consequent drying up of stimulus.

And in the world we have known since about the middle of the nineteenth century, the spirit of nationalism—so often a deliberately manufactured spirit—has rarely if at all entered into great creative performance. The art, the letters, the music, and the architecture we associate with celebration of the nation as a whole and of its capital is almost always deadly. We see such work at its worst when the nationalist mind is seized by war and its passions. This state of mind can be very destructive of art and thought, as in its depredations on works thought to be favorable to the enemy (the tearing out of German songs from American songbooks during World War I will serve as an example here), and its record of constructive achievement is dismal and frightening.

Any release, though, from the hold of nationalism in all areas is not likely to come easily or soon. I [have noted] the signal decline of the tie of patriotism in each of the Western countries, but it will not do to see in that decline the weakening also of the spirit of nationalism. For that spirit is sustained largely by centralization and collectivization of power, qualities which, as we have seen, continue to loom large in the conventional wisdom of the political clerisy. A whole philosophy of history—false, as I believe, but not the less powerful in its hold on the intellectual mind—tells us that progress has consisted in mankind's liberation from the smaller unities of village, town, and region, and in mobilization at the national level of loyalties which once went directly to them. To think, dream, plan, and hope in terms of the entire nation has been for a long time the mark of the political intellectual in whatever area he works—economy, education, or the arts and sciences. What Tocqueville wrote on the subject remains pertinent:

> I am of the opinion that, in the democratic ages which are opening upon us, individual independence and local liberties will ever be the products of art; that centralization will be the natural government.

Voluntary Association

Despite the American creed of individualism, which locates motivation and achievement in the recesses of the individual mind and character, human accomplishment in almost any form is the product of association, usually in small and informal structures whose essence is a high degree of autonomy. This is in no way to obliterate the fact of individuality, to deny the superlative powers which lie in certain individuals in all realms of culture and society; it is simply to call attention to the contexts in which individuals, even the greatest, thrive. What John Dewey wrote many years ago is eloquent and correct:

> Individuals who are not bound together in associations, whether domestic, economic, religious, political, artistic or educational, are monstrosities. It is absurd to suppose that the ties which hold them together are merely external and do not react into mentality and character, producing the framework of personal disposition.

It is only under the spell of the romantic individualism we have known for two centuries in the West that the myth of purely individual achievement—reflected in the enormous number of biographies written during the last hundred years or more—has achieved the commanding importance it so plainly has even at the present time. Only in the best of these, and even then the going can be difficult, do we come to sense the crucial importance in the life of even the most gifted creator or innovator of the tiny network of human attachments which is the true field of the creative impulse. Over and over, whether in literature, art, science, politics, economic enterprise, or technology, what we discover if we look carefully is not the lone individual obeying inner impulses but the human being who at some crucial point in his development has known, commonly in the most intimate and spontaneous of ways, a circle of other human beings brought together by common interests. That statement is as true of Darwin and Einstein as it is of Cézanne and Picasso. There is not a hint of social determinism in it; only recognition of the fact that it is in association—intimate, relevant, and free association—that individual energies become stimulated, strengthened, and, finally, focused.

Crucial are the *voluntary* groups and associations. It is the element of the spontaneous, of untrammeled, unforced volition, that is undoubtedly vital to creative relationships among individuals. Such associations have figured prominently throughout history, and we should no doubt know a great deal more than we do about them were it not for a historiography in the West that has been anchored for so long in the political state on the one hand and the individual on the other. Every city, every large, formal organization, when carefully examined, turns out to be a network of small, informal, voluntary associations. If cafes, taverns, and similar establishments have assumed importance in the history of culture, along with forums and town squares, it is because these are such natural environments for autonomous groups. It would be interesting to know whether, as the result of urban planning and contemporary styles of architecture, and also of skyrocketing of land values, there are as many such natural environments as there once were. I am inclined to believe that there are not, a fact that is bound to affect the nature of personality and the whole creative process.

But voluntary associations have an importance well beyond what they do directly for their individual members. Most of the functions which are today lodged either in the state or in great formal organizations came into existence in the first place in the context of largely voluntary association. This is true of mutual aid in all of its forms—education, socialization, social security, recreation, and the like. To say, as is so often said, that responsibility has passed from the *individual* to the state is a half-truth. It is much truer to say that responsibility has passed to the state from what were once voluntary associations. It is in the context of such association, in short, that most steps in social progress have taken place. To compare our bureaucratized, politicized age with some age in the past when individuals were obliged to look out for themselves, singly or in small households, is mere fantasy. Once we look carefully into the matter we are surprised by how many social groups, associations, and communities there actually were through which the fragility and precariousness of individual and family life were moderated.

It is impossible not to conclude that the impulse to form spontaneous and voluntary associations, of all sizes, has diminished in recent times. How could it not have? The whole thrust of modern society toward a politically managed social order; the well-recorded jealousy of governments, even democratic ones, toward such associations; and the incredible network of ordinances, zoning regulations, legal preemptions, and other emanations of the political order which hamstring the associative ethic—all these and other forces make voluntary association difficult indeed in our age, especially, it should be noted, when such association tries to deal with really significant social and economic problems.

There is a curious paradox in the legal position of voluntary associations today. In one sense they have a constitutional status they lacked in the past in this country. Yet it is not difficult to show that for political reasons their actual autonomy and mobility are less than in the past. Strangely, and regrettably, the Founding Fathers said nothing about freedom of association in their Constitution; the right to petition and freedom of assembly are very different from freedom of association. One can only conclude that the reigning political minds in this country were as uneasy at the thought of internal, private associations as were many European thinkers, *philosophes* included. The prized unity of the state, ideally resting on the people considered as a whole rather than as an assemblage of possibly discordant groups, made such associations unwelcome; for they all too easily become, it was thought on both sides of the Atlantic, conspiracies. Secret societies, even those in the form of lodges, were for a long time suspect on the ground of possible conspiracy. Very probably the law of conspiracy, to this day a powerful and enveloping law, has discouraged a great deal of voluntary association. An act that is relatively venial in individual conduct can become felonious when engaged in by two or more persons. Such is the state's fear of internal association, going back deep in modern political history.

In 1958 the Supreme Court in effect brought freedom of association up to constitutional level by affirming the right of the NAACP to carry on its regular activities in Alabama. According to Charles E. Rice, whose study of the relation of law to associations is seminal, this decision was the first in American history to give constitutional status to a freedom that has been widespread in America almost from the beginning.

Even so, one could wish for a specific, detailed amendment to the Constitution granting this intellectually and politically vital freedom. For, however welcome the Supreme Court decision is, it has to be seen among a whole thicket of other decisions, laws, and ordinances which by this time in our history make the actual act of voluntary association difficult. The paradox I mentioned above consists in the fact that while we do live now in the afterglow of a salutary Supreme Court decision, still the general combination of politicization of society, increasing recourse to bureaucracy and formal organization, and the predictably hostile attitude of the clerisy of power makes any really substantive freedom of association seem tenuous.

In the past freedom of association in this country was far from tenuous. Lack of constitutional sanction notwithstanding, proliferation of voluntary groups, associations, and societies was great throughout the nineteenth century, down, indeed, to World War I. Nothing seems to have impressed Tocqueville, and then later Lord Bryce in his own study of American democracy, more than did the great wealth of associations, constructed around a large variety of objectives and interests. Tocqueville well knew the status of such associations in France; a status that went back to the *ancien régime* and that had been given heavy confirmation by the Revolutionary law of 1791 which in effect forbade all voluntary associations. He knew too that nothing in the American Constitution specifically granted Americans this form of freedom, one that Tocqueville admired. He had already formed a strong opinion of the necessity of free voluntary associations to any free society, especially when that society is a democracy. He was as sensitive as Lamennais, Lacordaire, and Montalembert to the insufficiency of a merely individual freedom in the modern mass state. His firm belief in autonomous association, along with localism and decentralization, carried through indeed to his work on the Constitutional Commission in the Revolution of 1848, where, with Lamennais (whom he did not much like), he made every possible effort to embed these principles in the constitution.

It is of course in *Democracy in America* that we have the most eloquent and penetrating account of the value of voluntary association. There Tocqueville sets forth this value in political, social, and also psychological terms. Voluntary political associations are, of course, political parties, and Tocqueville, recognizing and lamenting somewhat the "decline" of great parties in the United States, declares political parties indispensable to the stability and the freedom of democratic life. Few things, he tells us, are more misunderstood by the sovereigns of Europe than the contributions that could and would be made to the stability of their kingdoms and republics by profuse political association. Political parties not only provide the seed ground for new and necessary legislation; they are also vital structures of opinion and sentiment which would otherwise become mere dust. The occasional danger that a political association may prove to be a conspiracy rather than a party is small by comparison with the dangers which ensue when there are no such associations.

It was, however, in the social, economic, and cultural realms that Tocqueville was most impressed by the remarkable proliferation of associations in American life. Here, in self-help, mutual-aid, and assurance associations, in organizations directed toward the accomplishment of some moral or spiritual end, and in the multitude of little societies for the furtherance of mind and taste, was a whole body of membership and behavior that Tocqueville thought utterly vital to freedom in a democracy. In earlier monarchical-aristocratic society, he tells us, the need for such associations was not so great, for in these the principle of social class, particularly of the aristocracy itself, along with the kind of local diversity that existed, went a long way toward providing society with that variegation and context of autonomy that was required by freedom. In modern democracy, however, the sheer weight of authority that is placed upon the people as a whole, the atomizing effects of democratic sovereignty upon traditional, especially class, distinctions, and the constant threat of public opinion limiting true individual freedom, all give special importance to the preservation of voluntary association. Each such association is a nursery of freedom, if only because it is built around a value or idea that men wish to be free to espouse. Voluntary associations are buffers between individual and state.

"Among the laws that rule human societies," Tocqueville wrote, "there is one which seems to me more precise and clear than all others. If men are to remain civilized or to become so, the art of associating together must grow and improve in the same ratio in which equality of conditions is increased."

I said above that the impulse to significant voluntary association in Western society has withered in recent times.

Yet as I write there are also faint signs of a possible resurgence of this impulse—to be seen among the varied reactions today to the failure of the political community in so many areas. The same pattern of forces that includes renewals of religion in certain manifestations, of ethnic loyalties, and of cooperative relationships in the smaller spheres of living, includes also, I think, a recrudescence of the spirit of voluntary association. It is noteworthy that more and more studies of the phenomenon are beginning to appear, that increased interest is clearly manifest among the younger age groups, and that objectives which only a decade or two ago would have been made the subjects of political action are at the present time nuclei of voluntary association. What would be immensely beneficial is the development of a clear philosophy of voluntary association that could take its place alongside philosophies—also to be hoped for—of the local community and of decentralization. Any such philosophy will, however, have to face the political clerisy's deeply seated aversion to any form of pluralism. The Renaissance-born, revolution-developed fondness for the unitary state based on an undifferentiated mass of citizens, availing itself of every possible technique of centralized power applied in nationalist-collectivist terms, will not disappear easily. To the mind of the political intellectual today, as in the age of the Italian humanists and in that of the Jacobins, nothing must seem more absurd, more reactionary, more at odds with the locomotive of history than what is private, voluntary, and social.

But one need only scan the pages of comparative social and cultural histories to be made aware of how often human societies have been rescued from political paralysis, from the boredom and apathy which go with homogeneity of life, and from the subjectivism that in time becomes the death of culture, by processes which are, at bottom, those of voluntary association turning itself imaginatively to new ways of life and thought.

A New Laissez-Faire

Basically, the problem is not one of any single type of group, community, or association. The essential problem to be met, whether by legislative and judicial design or by the forces of history, is that of creating a setting in which the social impulse will flourish. I mean the impulse to form associations of whatever kind in which significant function or role in the larger society can be combined with the sense of the social bond, of social authority, that is so fundamental in any of its significant forms. I have argued at length in this book that the greatest need in our age is that of somehow redressing the balance between political-military power on the one hand and the structure of authority that lies in human groups such as neighborhood, family, labor union, profession, and voluntary association.

What is required, obviously, is a form of laissez-faire that has for its object, not the abstract individual, whether economic man or political man, but rather the social group or association. I argued this a quarter of a century ago, although briefly, in *The Quest for Community*, suggesting there that only through such laissez-faire could the human need for community be met through ways other than politics—political action, political crusade, political Leviathan.

Nothing that has happened in twenty-five years indicates that the need for this kind of laissez-faire is anything but greater than ever. In an era of prosperity and opulence that could hardly have been imagined in 1950 we have seen the powers of government and bureaucracy steadily increase, to the corresponding moribundity of the social order. Mere economic affluence, we have discovered, can indeed be a virtual recipe for the widespread turning of responsibilities over to the ever-flowing revenue powers of government and for the consequent divorce between human beings and their ordinary, natural impulses toward social initiative.

What is required and what, on the evidence of history, periodically occurs is the establishment of a scene in which there is profound incentive to form, and to live in and by, associations or groups which are distinct from political government. It is absurd to say that such a scene exists at the present time. In countless ways, as I have indicated in the preceding sections, government, and also a whole attitude of mind supported by the political clerisy, discourages or makes difficult such associations. The police-sniffing in the name of conspiracy that goes on constantly is well accompanied by the kind of sniffing in disdain we find in the ranks of political intellectuals for whom anything worth doing is only worth doing through the political government. The blunt fact is, a large number of obstacles, starting with the mentality of the political clerisy, exists today so far as groups and communities are concerned, just as a large number of obstacles could be seen at the time Adam Smith, Turgot, and Ricardo proposed, in effect, a laissez-faire for individuals. I consider it just as important today as it was in these philosophers' time to stimulate through every possible means the liberty and creativeness of individuals. But our age is very different from theirs in the degree of strength that then existed, but now does not exist, in the social sphere.

It is not necessary to repeat what I have said in several connections in this book: that individual initiative and talent are rarely to be found outside the framework of some kind of moral and intellectual community. The point is simply that where an Adam Smith could rightly see in the sometimes too-abundant strength of the traditional social order occasional oppression of individual talent, in our own day the problem is that of finding the means of generating a social order within which the individual can live and derive a spirit of initiative. Nowhere, not in economy, state, or culture in any of its forms, do we in fact find aggregates of "individuals." What we find are human beings bound, in one or other degree, by ties of work, friendship, recreation, learning, faith, love, and mutual aid. That such ties can on occasion become constricting is not to be questioned. There are indeed ages, as I have noted, which are too strong in the social ties which in our own age in the West have grown so weak and attenuated. Nor do I doubt that there are a few individuals, by no means pathological, who, far more than most of us, desire solitude and liberation from the social bond in any form. Such individuals are not, however, elements of the problem we face at the present time.

Clearly, in an epoch of massive politicization, and with this of atomization of not merely numerous forms of association but also of the social impulse itself, we are in need of the creation, or recreation, of *intermediate* associations, of groups and communities which lie intermediate to individual and state and whose autonomy from either state or the political mentality is some measure of the allegiance they command in their members' lives. With such intermediate associations, those which exist normally in society, or those which might be created through legislation along lines both Emile Durkheim and Lord Keynes separately proposed, with maximum autonomy of operation once brought into being, a great deal of administration would be possible that would not be mired in the vast, imperial bureaucracies which now fill the political landscape. What has long been known as *indirect* administration would be possible in far higher proportion than exists at the present time. Of all the tragedies which have attended the effort to spread democracy without, however, altering the essentially Romanist form of the state that came into being in the Renaissance, the greatest, I am inclined to think, is the systematic flouting by government of the richly varied groups and institutions in the social order which could so easily become themselves the channels or instruments of governmental funding when this becomes necessary in time of crisis.

A single illustration will serve here: that embodied in

Milton Friedman's celebrated plan for a negative income tax on the one hand and educational vouchers on the other. From what labyrinths of bureaucracy we would be saved in the grim worlds of social workers and educational administrators had there been instituted in the beginning a system whereby a natural, already-existing social group—the household—would be the means of distributing public funds for welfare and for education. What better way of encouraging initiative in both family and in individual than through use of family as an indirect means of administration. Other organizations come to mind which, in appropriate circumstances, might also become such means or channels: private schools (so notably less expensive and more efficient than public schools), even churches, labor unions, cooperatives, neighborhoods, and so on.

There is nothing fanciful in this. The fact is that in some—now, alas, slight—degree we already engage in indirect administration. Nor should we forget the civilizations and the long ages in which, as in the cases of traditional China and the Western Middle Ages, the vastly greater part of administration was through kinship, guild, and other local groups. The proper way of distinguishing states in human history is not so much by the forms of manifest government as by the relationships which exist between government and the social order. Plainly, a government can be ostensibly "absolute" in its structure and yet, through broad and deep delegation of authorities to existing social groups, or through utilization of these in its administrative operations, be in substance a free government, or at least free society.

But the overriding objective of a new policy of laissez-faire would be that of stimulating *social inventions*. Since this idea is relatively unfamiliar, I must expand briefly on it.

All progress in civilization comes from inventions. It is wholly inadequate to make the word "invention" serve only the material and technological areas. There are also cultural inventions such as the epic poem, the tragedy and comedy, the novel, the essay, the painting, fugue, ballet, and symphony. We are prone to say these are outcomes of "cultural growth," but that is an evasion. Each is an invention. We invent forms of art just as we do mechanical things.

So are there social inventions: creations of structures which become elements of the social bond; some minute, others very large and widely diffused. I do not know why more attention is not paid in the larger study of change to this fact. The history of the social order is not some vague and continuous growth in time, analogous to the growths of plants and organisms, though there is of course a vast inherited symbolism to suggest that such growth is the very essence of society. Nor is the social order a mere emanation from man's biological, instinctual nature. Both the metaphor of growth and the extrapolation of instinct have done infinite harm to the understanding of the social order. We are prone to take something as complex as, say, primitive kinship systems and, because these involve sexual and procreative activities, assume that kinship structure is some kind of evolutionary exfoliation of biological instincts. No mistake could be greater. The origins of kinship in man's history are of course lost, but we would do better to conjure up a vision of some primitive Solon than of mere instinct in the fashioning of structures as ingeniously designed as clan, moiety, and tribe, with their complex requirements of endogamy and exogamy, and their delicate balancings of authority and responsibility.

If mankind's earliest social inventiveness is to be seen in kinship, the discovery of the agricultural and metallurgical arts about ten thousand years ago made possible a large number of other social inventions that in their entirety form what we call the social and economic and political orders. In every legitimate sense of the word the local community, with its often complex functions and roles, was a social invention. So, in due time, was the walled town and then, in rising occurrence, the guild, the trade fair, the marketplace, and the host of other social devices which were hit upon to facilitate handicraft and trade. It is impossible, and also needless, to list in any detail the social inventions which have made their appearances over the past few millennia. Suffice it to say that among them are the monastery, the university, the studio, the trading company, the mutual aid association, the labor union, and the economic corporation. The history of social organization comes down, basically, to the history of the rise and spread of social inventions—relationships among individuals which, once found useful and accepted, have in many cases gone on for thousands of years in a variety of civilizations.

History from this point of view is as checkered as the history of culture or any other area of human life. There have been periods of relative dearth of such inventions and other periods of relative fertility. If we look at the historical record in terms of efflorescence of social inventions we find certain ages very rich which we are often prone to think of as the opposite. Thus the Middle Ages—so long consigned to darkness by historians who took their cues from the Italian humanists or the French *philosophes*—is rich in social inventions, quite as rich indeed as we have discovered it to be in technological inventions. Monastery (in its distinctive Western form), village community, manor, fief, guild, university, parish: these are some of the more notable inventions—"developments" as we are more likely to say—of the medieval period. By comparison the following ages of Renaissance and Reformation were sterile as producers of social forms.

But there have been other periods of richness along these lines, such as the seventeenth century, with its creation of institutes and academies in the arts, letters, and sciences, all admirable as means of uniting the creative impulses of individuals in the areas represented. The eighteenth century is probably best thought of as a period of lull in social respects. This was, after all, the supreme century of development of the idea of the state from its absolutist to its popular form.

The nineteenth century, coming hard on the heels of the great political revolutions of the preceding century, confronted with the challenge of industrialism and its wrenching of so many human beings from the ancient ties of kindred and village, is also relatively rich in social inventions. The mutual aid society in new forms, the consumers' and producers' cooperatives, the assurance societies, the labor unions, and the business corporations were all without exception ingenious adaptations to problems presented by a new economic age. As I have noted, much conservative and radical thought alike saw in some of these structures the bases of a society that would not become devoured by militarism and political power. Nor should we overlook in this century the great wave of anarchist utopias, especially to be seen in the United States. On the frontier there were numerous adaptations along these lines: the storied logging and quilting bees, for example, only two of a significant number of social arrangements whereby the individual was rescued from ineffectuality or insecurity. We exaggerate the "individualism" of the frontier. It was in fact rich in social inventions, all of which were necessary to progress and protection.

I think the twentieth century has been singularly weak on the whole in social respects, and for reasons I have already given. The atmosphere of nationalism, of creeping bureaucratization of social life by the state, the political clerisy's adoration of those things which are done by the state alone have inevitably had a suffocating effect upon the desire to create in social as well as cultural ways.

Is a change becoming evident? I think it is, although it is too soon to be certain. Along with recrudescence of kinship, neighborhood, and local community, there are surely to be seen occasional signs of an inventiveness in social matters that reflects disenchantment with the state. The contemporary commune is, without question, one such sign. It is said that there are at present more than ten thousand communes. If so, there is much significance in that movement. Not very many years ago there were none except the outrightly religious ones, the monasteries. It is quite possible that other social inventions are to be seen coming into existence if we but look closely enough. In large degree social inventiveness and voluntary association are the same, but they should nonetheless be distinguished—such is the potential importance of each considered separately.

Intermediate association, indirect administration, and social invention are in no sense utopian fantasies; history, properly read, is filled with examples of all three. I not only think them worthy of deepest consideration as important avenues of calculated social policy; I believe that such is the widening in our time of the perceived impotence of political government in the scores of social, cultural and economic areas to which it has addressed itself during the past few decades that we are almost certain to see these ideas, along with revived localism, kinship, and voluntary association, being applied in human lives. Just as twilight ages are a recurrent phenomenon of Western history, so are ages of social replenishment, of reinvigoration of social roots, though less distinctly in our history as it is written. Human beings cannot long stand a vacuum of allegiance, and if, as seems evident enough, the political state in its present national, collective, and centralized form is no longer capable of fulfilling expectations and supplying incentives, human beings will surely turn, as they have before in history, to alternative values and relationships.

I do not, I think, underestimate the opposition that will be mobilized on every possible ideological ground against such an eventuality. The voices of the present political order are clamant and often powerful. But I believe they will be revealed, and perhaps before the end of this century, to be as ineffectual as the voices of another once-powerful clerisy in Western history, that of the Roman Catholic Church, proved to be in the fifteenth century.

I hope so. The drive of both clerisies is, and always has been, toward universality with its overtones of homogeneity, toward unity with its inevitable degeneration into uniformity, and toward authority that shortly degenerates into monistic power. Ideas do not entirely make history; social, economic, and military forces are required. But no force ever becomes ascendant apart from an idea or philosophy that gives it legitimacy and intelligibility.

The Image of Citizenship

In the end it all comes down, I suggest, to the way in which we conceive the nature of the citizen. In the Middle Ages the essence of citizenship was urban man's freedom from the exactions of obedience which existed in the more feudal countryside. One was a citizen by virtue of free association in the town, and although individual identity certainly existed in the towns and cities, there were nevertheless substantial contexts of kinship, occupation, religion, and other association which in effect put the individual at the center of a series of concentric circles. There was a great difference between the status of citizen and that of subject. The medieval expression "the city makes free" was apt description of the status, for the most part, of the citizen.

Over the centuries, however, the concept of citizen tended to become increasingly merged with that of political subject. In Hobbes' *Leviathan* and also his *Behemoth* one can see vividly the transition that takes place. The suspicious, even surly, view that Hobbes gives the claimed rights of citizens is part and parcel of the identical view he gives the historic corporate liberties of city, university, borough, and nobility. In Rousseau's *Social Contract* the whole matter is resolved by the absolute destruction of any individual or associative rights whatever and the assimilation of both into the monolithic General Will. In the French Revolution the title *citizen* became the highest possible form of address, replacing such ancient and honorable titles as *father, magistrate, scholar, priest,* and *lord.* Patriotism was now anchored in the state *une et indivisible.* The Revolution achieved what absolute monarchy had never been able to achieve; it swept with "gigantic broom," in Marx's words, all the smaller patriotisms away, leaving individual and national state as the two ascendant realities. The new citizenship, far from being based upon, rooted in, the social groups in which human beings actually live, was now the exclusive property of the unitary national state.

In substantial degree it has been this way ever since. Not, to be sure, in the United States for a long time, where a constitution recognized and guaranteed divisions of power, a hierarchy of authority, and local and regional contexts of citizenship which were almost feudal in certain respects. But, as I have suggested, the Civil War altered this in considerable degree, and World War I, with its war-based, totalitarian enthusiasm, its almost fanatic patriotism, did a great deal more to transform the nature of both loyalty and citizenship. Gradually the claims of locality and region waned. Add to this the popularity of the "melting pot" concept, with its inevitable derogation of regional as well as ethnic identities, and much the same flame of citizenship began to burn in this country that had burned so brightly in France at the time of the Revolution and had succeeded in melting so many of the ancient ties of association.

But that conception of citizenship is by now as obsolete, as moribund, as the kind of political state that gave it birth. We live, as is evident enough, in a world in which the ties of nationalism and patriotism threaten to be like museum pieces, in the West at least; in which the up-thrusts of ethnicity, localism, regionalism, religion, and kinship, small and scattered though they yet are, loom up as signposts to the future; in which the single most radical expression of youth is not political creed or crusade but communal retreat from politics. No doubt the conventional wisdom of the political clerisy sees the matter quite differently. The dream of the right President surrounded by the right aides, governing the right Congress, promulgating all the right laws, ordinances, regulations, and decrees, to take effect in all sectors of society, with a now disenchanted multitude converted overnight into a militant and centralized democracy of eager citizens—this dream is presumably an ineradicable one. But as the Reformation taught the West the expendability of one kind of clerisy, so, it seems evident, will this twilight of authority we are living in teach us the expendability of the political clerisy. In simple, blunt truth, the political intellectual is as obsolete as his religious prototype had become by the sixteenth century.

If citizenship is to be restored in any form at all in the Western nations it will be through the processes and structures I have described in the preceding sections of this chapter. Every voting study has shown us that the impulse to participate in politics, to the degree that it exists at all, is closely dependent *not* upon primarily political values and objectives but upon economic, social, and cultural ones. If there is to be a citizenship in the useful and creative sense of that word, it must have its footings in the groups, associations, and localities in which we actually spend our lives—not in the abstract and now bankrupt idea of *patrie*, as conceived by the Jacobins and their descendants.

There are two traditions of citizenship in the West and there have been since Plato and Aristotle. The one draws from the unitary state Plato so adored, with all loyalties other than that to state extinguished in the interest of the state. From Plato to Hobbes and Rousseau to the contemporary political clerisy, that tradition of citizenship has been a powerful one. I would not go so far as to declare it totally wrong, given certain historical circumstances, given times and places where ties of caste, occupation, and church may become oppressive with only the central government a means of some degree of individual liberation. Such conditions are, however, the very opposite of the dominant ones in the West at the present time, when the state in the form of Leviathan has become the overriding form of oppression and exploitation.

The second tradition of citizenship begins in Aristotle's notable criticism of Plato and the unitary communism of *The Republic*. Its essence is Aristotle's pluralist envisagement of the good society. He writes:

> The error of Socrates must be attributed to the false notion of unity from which he starts. Unity there should be, both of family and state, but in some respects only. For there is a point at which a state may attain such a degree of unity as to be no longer a state, or at which without actually ceasing to exist, it will become an inferior state, like harmony passing into unison, or rhythm which has been reduced to a single foot.

This is the tradition of citizenship that became in time the cornerstone of Burke's philosophy of government, but also of the philosophies of such disparate minds as Hegel, Tocqueville, Burckhardt, and Kropotkin—minds one and all committed to the view that citizenship must be rooted in the groups and communities within which human beings actually live. It was Burke who gave this view of citizenship its greatest expression. We find it toward the end of *Reflections on the Revolution in France* where he is commenting on the "geometrical" system of the Jacobins, on their effort to destroy all allegiances in any way competitive with the state, and their determination to re-place social diversity with a political monolith of virtue. Burke writes:

> We begin our public affections in families. No cold relation is the zealous citizen. We pass on to our neighborhoods and our provincial connections. These are our inns and resting places. Such division of our country as have been formed by habit and not by a sudden jerk of authority are so many little images of the great country in which the heart has found something it could fill. The love to the whole is not extinguished by this subordinate partiality.

> I cannot help thinking that any political society committed to that concept of citizenship, and to the structure of government and society, the plural structure, that must necessarily surround the concept, would find that crises, even those of war, could occur occasionally without fatally wounding the political community and the larger social bond of which it is a part.

CULTURAL DEBRIS: A MORDANT LAST WORD
Russell Kirk

As a tailpiece, the editor appends his own Last Word—originally published in a quarterly edited by him, *Modern Age,* and reprinted in his book *The Intemperate Professor, and Other Cultural Splenetics* (Baton Rouge, 1965), pp. 160-63. His book *The Conservative Mind* (1953) has been published in several editions and translations.

We live in a world that is giving at the seams. Sometimes, indeed—especially to a man who travels a good deal— there comes an uneasy feeling that the garment of civilization has already parted; and that if one were to tug even the least bit, a sleeve or a trouser leg of our social fabric would come away in his hand. In half the world, the decent draperies of the old order have been burnt altogether, and King Demos struts naked, like the emperor with his imaginary new clothes. When the garment of civilization is worn out, we are confronted by the ugly spectacle of naked power.

Yet cheerfulness will keep breaking in. At this hour when Communists and other totalists are busy ripping to shreds the "wardrobe of a moral imagination," certain people of a different cast of mind have turned tailors, doing their best to stitch together once more the fragments of that serviceable old suit we variously call "Christian civilization" or "Western civilization" or "the North Atlantic community" or "the free world." Not by force of arms are civilizations held together, but by the subtle threads of moral and intellectual principle.

Some years ago, I was in Europe participating in two international conferences, intended to help in this pious tailoring. Between sessions, I tramped about England and Scotland with an American friend, an executive in a great industrial corporation. Being something of a classical scholar, my friend collects sixteenth- and seventeenth-century editions of Latin works—particularly Cicero and Seneca—and pokes happily about Roman remains.

We found for his library, in the dusty caverns of Scottish secondhand bookshops, a number of admirable things at trifling prices. There lay the noble elephant folio of Strabo, in two immense volumes, at a mere thirty-five shillings; and the Strawberry Hill edition of Lucan, beautifully bound, at five guineas; and a twelve-volume set of Cicero for a pound. In an age of progressive inflation, one commodity alone remains stable, or increases little in price: classical works. At the devil's booth in Vanity Fair, every cup of dross may find its ounce of gold; but the one thing which Lucifer can't sell nowadays is classical learning. Who wants Latin texts? No twentieth-century Faustus disposes of his immortal soul for mere abstract knowledge. The copies of Strabo and Lucan and Cicero for which a Schoolman might have risked his life ten times over are now a drug on the market. As my friend remarked to me, "These things are cultural debris. It's as if a great ship had sunk, but a few trifles of flotsam had bobbed up from the hulk and were drifting on the surface of the great deep. Who wants this sea drift? Not the sharks. You and I are rowing about in a small boat, collecting bits of debris."

Whether our civilization really retains coherence sufficient for restoration to be possible may be made clear to all thinking men within a few years. If the fabric of our ancient society has declined to the condition of a mere scattering of debris, all the tailors in the world cannot put it aright—nor all the beachcombers live by raking the sand for its vestiges. The totalists say that the old order is a corpse, and that man and society must be fashioned afresh, in grim fashion, upon a grim plan. Yet there survive among us some people of intellectual power who hold that the wardrobe of our moral imagination is not yet altogether depleted.

Cant and equivocation dismissed, it seems to me that there are three great bodies of principle and conviction which tie together what is called modern civilization. The first of these is the Christian faith: theological and moral doctrines which inform us, either side of the Atlantic, of the nature of God and man, the fatherhood of God, the brotherhood of man, human dignity, the rights and duties of human persons, the nature of charity, and the meaning of hope and resignation. The second of these is the corpus of imaginative literature, humane letters, which is the essence of our high culture: humanism, which, with Christian faith, teaches us our powers and our limitations—the work of Plato, Virgil, Cicero, Dante, Shakespeare, and so many others. The third is a complex of social and political institutions which we may call the reign of law, or ordered liberty: prescription, precedent, impartial justice, private rights, private property, the character of genuine community, the claims of the family and of voluntary association. However much these three bodies of conviction have been injured by internecine disputes, nihilism, Benthamism, the cult of Rationalism, Marxism, and other modern afflictions, they remain the rocks upon which our civilization is built.

Well, presently my classics-collecting friend and I walked some miles of Hadrian's Wall, away at the back of beyond in Northumberland. Here, for centuries, *Romanitas* and *humanitas* looked northward into barbarism. It is an empty country still, much of it; Pictish hill forts still scowl almost within bowshot of the Roman masonry. To the men of the legions, garrisoned here generation upon generation, it must have seemed—even toward the end— that indeed Rome was immortal; and that the barbarian, however vexatious he might be in one year or another, never could give the death thrust to a civilization which extended from Mesopotamia to Pictland, from the Sahara to the Rhine.

Yet in the fullness of time, when the common faith of the Roman world had lost its virtue, the Picts came over the wall. The end of Roman civilization was as abrupt as its beginning had been slow.

In material accomplishments, the barbarians never equalled the Romans; nor had they need to. They possessed the will to endure, and in the end the Romans lacked that will. So all that remains of the material achievement of Roman civilization is some fragments of cultural debris: a few coins, a smashed helmet, scattered beads, a ruined wall, a battered stone head. And as for the Roman moral and intellectual accomplishment, it is sold nowadays for a price not much superior to that of waste-paper.

Once we put some value upon our Roman heritage, and I hope we may do so again. Among us there still are men and women enough who know what makes life worth living—enough of them to keep out the modern barbarian, if they are resolute. If they are enfeebled, and if they cannot make common cause, the garment of our civilization will slide to the rag bin, and the cultural debris of the twentieth century will drift down the rubbish heaps of the future. Not many years of indulgence, I fancy, remain to us. But—as Henry Adams was fond of saying—the fun is in the process.

BIBLIOGRAPHICAL
SUGGESTIONS

Even a selective bibliography of "conservatism" would have to include several hundred titles. Such a bibliography is appended to the several editions of Russell Kirk's study *The Conservative Mind,* readily available. The books recommended below, most of them still in print, are particularly useful studies of conservative thought and policy—although no selection from any of the following volumes happens to be included in this present anthology. For the most part, these books are expository and critical in character, rather than polemical or partisan.

Berthoff, Rowland. *An Unsettled People: Social Order and Disorder in American History.* New York: Harper & Row, 1971. A remarkably perceptive examination of the tension of order and freedom, by a conservatively inclined historian.

Cecil, Lord Hugh. *Conservatism.* London: Williams and Norgate, 1912. One of the earlier serious examinations of conservatism as a mode of social thought, as well as a political movement.

Hallowell, John H. *The Decline of Liberalism as an Ideology, with Particular Reference to German Politico-Legal Thought.* Berkeley: University of California Press, 1943. A learned impartial study.

Hearnshaw, F. J. C. *Conservatism in England.* London: Macmillan, 1933. An analysis extending from Tudor times to 1931.

Hogg, Quintin (Lord Hailsham). *The Conservative Case.* Harmondsworth, Middlesex: Penguin Books, 1959. A lively summary by an eminent British conservative politician.

Kirk, Russell. *The Conservative Mind, from Burke to Eliot.* Chicago: Regnery/Gateway, sixth revised edition, 1978. The most widely read study of conservative thought in America and Britain.

Kirk, Russell. *The Roots of American Order.* LaSalle, Illinois: Open Court Publishing Company, revised edition, 1978. A study of the sources of American social order, from the Hebrew prophets to the Constitutional Convention.

McDowell, R. B. *British Conservatism, 1832–1914.* London: Faber and Faber, 1959. Chiefly an examination of the Conservative Party, but taking account of ideas and social movements.

Minogue, Kenneth R. *The Liberal Mind.* New York: Random House, 1963. A professor of politics assesses the strengths and failings of liberalism.

Nash, George H. *The Conservative Intellectual Movement in America, since 1945.* New York: Basic Books, 1966. The chief account of conservative thinkers of recent years.

Starzinger, Vincent E. *Middlingness: Juste Milieu Political Theory in France and England, 1815–48.* Charlottesville: University of Virginia Press, 1965. A study of the weaknesses of the "middling mind."

Strauss, Leo. *Liberalism, Ancient and Modern.* New York: Basic Books, 1968. A learned study of the roots of "liberal" belief.

Wilson, Francis Graham. *The Case for Conservatism.* Seattle: University of Washington Press, 1951. A very brief but succinctly illuminating exposition.

Perhaps two score other books, of varying merits, concerned with conservative ideas, men, and measures have been published in recent years—studies, that is, possibly as deserving as the titles listed above. But doubtless the select list here will be found quite sufficient by most readers.

INDEX

Grateful acknowledgment is made to the following for permission to re-print copyrighted material:

Angus & Robertson Publishers: "What Must Be Developed?" from *The End of Modernity* by James McAuley. Copyright © 1959 by James McAuley.

Associated Book Publishers Ltd./Methuen & Co. Ltd. and Michael Oakeshott: "On Being Conservative," from *Rationalism in Politics* by Michael Oakeshott.

Edward S. Babbitt, Executor of the Estate of Irving Babbitt: "Burke and the Moral Imagination," from *Democracy and Leadership* by Irving Babbitt, 1924.

Doubleday & Company, Inc.: "The Informer" by Joseph Conrad. Copyright 1906 by Harper's Magazine; 1933 by Jessie Conrad.

Doubleday & Company, Inc., and John Lukacs: Excerpts from *The European Revolution and Correspondence with Gobineau* by Alexis de Tocqueville, edited and translated by John Lukacs. Copyright © 1959 by John Lukacs.

Doubleday & Company, Inc., The National Trust, Macmillan London Limited, and A. P. Watt Ltd.: "The Mother Hive," copyright 1908 by Rudyard Kipling from *Rudyard Kipling's Verse: Definitive Edition.*

Wm. B. Eerdmans Publishing Co., William Collins Sons & Co. Ltd., and the C. S. Lewis Estate: "The Poison of Subjectivism," from *Christian Reflections* by C. S. Lewis.

Faber and Faber Ltd., London, and Mrs. Valerie Eliot: "A Commentary" (on Marxist literary criticism) by T. S. Eliot, from *The Criterion,* Vol. XII, January 1933.

Gordian Press, Inc.: "Property and Law," from *Aristocracy and Justice* by Paul Elmer More.

Irving Kristol and Basic Books, Inc.: "Capitalism, Socialism, and Nihilism," from *Two Cheers for Capitalism* by Irving Kristol.

Louisiana State University and Mary Davidson Bell: "Some Day, in Old Charleston" by Donald Davidson, from *Still Rebels, Still Yankees and Other Essays* by Donald Davidson. Copyright © 1957, 1972 by Louisiana State University Press.

The Massachusetts Historical Society: A chapter from Henry Adams' *Democracy,* and Brooks Adams' "The Revolt of Modern Democracy Against Standards."

William Morrow & Company, Inc., David Higham Associates, Inc., and Malcolm Muggeridge: "The Great Liberal Death Wish," from *Things Past* (1978) by Malcolm Muggeridge, edited by Ian Hunter. Copyright © 1970 by Malcolm Muggeridge.

John Murray (Publishers) Ltd.: "Choice & Toleration," from *Perseus in the Wind* by Freya Stark.

John Murray (Publishers) Ltd., Houghton Mifflin Co., and Sir John Betjeman: "The Planster's Vision," from *John Betjeman's Collected Poems* by John Betjeman.

Oxford University Press, Inc., and Robert Nisbet: A selection from *Twilight of Authority* by Robert Nisbet. Copyright © 1975 by Robert Nisbet.

Mrs. Jacquetta Priestley (Jacquetta Hawkes): "The Woodpeckers and

A NOTE OF ACKNOWLEDGMENT

Several kindly and competent people helped in the laborious preparation of this anthology.

Mr. Wesley McDonald spent months in close collaboration with me, choosing the selections and finding accurate texts, and editing them.

Mr. and Mrs. Robert Rice supplied me with translations from the Latin and other languages.

Mr. Michael Jordan and Mr. William Buchanan prepared the index; also Mr. Jordan conducted much of the correspondence with authors and publishers, and read the proofs.

Mr. Robert Kamphuis, Mr. Keith Bower, and Mr. Charles Brown offered good advice on selections.

Mr. Warren Fleischauer, who has given me the benefit of his sagacity and sense of style in the writing of several of my books, took a substantial hand in this anthology.

At The Viking Press, Mr. Edwin Kennebeck was diligent and perceptive.

FOR THE BEST IN PAPERBACKS, LOOK FOR THE

In every corner of the world, on every subject under the sun, Penguin represents quality and variety—the very best in publishing today.

For complete information about books available from Penguin—including Pelicans, Puffins, Peregrines, and Penguin Classics—and how to order them, write to us at the appropriate address below. Please note that for copyright reasons the selection of books varies from country to country.

In the United Kingdom: For a complete list of books available from Penguin in the U.K., please write to *Dept E.P., Penguin Books Ltd, Harmondsworth, Middlesex, UB7 0DA.*

In the United States: For a complete list of books available from Penguin in the U.S., please write to *Dept BA, Penguin*, Box 120, Bergenfield, New Jersey 07621-0120.

In Canada: For a complete list of books available from Penguin in Canada, please write to *Penguin Books Ltd, 2801 John Street, Markham, Ontario L3R 1B4.*

In Australia: For a complete list of books available from Penguin in Australia, please write to the *Marketing Department, Penguin Books Ltd, P.O. Box 257, Ringwood, Victoria 3134.*

In New Zealand: For a complete list of books available from Penguin in New Zealand, please write to the *Marketing Department, Penguin Books (NZ) Ltd, Private Bag, Takapuna, Auckland 9.*

In India: For a complete list of books available from Penguin, please write to *Penguin Overseas Ltd, 706 Eros Apartments, 56 Nehru Place, New Delhi, 110019.*

In Holland: For a complete list of books available from Penguin in Holland, please write to *Penguin Books Nederland B.V., Postbus 195, NL-1380AD Weesp, Netherlands.*

In Germany: For a complete list of books available from Penguin, please write to *Penguin Books Ltd, Friedrichstrasse 10-12, D-6000 Frankfurt Main 1, Federal Republic of Germany.*

In Spain: For a complete list of books available from Penguin in Spain, please write to *Longman, Penguin España, Calle San Nicolas 15, E-28013 Madrid, Spain.*

In Japan: For a complete list of books available from Penguin in Japan, please write to *Longman Penguin Japan Co Ltd, Yamaguchi Building, 2-12-9 Kanda Jimbocho, Chiyoda-Ku, Tokyo 101, Japan.*